*B*ALANCHINE'S

COMPLETE STORIES OF THE GREAT BALLETS

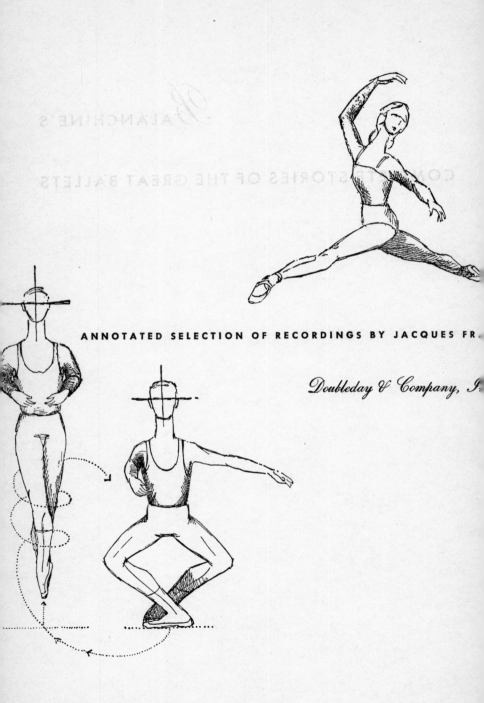

ANNOTATED SELECTION OF RECORDINGS BY JACQUES FR.

Doubleday & Company, I.

Balanchine's

COMPLETE STORIES OF THE GREAT BALLETS

BY GEORGE BALANCHINE

Edited by Francis Mason

DRAWINGS BY MARTA BECKET

Garden City, New York

Copyright © 1954 by Doubleday & Company, Inc.
All Rights Reserved
Printed in the United States

Library of Congress Catalog Card Number 54-5364

To the Ballet Audience of Today and Tomorrow

Dancing is an action, showing outwardly the spiritual movements which must agree with those measures and perfect concords of harmony which, through our hearing and with earthly joy, descend into one intellect, there to produce sweet movements which, being thus imprisoned, as it were, in defiance of nature, endeavor to escape and reveal themselves through movement. Which movement of this sweetness and melody shown outwardly (when we dance) with our person, proves itself to be united and in accord with the singing and with that harmony which proceeds from the sweet and harmonious song or from the measured sound we are listening to . . . The art of dancing is for generous hearts that love it, and for gentle spirits that have a heaven-sent inclination for it rather than an accidental disposition, a most amiable matter, entirely different from and mortally inimical to the vicious and artless common people who frequently, with corrupt spirits and depraved minds, turn it from a liberal art and virtuous science, into a vile adulterous affair, and who more often in their dishonest concupiscence under the guise of modesty, make the dance a procuress, through whom they are able to arrive stealthily at the satisfaction of their desires.

—Guglielmo Ebreo, *"William the Jew of Pisaro,"*
ITALIAN DANCING MASTER OF THE RENAISSANCE

Acknowledgments

Many people have helped in the making of this book. Genevieve Oswald of the New York Public Library's valuable Dance Collection worked tirelessly to seek out and verify many elusive facts. Roger Pryor Dodge generously permitted the use of photographs from the aforementioned Dance Collection. The Dance Archives of the Museum of Modern Art, Lydia Joel and Joanne Howell of *Dance Magazine*, Anatole Chujoy and P. W. Manchester of *Dance News*, Martin and Sally Kamin of the Kamin Dance Bookshop, Senia Solomonoff and the staff of his Ballet Book Shop and T. Wilde of The Dance Mart lent books, scores, and photographs and made available selections from their large collections of material on ballet. Anatole Chujoy's *Dance Encyclopedia* and the files of the following magazines have been invaluable for research: *Ballet, Dance Index, Dance Magazine, Dance News, Dance and Dancers*, and *The Dancing Times*.

The ballet reviews and articles of Richard Buckle in *Ballet*, Anatole Chujoy and P. W. Manchester in *Dance News*, Frances Herridge in the New York *Post*, Doris Hering in *Dance Magazine*, Margaret Lloyd in the Christian Science *Monitor*, John Martin in the New York *Times*, Walter Terry in the New York *Herald Tribune*, and Edwin Denby's collection of reviews, *Looking at the Dance*, have been crucial in the critical notes contained in this book.

These authors and publishers must be thanked for permission to quote from their works: Cyril W. Beaumont for his translation of *The Romantic Ballet as seen by Théophile Gautier*; Kamin Dance Bookshop for *An Elementary Treatise upon the Theory and Practice of the Art of Dancing*, by Carlo Blasis, translated by Mary Stewart Evans; Lincoln Kirstein, for his *Blast at Ballet*; Serge Lido for his *Ballet No. 2*; Little, Brown & Company, The Atlantic Monthly Press, and Bernard L. Schubert, Inc., for *Dance to the Piper*, copyright 1951, 1952, by Agnes de Mille; Macmillan & Co., Ltd., for "The Bumboat Woman's Story" from *Bab Ballads*, by Sir W. S. Gilbert; Pellegrini & Cudahy, Publishers, for *Looking at the Dance*, copyright 1949, by Edwin Denby; copyright 1936, 1937, 1938, 1939, 1940, 1941, 1942, 1943, by Modern Music; and *Stravinsky in the Theatre*, edited by Minna Lederman, copyright 1949, by Dance Index-Ballet Caravan, Inc.; Putnam

& Company, Ltd., Publishers, for *Reminiscence of the Russian Ballet,* by Alexandre Benois; Random House, New York, and Faber & Faber, Ltd., for *Age of Anxiety,* by W. H. Auden; Igor Stravinsky, for his *Stravinsky: An Autobiography;* Carl Van Vechten for "The Russian Ballet and Nijinsky," from *Interpreters,* by Carl Van Vechten.

The press representatives of the various ballet companies have been generous in responding to frequent requests: Samuel Lurie and Walter Alford of the Ballet Theatre; Philip Bloom and Wilbur Pippin of the New York City Ballet; Martin Feinstein, Bernice Richman, and Michael Swealy of the S. Hurok office (Sadler's Wells Ballet, Sadler's Wells Theatre Ballet, and the Agnes de Mille Dance Theatre); Isadora Bennett and Richard Pleasant of the Slavenska-Franklin Ballet; and Doris Luhrs of the Ballet Russe de Monte Carlo.

George Platt Lynes, who has collaborated with the author on photographing dancers and ballets so successfully over the years, and some of whose photographs grace this book, devoted a great amount of time to consultation with the editor and publishers, for which they are extremely grateful.

Betty Cage, Executive Manager of the New York City Ballet, has aided many aspects of the book's production.

For their interest, kindness, and assistance in numerous ways, grateful acknowledgment is made to Jane Allison, Baron, Cecil Beaton, Edward Bigelow, Natalie Bodanya, Charles Boultenhouse, Vida Brown, Bernard Buck, Josephine Cerasani, John Cornelius, Laurel Cutler, Stella and David M. Davis, Edwin Denby, Catharine de Bary, Fred Fehl, Felix Fonteyn, William Gorman, Sidonie Gruenberg, Albert Jackson, Marcus H. Jaffe, Mme. Tamara Karsavina, Arthur Kaufman, Lincoln Kirstein, Tanaquil LeClercq, Jack Landau, Hilary Masters, Fred'k Melton, Marianne Craig Moore, Wright Morris, Nathalie Molostoff, Constance Morgan, H. Roth Newpher, Eugenia Orousov, Walter E. Owen, Elise Reiman, Houston Rogers, Joan Sherman, Seymour N. Siegel, Ann Sloper, Maria Tallchief, Alfredo Valente, Roger Wood, Dorothy and Leo Paul Wren, and Lydia Zemba. The helpfulness of Patricia Michaels Mason—her reading of the manuscript and the proofs and her suggestions and criticisms—has been incalculable.

F.M.

Preface

I have been a choreographer and a ballet master now for almost thirty years. During this time, I have been asked many questions about ballet—not only by students, but by interested members of the audience who wanted to know my thoughts on dancing. When the idea of this book was first suggested to me, I immediately said that I was not a writer. But at the same time, I realized that a book would provide an excellent chance for me to answer these questions about dancing and choreography; it would allow me to present the ballets in current repertories; and it would provide me with an opportunity to write the comments I wished to make on my own ballets. I am indebted to Francis Mason for his valuable and indispensable assistance in putting this book together. Without such helpfulness the book simply would never have existed. And my thanks go also to Jacques Fray, the popular commentator and musician, for his section on ballet recordings. I believe that an acquaintance with the music of the ballet is necessary to complete enjoyment of the art.

I think we all agree that in the last ten years, and more particularly in the last few years, ballet has become an extremely popular art in the United States. It has become popular not only through frequent appearances of such companies as the Ballet Theatre, the Ballet Russe de Monte Carlo, the New York City Ballet, the Slavenska-Franklin Ballet, the Agnes de Mille Dance Theatre, and the Sadler's Wells companies from England, but has also achieved great popularity through motion pictures, musical comedy, and television.

People who have seen ballet on the stage or in the movies or on television for the first time have many questions about it. Perhaps the story they saw portrayed in dance form was not clear, perhaps they are interested in knowing what to watch for, in learning something more about the background of this art that has recently come to entertain them. Others have seen ballet, like it, know something about it, but want to know more. And there are those who have seen ballet and have not enjoyed it and have wondered why. Finally, there are dance students or young people who want to become students, and their parents, who are naturally interested in their children's pursuits. All of these people have questions about ballet, and I thought it important to try to answer them as best I could.

This book contains the stories of more than a hundred ballets in the repertories of ballet companies that perform in the United States. They have been chosen for the person who is going to see a ballet for the first time and wants to have some idea of what to expect, and they have been selected for today's ballet audience—the people who go to the ballet frequently and enjoy it. For this reason, most of the stories included are of ballets that can be *seen* today. All ballet companies boast of permanent repertories that list many ballets that are seldom, if ever, performed. Only when the unperformed works are likely someday to be revived, or are particularly interesting for their music or their significance in the history of the classic dance, have I included them. I don't think there's any point in wasting the reader's time with accounts of ballets that will in all probability never be performed again.

Some members of the ballet audience who are familiar with my own ballets might have occasion to wonder why this book is primarily devoted to ballet stories. Comparatively few of my ballets, it is true, tell stories in the usual sense. I think that dancing to music is entertaining alone; but other choreographers have thought stories extremely important and their work is naturally vital to the modern repertory.

Ballets have short lives. Compared to books, paintings, to plays, to pieces of music, their lives are very short indeed. Often, old ballets are revived by modern choreographers and danced by contemporary dancers, but these are the exceptions. The ballet audience, like every audience in the theatre, wants something new every year. When a ballet is a success, it sometimes remains one for three or four years, perhaps ten. Some of the ballets in this book will therefore be dated by the time it is published. Future editions will remedy this situation as much as possible.

I should like to thank Ralph Beebe, who originated the idea of this book and encouraged its completion. I am grateful to Lawrence Sherman, who guided the book's beginning and its early stages and who solved with rare understanding its initial problems. Marion Patton's suggestions, patience, and understanding have been invaluable. It is a pleasure for me to acknowledge my gratefulness to them.

GEORGE BALANCHINE

Contents

Halftone Illustrations

Part One

STORIES OF THE GREAT BALLETS

THE AFTERNOON OF A FAUN

Choreographic tableau in one act. Music by Claude Debussy. Choreography by Vaslav Nijinsky. Scenery and costumes by Léon Bakst. First presented by Diaghilev's Ballets Russes at the Théâtre du Châtelet, Paris, May 29, 1912, with Vaslav Nijinsky as the *Faun*. First presented in the United States by Diaghilev's Ballets Russes at the Century Theatre, New York, January 17, 1916, with Leonide Massine as the *Faun*.

The music for this ballet was written by Debussy as a *Prélude* to a poem by Stéphane Mallarmé. Nijinsky's idea of portraying a languorous faun whose rest is disturbed by beautiful nymphs is thus related to Debussy's inspiration. Mallarmé's poem is not simple, but a reading of it is essential to an appreciation of Nijinsky's apparently simple ballet. This is what happens in the ballet:

When the curtain rises, we see a faun idling away a hot summer afternoon. He lies on a hillock, playing the flute and eating grapes. It is apparent that his wants are simple and innocent. Dressed in light brown tights dotted with brown patches below the waist, he seems to be half boy, half animal.

A group of seven lovely nymphs on their way to bathe in a lake near by enter the faun's domain. They move in a line, forming a likeness to a Greek frieze, their bodies always turned to the audience, their faces always in profile. The faun has never seen such beautiful creatures before and climbs down from his hillock to observe the naiads with the golden hair and soft, gauze tunics more closely. The nymphs, in turn, are astonished by this creature who seems to be a handsome boy spotted like a goat with small horns growing from his forehead. What can he be? they wonder. Soon, as the playful faun leaps about them, the startled nymphs flee to the forest.

When they return, the faun tries to ingratiate himself with them. But still the naiads are frightened, and again they run away. All except one. This nymph is less embarrassed than her sisters and more anxious to discover the faun's secret. The faun is emboldened to make playful amorous gestures. The nymph allows him to touch her; she seems to respond to him, but then she eludes his grasp. She is frightened and rushes off to join the others. As she leaves, a silken scarf from her garment falls to the ground.

The faun, no longer playful, is sad at her departure. He picks up her scarf and holds it as if it were a treasure. He returns to the hillock, holds the scarf in his hands as if it were a woman's face, and touches it tenderly. Now he lays the scarf down softly and as he caresses it, imagines it to be the naiad he frightened away. With his possession of the scarf, the faun is content with his afternoon revery. It is as if the nymphs had never appeared, as if he had dreamed of their presence and in his dream possessed utterly the most beautiful of them all.

NOTES: *The Afternoon of a Faun* was Vaslav Nijinsky's first ballet. In its choreography and in its dancing the work completely rejected traditional forms. It was not a ballet in the accepted sense; it was a "choreographic tableau," a moving frieze, a work to be seen only from the front, a two-dimensional ballet. In his imitation of Greek paintings, Nijinsky was faithful to the spirit and to the letter; the traditional movements of classical ballet were altogether rejected in favor of an angular rigidity that would make possible a new expressiveness for the dancer's body.

Since Nijinsky's first performances, many dancers have taken the leading role in *The Afternoon of a Faun*, among them Leonide Massine, Serge Lifar, David Lichine, Igor Youskevitch, Leon Danielian, and Jean Babilée.

In 1936 Edwin Denby reviewed a performance by David Lichine:

"The *Faun* is an astonishing work. After twenty-three years it is as direct and moving as though it had been invented yesterday. It gathers momentum from the first gesture to the last like an ideal short story. From this point of view of a story, the way the veil is introduced and re-emphasized by the nymph is a marvel of rightness. From the point of view of visual rhythm the repetition of the nymph's gesture of dismay is the perfection of timing. It is, of course, because so few gesture motifs are used that one can recognize each so plainly, but there is no feeling of poverty in this simplification. The rhythmic pattern in relation to the stage and to the music is so subtly graded that instead of monotony we get a steady increase in suspense, an increase in the eyes' perceptiveness, and a feeling of heroic style at the climax.

"It is true that most of the gestures used have prototypes in Greek reliefs and vase paintings, but, in addition to that intellectual association with adolescence, the fact is that when the body imitates these poses, the kind of tension resulting expresses exactly the emotion Nijinsky wants to express. Both their actual tension and their apparent remoteness, both their plastic clarity and their emphasis by negation on the center of the body (it is always strained between the feet in profile and the shoulders *en face*)—all these qualities lead up to the complete realization of the faun's last gesture. The poignancy of this moment lies partly in the complete change in the direction of tension, in the satisfying relief that results; and the substitution of a new tension (the incredible backbend) gives the work its balance. But besides, the eye has been educated to see the plastic beauty of this last pose, and the rhythmic sense to appreciate its noble deliberateness. That it is so intensely human a gesture, coming after a long preparation of understatement, gives it, in its cumulative assurance, the force of an illumination. This force of direct human statement, this faith in all of us, is the astonishing thing about the *Faun*. It is as rare in dancing as in the other arts. These last moments of the *Faun* do not need any critical defense. But they have been so talked about that I am trying to point out for intellectuals that they are not a sensational tag, but that the whole piece builds up to them, and reaches in them an extraordinary beauty.

"The De Basil company danced the *Faun* beautifully. Lichine in the title role excelled. It is a part that demands exceptional imagination as well as great plastic sense. And Lichine had besides these a fine simplicity."

The Afternoon of a Faun was revived in a new version by Jerome Robbins for the New York City Ballet on May 14, 1953, at the City Center, New York. Tanaquil LeClercq and Francisco Moncion danced the ballet, which had scenery and lighting by Jean Rosenthal and costumes by Irene Sharaff. Louis Biancolli reviewed the ballet in the New York *World-Telegram* the next day:

"A brand-new version by Jerome Robbins of Debussy's *Afternoon of a Faun* brought repeated rounds of applause at last night's performance by the New York Ballet at the City Center.

"The novelty more than deserved the ovation. It was beautiful and tender, poetic and restrained, and highly imaginative.

"If you recall the old version, the romantic-minded faun spends a good part of the afternoon musing on real or imaginary meetings with a few nymphs the day before. This was Mallarmé's poem. Debussy put it to music, and Nijinsky made it come alive on the ballet stage.

"So much for history. Mr. Robbins has taken the faun out of Greek mythology and put him to work in a dance studio. He is shown stretching lazily about the floor and performing a modified version of Swedish calisthenics. It isn't hard to surmise where his thoughts really are.

"A ballerina wisps into the studio, glides about the floor, does one or two sequences at the practice bar lining the three walls, and then falls under the spell of the faun's unspoken desire.

"What follows is very proper—as compared with the old version. The faun fawns on the lady, of course, but with model finesse; they dance a little and eye one another shyly. He kisses her on the cheek, and she vanishes.

"It might all be a dream, or the gentle reality of a chance encounter between dance classes. It doesn't matter. There is perfect illusion of a sudden experience of beauty—and a perfect return to repose.

"Tanaquil LeClercq was splendid as the ballerina—a vision of silken loveliness floating into the daydream of a poetic idler. And Francisco Moncion was just as splendid as the lithe and gallant faun.

"One masterly stroke was the added illusion that the audience was actually serving as the fourth wall of the dance studio—that is the wall with the mirrors.

"When they stared blankly into the faces of the crowd the faun was really admiring his own reflection of a bronzed pagan god, and the lady could see in the mirror that she was no back number either."

Doris Hering in *Dance Magazine* said: "*Afternoon of a Faun* is a work of great awareness and wry insight and one that shimmers with atmosphere from beginning to end.

"The atmosphere begins to accumulate even before there is any dancing. When the curtain first rises, there is a fragile nylon drop downstage. The music stirs, and a light slowly rises behind the drop. The outlines of a dance studio are revealed. The nylon melts away, and one sees a tawny male creature asleep on the floor. He stretches. He arches his back and curves slowly from side to side. In mood he is very much like the faun of the old Nijinsky ballet. In appearance he is a boy alone in a dancing studio.

"The music draws him languidly to his feet. After a few tentative stretches, before a mirror (imagined on the audience side of the stage), he drifts to a corner of the room and curls on the floor, asleep again.

"Along a corridor behind the translucent back wall a female of unbelievable elegance picks her way on point. She glides into the studio, becomes aware of the sleeping male, but is more attracted by her own image in the mirror.

"The sleeper sits up like a startled faun. And slowly, hypnotically, with the music sifting through the space around them, they intertwine in a dance for two—or rather, for three. For the mirror is always there. After each moment of near-contact, they stare wide-eyed into its surface.

"Suddenly they drop to the floor, sitting in that ever alert manner of dancers and wild creatures. The boy brushes a kiss on the girl's cheek. She stares into the mirror, brings her hand slowly to her cheek, and leaves. The boy dances alone, trying to capture the atmosphere of her presence. As the music dies, he sinks slowly to the floor and sleeps.

"There is a wonderful sense of theatrical rightness in Mr. Robbins' choice of the antiseptic studio atmosphere for history of nascent love vying with narcissism—not only because dancers live in a world of mirrors, but because this particular format allowed him to concentrate on the rich mood relationship between the music and his own choreography. And instead of making a 'dance' in the formal sense of the word, he allowed the movement to flow out of the materials of the classroom, which are often more beautiful than their embellished stage versions. And he found two exceedingly sensitive performers in Francisco Moncion and Tanaquil Le Clercq."

THE AGE OF ANXIETY

Dramatic ballet in six scenes. Music by Leonard Bernstein. Choreography by Jerome Robbins. Scenery by Oliver Smith. Costumes by Irene Sharaff. Lighting by Jean Rosenthal. First presented by the New York City Ballet at the City Center, New York, February 26, 1950, with Tanaquil LeClercq, Francisco Moncion, Todd Bolender, and Jerome Robbins in the principal roles.

Inspired by Leonard Bernstein's Second Symphony, *The Age of Anxiety*, and the poem by W. H. Auden on which this music is based, this ballet concerns the attempt four people make to find themselves. The ballet follows the sectional development of the poem and music.

THE PROLOGUE: The curtain rises on a scene that might be a public place in any part of a large modern city. A man enters on the left and walks slowly to the center of the stage. A girl appears on the right and walks toward him. Two men join the couple. All are strangers. The four figures stand opposite each other to form a small square, as if they were standing about a table. They sit together, become acquainted, discover mutual interests and a common problem, and with quiet, implicit understanding agree to set out on a journey together.

It is clear that each of these four people has something to fear. Their gestures and smallest movements are timorous and tentative. Because they do not know each other well, they seem always to be seeking something in their relationship to make it seem less odd that four strangers should meet and instantly, instinctively, feel a need to share each others' thoughts. Strangers they certainly are, but in their immediate awareness of a common problem their relation assumes an interested tenderness, a feeling of relief that companionship is still possible. All are humble in the face of this unstated problem, which seems at first to be loneliness. The journey they take together is a metaphor, a figure in dance terms, of the long exploratory conversation they begin to have in order to learn more of themselves and their age. The dance mirrors their talk.

THE SEVEN AGES: The four characters show us the life of man from birth to death in a set of seven variations. In the first variation, one of the men learns to stand, to walk, to articulate. In the words of Auden's poem:

Behold the infant, helpless in cradle and
Righteous still, yet already there is
Dread in his dreams at the deed of which
He knows nothing but knows he can do,

The gulf before him with guilt beyond,
Whatever that is, whatever why
Forbids his bound; till that ban tempts him;
He jumps and is judged: he joins mankind . . .

The girl comes forward and dances the second age. Her movements are warm and open, joyously happy. The girl is not only conscious of herself, but conscious of life about her, and displays an eagerness to participate in that life: she sacrifices part of herself to the world.

In the third variation, the four strangers meet love—the inevitable consequence of knowing and discovering something outside the self. It is love on an elemental, physical level, the love of extreme youth that recalls Auden's lines:

Since the neighbors did,
With a multitude I made the long
Visitor's voyage to Venus Island . . .

The fourth age shows us the plight of social man, man thrust into the world of ambitions. Here he becomes aware for the first time of what he must do to climb the road to his ideal, how this road sometimes diverges and how he is perhaps deceived about his goal. Here he faces the problem of realizing a dream in an apparently dreamless world: which fork in the road shall he choose?

Now, in the fifth age, the dancers find material success and discover the price paid to achieve it. Here we imagine very easily a great modern city where nature is entirely absent, where everything moves on a fixed schedule, and where citizens are mere readers of timetables, conforming religiously to the demands of a huge machine that they have no power to control.

The sixth age shows us a reaction to this superhuman condition—disillusionment, a brief effort to rise above it, a danced argument as to which is better: to give in to the determinism of the city or to fight against it fearlessly. The four strangers split into two groups and take these differing points of view. At the end, one of the dancers tires. His fist moves to his mouth to stifle a yawn. He sits, curled up like a child.

In the final age, man has abandoned hope, abandoned his rage at human error, and ceased to have any reason to act. The dancer walks slowly, is ignored by passers-by. He reaches out, collapses, and is carried off. Slowly a figure moves across the stage, dragging behind him a long piece of crepe. The end has come. Man is dead and no longer a member of the minority.

THE SEVEN STAGES: The four figures come together again. They stand in a close line and move together awkwardly, reaching out in unison toward an invisible goal. They separate and look about, then start on a dream journey to find happiness.

Four figures dressed exactly like them, but with masks covering their faces, enter. Lines of masked creatures file in and dance between the four characters and their doubles, who imitate precisely the movements of the four.

One by one, and with different partners, the four strive for a goal where they will have no doubts and feel secure. They wander in a maze, lose their way, lose each other, then meet again safely. Nothing definite has been gained, but together they have had a harrowing common experience. They repudiate their doubles, pushing them aside. Now the four not only subconsciously know each other very well, but they are friends, too.

THE DIRGE: The four friends fall flat on their faces as the All-Powerful Father enters. This father symbol is depicted as a huge figure on stilts, a tin man of faith. He beckons to them with mechanical movements and stalks forward. They take courage and touch him. Other people enter and pay homage to the Father. It is interesting that he moves awkwardly, that he requires the assistance of his disciples. He is not so much a religious as a political figure: a representation of power that exists not through his own will alone. He sits on the shoulders of the crowd. The girl dances before him ecstatically, fascinated with the new-found rapid grace in movement his presence gives her. She reaches out to him supplicatingly. The Father responds to her plea by falling over, collapsing. The four regard him as the god that failed.

THE MASQUE: The exhausted girl falls against one of the boys. There is silence for a moment. Then carefree music blares out. The music simulates jazz, and the four characters cavort about the scene forgetting their problem in playful versions of jive. But soon their vigorous efforts to be cheerful begin to pall. One of them stops dancing and stomps in raging despair: it is the kind of protest of the half-intoxicated, the man who knew that drink would solve nothing at all. The girl curls up on the ground.

EPILOGUE: One of the men seems to die. The girl and another man go to him and help him. Now all four stand together as at the beginning of the ballet. They kneel together, then rise. The girl reaches out to the men, as if she wants to ask a final question the answer to which is very important to her. But they all have such questions. Gradually they turn and walk toward the four corners of the stage from which they came. Just before they exit, they turn and bow slightly to each other in gratitude for the faith they have given each other in the anxious age.

NOTES: W. H. Auden's *The Age of Anxiety: A Baroque Eclogue* was published in 1946. *The Age of Anxiety,* Leonard Bernstein's *Symphony No. 2,* for Piano and Orchestra, on which the ballet was also based, was first performed by the Boston Symphony Orchestra, Serge Koussevitzky conducting, on April 8, 1949. The composer was the piano soloist. At that time Bernstein offered a description of his work and its source, the poem by Auden. "The essential line of the poem (and of the music) is the record of our difficult and problematical search for faith. In the end, two of the characters enunciate the recognition of this faith—even a passive submission to it—at the same time revealing an inability to relate it personally in their daily lives, except through blind acceptance . . . If the charge of 'theatricality' in a symphonic work is a valid one, I am willing to plead guilty. I have a deep suspicion that every work I write, for whatever medium is really theatre music in some way . . ."*

Jerome Robbins, who had collaborated with Bernstein on two ballets for Ballet Theatre, *Fancy Free* (1944) and *Facsimile* (1946), was inspired by the music to choreograph a new work, his second as Associate Artistic Director of the New York City Ballet. Robbins has pointed out, however, that his ballet is different from both the poem and the score: "It is a ritual in which four people exercise their illusions in their search for security. It is an attempt to see what life is about." John Martin of the New York *Times* called the first performance of the ballet "one of the most important events of the dance season . . . If you are interested in seeing one of the most sensitive and deeply creative talents in the choreographic field at work, and tackling his most profound and provocative assignment with uncompromising vision, you will find the piece completely fascinating . . . Robbins' intuition is uncannily penetrating, his emotional integrity is unassailable, and his choreographic idiom is lean and strong and dramatically functional. He has a fine theatre sense, can evoke an atmosphere by means that are somehow never definable, and knows how to get from his dancers qualities that perhaps even they themselves are not aware of . . . The four leading figures are all admirably danced—by Francisco Moncion, Tanaquil LeClercq, Todd Bolender, and Mr. Robbins himself. Mr. Moncion, indeed, gives the most exciting performance of his career, both in terms of movement and the temperament behind it." Margaret Lloyd wrote in the *Christian Science Monitor:* "Because it reflects the tensions of our time, *Age of Anxiety* is a great and gripping ballet" (December 30, 1950).

In addition to the four original portrayals of the leading characters, Melissa Hayden, Nora Kaye, Hugh Laing, and Roy Tobias have danced principal roles in *The Age of Anxiety* with marked success.

DEL AMOR Y DE LA MUERTE
OF LOVE AND DEATH

Dramatic ballet in two scenes and an interlude. Music by Granados (from the opera *Goyescás*), arranged by Ernest Schelling. Choreography by Ana Ricarda. Scenery and costumes by Cecilia Hubbard. First presented by the Grand Ballet de Monte Carlo at the Théâtre de Monte Carlo, April 1949, with Tamara Toumanova as the *Duchess*, George Skibine as the *Torero*, and Ana Ricarda as *Manola*. First presented in

*Program notes of the Philharmonic-Symphony Society of New York, 1949–50.

the United States by the Marquis de Cuevas' Grand Ballet at the Century Theatre, New York, November 1, 1950, with Marjorie Tallchief, George Skibine, and Ana Ricarda in the principal roles.

Gay Spanish music and peasants dressed in their finery place the scene of this ballet in an old Spanish village at *fiesta* time. The light is bright over the plains that stretch into the background, and behind the dancers, under a large, shady tree, sits a man who accompanies the festival dancing with his guitar. Six couples fill the scene, the girls in front, across the stage, turning to show the beauty of their full skirts. Toward the back, one of the girls flies a kite with a grotesque decoration. As the dance finishes, a torero joins the group and all stand back as he runs diagonally across the stage from the right, bragging of his skill by alternately kneeling and then jumping high, his legs thrust out straight before him in mid-air. He is dressed in white with a handsomely embroidered gold coat, and all the girls rush to surround him when he has finished his dance. They wish to keep him among them and blindfold him for a game of blindman's buff. The torero is reluctant, however, to join their festivities. He impatiently exits. Almost before we have missed him, he is back again, and now we understand his impatience, for he brings with him the girl for whom he has been waiting all along, the dark and stunning Manola.

To the rhythm of her castanets Manola dances a rapid variation on Spanish dance themes for her lover and the admiring crowd. When she has finished and won the applause of the assembled villagers, we see that the day has grown late. The lights have gone down, and the torero turns expectantly to Manola. They dance together now, the company circling around them.

Toward the back of the stage, behind the great tree, we make out a strange new figure, a woman. She is dressed in black, wears a high black hat, and a black fan covers her face. This is the duchess, accidentally mixing with the common folk on the festival day. She walks among the crowd with haughtiness, and everyone is still as they admire her beauty. The torero is fascinated and slowly, as if in a trance, walks toward her. He throws his bright red cape on the ground for her to step upon. The duchess touches the cape lightly with her shoe and turns away beguilingly, inviting flirtation. She drops her fan. The torero picks it up, but no sooner has he done so than the duchess' husband enters slyly and observes her indiscretion. The duke crosses the stage in the back, accompanied by two black-cloaked servants. Men from the village commence a gay dance during which they beat long wooden sticks in the air in a suggestion of warning, and the torero is left alone.

He throws his red cape across a seat at the foot of the tree and muses about the black fan and the lady who left it. He dances alone for a moment, repeating the steps that marked his entrance, then dreams again. His dream achieves an interlude of reality as the duchess enters swiftly, all in white. She rests her hand on his shoulder and poses in arabesque. Then she begins to dance before him, and soon the torero joins her, and together they dance a long and flowing adagio. He lifts her high in the air, her body falls back over his shoulder, and the torero carries her toward the back of the stage. As he moves forward again, her legs open wide, and as he pauses, her body slips down, her right *pointe* touches the ground, and her left leg is extended behind her. After the lovers have embraced, the torero turns dreamily away and sits down again to look again upon the duchess' fan. She touches his shoulder and poses gracefully over him, and the interlude is ended.

A drop curtain that portrays a frightening and gigantic owl in startled flight is lowered as the scene is changed. When this curtain rises, the stage is completely dark save for a small orange light. The scene is gradually bathed in a soft blue haze, and we see that the orange light belongs to a lantern that hangs on the portico of a tavern. Standing in the center of the stage is Manola in a long black dress, and standing about her are four men in bright blue suits and white stockings. Manola begins to dance, and here her castanets imply a suppressed and frantic rage. Her feet stomp the ground in a determined rhythm, and the men join in. Four girls enter, and when Manola's other friends leave, the five women dance sensuously to a slow tempo. In the midst of their dance, the torero enters. Manola ignores his presence, but he comes close to her. Knowing that he loves another, Manola turns her back, rejecting him. The torero leaves the scene hurriedly, and Manola and her companions increase the tempo of their dance and build to a frenzied speed. Then they all leave the scene.

The duchess enters, dressed in black, as she was when we first saw her. She seems to be searching for her lover and leaves the stage just as the torero arrives. He looks about for her, and suddenly she is back again. He lifts her high, as he did in his dream of their meeting, and the two dance with mounting passion. They kneel and embrace in final fulfillment of their love as the duchess' husband enters to expose them. The duke brings with him two servants, who attack the torero. The torero fights back, but as he runs between the two men he is stabbed mortally. He reels at the pain of the wound and falls against the portico. Defying her husband, the duchess turns to him and places her lips on his as he dies. The duke turns away in disgust. The villagers come on the scene, carrying with them a large black flag signifying the end of the *fiesta*. They cross the stage slowly. The duchess runs forward to execute a series of fierce *fouettés* as the curtain falls.

L'AMOUR ET SON AMOUR
CUPID AND HIS LOVE

Ballet in two scenes. Choreography by Jean Babilée. Music by César Franck. Settings and costumes by Jean Cocteau. First presented by Les Ballets des Champs-Elysées, at the Théâtre des Champs-Elysées, Paris, December 13, 1948, with Jean Babilée and Nathalie Philippart in the title roles. First presented in the United States by Ballet Theatre at the Metropolitan Opera House, New York, April 17, 1951.

The story is told in mythology of Psyche, the daughter of a great king, who was so beautiful that the goddess of love became jealous of her. Wrathful Venus thereupon sent to earth her son, Cupid, to excite the girl with a passion for a hideous and hateful man, as a penalty for thus emulating the most beautiful of all the goddesses. Cupid came to Psyche to fulfill Venus' designs, but was so enchanted by the girl's loveliness that he fell in love with her. Secretly he came to earth every night to visit Psyche, taking leave of her before the break of day to conceal his identity, lest Venus discover his treachery in love.

Psyche's sisters knew of these visits and in their jealousy instilled doubts within the girl's heart: why should a lover conceal himself in the dark? The next night Psyche vowed to see her lover. As he slept, she lighted a lamp and saw the handsome god. But a drop of oil from the lamp fell on Cupid's shoulder, and he awoke to see her watching him. The youthful god rose up, told Psyche that her lack of faith had spoiled their love, and vanished into the night.

The desperate girl waited night after night, but her lover never returned. She went in search of him, beseeching the help of all the gods and goddesses. At last she came to the temple of Venus and humbly invoked her aid. The goddess swore vengeance and devised for Psyche a series of tasks she must accomplish before she could find her love. Venus' instructions were so difficult to carry out that Psyche almost died in her efforts to fulfill them. But Cupid, observing her plight, encouraged and aided his love from afar.

Venus became reconciled to the girl's beauty and no longer despised her. Psyche joined Cupid in the heavens, and the two lived happily ever after. Psyche is the Greek word for soul, and the girl in this myth thus represents the human soul that strives and labors through insuperable difficulties to reach the supreme happiness of Olympus.

L'Amour et Son Amour does not recount the details of this story. Instead, the ballet strives to present the quality of the love that gave rise to the myth, to portray in movement the reunion of the god with the earth-bound girl and the attachment that made that reunion possible. The ballet carries a motto by Jean Cocteau: "Love has no explanation—do not seek a meaning in love's gestures." The music is César Franck's *Psyché* Suite.

The subdued music begins slowly. A drop curtain, white against a misty violet, depicts the profile of a youth whose eyes are directed toward a small opening in the painted frame that contains his image. The music heightens slightly and subsides again as the violet of the curtain changes to green. The curtain rises. A bright backdrop, painted in the sunny colors of the Mediterranean, pictures an imaginary map; it is framed by a Greek design. The scene is earth.

Psyche enters on the right. A flesh-color, skintight bodice reveals the beauty of her body. About her waist she wears a dark net skirt. Her long dark hair reaches to her shoulders. She moves slowly, almost listlessly. The graceful poses she assumes become an impressionistic rendering of the flow of the music. She moves as in a dream.

A man enters on the left, then another. The two approach Psyche, kiss her hands, and pay tribute to her beauty. They lift her gently, and the girl moves in mid-air between them. They hold her as she poses ethereally, like a drifting cloud. She stands alone for a moment, enchanted by some distant reality the men know nothing of. They come close to her again, and the three dance. The girl's arms stiffen. Holding her hands, one of her partners lifts her to the other. Psyche leads the dance with soft gestures, as if to instruct her admirers in the realm of her imagination. Her arms gesture with tender voluptuousness.

The men leave her, and Psyche stands alone, her arms at her sides. The music whirs to announce the arrival of seven zephyrs, who enter breathlessly. Their misty green gowns float in the air behind them. They surround Psyche in a wide semicircle. She responds to them with a gesture of sudden awakening. The zephyrs kneel and bow their heads, and Psyche dances alone. The zephyrs rise, and she dances among them, taking their hands as they weave in and out into a close circle that encloses her. Their hands flutter over Psyche's head to the accompaniment of the harp. Psyche falls back in the arms of one of the zephyrs. Another comes and lifts her legs, and three zephyrs carry her off toward Olympus. The other zephyrs fly into the twilight. The drop curtain falls.

After a brief interlude, the scene changes. Now we are high in the heavens. It is night. White lines sketch in the outlines of great constellations made by twinkling stars. The sky is warm, midnight blue. Psyche enters on the left. She marvels at the spacious beauty of the scene, its limitless starry light. The zephyrs stand behind her as she dances with them. Psyche senses that her dream is about to come true. The zephyrs rush her off.

Cupid leaps in, seemingly sustained in the air by the white wings he wears. He circles the stage in bold and daring flight. He becomes thoughtful and kneels. He looks toward the left and beckons with a noble godlike gesture toward the light. He leaves the scene. Just as he steps off, Psyche enters with the zephyrs; she moves in retarded, slow motion. The glow of the sky darkens. Psyche lies down. The stars black out.

Cupid appears in a circle of soft white light that seems to emanate from his person. He moves his arms slowly, as if he were pulling effortlessly invisible wires. Psyche attempts to rise. Cupid goes to her. Now she stands, holding onto his shoulder for support. The young god puts his arm about the girl's waist in recognition, and the two dance, softly and slowly, backward and forward. The music mounts to a crescendo. The two lovers kneel together. Cupid rises, turns with tremendous speed. Psyche imitates his movement. He holds out his arms, and the girl rushes toward him. He catches her foot in his hands and carries her back swiftly as she hovers over him.

Psyche steps down and poses against Cupid's back. He kneels, and the girl walks around him as he holds her hand. The music gradually loses its intensity. The two dance together gently. The light dims. Cupid holds up his left hand. The girl circles the stage and disappears. The light fades. Cupid stands in his domain, governing the light of the stars with his hands. The stars lose their luster; the circle of light about the god narrows to a pin point.

NOTES: *L'Amour et Son Amour*, Jean Babilée's first ballet, was created by the choreographer for his wife, Nathalie Philippart, and himself. The music is César Franck's *Psyché* Suite, which Babilée had long admired and had no hesitation in choosing for his first choreography. Writing soon after the ballet's first performances in London in 1949, Richard Buckle said in *Ballet*: "I have heard that certain agreeable sensations can be infinitely prolonged by the taking of haschisch, and that is what the music suggests to me . . . Babilée has invented an indefinite and dreamy slow-motion choreography, which only becomes a little more agitated towards the end when the music mounts to a climax . . . There are lovely moments in the ballet . . . It is an effective vehicle for the beauty and personality of the two chief dancers." Walter Terry wrote in the New York *Herald Tribune* after the American *première* of *L'Amour et Son Amour* that it was "a ballet of delicate beauty and fleeting fantasy . . . in truth, a heavenly ballet which traces lyrically the meeting and union of a sky being with an earth maiden . . ."

APOLLO, LEADER OF THE MUSES
APOLLON MUSAGÈTE

Ballet in two scenes. Music and book by Igor Stravinsky. Choreography by George Balanchine. Scenery and costumes by André Bauchant. First presented by Diaghilev's Ballets Russes at the Théâtre Sarah

Bernhardt, Paris, June 12, 1928, with Serge Lifar as *Apollo*, Alice Nikitina as *Terpsichore* (Alexandra Danilova alternated with Nikitina in this role in the original production), Lubov Tchernicheva as *Polyhymnia*, and Felia Dubrovska as *Calliope*. First presented in the United States by the American Ballet at the Metropolitan Opera House, New York, April 27, 1937, with scenery and costumes by Stewart Chaney. Lew Christensen was *Apollo*; the three *Muses* were danced by Elise Reiman, Holly Howard, and Daphne Vane.

To the Greeks, the god Apollo was many things: he was the god of prophecy, the god who punished wrongdoers, the god who helped those in trouble, the god of vegetation and agriculture, and the god of song and music. Apollo received different epithets, different names, for each of his various powers. Because of his powers of song and music, he was also closely associated with the Muses, goddesses who represented the different arts and derived inspiration from Apollo's teaching. This ballet concerns itself with Apollo, leader of the Muses, the youthful god who has not yet attained the manifold powers for which he will afterward be renowned among men.

The three Muses of the ballet were selected for their appropriateness to the choreographic art. In the words of the composer, "Calliope personified poetry and its rhythm; Polyhymnia represents mime; Terpsichore, combining in herself both the rhythm and the eloquence of gesture, reveals dancing to the world and thus among the Muses takes the place of honor beside Apollo."*

The ballet begins with a brief prologue that depicts the birth of Apollo. Before the opening curtain, the string orchestra intimates the theme that will become identified with the god as the ballet progresses. This theme receives a rhythmic accompaniment from the lower strings, and the curtain rises.

The scene is Delos, an island in the Aegean Sea. It is night; stars twinkle in a dark blue sky. Back in the distance, in a shaft of light, Leto gives birth to the child whom the all-powerful Zeus has sired. She sits high on a barren rock and holds up her arms to the light. The music quickens, the woman buries her face in her hands, a hurried crescendo is cut off sharply, the strings are plucked, and Apollo is born. Leto disappears, and in the shaft of light at the base of the high rock stands the infant god, wrapped tightly in swaddling clothes. He hops forward stiffly to a swift, flowing melody.

Two handmaidens leap softly across the stage and come to Apollo. The newborn god falls back in their arms; his mouth moves in an inarticulate cry for help, and the two women begin to unwrap his swaddling clothes. They circle the god, unwinding the rich cloth, but before they can finish, Apollo spins suddenly and frees himself of the garment and looks about the dark world, not seeing clearly, not knowing how to move. After this burst

*From Stravinsky: *Chronicle of My Life*.

of energy, he is frightened. His head is crowned with golden vine leaves and his body is endowed by nature with sinuous strength, but the young god is bewildered.

The two handmaidens bring to him a lute, sign of his future greatness in music. Apollo does not know how to hold the instrument. They place it in his hands and stand behind him, reaching out their hands to pluck the strings. Apollo follows their example and finds the first clue to his immortality. There is a black-out.

The musical statement that marked Apollo's birth is repeated sonorously. When the lights come on again, the scene is brilliant, as if a flash of lightning had been sustained and permanently illuminated the world. Apollo, dressed now in a short gold tunic, stands in the center of the stage. To the music of a solo violin, he plays upon the lute. He whirls his arm around and around in a large circle over the strings, seeming to draw music from the instrument with his youthful strength. Other strings now accompany the solo violin softly. Apollo places the lute on the ground and dances alone. He reaches out to the lute for inspiration and moves tentatively, carefully, but with a new-found ease. Now that he has proved his potential grace in movement, Apollo picks up the lute again. He turns slowly in attitude, holding the lute before him. The solo violin concludes the theme.

Three Muses appear to Apollo, walking slowly and respectfully toward him from three corners of the stage. With a godlike gesture, the god welcomes them. The young goddesses bow to him, then in unison bend in low arabesques about the lute he holds high in his hands. They break this pose and stand together. The melody is strong yet moving, vigorous yet simple, like the youthful, inexperienced quality of the dance that now begins.

Apollo reaches out and, touching their hands gently, draws the Muses close to him. The three girls stand close together, one behind the other. Apollo takes their hands one by one. They pose in arabesque for an instant and move to the center of the stage. He motions two of the girls aside; Terpsichore, Muse of song and dance, falls back in his arms. He leaves her kneeling alone and, enclosing the other two girls in his arms, he lowers them slowly to the ground so that they also kneel.

Terpsichore rises and, dancing on point, slowly takes the hands of her sister Muses and encircles their kneeling figures. Now the three Muses stand again in a close line. The lower strings play the poignant theme with deep strength, and Apollo circles the stage in broad, free leaps as the girls move their arms in rhythm to the music.

The god returns to the Muses and supports each as she turns close to the ground. The girls form a line behind Apollo and move across the back of the stage, their bold, youthful figures imitating the dance of their leader. The girls pause and kneel, then rise at once. Apollo, arms outstretched, supports them as they hold hands and form a circular tableau.

When this tableau is broken, the Muses form a close line in front of

Apollo. This line moves backward as one, the young god and goddesses shuffling awkwardly on their heels. The line comes to a rest. The three girls stand motionless; Apollo bends down and tenderly pushes them into motion with his shoulder. Led by Terpsichore, the Muses dance alone. The melody ends.

Apollo presents each of the Muses with the symbol appropriate to her art. To Calliope, Muse of poetry, he presents a tablet; to Polyhymnia, Muse of mime, a mask that symbolizes unearthly silence and the power of gesture; and to Terpsichore, Muse of dancing and song, he gives a lyre, the instrument that accompanies those arts. The Muses accept these gifts with delight and respect, form a line, and hop like pleased children to the side of the stage. Apollo commands the Muses to create and sits to watch what they will do.

Calliope comes forward with her tablet. She holds it out before her, then clutches it to her heart. Placing the tablet on the ground, she dances. The melody she moves to is based in form on the Alexandrine, the classical heroic measure of French poetry. Her dance is emotional, yet not weakly so; as she circles the stage before Apollo, her leg boldly sweeps the air before her. She is scribbling hastily on the palm of her hand when her dance nears its end, wondering if she has done well. She becomes a little sad, the music seems to cry out softly with her, and she goes to show Apollo what she has written. He does not approve.

Brilliant chords herald the dance of Polyhymnia, who soon puts her mask aside and dances rapidly to a sprightly, rhythmic melody. The girl holds her finger to her lips throughout the dance, as she tries to maintain the dignity of her mask, but her youthful enthusiasm gets the best of her: she forgets—as she responds to the happy, worldly music—and before she knows what has happened, her lips have moved and she has spoken. Terrified, she claps her hands over her mouth, punishing her own naughtiness, but Apollo sees what she has done and censures her.

Terpsichore comes forward and dances in profile with her lyre. She holds the instrument high above her head, her curved arms suggesting the shape of the lyre, and her feet pluck at the ground as if they played upon it. She moves adroitly and sharply, with assured grace; the gestures she makes with her arms as she poses in a series of balanced arabesques show us that her whole body is co-ordinated to beauty. The music she dances to is similar in melody to Calliope's, but the rhythm is different; like her dance, it is more pointed, less romantic. Of all the Muses, she alone dances perfectly, and Apollo commends her.

Now the young god dances alone. Majestic chords announce the theme of his variation. He reaches his arms up toward Olympus, leaps grandly into the air, then kneels. To the quiet rhythms of the music, Apollo performs with ideal perfection, setting an example to the Muses and reminding us that he himself has acquired the skill he demands of them.

As his dance ends, Apollo sits on the ground in a graceful, godlike pose.

Terpsichore appears before him and touches his outstretched hand. The young goddess steps over his arm and bends low in extended arabesque beside him. Now the girl rises and sits on Apollo's knees. He holds his arm up to her, she takes it, and both rise to dance a muted *pas de deux*. The melody is softly lyrical, but at the same time strong; it depicts in sound an awakening of Olympian power and strength, beauty and grace.

Apollo supports Terpsichore in extended arabesque, lifts her daringly high so that her body curves back over his shoulder, holds her as she extends her legs and sinks on the ground to rise on point in graceful extensions. She pirouettes swiftly and sharply in his arms then entwines herself around Apollo. The music brightens, they separate, dancing playfully, then meet again. Both kneel. Apollo puts his head in Terpsichore's open hands. Now, at the end, she falls across Apollo's back as the god bends down to give the Muse a short swimming lesson as a reward for her beautiful dancing. Her arms push the air aside as if they were moving in the water. When Apollo rises, Terpsichore's body is curved against him.

Calliope and Polyhymnia rush in and join Apollo and Terpsichore in a joyous *coda* in which the Muses surround Apollo with their new-found pleasure in movement. The young god, in their midst, holds out his arms; two of the girls grab hold, and he swings them through the air. The quick grace of the Muses is accompanied by lively, shifting rhythms in the music that rushes to a finish. Apollo takes them by the hand and drives all three across the stage in a swift chariot race. As the music ends, Apollo stands alone. The three girls walk toward him together and in unison clap their palms. Apollo leans down and places his head against their hands.

From on high, Zeus calls his son Apollo home with mighty crescendos of sound. Apollo stands motionless, as if under a spell, listening. The three Muses sit upon the ground. Apollo walks slowly around them. As he stands in back of them and reaches out over them, the three girls lift their feet to meet his hand. Apollo blesses them with a noble gesture. The Muses reach their arms up, and Apollo lifts them up beside him. For a moment the arms of the four figures are entwined, then the three Muses pose in arabesque behind Apollo's profiled figure to form a tableau in which the goddesses are as one with him.

Now Apollo takes their hands and draws them like a chariot across the stage. He takes them to the foot of the high rock, then walks forward and begins to climb to the summit, pointing the way to Olympus. The Muses follow. The four figures are silhouetted against the sky, holding out their arms to the sun. Leto, Apollo's mother, falls back in the arms of his hand-maidens as she reaches up to her son in farewell.

NOTES: *Apollo* is not the kind of ballet most people expect to see when they know its name. When the ballet was first performed, a French critic said that this was not Apollo at all, that the choreographer had cultivated the deliberately odd, that Apollo would never have done this, or this, or this, etc. When the critic was asked how he knew what Apollo would have done, he had no answer. He was thinking of some familiar statue of Apollo, the Apollo Belvedere perhaps, and imagined that a ballet about the god would personify sculptural representations. But *Apollon Musagète* is not Apollo Belvedere; he is the wild, half-human youth who acquires nobility through art.

Stravinsky's *Apollon Musagète* was originally commissioned by Elizabeth Sprague Coolidge and received its first performance at the Library of Congress in Washington on April 27, 1928, with choreography by Adolph Bolm, who danced the principal role. Ruth Page (Terpsichore), Elise Reiman (Calliope), and Berenice Holmes (Polyhymnia) were the three Muses. After this first performance, Stravinsky offered the score to Diaghilev, who assigned the ballet to me.

This was the second time I had worked closely with Stravinsky's music (*Le Rossignol* was a first attempt, an exercise set me by Diaghilev in 1925). *Apollo* was a collaboration. As I wrote in *Stravinsky in the Theatre*, "I look back upon the ballet as the turning point in my life. In its discipline and restraint, in its sustained oneness of tone and feeling, the score was a revelation. It seemed to tell me that I could, for the first time, dare not use all my ideas; that I, too, could eliminate. I began to see how I could clarify, by limiting, by reducing what seemed to be myriad possibilities to the one possibility that is inevitable.

"In studying the score, I first understood how gestures, like tones in music and shades in painting, have certain family relations. As groups they impose their own laws. The more conscious an artist is, the more he comes to understand these laws and to respond to them. Since working with Stravinsky on this ballet, I have developed my choreography inside the framework such relations suggest."

Stravinsky, in *Chronicle of My Life* (1936), notes that the invitation to compose a ballet for a contemporary music festival in Washington gave him an opportunity to carry out an idea that had long appealed to him, "to compose a ballet founded on moments or episodes in Greek mythology plastically interpreted by dancing of the so-called classical school . . . I had especially in my thoughts what is known as the 'white ballet,' in which to my mind the very essence of this art reveals itself in all its purity. I found that the absence of many-colored effects and of all superfluities produced a wonderful freshness. This inspired me to write of an analogous character. It seemed to me that diatonic composition was the most appropriate for this purpose, and the austerity of its style determined what my instrumental ensemble must be. I set aside the ordinary orchestra because of its heterogeneity . . . and chose strings.

"On June 12, 1928, I conducted the first production of *Apollo* . . . in Paris. . . . George Balanchine, as ballet-master, had arranged the dances exactly as I had wished—that is to say, in accordance with the classical school. From that point of view it was a complete success, and it was the first attempt to revive academic dancing in a work actually composed for the purpose. Balanchine . . . had designed for the choreography of *Apollo* groups, movements, and lines of great dignity and plastic elegance as inspired by the beauty of classical forms. . . .

"As for the dancers, they were beyond all praise. The graceful Nikitina with her purity of line alternating with the enchanting Danilova in the role of Terpsichore; Tchernicheva and Dubrovska, those custodians of the best classical traditions; finally, Serge Lifar, then still quite young, conscientious, natural, spontaneous, and full of serious enthusiasm for his art—all these formed an unforgettable company."

The importance of *Apollo* to the history of ballet has been described by Lincoln Kirstein: "*Apollon Musagète* introduced to ballet in its time a spirit of traditional classicism absent since Petipa's last compositions almost 30 years before. It demonstrated that tradition is not merely an anchorage to which one returns after eccentric deviations but the very floor which supports the artist, enabling him securely to build upon it elements which may seem at first revolutionary, ugly and new both to him and to his audience. *Apollon* has now lost for us the effects which offended, irritated or merely amused an earlier public. We forget that much of the 'modernism' of adagio movement in our classic dance derives directly from *Apollon;* that many ways of lifting women, of turning close to the floor, of subtle syncopation in the use of *pointes*, of a single male dancer supporting three women, were unknown before *Apollon*. These innovations horrified many people at first, but they were so logical an extension of the pure line of Saint-Léon, Petipa and Ivanov that they were almost immediately absorbed into the tradition of their craft.

"Glenway Wescott said that instead of *Apollo, Leader of the Muses,* the ballet should have been entitled *Apollo's Games with the Muses*. The mimed athletics, the strenuous atmosphere of violent physicality recall the nervousness of runners before a race. Each variation seems a training for the final translation to Olympus. In the chariot-race finale which evokes memories of the profiles on Roman coins and cameos and of the decathlon, visualized in the newly extended idiom of Russian ballet, a transformation of the Olympic games into contemporary dancing takes place. Of all Balanchine's works *Apollon* is the most significant historically, the most compact, the most influential . . ." (In "Balanchine Musagète," *Theatre Arts,* November 1947.)

Apollo has been staged in Denmark (1931), New York (1937, 1943, 1945, 1949, 1951), Rio de Janeiro (1941), Buenos Aires (1942), and again in Paris (1947). It has also been staged in Mexico City. It was performed in Europe during Ballet Theatre's European tour of 1950. André Eglevsky,

Igor Youskevitch, and Nicholas Magallanes have danced *Apollo* in American revivals. Among those who have danced the three Muses in revivals of the ballet are: Vera Zorina, Rosella Hightower, and Nora Kaye (Ballet Theatre, 1943); Alicia Alonso, Barbara Fallis, and Nora Kaye (Ballet Theatre, 1949); and Maria Tallchief, Tanaquil LeClercq, and Diana Adams (New York City Ballet, 1951). In the revival at the Paris Opéra in June 1947, Michel Renault was Apollo; Maria Tallchief, Terpsichore.

APPARITIONS

Dramatic ballet in three scenes with prologue and epilogue. Music by Franz Liszt. Choreography by Frederick Ashton. Book by Constant Lambert. Scenery and costumes by Cecil Beaton. First presented by the Sadler's Wells Ballet at the Sadler's Wells Theatre, London, February 11, 1936, with Robert Helpmann as the *Poet* and Margot Fonteyn as the *Woman in Ball Dress*. First presented in the United States by the Sadler's Wells Ballet at the Metropolitan Opera House, New York, October 25, 1949, with the same principals.

The inspiration of a poet is the subject of this romantic ballet. Here the poet derives his work not from real life, or from anything connected with it, but from the realm of the fantastic imagination, from apparitions. The ballet thus depicts the poet as character rather than creator, as a victim of the apparitions he finds it necessary to invoke. The scenario of *Apparitions* was suggested by the synopsis Hector Berlioz wrote for his *Symphonie Fantastique*. The music, orchestrated by Gordon Jacob, was selected from the later works of Franz Liszt by Constant Lambert.

PROLOGUE: The curtain rises on a scene representing the poet's study. It is an immense, dark, high-ceilinged room with great leaded windows—the kind of room in which we think instantly of hidden shadows lurking in the corners. It is night. On the right, a lamp stands upon a desk. Seated at the desk is the poet. He is evidently engrossed in composition, for at first he does not look up. Soon, however, he rises and gestures impatiently. His poem is not progressing as he would wish; he seems to require a fresh stimulus to continue.

The poet is astonished as light appears outside the windows. He is amazed further when he observes in the window frames mysterious apparitions. There stands a beautiful young woman in a formal ball dress, there a handsome hussar, and there a monk. Immediately the poet is enamored of the woman, who smiles at him in recognition. He sees in her an idealized version of all women, a picture of the perfect romance, and for a few moments he imagines that he has the key to the end of the poem he has been writing. But the woman and the other figures disappear. He reaches out toward them, then turns and sits again at his desk. Now his inspiration is so intense that words will not come. His mind is preoccupied with the source of his inspiration rather than the lines she might assist him to create. His mind whirls with romance. He gives up in impatience, abandons the poem, and takes a potion to induce sleep. The curtain falls.

SCENE ONE — A BALLROOM: Now the scene shifts to the locale of the poet's dream. The curtain rises on a ballroom, where fashionable couples are dancing. The poet enters, observes the scene, and wishes to participate in the discreet gaiety, but the dancers look through him as if he were the empty air. At a pause in the dancing, the lovely woman in the ball dress enters the room. All the men—particularly a handsome, swashbuckling hussar—are deferential to her dark beauty and vie for her favor. The dancing recommences. In this new dance, the women change partners constantly, and suddenly the poet is holding in his arms the apparition that delights him. But she is unaware that she has seen him before and turns her head away to catch sight of the hussar. She leaves the scene when the hussar rejoins her, and soon the ballroom is empty. The poet, alone, despairs.

SCENE TWO — A SNOW-CLAD PLAIN: The dream changes, and the poet finds himself in the lonely winter forest. He longs for the reappearance of the woman, but imagines that she will again reject him. He hears bells in the distance, wonders what they are for, and dancers who wear skirts shaped like bells move around and around him, giving vivid expression to his romantic hallucination.

A funeral procession enters. Cloaked figures carry the body of the deceased on a bier. The poet is startled to see that the procession is led by the monk who appeared in the window of his study. Now he has seen again all three: the girl, the hussar, and the monk. Is this the end? What will happen? Will his dream be resolved?

He is drawn to the bier. Before the monk can prevent it, he snatches away the burial cloth and discovers the face of his beloved. Again he despairs. The monk reprimands him. The procession moves on. The poet falls to the ground to weep and to pray.

SCENE THREE — A CAVERN: The scene now is a dark, secluded cavern. Creatures in red costumes have gathered here to practice some secret, magical rite. The poet joins them, seems to be accepted among them, rejoices, then falls back aghast as he sees before him the creature of his imagination, her face defaced, grotesque, ugly. The poet disclaims responsibility for his dream and seeks to escape. The woman is now attracted to him and will not let him go. The poet faints. As he passes into deep unconsciousness, her face miraculously takes on its previous apparent beauty.

EPILOGUE: The final curtain rises on the poet's study. He is still asleep. Gradually he wakens. He cannot shake off his dream, and as he pieces it together, he sees the dream as a telling, romantic poem on his own pursuit of romanticism—a perpetual destruction of the self in the seeking of the unattainable. He kills himself.

The woman of his imagination enters and grieves. She turns her face away as cloaked figures take up the poet's body.

ASSEMBLY BALL

Classic ballet in four parts. Music by Georges Bizet. Choreography by Andrée Howard. First presented by the Sadler's Wells Opera Ballet at the Sadler's Wells Theatre, London, April 8, 1946, with June Brae and Leo Kersley as the principals. First presented in the United States by the Sadler's Wells Theatre Ballet at the War Memorial Opera House, San Francisco, California, December 13, 1951, with a cast headed by Svetlana Beriosova, David Blair, and Patricia Miller.

Assembly Ball has no story; it is simply a ballet about young people dancing together at a formal party. Because they are young, this formality is somewhat strange to them, but throughout the party they nevertheless discover that youthful spirits are ideally expressed in such surroundings. In most nonstory ballets, an audience is apt to find a particular quality or mood that sets the work apart from other ballets of the same kind. Like the ballet entitled Symphony in C, Assembly Ball is set to the Symphony in C of Bizet, and we have a chance here to observe the different effect of the same music on two choreographers.

ALLEGRO VIVO: The curtain rises on Assembly Ball before the music begins. The stage is dark. A bright spotlight catches a boy turning rapidly with the first chords of the symphony, and gradually the scene brightens. The boy, dressed in a long red coat, is the master of ceremonies for the coming ball. The back wall of the room is festooned with garlands of flowers, and benches stand at the side and the back.

Two girls in yellow dresses appear in large windows at the back that look down on the ballroom from a low balcony. They pass from view and then enter. They join the master of ceremonies for a pas de trois. At the four corners of the room, four girls in white come in and, with the girls in yellow, circle about the master of ceremonies. Other dancers appear on the balcony, and as the girls form a diagonal line, the heroine enters with two boys.

The master of ceremonies welcomes this beautiful girl and begins to dance with her. The net of the girl's dress floats about her as she is lifted by her partner. She leaves the stage, and the boy dances alone, leaping about the room to express his admiration for her. An elderly gentleman enters, looks about the room, and departs.

Now the master of ceremonies hails four couples who enter at the corners of the stage. The four girls in white sit on the benches and watch the couples follow the lead of the master of ceremonies in a dance. Soon the girls in yellow rejoin the leader for another *pas de trois*. As the lively first movement ends, the dancers tire; with its last chords, all but two of the couples are resting on the benches.

ADAGIO: The lights dim. The master of ceremonies looks about the room as the quiet music begins. They all sense some other presence, and there is an air of expectancy. The ballerina is carried in, held aloft by two cavaliers. The master of ceremonies goes to her, her cavaliers retire, and a warm, slow *pas de deux* begins. When the tempo of the music brightens, the two lovers pass each other in leaping diagonals.

The old man wanders into the room again. The two girls in yellow rise from the benches and dance with him. He is delighted that he can keep up with these youthful creatures and begins to enjoy himself. The slower, romantic music returns; the ballerina dances a wistful variation. Now the master of ceremonies joins her, turns her in arabesque, and kneels before her. The heroine bends down and kisses him. Her cavaliers return and lift her off into the wings.

ALLEGRO VIVACE: The scene brightens. Four boys enter, and in their midst the master of ceremonies dances a dashing, brilliant variation. As his dance finishes, he spins in the air and falls to the floor, where he simulates a pensive, romantic pose. Four girls join the boys, and the couples dance about him. He rises and leaps high over a line of kneeling girls.

The old man returns and becomes dizzy as he tries to keep up with the accelerating music. He and the master of ceremonies dance together briefly, all the young people clap hands, and the ball is now at its height. The ballerina enters and bows sweetly to the old man. The master of ceremonies presents a bouquet of roses to the ballerina. Three of the girls dance with single roses that are presented to them. A fourth girl snatches a rose away from one of them, and while the old man comforts this girl, she takes her place on the dance floor. The master of ceremonies dances with the ballerina again, and the other couples respond to their obvious happiness with youthful and joyous movement.

ALLEGRO VIVACE: In the last movement, as the music matches the sprightly spirits of the dancers, the master of ceremonies and the elderly gentleman dance with the ballerina, after which all the guests join hands and line up, on the left and right. The two girls in yellow and their partners bring the ball to a whirling conclusion.

The lights begin to fade. The ballerina and the master of ceremonies pirouette into the wings, and the couples begin to depart. Soon the stage is empty. In the back, we see the old man bowing to the young dancers as he bids them good night.

LE BAISER DE LA FÉE
THE FAIRY'S KISS

Ballet-allegory in four scenes. Music and book by Igor Stravinsky. Choreography by George Balanchine. Scenery and costumes by Alicia Halicka. First presented by the American Ballet at the Metropolitan Opera House, New York, April 27, 1937, with Gisella Caccialanza as the *Bride*, William Dollar as the *Bridegroom*, and Kathryn Mullowney as the *Fairy*.

Stravinsky dedicated this ballet "to the memory of Peter Tchaikovsky. . . . It was his Muse (like our Fairy heroine) whose fatal kiss, imprinted at birth, made itself felt in all the work of that great artist, and eventually led him to immortality. Thereby does our ballet (with a similar tale) become an allegory." The story of the ballet is derived from a tale by Hans Christian Andersen—"The Ice Maiden." Stravinsky selected elements from this long and beautiful fairy tale to compose his scenario. Here, the Ice Maiden comes down from the sky to claim for her own a hapless youth. When he is a child, abandoned in the snow, the fairy kisses the boy coldly with a fatal kiss that seals his eternal devotion to her. The babe becomes a man and, with no recollection of the fairy's power over him, is engaged to be married. The Ice Maiden returns to fulfill the prophecy of her kiss and to carry him away to the ends of the earth.

FIRST TABLEAU—PROLOGUE—THE SNOWSTORM : The curtain rises soon after the orchestra has begun to play softly a lilting lullaby. The scene is deserted, barely lit. Snow begins to fall. A woman enters, carrying a child. She dances across the stage, her hood flowing behind her. She lifts the child in her arms lovingly and covers it with her cape. At first she does not appear to be alarmed at the snow, but the lullaby to which she dances changes to an ominous melody presaging a severe storm and the woman is frightened for her child. She covers it more carefully, holds it close to her breast, and continues on her way. Winds leap across the stage from right and left, passing close to her, then circling about her as if to enclose her with their freezing force. She cowers in terror. Myriad snowflakes enter behind her, hover over her, and leave her shivering on the ground. The piercing winds return, their frigid capes streaming from their shoulders; the snowflakes re-enter and surround the mother. She rises helplessly and attempts to flee, but the snowflakes divide into groups and block her escape. The music increases its ominous force. The snowflakes force her to the front and drown her with freezing snow. As the mother cowers beneath them, she thinks only of her child. She dies. The winds remove her body, and the child is abandoned to the snowflakes, who pass over the pathetic bundle as they vanish.

The winds pull in a swift white sleigh that brings onto the scene a beautiful fairy, the Ice Maiden. A spotlight catches her imposing figure. She stands in statuesque pose, holding high a wand of ice; her noble head is crowned with a star of white jewels; her dress is white, long, and full. She steps down from the sleigh, presents her wand to her escorts, and directs them away. Immediately she begins to dance. Each one of her open, flowing movements is imitated by a figure in black, who stands in the distance like a shadow to remind us that the beauty of the fairy is bewitching. The fairy dances close to the child. She stands over him; her flowing white dress seems to cover him as she turns brilliantly on point. She bends over the child, reaches out, draws him close to her face. She kisses him tenderly, yet coldly, and places the child on the ground. Now that she has sealed the fate of the helpless child, the fairy dances away slowly on point. Her shadow disappears with her.

The scene darkens. A peasant enters, carrying a lantern. He is followed by a group of mountain climbers, who help him as he seeks to recover the lost child. The music imitates their anxieties. At last one of the men sees the small bundle in the snow. The light is brought nearer, and the other men hold him as he reaches down and picks up the child while the orchestra sounds climactic chords of pathos. The scene blacks out as they hurry off.

SECOND TABLEAU—THE VILLAGE FESTIVAL: Twenty years have passed. Befriended by peasants, the child has grown up to become the most popular young man in the village. He is to be married soon to the miller's daughter.

After a brief orchestral interlude, the lights come up on a colorful mountain scene overhung with fir trees; snow-capped peaks are seen in the distance. Boys and girls of the village dressed in gay Swiss costumes stand in a wide circle dancing a folk measure to a rhythmic, holiday tune. A group of boys then move to the center, where they are surrounded by the smiling girls. They all gather behind the village bandsmen and parade around the stage.

A high-spirited boy carrying a gun runs into the crowd. This is the bridegroom. Everyone welcomes him, particularly the girls, and it is clear that he has the affections of them all. He dances forward with two of the girls to the light rhythm of the music, which soon becomes strong and robust. Everyone joins them in their youthful dance. When the dance is over, the young man calls one of his friends and directs him to shoot at a distant target. The boy aims and misses. Another boy tries and misses. The bridegroom seizes his gun, shoots, and hits the target, to the delight of the girls, who playfully congratulate him.

The bride enters, surrounded by six of her bridesmaids. She dances briefly before the company, and then the boy joins her for a happy duet that reflects their mutual joy. Several of the village girls start a yodeling contest, which is interrupted for a final festival dance by the bride, the bridegroom, and all their friends. The peasants encircle the bride and bridegroom and begin to leave the stage. The bride goes off with her friends. The boy seems to depart with the rest, but as the stage empties, we see that he has remained. He sits on the ground in quiet meditation. One of his friends tries to persuade him to continue with the celebration, but the boy refuses. He is alone.

On the right a beautiful gypsy enters. She is dressed in black and white. The boy does not notice her as he looks at the ground thoughtfully. The gypsy crosses the stage in a determined stride, her arms gripped at her sides. The jewel she wears on her forehead catches the light for an instant; her face is a frigid mask. It is the face of the Ice Maiden, who has disguised herself to discover the boy. She approaches him, circles him several times, as if to be sure of his identity, then sits down close beside him and looks up straight into his face. The orchestra sounds a sharp chord; she grips his wrist fiercely and examines his open palm to foretell the fate she herself has planned for him.

The boy is completely passive to the strange gypsy fortuneteller. His body falls back as she circles his hand before her savagely. She rises, throws his hand away from her in a gesture of triumphant recognition, and dances before him. The boy watches as she steps with fascinating, malevolent vigor, flinging her loose black hair over her face. He responds to her exotic dynamism and comes to her. He holds the gypsy obediently while she walks forward as if she were driving her points into the ground. Now they cross the stage to the right, the gypsy whirling rapidly, the boy following and falling at her feet as she extends her leg to lash the air above him. He rises to embrace her, but she shoves him away contemptuously, then seizes him violently and passionately. The boy is obedient to her every gesture as he realizes her power to fulfill his fortune. She turns him around, stands in back of him, points her arm forward over his shoulder, and pushes him in its direction. The boy does not resist; he walks in a dream as the gypsy directs him toward his destiny. Black-out.

THIRD TABLEAU—INSIDE THE MILL: A group of peasant girls are arranged in an open triangular tableau as the lights illuminate the interior of the bride's home. The rough wood walls are decorated with wreaths; candles hang low from the ceiling; there are two large windows at the back. The scene is framed with old Swiss lace. The day of the wedding is approaching, and all of the bride's friends have gathered to prepare for the occasion. The peasant girls dance gaily to a blithe melody, led by a girl in a bright yellow skirt, whose energy and enthusiasm are expressed in precise, rapid steps.

The bride enters and dances in front of the group. Dressed all in white, she wears a small wreath of white flowers in her hair. The girls in back of her imitate her movements. The bride walks back to welcome her friends;

some of them form a circle around her. She bows, then bows to another group that surrounds her. She blows kisses to them all and exits.

The peasant girls dance again; the bride returns just before the music ends and she stands in the center of a beautifully posed group her friends form about her. The girls run off and leave the bride alone. The orchestra begins to play quietly a lovely, sweeping melody. The bride circles the room, goes to the window, looks out expectantly, but sees nothing. She is waiting for the bridegroom. She walks over to the other window, her back turned to the room. The bridegroom enters. The bride does not see him. He circles the room looking for her. She moves away from the window as if she felt his presence, but does not find him, for the boy has walked behind her. Both stand in the center of the room, their arms held out, seeking. Their backs almost touch and they move away in opposite directions to circle the room again. The boy kneels. The girls sees him, runs up behind him softly, and leans over his shoulder to welcome him playfully. He rises. Their *pas de deux* begins.

The couple cross the front of the stage together, extending their arms to the side in rhythm to the flow of the music. The bride falls back in the boy's arms. The music changes, as a clarinet states the theme of their adagio. The boy holds the girl about the waist as she dances quickly but softly, like a sylph. He lifts her as they move together, and her points continue their dance in the air. The bride kneels and watches the boy dance. Then both circle the stage. The girl beckons to him and whispers something. They stand together in the center of the stage. They bow low to each other. The boy holds out his hand and, as the orchestra states the climax of the theme, the girl takes his hand and poses in a low, deep arabesque. She rises and falls back against his arm. He raises her off the floor with low lifts in which the girl bends her knees softly. He holds her under her arms, and the girl sits on his knee, smiling happily, her legs extended before her.

The bridegroom stands aside and watches the girl dance alone to a fresh, piquant theme. She dances flirtatiously, flouncing her skirt high. She mimes her intense happiness, feigning intoxication from her joy. The black shadow of the Ice Maiden suddenly appears before her and points menacingly. The boy does not see the apparition, who disappears before the girl has rushed backward into his arms. The bride looks toward the vanished shadow and moves her hand in front of her face in innocent, unbelieving astonishment.

A pounding drum announces a sharp, accelerating dance melody. The peasant girls re-enter to take up its rhythm, and the bride and bridegroom leave the stage. The bridegroom returns to dance a short, brilliant variation. He is followed by the bride, who comes down the stage diagonally, dancing smartly on one point, extending her other leg straight out to the side with every step. She finishes her dance with a series of rapid turns that delight the whole company, then runs across the stage at full speed toward the bridegroom, who catches her daringly in mid-air.

The couple leave the stage to the dancing peasants for a moment, then return to join them in a final ensemble. At its conclusion one of the girls brings out the bride's veil and throws it playfully over her head. The girls gather about the bride and separate the two lovers. The bride leaves the stage with her playful friends. The bridegroom remains alone. The light dims.

The bridegroom turns rapidly; as he comes out of his spin, he sees on the right a girl dressed in white, her head and shoulders covered with a long white veil. As he recognizes his fiancée, he seems also to be remembering slowly and with effort that he must have known her like this always—tall, beautiful, and in white. He moves toward her, fascinated by his illusory recollection and the new loveliness she has for him. The girl does not move; she remains motionless, drawing the boy toward her with mysterious and bewitching magnetism. He stands in front of her, reaches around her strongly, and holds her tightly by the waist, his face buried in the frigid whiteness of her veil. Thus holding her, he lifts her feet off the floor; her body arches back, and he carries her walking slowly backward. Now the orchestra states fully but quietly the melody of Tchaikovsky's "None But the Lonely Heart," which was suggested softly at the beginning of the scene.

The boy lets the girl down gently and falls helpless against her. His limp body falls to the floor at her feet. The girl bows over him, opens her arms wide, takes his hand, and pulls him up as she circles about him. They move a short distance together; then the boy kneels. He stretches his arms back; the girl takes his hands. He crawls forward. The girl stands against his back, her body in arabesque, her face falling over against his. Her white veil envelopes his face in a glacier of tenderness. The tragic melody, now at its height, accompanies them as they move across the stage.

The boy falls forward on the ground. The girl bends down and covers him with her veil. He rises under it, throws the veil back over her head, and stands transfixed as he beholds her face—the face of the Ice Maiden and gypsy in one. The Ice Maiden stands regally as we saw her in the first scene, her lovely, noble head crowned with a star of shimmering crystals. The boy backs away from her in terror at his recognition, then draws close to her again in helpless, passionate longing. He rests his head on her breast. The Ice Maiden stands rigid, head back, her arms stretched out behind her. Slowly she lifts her arms and touches the boy's head with a retarded and considered gesture that seems to freeze the gentleness of her touch and turn him to ice. Now she moves her hand down the boy's trembling arm, takes his hand, and leads him away. The scene blacks out.

FOURTH TABLEAU—EPILOGUE: The lights come up on the same scene. The bride enters the room, searching for her fiancée. She circles the stage, looks out of the windows from which she has so often seen him come to the mill. He is nowhere to be found. She waves her veil over her head sadly and begins to despair. Then suddenly, in the back, the wall of the room disappears and the bride beholds in the sky a scene that makes her tremble. High up, far away in the distance, the Ice Maiden sits in the cold blue winter sky holding out her arms to the bridegroom, who strives to reach her. He stretches out his arms to the magical fairy, who seems to enfold him. They rise together in the sky. The bride kneels and, weeping, waves her wedding veil in farewell.

NOTES: At the end of 1927, when he was finishing the music of *Apollo, Leader of the Muses*, Igor Stravinsky was asked by Madame Ida Rubinstein to compose a ballet for her. Bronislava Nijinska was to be the choreographer, Alexandre Benois the designer. Stravinsky writes, in his autobiography: "The idea was that I should compose something inspired by the music of Tchaikovsky. My well-known fondness for this composer, and, still more, the fact that November, 1928, the time fixed for the performance, would mark the thirty-fifth anniversary of his death, induced me to accept the offer. It would give me an opportunity of paying my heartfelt homage to Tchaikovsky's wonderful talent.

"As I was free to choose both the subject and scenario of the ballet, I began to search for them, in view of the characteristic trend of Tchaikovsky's music, in the literature of the nineteenth century. With that aim, I turned to a great poet with a gentle, sensitive soul whose imaginative mind was wonderfully akin to that of the musician. I refer to Hans Christian Andersen, with whom in this respect Tchaikovsky had so much in common. To recall *The Sleeping Beauty, The Nutcracker, Swan Lake, Pique Dame*, and many pieces of his symphonic work is enough to show the extent of his fondness for the fantastic.

"In turning over the pages of Andersen, with which I was fairly familiar, I came across a story which I had completely forgotten that struck me as being the very thing for the idea which I wanted to express. It was the very beautiful story known to us as the 'Ice Maiden.' I chose that as my theme and worked out the story on the following lines. A fairy imprints her magic kiss on a child at birth and parts it from its mother. Twenty years later, when the youth has attained the very zenith of his good fortune, she repeats the fatal kiss and carries him off to live in supreme happiness with her ever afterwards. As my object was to commemorate the work of Tchaikovsky, this subject seemed to me to be particularly appropriate as an allegory, the Muse having similarly branded Tchaikovsky with her fatal kiss, and the magic imprint has made itself felt in all the musical creations of this great artist.

"Although I gave full liberty to painter and choreographer in the staging of my composition, my innermost desire was that it should be presented in classical form, after the manner of *Apollo*. I pictured all the fantastic roles as danced in white ballet-skirts, and the rustic scenes as taking place in a Swiss landscape. . . ."

The ballet was performed for the first time November 27, 1928, at the Opéra, Paris, with the composer conducting. It was performed in other European capitals and, in 1933, at the Colon Theatre in Buenos Aires. November 26, 1935, Frederick Ashton choreographed a new version of the ballet for the Sadler's Wells Ballet. This version, designed by Sophie Fedorovitch, featured Pearl Argyle and Harold Turner. In 1937 I staged *The Fairy's Kiss* for the American Ballet's Stravinsky Festival at the Metropolitan Opera House. This was the work's first performance in the United States.

Certain parts of the story of the ballet are hard to make clear on the stage. At the beginning of the Second Tableau, for example, how is the audience to know that the bridegroom is the child of the Prologue? Believing that everything must be clear on the stage, I have tried to indicate this in a number of ways in different revivals of the ballet, as I have also endeavored to make it obvious that the gypsy is, in reality, the fairy disguised. The finale of the ballet also presents a mechanical difficulty. Ideally, the ending should have a magical effect: the fairy should appear to be suspended and the bridegroom, just below her, must seem to be swimming through space, as it were, to reach her. At the end of Andersen's original story, the Ice Maiden drags the boy down into the lake with her, and in recent revivals I have tried to indicate that the two figures are moving together in the water, but limited audience visibility of the back of the stage has prevented this plan from attaining real success. There is no question but that the final Tableau requires a stage high and deep for the achievement of full illusion.

The Fairy's Kiss has been revived twice by the Ballet Russe de Monte Carlo: on April 10, 1940, at the Metropolitan Opera House, with a cast headed by Alexandra Danilova as the bride, André Eglevsky as the bridegroom, and Mia Slavenska as the fairy; and on February 17, 1946, at the City Center, New York, with Alexandra Danilova, Frederic Franklin, and Maria Tallchief. It was staged for the Opéra, Paris, July 2, 1947, when Tamara Toumanova, Alexandre Kaliujny, and Maria Tallchief took the principal roles. At its revival by the New York City Ballet on November 28, 1950—but for one day, the ballet's twenty-second anniversary—the leading roles in *The Fairy's Kiss* were danced by Tanaquil LeClercq, Nicholas Magallanes, Maria Tallchief, and Patricia Wilde.

The Fairy's Kiss has been called by Edwin Denby, in *Looking At the Dance*, "Ballet at its grandest. It has a range of expression that includes the brutality of the peasant dances, the frightening large mime gestures of the fortunetelling scene, the ominous speed-up of the wedding party, the hobbled tenderness of the bridal duet, the clap of thunder entrance of the veiled Fairy, the repulsive dissolution of the last scene; all of it fascinating and beautiful. Its images of destiny, its tragic illuminations are as convincing as any I know in literature . . . *Baiser de la Fée* is poetic theatre at its truest."

BALLADE

Dramatic ballet in one act. Music by Claude Debussy. Choreography by Jerome Robbins. Scenery and costumes by Boris Aronson. Costumes executed by Karinska. Lighting by Jean Rosenthal. First presented by the New York City Ballet at the City Center, New York, February 14, 1952, with Tanaquil LeClercq, Janet Reed, Nora Kaye, Roy Tobias, Robert Barnett, Louis Johnson, John Mandia, and Brooks Jackson.

This ballet's program note reminds us that a *ballade* (or *ballad*) is "a musical composition of poetic character . . . a dancing song, a poem of unknown authorship which recounts a legendary or traditional event and passes from one generation to another." The legendary or traditional event in the ballet is enacted by the legendary and traditional characters Harlequin, Columbine, and Pierrot, who find themselves in a band of other, more modern, theatrical characters. The music for *Ballade* is Debussy's flute solo *Syrinx* and the same composer's *Six Antique Epigraphs*, orchestrated by Ernest Ansermet.

Snow is falling on a quiet scene as the curtain rises. Seven people lie asleep in chairs that are grouped about the stage. In the back is a drop curtain that depicts the sun and moon surrounded by clouds of ice. The people take no notice of the snow; their bodies lie limply in the chairs, and they seem like so many rag dolls.

To the quiet music of a flute, a strolling musician enters, carrying balloons. The snow stops falling. Slowly he goes to each of the chairs and at each one he leaves a balloon. When he has distributed balloons to all seven, he watches as the hands that hold them are drawn mysteriously upward. Gradually all the figures waken and rise toward their balloons. They bow to the strolling player and look up at the balloons he has left them as he leaves the scene.

One of the girls steps out. She is dressed in Harlequin's traditional costume of varicolored diamond patches. Slowly she turns; the others move the chairs back and run about the stage with their balloons. Now they tie the balloons to the chairs and come forward to dance in a semicircle.

The rest of the group retire as three boys dance forward rapidly and, like clowns and tumbling artists, execute a rushing, circusy number. When they finish, the girl dressed as Harlequin comes forward. She reaches down, takes her foot in her hand, brings it around behind her back, and turns. Now she somersaults and her movements take on an angular quality. As the music becomes faster, she leaps wildly, circles the stage, revolves in bouncing turns, and goes back to her chair.

A girl in pink, her cheeks spotted with circles of bright red rouge, begins to dance. This is Columbine. A boy, also dressed in pink, kisses her hand. He kneels before her as she begins to dance to quick, subtle music. The girl is indifferent to the boy and wanders almost accidentally into his arms. He tries to get some reaction as he declares his love, but the girl, like a rag doll, looks at him stupidly. Finally he embraces her and kisses her throat. The girl reaches into her dress to find her heart and brings out a handful of sawdust. The astonished youth retires, and the girl sits on the floor at the left.

Now a girl representing Pierrot takes the center of the stage briefly. The melody sounds hauntingly. Pierrot collapses and dies. Two boys take up her loose, disjointed body and carry her. The others grieve. Pierrot is given a balloon and slowly she rises. She wonders at the balloon's magical force in bringing her to life again. The strange figures watch breathlessly as she ponders this mystery and makes a decision. The music stops. Pierrot stares up at the balloon, then deliberately allows it to slip through her fingers. In stunned silence her fellow actors imagine that she has sacrificed her life. Everyone watches as the balloon disappears overhead.

Forgetful of Pierrot's sacrifice, the whole troupe dances a happy ensemble. Suddenly the lights begin to go down. The strolling musician returns, and the players return to their chairs. As he takes their balloons away, each collapses and becomes lifeless again. The strolling musician stares at Pierrot, who stands alone without a balloon. Slowly he leaves the scene. Pierrot looks after him for a moment, then goes to each of the chairs, trying to waken their occupants. She cannot stir them. Snow begins to fall again, and the curtain descends as Pierrot, sad that she alone possesses a life outside the magic of the theatre, stares off into the distance.

BALLET IMPERIAL

Classic ballet in three movements. Music by Peter Ilyich Tchaikovsky. Choreography by George Balanchine. Setting and costumes by Mstislav Doboujinsky. First presented by the American Ballet at the Hunter College Playhouse, New York, May 27, 1941, with Marie-Jeanne, Gisella Caccialanza, and William Dollar in the principal roles. Revived by the Ballet Russe de Monte Carlo at the City Center, New York, February 20, 1945, with Mary Ellen Moylan, Maria Tallchief, and Nicholas Magallanes in the leading roles. Revived by the Sadler's Wells Ballet at the Royal Opera House, London, April 5, 1950, with scenery and costumes by Eugene Berman and a cast headed by Margot Fonteyn, Michael Somes, and Beryl Grey. Revived by the Ballet of La Scala, Milan, with scenery and costumes by Eugene Berman, March 25, 1952, with Olga Amati, Gilda Maiocchi, and Giulio Perugini in the principal roles.

Great ballets of the past are directly associated with great composers of the past. *The Sleeping Beauty*, the masterwork of the great nineteenth-century choreographer Marius Petipa, survives not only for its dancing, but also for its music. Petipa created more than sixty full-length ballets during a half century of work as Ballet Master at the Imperial Russian Theatre. Few of these works are performed today. This is not because the dancing in these ballets was not good; it is because their music was not good enough to inspire the dancing to new heights. Audiences have wished to forget the bad music and, consequently, the dances that went with it.

Since the death of Petipa, in 1910, much has happened to the classical dancing he developed into so high a form in his famous ballets. The basic vocabulary is the same, but we have added new words, new phrases; classical dancing today is much more difficult, more complex, more intricate, more demanding. Oftentimes people are inclined to think that the great dancers of the past were incomparable and that dancers today are as nothing beside them. This is not true. The great dancers of the past were incomparable for what they did. Today we do something else.

Ballet Imperial is a contemporary tribute to Petipa, "the father of the classic ballet," and to Tchaikovsky, his greatest composer. The ballet is set to Tchaikovsky's *Piano Concerto No. 2, in G.* It is a dance ballet and has no story.

FIRST MOVEMENT—ALLEGRO BRILLANTE: The orchestra and piano introduce the opening theme, a brilliant and noble melody. The piano develops this theme alone, and a quick rush on the strings signals the second theme. The curtain rises. Eight couples in classical costume stand in a diagonal, the boys facing the girls some distance apart. They begin to dance. The stage frame is draped with blue velvet trimmed with ermine. We are in the room of a palace. In contrast to this sumptuous warmth, in the distance there is a view of the snow-covered Fortress of Peter and Paul. The royal gates that direct our eyes to this view are embellished with the imperial eagle. The dancing is quick and formal, bright and dignified.

Eight girls join the eight couples, and after them comes a soloist, a beautiful young girl who prepares the stage for the ballerina. The ballerina enters, dances to a piano cadenza, and by her loveliness in performance convinces us that we are watching a queen among dancers. At first she dances alone, finishing her variation in open rapid turns that encircle the stage. The music is softer, has now a stately romantic quality, and the ballerina dances with a cavalier. Now the ballerina and the *corps de ballet* leave the stage and the soloist performs a *pas de trois* with two boys. The second theme has returned with the same signal from the strings, it has merged with the first, and the music gathers to a flourishing finish. The ballerina and the *corps de ballet* dance to this music with young, regal splendor, and the movement is over.

SECOND MOVEMENT—ANDANTE NON TROPPO: After a brief introduction, the piano plays alone the principal theme. This is music of sentiment, pathos, and high feeling—slow, almost retarded, in its romantic commitment. A solo violin plays the theme accompanied by the piano. The ballerina enters with her cavalier. Eight girls form a maze through which the ballerina and her partner move. Now she and her partner are lovers. They appear to be happy, but then the man pleads with her intently and we understand that their love is not perfect. But soon the ballerina responds to her lover's plea and dances with tender intimacy. The *corps de ballet* dance protectingly around the couple and lead them gently into the wings.

THIRD MOVEMENT—ALLEGRO CON FUOCO: The music is gay and assertive with a fiery brightness and crispness. The ballerina is carried in high on the shoulders of her partner. He sets her down softly, and she dances with ravishing quickness to the brilliant music. She and her partner leave the stage for a moment to the *corps de ballet*, but return again and again to lead the dancing. The ballerina's partner dances a variation, the soloist is seen briefly leading the crowded stage of dancers, and the ballerina comes back to finish with her court the final, electric flourish of ensemble movement.

LE BEAU DANUBE

Ballet in one act. Music by Johann Strauss. Choreography by Leonide Massine. Scenery and costumes by V. and E. Polunin, after Constantin Guys. Costumes by Comte Etienne de Beaumont. Book by Leonide Massine. First presented in a two-act version by Comte Etienne de Beaumont's Soirée de Paris, Paris, May 17, 1924, with Lydia Lopokova as the *Street Dancer*. First presented in the final one-act version by the Ballet Russe de Monte Carlo at the Théâtre de Monte Carlo, April 15, 1933, with Alexandra Danilova as the *Street Dancer*, Leonide Massine as the *Hussar*, Tatiana Riabouchinska as the *Daughter*, Irina Baronova as the *First Hand*, and David Lichine as the *King of the Dandies*. First presented in the United States by the Ballet Russe de Monte Carlo at the St. James Theatre, New York, December 22, 1933, with the same principals.

This famous character ballet takes place in a public park, the Prater, in old Vienna. Nowadays we are somewhat used to ballets that are set in parks —where policemen romance with governesses, where children rollick and get into mischief, and where the perennial gigolo tries to interest the young, innocent girl. These are all adaptations of *Le Beau Danube* (*The Beautiful Danube*) and a tribute to its popularity. Roger Désormière arranged and orchestrated the pieces by Johann Strauss that make up the ballet's score.

The curtain rises on a charming wooded park in Vienna. It is Sunday afternoon, about a hundred years ago. A gardener is tidying up the grounds, a young artist is painting at an easel; we hear the sound of a Strauss waltz and we believe the pretty picture we see on the stage. Strollers soon enter and enjoy the beauty of the scene: a family with two daughters, ladies of the town, seamstresses and dandies.

The artist is attracted to the first hand, the seamstress, and flirts with her as he sketches her portrait. The girl is pleased with the artist until the King of the Dandies rushes in and whisks her away from him.

Now a dashing hussar, in immaculate uniform, promenades with one of the daughters of the family. He is deferential to her family and is apparently formally engaged to her, for when he dances a mazurka with the girl their romance appears to be permanently happy. They leave the scene hand in hand.

A small band of street entertainers enter and set up to amuse the crowd that has gathered. The manager of the troupe points with pride to his principal artiste, a dancer, and the beautiful girl begins a lively solo that thrills the crowd. The manager and an athlete with bulging muscles join her; the dance becomes hilarious and everyone applauds them.

The hussar and his fiancée stroll back into the park at this point, and the hussar is embarrassed to see his past catch up with him. The street dancer instantly claims him as a former devoted lover and, to his fiancée's horror, pretends that the hussar has deserted her! The poor girl swoons during this scene of simulated jealousy and her family escort her out of the park, vowing vengeance on the ne'er-do-well hussar. The street dancer, not to be outdone by her rival, pretends to swoon also.

The hussar is distressed at what has happened, but he could hardly control the whims of the street dancer and there is nothing else for him but to take up with her again! The crowd wanders off and they are alone. The first familiar bars of the *Blue Danube* Waltz are heard. The hussar is moved to dance; quietly and slowly the music accompanies his recollection of his romance with the dancer, and he opens his arms to her. He waits, not moving. She too remembers. She feels false jealousy no longer, and they begin to dance, their initial restrained steps building gradually to an ebullient and joyful whirling with the persistent swell of the waltz.

But just as the former lovers seem to be reunited, the hussar's fiancée returns. She has run off from her raging family and insists on claiming the hussar: after all, she loves him. Why should she give him up so easily? The hussar, who has never seen such determination in a woman, is charmed by her completely and again forgets the street dancer. The *Blue Danube* has ended.

The young girl's family race in and try to separate their daughter from the fickle hussar, but the younger daughter steps in, cajoles and persuades, and tears turn to laughter. The hussar is properly deferential again to his fiancée's family; the father blesses the handsome couple; and the crowd in the park dance in celebration of the happy resolve. The street dancer, too, congratulates them with a final display of high-spirited dancing, and the charming park becomes a place where nothing unpleasant can ever happen.

BEAUTY AND THE BEAST

Dramatic ballet in two scenes. Music by Maurice Ravel. Choreography by John Cranko. Scenery and costumes by Margaret Kaye. First presented by the Sadler's Wells Theatre Ballet at the Sadler's Wells Theatre, London, December 20, 1949, with Patricia Miller as *Beauty* and David Poole as the *Beast*. First presented in the United States by the Sadler's Wells Theatre Ballet at the Denver Auditorium, Denver, Colorado, November 14, 1951, with the same cast.

Ravel's *Mother Goose* Suite is made up of five movements, each based on a famous fairy story. The familiar tale of "Beauty and the Beast" inspired the fourth movement of the suite, but the English choreographer John Cranko has been inspired to use this dramatic theme as an accompaniment to almost all of Ravel's score.* The ballet is an intimate drama, actually a long *pas de deux* for the two principal characters.

The curtain rises soon after the music has begun. The scene is the forest where the beast is king. The light, almost transparent, cloth on which the trees of the forest are painted is cut into strips, giving a jungle effect. The light is dim. The beast reclines alone in the forest. He seems to be sleeping; he wakens and rubs his eyes with his long, clawlike hands. Then we see that he is weeping. His whole body shakes with violent sobbing.

Behind him, a beautiful young girl enters the forest. The beast does not see her, and the girl, unaware that she has happened upon a dangerous wood, moves in and out among the trees. The beast rises, sensing a strange presence. He wishes to welcome the girl, but knows he will frighten her. As her back is turned, he reaches out to her plaintively. The girl moves off into the forest, and the beast follows her. She begins to feel that she is not alone.

The ragged trees rise, and the scene changes to another part of the forest. Here in the center of the jungle is a dark clearing. A little light penetrates the darkness through an entrance formed by curving trees. Here the girl enters. Now she is thoroughly lost and frightened and she does a little dance to allay her fear—a kind of whistling-in-the-dark variation. Gradually she tires and sits down to rest. Soon she falls to the ground and sleeps.

Light begins to fill the jungle through the grottolike entrance formed by the trees. The girl wakens and looks about. She observes birds in the trees, dances happily, gesturing lovingly to the surrounding forest. She ap-

*The section *"Laideronette, Impératrice des Pagodas"* is omitted in the ballet.

proaches one of the trees to pick fruit. As she takes the fruit, she sees that it is held in the hairy paws of the beast, who has been observing her secretly.

The girl faints. The beast picks her up and holds her carefully. The girl sobs in his arms and releases herself. She attempts to flee the forest, but at the entrance, branches of trees reach out to restrain her. The door of the cage has been shut, and the girl looks at the beast in terror.

The beast tries to convince her that he means no harm. Gently he kneels before her and holds out a red flower. Again the girl wishes to escape. The beast grovels on the ground, then crawls helplessly. He drops the flower and begins to cry. The girl goes over to him, but she is still too frightened to indicate her pity. She turns to run through the entrance, where the confining branches have disappeared. She passes through, out into the light, but her hand still holds the side of the entrance: she is uncertain and returns.

She dances back into the jungle. Now she is completely unafraid. She stands over the beast and helps him rise. He lifts her high in his arms and holds her so that she almost stands above him. The girl reaches down and holds his face in her hands. The music rushes magically; the beast releases her; and we see that his face is no longer the fierce mask of a ferocious beast, but the face of a handsome young man. The girl caresses his face, and the two lovers dance a flowing *pas de deux* in which the changed beast holds the girl secure as her feet gently touch the ground. At the end, the lovers reach out to each other and the curtain falls.

LES BICHES

Ballet in one act. Music by Francis Poulenc. Choreography by Bronislava Nijinska. Scenery and costumes by Marie Laurencin. First presented by Diaghilev's Ballets Russes at the Théâtre de Monte Carlo, January 6, 1924, with a cast that included Vera Nemtchinova and Anatole Vilzak, Alexandra Danilova, Bronislava Nijinska, Felia Dubrovska, Ninette de Valois, Alice Nikitina, Lubov Tchernicheva, Nicholas Zverev, and Leon Woicikowski. First presented in the United States by the Marquis de Cuevas' Grand Ballet at the Century Theatre, New York, November 13, 1950, with a cast headed by Marjorie Tallchief, George Skibine, and Olga Adabache.

Two ballet companies have preferred to call this ballet *The House Party* and *The Gazelles.** It is certainly about a house party. There is a hostess, a woman considerably older than her youthful guests; she seeks to form an attachment with one of the young men at her party. The relations of some of her guests are similarly romantic. The ballet thus has a romantic theme rather than a specific plot; the characters are dancers. The ballet is in eight

*Literally, *les biches* means *the hinds*, but colloquially it also means simply *girls*, or *young ladies*.

parts, corresponding to the divisions of the score: "Rondo," "Chanson dansée," "Adagietto," "Jeux," "Rag Mazurka," "Andantino," "Chanson dansée," "Finale."

Before the curtain rises, the orchestra plays a short introduction; slow at first, the music becomes smartly quick and pulsating and reminds us of the vitality of youth. The curtain rises on an enormous room that bears the mark of the fashionable interior decorator. Painted blue curtains at the back enclose a window. A large blue couch stands at the rear. Twelve girls enter and dance pertly to the rhythm of the music. Their long, cool pink dresses whirl about them in innocent contrast to the sophistication of their steps. The girls kneel, rise, circle on point, bend back seductively, and choose partners as the music hastens to a brisk finish. They run off in gushing, schoolgirl fashion.

Three boys in bathing trunks enter to the strong, choppy beat of the "Chanson dansée." They dance in a line; their movements are assertive and angular. They thrust out their chests and display their biceps in a dance that stylizes athleticism. The two boys on the side imitate the turns of the dancer in the center. They kneel. The twelve girls run in. The boys continue their dance for the girls' benefit, while the girls try to attract them. They surround each of the three boys, then stand in a semicircle behind them. The boys kneel before the girls, but seem to be disinterested.

A girl dressed like a page boy in white tights, blue tunic, and white gloves enters on the right and interrupts the scene. She crosses the stage on point, holding her hand up stiffly, as if she were on some secret errand. She takes no notice of the guests, but the boys are fascinated. The girl leaves and, abandoning all hope of winning the boys, four of the girls flounce away and arrange themselves decorously on the sofa. The others continue their flirtation with the boys, who abandon them again when the girl enters as before. One of the youths is attracted to her; she dances off, and the flighty girls take up with the other two boys. The strange girl recrosses the room, but pauses this time to dance briefly. Her hands are joined and she holds out her arms as she poses; her movements are softly angular. Two of the boys have gone off with the girls in pink, and one of the boys watches the girl in blue as she dances alone, apparently oblivious of his presence. He comes up behind her as she finishes her variation, comes close and holds her arms; the two exit together.

The two boys return with the girls and begin a rollicking game. The boys slide the couch forward. They stand on it, lifting the girls over it; then the girls dance across the couch one by one and hop off the arm onto the floor. The boys walk off. The sofa is turned with its back to the front, and the girls hide behind it as the girl in blue re-enters with her partner. They dance briefly and exit when they see they are being watched. The boys come back to find the girls. They move the couch back near the window, and all leave the stage.

A woman in an elaborate yellow dress enters and crosses the stage with mannered steps. This is the hostess. She brandishes a long cigarette holder pointedly, as if she were posing for a stilted advertisement, and at the same time nervously belies her pose by playing with her long pearl necklace. Her hands are constantly in motion; she cannot remain still for an instant. Her dance is the dance of a woman who can never imagine herself alone; it is the perpetual and desperate performance of a woman who has to be seen to appreciate herself. No one interrupts her parody of a youthful dance, and she stops. She arranges herself languidly on the couch.

The two young men enter suddenly. They dance proudly, asserting their masculine strength. They approach the hostess, stomping their feet. She is delighted and joins them in a dance to the "Rag Mazurka." Vigorous at first, their *pas de trois* slows down. The hostess is enamored of both her partners. Both boys offer their arms. She doesn't know which to choose. She takes a chance and breaks free. Both boys follow her off.

The girl in blue meets her partner in the center of the stage for a *pas de deux* to the "Andantino." Their gestures and steps are strangely discontinuous; they move, pause, move again—formal, but intimate. Their dance ends as the boy holds the girl straight in his arms; then, with an intricate twist of both their bodies, the girl is poised high on his shoulder. They leave the stage.

To a sprightly tune two young girls enter and dance a lively duet in which each tries to outdo the other in expressing their attachment. Their dance becomes secretive when they imagine they are not alone. They blush and exit hurriedly.

In different groups that turn rapidly as they cross the stage, the entire ensemble gradually returns for the finale—first the girls, then the boys, followed by the hostess and the girl in blue. All romantic attachments seem to be forgotten as the ensemble joins together for a final fling.

NOTES: One of the popular ballets of the Diaghilev era, *Les Biches* is regarded by its choreographer as the modern equivalent of *Les Sylphides*. It has been revived since its first production by the Markova-Dolin Ballet, when Alicia Markova danced the part of the girl in blue and Anton Dolin danced her partner; and by the Grand Ballet of the Marquis de Cuevas, where the production has met with critical and popular approval, both in Europe and New York.

The composer, Francis Poulenc, noted in the English magazine *Ballet* (Volume 2, No. 4) that *Les Biches* "is a ballet in which you may see nothing at all or into which you may read the worst . . . In this ballet, as in certain of Watteau's pictures, there is an atmosphere of wantonness which you sense if you are corrupted but which an innocent-minded girl would not be conscious of."

It is to be noted that among the many dancers in the original production of *Les Biches* who afterwards became famous as ballerinas was a soloist who was to become famous in another sense: Ninette de Valois, who has been director of the Sadler's Wells Ballet since its inception.

BILLY THE KID

Ballet in one act. Choreography by Eugene Loring. Music by Aaron Copland. Book by Lincoln Kirstein. Scenery and costumes by Jared French. First presented by Ballet Caravan at the Chicago Opera House, Chicago, October 16, 1938, with Eugene Loring as *Billy*, Marie-Jeanne as the *Mother* and *Sweetheart*, Lew Christensen as *Pat Garrett*, and Todd Bolender as *Alias*.

The story of Billy the Kid is already a legend in America, a part of the larger legend we know as the Opening of the West. The facts known about him— that his real name was William H. Bonney; that he was born in New York City in 1859; was taken to Kansas when he was three; killed his first man in Silver City, New Mexico, when he was twelve; and by the time he was hunted down and shot, at the age of twenty-one, had killed a man for every year of his life—these facts remind us of a gangster movie. But actually these facts do not tell us the whole story of the Kid. They do not tell us that, although Billy the Kid was regarded as the most dangerous desperado of his time, he was loved and admired as much as he was feared, and that the Far West after the Civil War was a place where these emotions could interchange and resolve—to make of his life the heroic myth it has since become. This ballet is not, therefore, a simple biography of a wild West killer: it is the story of the life of Billy the Kid as it became a part of the life of his time.

PROLOGUE: The first, slow notes of the music are subdued and eerie, like sounds in the wilderness at night. The curtain rises. Across the front of the stage a spotlight shines, making a path of brilliant orange light. The rest of the stage is suffused in a semidark glow, as if bathed in the light of the golden sun. An arid khaki-colored desert and tall, branching cacti are seen in the distance. From the right, a man dressed in a cowboy outfit steps boldly into the path of light. Later we shall learn that this is Pat Garrett, the sometime friend of Billy the Kid who becomes sheriff and kills him. But at the moment he is simply any American pioneer, moving westward toward the blaze of the setting sun. He moves stiffly, with determination; for each step forward he will take none back. Then his progress becomes a dance, the movements of which remind us of the frontiersman's work: he circles his arm high over his head to lasso invisible cattle; he pulls back roughly on invisible reins to halt a covered wagon, then drives the horses on with a lash of a whip; he kneels motionless, gun pointed, to catch the imaginary Indian. The music gains in strength with his vigorous movements. It becomes stronger still, as Garrett is followed by another man and a woman. The man copies every one of his leader's gestures, while the woman sets a dance pattern for the pioneer mother who rocks her children to sleep even when danger surrounds her. Other couples enter, and the orchestra builds gradually to sound a mighty processional as the pioneer figures follow their leader in this formalized march to the West. Now Garrett thrusts his arms forward, pushing back the frontier. He faces directly into the light. He pirouettes rapidly, spine in the air, and repeats these movements as all the men in the caravan follow his lead. All the dancers catch the full vitality of the music, which itself pushes forward to a resistless, persistent climax. Then, at its fullest volume, the music is cut off sharply. There is a black-out.

STREET SCENE: When the lights come up again, the backdrop still depicts, as it will continue to do, the same arid desert, but before the curtain move a group of particular characters—not pioneers simply—who place this episode in the hot and sunny main street of an early Western town, just north of the border. Woodwinds play an old Western tune that the rest of the orchestra takes up gaily and playfully. A smiling, sinuous Mexican in a wide-brimmed hat struts about, pawing the street with his boots like a tame but unbridled stallion. Pioneer women, dressed for the town in close-fitting bonnets, pass him by, their arms crooked to carry invisible burdens. The Mexican ignores them. Cowboys ride across the scene, spurring on the imaginary horses they straddle. Three dancing girls enter, their hands on their tightly corseted hips in an impudent attitude. Two women look them up and down and, noting their high-buttoned gold shoes and garish red tights, turn up their noses in disapproval, sniff at the air, and walk away. Eight cowboys ride on, and there is a short rodeo. At the end three of them stop and take up with the dance-hall girls. A group of lovely Mexican girls come onto the scene, and now the street seethes with activity. The people stand about, some talking, some flirting, others going about their private business.

Then suddenly the music is quiet. An oboe sounds a theme, and on the left a small, attractive woman comes in. She is dressed in city clothes and is clearly a stranger to the community. A big, gangling boy, dressed only in overalls and a straw hat, hangs onto her skirts, and they move through the crowd. This is Billy the Kid. The boy looks about and appears to want to stop, but his mother walks on ahead and they exit. The Mexican and the four Mexican girls dance together briefly, and then the Kid and his mother return. This time the Kid shows off his strength by softly lifting his mother around for several measures. She pushes his cheek to tell him how silly he is, and he turns his face away, blushing, but he persists at the game and the two waltz off.

Meanwhile something has happened to the crowd. They stand closely packed together, watching an argument between the Mexican and a man in red. The argument becomes a fight. They hit each other in slow motion, neither falling. The music accompanies their blows with retarded rhythm that increases in volume and speed as the fight becomes serious. The people in the crowd begin to sense that they should stand back. Now, as a trumpet sounds the theme militantly, the Kid enters with his mother. Both of them are fascinated by the brawl and stand on the fringe of the crowd. Just as they join the group, the Mexican pulls a gun. The man in red turns quickly to defend himself and steps against the crowd, right next to Billy and his mother. The Mexican fires. He misses. Billy's mother doubles up in agony. She falls against her son, who stands transfixed, staring straight ahead, not comprehending. She grasps his arm, slides down slowly to the ground, and dies. The people are horrified, but they, too, are motionless. They remain still and shocked as the Kid shakes off his dream, grabs a knife, and dashes over to the Mexican. Billy kills him with one quick stab in the back. He topples over. Everyone steps back, unbelieving. Billy looks about wildly, wondering where to go. Pat Garrett steps in to help him, but the Kid ignores him and runs off. Already he has chosen his way.

One of the men stoops to pick up the body of the Kid's mother, and the whole crowd leans over in unison, expressing the common grief. Another man kneels down beside the dead Mexican, throws him over his shoulder, and carries him off. But the Mexican will reappear. He becomes Alias, a character of many disguises who haunts the Kid constantly throughout his life and finally helps to kill him.

The crowd begins to disperse. Couples walk away, shaking their heads, still stunned by the two murders. But instead of leaving the stage, they mill about, circling slowly, and we see after a few minutes that perhaps they are not the same men and women who saw Billy the Kid's first crime. The men lift their women affectionately, just as Billy lifted his mother, but everyone is wary and suspicious. The people have changed. They have grown older and, as we have been watching them, years have passed in the street. Finally, one by one, the couples leave and the stage is empty.

THE DESERT: The Kid enters in the back. He is no longer a child. He is dressed in black and white striped riding breeches, boots, a wide-brimmed hat; there is a skull on his shirt pocket. He dances alone. In this dance we understand a little of how the Kid has grown up. The proud pose that begins and ends the dance is confidently self-assertive, and in between the Kid performs a series of difficult movements with ferocity rather than grace. He stomps loudly with his heavy boots, circles an imaginary foe with his gun ready to fire, spins swiftly in the air, lands, and kicks out at his victim. He is going through the only vocabulary he possesses, and we realize that all of his life, every waking moment, is a practiced preparation for the next time he will have to kill. His dance gesture for shooting is a quick aim at the target, then a spin in the air that matches the speed of a bullet, and finally a vicious kick. It is the gesture of a man who hates his dead foe and the whole world. And there follows inevitably the same pose of self-assertion. Never does this man doubt that he has done the right thing, never has he supposed himself guilty of a crime. Shooting happens to be his way of living: a murder is just like lighting a cigarette.

As the Kid nears the end of his soliloquy, he is interrupted by the arrival of a small posse. Three men canter across the stage in formation, circle, and try to close in on the Kid. He hides. Then he aims, spins, and kicks. The leader of the three men falls dead. The Kid prances slowly and softly, then draws himself up to his full height and stands triumphant. The scene blacks out.

A spotlight at the front of the stage comes on. Sitting close to the footlights, around a campfire, the Kid and Pat Garrett are playing cards. Garrett is now sheriff, but still a friend to the Kid. The light from the fire makes enormous silhouettes of their figures against the backdrop. The orchestra plays a quiet, wistful melody. The Kid shuffles the cards and deals. The two men draw their cards. A man and two cowgirls, all friends of Billy, approach the fire. The man stoops down to watch the card game. Garrett is distracted for an instant, but turns back to find the Kid cheating. He protests. The Kid is patient with him at first, denies cheating, and attempts to humor him. Pat continues to protest, but when he sees that the Kid will not accept his friendship, will not even admit to overt cheating, he rides off into the night. Billy's three friends gather about the fire and take up the cards while the Kid stands aside. His rage mounts. Pat has got the better of him. He stomps angrily, regretting that he did not kill his friend. The group at the fire turn and stare at him; they are frightened at what he may do. But the Kid does not have time to act. Shooting is heard in the distance, and before he can flee, the stage fills with people. The drums boom with gunfire as Pat Garrett leads a posse on in pursuit of the Kid. Billy moves to defend himself, shoots wildly as his friends gather about him and his attackers fall on their faces to protect themselves. A fierce gun battle ensues, during which the Kid continues to shoot out indiscriminately at all comers. He and his friends are hemmed in by two lines of gunfire. They are all killed except Billy. As he is about to fire another round, he trips over the body of one of his own men. Two men move in to hold him. One of them is Alias. The Kid kills Alias. The other is Pat Garrett. Pat is quick: he sticks a gun in the Kid's back and rides him off to jail. The Kid does not seem to care in the least.

The posse that has helped capture Billy—cowgirls and cowboys—now join together to celebrate and dance joyfully. In the midst of their frolic, the Kid's sweetheart, a beautiful Mexican girl, walks in and tries to find her lover. No one pays any attention to her. She leaves the scene disconsolate. The celebration is blacked out.

THE JAIL: Billy stands on one foot, shuffling cards. Naked above the waist, he wears a kerchief about his neck, arm bands, and black riding togs over white tights. His jailer, Alias, stands at his side, ready to receive his cards. Billy bides his time, shuffles the cards slowly, and shifts to the other leg. The jailer grows impatient and turns away for an instant. Billy moves openly to grab his gun, as if the jailer expected him to. The jailer, of course, sees the move but ignores it. He suggests that it is all part of the game and that Billy won't do anything wrong. He walks away. The Kid sneaks up on him softly and this time does grab his gun. The jailer turns back, expecting the Kid to hand it over. The Kid laughs. He kills the jailer and stands again triumphant. Black-out.

THE DESERT: The Kid gallops across the stage to his hide-out. He disappears. A posse follows, but they are unable to pick up the trail. Billy enters again, screened by two Mexican girls, who stand between him and the posse. Alias, now disguised as an Indian guide, leads him away. The Kid arrives at a quiet spot, and Alias leaves him. Pat Garrett and his riders pass by, but see nothing. Billy takes his hat off and undresses to go to sleep. He is so tired he seems to be asleep already. He crouches on the ground to the right and stacks his clothes automatically, as if in a dream. His sweetheart enters on the left, behind his back. She dances on point, formally. He does not turn and see her, but looks up, seeing her in his mind's eye. He looks back down at his clothes. The girl touches his shoulder and poses briefly. He stirs, first swings his right leg out and back from his crouching position—a movement in stylized keeping with the girl's remote intimacy. She stands close beside him, but he is never aware of her real presence. He rises, stretches; the girl holds onto him and poses again beautifully, and they begin a short *pas de deux* to a sensuous waltz. He lifts her gently and swings her body slowly, not looking at her at all; he might be dancing with any girl and she with any man. Almost immediately he abandons her and goes back to stretch out to sleep. The girl dances off as quietly as she came, with no protest. The dream is over.

Pat Garrett, led by Alias, comes in and watches Billy asleep. Billy has not heard them, but wakes up as if warned by something. He reaches for his gun, holds it ready. The night is black: he sees nothing. For an instant he is afraid. Garrett and Alias stand stock-still, holding their breath. Billy calls out "¿*Quien es*?" ("Who is it?"), his voice hoarse with fear. There is no answer. He waits. Still no sound. He laughs to himself, silently. To reassure himself, he laughs harder; his body shakes with laughter. He stops, takes out a cigarette, strikes a match, and illuminates his face for a flickering moment. Garrett fires. Billy falls. He is dead.

Long-robed Mexican women enter and stand over his body. They pass by slowly, mourning, to music of lamentation, and the light fades.

EPILOGUE: The setting sun shines across the stage, and Pat Garrett walks in boldly, as he did at the beginning of the ballet, leading a host of pioneers. All march facing west, then turn back east, then west again, as the music impels them forward.

BLUEBEARD

Comic ballet in two prologues, four scenes, and three interludes. Music by Jacques Offenbach. Choreography by Michel Fokine. Book by Michel Fokine. Scenery and costumes by Marcel Vertès. First presented by Ballet Theatre at the Palacio de Bellas Artes, Mexico City, Mexico, October 27, 1941, with a cast headed by Anton Dolin as *Bluebeard*, Alicia Markova as *Hermilia*, Irina Baronova as *Boulotte*, Ian Gibson as *Prince Sapphire*, Antony Tudor as *King Bobiche*, Lucia Chase as *Queen Clementine*, Miriam Golden, Jeannette Lauret, Nora Kaye, Rosella Hightower, and Maria Karnilova as *Wives of Bluebeard*, and Dimitri Romanov, Donald Saddler, Annabelle Lyon, Jerome Robbins, and Hugh Laing as the *Queen's Lovers*. First presented in the United States by Ballet Theatre at the Forty-fourth Street Theatre, New York, November 12, 1941, with the same principals.

Bluebeard is a comedy with a double plot. Its characters are everywhere at once, and if you don't have a clear idea of who they are and what they're up to, the ballet doesn't turn out to be as funny as it might be. The music, arranged and orchestrated by Antal Dorati, is taken from Offenbach's operetta *Barbe-Bleue* and other scores by that composer. The time is the beginning of the sixteenth century; the place is the mythical kingdom of King Bobiche.

FIRST PROLOGUE: There is a rousing, thumping overture. The curtain rises. King Bobiche, a tottering old man in purple robes and ruby crown, enters the scene carrying an infant. This is his daughter, Hermilia, who must be exiled because she is not a son. The old king doesn't know quite how to go about this, but he is determined that the child's birth shall be kept secret. Count Oscar, his chancellor, brings on a basket. The dejected monarch secures a necklace about the child's throat to identify her royal lineage; the two men place her carefully into the basket and sneak off to set her adrift in the river. Black-out.

SECOND PROLOGUE: Count Bluebeard sticks his head through the curtains and steps out quickly. He tweaks his beard, rolls his eyes, smacks his thigh, and appears to be a real devil of a fellow. He embraces a girl who comes along and kisses her so passionately that she collapses. This is his first wife. The same thing happens to two other maidens. A fourth girl is so overcome by the mere sight of Bluebeard that she falls in a trance before he can grab her. The fifth wife drinks with her husband. When she dies of the poison prepared by Bluebeard's henchman, Popoloni, Bluebeard stands over her body with an eager and how-was-that-for-killing-them-off leer.

ACT ONE — THE PALACE OF KING BOBICHE: The drop curtain rises on a medieval castle. Huge battlements rise up in the distance. It is night, some eighteen years after King Bobiche cast his daughter into the stream. On the right is a garden bench.

Queen Clementine dances in, followed by a page of the court. The page immediately begins to make love to the queen on the garden bench. The queen does not seem to care in the least. Bobiche interrupts them, parts the two lovers as if he'd spent his life dealing with his wife's infidelities, and then storms about with pretentious jealousy.

The queen pleads with him, but the king is adamant and orders that the page be hanged. When the poor lad is dragged off by the king's soldiers, the king chases his queen about the garden. They disappear for a moment. By the time the queen returns, two more suitors, dashing Spaniards with castanets and guitars, are ready to pay court to her. She is enchanted and watches with pleasure as the two men draw swords and fight for her affection. The two men readily see, however, that the queen is generous and can love them both. They put down their swords and alternately she kisses them as she joins them in a *pas de trois*.

Again the king interrupts and again we have tears, royal insistence, and an order for two more executions. This process goes on until five of the queen's many lovers have been caught in the act and sent off to be hanged. But still the king is not satisfied. He can certainly not expect his wife to love him and his mind goes back to the daughter he might have loved so much. He turns his back on the queen and weeps. He must get his daughter back, if by some miracle she is still alive!

The king orders his chancellor to search every corner of the kingdom for Hermilia and then condescendingly takes the hand of the queen. Members of the court kneel as the royal pair leave the garden. The drop curtain falls.

FIRST INTERLUDE — A CITY STREET: On his way to carry out the king's order, Count Oscar encounters the lovers of the queen, who are being led by their executioner to the gallows. He takes pity on them and inquires if they have any money. Luckily, they have. Good old Oscar empties their pockets and pardons them. The five men dance for joy while the chancellor counts his money.

ACT TWO — THE COUNTRYSIDE: With a roll of the drums, the curtain rises on a bright scene in the country. Scarecrows look out over the wheat fields in the distance, and the sun shines with an intense, glowing yellow. Peasant girls and boys dance together happily, circling and forming a chain, moving in vigorous, youthful harmony. One of the girls we notice right away because she is the prettiest of them all and because everyone seems to admire her. This is Floretta, in reality Hermilia, the daughter of King

Bobiche. As if this weren't enough, the shepherd with whom she dances a romantic *pas de deux* is actually no shepherd at all but Prince Sapphire!

As Floretta sits on her shepherd's knee, a stunning blond girl comes in and berates the shepherd. She brags of her jealousy in a big emotional display, stamps her foot at Floretta, and the two lovers fly from her rage. Boulotte follows them.

Popoloni, the old alchemist who has helped Bluebeard kill off his wives, comes onto the scene. He tells the peasant girls that Bluebeard needs a new wife and that he will choose one of them for his bride. Bluebeard follows him almost immediately in an absurd chariot, and the girls quake at the sight of him. A few of the more courageous girls surround him, while others manage to form a line. Bluebeard looks the girls over one by one as if he were examining fresh meat. He doesn't like what he sees and pouts. As all the girls circle him, Boulotte re-enters. Bluebeard is just another man to her. She smacks him on the back, tweaks his beard, and treats him as if he were a rough and ready peasant. Ready Bluebeard obviously is: no woman has been so bold with him in years. He dances with her and soon proposes. Boulotte instantly consents, and Bluebeard carries her to his chariot. All wave as they exit.

Now the two plots of the ballet cross. Count Oscar, the chancellor, enters with one of the king's men. He is searching for the king's lost daughter. Popoloni engages Oscar in conversation, and as they talk, Floretta and her shepherd pass by. The shepherd bids the girl a hurried good-by as soon as he sees the count, who would expose his disguise. Count Oscar approaches her, asks politely to see her necklace, and Floretta is revealed as Princess Hermilia! Floretta fears that her shepherd might not love a Princess and wants to make sure of his affections. But, of course, Prince Sapphire is off sulking with similar thoughts. The drop curtain falls.

SECOND INTERLUDE: Bluebeard and Boulotte are racing across the stage to celebrate their marriage when their chariot passes Count Oscar and Hermilia. The fickle Bluebeard eyes the princess, and already he has had enough of the bouncing blonde. He must marry her, he decides, and vows to set a new plot in motion.

ACT THREE — A CELLAR IN BLUEBEARD'S CASTLE: The scene is dark as a dungeon. This is the laboratory of the alchemist Popoloni. On the left, at a table, chemicals burst into flame as he mixes them together. He chuckles to himself, delighted that his master has given him a new project. On the right are five vaults, each bearing the name of one of Bluebeard's dead wives! A sixth grave, as yet uncovered, is ready to receive another wife.

Bluebeard stalks in to give Popoloni his final orders: Boulotte must die! Boulotte enters and slaps him on the back. Bluebeard, out of all patience, tells Popoloni to be hasty. Boulotte takes one look at the five graves and clasps Bluebeard frantically in her arms. He pushes her off and Boulotte rolls about on the floor in despair. She rises and hangs on Bluebeard's neck, pleading with him to save her. "No!" he answers, and leaves her alone with her poisoner.

Boulotte goes over to Popoloni and tries to flirt with him. But the old man pushes her off his knee and tells her to leave off. He tells her that he has something for her and bids her drink from two goblets. Boulotte looks toward the open grave and refuses to drink. When Popoloni turns his back for a moment, she picks up a goblet from his table and drinks that one, instead. Poor girl, all the goblets are filled with the same poison! She falls to the floor.

Popoloni pretends grief; he is joined in his sorrow by Bluebeard, whose body shakes with sobs. He kneels beside his beloved and then, suddenly, he is up dancing as if he is absolutely delighted! He leaps over the body and dashes off in pursuit of the Princess Hermilia.

Old Popoloni's grief turns out to be genuine. He takes a feather, touches it to Boulotte's face, and she is alive again. Then, at a clap of his hands, all the graves open and we see that all the other wives have been similarly brought back to life by the alchemist. Bluebeard's first five wives surround Boulotte and pay tribute to the kindly Popoloni in a happy dance. The scene blacks out.

THIRD INTERLUDE: Bluebeard, too, has his qualms. The ghosts of his murdered wives circle around him as he recalls his crimes. For a moment, he is sorry.

ACT FOUR—THE COURT OF KING BOBICHE: King Bobiche leads his queen to their great, ermine-draped throne, and both prepare to welcome the Princess Hermilia to her true home. They embrace their daughter, who is strangely unhappy. They find out why when the king proposes that she marry a prince named Sapphire. Hermilia doesn't want a prince; she wants her shepherd. She storms about the court, refusing to consent to her father's wish. In despair, the king calls for Prince Sapphire, and when he appears, Hermilia cannot believe her eyes. Everyone rejoices.

But not for long. Bluebeard, no longer remorseful, is determined to wed Hermilia. He dashes in and flourishes his sword. The king is terrified and hides behind the throne. Prince Sapphire, the only fearless member of the court, suggests a duel. They begin to spar with their swords. Bluebeard tricks the prince and stabs him in the back. Bluebeard chuckles as his rival falls dead. Hermilia mourns her lover while the heartless Bluebeard wipes his sword and turns to her. Now, indeed, she must marry him!

Popoloni enters the court leading five masked women. Bluebeard is so busy sitting in Hermilia's lap that he doesn't pay much attention. Poor Hermilia can do nothing but cry. When Bluebeard looks up, the five women unmask: he sees all his dead wives! He leaps high into the air and runs for his life. The wives close in and beat him soundly. He frees himself and threatens Popoloni. But he observes that one of his former wives was really worth saving, after all. He drops the sword and goes to embrace her.

But King Bobiche has other ideas. The queen's five lovers have returned from the dead, too, and something must be done quickly: so he pairs them off with Bluebeard's wives. Old Popoloni recalls Prince Sapphire to life, and Hermilia is happy. The royal couple parade with Bluebeard and Boulotte, trumpets blare, Boulotte whirls around and around and around, and the colorful assembly of courtiers and peasantry rejoice.

BONNE-BOUCHE
TIDBIT

Comic ballet in three scenes. Music by Arthur Oldham. Choreography by John Cranko. Book by John Cranko. Scenery and costumes by Osbert Lancaster. First presented by the Sadler's Wells Ballet at the Royal Opera House, Covent Garden, London, April 4, 1952, with Pauline Clayden as the Young Girl, Brian Shaw as the Lover, John Hart as the Rich Old Neighbor, Alexander Grant as the Black King, and Gilbert Vernon as the Officer, among the principals.

In the London of the early twentieth century there were, as always, socially ambitious mothers who designed endlessly for their daughters' success. This amusing ballet treats of this time and shows us what happens to a young girl whose mother can never make up her mind just who is good enough for her beautiful child.

SCENE ONE—SOUTH KENSINGTON—MORNING: The curtain rises on a public square in the London borough of Kensington. A squat, ugly church dominates the background; to the left and right are houses, with porticos opening on to the square. A lovely young girl comes out of a house on the left, and almost immediately two of her suitors cross the square. First, a young officer, who salutes her; next a good-looking young man, who nervously gives her flowers and an engagement ring.

The girl's mother, an obvious busybody who could not think of minding anything but her daughter's business, joins her and approves of the ring, whereupon the happy girl and her fiancé go for a stroll. All this time the girl has been observed by an old man from a house opposite, who peers at her lecherously through a telescope. When she has disappeared with her young man, this old fool hobbles over to pay a call on the girl's mother. Mother is upset. She thinks the man too old, too unattractive, and for once she is right. She does not know, however, that he is also rich. The man orders his butler to fetch something, and when the servant brings back a diamond necklace, the mother is convinced that neither age nor infirmity can stale this suitor's charms.

When the daughter returns, the mother seizes her engagement ring and allows the rich old man's necklace to be placed about her neck. Daughter is a little bewildered, but—admiring the diamonds—allows her mother to proceed apace with the wedding ceremony. Time, after all, is essential, with such a bridegroom.

No sooner has the wedding party entered the church than the rich old man is carried out. He dies and is carried back in. Mother and daughter weep over their lost luck.

Daughter's first fiancé returns, bent on suicide. He doesn't know the girl isn't worth it and tries to hang and shoot himself. He bungles both attempts and rejoices when the girl comes to him and says that they can be as before, that she has loved *him* all along. The lover joyously consents and, after an ensemble dance with the neighbors, the daughter sends him off.

The real reason she has dismissed him is soon apparent. The young officer who saluted her so gallantly earlier in the day has come back. The lover watches this scene from a hidden position. When the officer proposes, the fickle girl instantly consents. Her bridal veil is brought again, and again we have a procession to the church. And again fate intervenes. The officer is accosted by a woman with several children, who accuses him publicly. The officer runs off, and the girl is alone, once more sans fiancé.

Her lover confronts her with her faithlessness, and the girl tries to laugh off both her intended marriages. He is not consoled, however, and after the daughter has gone into her house, takes refuge in joining a band of militant soul savers, the League of Light, who have invaded the square with a brass band. Daughter and mother urge the lover to remain with them, but the twice-disillusioned young man has had enough and goes off with the metropolitan missionaries. Everyone on the scene—with the exception of mother and daughter—has sense enough to applaud his lucky escape, and the curtain falls as daughter weeps and mother comforts.

SCENE TWO—AFRICA—SOME WEEKS LATER: A witch doctor, with an appropriately grotesque mask, is performing a weird dance as the curtain rises. Water is seen in the background through the thick trees, and beyond the water is a peninsula with palm trees. The witch doctor's lord and master, the cannibal king, is about to leave the jungle for a trip to London. Soon the king himself appears. He wears a strange military uniform of yellow and gold; epaulets and earrings embellish his costume. He condescends to pause for a moment on his journey to the nearest port, then climbs on a leopard-skin litter to be borne off. His black slaves follow behind, carrying elegant modern luggage.

Now abandoned by its ruler, the jungle is invaded by representatives of a higher civilization. The League of Light, led by the girl's jilted lover, marches in on a crusade. The missionaries are somewhat the worse for wear after their long trek from London, and in no time at all beasts of the jungle— snakes and crocodiles and dark, unseen creatures—gobble up the whole brass band. The lover is alone. He sleeps and dreams of his lost love in the lovely, sunny Kensington square. The girl advises him in the dream to wake up and dig where he lies. When day comes, the young man is astonished to see a spade lying near by. He is reminded of his dream and begins to dig. He finds gold, vast quantities of it! The curtain falls.

SCENE THREE—SOUTH KENSINGTON—SOME MONTHS LATER : The drop curtain rises on the first scene, which is altered only in its decorative preparations to welcome the cannibal king, the new resident of the square. The house occupied by the rich old gentleman is now ready to receive him, and the square is aflutter with the preparations of neighbors and those Londoners who are naturally curious to see a real African potentate. Mother, indomitable, watches the scene from her balcony with her daughter.

The cannibal king finally enters with his entourage. He does not appear to be very happy in South Kensington, but perks up as soon as he spies the young girl on the balcony. He flirts with her, and the girl descends to the street. Now he dances with her happily and escorts her into his new house.

Now the old lover enters. He is no longer a member of the League of Light, but a flashy young man whom the mother would no doubt delightedly call *nouveau riche*. His attire, his diamond stickpin, attests to his new-found wealth, and he enters the square in triumph. He goes directly to the mother and inquires after his former sweetheart. Mother replies that daughter has found an even better match and points with pleasure to the cannibal embassy. As she enjoys this brief moment of triumph over the young man, the cannibal king steps out onto his balcony, rubs his belly with great satisfaction, and belches with sonority. He apologizes and retires.

The lover is aghast that the girl has chosen the cannibal beast and prepares to break down the door of the king's house. He gains entry and returns to the square carrying a great covered silver dish. The bystanders wonder what is afoot and gather round. The lover takes off the cover and peers into the huge dish through the escaping steam. He examines the contents carefully and then, to the amazement of all, takes out all that is left of the daughter: the rose that she wore, the diamond necklace, and, unkindest cut of all, the engagement ring he gave the girl so many suitors ago! No one seems to understand the import of these remains except the lover and the police, who attempt to rout out the cannibal king. The king, his appetite satisfied after his long, starving trip, easily eludes them. The neighbors finally understand what has happened and join the police in the chase. The king and all escape, and the mother, poor mother, is the only one who weeps. The lover, thrice disappointed, walks across the square to the statue of a goddess that adorns a fountain standing in front of the church. Disconsolate, weeping, he hangs the diamond necklace about the statue's neck and places on her finger his own tarnished engagement ring. In stone, the daughter is more real than she ever was in the flesh. The lover wipes away his tears, and the curtain falls.

BOURRÉE FANTASQUE

Classical ballet in three parts. Choreography by George Balanchine. Music by Emmanuel Chabrier. Costumes by Karinska. Lighting by Jean Rosenthal. First presented by the New York City Ballet at the City Center, New York, December 1, 1949, with Tanaquil LeClercq and Jerome Robbins, Maria Tallchief and Nicholas Magallanes, Janet Reed and Herbert Bliss as the principals.

This dance spectacle in three movements has no story, but each of the three parts has its own special character and quality of motion to match the buoyant pieces by Chabrier that make up the ballet's score. Each movement of the ballet is danced by a different *premier danseur* as principals. The "Joyous March" that serves as the overture sets a festival pace for the proceedings: loud, cheerful chords, crashing cymbals, and themes so blatantly vivacious that our senses are prepared for the high-spirited geniality with which the ballet both begins and ends.

BOURRÉE FANTASQUE: The curtain rises just before the overture finishes its final crescendo. Transparent white gauze curtains are draped across a blue background, and from the ceiling of the stage hang three black chandeliers, each holding differently colored candles. To the extreme right, standing in a straight line at right angles to the footlights, are four couples waiting for their cue. They are dressed in smart, crisp black; the girls fan themselves with small black fans. The sprightly music begins. The couples join arms and dance across the stage with jaunty, playful steps. The boys encourage the girls, who turn rapidly as their movements become more complicated. Four girls enter at the back; the couples stand back on either side as the newcomers move downstage, dancing in unison a series of bright, high steps. All the dancers are manifestly enjoying themselves immensely as they execute the precise, sparkling routine, yet they all maintain a firm, dead-pan expression, which makes their dancing absurdly comic. The boys leave their partners and pull the girls into their line. Everyone bows low.

A tall girl and a boy much shorter run out onto the stage and dance together briskly. The girl wears flowers high in her hair and fans her face impatiently. They stop suddenly; the music hesitates. The girl turns her back on the boy and looks down at her fan, which clearly amuses her more than he does. The boy tries to make a graceful pose and grabs hold of the ballerina's waist for support. She looks down at him with bored contempt; apparently he will think anything funny. He puts out his leg and looks on incredulously as the ballerina steps across it with little, mincing steps. He smiles at her gratefully; every one of her gestures is marvelous to him. She collapses in his arms and dances frantically. She holds her leg high, and he obligingly supports it under the knee. He stoops down close to the floor to watch her feet closely. The ballerina is determined to exploit his patience at every opportunity and when the boy supports her in attitude, she throws her leg up behind him and kicks him in the back of the head. The boy continues, however, to fancy that she is perfection itself. He moves to sit down, but the ballerina jumps into his lap before he reaches the floor. He tries to engage her flirtatiously, but she will have none of it; he nods his head beseechingly, but she shakes her head insistently. They rise and exit with a flourish.

The eight girls and four boys dance briefly. Like the ballerina's partner, the boys crawl on the floor to admire the girls' dancing feet. Then they move between the two rows of girls and join them in witty steps to the staccato verve of the music.

The ballerina and her partner return and enliven the fun to a high pitch of merriment. The boy holds the ballerina about the waist and squats low behind her as she hops toward the back on one point. Then he joins the other four boys in a dance that becomes intensely brisk. The ballerina fans herself calmly. The girls come forward and rejoin the boys, and the ballerina's partner twirls her about. He catches her in a tight embrace, but she bends her body back, trying to escape. He attempts to put his arms around her neck, but she holds his hands; their arms tangle hopelessly. The two move close to the footlights and forget all classical pretensions as they turn swiftly around and around on one foot, like circus performers. They both stop this exhibition simultaneously and join the group in a final round of merriment that ends abruptly on a note of rampant gaiety.

PRELUDE: The gauze curtains are pulled slightly higher over the empty stage. Eight girls enter from the wings and cross the stage fleetingly, softly, devising a fragile, romantic mood to the new sensuous melody. They arrange themselves in two striking poses about their leaders. A lovely girl walks out slowly from the back. She is looking for someone; she approaches like a sleepwalker and notices no one. A boy emerges from the opposite side. He, too, moves as if he were in a dream. The boy and the girl wander in different directions, weaving in and out among the other dancers as if caught in a labyrinth that will never lead them to each other. Each appears to sense the other's presence, but as they pass closely, their hands almost touching, their reverie does not allow them to see and after a pause they continue on their search.

At last the boy discovers the girl. Her back is turned to him. He places his hand on her shoulder; at his touch she poses gracefully. The boy takes his supporting hand away; the girl stands motionless on point for an instant until he has moved in front of her. She places her arms on his shoulders, and the boy assists her as she displays her comeliness in open turns that cause her black dress to flow about her. Their contact is intimate but also remote, warm yet formal; they recognize each other only in the perfection with which they dance together. She falls back in his arms.

The boy turns briefly to support two of the other girls, but returns to the ballerina. She pirouettes rapidly with her arms high over her head; the boy catches her still turning figure and circles with her. He lifts her tenderly. Momentarily, he is separated from the ballerina and the other girls group themselves around him. He kneels and they cover his head with their arms possessively so that he does not see his lover approach him. She moves away listlessly, returns, retires, then moves back toward him determinedly, in a running leap. The boy looks up and catches her falling body tenderly as the other girls back away. He lifts the ballerina high, and they move forward diagonally across the stage, two girls following along closely, their arms stretched up to clasp the ballerina's outstretched hands. The other girls move by in the opposite direction, passing under their arms swiftly and creating an impression of effortless speed. Now the boy moves backward with the ballerina and the group moves forward beneath her. He lifts her down and for an instant he loses her. The sumptuous music nears its fullest statement as he finds her again. He holds her hand, she rises on point and extends her leg slowly but firmly. Her extended point seems to pierce the richness of the melody.

With an elegant flourish, the ballerina bends low before the boy in a formal gesture of gratitude and acceptance. She rises to turn rapidly in attitude; the boy steps forward quickly and catches her about the waist as she turns full circle. The movement is repeated several times, after which the lovers stand close together, her head on his shoulder. They move apart; the girls glide in between them, forming the same intricate pattern that separated them at the beginning. They look about, seeking, wandering in and out; they pass, pause, but do not find. Both walk off as they came, preoccupied with their private dreams. The others dance slowly into the wings.

F Ê T E   P O L O N A I S E : To the tune of a lively fanfare, a girl and a boy run out onto the stage. The boy kneels, takes the girl's hand, and holds her secure as she races around him. They are followed by three couples, who repeat this routine while the orchestra hurries its preface to the principal theme. Two other couples join the group. These two girls place their hands on their hips and look out into the audience with the gay impudence of chorines. A loud beat is sounded on the drum, and the exhilarating polonaise begins as the two girls are thrown high by their partners.

The other couples join the dance; the boys kneel around the girls in a circle and with a whipping motion encourage their cavorting. Directly all the dancers have caught the vivacity of the music, the ballerina enters to make the scene more animated still. Her grace and high good humor infect the dancing with fresh lightness. She seems astonishingly light as her partner swings her high about him. Finally, he catches her in a breath-taking leap and the two exit.

There are now eight couples on the stage, who dance together briefly before the ballerina and her partner return. This time the boy swings the ballerina about him on one arm; her legs beat together in mid-air. The girls circle them; the ballerina is turned rapidly by her partner as the girls dance around them; then she kneels. She leaves the stage, and the romantic ballerina of the prelude enters with her group of dancers. Soon all three ballerinas and their partners are assembled with the entire *corps de ballet*. The *corps de ballet* form concentric circles about the romantic ballerina, who is lifted high above them, and for a few moments the entire scene whirls with movement as each circle of dancers runs around and around.

All the boys dance a short routine with boundless energy, and the three ballerinas come to the front of the stage with their partners. Now it is almost like a competition between them. The ballerinas gather with their different groups. They take turns leading the groups of eight girls across the stage diagonally with broad, running jumps. The groups crisscross in mid-stage as the music nears a climax of jubilation. Then all the ensemble is reunited for the height of the festivity. Their ensembles are grouped behind the three ballerinas in a spectacular pose as the music ends and the curtain falls.

LA BOUTIQUE FANTASQUE
THE FANTASTIC TOYSHOP

Ballet in one act. Music by Gioacchino Rossini, arranged and orchestrated by Ottorino Respighi. Choreography by Leonide Massine. Scenery and costumes by André Derain. First presented by Diaghilev's Ballets Russes at the Alhambra Theatre, London, June 5, 1919, with Enrico Cecchetti as the *Shopkeeper*, Lydia Lopokova and Leonide Massine as the *Cancan Dancers*, and a cast that included Lydia Sokolova, Leon Woicikowski, Stanislas Idzikowski, Vera Nemtchinova, Lubov Tchernicheva, and Serge Grigoriev. First presented in the United States by the Ballet Russe de Monte Carlo at the Majestic Theatre, New York, March 20, 1935, with a cast that included Alexandra Danilova and Leonide Massine (*Cancan Dancers*), Eugenia Delarova, Tamara Grigorieva, Nina Verachinina, Yurek Shabelevsky, Roland Guérard, David Lichine, and Serge Grigoriev.

Like *Coppélia*, *La Boutique Fantasque* is based on the charm of the mechanical doll. Here, in a great fantastic toyshop in southern France, dolls from all over the world entertain customers from all over the world, who have come to see the detailed and charming workmanship of a master dollmaker. The time is the 1860s.

At the rise of the curtain, the sunny shop is empty. It has been closed for lunch. The shopkeeper and his helper return and open the doors for business. While they are busy preparing for their work, a dirty little boy comes in and attempts to steal gold lace from one of the shopkeeper's prize dolls. The thief is apprehended and, fleeing, bumps into two prospective customers, an English old maid and her companion.

The old maids want to see the best dolls and when the shopkeeper has shown them the mechanical peasant dolls on display, they ask to see more. New customers, an American family with two children, charge in. The family know the English ladies and after all the customers have exchanged greetings, the American turns to the shopkeeper and asks to see his dolls.

The shopkeeper obsequiously consents, and two tarantella dancers are wheeled in. When the customers have examined them, the two dolls, an Italian girl and her sweetheart, break into an animated tarantella to the lively accompaniment of rattling tambourines. Then, as if their mechanism had run down, the dancers collapse.

Next there is a mazurka, danced by dolls representing the Queen of Clubs, the Queen of Hearts, the King of Diamonds, and the King of Spades. A Russian couple enter with their four children. The English ladies resent the intrusion of these foreigners and take their leave.

The next set of dolls displayed by the shopkeeper represent a snob and a melon hawker, a combination of the rich and the poor. The snob bustles about busily while the melon hawker slices a melon and presents it to him. Then the melon hawker shines the shoes of the snob, who trips over the hawker, only to rise again in a mechanical miracle.

The customers are now convinced that they are seeing a great and marvelous entertainment. Their mutual enthusiasm makes them all friendly and they watch with delight as more dolls perform.

Five Cossack dolls led by a chief perform a rapid dance next. Then the chief Cossack is joined by a Cossack girl doll, who kisses him while the soldiers snap to attention. The porters of the fantastic toyshop drill the Cossacks off.

Now two dancing poodles display their skill by walking on their hind legs. The female dog tries to attract the male dog by her cavortings and the male dog, in his enthusiasm for her dancing, rushes around and around her. The American couple are shocked at this amorous display and blindfold their children.

The shopkeeper now informs his prospective customers that they are about to see the most ingenious dolls of all: the cancan dancers. The couple who are wheeled in dance with such gusto that all the spectators are bound to agree. As the girl doll abandons herself in the cancan, her partner is so delighted that he performs marvelous gravity-defying tricks.

Now both families who have been watching the dolls want to buy the cancan dancers. The American children like the male doll best, the Russians the girl. Their fathers talk to the shopkeeper, agree to pay his price, and leave, saying that they will call for the dolls in the morning.

Night has fallen. The shopkeeper and his assistants lock up and leave.

Now that they are alone, all the dolls in the shop emerge from their boxes and become more animated than ever. They are very happy to be dancing so freely, but they are also sad. The cancan dancers are to be separated tomorrow. The two lovers dance together for what seems to be the last time, and the other dolls dance about them, celebrating their love. At the end of the revels there is a general cakewalk, danced by all the dolls.

When morning comes and the shop is reopened, all appears to be as it was the night before. But when the American and Russian families call to pick up the dolls they have engaged to buy, something is amiss: the cancan dancers have disappeared from their boxes! The children howl, the fathers berate the shopkeeper, and the mothers rage. The shopkeeper and his assistants are beaten, and the whole toyshop is attacked by the disappointed customers.

Just when it seems likely that the irate foreigners will destroy the shop completely, the toy dolls come to the rescue. The poodles attack the Russian mother; her husband and children are set upon by the card toys; and the Americans are routed by kicking ballet-dancer dolls. Finally the Cossacks drive the customers from the shop.

Unbelieving, the Americans and Russians stand outside and look back through the window. They see all the dolls in the shop dancing together a brilliant ensemble, a final happy dance. The shopkeeper and the cancan dancers shake hands. All the dolls rejoice that the two lovers are still together.

THE CAGE

Ballet in one act. Music by Igor Stravinsky (*Concerto Grosso in D for Strings*). Choreography by Jerome Robbins. Costumes by Ruth Sobotka. Lighting by Jean Rosenthal. First presented by the New York City Ballet at the City Center, New York, June 10, 1951, with Nora Kaye as the *Novice*, Yvonne Mounsey as the *Queen*, and Nicholas Magallanes and Michael Maule as the *Intruders*.

This ballet is a dramatic demonstration of a phenomenon common to insect and animal life and to Western mythology too: the phenomenon of the female considering the male as prey. The mantis devours her partner after mating; the spider kills the male unless he attacks first; and the Amazons, in Greek mythology, were a cult of warlike females who did not associate with men, except for procreation. The Amazons despised their male children and maimed or destroyed them. Woman was sufficient; Man was accidental. *The Cage* shows us such a tribe of women.

Before the ballet begins, the auditorium is completely dark. The footlights come up before the curtain, then go out; the lights in the orchestra are extinguished. There is no music. The curtain rises. The light is obscure and misty, but we see hanging over the stage a tangle of multicolored strands, like the web of some huge spider. Mysteriously, as if it were a living thing, the web rises, stretches, and hangs over the floor. On the left stand a group of female figures arranged in a tight tableau; they are clustered together like bees in a hive.

The music begins with three notes sounded sharply on the strings. The women stir. In the center of the group sits the queen of the tribe. The lights come up gradually. A still, shrouded creature is drawn out from between the queen's legs; the novice has been born. The queen strips the confining membrane from the novice's body. The new member of the tribe crouches slightly. Her body is marked with endless, tangled viscera. Her face is still covered. She is motionless. The queen stands behind her, extending her arms grotesquely, seeming to enclose the novice with her long talons.

The orchestra begins a vibrant march. The twelve members of the tribe turn their backs, rise on point, and commence a grotesque ceremonial dance. As their bodies turn, we see that their backs are insectlike: strands reach out from their black spines to cover their backs, and they seem to resemble scuttling beetles. The queen leaves the novice and dances among the tribe. The women circle her and bow low obediently as she dances. The novice remains inert.

Now two of the women go to the novice and drag her to the center, before the queen. The queen tears off the membrane covering her face. The novice's hands reach up to protect her eyes from the sudden light. Her face is a mask; her hair, dark and wet, clings to her head. The queen is well pleased at her ugliness. The birth rite is over; the queen and her creatures leave to watch the novice from the surrounding darkness. Just as she departs, the queen touches the novice's dark head in blessing.

The melody changes; the music slows in tempo. The novice's untrained limbs do not yet know how to move and she squats alone. She tests her arms and legs, pushes her body up on them, rises on point. Her gestures are sudden and sharp, her body angularly contorted. Her fingers are clawing and knifelike blades cutting at the air tentatively; her arms are sinuous, serpentine. She walks with knees open and bent, arms ready to enlace her prey.

The music breaks into a loud, rapidly rhythmic burst of sound. A man rushes in and seizes the novice by the waist. She twists away in revulsion. The intruder attempts to pull her close to him and falls to the ground. The novice falls upon him, and they roll over together. The exhausted intruder lies quiet as the novice rises and steps upon his chest with the sharp point of her foot. Now she straddles his body, grabs his head between her legs, clenches her fists, tightens and twists her body, and cracks his neck with her knees. He is dead.

The music quietens. The novice kicks the body over on its face. As the orchestra resumes the opening march, she dances alone, her knees rising high, driving her feet hard against the ground. Her head is thrown back and her mouth hangs open in a shriek of triumph.

The queen leads the tribe back to the novice. The hideous women stalk into the light, surround the novice, and congratulate her. She has met the test, her instinct has obeyed the law of the tribe: she has killed her first male. The novice kicks at his body contemptuously, and he is dragged off.

The queen embraces the novice. Other women in the tribe pair off and rest together. The women are content with their own society and relax without fear of intrusion. Then the music sounds a warning. The couples separate. The light dims. The queen signals the others to hasten away. The novice, suddenly afraid, is running off after them as her swift body is caught up in the arms of a dark, handsome intruder. Her legs try to kick her body free as he holds her, but she cannot loosen his grasp. The warning in the music ceases; the melody flows yieldingly. The novice is now unsure. Gradually she succumbs to the superior strength of the intruder and dances with him a romantic love duet. He holds her on his knee, and she sharpens her claws together, not for battle now, but for love. Their bodies separate and their fingers approach and entwine like bristling antennae. She tries to make herself graceful as she dances and falls back into the intruder's arms. He catches her body between his legs; her face turns up toward his, and their arms embrace in a cocoon. The novice's feet beat at the floor as the intruder becomes her lover.

The lights go down for a moment. The music whirrs ominously. The frightened intruder moves and the woman falls to the ground. The two lovers cower together, trying to conceal each other in the darkness, as the queen and the tribe enter. Then, as the intruder sees the women who would claim the novice, he revolts and pushes the woman, now hideous to him, into the arms of her Amazon queen.

This is what the tribe have waited for. The queen directs her creatures to attack the intruder as the novice is held secure. The women climb upon the intruder like ants on a stick of candy. He is released briefly and rolls helpless on the ground. The novice's native instinct begins to return. She falls upon him, straddles him, and slides her body over the passive male. She squats guiltily as the women seize him and carry him aloft. The queen orders her fellow creatures to carry the novice on their shoulders and hold her poised above him. The novice's claws are straight and sharp for the kill. She aims carefully and deliberately and slashes.

The body of the intruder lies again on the ground. The hungry women crawl over him, devouring his limbs. The novice strangles him between her knees. His body curls for a moment, then straightens. He is dead. His body is rolled across the stage. The victorious women leap over it as they dance triumphantly.

The novice cleans her talons. The queen joins her to accept her as a true member of the tribe. The two grotesque figures whirl together, then stand motionless, their deformed bodies dominating the dark cage. The music stops. The great spidery web loosens and falls about them to the ground.

NOTES: Anatole Chujoy wrote in *Dance News* after the *première* of *The Cage* that this ballet "is not a pretty work and not for children. It is outspoken, bitter and violent. The implications of its comment are wider than the abstracted insect kingdom it deals with, and these implications are not pleasant to contemplate. It is also a tremendously exciting work, beautiful in the savagery of its contents, thrilling in its choreographic development. It is probably the most powerful work Robbins has ever done and choreographically it is the most mature. Nora Kaye dances the novice with the great dramatic power she has always commanded, multiplied many times. She resorts to no histrionics, no tragic outbursts. Her force here is in the charged intensity of her movements, in the . . . practically immobile features of her face, her expression of animalism, which all combine to produce a superb performance that will be long remembered." John Martin of the New York *Times* found Nora Kaye "totally magnificent. She is beautiful and terrifying. Her very stillness takes command of the stage . . . Her tremendous theatrical power has rarely been more masterfully exercised."

It is interesting that during rehearsals for *The Cage* the choreographer and the dancers frequently remarked the new ballet's similarity to *Giselle*, Act II, in which the relentless Wilis contrive to force the heroine of the ballet to cause her lover's death.

Melissa Hayden and Francisco Moncion danced the principal roles in *The Cage* for the first time on November 6, 1952, at the City Center, New York.

CAKEWALK

Ballet in three parts. Music adapted and orchestrated by Hershy Kay after music by Louis Moreau Gottschalk. Choreography by Ruthanna Boris. Scenery and costume by Robert Drew. Lighting by Jean Rosenthal. First presented by the New York City Ballet at the City Center, New York, June 12, 1951, with a cast headed by Janet Reed, Patricia Wilde, Yvonne Mounsey, Herbert Bliss, Frank Hobi, Tanaquil LeClercq, and Beatrice Tompkins.

Cakewalk is an American ballet based on the minstrel shows. The great era of the minstrel show began to end toward the turn of the century, but this ballet reminds us of why this form of entertainment, native to America, was once so universally popular: like the original, it has humor, sentiment, magic, and liveliness. *Cakewalk*, being a ballet, doesn't have the two sets of bones, the two banjos, the two tambourines, and the singers that every real minstrel show used to have. These musical elements are taken care of by the orchestra, which plays in special arrangements a group of pieces and songs by Louis Moreau Gottschalk, the American composer and pianist whose music was so popular among original minstrel show artists: such works as "Bamboula," "Maiden's Blush," and "Won't You Buy My Pretty Flowers?" On stage, the dancers imitate the conventional minstrel show turns in dance terms that combine folk dancing with an enlivened classical technique. Like all proper minstrel shows, *Cakewalk* is divided into three parts.

PART ONE : The orchestra strikes up a loud, ebullient overture. The curtain rises. At extreme left and right are entrance doors on to the stage. In the back hangs a drop curtain that shows a huge Mississippi side-wheeler plying up the stream. Already, before the dancers appear, we have a vivid sense of the atmosphere in which the original minstrel show flourished.

One by one, the performers make their entrance to begin the "Grand Introductory Walkaround." They strut across the stage rapidly, led by the interlocutor, giving us a hint of the novelties to come. Finally, when all have disappeared in the door at the left, the drop curtain rises and we see the stage set for the minstrel show. In the back stands a long platform with ramps leading forward down to the stage. Gold chairs and torches are lined up on stage and platform. The "Grand Introductory March" reaches a climax of happy anticipation, and the artists—the center performers, the semicircle, the auxiliary ladies and gentlemen, and the two end men—move to their seats. A tambourine claps for order as all sit down at the interlocutor's signal.

The interlocutor leads forward a dainty girl, whose old-fashioned curls and somber countenance presage a dance of great seriousness. The orchestra sounds the first notes of a "Pathetic Ballad" in slow waltz time; the girl moves forward on point and renders a dance of absurd tragedy. She is all alone; the four boys who dance with their partners in a semicircle around her will not pay any attention to her. She is doomed to be a perpetual wall-flower. Yet all the time the girl maintains in her steps and gestures an indifference to ordinary mortals that exposes her addiction to pathos. She loves to be sad, and sad in the grand manner. She clasps her hands and raises them in supplication; she kneels, begging for help in her distress; she turns beseechingly to the happy couples for succor. No one will help her! The girl raises a pointed hand to her temples and fires. The saccharine music expires, and the unfortunate creature is free to be happy again. She takes her seat, rises disconsolately to the audience applause, and sits down again, her eyes downcast.

The interlocutor, his black cane in hand, comes forward and performs "Sleight of Feet," a rhythmic jumping specialty that makes him a magician in movement. He tries to attract our attention to his hands, his coattails, and his cane as his feet perform quick marvels. The end men run forward with a chair, and he falls back, exhausted by triumph.

The interlocutor is followed by the two end men, one short, the other tall, who rise from their places at each end of the line and dance "Perpendicular Points." This number displays their adroit sharpness in dancing almost continually on their toes to curtly paced music that would trip them up if it could. Their long swallow-tailed coats bounce in the air as their points hit every beat of the music. As their number ends, they rush over to the left and end up sitting in the lap of the surprised interlocutor.

The lights go down. A bright spotlight catches a girl in a shining red dress who rushes out and dances a vigorous "Freebee" to a fresh, rousing theme. All the performers clap their hands in rhythm to the music; the girl dances faster; the whole troupe catches the contagious liveliness of her movement and the members come forward to join her. They parade across the platform as the girl in red is lifted high between two boys and carried around the stage. But the instant her feet touch the floor, she is on fire again with movement and leads all in a jumping, turning ensemble that increases in speed and dizziness. All fall flat on the floor, exhausted.

PART TWO: The dancers rise and carry out the chairs and benches. The drop curtain falls, and some of the performers come forward and sit to watch the show themselves. The stage is now empty and dark. The music warns of mysterious events. Three capes—red, green, and purple—seem to move across the stage unsupported, sweeping the air before them. Then the capes are dropped and we see that they are worn by Louis, the Illusionist, and his two assistants, Moreau and Lessau—the interlocutor and the two end men in disguise.

Louis and his two assistants make magic signs, gather close in a line, their capes before them. The drop curtain rises. The three cloaked figures slide off into the wings, miraculously leaving before us, in the center of the stage, the goddess Venus, gamboling on the green with three Graces. When they have danced their bit, the magician and his helpers return. They enclose the four mythical figures in their capes and they disappear.

Next Louis brings forth a wild pony, transmigrated from its native hills. The wild pony, danced by the leader of the frenzied "Freebee," cavorts and bucks about her unnatural surroundings with stubborn, bold abandon. The magician tries to tame her, pulling the reins taut, but the pony's mane switches the trainer's face and he at last releases her.

Tinkling music is heard. Perched on a seat hung with flowers, Hortense, Queen of the Swamp Lilies, swings into view and off again. Her garlanded swing brings her back, however, and she is lifted down to earth by Harolde, the young poet, who joins her in a *pas de deux*. To the music of a solo violin and the harp, the idealized lovers dance with considered, prolonged languor, never hurrying, never reaching their goal.

PART THREE: The lights come up. The magician has materialized his last illusion and he and his assistants leave the scene stealthily, their cloaks wrapped about them. The orchestra begins a catchy march, and all the participants parade the stage in a spirited, strutting, gala cakewalk that moves rapidly to a boisterous, rollicking conclusion. All the dancers wave responsive greetings to the audience as the curtain falls.

CAPRICCIO ESPAÑOL

Ballet in one act. Music by Nikolai Rimsky-Korsakov. Choreography by Leonide Massine, with the collaboration of Argentinita. Book by Leonide Massine. Scenery and costumes by Mariano Andreù. First presented by the Ballet Russe de Monte Carlo at the Théâtre de Monte Carlo, May 4, 1939, with a cast that included Argentinita, Alexandra Danilova, Michel Panaieff, and Leonide Massine. First presented in the United States by the Ballet Russe de Monte Carlo at the Metropolitan Opera House, New York, October 27, 1939, with Mia Slavenska, Alexandra Danilova, André Eglevsky, and Leonide Massine in the leading roles.

Capriccio Español is a ballet about Spain, rather than a Spanish ballet. Just as Spanish dance themes provided Rimsky-Korsakov with melodies for a bright and colorful orchestration, the choreography here uses Spanish dance steps to create a romantic and colorful representation that some of us might imagine to be Spain. The ballet, therefore, has no particular story to tell; instead, it tries through a series of dances to create an atmosphere, a feeling that something real has been touched.

The ballet begins with a dance called the alborada, a morning serenade. We find ourselves in the public square of a small Spanish town whose inhabitants are preparing for a festival. The music is almost uncontrolled in its loud, blaring enthusiasm. Boys of the village dance with wild abandon to this music. Soon they are joined by a group of girls. But instead of choosing the boys for their partners, the girls turn to the elders of the village and dance with them playfully and charmingly. The girls are aware that only these older men, who have seen so many beautiful women in their lives, have a real and knowing appreciation of their loveliness, and the older men, in turn, are charmed by the fact that the girls know this. The music is quieter, occasionally bursting into crescendos, as it varies the more gentle secondary theme.

The turbulent first movement is now repeated, and the boys again take up their dance. There is a roll on the drum, which the brasses build into a fanfare, and a stunning gypsy comes into the square. This is the fortuneteller. She begins to dance, enchanting all the village with her fiery, sinuous movements. A gypsylike melody inserts itself between solos for various instruments as the fortuneteller continues to hold everyone's attention. She is joined by a partner and in the rapid stampings, quick whirls, and persistent rhythms of their dance, the bodies seem to make the whole square vibrate. The strings are plucked like guitars, and the couple bring their duet to a close with a fandango.

Another couple come forward and, in the midst of the excited crowd, now overflowing with the spirit of the festival, this peasant boy and girl lead all the natives in a tempestuous ensemble. The fortuneteller returns with her partner to join the peasant couple as the festival reaches a peak of excitement. All the people have now forgotten that they are moving in a dance, for their dancing derives from a holiday impulse that makes everything but dashing and turning movement impossible. Inspired by the dazzling display of the two lead couples, the villagers become intoxicated with joy at their own brilliant facility and dance with their leaders a final, uproarious ensemble as the opening theme of the ballet triumphantly returns.

NOTES: *Capriccio Español* has been frequently revived in Europe as well as in the United States. The ballet was revived for Ballet Theatre in 1943 and for the Ballet Russe in 1951. Massine appeared in both these productions. In the part of the fortuneteller, Mia Slavenska, Nathalie Krassovska, Nora Kaye, and Nina Novak have succeeded the late Argentinita. In 1941 *Capriccio Español* was made into a Technicolor short subject by Warner Brothers. The name of the movie was *Spanish Fiesta;* its stars were Tamara Toumanova and the choreographer, Massine.

CAPRICHOS

Ballet in four episodes. Choreography by Herbert Ross. Music by Bela Bartók. Costumes by Helene Pons. First presented by the Choreographers' Workshop at the Hunter Playhouse, New York, January 29, 1950. Presented by Ballet Theatre at the Center Theatre, New York, April 26, 1950, with Charlyne Baker, Jenny Workman, Nana Gollner, John Kriza, Ruth Ann Koesun, and Mary Burr as the principals.

This ballet derives its inspiration from the comments the Spanish artist Goya made on a series of his etchings. The choreographer has taken four of these comments and visualized opinion. The ballet is performed to Bela Bartók's *Contrasts for Piano, Clarinet, and Violin.* A blue backdrop is the only scenery.

There are two girls on stage as the curtain rises. They are dressed in brief white nightgowns. They wear black crucifixes about their necks and long black gloves. Goya's comment is: "These good girls have seats enough and nothing to do with them better than carry them on their heads." The girls are not good at all. Their principal pleasure consists in pulling their dresses up to their necks as often as possible. They carry two stools and try to amuse themselves by playing with them as they cavort about the stage. Finally the girls realize that they are boring themselves to death. One stands holding a stool on her head; the other falls to the ground in an idiotic posture.

"No one ever escapes who wants to be caught" is Goya's second comment. The two girls remain on stage to watch. One fans her dress back and forth to cool her body; the other relaxes with her head in her hand. A woman in black enters, her head concealed by a blue shawl. She is followed by two men in cloaks. The woman moves over to the two girls, who observe her with preoccupied, gum-chewing expressions. The woman begins to dance. The men close in. She pretends to detest them and to want to be alone. The men are delighted by the pretense at resistance and allow her to fascinate them. They move in and caress her boldly, and the three dance together, the woman clapping her hands with simulated Spanish pleasure. The two men lift her up to their shoulders, then each holds her and swings her body around and around. As one of the men embraces her, the other picks up her feet. They lay the woman on the ground. Now something has happened that the two girls can understand; they move over to the woman. The men walk away. The girls frolic about the stage. The woman rises and disappears, her blue shawl whirling with her movement.

The girls are dejected again. A young widower enters. He mourns his dead wife and holds his hand before his eyes as he sees the lascivious girls. He moves over toward them, his face determined to be sad. Then he goes to the back of the stage and stands close to the wings. He holds out his arms in supplication. Suddenly, as if he were holding out his arms to catch a potato sack, his dead wife falls into his arms. Her body is limp, absolutely lifeless. The man kneels. He attempts to bring his love to life, but her loose body resists his efforts. If he does not hold her, the girl falls over on her face. The young man gets a little annoyed and tries to dance with his rag doll of a wife. He is forced to push her legs ahead of him. Now he is embarrassed. He shows the girls that his wife really is dead. There is no use pretending. Goya's comment is: "If he were more gallant and less of a bore, she would come to life again." He carries his wife off.

The color of the backdrop changes to a bright green. The two girls rise from their siesta as four hooded figures enter slowly, carrying long brooms of straw. The girls are suddenly respectful in the presence of these mysterious, religious men. Two of the men carry a plank; a woman sits upon it, resigned to her fate. ". . . They are determined to kill this saintly woman. After judgment has been pronounced against her, she is dragged through the streets in triumph. She has indeed deserved a triumph, but if they do it to shame her, they are wasting their time. No one can make her ashamed who has nothing to be ashamed of . . ."

The triumphal procession is over. The men stand the plank upright and fix its base in the ground. The girls stand on their stools at the back to see better. The saintly woman is tied to the plank. Red light appears at her feet, and from the movement of her toes it is apparent that she is uncomfortable. She tries to escape the licking flames by lifting one tortured foot, then another away from the fire. One by one, the four men toss their brooms of straw at her feet. The woman trembles all over. The light on the backdrop becomes brilliantly red. With a hideous gesture, the woman at the stake claws at her flesh, seeming to pull it up over her face like a mask. One of the men stands behind the stake and extends his arms straight out, sanctifying the project. The woman's body falls forward. Her bonds still hold her to the stake. Everyone is still but the two girls, who move about slowly. One finally rests on her stool and amuses herself alone. The other girl, on the right, imitates crudely the sufferings of the saintly woman. The curtain falls. A voice says, "*El sueño de la razón produce monstruos*" ("The dream of reason produces monsters").

CAPRIOL SUITE

Ballet in one act. Music by Peter Warlock. Choreography by Frederick Ashton. Scenery and costumes by William Chappell. First presented by the Marie Rambert Dancers at the Lyric Theatre, Hammersmith, London, February 25, 1930. First presented in the United States by the Sadler's Wells Theatre Ballet at the War Memorial Opera House, San Francisco, California, December 5, 1951, with a cast that included Patricia Miller, Donald Britton, and David Poole.

This entertainment ballet is a twentieth-century version of dances that were popular four hundred years ago. In 1588, the Frenchman Thoinot Arbeau set down in writing a record of sixteenth-century dances with the music that accompanied them. This book, called *Orchesography* (writing dancing), appeared seven years after the presentation of the first modern ballet, the first ballet to unify in one entertaining spectacle the theatrical elements that had amused the courts of Europe for many centuries.

Arbeau's book is a dialogue, in the classical manner. He and a novice at the dance, a young man named Capriol, talk about dancing—how it came to be so popular among mankind, the different kinds of contemporary dancing, and the proper music to accompany the different forms. Peter Warlock, the English composer, arranged a number of the tunes set forth by Arbeau in an orchestral suite, and Frederick Ashton, in turn, devised the appropriate sixteenth-century dances as described by Arbeau to young Capriol.

The curtain rises and the orchestra begins a sprightly tune. The setting is simple and formal: a low stone railing topped with urns curves about the back of the stage. The back cloth is light green. Two couples dressed in the sixteenth-century French fashion perform a *basse danse*, a light but dignified measure. When they finish, the lights dim and two boys lead on a girl dressed in a long skirt. The orchestra plays a stately pavane, and the girl begins to dance between her escorts. Soon she pauses and sits on the knee of one of the boys. He presents a red rose to her. She sweetly refuses to accept it and when the other boy offers her a scroll, upon which he has written a poem to her, she will have none of him. She rises, and the boys stand on each side of her contemplating the gifts she has rejected.

The lights brighten, and to gay, bouncing music a girl and a boy dance a tordion, a court dance that is nevertheless playful and uninhibited in enthusiasm. The dancers who performed the pavane watch the dancing couple. Another girl enters. When the tordion finishes, those two couples come forward. The dancing, which has mostly been confined to the floor, now rises as the boys perform *pieds en l'air* to entertain the girls. When the dance is over, the boys kneel and the girls fall back over their shoulders. They leave the stage.

The music becomes bright and brisk. Four boys jump out onto the stage and dance a mattachins, a vigorous sword dance. Three of the boys lift the victor high over their heads as this dance ends. Gradually all the dancers return and perform different versions of the branle, a sixteenth-century court dance so popular that there were different versions for different age groups. The music increases in gaiety. The more ebullient dancers enclose in a moving circle the more stately couples, and the curtain falls.

NOTES: *Capriol Suite* is the earliest work by the distinguished English choreographer Frederick Ashton in the current ballet repertory. It is his sixth ballet. *Capriol Suite* was revived for the Sadler's Wells Theatre Ballet on November 5, 1948, at the Sadler's Wells Theatre, London.

CARACOLE

Classic ballet in five parts. Music by Wolfgang Amadeus Mozart. Choreography by George Balanchine. Costumes by Christian Bérard. Lighting by Jean Rosenthal. First presented by the New York City Ballet at the City Center, New York, February 19, 1952, with a cast headed by Maria Tallchief, Tanaquil LeClercq, Melissa Hayden, Diana Adams, Patricia Wilde, André Eglevsky, Nicholas Magallanes, and Jerome Robbins.

The name of this ballet is taken from the French term *caracole*, meaning a twisting or turning in compact form. To the equestrian, a *caracole* is a half turn to right or left in the riding ring, or any turn or twist that the horse might make in capering about the ring in a zigzag course. The word is not used here literally—the ballet does not consist simply of twistings and turnings—but in a larger sense, to indicate the inherent design any dance must have as it fits itself to a compact piece of music that is both humanly happy and sublime.

This piece of music is a work Mozart composed when he was twenty-one years old: the *Divertimento No. 15, in B-flat major* (K.287), for strings and two horns. Mozart wrote many such divertimentos and serenades—works designed for immediate occasions: large garden parties, carnivals, formal evening gatherings. All these pieces were written to divert and charm audiences that expected to be entertained. Very often people danced to them. This particular divertimento is probably the greatest of its kind. It represents Mozart at his best, infusing a familiar form of court music with warm dignity, playfulness, and tender, lyric beauty.

The ballet follows the different movements of the score. There is no story. *Caracole* is designed for a constellation of five ballerinas, three *danseurs*, and a *corps de ballet* of eight girls.

FIRST MOVEMENT—ALLEGRO: The strings curtly and brightly announce the happy opening theme. The curtain rises. Two ballerinas stand on either side of a tableau formed by the *corps de ballet*. Some of the girls stand in a close semicircle; the others kneel before them. They are dressed colorfully in white and various shades of red. The ballerinas wear stately white costumes and headdresses of high white plumes.

The girls in the *corps de ballet* nod their heads and move their arms to the music, and the ballerinas begin to dance before the group. As the group forms circles, diagonal parallels, and moving, converging lines, the soloists dance around and between them. The three male soloists rush in and dance to the bold and rapid strings as the ballerinas leave the stage. The music becomes dainty and piquant, and the three cavaliers give way to the entry of the final three soloists. The ballerina in the center bows her head to her two sisters, and the three dance. The boys go to them, and the six soloists perform in front of the *corps de ballet*. The first two ballerinas join them, the boys retire, and the five girls dance in a line. Their cavaliers return, everyone bows, and the movement seems to be over, but the boys, changing partners, now support the girls in rapid turns that end the first section with a flourish. The *corps de ballet* leaves the stage.

SECOND MOVEMENT—ANDANTE GRAZIOSO—THEME AND VARIATIONS: The theme is played softly on the strings, and two of the *danseurs*, taking turns, state the theme in dance terms before the soloists. After this brief introduction all leave the stage, and now, one by one, the other soloists dance alone to six variations on the theme.

The ballerina who dances the first, brilliantly accented variation moves with quick, dazzling elevation. The second variation on the theme is soft and lyric with distant whirring strings, and to this music another girl dances, her foot trembling to the tender joyousness of the music. The horns herald the brighter, lightly militant third variation, which is performed by a third ballerina. Now the theme is varied with an alternating rhythm of shifting volume, to which a fourth ballerina dances a solo.

The *premier danseur* now comes forward and dances a spectacular aerial variation to strongly accented chords that are answered plaintively by the strings. The *prima ballerina* takes his place, as the music gathers in tempo, and proceeds at whirlwind speed with the final variation. She turns with increasing momentum to the demanding acceleration of the theme's last statement and finishes the series of variations with a delicate, precisioned display of virtuosity.

When her variation ends, all the soloists return to the stage. The girls and the *premier danseur*, in a line, bow to the boys opposite them who first stated the theme, and all retire to the wings.

THIRD MOVEMENT — MINUET: The stately minuet is danced by the *corps de ballet*. Here the eight girls divide themselves into couples and quartets that respond to the graciousness and formality of the music with varied formal patterns. At its conclusion, they leap off into the wings.

FOURTH MOVEMENT — ANDANTE: The beautiful slow movement, a concerto for solo violin and orchestra, is danced by all the soloists. This is a grand adagio not for one but for five ballerinas. At the beginning the stage is empty—a boy leads on one of the ballerinas, who moves across the stage on *pointe*. He lifts her gently, then lifts her just off the floor as he moves in a swift diagonal. One by one the girls make their entries with their attendant cavaliers.

The *premier danseur* now brings in the *prima ballerina*. He lifts her forward. Alternately, all five girls dance alone, then each moves in turn supported by one of the cavaliers. As the tender melody ends, the girls form a diagonal line. Their cavaliers bow to them, and the movement is over.

FIFTH MOVEMENT — ALLEGRO MOLTO — ANDANTE: The gay and sprightly music here is based on an old German popular song. Mozart treats the melody playfully. Two by two, the *corps de ballet* run on and by their swift, ebullient dancing respond to the joy of the music. One of the solo couples joins them. The boy abandons one ballerina for another who dances onto the scene swiftly. They are followed by a *pas de trois* of two ballerinas and a male dancer. The eight girls of the *corps* form a close square, bow to each other, and kneel.

The *prima ballerina* now takes the stage. The music gathers to a lively, rushing climax. Soon all the soloists are on stage with the *corps de ballet*. When the lively music is interrupted by a serious, elegant recitative that sounds in amusing contrast to the popular melody, the cavaliers take turns supporting each of the ballerinas in final slow movements. The playful melody suddenly returns, and all the ensemble circle the stage in a rushing spiral and leap off into the wings.

NOTES: The New York City Ballet did not originally intend to present a new musical ballet like *Caracole* during its tenth New York season, in February 1952. I had planned instead to produce for this season *Don Juan*, using the score by Richard Strauss, as a companion piece to *Tyl Ulenspiegel*, which was already in the repertory. I made plans for *Don Juan* in some detail, cast the ballet, and began rehearsals. I soon discovered, however, that the score could not accommodate the ideas I had in mind and was compelled to drop the subject.

Since it was important that another ballet be substituted for *Don Juan*, I set to work on another idea. I chose to do a classic ballet to Mozart's *Divertimento in B-flat*, a work I had long cherished as one of the most beautiful pieces of music in the world. The ballet was cast, rehearsed, and completed within a week.

CARD GAME
JEU DE CARTES

Ballet in three deals. Music by Igor Stravinsky. Choreography by George Balanchine. Book by Igor Stravinsky, with the collaboration of M. Malaieff. Scenery and costumes by Irene Sharaff. First presented by the American Ballet at the Metropolitan Opera House, New York, April 27, 1937.

The characters in this ballet represent the cards in poker hands. There are twenty-six cards for the whole ballet, representing portions of the four suits, plus the joker. Fifteen of these cards—one always the joker—are dealt out to make up three separate hands of poker for each of the three scenes in the ballet. The ballet is prefaced by this translation from a poem by La Fontaine:

One should ever struggle against wrongdoers.
Peace, I grant, is perfect in its way,
But what purpose does it serve
With enemies who do not keep faith?

FIRST DEAL : The orchestra plays a sonorous and playful march. The curtain rises on an empty stage. The scene is enclosed in a green felt façade. A great crystal candelabra stands at the left, representing one corner of a card table. The green table top stretches back up against the backdrop, where another candelabra is suspended at the opposite corner of the table; the stage thus becomes the table itself.

Fifteen dancers trip out from the right and form in a line straight across the stage. All hold large yellow-striped cards before them, concealing their identity. The joker is among them. Easily identified by his yellow costume striped with bright orange and his silly fool's cap, he steps out of line and runs about, trying to find the best hand. The cards turn and move close together in a shuffling movement. Then the hands are dealt out by an invisible player. The first five cards on the left jump out of line over to the left; the remaining cards form hands at the center and on the right. All the characters still hold the cards before them, but the joker can be distinguished in the hand on the left.

The hand on the right throw the placards over their heads to reveal themselves as the Ace and Queen of Hearts, the Queen of Clubs, the Jack of Spades, and the Jack of Diamonds—a two-pair hand. All the cards are easily identifiable in their resplendent costumes. The Ace of Hearts, his head covered like some medieval armored knight, flourishes his powerless sword in the air, and the smiling Queen of Hearts is surrounded by her dancing partners. The cards fall back in line and bow to the hand at the left.

The second hand turns out to be two kings and two eights—with the joker, a full house. The four cards and the joker step out proudly, the joker flagrantly boasting about the two kings. Now the members of the back hand throw off their placards. The joker holds his nose in contempt as he sees a pair of sevens, but he is stunned along with everyone else as they see three aces with the two sevens—another full house, which beats the joker's hand unaided! The joker comes forward, laughing hilariously to music that accompanies his dance. He grips his sides and bends over as he laughs. His loose, disjointed figure cavorts about the stage in short, jerky steps, running to the left, then to the right. He pirouettes like a top and circles the stage in wide, distorted leaps, turns in the air, slaps the table with his hands, and exits. The three hands spread out and close. All the cards choose partners and slowly dance off. The last couples to leave the stage are the two disconsolate kings with their two eights hanging limply on their arms.

SECOND DEAL: The introductory march to the ballet heralds the second scene. A new line of cards run out from the left, holding up before them large blue-striped placards. They form in a line down the center of the table, shuffle, and form three hands as before. From the hand at the left two jacks step out and dance. They bow and scrape before the three kings in their hand, carrying their trains and saluting them endlessly to a comic martial tune. They fall back into line and bow ceremoniously to the right after they have danced a courtly measure.

The Queen of Hearts steps out of the second hand, bounces in royal attitude, and dances a sprightly variation to a vivacious tune while throwing kisses gaily to everyone. She resumes her place, and the Queen of Clubs emerges and dances alone. She spins rapidly with her arms extended and as the whirring tune finishes, she stands with her hands on her hips while the Queen of Diamonds performs a difficult series of steps to a fresh melody. The Queen of Spades follows her, and then all four queens stand and watch the Jack of Hearts, their one remaining card, perform his variation. He bows to the queens; they all dance together and resume their places. They gesture toward the hand arranged in the center. Four aces and the ubiquitous joker come forward, the joker walking arrogantly, congratulating himself on the good luck he brings. But his hand has won the deal on its own merit, without his help.

The joker dances with the four queens as all the other cards leave the stage. He pulls them around in a line as he kisses the hand of the Queen of Hearts, then tags onto the end of the line. The joker stands in the middle of the line and dances lackadaisically with the queens, amusing himself at their silly posturings and leading them in a dance that burlesques their charm. Finally he pushes them all into the wings.

THIRD DEAL : The same march begins the third deal. A line of cards, their identities concealed as before, file out from the right; the cards are dealt into three hands. The hand on the left—a flush of Hearts, the five, six, seven, eight, and nine—walk to the front and dance pertly but modestly. They retire, and the joker dances forward with the hand on the right—the seven, eight, nine, and ten of Spades—with the joker, a higher flush than the first hand. The joker tries to play off his Spades against the Hearts, but the first hand moves away to stand in front of the final hand, which is still unrevealed. The joker and his Spades form a huddle to decide on the best method of play, then the five cards form a line, with the joker at the end. He bumps the girls forward and dances with them playfully as the orchestra mimics a bright melody of Rossini's.

The Hearts move forward; the joker and his Spades run back to see the final hand and stand aghast as they behold a royal flush: the ten, Jack, Queen, King, and Ace of Hearts! The joker grips his head in despair: he can laugh no longer when the joke is on him. He falls on his back, the music laughs at him, he rolls over and crawls off.

The royal flush marches forward to a delightful tune. The jack holds up his hand, trumpeting their arrival; the king and queen raise their hands in greeting and congratulate each other that the royal family is reunited. The queen jumps and everyone jumps. All the cards in the three deals gather behind them. They blow kisses to all her family and everyone else in sight and they all bow to her in mock humility. The other cards come to shake the hands of the lucky hand, and the king and queen welcome them. The king orders all the Hearts in the deck to come forward with the royalty. The other suits form lines behind the Hearts and all dance a courtly measure to the king's command. The deck of cards form a tableau about the queen. She is lifted high above them; the surrounding multitude fall forward in obeisance to her; and as the lights go out, all the cards are seen scrambled together in the middle of the table, shuffled together for a new game.

NOTES: *Card Game* was the first collaboration between Stravinsky and myself in the United States. In 1936, when Lincoln Kirstein and I decided upon a Stravinsky Festival for the American Ballet, we wanted to present a new Stravinsky ballet. We wrote to Stravinsky in Paris, commissioning him to write a new ballet. We told him to write anything he wanted. He decided on a dance with playing-card characters, a poker-game ballet.

Soon after the score arrived in New York and I had begun rehearsals on the new ballet, Stravinsky himself arrived. As always, the ballet was a collaboration. Lincoln Kirstein has noted that Stravinsky possesses "the profound stage instinct of an amateur of the dance, the 'amateur' whose attitude is so professional that it seems merely an accident that he is not himself a dancer."

In *Card Game*, Stravinsky and I attempted to show that the highest cards—the kings, queens, and jacks—in reality have nothing on the other side. They are big people, but they can easily be beaten by small cards. Seemingly powerful figures, they are actually mere silhouettes.

Card Game was revived by the Ballet Russe de Monte Carlo at the Fifty-first Street Theatre, New York, October 14, 1940, with Frederic Franklin as the joker and a cast that included Alexandra Danilova, Nathalie Krassovska, Alicia Markova, André Eglevsky, and Igor Youskevitch. In the most recent revival by the New York City Ballet (first performance February 15, 1951), Todd Bolender and Janet Reed have danced the joker and leading parts have been danced by Janet Reed, Patricia Wilde, Doris Breckenridge, Jillana, Francisco Moncion, Frank Hobi, Michael Maule, and others.

Another version of Stravinsky's score was choreographed in 1945 by Janine Charrat and had its first performance by the Ballets des Champs-Elysées in Paris, with Jean Babilée as the joker.

CARMEN

Dramatic ballet in five scenes inspired by the opera by Meilhac and Halévy. Music by Georges Bizet. Choreography by Roland Petit. Scenery and costumes by Antoine Clavé. First presented by Les Ballets de Paris de Roland Petit at the Prince's Theatre, London, February 21, 1949, with Renée Jeanmaire and Roland Petit in the principal roles. First presented in the United States by Les Ballets de Paris at the Wintergarden, New York, October 6, 1949, with the same principals.

SCENE ONE—A PUBLIC SQUARE IN SEVILLE: What seems to be a building with an outside staircase stands at the back of the square, and from it a long clothesline hung with multicolored garments suggests that it is a cheap public square. Three men play at cards on a plank that has been set up between two high ladders. Couples mill about the square in a casual and desultory manner, smoking, dancing occasionally with simulated high spirits, but in general implying that if they wait about long enough, something important may happen. They are not disappointed. Upstairs in the building someone is making a ruckus. Everyone listens attentively. Down the stairs runs an unfortunate girl who is clearly having difficulty with her pursuer. We understand why when we see that her pursuer is Carmen.

Everyone in the public square knows Carmen, every woman and especially every man. By experience and reputation fierce in love, Carmen is also fierce in jealousy, and although no one knows or cares what she is fighting with this other girl about, all the people in the square assume that the fight is worth watching. They take sides. Between two groups who egg them on, Carmen and the girl scratch each other and tear each other's hair out and kick each other around. The crowd is delighted with their ferocity and cheers spitfire Carmen when she succeeds in throwing her opponent to the ground. Just as they begin to express their enthusiasm for her victory, Don José, cape flying, enters on the run. Everybody seems to know him, too.

Don José is an official of some sort, a man from another part of the town, perhaps a policeman in mufti. He does not approve of what is going on and tries to break up the crowd. He takes pity on the prostrate girl, but then he sees her conqueror. The music sounds an ominous theme; the drum beats warningly. Don José is transfixed, immediately attracted to Carmen, as all the men seem to have been. He takes in her long and supple body, her boyish bob, her defiant eyes, her wide red mouth that seems a brilliant slash across her white round face, and doesn't know what to do. Then he remembers his duty. He seizes Carmen by the shoulder, coldly, officially, to admonish her. Carmen responds by glaring up at him and yanking down her blouse to expose the voluptuousness of her other shoulder. Don José is confused. Instead of arresting her, he allows Carmen to make a rendezvous with him. He dashes off, and the spectators nod to themselves knowingly.

SCENE TWO—A TAVERN: The stage is dark as the curtain rises on the second scene. Gradually a line of paper lanterns light up across the scene, and behind the lanterns is a tavern: tables and chairs, a bar in the back, and steps leading to an upstairs room. A number of steady customers are disposed about the tavern. A couple are making love, indifferent to their surroundings, and other habitués sit on the wooden chairs in an attitude of boredom. Some of them get up and start a kind of dance—wiggling and stomping and turning cart wheels and revolving the chairs on one leg—signifying their willingness to make the evening a deliberate, if not a spontaneous, success. Back near the bar, a man cloaked in black dozes.

Don José enters the room. He enters it just as he entered the public square: officiously, disapprovingly. But in the tavern, he senses that this will not be tolerated. After all, he has come on his own account, not on any official business, and everyone happens to know his particular business. And so, he joins the steady customers to prove that he is a regular fellow. He dances all by himself to prove also that he is a dashing fellow, while the crowd stands back and sings to the rhythm of his stomping the "Habañera." Although this song, with its warnings of rebellious love that can never be tamed, accompanies Don José's solo, he is sensitive only to its rhythms, which the spectators accentuate with militant clapping of hands. Don José is thinking of his meeting with Carmen.

Carmen has apparently been hiding behind the bar all this time. Suddenly, we see her sitting on top of it. Two gallants lift her down, and she commences a dance of her own. She carries a small black fan, which she holds close to her breasts. Her naked shoulders and her hair are covered with shiny spangles that fall from her body as she turns in powerful spins. Carmen's dance has more dash and strength than Don José's, and everyone watches her long legs as she traverses the tavern with steps that reveal her character as an untamable lover. Don José observes her more intently than the rest. At the end of her dance, Carmen kneels at his feet, her arms open in a gesture of welcome that is both public and intimate.

Don José goes to her. Carmen pretends that she is indifferent and fans herself nonchalantly. A pickpocket tries to rob Don José, but he brushes him aside. He picks Carmen up, holding her knee in his arm. He carries her closely, possessively, as if she had never been carried by a man before. He turns and carries her upstairs; Carmen relaxes in his arms.

When the two lovers have disappeared, two men and a girl begin a tempestuous dance that attracts all the customers. All join in the dance and whip themselves into a frenzy of happiness. Carmen's rendezvous has been a success, Don José has been seduced, and there is cause for rejoicing: they need fear officials no more. Carmen and Don José run down the stairs and lead the dance. The crowd fall on their knees around the lovers and beat the floor to the hysterical rhythm of their feet. At the climax of the music, Don José enfolds Carmen in his cape and runs off with her.

SCENE THREE—CARMEN'S ROOM: IT IS THE MORN-ING AFTER: Don José pulls back the yellow curtains that conceal the boudoir from the audience, and bright sunlight from an open window fills the room. Carmen lies on a disordered iron bed, sucking a plum. She rises lazily, stretches, and slowly goes into a dance. Don José pours water in a basin, washes his hands, dries them on the curtains, and seems not to notice the increasing sensuous pleasure Carmen derives from her own seductiveness. He sits and watches her disinterestedly. She caresses her body, her hands moving from her hair over her face to her shoulders, her breasts and her thighs, and up again to her face. Don José shows no signs of interest and, tired of self-love, Carmen turns away with disgust toward the balcony outside the window. The noise of the street attracts her. Instantly, Don José is on his feet. Really, he isn't tired at all. He wishes her to stay! Carmen moves to leave the room, but Don José pulls her back. Carmen, however, will be detained only by love. The lovers kiss and begin a dance together.

Don José lifts Carmen up to his shoulder, then holds her as her body comes down full length in his arms. Carmen's interest in him is renewed and gradually she compels Don José to share her passion. His body falls back to the floor and he braces himself on his arms and legs as Carmen poses aggressively above him, her knee resting between his. Carmen's breathing is now as lusty as her movements, and Don José responds fully. The climax of her passion approaches. She lies upon him. Don José raises his knees, and Carmen's legs stretch out straight from her curved body in an attitude of diving. The tenseness in their bodies relaxes as the music ends and the two lovers lie exhausted.

Barely has their passion subsided than three of Carmen's friends enter to persuade them to come out into the street. The friends whisper secretively to Carmen, and she motions to Don José to follow them. Now he will follow her anywhere.

SCENE FOUR—A STREET IN SEVILLE: It is night again. The scene is abandoned. Old cart wheels stacked against posts constitute the only scenery. Carmen and Don José, followed by her friends, walk on carefully, not wishing to be overheard. Cloaks disguise their identity. There is a brief conference. They are giving Don José his final instructions. Carmen puts a dagger in his hand. He listens and nods; the others leave and he is alone. The orchestra again sounds the theme that marked the first, fateful meeting of Carmen and Don José, and the drum now beats the rhythm of death. Don José stomps his feet in unison with the drum and waits. On the right, a man in a purple cloak enters. Don José seems to recognize him, stands motionless as he passes, then throws himself upon him. He stabs the man in the back. The man falls flat on his face. Don José reaches for his purse. Carmen and her bandit friends run out from hiding, grab for the money, and run off. Don José kicks the body over and follows them.

SCENE FIVE—IN FRONT OF THE PLAZA DE TOROS: Now that Don José has become a part of Carmen's life and has made the ultimate sacrifice and killed for her, Carmen begins to lose interest in him. She must always be taming someone to her will; once they have given in, she must seek new conquests. At the beginning of the fifth scene a crowd of lovely girls dressed colorfully but formally stand outside the arena, the Plaza de Toros, waiting for the bullfight to start—but waiting, too, for the arrival of the handsome toreador. The toreador, brought in on the shoulders of his admirers, gets down smartly and welcomes the greetings of the girls. As he flirts with them, he notices Carmen standing away from the crowd. She stares at him. She wears a veil, and the toreador prefers her indifference to the open affection of the young ladies. Don José enters and observes this silent exchange between Carmen and the toreador. The bullfight is about to begin; the toreador turns away from Carmen regretfully, and the crowd follows him into the arena. Carmen starts to join them.

Don José rushes up to her, tears off her veil, and grasps her throat in a passion of jealousy. He holds her face between his hands, and Carmen defies him. They separate, take positions at either side of the stage, and stand for a moment facing each other with so deep an anger that they become animal in their hatred. One of them must tame the other. The drum sounds slowly in a staccato beat; spotlights magnify and double the shadows of Carmen and Don José against the side of the arena. They approach and separate in a manner very similar to the fight in progress inside the ring, daring each other on, determined that one of them shall die. The drum beats faster and louder; Carmen circles Don José. He pulls out the dagger, rushes her quickly, and stabs her in the heart. He holds her about the waist as her body writhes back. She reaches up a trembling arm and caresses the face of her lover. She can stand no longer. Don José holds her to him still, and her legs vibrate with her heart's last beat. She falls limp. The music sounds brilliantly. Hats are thrown in from the arena. The fight has been won. The love has been lost.

NOTES: Soon after *Carmen's* London *première*, Cyril W. Beaumont wrote in *Ballet:* "As a conception for the theatre, *Carmen* is superb. Vigorous, racy, dramatic, it glows and throbs with passion. The *pas de deux* in Scene III is a remarkable stylization of the course of passionate love rendered with the insight and subtlety of a combined Stendhal and Choderlos de Laclos. Indeed, the whole *pas* is so bold that success or failure is balanced on a knife-edge. It could so easily evoke ribald mirth or cries of shocked protest; yet, interpreted with the tact, skill, and artistry of Jeanmaire and Petit, it is a masterpiece of emotional experience . . . Petit gives a fine performance as Don José, not only as dancer and mime, but also as cavalier. . . . Jeanmaire's Carmen is a magnificent creation . . . What a dancer! What an actress! What vitality! What power to portray subtle shades of varied emotions! And how intensely she feels each change of mood, forcing the spectator to share in her loves and her hates, her moments of gaiety and her moments of fear! Whatever Jeanmaire may achieve in the future, I shall never forget her Carmen. . . ."

CARNAVAL

Romantic ballet in one act. Music by Robert Schumann. Choreography by Michel Fokine. Scenery and costumes by Léon Bakst. Book by Michel Fokine. First presented at Pavlova Hall, St. Petersburg, 1910, with Tamara Karsavina as *Columbine*, Vera Fokina as *Chiarina*, Ludmilla Shollar as *Estrella*, Bronislava Nijinska as *Papillon*, Leonide Leontiev as *Harlequin*, Vsevolod Meyerhold as *Pierrot*, Enrico Cecchetti as *Pantalon*, and Joseph Kchessinsky as *Florestan*. First presented in Western Europe by Diaghilev's Ballets Russes at the Théâtre National de l'Opéra, Paris, June 4, 1910, with the same principals except for the following substitutions: Vaslav Nijinsky as *Harlequin*, Adolph Bolm as *Pierrot*, and Ivan Kussov as *Florestan*. First presented in the United States by Diaghilev's Ballets Russes at the Century Theatre, New York, January 1916.

First performed as a *divertissement* for a benefit in St. Petersburg, *Carnaval* was later revived and presented in Paris by Diaghilev. It became one of the most popular ballets in his repertory and one of the most popular works in the repertories of ballet companies that have since performed it, though it must be admitted that contemporary revivals have hardly retained the spirit of the original. The music is an orchestration of Schumann's *Carnaval* Suite for piano. The principal characters—Pierrot, Columbine, etc., are drawn from the *commedia dell'arte*, the popular early Italian street comedies.

The scene is an antechamber to a ballroom. At the rise of the curtain, we are introduced to the atmosphere of the ball that is taking place in the next room. Girls run by, pursued by their escorts. Dancing couples from the ball take refuge in the empty spaces of the anteroom and waltz. Chiarina and Estrella, two charming girls, enter with their partners. Two lovers kiss in passing and return to the ball.

Pierrot, the sad clown, pokes his head into the room. He steps into the room carefully, lest anyone hear or see him, his long, loose sleeves flapping dejectedly at his sides. He moves with slow melancholy; he seems to be saying that he is the only one in the world who will not dance and enjoy himself at the ball. Aware of his ugliness and awkwardness, he is filled with self-pity.

Harlequin bounces in, notes the melancholy Pierrot, and taunts him for not joining in the fun the music calls for. Unmercifully the energetic Harlequin pokes at the helpless clown, who falls to the floor. The irrepressible Harlequin leaves him in disgust.

Couples from the ball dance through the anteroom again. Pierrot looks at them and takes himself off before he can be chided once more.

Now the romantic poet Eusebius enters. He sits on a settee and wistfully contemplates a vision he has of an ideal lady. The lady materializes in the form of Chiarina, who gives him a rose. Estrella, ambitious and flirtatious, enters pursued by the eager Florestan, who beseeches her to grant him the favor of some small attention. Estrella pretends to disapprove of his advances, but then links her arm in his; the two exit for a dance.

Eusebius and Chiarina dance, or rather Chiarina dances and Eusebius observes her with adoring eyes. They leave the scene together.

Papillon, a girl whose varied, busy movements suggest a perpetual giddiness, rushes in. Pierrot discreetly follows her, hoping to make a conquest at last. He watches her from behind a settee, then bounds out into the room to catch her. When poor Pierrot thinks he has finally found a partner, Papillon escapes his grasp and leaves. The helpless clown is alone again.

Now there is an interval of dancing by Chiarina and two of her girl friends, who are masked. Florestan, still in pursuit of the coquettish Estrella, comes into the room. The girls playfully try to detain him, but the determined youth flees.

Columbine, gay and flirtatious, enters with Harlequin. They play together amorously. Though she seems to like him very much, the girl refuses Harlequin's invitation to elope. Their rendezvous is interrupted by the foppish Pantalon, who sits on a settee and reads with relish a note. Columbine goes to the back of the settee and puts her hands over Pantalon's eyes, while Harlequin snatches the note away from the intruder.

Pantalon, who was only reading the note to attract attention, tries to ingratiate himself with Columbine, who toys with him amusingly and then suggests that he join her and Harlequin in a *pas de trois*. At the end of the dance, she and Harlequin send Pantalon on his way.

Harlequin sits on the floor and indicates to Columbine that his heart lies at her feet. The fickle girl goes to the settee, where Harlequin sits adoringly in front of her.

The dancers return and, observing Harlequin and Columbine, congratulate them on their love. Columbine is suddenly nice to everyone. She comforts the pompous Pantalon and permits poor Pierrot to kiss her hand. All join in a happy dance.

The joviality is cut short by a crowd of busybodies, proper people who think that the people in the anteroom are not behaving with decorum. The gay dancers mock them and shove them about until they take flight. In the melee, the trickster Harlequin sees that Pierrot and Pantalon are pushed together. Before the two can separate themselves, Harlequin has tied Pierrot's long sleeves together around Pantalon. While Pantalon tries to release his bonds, all the other dancers gather about Columbine and Harlequin to form an admiring tableau.

CHECKMATE

Dramatic ballet in one scene with prologue. Music by Arthur Bliss. Choreography by Ninette de Valois. Scenery and costumes by E. McKnight Kauffer. First presented by the Sadler's Wells Ballet at the Théâtre des Champs-Elysées, Paris, June 15, 1937, with June Brae as the *Black Queen*, Robert Helpmann as the *Red King*, Pamela May as the *Red Queen*, Harold Turner and William Chappell as the *Red Knights*, Richard Ellis and Michael Somes as the *Black Knights*, Frederick Ashton and Alan Carter as the *Two Players*, and a cast that included Margot Fonteyn and Leslie Edwards. First presented in England by the Sadler's Wells Ballet at the Sadler's Wells Theatre, October 5, 1937, with the same principals. First presented in the United States by the Sadler's Wells Ballet at the Metropolitan Opera House, New York, November 2, 1949, with Beryl Grey as the *Black Queen*, Leslie Edwards as the *Red King*, Gerd Larsen as the *Red Queen*, Alexis Rassine and John Field as the *Red Knights*, Kenneth Melville and Philip Chatfield as the *Black Knights*, and a cast that included Pauline Clayden, Rosemary Lindsay, Rowena Jackson, Kenneth Macmillan, and John Cranko.

Checkmate is an allegory, a story of the battle between love and death told in terms of a chess game. It is apparent from the beginning who will win, but the contest, with its determined conflicting forces, creates a dramatic situation that often precludes prediction and the spectator, like the quiet chess player, finds himself deliberating the outcome.

The terms of the allegory are introduced in a prologue. The music is ominous, doomful, without relief in its projection of the battle to come. The curtain rises on a chess game. Two players in armor, Love and Death, sit opposite each other at a small table in the center of the stage. The chess game begins as Love makes a move. Death watches, deliberates, and moves his skeletonlike hand over the table. He moves. Love tries to analyze the situation, will not move again as he sees that the situation is hopeless: it is checkmate and there has not been any game at all. Black-out.

A backdrop rises, and we see that the stage is covered with black and white squares, as on a chessboard. The red chessmen enter and begin to take their places on the board. First come the eight pawns, danced by girls, gay and lighthearted pages to the royalty to come. The two red knights march in from opposite sides of the board and practice their fierce skill in combat. Two black knights, sent by the enemy to report on the strength of the other side, herald the entry of the black queen, whose omnipotence over all the pieces on the board is soon apparent. She beats off one of the red knights who will not submit to her attractions. To make himself attractive to her, the other red knight dances a vigorous mazurka. When he finishes, she rewards him with a red rose—Death's symbol of the blood she will spill before she is through. The pawns leave the board, followed by the conquering black queen and the black knights. In their absence, one of the red knights dances the praises of the black queen. Two red bishops parade in ceremoniously, followed by two red castles. Finally the red king and queen enter. Both knights salute them. The red king, old and doddering, can hardly make his way about the board and it is clear he can win nothing, while the queen is anything but a matriarch. The red pieces are now all in place, and the game begins in earnest.

The black queen leads the onslaught. The red king tries to maneuver his forces to prevent a frontal attack, but the black queen sees an opening and dashes through the enemy line. Even the two red bishops cannot hold off the black pieces. The red queen begs for mercy for her king, but the relentless black queen delivers her into the hands of her two knights.

The red knight, who imagined himself powerful in love, even with the black queen, attempts to rally his king's forces. For a time the contest is equal, for the knight's love of his king appears to be a match for his passion for the enemy queen. But when he must choose, when he has the chance to slay the queen, when she is kneeling helpless before him, he naturally hesitates. The black queen laughs in his face and cuts him down. The red king despairs. Death enters. The body of the defeated red knight is held high by the red pieces, and Death leads the cortege off the board.

The red king has been abandoned; he is alone on the board with the black queen. She toys with him like a snake. He cannot escape: wherever he turns, a new black piece appears to block his path. He makes a pathetic figure—but then, from the beginning he has seemed weak and powerless—and the black queen's game with him becomes a protracted mercenary exhibition of power. She looks at him as if wondering whether the game were worth winning after all, he being such a contemptible creature. He is backed into his throne. Now, with nothing to lose, the king fights back with vigor for a brief moment. The black queen admires his mettle so much that she condescends to kill him. It is checkmate indeed.

NOTES: *Checkmate*, long in the repertory of the Sadler's Wells Ballet, was one of this company's first modern productions to be introduced to the American audience. On the occasion of its New York *première*, Walter Terry wrote in the New York *Herald Tribune* that *Checkmate* was "a superbly composed dance work by the company's director, Ninette de Valois. 'Composed,' I think, describes it accurately for . . . its major virtue is its dance invention. Miss de Valois has created an impressive array of dance patterns, strong and sharp and fresh."

CINDERELLA

Ballet in three acts. Music by Serge Prokofiev. Choreography by Frederick Ashton. Scenery and costumes by Jean-Denis Malclès. First presented by the Sadler's Wells Ballet at the Royal Opera House, Covent Garden, London, December 23, 1948, with Moira Shearer as *Cinderella*, Michael Somes as the *Prince*, Robert Helpmann and Frederick Ashton as *Cinderella's Stepsisters*, Pamela May as the *Ragged Fairy Godmother*, Nadia Nerina, Violetta Elvin, Pauline Clayden, and Beryl Grey as the *Fairies*, and Alexander Grant as the *Jester*. First presented in the United States by the Sadler's Wells Ballet at the Metropolitan Opera House, New York, October 18, 1949, with Margot Fonteyn as *Cinderella* and the same principals.

Cinderella is a story everybody knows and in the past it has attracted a great number of choreographers—French, Russian, and English. This particular ballet on the story, however, is important for a special reason: it is the first classic English ballet in three acts, the first full-length English work in the style and manner of the great nineteenth-century classics. But *Cinderella* is entertaining as well as important. Here the familiar tale is embellished with dramatic and comic differences, with *divertissements*, and with the grace and warmth of the grand academic style.

ACT ONE: A room in the house of Cinderella's father. The curtain rises on a somber scene. Cinderella crouches on the hearth of a high stone fireplace on the right. On the left, at a plain table, her father sits reading. Near him sit Cinderella's two stepsisters, busily sewing a scarf. They are elderly and hideous, and there is an obvious tension in the room. Cinderella is sitting by the fireplace because she is not allowed to sit anywhere else. Dressed in worn, unbecoming brown, she makes a pathetic figure. The light shines on her face and, despite her sadness, we note that she is beautiful. The music is quiet but expectant; strings are plucked rapidly to sound curiously like the clicking of knitting needles.

The stepsisters, old maids that they are, have been invited to a ball this very night and they work at their sewing with some haste. They finish the scarf and begin to fight about who shall wear it. Cinderella glances at them as if their bickering were all too familiar: in this house there is either quarreling or silence. But she is afraid to interfere. She is no longer the daughter of the house but its servant. The daughters of her father's second wife now rule the house, and she, like her father, can exist only by conforming to their wishes.

The father tries to calm his stepdaughters, but abandons hope when they ignore him. Each tugs at her end of the scarf, and it is torn in two. The stepsisters leave the room, still quarreling, and he follows after them despondently. Cinderella is alone. She takes up a broom and moves wistfully about the room, posing gracefully. She is thinking of happier days, when her mother was alive and there was love for her to respond to. She picks up a piece of the scarf her stepsisters have left behind and puts it around her shoulders: now she is a lady, the lady her mother would have wanted her to be. She takes a candlestick from the table, crosses the darkened room, lights the candle at the fireplace, and holds it high to look upon her mother's portrait, which hangs above the mantel. The father returns, sees his daughter's despair, and attempts to cheer her. But he, too, is sad. The ugly stepsisters come in and reprimand him for keeping Cinderella from her housework. They warn the girl to return to her cleaning.

The orchestra sounds a new, magical melody. The stepsisters hear it, too. Cinderella looks up expectantly, and into the room hobbles a hunchbacked woman in rags. Her face is grotesque, her rags are filthy, but Cinderella seems to welcome her. The old hag begs for money, and the two stepsisters go into a tizzy of silly fear, running away to the other side of the room. Cinderella would like to comfort the old hag, but she knows that she has nothing to give. When the woman begs from her, Cinderella can only give her a bit of bread. The elder stepsister is annoyed at this generosity and threatens the woman. But, like an omen fulfilled, she is suddenly seized with a toothache and flees back to her sister. As Cinderella watches, wishing she could help more, the old hag glances at her gratefully and gently and disappears.

No sooner has the father reminded his two stepdaughters that they must begin to dress for the ball, than purveyors arrive—a tailor, dressmakers, a shoemaker, a jeweler, a hairdresser, a dancing master, each taking advantage of the sisters' new-found popularity to sell all their wares and talents. The old women are delighted at this attention, costly as it may be, and titter constantly like debutantes. Soon they are decked out in extravagant dresses. At this point the dancing master reminds them of the courtly steps in which they must be perfect. The women practice their bows and try to dance, as two violinists play a gavotte. The elder stepsister, old as she is, manages to execute the gavotte more or less to the dancing master's satisfaction, while the meek, shy sister despairs of learning. The dancing master sees that neither will ever learn and finally pretends that both are perfect.

The time of the ball is drawing near, and the stepsisters hurry with their make-up, primping extravagantly, as if all the powder and rouge in the world would reduce their ugliness. Their coach is announced, there is a final flurry of activity, and the sisters, absurdly proud in their bearing, depart.

Again Cinderella is alone. She looks into the fire. The women did not even bother to say good night to her. She wonders what the ball will be like, what any ball is like. She dances again with the broom, holding it before her as if she were not waltzing alone, and moves happily about the room, imagining herself at the ball. Soon she sees how silly she is being, puts the broom down, and goes back to sit at the hearth.

The harp is plucked gently, and again the eerie, high, piercing cry that heralded the arrival of the old beggarwoman causes Cinderella to look up and smile. The music is magical, like the loveliness of a dream; it grows in volume as the lower strings sound a full, promising melody. The room in which Cinderella sits seems to disappear, its walls vanishing. The old woman stands in the center of the room. She looks at Cinderella, and then something more extraordinary happens. In a flash, the old hag is transformed into a lovely, kind fairy: the ragged cretin becomes a beautiful creature dressed in a shimmering gown.

Cinderella cannot believe her eyes and when her fairy godmother tells her that she must prepare for the ball, that now, really, she *is* going to the ball, the lonely girl almost cries with happiness. The fairy godmother waves her wand, calling forth four fairies to dress Cinderella for the ball.

First comes the fairy Spring, then the fairies Summer, Autumn, and Winter. One by one, the fairies each dance a variation. After each one appears, the accompanying backdrop vanishes and Cinderella's room stretches back into the distance farther and farther. The scenery is transformed completely for each fairy, changing in color from green to icy blue, in surroundings from abundant garlands to a pinnacle of ice, and the fairies and their attendants are dressed charmingly in the habits of their seasons.

Cinderella sits on the floor at the feet of her fairy godmother, taking in the full magic of her great powers. Now she understands. The fairy godmother tells her to bring a pumpkin. Before the girl's astonished eyes, she changes the pumpkin into a magnificent coach. Cinderella is surrounded by the fairies, who present gifts to her and dress her for the ball. Almost at their touch, the lonely girl becomes as beautiful as a fairy tale princess, dressed splendidly in white and gold, wearing a crown and a long, flowing cape with a high pearl collar that encloses her shining face.

Her godmother tells Cinderella not to delay, that a new-found happiness awaits her at the ball. But she warns the girl that she must leave the ball before the clock strikes twelve. If she remains after midnight, the magic will vanish as mysteriously as it came and she will be just a lonely girl again, dressed in shabby clothes. Cinderella promises that she will not tarry and bows to her in gratitude. The fairies and a multitude of stars surround Cinderella as she goes to her coach and proceeds to the ball.

ACT TWO — A BALL AT THE PALACE : The ball has already begun when the curtain rises. Members of the court are dancing a formal measure in a ballroom that has been set up in the palace garden. Two great trees and their overhanging branches enclose the festive scene. To the left and right, spectators watch the ball in low stage boxes. In the back, on either side of a flight of low steps, are two high elegant structures, pavilions set up especially for the ball. On the ground floor of these pavilions we can see other guests amusing themselves. Farther back, by the light of a distant chandelier, we can make out a splendid formal garden. At the top of the steps is the prince's throne. The prince has not yet arrived, and the court jester sits on the royal stool.

Cinderella's stepsisters make an absurdly grand entry in keeping with the elegance they have assumed for the occasion. Cinderella's father accompanies them and is made visibly ill at ease by their pretensions. The older sister is determined to enjoy herself and acts unimpressed by the beauty of the palace garden: it is all her due, designed for her enjoyment, and she imagines herself attractive. The younger sister is more honest and cannot so easily disguise the fact that all this elegance is strange to her. She tugs plaintively at her sister's dress and wants to go home. She is, of course, refused and resolves to see the evening out only when a courtier begins to pay her some attention, thus reviving her spirits. She is disenchanted when her jealous sister takes her suitor away.

Now, as another courtly dance commences, the two sisters have a chance to perform the measures the dancing master taught them. The older sister watches with disgust as the younger dances. She starts out well, and for a moment we think she is really going to make it, but her steps become tentative and it is soon apparent that she's forgotten every step she knows. The older sister laughs, executes the dance with grotesque accuracy, and then, to show off, tries to balance on one foot. The younger sister is terrified, and, of course, the show-off begins to topple over. The jester catches her as she stumbles about trying to keep from falling flat on her face.

Four friends of the prince enter and prepare the guests for the arrival of their host. The handsome prince enters with a regal but lively flourish, and all the guests bow to him. The two sisters attempt to make their reverence so that the prince will take particular notice of them, but he does not even glance at them. The prince's companions dance a *pas de quatre*, which is followed by another general dance by the court.

One guest has not yet arrived. The light, mysterious music that heralded the first appearance of Cinderella's ragged fairy godmother interrupts the court music, and everyone pauses. The jester, at the prince's order, goes to welcome the newcomer in the garden. The twelve girls representing stars and the four fairies with their pages enter at the rear, and the court wonders what to expect with such an elaborate preparation. All look toward the entrance to the ballroom as the prince awaits the guest. Finally the royal coach of Cinderella draws up to the garden gate. The girl steps out, and all are dazzled by her natural beauty and the loveliness of her costume. The prince, who is immediately charmed, takes Cinderella's hand and leads her forward. Two pages hold Cinderella's train while the stars and fairies kneel about their mistress. Wishing to discover more about this ravishing girl, the prince escorts her for a walk through the palace grounds.

The other guests, who have watched the entrance of Cinderella from the boxes at the sides of the ballroom, now mingle on the dance floor and begin a masked dance. The ugly stepsisters, of course, have not recognized Cinderella and accept her simply as visiting royalty. Soon the prince returns alone and dances a variation, after which he leaves the scene. Now Cinderella dances and in her movements she conveys the youthful and tender joy she feels at the ball. It is as if she belonged there, for she is unembarrassed and confident in her natural graciousness.

The two sisters, alone for a moment, spend their time gossiping about the unattractive girl who has gained the prince's favor. The two lovers return. The harp is plucked against a deep, flowing melody, and they begin a *pas de deux*. The dance is soft and considerate, yet strong in its regal elegance and the personal elegance of the handsome young pair. The prince kneels before Cinderella as their dance finishes. She responds to his love by dancing a variation that reflects her new-found pleasure in loving and being loved. She is so happy that she has no memory of her misery at home; she pirouettes rapidly, and her two stepsisters are a million miles away.

A Negro page brings to the prince an orange on a silver tray. This is the most highly prized fruit in all the kingdom and the finest gift he can give Cinderella. She accepts it graciously. Then the prince turns to the ugly stepsisters and bestows an orange on each of them. Instantly they begin to quarrel about whose orange is larger, and the dominating sister snatches the choice one away from the timid creature.

Cinderella and the prince lead the court in an ensemble dance. The music is a bright, sparkling waltz that gradually gains in sonorous force, and all the guests are caught up in the spirit of romance. Suddenly—as the waltz gains relentless force, cymbals shimmer, and we hear the loud ticking of a clock—a flourish of trumpets announces the approach of midnight. The cymbals crash, to warn Cinderella that she must hasten. The girl rushes from the prince's arms. He watches, astonished, as she tries to make her way through the crowded guests to the gate. The girl is desperate lest her secret be discovered. When she arrives at the gate, midnight has come. Her beautiful dress becomes her ragged work clothes, and she flees into the night, leaving behind one of her slippers. The prince cannot understand; he looks after her as the orchestra restates the theme of their *pas de deux* and the curtain falls.

ACT THREE, SCENE ONE—AFTER THE BALL: When the curtain rises on the first scene, again Cinderella is seen sitting by the fire in her father's house, just as she was at the entrance of the fairy godmother. She is asleep. She wakens, looks about, and thinks she has dreamed of the ball. Only the slipper she finds hidden in her apron convinces her that she really was there, that there was a handsome prince, and that he did love her. She dances again with the broom, reflecting in her steps her unhappiness before the ball, her recollection of her first love, and her resignation to her everyday life.

Her sisters return. They are so tired that they don't even wish to gossip until they have undressed and cast off the weight of their excessive finery. They sigh as they remove their shoes from their swollen feet. But soon they are taunting Cinderella with tall tales about the ball, the prince, and his attentions to them. They toy with the oranges he gave them, and Cinderella is thinking too much of what the ball was really like to care much about their prattling.

The women hear a disturbance in the street. Townswomen rush in and excitedly announce that a royal procession is waking everyone up, that the prince, enamored of a girl he cannot find, is determined to discover the owner of a shoe left behind at the ball. He vows that he will marry the girl whom the shoe fits.

The sisters are apprehensive lest the prince visit their house when they are not fully dressed and scurry about putting on their formal gowns and their tight shoes again. The prince enters with the jester and an entourage. He holds Cinderella's lost slipper in his hand and declares that the woman it fits shall become his wife. He does not notice the girl in rags who crouches at the fire. The stepsisters do obeisance before the prince, who responds to them so graciously that they imagine one of them might be the chosen one. First, the shy stepsister tries on the shoe. She knows it is silly to pretend that it will fit and gives up wistfully. The other sister is delighted at her failure, but has no more luck herself, despite much straining and pinching in an effort to force her foot into the shoe.

When it is apparent that she, too, is a misfit, Cinderella helps her pull the shoe off. As the girl kneels before her sister, the other slipper falls from her apron pocket. The prince sees it and asks the girl if she will try on the shoe.

Her stepsisters rail at her, but the prince insists. The shoe fits perfectly. At first the sisters cannot believe it, but when the prince announces that Cinderella will be his bride, they attempt in several reverential gestures to make up for the years of misery they have caused the girl. Cinderella understands them, pities them, and touches them lovingly as they bow before her. The prince and Cinderella embrace. The fairy godmother appears and raises her wand.

ACT THREE, SCENE TWO—AN ENCHANTED GARDEN: The scene is transformed. We find ourselves in a magical place, a colorful garden where the light seems to sparkle. There a great boat awaits the arrival of the lovers. The prince's friends and the fairies dance together, and Cinderella and the prince enter. Six of the stars surround them as they dance, the fairies pose gracefully with their cavaliers, and the music sounds soaringly the theme of ideal romance that marked the couple's first recognition of love. The fairy godmother and all the magical creatures wish the lovers godspeed, and they step into the waiting ship. The surging music falls off into soft measures that predict eternal joy. The prince holds Cinderella in his arms as they sail off on a happy voyage that will never end.

NOTES: *Cinderella* is the first all-English three-act classical ballet. The success of the Sadler's Wells productions of *The Sleeping Beauty* and *Swan Lake* suggested that this form of entertainment might well match the popularity of the conventional ballet program consisting of three or four different ballets. The acclaim with which *Cinderella* was greeted in England after its first performance confirmed this notion and led incidentally to the second all-English evening-long ballet, *Sylvia*, in 1952.

In the English magazine *Ballet*, the American critic Edwin Denby wrote of the *première:* "*Cinderella* lasts two hours and a half and doesn't seem long. The current that carries it is easy and gentle. Its hold on one's attention is so mild that an American like myself is hardly aware of being in the theatre. The spell it creates doesn't crystallize in a climax or a specific dance image but no mean gesture breaks the continuity of it. English is the lightness of its fragrance, the charm it holds is a grace of spirit, an English sweetness of temper. It doesn't excite, it ever so mildly refreshes. To keep in a three-act ballet such a tone, to sustain it without affectation or banality, shows Ashton's power, and he shows this in doing it as simply as possible, by keeping the dancing sweet."

Margot Fonteyn, for whom the title role in *Cinderella* was originally designed, fell ill before its first performance. Her part was taken by Moira Shearer and, later, by Violetta Elvin until Fonteyn recovered sufficiently to dance it.

The score by Prokofiev for *Cinderella* was composed between 1941 and 1944 for a Soviet production of Perrault's famous fairy tale.

CON AMORE

Classic ballet in three scenes. Music by Gioacchino Rossini. Choreography by Lew Christensen. Libretto by James Graham-Luhan. Scenery and costumes by James Bodrero. Scenery executed by James Martin. First presented by the San Francisco Ballet, March 10, 1953, at the War Memorial Opera House, San Francisco, with Sally Bailey, Nancy Johnson, and Leon Danielian in the principal roles. Presented by the New York City Ballet at the City Center, New York, June 9, 1953, with a cast headed by Sally Bailey, Nancy Johnson, Herbert Bliss, and Jacques d'Amboise.

Con Amore is a ballet about love as it was frequently depicted in nineteenth-century European engravings. It is about love as it was regarded a hundred years ago and about love as it is frequently still regarded today. The ballet is in three scenes, each of which has for its music an overture by Rossini: the overtures to La Gazza Ladra, Il Signor Bruschino, and La Scala di Seta.

SCENE ONE — THE AMAZONS AND THE BANDIT: After a musical introduction, the curtain rises on a stylized rustic scene. Here a company of Amazons, handsome and robust girls in smart military uniforms, are drilling under the command of their captain and her lieutenants. The girls move briskly and sharply, and it is apparent from their severe military bearing that they have never known love and wouldn't even entertain the idea of it. They are perfectly happy watching their beautiful captain as she sets an example of the brilliant skill in dancing and drill that they themselves hope to attain.

Love, however, asserts itself. A bandit invades the wood and dances among them. The girls treat the handsome intruder with disdain at first, but his uncontrolled gaiety and charm eventually pierce their hearts. But the vagabond bandit will have none of them. He will not be tied down by love and spurns their affections. He even dares to resist the charms of the lovely captain. At this point the perennial wrath of woman scorned holds the bandit at bay. The Amazons aim their muskets at him and he kneels before them, helpless. Black-out.

SCENE TWO — THE HUSBAND'S RETURN: After a short musical interlude, the curtain rises on the boudoir of a fashionable lady. She is alone in the room and is obviously preparing for a tryst. This turns out to be a series of trysts. The lady's husband is away at the moment, and all of her suitors have chosen this night to visit her.

First, a man about town knocks at her door. The lady admits him. The man attempts to embrace her, but the lady eludes him. It is clear, however, that she does not wish to elude him long. But before she can succumb, there is another knock at the door. The man about town hastily conceals himself, and the lady admits a sailor, who relentlessly chases her about her apartment, breathing lustily. He has almost worn the lady down when there is still another knock. The lady hides the sailor in her closet and admits a young student. This lad, instead of being eager for the lady's affections, finds her charms distasteful. She is obliged to make the advances, which the young man, knees quivering, just manages to escape. The man about town and the sailor, who have been watching all this, emerge from their hiding place to berate the student and resume their attack. There is another knock at the door. The lady's husband enters. He sees his wife with the three men and stares at them with his mouth open in astonishment. Black-out.

SCENE THREE—A TRIUMPH OF LOVE: In the final scene, we return to the finale of Scene One, where the bandit still kneels at the mercy of the angry Amazons. Amore (Cupid) enters in a chariot and with her skill attempts to remedy the situation. Hardly has she begun to do so than we are again presented with the dilemma of the finale of Scene Two. What is Amore going to do with all these men who seem to be in love with the same woman? But Amore solves everything. She draws her bow; her arrows pierce the hearts of all the men. As the curtain falls, the bandit, smitten finally with love for the Amazon captain, holds her in his arms; the lady is reunited with her husband; the man about town and the sailor embrace the Amazon lieutenants; and the timorous student, struck by love at last, rushes to claim Amore herself.

CONCERTO BAROCCO

Classic ballet in three movements. Music by Johann Sebastian Bach. Choreography by George Balanchine. Scenery and costumes by Eugene Berman. First presented by the American Ballet at the Theatre of Hunter College, New York, May 29, 1940, with Marie-Jeanne, Mary Jane Shea, and William Dollar in the principal roles.

The only preparation possible for this ballet is a knowledge of its music, for *Concerto Barocco* has no "subject matter" beyond the score to which it is danced and the particular dancers who execute it. Set to Bach's *Concerto in D minor for Two Violins*, the ballet tries to interest the audience only by its dancing, its treatment of the music, just as Baroque art and architecture interested people not because of their subjects but because of the decorative treatment that embellished those subjects.

Bach's great concerto can stand alone. Some people then wonder, why arrange a ballet to such music? Why not arrange ballets to music that is more dependent, music that dancing can "fill out"? The answer is that bad music often inspires bad dancing, bad choreography. It is not an accident that the dance masterpieces of Saint-Léon, Petipa, and Fokine all have scores that are also masterworks. *Coppélia, The Sleeping Beauty*, and *Petrouchka*, with their scores by Delibes, Tchaikovsky, and Stravinsky, suggested to each one of these choreographers an advance in the development of ballet.

Choosing pieces of music for dancing is a matter for the individual choreographer. A choreographer disinterested in classical dancing will not care to use scores by Bach and Mozart except for theatrical sensational reasons; he will select music more to his immediate purpose. But if the dance designer sees in the development of classical dancing a counterpart in the development of music and has studied them both, he will derive continual inspiration from great scores. He will also be careful, as he acts on this inspiration, not to interpret the music beyond its proper limits, not to stretch the music to accommodate a literary idea, for instance. If the score is a truly great one, suitable for dancing, he will not have need of such devices and can present his impression in terms of pure dance.

FIRST MOVEMENT — VIVACE : The curtain rises. The music begins. There are eight girls on stage. Dancing variously as one group, as two groups, and in duets, the girls correspond to the music the orchestra plays, but not in any strict or literal sense; they do not mirror the music, rather they move in accordance with its length, the space between its beginning and end being filled by a dance picture of the music. Just as the portrait is different from the news photograph, so the dance picture tries to tell something independent of an exact, bar-by-bar, rhythm-by-rhythm, mirror image of the music.

As the two violins take up their parts in the music, two soloists enter. Singly, together, and with the *corps de ballet*, they become a part of the dance orchestration. They support each other as the music of one violin entwines the other; they depict and develop dance themes that recur with the repetition and development of themes in the orchestra.

SECOND MOVEMENT — LARGO MA NON TANTO : Now the soloists leave the stage. The orchestra sounds the touching, lyrical melody. One of the soloists returns, accompanied by a male partner, who lifts her softly and slowly, turns her as the *corps de ballet* bend low before her, and leads her in and out of a maze formed by the *corps*. The music is tender, but it possesses a warm nobility and strength that the ballerina's partner allows her to imitate as its development proceeds. When the music gathers toward a full statement and the theme repeats again and again, climbing with each repetition to a climactic rest, the ballerina's partner lifts her without pause high over his head, over and over again, to the accumulating sound. Then, toward the end of the movement, the boy slides the girl low across the floor in three daring movements. The ballerina rises each time in an open pose that reflects the strength underlying the lyricism of the theme.

THIRD MOVEMENT — ALLEGRO : The music is now quickly rhythmic. All ten dancers seem to respond to it spontaneously, marking the beat of the music with soft, light jumps, crisp arm gestures, and syncopated groupings. As the joyous music ends, all the dancers kneel.

NOTES: When the American Ballet and Ballet Caravan merged in 1941 to become the American Ballet Caravan, *Concerto Barocco* was one of the works mounted especially for the new company's Latin-American tour, March–November 1941, sponsored by a contract with the Office of the Co-ordinator of Inter-American Affairs (Nelson A. Rockefeller, Co-ordinator).

The American Concert Ballet revived *Concerto Barocco* at the Y.M.H.A., New York, November 14, 1943, with Mary Jane Shea, Lillian Lanese, and Francisco Moncion in the leading roles.

On September 9, 1945, the ballet was again revived, by the Ballet Russe de Monte Carlo at the City Center, New York, but without the original Berman *décor* and costumes. Marie-Jeanne, Patricia Wilde, and Nicholas Magallanes danced the principal roles. Ruthanna Boris, Patricia Wilde, and Frank Hobi later danced *Concerto Barocco* in the Ballet Russe production.

The ballet was staged for the Marquis de Cuevas' Grand Ballet de Monte Carlo in Europe in 1948. Marjorie Tallchief, Ethery Pagava, and George Skibine were the principals at the first performance.

On October 11, 1948, *Concerto Barocco* was done by the New York City Ballet at this company's first performance at the City Center, New York. The original *décor* and costumes were restored. Marie-Jeanne danced the principal role. On September 13, 1951, the New York City Ballet presented a new production of *Concerto Barocco*, which had been absent from the repertory for several seasons. Maria Tallchief, Diana Adams, and Nicholas Magallanes took the principal roles. At later performances of this ballet, the principal roles were taken by Tanaquil LeClercq and Patricia Wilde. The ballet was danced in black practice costumes against a blue cyclorama.

CONSTANTIA

Classic ballet in three movements. Music by Frédéric Chopin. Choreography by William Dollar. Scenery by Horace Armistead. Costumes by Grace Houston. First presented by Ballet International at the International Theatre, New York, October 31, 1944, with Marie-Jeanne, William Dollar, and Yvonne Patterson in the principal roles. Revised and presented by Ballet Theatre at the Metropolitan Opera House, April 9, 1951. Scenery and costumes by Robert Davison. Lighting by Peggy Clark. Alicia Alonso, Igor Youskevitch, and Norma Vance danced the leading roles.

Constantia is a ballet based on Chopin's *Piano Concerto No. 2, in F minor.* As its title indicates, however, it is not a purely "abstract" ballet. Constantia

Gladkowska was a young singer at the Warsaw Conservatory much admired by Chopin. The composer was completely under her spell at one time, adored her passionately, yet he never actually met her. He dedicated the second movement, the Larghetto, of his second piano concerto to the young Polish singer to express his admiration. Although he never met her, his love remained so powerful that he wrote a friend saying that "unbearable longing" had driven him into exile.

Thus the ballet *Constantia*, while tracing in dance the lines of the piano concerto, also aims to evoke the fervor of Chopin's romance. It is pure dance touched with the pure romance that the composer felt for Constantia.

FIRST MOVEMENT—MAESTOSO: The ballet is danced by two principals—a ballerina and the *premier danseur*—a principal soloist, four secondary soloists, and eight couples. These dancers perform before a decorative green backdrop expressive of the spirit of spring. Their costumes are colored in light tints, fragile shades appropriate to youthful, idealistic romance. Here in the first movement, all the dancers are introduced. First, the four girls (secondary soloists) and the eight couples set the stage for the arrival of the principals. The first soloist leads the eight girls and they make patterns with the line of the music.

The ballerina enters with her partner. They meet, dance briefly, and the girls re-enter to separate them. The *premier danseur* performs a variation. In the background, the boys imitate his steps. The ballerina returns to him; he slips his arms through hers and carries her off.

The couples dance fervidly and rapidly, the romance of the principals serving as the ideal.

SECOND MOVEMENT—LARGHETTO: The lights dim. The principals enter as the orchestra sounds a lovely, soft lyric. The *premier danseur* holds the ballerina gently and lets her down to the floor. He sits beside her. They are oblivious to the dancers who surround them. As the trembling melody ends, the ballerina is lifted off into the wings by her lover.

THIRD MOVEMENT—ALLEGRO VIVACE: The lights come up, and the stage is filled with dancing couples. The ballerina enters alone. The boys and girls leap around her as she dances a light, vivacious solo. When she leaves the scene, the principal soloist performs a variation. Now the ballerina returns with her partner and they dance together, turning alternately, then together. He lifts her to his shoulder; as they leave the stage, the *premier danseur* turns around and around, the ballerina poised gracefully against him.

The music gathers its strength and moves toward an effusive and happy finish. A girl is lifted down a long diagonal of boys, the couples return, the *premier danseur* dances a final variation, the whole cast fills the stage, and the ballerina rejoins her lover for a final dance that ends in a graceful, romantic tableau.

NOTES: *Constantia* has a considerable stage history. It was the first ballet by the American choreographer William Dollar, creator of *The Duel*, *Five Gifts*, etc. The ballet's history began in 1936, when Dollar, then a principal dancer with the American Ballet at the Metropolitan Opera House, choreographed with me a ballet called simply *Classic Ballet*, to Chopin's Second Piano Concerto. Dollar was responsible for the first and third movements, I for the second.

In 1944, when Dollar staged *Constantia* for Ballet International, *Classic Ballet* was revised by Dollar into a unified work. Again, in 1951, the work was completely revised for Ballet Theatre. Originally entitled *Concerto* when it became a part of the Ballet Theatre repertory, the ballet later assumed its earlier name, *Constantia*, to prevent confusion with *Schumann Concerto*, the work that was first performed by Ballet Theatre the following season. *Constantia* is not to be confused with *Chopin Concerto*, the ballet by Bronislava Nijinska that was danced at one time by the Ballet Russe de Monte Carlo.

COPPÉLIA
or
THE GIRL WITH ENAMEL EYES

Classic ballet in three acts. Music by Léo Delibes. Choreography by Arthur Saint-Léon. Book by Charles Nuitter and Arthur Saint-Léon, after a story by E. T. A. Hoffmann. First presented at the Théâtre Impérial de l'Opéra, Paris, May 25, 1870, with Giuseppina Bozacchi as *Swanilda* and Eugenie Fiocre as *Franz*. First presented in the United States by the American Opera at the Metropolitan Opera House, New York, March 11, 1887, with Marie Giuri and Felicita Carozzi in the leading roles. First presented in England at the Empire Theatre, London, May 14, 1906, with Adeline Genée as *Swanilda*.

Just as *Giselle* is ballet's great tragedy, so *Coppélia* is its great comedy. Both ballets are love stories and both have their roots in real life as well as in fantasy. In *Giselle* there are ghosts to test the quality of the hero's love for the heroine, and in *Coppélia* there is another romantic device by which the heroine makes sure of her lover's devotion. This device is the beautiful, lifeless doll, whose quiet, mechanical beauty contrasts with the charming liveliness of the real-life heroine. Because the hero in *Giselle* can only meet his lost love briefly in fantasy, and thereafter she is lost to reality, the ending of the ballet is tragic. But in *Coppélia* the inadequacy of the fantastic wax doll leads the hero back to his real love, and the ending is happy. And where Albrecht in *Giselle* learns an unhappy lesson from which he will never completely recover, Franz in *Coppélia* learns a lesson that makes his life happy forever after.

ACT ONE — THE SQUARE : A spacious overture sets the tone for the whole ballet. The music begins with a melody of quiet dignity, first stated by the horns, then swept up by the strings. A muffled drum sounds, and the mood changes spontaneously to open gaiety as the orchestra plays a spirited, robust mazurka. At its conclusion, the curtain rises.

The scene is a square in any small town in Central Europe; the time is a sunny afternoon several hundred years ago. A small house in the back faces the audience; on the side, a higher dwelling with a balcony projecting from the second floor dominates the street. Other buildings cluster about the square in a pleasantly haphazard fashion. All the façades are clean and painted in bright colors, and the walls and roofs seen in the background confirm our impression of an old village whose charm has not been worn away by changing times. The square is empty. An old man, bent with age, hobbles out of the door of the house on the right. This is Dr. Coppélius, the town's most mysterious citizen. He is said to dabble in alchemy and magic, but no one knows precisely what he does. Coppélius looks up at the balcony of his house, and we see that a lovely young girl is sitting there, reading a book. She is hidden a little from the full light of the sun, is wholly preoccupied with her reading, and takes no notice of the old doctor. Coppélius points up at the studious girl, rubs his hands with satisfaction as if he were a delighted chaperone, and re-enters his house.

The door of the little house in the back opens in a moment, and Swanilda emerges. She is dressed in bright colors particularly becoming to her dark beauty. From her movements, we know almost immediately that she is very young and very much in love. The music to which she dances is piquant in the unembarrassed fullness of its melody, and Swanilda dances to it with obvious pleasure at some inner happiness. She walks rapidly on point, looking about the square anxiously to see that she is alone. She is expecting someone, but has some business of her own to attend to first. She glances up at the balcony of the large house and sees there the charming young girl, just as attractive as she is. The girl is intensely occupied and, holding the book rigidly before her, she does not look down to see Swanilda waving to her. Swanilda is annoyed. First of all she is annoyed because the girl is clearly snubbing her, but she is chagrined mostly because she has noticed that Franz, her fiancé, has also waved at this strange girl and has never mentioned it to her. Everyone calls the girl Coppélia. She is said to be the old man's daughter, but Coppélius has never appeared with her in the streets of the town and their relationship is just as unfathomable as Coppélius himself. Swanilda imitates her, holding an imaginary book before her. Then she bows low to Coppélia, in mock ceremony. Still the girl will not notice her. Swanilda stamps her foot in annoyance and dances briefly. She does not understand why Coppélia sits there reading on such a beautiful day and suspects she might be in a trance. On the other hand, she might be waiting for Franz! Swanilda approaches the house to see the girl more closely, shakes her fists at her, but quickly turns away as she hears Franz coming down the street. She is carefully hidden by the time he enters and she observes him secretly.

Franz is a high-spirited young peasant dressed in country costume. Like Swanilda, Franz is open and carefree by nature, but his heartiness masks a certain conceit: he seems not to have a care in the world and would not think it odd if every girl in the village adored him as much as Swanilda does. He does not go directly to Swanilda's door, but strides over to the house of Coppélius. After making sure that he isn't being watched, he glances up at the balcony. He waves to Coppélia flirtatiously, but also casually, as if he were in the habit of greeting her every time he passed. He points to Swanilda's door and remembers his love for her in the midst of this new infatuation. He clearly enjoys not knowing which lovely girl to choose. He clutches his heart as he looks up at Coppélia, then blows a kiss to her. Swanilda's worst suspicions of Franz's fickleness seem to be justified. Her suspicions become fears when Coppélia looks up from her book and waves back to Franz. Neither she nor Franz can see that behind the girl Coppélius stands concealed. He watches the flirtation with obvious disapproval, steps forward quickly, and closes the window curtains in Coppélia's face. Franz is abashed by this sudden disappearance of his new love. He is so distressed that he doesn't notice Swanilda, who has come into the square and stands right behind him. Swanilda refuses to attract his attention when he won't even turn away from the balcony; she walks off.

Now Franz consoles himself by remembering his rendezvous with Swanilda. But he does not have time to reach her door before Swanilda returns, bringing a beautiful butterfly she has just caught.

Franz takes the butterfly from her and pins it to his shirt. To Swanilda, this harmless gesture is a stab at her own broken heart. She bursts into tears and angrily accuses Franz of being unfaithful to her. He demurs, but she has no patience with his offhand answers and suggests that they come to him just as readily as his flirtations. Now that he sees how serious she is, Franz sincerely denies that he loves anyone else. But Swanilda is firm in her disbelief; she will not listen. Now Franz begins to lose his temper: how can she fail, he wonders, to see that he loves only her? Swanilda leaves the square, and Franz hails a party of peasants, their friends, who are unaware of the tension between the two lovers. They dance the rollicking mazurka that the orchestra first played in the overture, and when Swanilda joins them, her anxieties are momentarily dispelled. But she is determined to keep clear of Franz and, even at the sacrifice of her happiness, will accept no explanations.

The dancing of the peasants halts as the burgomaster enters the square. Everyone stands aside to make room for him and listens attentively as he tells them that on the next day the village will receive a great new bell for the town clock as a gift from the lord of the manor and that they must prepare themselves for the celebration attendant upon the ceremonies. The peasants are delighted at the idea of an unexpected festival. Their pleasure is so great that they do not pay much attention to strange noises emanating from the house of Coppélius.

The burgomaster goes on to say that the gracious lord will present handsome dowries to the girls who marry on the festival day. Several couples look at each other expectantly, but Swanilda is unmoved. Franz watches her closely. The burgomaster turns and asks her if she will be wed tomorrow. Unwilling to expose her broken heart to her friends and perhaps still hoping that she may be wrong about Franz's love, Swanilda resorts to fate and takes up an ear of wheat which the burgomaster offers her and shakes it near her ear, looking at her fiancé. The custom is—if she hears anything, her lover "loves her true"; if the wheat is silent, her lover "loves her not." Franz supports Swanilda in lovely deep poses as she bends low to listen to the wheat. Swanilda hears nothing. Franz, who thinks this pretense is silly, also hears nothing. She beckons to a friend and shakes the wheat again. The friend claims there is a sound, but Swanilda will not believe it. She throws the straw to the ground and announces that she and Franz are no longer engaged. Franz stalks away in disgust at the ways of women, while Swanilda joins her friends to dance a bright, gay tune as if nothing had happened to disturb their good time. A drum roll sounds, and Swanilda's friends dance a czardas, a Hungarian folk dance that starts out with slow, formal dignity and then increases in both speed and humor to become delirious with joy. The light grows darker and the group soon disbands. The stage is empty as night falls.

The door to Coppélius' house opens, and the wizened old man totters out. He pulls out a large key, locks the door, tries it several times, puts his key away, pats his pocket, and proceeds slowly across the square, leaning heavily on his cane. Obviously reluctant at leaving his house, Coppélius is easily frightened by a band of pranksters who rail at him good-humoredly, dance about him, and boisterously try to overcome his reluctance to join in. He loses his temper, which only encourages the fun. As they push him about, Coppélius drops his key. The villagers do not notice this and soon leave him. He shuffles across the street on his errand, shaking his head at their impertinence.

Swanilda and a group of her friends pass him as they enter on their way to supper. Swanilda is delighted to find that he has lost his key. She looks back toward Coppélius, who has now disappeared, and then at his house. Her friends easily persuade Swanilda to try the key in Coppélius' door. At last she will discover the illusive Coppélia alone! She goes to the door, fits the key to the lock, and signals pleadingly to her friends to follow. She steps in. She backs out hurriedly, frightened at her own audacity and the dark interior. Her friends line up behind her in single file, trembling with fear, and one by one they enter the house.

The square is deserted for a moment, then Franz comes in, armed with a ladder. The petulant youth is determined to have his love acknowledged

by Coppélia, now that Swanilda has renounced him, and he places the
ladder against the house. He is climbing up to a window when Coppélius,
who has finally missed his key, rushes in to look for it. He apprehends Franz,
attacks him with his walking stick, and chases him off. He then continues to
search for the key. When he fails to find it and discovers that his door is
wide open, he throws up his hands in despair and with great agitation runs
into the house. The persistent Franz re-enters, places his ladder again, and
climbs toward the mysterious Coppélia. The curtain falls.

ACT TWO—COPPÉLIUS' HOUSE: The scene is a large room
with dark walls. There is a large window at the back, and on the left is a
curtained enclosure. Curious immobile figures, staring straight ahead, sit and
stand about the stage in fixed attitudes, each as if cut off in the middle of
a gesture. But there is not time to observe them before Swanilda and her
friends walk in on tiptoe. The girls take in the weird room and are clearly
sorry that they have let Swanilda talk them into coming. A small light throws
their shadows against the walls, and they retreat into the center of the room.
More curious than afraid, but still treading softly, Swanilda roams about
looking at the woodenlike characters.

They seem to be dolls, but they are all life-sized and the suspended
gestures in which they are fixed are alarmingly human. On the right, seated
on a cushion, sits a tall Chinaman dressed in a richly embroidered native
costume. A one-man-band in resplendent parade dress stands with arm out,
ready to strike the huge drum he carries. An astronomer in long black robes
and a high, peaked hat, a poised juggler in the middle of one of his tricks, a
Harlequin in typical diamond-patched costume, and a king holding scepter in
hand—all these characters occupy Coppélius' room as if it were their home.
[In the Sadler's Wells Theatre Ballet production, the figures are a Chinaman, a Crusader, Pierrot, an astrologer, and an Oriental dancer.] They are all
individuals, each seems to exist apart from the others, yet to Swanilda and
her friends the silent, still figures have no animate existence at all and
resemble nothing so much as oversized dolls. Still, the girls are terrified by
the darkness and the strange silence. Swanilda is instinctively moved to
investigate the curtained alcove, for nowhere does she see Coppélia. She
goes over, starts to peep through the curtain, and then runs back to her
friends. Her knees are trembling so much that one of the girls holds her
shaking legs. The girls force Swanilda to return to the curtain, and this time
she is a little bolder. She looks behind the curtain, runs back to her friends,
and gestures with automatic movements to music that might accompany
the dance of a mechanical toy! Coppélia is a doll! One of the girls accidentally collides with the sitting Chinaman, and the interlopers are aghast
as the Chinaman throws out his arms like an automaton, wags his head
knowingly, and does a little rhythm act. The terrified girls approach him
carefully, but the Chinaman does not change his position. He is a doll, too,
but a wonderful mechanical doll, so close to reality that the girls have never

imagined his like before. They stare rapturously at his jerky, automatic gestures, laugh delightedly, and search for the hidden clockwork that makes him move. They find nothing. The music peters out. The doll stops as he began.

Swanilda and her friends examine the doll Coppélia. Swanilda reaches out tentatively and touches her. Coppélia is cold as ice, utterly lifeless, a wax doll like all the rest! Swanilda takes her book away, and the frozen girl sits as before, her stilted hands grasping nothing. Swanilda can make neither head nor tail of the book and turns back to be absolutely certain that the lovely girl will not look up and wave to her, as she did to Franz. She leans over to feel her heart. She feels nothing. Sure now that the charming creature of whom she was so jealous is merely an absurd doll, Swanilda gathers her friends about her and laughs with glee at the prospect of Franz paying court to her.

All the girls are tremendously relieved that they have no one to fear in the empty house and prankishly run to each one of the dolls. They wind the dolls up, and soon all the mechanical creatures are in motion. The one-man-band plays his music, the juggler commences his act, the astronomer lifts a telescope to his eye—and the fascinated girls can't decide which they like best. They are so enchanted by the dolls that they do not hear Coppélius enter. The music imitates his fierce anger.

He runs in, cape flying behind him, speechless with rage. He shakes his stick at the intruders and rushes about to catch them. All the girls retreat toward the door—all of them except Swanilda, who sneaks into Coppélia's booth while the toymaker shakes his stick at her fleeing friends and pulls the curtains closed. Coppélius comes back into the room and makes straight for the curtains to see if the girls have harmed his most cherished creation. A window opens at the back, and Coppélius stops. Another intruder! He stands close against the back wall, ready to pounce on the stranger. Franz climbs into the room. Coppélius waits patiently until the youth cannot return to the window and then sets upon him. Franz pleads that he means no harm, that he has entered merely to see the girl he loves, and that he will die unless he talks with her.

Gradually Coppélius realizes that Franz is quite serious and he ceases to threaten him. He wants to hear more and astonishes Franz by becoming quite friendly. Coppélius insists that he stay, telling him that his daughter will be in very shortly, and invites the unbelieving youth to sit down and have a drink. When the drink is poured, Franz has no more apprehension and accepts it with relish. The toymaker chatters constantly, pretends to drink too, and Franz—gloriously happy now that he has neared his goal— fails to see that Coppélius is providing him with one drink after another. He tries to describe the beauties of Coppélia to the old man with drunken gestures, and his host nods repeatedly in agreement as Franz's intoxication is increased by a potion he has poured into the drink. Franz's head falls back.

against the chair, his arms hang limp in sleep, and in this room filled with dolls he is almost like a doll himself.

Coppélius checks to be sure that he is unconscious and wrings his hands in glee in anticipation of his next move. He takes out a huge leather volume, puts it down on the floor, and hurriedly leafs through the pages looking for a secret formula he has never used before. He finds it, leaps up, looks back at Franz, and approaches the drawn curtains of Coppélia's closet. He yanks back the curtains, peers in, and examines carefully every feature of Coppélia's face and dress. The clever Swanilda no longer resembles herself as she sits rigidly in Coppélia's costume, holding up her little book. Coppélius goes behind her chair and wheels Swanilda into the middle of the room as the orchestra sounds a beautiful melody on piercing, muted strings. He glances down at the book and makes magical gestures in Swanilda's face. Swanilda does not blink. Now the toymaker runs over to Franz and, moving his hands down the youth's body from head to foot, seems to pull the power of life from him like a magnet. Coppélius holds the life force tight in his hands and goes back to the doll, whom he tries to endow with this potency. He consults the book again and repeats the ritual. To his astonishment and happiness, Swanilda tosses away the book, and Coppélius believes his wooden doll has actually come to life.

Swanilda's arms move stiffly as the music mimics the mechanics of her strength. She raises her head and stands up, her body still bent over in a sitting position. The delighted Coppélius straightens her up, and she stands still for a moment. Her face is expressionless. Then she begins to try out her arms and legs, pushing her feet out before her in a simulated walk. Coppélia's master encourages Swanilda's every step with more incantations; the girl is excited at her success in deceiving him. She looks over at Franz and can hardly wait until he wakens. Meanwhile she lets Coppélius imagine that he alone is responsible for her new-found vitality. Her stance is rigid and her face assumes an equally artificial smile. At Coppélius' command, her legs move less mechanically, and soon she is dancing to a light, sparkling waltz, perfecting her steps as she circles about. Now that he has taught her to dance, the toymaker wishes her to continue showing off his magical powers. The doll smiles ingratiatingly, but instead of dancing she walks about the room, as if she were exploring it for the first time. She goes over to Franz, shakes him, sees the discarded wine mug, and raises it to her lips. Coppélius snatches it from her in the nick of time. He is beginning to find out that this live doll can be as exasperating as any young girl.

Swanilda keeps up her fun with him, but still maintains her mechanical characteristics. Like a child, she pretends in each one of her tricks merely to be doing what her teacher has told her to do in the first place. The tormented Coppélius beseeches her to dance again; she stares at him dumbly. Finally, to keep her out of any more mischief, he distracts her by placing a black mantilla about her shoulders. Swanilda responds instantly by dancing a bolero. The music is subdued, but the girl intensifies the impassioned Spanish dance as the tempo mounts. Coppélius now supposes that there is nothing he cannot make her do; he experiments further by investing the doll with a Scottish plaid. Sure enough, as the orchestra pipes a sprightly jig, she follows its rhythms like a good Scottish lass. At the end of this dance, however, Swanilda has had enough. She kicks the pages of his magic book and runs berserk about the room.

She tries to awaken Franz from his stupor. Coppélius, fraught with anxiety lest she harm herself as well as the other dolls, finally succeeds in grabbing her. He sets her down hard on her chair, shakes his finger in her face, and rolls the chair back into the curtained alcove. Franz stirs, stretches, and looks about. Coppélius allows him no time for questions and tells him to get out. Franz leaves eagerly, climbing back out of the window. Swanilda, no longer a doll, pushes the curtains aside and dashes about the room knocking over every one of Coppélius' precious toys except the king, who stands in ridiculous majesty over the chaotic scene. Then, all too lifelike, Swanilda escapes through the door to catch up with Franz.

The shocked Coppélius cannot believe his eyes. He pulls back the curtains, and there, thrown across her chair, he sees the naked, limp body of his beloved Coppélia.

ACT THREE—THE WEDDING: The festival day has arrived, and all the villagers have gathered in the sun on the manor house lawn to take part in the celebration. The town's new bell has been blessed, and the lord of the manor awaits the presentation of dowries to those who will marry on the holiday. Swanilda, radiant in her wedding costume, and Franz, also in formal array, approach the lord with the other couples. Franz cannot take his eyes off Swanilda, who has taught him the lesson he unconsciously yearned to know. He knows now that, as his wife, she will be to him all women— all the other girls the beautiful Coppélia represented. The assembled villagers share the exuberant joy of Franz and Swanilda. The lord of the manor congratulates them and presents the dowries.

The irate and pathetic Coppélius marches in and upsets the happy throng by reminding them of the damage he has sustained. Coppélius is so intent on securing compensation, rather than explanations and apologies, that the crowd does not sympathize with him readily. The only one who sympathizes is Swanilda, who steps forward understandingly and offers him her dowry. The sullen Coppélius is about to take it, but the lord of the manor motions Swanilda away and rewards the toymaker with a bag of gold. The old man leaves the scene, wondering whether it will ever be possible for him to create a doll as lovable as his ill-fated Coppélia.

The pageant of the day now commences. The peasants dance the familiar "Dance of the Hours," in which the arrangement of the performers imitates the progress of the hours around an enormous clock as the hurdy-gurdy music tinkles the time away. The twelve girls form a circle like the face of an enormous clock, kneel toward the center, and one by one rise, pirouette, and kneel again, telling the time away.

Soft woodwinds herald the arrival of Dawn, danced by a lovely young girl. Her dance, with the music, is at first slow and tentative, like the gradual approach of light; then her body responds to bright wakening music and she celebrates the rising sun.

Now Prayer—a demure girl who clasps her hands before her and turns slowly in deep arabesques—delights the villagers. She kneels as the harp ends the music for her dance.

A peasant couple perform a vigorous betrothal dance to rhythmic, piping music. They bow to the lord of the manor, and all await the arrival of the bride and groom.

Franz bows and holds out his hand to Swanilda. Together they dance a moving adagio to a deep melody from the strings. Franz carries Swanilda high on his shoulder, sets her down gently, and the girl kneels before him. She rises on point, pirouettes swiftly in his arms, is lifted again, released, and caught as her lover holds her across his knee. He turns her in arabesque, and the dance that symbolizes their reconciliation and pledged happiness comes to an end. Their dance together and the variation each now performs alone reveal the youthful strength and tenderness each possesses for the other. When they have finished, all the villagers join the smiling couple in a fast, constantly accelerating dance in which the whole company becomes a part of the breathless happiness reflected in the shining faces of Swanilda and Franz.

NOTES: *Coppélia* is the first music-dance drama of uniform excellence. No part of the ballet is subservient to any other, and, most important of all, ballet music in *Coppélia* participates in the dance drama as never before. Delibes' charming and melodic dramatic music assists the plot and gives new dignity to the dance, which had for the most part been previously supported by music of a prescribed rhythm and length. Before *Coppélia*, no one listened to ballet music except in the theatre; ballet music was simply a pretext for dancing and, in itself, valuable only for sentimental reasons. The composer was the servant of the choreographer. But with Delibes' masterful scores to *Coppélia* and *Sylvia*, music and dance became unified; collaboration between choreographer and composer was necessary. Tchaikovsky was directly inspired by Delibes' ballet music to write his own. Delibes is the first great ballet composer; Tchaikovsky and Stravinsky are his successors.

But the story of *Coppélia*, based on a tale (*Der Sandmann*, also the basis of Act I of the popular opera *Tales of Hoffmann*) by the German master, E. T. A. Hoffmann, the choreography of Saint-Léon, and the dancing of the first performances were of a quality to match the innovations of the music.

Giuseppina Bozacchi was the first to dance *Swanilda*. She secured the role by accident. The director of the Paris Opéra had engaged for the part the Russian ballerina Adela Grantsova, who had begun rehearsals when she sprained her foot and became ill with typhoid fever. A substitute had to be found quickly, for the Opéra had not produced a ballet for some years; *Coppélia* could not be indefinitely postponed.

The director found the dancer he wanted in Bozacchi, an Italian girl who had come to Paris when she was ten to study dancing. She was sixteen when she made her debut as Swanilda at the first performance of *Coppélia*. The director, Delibes, and Saint-Léon had worked with her for many months on the role, and at the *première* she justified all their hopes. The ovation she received that night made her the first dancer of ballerina status to grace the Opéra stage in seven years.

Bozacchi had danced eighteen performances of *Coppélia* when the Opéra was closed down because of the national emergency created by the Franco-Prussian War. Paris, under Prussian siege, became a stricken city, and thousands perished from want of food and warmth. Giuseppina Bozacchi was one of these. She died of fever on the morning of her seventeenth birthday, six months after her triumph in *Coppélia*.

When *Coppélia* was revived at the Paris Opéra, October 16, 1871, Léontine Beaugrand, for whom Nuitter, the ballet's librettist, had intended the role of *Swanilda*, assumed the principal role. It is to be noted that in the original French production, and in many subsequent French revivals, the part of Franz, the principal male role in *Coppélia*, was danced by a woman.

In 1884 *Coppélia* was presented in St. Petersburg, which had become the center of the ballet world. Marius Petipa, who was responsible for the Russian ascendancy, presented his version of Saint-Léon's original choreography. The Russian painter and designer Alexandre Benois saw this first Russian production in St. Petersburg. This is what he writes about its music, its dancing, and its story, in *Reminiscences of the Russian Ballet*:

"Delibes' works are not numerous and unfortunately one of his masterpieces—the opera *Lakmé*—has become vulgarised. *Coppélia*, with the exception of individual pieces, has escaped the fate of *Lakmé* and the music is still delightfully fresh, expressive and genuine. How perfectly wonderful this masterpiece must have seemed when it was first given. The ballet world of St. Petersburg received the new ballet with patronising approval; *Coppélia* was usually alluded to as 'a very nice little ballet with very nice music,' and the artists all agreed that 'the music was easy to dance to.' But there were some who immediately recognised *Coppélia* as something out of the ordinary, something as striking in its own way as *Carmen*, recently produced at the St. Petersburg opera. Among these enthusiasts were several musicians —headed by Tchaikovsky. Both my elder brothers, Albert and Louis, had appreciated *Coppélia*, which was all the more surprising as one of them was more or less indifferent to the theatre, while the other liked only Italian Opera.

"I went to see *Coppélia* for the first time after having played through the music on the piano—following the advice of my brother Louis. But when I first heard the ballet in the theatre, it seemed somehow to move and delight me to the very depths of my soul. It is true that there was much that was delightful in the ballet besides the music. The part of Swanilda was charmingly danced by the pretty and graceful Varvara Nikitina, who was in those days one of the chief adornments of the Imperial stage. The famous Stukolkin was amusing and mysterious as the old Coppélius, while Gerdt made a delightful Franz, Marussia Petipa danced her *czardas* and *mazurka* most brilliantly, flashing her beautiful eyes in all directions. The mimed scenes in the first and second act were performed with both humour and taste and lastly, every individual number in the final act was a real *chef-d'oeuvre* of the ballet-master's inexhaustible imagination. But such merits are common to nearly all the famous ballets. In *Coppélia* there seemed to be something new, something that raised it on to another plane. The whole performance seemed to be dominated by some higher inspiration, to be penetrated with the essence of poetry; the artists themselves to have achieved unconsciously a greater vitality and an unusually noble demeanour in their gestures and dancing. This metamorphosis was *entirely due to the music*.

"I saw *Coppélia* for the first time in December of 1884 and after that Volodia Kind and I never missed a single performance, taking care to reserve good seats in advance. In those days tickets were not so difficult to get, and both the stalls and the boxes had many empty gaps. Ballet in that period had not yet gained a great popularity with the general public, and the *balletomanes* only filled the first three rows of the stalls. My friend and I were bent on getting places in those privileged rows and to obtain them a little diplomacy had to be practised and friendly relations maintained with the box-office cashier.

"I must say that our enjoyment of *Coppélia* was purely artistic. After Marussia Petipa's dances in the first act, the excitement they had aroused would change into pure artistic delight at Zhukova's wonderful gracefulness and the 'old' Kshesinsky's brilliant, characteristically Polish way of dancing the *mazurka*. Another extremely vivacious dancer was the Hungarian Bekeffy, who, though known to be very gloomy in everyday life, became on the stage one of the most thrilling dancers to watch, firing both his partner and the public with his own enthusiasm. My 'passion' for Marussia Petipa now began to wane, for when I compared her dancing to that of these first-class artists the verdict was not in her favour.

"The delight I experienced from the very first act of *Coppélia* continued to grow as the drama developed, and this again was due to the expressiveness of the music. It was impossible not to believe that Swanilda and her companions had really penetrated into Coppélius' gloomy panopticon, that the silent, immobile figures were not really made of wood or of wax, that one of the girls had not accidentally touched the springs and thus started the automatons on their absurd repetitive gestures: the Chinaman nodding his head and making rhythmic, jerky movements, the astrologer moving his telescope from one side to the other, the knight in armour sheathing and unsheathing his sword. How charming were Swanilda's girl-companions in their fright and how quickly they became reassured that the figures were nothing but dolls! How infectious was their laughter and how gracefully they danced, stepping daintily on their points, in and out between the figures, to the sounds of the snuff-box tune! This contrast of automatic, senseless movement with the playfulness of living people is one of the most charming *trouvailles* in the whole of ballet literature.

"But there were other musical joys still in store for us. The scene where old Coppélius catches Franz as he climbs in through the window is really brilliant, particularly when the old man is struck by the great idea of extracting the vital force from the young lout in order to transfer it to his doll. Every theme in this part of the music is a gem and they follow each other naturally and logically; the music describing the angered Coppélius is succeeded by another melody which expresses the mask of benevolence he puts on in order to coax Franz into drinking the magic draught. As Franz listens to the gay sounds of the *Brindisi*, he gradually becomes completely drunk and in the end unconscious. Even to this day, though I know it is *nicht ernst gemeint*, whenever I hear this part of *Coppélia* I get 'the creeps.' The scene used to be acted by Stukolkin in the real Hoffmann manner, and inspired in me a love for 'Hoffmannism,' though I had not then read a line written by the author of *Kater Murr* and *Der goldene Topf*.

"The spirit of Hoffmann lives in *Coppélia* in spite of the fact that the libretto is only a humourous parody of his gloomy fairy tale '*Der Sandmann*.' I am not certain whether Stukolkin himself was acquainted with Hoffmann's works, but I have no doubt that he did not merely act his part, but was actually transformed, body and soul, into the ridiculous and weird magician. It was ten years later, while acting this part, that Stukolkin collapsed and died from a fatal heart attack. The old man must surely have been in a trance; he always *lived* his part and was profoundly affected by everything the music made him feel.

"I have dwelt somewhat longer on this scene not only because it is the climax of the whole ballet but because it made so deep an impression on me, that later on in life, when I created my ballets *Le Pavillon d'Armide* and *Petrouchka*, I seemed to be fulfilling ideas that had been born in me in the days of *Coppélia*."

Soon after the Russian production, *Coppélia* was mounted by the Royal Danish Ballet in Copenhagen, where, as in Paris, it is still a part of the permanent repertory. Also, as in Paris, the Danish *Coppélia* remains close to the Saint-Léon original; it has not been influenced by Russian revisions. Richard Buckle wrote of the Danish *Coppélia* in *Ballet* in 1951: "I have seen the old ballet danced by half a dozen or more companies, in Paris, Rome and London, but I have never seen it done as well as this." And P. W. Manchester wrote in *Chrysalis* in 1952 that the Danish *Coppélia* "as it now stands is so completely excellent in its own way that, with this company's almost fanatical loyalty, it is likely to remain as it is from now on."

The first American production of *Coppélia*, though greeted with applause by press and public in 1887, was not as important as a later one, that of February 28, 1910. Carl van Vechten reviewed this performance in the New York *Times*:

"More than two-thirds of the boxes at the Metropolitan Opera House were still filled with their occupants at half after 12 last night. It was not a performance of *Götterdämmerung* without cuts that kept a fashionable Monday night audience in its seats, but the American debut of Anna Pavlova, the Russian dancer from the Imperial Opera in St. Petersburg. Mme. Pavlova appeared in a revival of *Coppélia*, which was given at the Metropolitan for the first time since the season of 1904–05. As this was preceded by a performance of *Werther*, the ballet did not commence until after 11, and it was nearly 1 before it was finished.

"However, Mme. Pavlova easily held most of her audience. It is safe to say that such dancing has not been seen on the local stage during the present generation. If Pavlova were a regular member of the Metropolitan Opera Company it would also be safe to prophesy a revival of favor for the classic ballet.

"The little dancer is lithe and exquisitely formed. When she first appeared just after the curtain rose there was a dead silence. She received no welcome. She wore the conventional ballet dress and her dark hair was bound back with a blue band.

"After the first waltz, which immediately follows her entrance, the audience burst into vociferous applause, which was thereafter repeated with every possible opportunity. Pavlova received an ovation of the sort which is seldom given to anybody at this theatre.

"And her dancing deserved it. To begin with, her technique is of a sort to dazzle the eye. The most difficult tricks of the art of the dancer she executed with supreme ease. She even went further. There were gasps of astonishment and bursts of applause after several of her remarkable feats, all of which were accomplished with the greatest ease and lightness.

"Grace, a certain sensuous charm, and a decided sense of humor are other qualities which she possesses. In fact, it would be difficult to conceive of a dancer who so nearly realizes the ideal of this sort of dancing.

"In the first act she was assisted at times by Mikhail Mordkin, who also comes from St. Petersburg, and who is only second to Pavlova as a remarkable dancer. Their *pas de deux* near the end of the act was perhaps the best-liked bit of the evening. It was in the second act in her impersonation of the doll that Pavlova disclosed her charming sense of humor.

"At this time it is impossible to write any more about this dancer, but there is no doubt that she will prove a great attraction while she remains in New York."

The following night at the Metropolitan, Pavlova and Mordkin danced a program of *divertissements,* and on March 18, 1910, at the New Theatre, Pavlova performed for the first time in the United States *Le Cygne* (*The Dying Swan*), which Van Vechten called "the most exquisite specimen of her art which she has yet given to this public."

Catherine Geltzer, who was to dance the first American production of *Swan Lake,* danced *Coppélia* at the Metropolitan in 1912, and Adeline Genée, who had achieved great success with the part of Swanilda in London (1906), danced it in New York in 1913. New York was not to see another full production of *Coppélia* for twenty-five years.

The Russian production of 1884 has been the basis for modern productions of *Coppélia* familiar to the English-speaking world: for the production of the Ballet Russe de Monte Carlo, Ballet Theatre, the Sadler's Wells Ballet, and the Sadler's Wells Theatre Ballet. These productions have been founded, in other words, on Saint-Léon's original, via Petipa's initial revision, emendations by Lev Ivanov and by Enrico Cecchetti, reconstructions of these "originals" by Nicholas Sergeyev, and additions by contemporaries such as Massine, et al. Contemporary productions have varied in completeness and length.

The first of these was presented by the Sadler's Wells Ballet (then the Vic-Wells Ballet) on March 21, 1933, at the Old Vic Theatre, London. William Chappell designed this production, in which Lydia Lopokova and, later, Ninette de Valois danced Swanilda. Walter Gore appeared as Franz.

The second was staged by the Ballet Russe de Monte Carlo in London in September 1938 for Alexandra Danilova, who made such a hit in the role of Swanilda that she has been associated with the part ever since. Danilova first danced *Coppélia* in the United States at the Metropolitan Opera House on October 17, 1938. Michel Panaieff was her partner as Franz. Another dancer in the ballet was later to dance with Danilova hundreds of performances of *Coppélia*—Frederic Franklin. Edwin Denby wrote in the New York *Herald Tribune* in 1944: "In the Monte Carlo production the choreography and the decoration are—like the music—distinguished, gracious and light . . . I noticed with some surprise that if you follow the action quite literally, it isn't a silly story, as people claim it is. A part of *Coppélia's* secret is the serious good sense with which it treats a serious subject—the basis for a good marriage . . . Danilova . . . is the most wonderful *Coppélia* heroine in the world."

Ballet Theatre presented a short version of the ballet in October 1942, with Irina Baronova and Anton Dolin as the principals. Baronova and Dolin were later succeeded by Rosella Hightower and André Eglevsky in this production.

In 1946 the Sadler's Wells Ballet restaged *Coppélia* at the Royal Opera

House, Covent Garden, with Margot Fonteyn. The *décor* and costumes were again by William Chappell.

The Sadler's Wells Theatre Ballet staged a new production on September 4, 1951, at the Sadler's Wells Theatre, London. Elaine Fifield and Svetlana Beriosova alternated in the role of Swanilda. This *Coppélia* was first performed in the United States at the Buffalo Theatre, Buffalo, New York, October 22, 1951, with Svetlana Beriosova and David Blair in the principal roles. Beriosova and Blair also introduced this production to New York, at the Warner Theatre, March 27, 1952. In *Dance and Dancers* Clive Barnes wrote: "Beriosova is the most delicious Swanilda to be seen in London for years. She was gay and charming, dancing with terrific spirit for the sheer joy of living."

In addition to the dancers already named, Vera Nemtchinova, Mia Slavenska, Moira Shearer, Ruthanna Boris, Nadia Nerina, and Maryon Lane are among the ballerinas who have danced Swanilda in various productions. Frederic Franklin, André Eglevsky, Igor Youskevitch, Leon Danielian, Alexis Rassine, Donald Britton, and Pirmin Trecu are familiar for their portrayals of Franz.

LA CROQUEUSE DE DIAMANTS
THE DIAMOND CRUNCHER

Dramatic ballet in four scenes. Score by Jean-Michel Damase. Choreography by Roland Petit. Book by Roland Petit and Alfred Adam. Songs by Roland Petit; lyrics by Raymond Queneau. Scenery and costumes by Georges Wakhevitch. First presented by Les Ballets de Paris at the Théâtre Marigny, Paris, September 25, 1950, with Renée Jeanmaire, Roland Petit, and Gordon Hamilton in the principal roles. First presented in the United States at the National Theatre, New York, October 31, 1950, with the same principals.

This "fable of Paris" tells the story of a beautiful woman who steals diamonds not from avarice but from—actual hunger! She simply likes to eat them and can survive on nothing else. This fabulous creature in the ballet never would have been discovered had it not been for a curious incident.

SCENE ONE—THE PARIS MARKET: The setting for the incident is Les Halles, the great market in Paris, where early every morning dealers and vendors come for their daily supplies. It is still dark when the curtain rises. A girl stands alone near a bar that has not yet opened its doors. Nattily dressed thugs approach her for favors, but seem to be more interested in a private business of their own. Three thieves walk in with cocky strides. Someone whistles. Over near the bar, one of the thugs strikes a match for one of the thieves. As the thief leans over to light a cigarette, a long white arm reaches out from the wall and picks his rear pocket. This ruse is repeated with another thief: whistle, light, take, and the robbers start to fight among themselves over their losses. They accuse the girl. She takes a light and loses her purse.

The *bistro* proprietor comes out to take down the shutters and open for business. He dances about the street like a sprite, full of cheer and elation. A girl pushes on a cart loaded with vegetables for sale; a number of other market girls follow her and sing a risqué song about how they sometimes interest dealers in their groceries.

By the time the song is ended, many people have gathered in the street. The three girls dance around the crowd and stop only to hail the arrival of a delivery truck that chugs up to the *bistro* loaded with a crimson couch. A boy wearing a gray cap and a black alpaca coat gets out of the driver's seat and dances for his own amusement and the amusement of the crowd. Everyone seems to be unusually ebullient this morning, as if a festival were about to take place. They help the driver unload the couch. The bartender is beside himself with joy at the new piece of furniture he has ordered for his *bistro* and sings a song about it. The girls and boys hide behind the divan and peek over the top, then surround the barkeeper as he ends his number with a dance. Four toughs come in as he finishes. Over near the bar, they give the delivery boy a light. He leans down to take it; the long, shapely arm reaches out again. The boy feels the hand robbing his back pocket and turns to see whom it belongs to. He caresses the beautiful arm as it withdraws into the wall.

SCENE TWO—A BISTRO: The scene changes to the inside of the bar. Three couples are dancing, while the bartender serves drinks. The delivery boy jumps over the couch, which is halfway in the door, and goes to the bar. He has a drink, seems to enjoy it, then goes over and looks out the window as if he were miserable. The girls notice him and pull him into their circle. He sings, in French and in English! Then he does a little dance which pleases the girls particularly. A policeman looks into the bar and wonders how long the bartender is going to keep the couch half inside, half in the street. It is brought into the *bistro*, and the bartender lovingly supervises its placement. He thought it would fit along a certain wall, but it is too long. It won't fit anywhere! He is about to give up in despair when someone pushes the wall in with the couch and it fits beautifully. The bartender is delighted and thanks everyone. They all go off, but the delivery boy stays behind to catch a little rest on the new couch. He closes his eyes and relaxes. A hand comes through the wall, moves over his face gently, and disappears. He starts and sits up. The bartender asks if he wants anything more to drink. The delivery boy thinks he has had too much already and lies down again. The mysterious hand again caresses his face and vanishes. Now the boy thinks maybe he has not had enough to drink. He drinks down a glass quickly, hoping that his hallucination will pass, and turns back to the couch. He lies down, and the whole couch is pulled through the wall. The hallucination has just begun!

SCENE THREE — THE DEN OF THE DIAMOND CRUNCHER: The scene in the bar blacks out. When the lights come up again, the couch is on the other side of the wall, in a kind of junk room filled with closets. The boy sits on the couch holding his head. The same white hand comes over the back of the couch to tease him. This time he grabs it. Its owner emerges. She is a long-legged *gamine* in a tight, brief bodice and black tights. She runs to open all the closets, and out come the thugs we have seen before in the street. Outside, someone whistles. The boy hides behind a cupboard and watches the girl as she reaches her hand through the outside wall and brings it back filled with jewels. The girl's teeth shine as brilliantly as the gems she holds to her face. She wants them all for herself. Her partners in crime disagree and pound on the table for their share. She surrenders a few of the jewels. They want more. She gives up a few more. Then she leans against the back wall in a relaxed pose. She holds the jewels up, her eyes glisten with anticipation, and she throws diamonds into her mouth and chews them like salted peanuts. Then she sings a song, to explain how she just likes the way the things taste. She dances with each of the thieves in turn, slowly and beguilingly. Another whistle is heard. The thieves scamper off and La Croqueuse is left alone with the delivery boy, who comes out of hiding to join her in a dance. He kneels before her, fascinated, and she falls across his shoulder. He lifts her up and assists her in rapid movements that charm him even more. La Croqueuse is also attracted to the boy, and their dance ends in an embrace that is broken only by the sound of the whistle. She springs to the wall, extends her hand, and brings it back filled with diamonds. The thieves re-enter and assault her, turn her upside down, and demand the loot. The delivery boy tries to fight them off, and, in the confusion, La Croqueuse passes the diamonds to him. He dashes out into the street. The scene blacks out.

SCENE FOUR — OUTSIDE THE BISTRO: Now we are in the street again. It is night. A drunken man about town, formally dressed and bewildered by his surroundings, is comforting his lady over the loss of her jewels. The delivery boy returns the diamonds—apparently all of them. Market girls carry in baskets filled with fresh cabbages. The boy hides a jewel in one of the cabbages when the crowd isn't looking. He whistles. La Croqueuse comes out through the wall in a state of delirious anticipation. The delivery truck rolls in. All the cabbages are piled onto it, and the market girls climb up on the back. The boy gets into the driver's seat; La Croqueuse jumps in and stands beside him. The curtain falls as we see her take out the diamond, throw her head back, and dangle the jewel over her mouth.

NOTES: After the New York *première* of *The Diamond Cruncher*, Walter Terry reported in the New York *Herald Tribune* that "Mr. Petit has told his story with great wit, both in movement and in song. The street dances outside the café are wonderfully inventive . . . and represent a thoroughly satisfactory blending of academic ballet, modern dance and contemporary swing . . ."

Writing of Jeanmaire's performance in the title role, John Martin remarked in the *Times* that "compared with her *Croqueuse*, her *Carmen* was cold, dull and dowdy."

DANSES CONCERTANTES

Classic ballet in five parts. Music by Igor Stravinsky. Choreography by George Balanchine. Scenery and costumes by Eugene Berman. First presented by the Ballet Russe de Monte Carlo at the City Center, New York, September 10, 1944, with a cast headed by Alexandra Danilova and Leon Danielian.

Stravinsky's *Danses Concertantes* was first performed as a concert piece, but the composer had conceived the work with the choreographer and had intended his score to be used in the theatre. When the work was first played (1942), it was apparent that the music embodied dancing—not only dance rhythms, but specific poses and gestures for a group of dancers—so that to hear *Danses Concertantes* was also to visualize a ballet. The plot of the ballet *Danses Concertantes* is the plot of the score: "Introductory March," "*Pas d'Action,*" "Four Variations on a Theme," "*Pas de deux,*" and "Concluding March."

The curtain rises on a handsome, ornate drop curtain. Between two high columns draped in rich cloth, the legend of the ballet is sketched out and we read the name of the ballet, its composer, choreographer, and designer. The orchestra commences a rhythmic, witty march. The dancers, in bright costumes, parade before the curtain at the music's command. There are fourteen of them—eight girls, four boys, and the *premier danseur* and the ballerina, who enter toward the end of the march and finish it with a flourish.

The drop curtain rises. The ballerina dances before the *corps de ballet*, which is arranged in four groups, in each of which a boy partners two girls. The colorful, spangled figures of the dancers are outlined boldly against the dark back cloth. The ballerina dances with sweet, lyric grace, but also with humor, for the music contrives to interrupt and cut short its soft melody with sharp accents in surprising places. You get the impression that you might get from reading a lyric poem whose lines are sometimes truncated in the middle of words but nevertheless flow on to graceful conclusion.

The majestic opening of this second section is heard again, and the full orchestra plays a lively, precisely accented conclusion that merges directly into a new theme that is quiet, tender, and romantic. The ballerina has left the stage, and each of the four groups of dancers comes forward and dances a *pas de trois* to variations on the theme.

The first and second variations are rigorous in rhythm, and the musical phrases seem to balance about a center, as the two girls cluster and move away from the boy. The third variation, Andantino, is softer, more wistful; the fourth, happy and boisterous.

The dancers now leave the stage to the ballerina and her partner, who dance a *pas de deux*. The dancers are almost personified in the music, which demands at first beauty in slowness, then a quiet, pointed wit that ascends to an elevated, noble manner. The *pas de deux* ends on a note of tenderness.

All the dancers return. The opening march is resumed, and the entire group dances to its buoyant rhythm. The music ends sharply and unexpectedly. All rush forward and bow low to the audience as the curtain falls behind them.

NOTES: Frederic Franklin later took the role first danced by Leon Danielian. Maria Tallchief, Ruthanna Boris, and Mary Ellen Moylan were among the dancers in the first performance.

DANTE SONATA

Dramatic ballet in one act. Music by Franz Liszt. Choreography by Frederick Ashton. Scenery and costumes by Sophie Fedorovitch. First presented by the Sadler's Wells Ballet at the Sadler's Wells Theatre, London, January 23, 1940, with Margot Fonteyn and Robert Helpmann among the principal dancers. First presented in the United States by the Sadler's Wells Ballet at the Metropolitan Opera House, New York, September 23, 1950, with Margot Fonteyn, Moira Shearer, and Michael Somes among the principals.

This ballet is based on appreciations of Dante's *Divine Comedy* by the poet Victor Hugo and the composer Franz Liszt. Liszt used Hugo's poem *After a Reading of Dante* as an eloquent statement of his own appreciation of that poet and wrote a composition for piano on its theme. This ballet, like Liszt's music, depicts an embattled conflict between the forces of good and the forces of evil.

The curtain rises on a decorative backdrop that indicates with a few white lines the fiery fumes of purgatory hovering above parallel lines reminiscent of ascending steps. There are two groups of people in the ballet: the Children of Light and the Children of Darkness. The former are dressed in innocent white, most of the latter in black. Black, shining snakes coil about the bodies of the two principal Children of Darkness, a man and a woman.

The Children of Light, apparently those who have understood their sins and repented, dance joyfully alone. Soon they are invaded by the Children of Darkness. The evil men and women attack the purified ones with determined concupiscence. The Children of Light try to beat them back, but some are seduced.

The Children of Light move flowingly, without suddenness, while their opposites fill the stage with violence. The efforts of the innocent to save themselves, to prevent any one of their number from yielding to this violence, enforce a constant tension. But finally their resistance is in vain: physically they become slaves to the powers of evil.

The Children of Darkness are not enlightened by their triumph and regard it with displeasure even as it is achieved. The curtain falls as the leaders of the Children of Light and the Children of Darkness, on opposite sides of the stage, are held up by their fellows in simulated crucifixion, their limbs twitching with agony.

DAPHNIS AND CHLOË

> Dramatic ballet in three scenes. Music by Maurice Ravel. Choreography by Michel Fokine. Book by Michel Fokine. Scenery and costumes by Léon Bakst. First presented by Diaghilev's Ballets Russes at the Théâtre du Châtelet, Paris, June 8, 1912, with Tamara Karsavina as Chloë, Vaslav Nijinsky as Daphnis, and Adolph Bolm as Dorkon. Revived, with choreography by Catherine Littlefield, for the Philadelphia Ballet, 1937. Revived, with choreography by Frederick Ashton, by the Sadler's Wells Ballet at the Royal Opera House, Covent Garden, London, April 5, 1951. Scenery and costumes by John Craxton. Margot Fonteyn, Michael Somes, Violetta Elvin, John Field, and Alexander Grant danced the principal roles.

The two orchestral suites Daphnis and Chloë, now so familiar to us, are derived from an original ballet score designed for this ancient tale of youthful romance. Actually, two suites Ravel made of this music were performed in concert form before the ballet was produced. Suite No. 1—"Nocturne," "Interlude," and "Warriors' Dance"—begins at the end of Scene One of the ballet, after Daphnis has collapsed, and concludes with the end of the general dance of the pirates in Scene Two. Suite No. 2—"Daybreak," "Pantomime," and "General Dance"—is the music for the whole of Scene Three.

In its outlines, Daphnis and Chloë is not radically different from many ballets with stories that relate the love of young people who are finally reunited after some difficulty, some obstruction, has seemed to rule out a happy ending. This is naturally the way of ballet stories, as it is with all fiction, for unless there is some kind of obstruction, we are not apt to have a story:

love, alone, is not enough. But it is the different quality of the love—the difference in the affection of Tristram for Iseult in *Picnic at Tintagel*, of Franz for Swanilda in *Coppélia*, of Amyntas for Sylvia in *Sylvia*, and in the way these lovers react to any interference—that make all these stories interesting. If we care about the kind of affection these lovers have for each other, what their gestures are, and how they look together, we are apt to be disturbed if any obstruction is put in their way and we are delighted at the end if the lovers seem to be happy and forgetful in their understanding of what has come between them. The two lovers in the story *Daphnis and Chloë* are very young; they are youthful innocents. We are made to see this and resent immediately the interference they endure. We are happy at the end because their initial innocence is not seriously violated: they still love, but with a difference that will make them happier.

SCENE ONE—A SACRED GROVE: On this day young people of a Mediterranean isle are paying tribute to the god Pan and his nymphs, whose grotto stands at the left. Daphnis, the handsome shepherd, and Chloë, the girl he has loved all his life, are among the worshipers. Their affection has become so accepted by the other young people that some of the maidens don't seriously believe in it. Still hoping that Daphnis will notice one of them, the maidens join him in a dance. Chloë reacts with appropriate jealousy and does not repulse the advances of another shepherd, Dorkon. All this is in the spirit of fun; the lovers have taken a vow to be faithful to each other, and their friends are amusing themselves a little because of the seriousness of the romance. Dorkon, however, is serious too, and Daphnis tells him to leave his girl alone. But Dorkon is not to be easily routed. Daphnis becomes angry, and his friends try to make light of the situation by suggesting that the two begin a dancing contest for Chloë's favor.

Dorkon's dance is as crude and awkward as his advances toward Chloë have been, and Daphnis, in a splendid dance with his shepherd's crook, easily defeats him. Chloë rewards Daphnis with a kiss, Dorkon departs, and her friends take Chloë away.

Daphnis is alone. He lies down on the ground and daydreams of his perfect love. He has almost fallen off to sleep when he is joined by the temptress Lykanion. Daphnis is indifferent to her beauty, but strangely attracted also. Lykanion is sure of her knowledge of love, and the inexperienced youth is disturbed. But Lykanion is too anxious to instruct Daphnis. He senses instinctively the evil in her advances and dismisses her.

Now the youth is roused by a battle cry. A band of pirates have invaded the island, and the natives have risen in arms against them. The defenseless girls seek the safety of Pan's grotto, but the pirates, disrespectful of the god, pursue them. Bryaxis, leader of the pirates, captures Chloë and carries her off swiftly before Daphnis can act. Daphnis cannot understand how this has happened. He despairs and rails at the power of gods who would permit her abduction.

The music is quiet and mysterious. Suddenly one of the stone nymphs of the grotto comes to life in a magical blaze of light. As the chorus begins to chant along with the music, this girl and two other nymphs begin to dance. Daphnis does not see them. Now they go to him, rouse him, and lead him before the grotto of Pan. At the nymphs' call, an image of the god fills the sky. Daphnis prays that the powerful god will restore Chloë to him.

SCENE TWO—THE PIRATES' HIDE-OUT: On the shore of another island, the pirates are celebrating their victory at night. They dance joyfully and divide among themselves the day's profits. Chloë, her wrists bound together with rope, is brought in, and Bryaxis, the pirate captain, commands her to dance. The helpless girl is afraid to refuse, but soon, as she dances, she lifts her bound wrists in supplication, begging to be released. Bryaxis only laughs at her. The terrified girl trembles at the thought of intimacy with such a man. Bryaxis is about to approach her when the seacoast is suddenly illuminated by brilliant, flashing light. The pirates cower at this miracle and stare, astonished, as the great god Pan appears in a vision. He orders the pirates to free Chloë. The brigands flee to the hills.

SCENE THREE—ANOTHER PART OF THE SACRED GROVE: The orchestra is silent as the curtain rises. Daphnis, lying alone, grieves over Chloë's loss. Gradually the music imitates the sounds of the breaking day; the sun rises. Fellow shepherds come seeking Daphnis. But he does not wish to join them; only by praying to the god may he help his love to be rescued. Chloë's friends appear and tell him that she has returned. The ecstatic Daphnis searches for her. At first sight of Daphnis, Chloë runs into his arms, and the two lovers rejoice.

Lammon, an old shepherd, tells Daphnis that his prayers have indeed been answered but that Pan acted in his favor because of the god's memory of his own love for the Syrinx. Daphnis and Chloë, in their gratitude for Pan's intervention, re-enact the god's romance for their friends. Daphnis, as Pan, vainly pursues the lovely nymph, who flees from him. He pleads with her, but she will not acknowledge him. She hides and, at Pan's persistence, casts herself into a brook and drowns. The god takes a reed from the brook and makes of it a flute, which he names for Syrinx. He plays upon the flute. At its sound, Chloë begins to dance with tenderness and joy.

The ensemble joins the two lovers in a final general dance that celebrates their reunion and their lasting love.

NOTES: Serge Diaghilev commissioned Ravel to compose a ballet in one act on the story of Daphnis and Chloë. The work was to be performed in 1911, and during the ensuing delay, Ravel arranged two suites from his score, both of which were performed in the concert hall before the ballet's first performance. The ballet at last saw the stage June 8, 1912, with Tamara

Karsavina and Vaslav Nijinsky in the title roles. Fokine, the choreographer, had had in mind a ballet on the Daphnis and Chloë legend for eight years. In 1904, in St. Petersburg, he had submitted a scenario for such a work to the director of the Imperial Theatre, along with a preface that detailed the reforms to be embodied in his work, reforms that he regarded as crucial for the art of ballet: "The dance need not be a mere *divertissement*, introduced into the pantomime. In the ballet the whole meaning of the story can be expressed by the dance. Above all, dancing should be interpretive. It should not degenerate into mere gymnastics. It should, in fact, be the plastic word. The dance should explain the spirit of the actors in the spectacle. More than that, it should express the whole epoch to which the subject of the ballet belongs. . . . The ballet must no longer be made up of 'numbers,' 'entries,' etc. It must show artistic unity of conception . . . a unity which is made up of the three elements—music, painting, and plastic art. . . . The great, the outstanding feature of the new ballet . . . shall be but one thing—the aspiration for beauty . . ."

But the reforms suggested in Fokine's manifesto were largely ignored and his project for a ballet was refused. Part of his original scenario was staged for the Diaghilev Ballets Russes after many of his reforms had been realized, in *Les Sylphides*, *Firebird*, and *Petrouchka*.

This production of *Daphnis and Chloë* was a considerable success. Tamara Karsavina, who created the part of Chloë, has written* that the ballet was, to her mind, Fokine's masterpiece. "In it, Fokine explored to the full the recesses of neo-Greek choreography as originally revived by Isadora Duncan."

Successful as it was, however, the production of *Daphnis and Chloë* created a quarrel between the choreographer and the impresario. Fokine had difficulty obtaining adequate rehearsal time and new costumes for his new ballet, and since Nijinsky, in his staging of *The Afternoon of a Faun*, was being rewarded with both, the older choreographer felt slighted. Soon after, he left the Diaghilev company for two years.

The *Daphnis and Chloë* of Catherine Littlefield, pioneer in American ballet, was a completely new choreographic venture, first produced in 1937 for her Philadelphia Ballet.

The new staging of *Daphnis and Chloë* by Frederick Ashton for the Sadler's Wells Ballet was the first of two new works commissioned of this choreographer for the Festival of Britain.

Ballet, Vol. 11, No. 5, June 1951.

LES DEMOISELLES DE LA NUIT
THE LADIES OF MIDNIGHT

Dramatic ballet in three scenes. Music by Jean Françaix. Choreography by Roland Petit. Book by Jean Anouilh. Settings and costumes by Léonor Fini. First presented by Les Ballets de Paris at the Théâtre Marigny, Paris, May 21, 1948, with Margot Fonteyn, Roland Petit, and Gordon Hamilton in the leading roles. First presented in the United States by Ballet Theatre at the Metropolitan Opera House, New York, April 13, 1951, with Colette Marchand, John Kriza, and Eric Braun.

This ballet rightly assumes that when a young man marries a cat, things are going to be pretty difficult around the house. How the young man meets the cat, how he is enamored of her feline grace, how his love transforms her for a time into a beautiful young girl, and how, despite his love, his wife is unable to conquer an irresistible inclination to scamper on the rooftops, the ballet chooses to relate in three scenes.

SCENE ONE—A HOUSE IN THE COUNTRY: Low, moaning music is heard from the orchestra as a brief overture begins. The curtain rises. The scene is a large, high room whose walls are papered with yellowing, peeling newspapers. Cats sit about the room in relaxed attitudes: some polishing their nails, some resting against a ladder. A black kitten reclines on a white couch at the right. On the wall, partially obscured by a wispy rag, hangs a portrait of a big, beautiful white cat. A doorway in the center is hung with tattered and torn cloth; innumerable cats must have sharpened their claws on it.

A young musician enters. He pushes aside the dusty drapes and steps carefully into the room. He has been invited to this house in the country to play at a wedding and is astonished to see that no ordinary preparations for such an occasion have been made. He observes the curious cats and walks over to the portrait. He turns in the air in surprise at what he sees there. The entire house is occupied by cats!

Two black-and-white cats in handsome livery, pages to the household, dart out and grab the musician's hat. The tempo becomes brisk. The light brightens. He chases after them unsuccessfully. The black cat rises from the couch; she and three of the kittens surround the musician. The cats dance about the boy, scratching at his face. The black cat curls up at his feet. He dances for a short time with the kittens. They leave. Agatha, the beautiful white cat at whose portrait the musician has marveled, enters quickly, expectantly. Agatha is the bride of the month. The cat baron who rules over the house marries one of his harem every month, and it is Agatha's wedding that the musician has been invited to attend. Tall and graceful, with long, lithe legs, she immediately attracts the young man. She is dressed in white, with short gloves; a blue ribbon is tied about her throat. The music changes; an oboe plays a wistful, yet playful, melody to the accompaniment of plucked strings.

Agatha begins to dance. The musician watches, fascinated. The music becomes rhythmic. He compares the cat to her portrait. He goes up to Agatha. She circles him on point, and the strings commence a flowing theme. The boy turns swiftly and kneels at her feet. Now he rises and holds her close. The cat responds experimentally. Gradually Agatha becomes as interested in the musician as he is in her. He lifts, holds, and embraces her for a duet that lasts five minutes. The music whines plaintively. The other cats look on with horror. What will the cat baron do? They attack the boy and try to pull him away, but Agatha climbs up on his back. Cymbals and brass simulate the contest. The boy embraces the cat. The music is silent for a moment.

The cat baron enters, his fur bristling. A lovely black cat, whose costume is embellished with the skeleton of a fish, separates the lovers rudely. She is evidently the cat baron's principal aid. Footlights throw the shadows of the two lovers and the jealous cat baron against the back wall. The baron dances in gleeful anticipation of his wedding. Agatha dances with him, not unwilling at first, but she breaks away and gestures to the boy, who stands on the opposite side of the stage, holding out his arms to her plaintively. She goes to the boy. The cat baron pulls them apart and dances furiously. He threatens the musician with his long claws.

The black cat takes Agatha's hand and pulls her toward the baron. A white veil is thrown over the bride's head before she can protest. Daringly she pulls it off and rejoins the boy. The cat baron makes a last effort to dominate her passions. The pages hold the cat couple high on their shoulders in a wedding parade. But Agatha falls down into the musician's arms. The desperate cats scuttle off. Suddenly Agatha is no longer a kitten; her face is the face of a beautiful girl.

SCENE TWO—AT HOME: The orchestra plays a protracted interlude of hurried music. The curtain rises on a boudoir scene. A white bed canopied in white gauze stands on the left. At the right is a large window, looking out on to a dark-blue night. A bird cage stands near the window. Agatha, in a becoming white costume, her light hair shining, stands alongside her new husband. They embrace. The girl goes over to the bird cage, takes out a bluebird, fondles it, and dances as she holds it before her. The boy sits at the foot of the bed and watches her adoringly. Odd, this passion of hers for birds.

He rises, stands by the window, then goes over to the right wall. As he steps back into the room, the cat baron follows him closely. Agatha is agitated. Her lover tries to throw the intruder out, but the baron is so delighted to see his sometime fiancée again, even if she is a real girl now, that he forces her to dance with him. When the boy separates them, the cat jumps up onto his back and scratches at him fiercely. Both claim Agatha. Finally the musician succeeds in throwing the baron out.

Agatha seems to be grateful. To a quiet, deep melody, she stands behind the boy and wraps her arms about his neck. They begin to dance. In the midst of their *pas de deux,* the girl's limbs seem to quicken. The boy takes her to the bed. There he lifts her high on his shoulder. He lets her down slowly, and the girl's body curves backward. He rocks her back and forth, his knee a fulcrum to her seesawing body. The boy falls back, exhausted. Agatha falls over his knees.

Prolonged, mournful cat calls are heard. Agatha raises her head. The sounds persist. As she moves off the bed onto the floor, a cymbal crashes. Her movements are catlike. She looks back at her lover, despairs, and climbs out the window. The musician awakens. The orchestra plays the haunting music of the ballet's overture. Where has Agatha gone? Out on the roof again, presumably. He takes a candle and follows her.

SCENE THREE — THE ROOFTOPS: The theme of the overture persists throughout the interval. The scene, as the curtain rises, is a red rooftop against a blue sky. Four dormer windows penetrate the roof from within. There is a gutter at the front. Agatha and the cat baron stand poised against two of the windows. They run to each other and embrace in the gutter. The musician climbs onto the roof through the window at the left. Other cats crawl over the roof and stand ready to attack him behind the window. They pounce on him. The boy falls. Agatha and the cat baron lead a train of cats over the roof, in and out among the windows. The boy tries to follow and slides into the gutter. When he rises, the cats gather behind each of the windows and menace him as he tries to gain the top of the roof. He holds Agatha desperately for a brief moment. The cat baron pulls her away and leads her to the peak of the roof. There the other cats place her on the baron's back. He races down toward the gutter. Agatha falls. The musician has been slapping about in the gutter like a fish fresh out of water. He squirms over to the girl. He sits up. Agatha poses against him; then both fall back. Their bodies arch away from each other, their hands and feet joined. They move close and lift their legs so that their toes touch. The boy dies. The girl looks down at him and dies. Their heads fall back and their arms dangle over the edge of the roof. Their curious love is happy in death.

NOTES: After its first performance by Ballet Theatre, *Les Demoiselles de la Nuit* was called by John Martin of the New York *Times* "in many ways the best of Petit's ballets to be seen in this country. Though it has his characteristically theatrical approach, it has also much more of a choreographic basis than any of his other pieces." Petit had originally planned to include this ballet in the repertory of his own Ballets de Paris during one of its New York seasons, but had been unable to do so. Colette Marchand had succeeded Margot Fonteyn in performances of the principal role in Paris when the ballet was first produced; in New York, Marchand repeated her earlier success. The ballet has been considerably revised since its first American performance. Mary Ellen Moylan has danced Agatha with both critical and popular approval.

DESIGNS WITH STRINGS

Music by Peter Ilyich Tchaikovsky. Choreography by John Taras. First presented by the Metropolitan Ballet at Wimbledon, England, February 6, 1948. First presented in the United States by Ballet Theatre at the Center Theatre, New York, April 25, 1950, with costumes by Irene Sharaff.

Designs with Strings is a dance ballet to the second movement of Tchaikovsky's Trio in A minor, arranged for piano and string orchestra. Instead of a story it has a mood, a character that arises from the dancing. There is no scenery; all the dancers wear simple black classical costumes and it is only in what they dance that they become individuals rather than performers.

The piano plays the stately, sentimental opening theme. There are six dancers—two boys and four girls. When the curtain rises, they are grouped together and stand motionless in silhouette against a plain backdrop. Their arms are extended slightly as they stand together; all the dancers appear to have a common relation and when they respond to the music and begin to move slowly in and out among themselves, they create an impression of unwinding of latent, quiescent energy.

The lights come up, the full string orchestra takes up the theme, and three of the dancers leave the stage. The remaining three, a boy and two girls, dance softly to the music. Their movement, like the melody, is romantic —a little sad, a little wistful. Their three companions return and circle the stage rapidly, as if to show that there is happiness in romance also. All six dance together briefly, and suddenly the melody quickens and the music becomes tinkling and light and gay. The dancers duplicate this change of pace and temper with whirling acceleration and with steps that are sharply fast and precise.

At the climax of this openly joyous sequence, the dancers leave the stage and a girl dances with a boy alone. The theme changes for this pas de deux, which is not at first so much romantic as it is matter-of-fact. But the dancing soon alters this, and we see as they move together that the girl and the boy are surprised and pleased to be by themselves, apart from the group.

He lifts her off into the wings on the left; the first theme returns accompanied by a newly accented rhythm. Three girls rush out and dance brightly for a moment, to break the romantic spell, and leave the stage.

Another theme, noble and lowing, is heard on muted strings. The ballerina returns with two boys, who support her in a short dance. The wistfulness and playfulness have disappeared; the ballerina and her partners display a proud, youthful dignity. The new-found dignity breaks into pathos, however, upon the return of the other dancers. The six try to dance together as before, first the girls, then the boys. The first theme is heard again, poignantly on piercing strings. The ballerina separates herself from the group, and a boy supports her in a series of slow, extended movements across the stage. The other dancers move forward and separate them. The girl runs to the boy, seeming to plead with him and to claim him. But when she places her arms on his shoulders, he slips away from her and goes to rejoin the others. Slowly the girl follows him. The lights go down. The dancers stand as they were at the beginning, their figures silhouetted in a close group that seems now inseparable.

DIVERTIMENTO

Classic ballet in five parts. Music by Alexei Haieff. Choreography by George Balanchine. Lighting by Jean Rosenthal. First presented by Ballet Society at the Hunter Playhouse, New York, January 13, 1947, with Mary Ellen Moylan and Francisco Moncion in the leading roles.

Divertimento has no characters, no narrative, no plot. It is purely a dance ballet. The music and dancing combine to make a progression—a beginning, middle, and end for the stage situation—but no "meaning" was intended. What is entertaining here is to be found in the dancing. There is no real story: we simply watch a young girl going from one party to another.

The five parts of the ballet, corresponding to the divisions of the music ("Prelude," "Aria," "Scherzo," "Lullaby," and "Finale"), are danced continuously, without interruption. There is no scenery, only a plain black backdrop.

PRELUDE: Four young couples and a boy are on stage when the curtain goes up. The girls wear short white tunics, the boys white polo shirts and black tights. The boys bow to the girls slowly and formally, as if the gesture signified the beginning of a serious kind of game. The girls return the bow, and the couples begin to dance.

The boy who has no partner looks about, waiting. Finally his girl comes. She looks down at him gently as he bows to her. The other couples watch, see that these two want to be alone, and leave them.

A R I A : The boy and girl stand hand in hand for a moment, then begin to dance a *pas de deux*. The dance is at first open and playful, in keeping with the animated music. As the tempo falls off, the dance becomes slow and sinuous, intimate. At the end the two lovers hold hands; the girl looks down modestly.

S C H E R Z O : The lovers leave the stage. The four boys return, each dancing a short variation alone. Their girls join them; they all dance together.

L U L L A B Y : Here the girl is alone. She walks to the center of the stage and stands absolutely still. She lifts her arms slowly, languorously, as the orchestra begins a haunting lullaby. She dances now as if she were not at a dance but alone, in a private room, proving something to herself. Her movements are slow and balanced; the dance is difficult, but she does it perfectly, even though there is no one to see. For a brief moment at the end, she opens her arms wide and seems to waken from a reverie. Then she relaxes completely and stands in repose.

F I N A L E : Four girls enter, and the girl who has danced alone joins them. The music is vivacious, the dance light and amusing. Their partners enter, and all dance together; the girls take turns showing off in a brief contest, and everyone is happy. Just as the boy who has danced with the girl imagines that she is his alone, she walks away coquettishly. She looks back for an instant, then leaps into the wings.

NOTES: The composer, Alexei Haieff, has written that each movement of *Divertimento* is "dedicated to a friend of mine. The *Lullaby* was composed for my friends' babies, who were being born in abundance in 1944." The piece was composed originally for piano, which was the form in which I first heard Haieff play it, though it had already been performed as an orchestral suite. I liked it very much when I heard it the first time, but I didn't at first think of it as music for a ballet. I soon found I couldn't get the piece out of my head; within a week *Divertimento* became a ballet. People have told me that *Divertimento* is very "American." It is American only because the classic style is new here. The movements are not American at all—it's the way they are done.

The leading role in *Divertimento* has been danced by Mary Ellen Moylan, by Maria Tallchief, and by Tanaquil LeClercq. Francisco Moncion and Nicholas Magallanes have taken the principal male roles. Cyril W. Beaumont, in the *Sunday Times* (London), August 6, 1950, wrote: "The chief interest of this work is the *adage* rendered by Tallchief and Moncion, an extremely interesting composition in which the ballerina moves *sur les pointes* almost *sur place*, the dance being conveyed by subtle inflections of the movement made by one raised leg, by the execution of sweeping curves, and by constantly varying the torso line in relation to the pose of the head and limbs . . . Of noble bearing and invariably well-groomed, Maria Tallchief exhibits an excellent technique and control, but remains serene and unruffled throughout the most testing *enchaînements*. She is clearly possessed of a fine sense of line and subtle appreciation of quality of movement and radiates that rare style in movement which proclaims the genuine artist."

DONALD OF THE BURTHENS

Dramatic ballet in two scenes. Music by Ian Whyte. Book by Leonide Massine. Scenery and costumes by Robert Colquhoun and Robert Mac-Bryde. First presented by the Sadler's Wells Ballet at the Royal Opera House, Covent Garden, London, December 12, 1951, with Alexander Grant as *Donald* and Beryl Grey as *Death*.

The tragic story this ballet tells is an old Scottish version of the Faust legend. The ballet is made up of Scots music, Scots scenery and costumes, and choreography based on Scottish folk dances. The title of the ballet refers to the hero's occupation: he is a woodcutter, his burthen is wood.

SCENE ONE—THE FOREST: Young girls dance a "Waulking Song" soon after the curtain rises. Donald, a young woodcutter about his business, enters carrying his burden of wood. The girls laugh at him for spending his days in carrying wood. A strange woman dressed in scarlet appears to him. She tells him that she is Death and that she can do much for him. Donald is weary of carrying wood and wishes to become a doctor. Death tells him that he can become a doctor through her aid, but that at no time must he abandon the faith in her and pray to another god. For should he pray to another god, he will automatically deliver himself to her will.

Donald marvels at her power and asks Death how she shall make him a doctor. She replies that it is very simple: she knows who is going to die and who will recover. If he sees her standing at the head of a patient's bed, he should do nothing for the patient, for he will die, but if she stands at the foot, he will get well.

Donald thereupon makes a bargain with her and places his life in her hands. Soon he is a very successful doctor, indeed. He prognosticates accurately, and people are astonished at his knowledge of whether his patients will live or die. He cures a sick child and three men who think they have been changed into goats by some evil power.

SCENE TWO—THE KING'S CHAMBER: Donald's fame has spread throughout the land, and when the king falls ill, the young doctor is sent for. The king lies on a great bed in a huge, cold hall. Four men kneel in prayer at his bedside, while the women of the court lament his illness. Donald enters to examine the king and discovers that death is standing at the head of the bed! The king will die!

Donald does not wish his king to die and arranges for the bed to be

Nijinsky in Diaghilev's Ballets Russes production of *Afternoon of a Faun.*

LEFT: Nijinsky as Petrouchka in Diaghilev's Ballets Russes production. RIGHT: Nijinsky in Diaghilev's Ballets Russes production of *Scheherazade*. BELOW: *Giselle* (Act II): Tamara Karsavina and Vaslav Nijinsky in Diaghilev's Ballets Russes production.

Anna Pavlova: a portrait study.

LEFT: Anna Pavlova in *The Dying Swan*, 1915. BELOW: Olga Spessivtzeva in *Giselle*. RIGHT: *Pas de Quatre*, London, 1845: Carlotta Grisi, Marie Taglioni, Lucile Grahn, and Fanny Cerito. BELOW RIGHT: *Pas de Quatre*, London, 1951: Nathalie Leslie, Alexandra Danilova, Alicia Markova, and Tatiana Riabouchinska. Festival Ballet production.

The Dance Ma

Bettmann Archive

LEFT: *Coppélia*: Alexandra Danilova and Frederic Franklin in the Sadler's Wells Ballet production.

BELOW: *Petrouchka*: Alicia Markova and Leonide Massine. Festival Ballet, London, 1950.

©Baron-Pix

©Baron-Pix

Alicia Markova.

André Eglevsky in *A la Françaix*, New York City Ballet.

turned around so that Death now stands at its foot. Immediately the monarch begins to recover. Death, furious at Donald's trickery, goes again to the head of the bed. Again Donald has the bed turned. Finally Death is outwitted and leaves the scene. The king is now completely well, and the women leave off their lamentations. A sword dance is performed by young men, who pay tribute to the king. This is followed by a country dance for four girls and, finally, by a joyful general dance.

Children come to the court and ask the famous doctor to teach them a prayer, the words to which they have forgotten. Donald obliges them, upon which Death, who had warned him never to pray, appears to declare that the jig is up: he has broken his part of their bargain. Donald falls to the ground. Death stands at his head: he dies. The king, his knights, and all the people mourn Donald's passing, but Death forces them to dance in celebration of her power.

THE DUEL

Ballet in one act. Choreography by William Dollar. Music by Raffaello de Banfield. Costumes by Robert Stevenson. Lighting by Jean Rosenthal. First presented by the New York City Ballet Company at the City Center, New York, February 24, 1950, with Melissa Hayden and William Dollar, Val Buttignol, Walter Georgov, Shaun O'Brien. This ballet is an extensive revision of the same choreographer's *Le Combat*, which was performed for the first time in the United States by Les Ballets de Paris at the Winter Garden, New York, October 6, 1949.

This short, dramatic ballet tells the story of the brave Christian warrior Tancred, and the pagan girl Clorinda: how they meet, fall in love, separate, and meet again for a final, fatal encounter. A low beating of the drum and subdued fanfares—heard as if from some distant battlefield—introduce the warlike rhythms that dominate the ballet.

The curtain rises on a scene that might represent any barren field. Rocks are clustered on the left, there are no trees, and a bright sky exposes the wasteland. Four Crusaders stand poised for action against any intruder. All are armored and wear high-plumed helmets with visors that conceal their faces. One of them, the warrior in red, is the leader, Tancred. They begin to dance, holding out their arms to control invisible reins, jumping and turning, practicing their skills in battle. They are all obedient to Tancred's command.

A strange warrior enters and approaches. The four Crusaders stand in line, ready to attack. The stranger is dressed in black. This is Clorinda, the beautiful Saracen. From her golden helmet streams a green scarf lined with red. Her movements are direct and unafraid; she is not in the least terrified of the enemy. She comes nearer to the group. The men stand motionless until finally the daring Clorinda challenges one of the Crusaders. He moves out of line and engages her in battle; the other men observe their code of honor by refusing to assist him. The two warriors rush each other swiftly, jumping high as they pass back and forth. Clorinda gains the upper hand and wounds her opponent mortally; and he falls over on his face. She dances around his body on firm points, her head held high. During the duel, her helmet had fallen off, and the long black hair that hangs down to her shoulders accentuates her proud beauty. Tancred walks toward her, obviously moved both by her bravery and her loveliness. He takes off his helmet and bows in tribute. Clorinda does not respond. She leaves the scene. Black-out.

Tancred enters alone. He dances, to reveal his superior strength and agility as a prince of warriors, and exits. Clorinda follows him. Now she is dressed in full battle array, with a visored helmet topped with a black plume. She leaps around the stage lightly, glorying in her own adroitness. Suddenly she stops; she senses danger. Two Christian warriors appear before her. She leaps into the air as they rush by closely, trying to enclose her. The drum beats in staccato rhythm. Clorinda does not hesitate in her attack, and soon the Crusaders weary of their effort to maneuver her into a dangerous position. She drives them off.

Clorinda relaxes for a moment and briefly shows herself to be a beautiful and pathetic girl, exhausted by the strenuousness of war. She holds her hand up beseechingly and opens her arms wide, as if she were praying for relief from the life she has chosen. She holds her head in her hands despairingly for an instant, but then she is alert again, listening for anyone who might be watching her. She crosses the stage slowly in an arrogant posture. A drum beats, loudly and suddenly. Clorinda leaps off.

Tancred enters, seeking out the enemy. He follows Clorinda. She re-enters the field, the Crusader close behind. Neither recognizes the other. They begin to fight, standing close together at first, then separating to each side of the stage, then approaching each other warily. Tancred supports Clorinda and turns her as she assumes first a tight, aggressive pose, then an open arabesque. Now the duel becomes earnest as the two adversaries dodge and jump aside from their strong thrusts. Clorinda wounds Tancred, but this only encourages the Crusader. He stabs the girl as they engage in close contest. She falters in pain. They separate, preparing for the finish. They approach slowly. The girl falls. Tancred stands back. She pulls off her helmet. He sees her face; his own face is shocked with recognition. He holds out his hands helplessly, then takes off his own helmet and goes to her. He lifts her to him, and in her agony and love Clorinda's body curls in his arms. Tancred stands and pulls Clorinda up. She leans against him, her head on his shoulder, and he turns her in arabesque. Her movements are now automatic. She seems not to have the strength to move at all, and yet she wishes to reassure Tancred of her own love. But she is tired. He carries her in his arms; her body stiffens, her legs beat in a final spasm, and she is dead. Tancred places her body on the ground softly and stands over her. As he grieves, he remembers the long battle he has just begun. He picks her up and carries her off.

NOTES: *The Duel* is a revision of *Le Combat*, a work mounted by William Dollar for Roland Petit's Ballets de Paris, June 28, 1949, at the Théâtre Marigny, Paris. Colette Marchand took the leading role, as she did at the first American performance of *Le Combat* by Petit's group, four months later.

The Duel embodied the choreographer's original intentions for the ballet, intentions that he had not been able to execute because of the circumstances surrounding the production of *Le Combat*. The latter was, in effect, a *pas de deux; The Duel* has two central figures in a larger cast.

After the *première* of *The Duel*, John Martin wrote in the New York *Times:* "What Mr. Dollar has evolved choreographically is very distinguished indeed . . . He has devised at the end one of the most brilliant of adagios . . . It is danced magnificently by Melissa Hayden, who brings a tremendous dramatic strength onto the stage with her, as well as a technique that is lithe, powerful and supremely controlled."

Francisco Moncion succeeded the choreographer in the principal male role in *The Duel*. The heroine has also been danced by Patricia Wilde.

LES ELFES
THE ELVES

Ballet in one act. Music by Felix Mendelssohn. Choreography by Michel Fokine. First presented by Fokine's American Ballet at the Metropolitan Opera House, New York, February 26, 1924.

Although this ballet does not pretend to tell a story, it is not based on the music alone. Instead, there is a kind of atmosphere, a mood, which the music possessed for the choreographer, and it is this impression that the dancers represent on the stage to the music's accompaniment. The music for the ballet is in three parts: the well-known Overture to *A Midsummer Night's Dream,* and the Andante and the Allegro from the *Concerto in E minor for Violin.* In addition to the ballerina and her partner, there are twenty-four dancers in the ballet: eighteen girls and six boys. There is no scenery.

Les Elfes has been revived a number of times. The first revival was by René Blum's Ballet Russe de Monte Carlo, with scenery and costumes by Christian Bérard. With Mia Slavenska and Igor Youskevitch in the leading roles, this company presented *Les Elfes* in New York in 1939. The most recent revival was by the Ballet Russe de Monte Carlo at the Metropolitan Opera House, New York, April 20, 1950, with the Bérard costumes and a cast headed by Mary Ellen Moylan and Frederic Franklin.

OVERTURE: The curtain rises slowly, and directly the music has begun. The light is obscure and romantic. A group of girls, attired in light green gossamer, lie curled up on the stage, asleep. They raise their heads and listen as the music comes to life; they kneel and flutter their arms in unison, as if preparing for elfin flight. Gradually they rise, intermittently agitating their wings, and seem to fly off lightly into the night as they leave the scene.

Two principal dancers enter swiftly. The girl is lifted to the rhythm of the music, then turns rapidly. Her partner holds the ballerina high as they exit on the right. Two girls dance across the stage airily. A group of boys forms on the right, and one by one the boys leap diagonally downstage to the music and disappear into the wings. The sprightly elves return in a large ensemble and dance gaily. The boys join them, and a triangular tableau is formed with the *corps de ballet* reclining and pointing toward the principal dancers.

The ballerina and her partner come forward and dance. Another couple joins them, to dance similar movements; seven boys lift their partners up to their shoulders; the elves flutter their arms brilliantly. Even as they stand on the stage, they seem to seek the freedom of the air.

ANDANTE: The stage is empty for a moment, then four elves return. They leave the scene and are followed by a circle of twelve, who dance briefly, yielding the stage to six. The six girls kneel, and the *premier danseur* enters to dance a variation alone. The girls come back when he has finished; two of them bring with them the ballerina. She pirouettes off the scene to the right, but soon returns, and the ensemble dances.

ALLEGRO: The groups of elves fill the stage. The boys kneel in a line behind them. All the girls kneel, too, then row by row rise, flutter, and dance. The girls in the front row spin, and the boys come forward to support them. Six couples arrange themselves in the center of a moving tableau. Their partners lift them high, and as the curtain falls, the elves are still fluttering.

FAÇADE

Ballet in one act. Music by William Walton. Choreography by Frederick Ashton. Scenery and costumes by John Armstrong. First presented by the Camargo Society at the Cambridge Theatre, London, April 26, 1931, with a cast that included Lydia Lopokova, Alicia Markova, and Frederick Ashton. First presented in the United States by the Sadler's Wells Ballet at the Metropolitan Opera House, New York, October 13, 1949, with Moira Shearer and Frederick Ashton in featured roles.

The music to *Façade* was originally written as a setting to certain poems by Edith Sitwell. The poet recited her verses accompanied by the music. The ballet has nothing to do with the poems and uses only the music, to which the choreographer has arranged a series of nine comic *divertissements* that poke fun at their subjects. The scene shows the façade of a large, light-colored house of the Victorian era.

First, two girls and a boy amble out on stage and dance a "Scottish Rhapsody" in appropriate native costume. This is followed by a number called "Yodeling." A milkmaid enters with a stool. Soon she is disturbed by three mountaineers, who turn her around as she stands posed on the stool and pay tribute to her fresh beauty. There is a yodeling contest, in which the girl enters with gusto. The music ripples and laughs with the happy young people. Next comes a "Polka," danced by a smart young lady.

Now two couples dance a "Fox Trot," which is followed by a "Waltz" executed by four girls. Two vaudeville dandies take up the "Popular Song" and perform it with quick, funny precision. The "Country Dance" features a silly country girl, a yokel, and an irate squire. A gigolo, overslickly dressed in evening clothes, and a debutante, who wears a long red dress and an absurd feather in her hair, now come forward and dance the "Tango." The gigolo bends the debutante backward, dips her low, runs a scale down her back with his fingers, and with a devilish air tries to overexploit her good nature. The debutante is amenable to any treatment, however, and finishes the dance considerably disheveled. All the dancers come forward now and join in a "Tarantella Finale."

FACSIMILE

Choreographic observation in one scene. Music by Leonard Bernstein. Choreography by Jerome Robbins. Scenery by Oliver Smith. Costumes by Irene Sharaff. First presented by Ballet Theatre at the Broadway Theatre, New York, October 24, 1946, with Nora Kaye, Jerome Robbins, and John Kriza.

A naturalistic ballet of ideas, *Facsimile* takes up a problem which is not only contemporary, but ageless. It is the problem of what modern man shall do with his time. Often apparently immune to authentic feeling, he takes refuge in the constant company of his fellow men, where he can conceal his lack of security. He arranges his life not only to conceal his real identity from his friends, but to hide it from himself. The ballet's program note reads: "Small inward treasure does he possess who, to feel alive, needs every hour the tumult of the street, the emotion of the theatre, and the small talk of society."

The scene of the ballet is a lonely stretch of beach. There is an improvised bathing tent at the left. On the right, disappearing in the distance, is an irregular line of pilings, marking the shore line. When the curtain rises, there is but one figure on stage: a woman in a bathing suit, who is idling away her time. The music is quiet and as lonely as the scene.

We see that the woman is bored. She seems to have nothing to wait for and walks about trying to find something to amuse her. She takes no pleasure in the scene and tosses away inanimate objects. Finally she goes over to her bathing tent, pulls the awning across it, and amuses herself slightly by watching her own shadow. Her own shadow is better than no society at all.

The woman turns and looks down the beach. Someone is coming! She is delighted and childishly runs behind the awning to surprise the stranger. A man strolls onto the scene. He does not see the woman and, just as she has done, tries to find something to amuse him. He plays with his beach towel, looks up and down the beach, thinks of nothing. He wonders why he is there. Now he sees the woman's shadow on the awning.

She steps out coyly. Both these vacuous personalities try to make something of themselves. Alone, they may be nothing, but together, they must pretend that this is not true. They introduce themselves, chatter, begin to flirt. They have nothing else to say to each other and grasp at flirtation like a straw. They therefore take their love very seriously.

But soon they tire even of this recourse. They come to life again as another man strolls toward them. Both imagine that the newcomer might be self-sufficient enough to amuse them. He turns out to be just as insecure as they are.

Now that they are a triangle, one woman and two men, the idlers try to make something out of nothing. The first man pretends to be annoyed at the intrusion of the second and claims the girl's whole attention. The girl plays along with him, and the intruder sees that this might be an interesting game after all. He flirts with the woman and tries to win her from his rival.

The woman now has a situation that amuses her immensely. She plays with the two men adroitly and watches closely to see their reactions. She knows that the important thing is to be so charming that the game will never end, for if either suspects that she is insincere, both will desert her. The men participate in the game for a short while, but the first man finally insists that she stop this nonsense and be his. The woman says, "No." Finally she has to take some way out and confesses that she likes the second man best. Her first lover storms at her and acts furiously jealous. He takes the woman and his rival and drags them across the beach. Soon all three are fighting together, their bodies tied in a writhing knot on the beach.

The woman is through. She cries out, "Stop!" The three figures untangle themselves, and when they see that the girl is really serious and actually prefers neither one of them, the two men leave the scene. The first man acts as if he had been hurt and misunderstood; the second tries to shrug off the incident: what difference could it possibly make to him? Now the woman is alone again. The incident has not made any difference to her, either. As she strolls away from the beach, there is a real question as to whether anything will ever make any difference to her.

FALL RIVER LEGEND

Ballet in eight scenes, with prologue. Music by Morton Gould. Choreography by Agnes de Mille. Scenery by Oliver Smith. Costumes by Miles White. First presented by Ballet Theatre at the Metropolitan Opera House, New York, April 22, 1948, with a cast headed by Alicia Alonso, Diana Adams, Peter Gladke, and John Kriza.

This modern melodrama is founded on fact. Fall River, Massachusetts, in the summer of 1892 was the scene of a hideous crime that attracted the attention of the nation. In that city, a respectable spinster by the name of Lizzie Borden was said to have hacked to death with an ax her father and her stepmother. Lizzie Borden was subsequently tried for this double murder. The jury, however, acquitted her, and she went back to her father's house and lived as a recluse until she died. The murderer was never found.

In *Fall River Legend*, Lizzie Borden is hanged. Here she is called the Accused, and in the prologue of the ballet she faces the gallows.

PROLOGUE: Before the curtain rises, the music begins with loud shrieks of sound that forebode terror. The orchestra quiets down, the curtain rises, and we are about to be witnesses at an execution.

The gallows stands stark and bare, its rope dangling, against a dark, blue-green sky. The Accused, in black, stands on the right with her pastor. Near them is a black, leafless tree. On the left, the speaker for the jury mechanically intones the jury's bill: that the jurors on oath present that on August 4, 1892, the Accused with a certain weapon, to wit, an ax, did assault and kill her stepmother and father with twenty mortal wounds. The Accused stands in a spotlight on the right. She holds the pastor's hand and seems immune to feeling. The speaker for the jury recalls aloud that the house where she committed these murders was the house where she was born. As he remembers that she lived there once with her father and mother in happiness, the drop curtain rises, the gallows slides back to support a corner of the house, and the lights rise on a typical Victorian home set back off the street. Except for the stoop and the front door, the façade of the house is torn away to expose the interior. On the left, we notice a tree stump set for chopping wood. We are to see the Accused in her childhood.

SCENE ONE—THE HOUSE OF THE ACCUSED—THE PAST: The sky that hangs over the house is washed in hideous green. The Accused, dressed now in dark green, stands before her room and watches time go back to the days of her girlhood. Old neighbors and townspeople pass by. Her father and mother are there. The Accused holds out her hands to them longingly, trying to claim their attention, but they do not notice her. A young girl in white appears. We know immediately that she is the Accused as a child. The Accused goes to her, hovers over her as if to protect her, and follows her girlish dance steps to hurdy-gurdy music.

The child runs to her mother. The mother caresses her daughter; the Accused pathetically fingers her mother's white shawl. A strange woman enters. Her back is straight as a ramrod, her chin is held high; she is dressed in severe black with a black boa about her shoulders. This woman marches, rather than walks, and watches with the determined interest in everyone else's business that only the spinster can have. The child is frightened of this woman; the Accused articulates this fright in a sudden tightening of her gestures: as the mature child, she is not only afraid, she knows why she fears. Instinctively the Accused goes to her father and kneels before him to guard him against this woman. But the adamant spinster comes forward; the father welcomes her and shakes her hand, not seeing his daughter as she kneels between them.

The spinster turns on the child and scolds her, apparently for no reason at all, but we see instantly that the spinster is acutely aware of the child's hatred that the Accused has expressed. Just as we note the woman's rudeness in scolding the girl in the presence of her mother, we see that the mother is indifferent. She is ill. She clutches at her heart and faints. A crowd gathers. The father and the child rush to her and hold her lovingly; they are helpless in their fear and shock. The spinster orders the child away from her mother and takes charge like a schoolteacher. The Accused, who has seen it all before, trembles; she holds her hands in front of her face to erase this memory. The child cries.

The mother recovers slowly from the attack, and the father leads her to the house. He turns at the door and bows to the spinster. The crowd disperses. The spinster walks proudly and primly down the street alone. The Accused turns her back on this woman.

The lights go down and a little time passes. When the stage is lit again, we see the child sitting on the steps by the door watching her mother and father dance. The Accused watches, too, as her parents move gracefully in a soft love duet. The child goes to her father, who holds her tenderly; then the mother lifts the girl into her arms. We are watching the ideally happy family. The Accused joins in the reliving of her childhood and with the girl dances gaily about her loving parents. She seems to lose all her hardness and bitterness; she forgets about the future as she and the child become one in their movements and one in their affection for the mother and father.

But the joyous dance is too much for the mother. She has another attack. Two passers-by run for help. The father lifts her carefully and carries her into the house. The Accused and the girl pray together for their mother. The spinster enters and goes immediately into the house. Two women come to the girl and dress her in black: her mother is dead. The Accused clutches the side of the house, hides her agony, and represses the hatred that must soon be asserted.

The father comes out into the street, looking for his daughter. The spinster stands beside him. The child runs to her father's arms and weeps. He attempts to console her, but the child breaks away from him and moves to enter the house. She cannot go in: the spinster, now in complete control, stands in the doorway.

The child returns to her father and kneels at his feet, begging him to allow her to see her mother. The woman in black marches up to the child and, taking her shoulders in her hands, shakes her viciously. The grieving father does not understand. He tries to separate them, then buries his face in his hands. He bows to the woman's authority and falls on his knees at her feet.

In the background, the Accused has turned to watch. Her grief and indignation are uncontrollable; her body writhes obscenely. The spinster sees the mother's white shawl lying on the ground. She goes to pick it up. As she does so, the Accused runs across the stage and leaps to her father's back, claiming him, denying him everything but grief. But he does not feel her presence. The spinster puts the white shawl over her shoulders. The father lifts her in his arms and takes her across the threshold. The door slams shut in the face of the Accused.

SCENE TWO—THE HOME OF THE ACCUSED—THE PRESENT: Many years have passed. The child has disappeared, and the Accused now lives her own part in the tragedy. She is a woman now, a young woman who ought to have been married years ago. As the lights come up, we see her father and her stepmother in the living room of the house. They sit opposite each other, rocking back and forth, reading books that they hold out stiffly in front of them. There is no music. In this oppressive silence, the Accused enters. She takes a chair between the two. All three rock in unison. The silence becomes taut and music begins quietly.

The house is moved forward to the front of the stage. The Accused rises from her chair and snaps her fingers desperately, demanding an end to this sitting and staring. Her father and stepmother do not pay any attention to this outburst. For a moment the Accused sits down again, then, nervously, almost without control, she runs up the stairs and down again, apparently for no reason at all. The stepmother glances up knowingly from her book and whispers to her husband. The Accused returns to sit and rock and stare. She gets up to look out of the window, but the woman in black follows her and snaps the window shade shut in her face. The Accused goes to her father and embraces him, but the woman pulls her away.

The Accused can bear it no longer; she goes out into the yard. The suspicious stepmother follows her for a moment, but sees she is alone and returns to the sitting room. Her husband places the white shawl about her shoulders and stands behind her chair.

In the yard the Accused meets her pastor. He is young and pleasant-looking, slightly deferential to her, and she is plainly attracted to him. They dance together, the girl participating in the dance with a kind of desperate and abandoned joy. She has no other companionship, no one knows the secret agonies and longings of her heart, and she does not know how to be happy in a normal way. The pastor is sufficiently acquainted with her family situation to be sympathetic and kind. The dance over, the two shake hands formally, both of them a little conscious of the absurdity of this convention.

The father opens the door and comes out to look for his daughter. He has acquired now the sternness and brusqueness of his wife. He disapproves of the rendezvous and tells the girl to come in. She does so reluctantly, and the pastor leaves the scene.

Back in the parlor, the family sit rocking again. The Accused moves from her chair and goes into the back hall. She re-enters the room with an ax in her hand. The orchestra sounds a sharp shriek on the strings. The step-mother cringes and seeks protection from her husband. The girl does not understand why she should be afraid and smiles to herself. She goes out into the yard, chops wood, and buries the blade of the ax in the chopping block. She goes back into the house with the wood, wipes her hands, and sits down again. Everything is still the same.

SCENE THREE—THE STREET BEFORE THE HOUSE: The house is moved back. We hear light and gay music, and young happy couples fill the street and dance together. The Accused opens the door and comes out to watch; her family remain seated in the parlor. Sitting on the doorstep, the girl observes wistfully the open happiness of youth. A soft and romantic *pas de deux* is danced by one couple who find themselves alone for a moment; then they are joined by other couples and leave the stage.

The Accused is alone and despondent. She thinks she must hate what she cannot have. The music snarls; she rises, leaps, and turns down the stage in a rapid diagonal. She almost runs into the ax, which still stands buried in the tree stump. She touches the handle. The music cries out in warning, and the girl creeps away from the ax in terror. She falls to the ground. As she rises, her eyes turn, fascinated, back to the ax. She moves toward it; her hand trembles. She is revolted by her thoughts and moves away.

Just as she does so, the young pastor enters with a bouquet of red roses. The music is low and tender. The girl takes the flowers and smoothes her hair. The pastor picks her up and holds her briefly as if she were a child. They begin to dance, and the girl forgets that romance seemed impossible for her five minutes before. The pastor asks her to come with him on a church picnic, and the girl responds eagerly.

Her happiness is short-lived. Her father and stepmother come out of the house and see her with the pastor. The parents creep up on the innocent lovers. The stepmother stares at the girl. The Accused falls to the ground and kicks her feet in an uncontrolled, childish tantrum. She rolls across the stage and finds herself looking straight at the ax. Meanwhile the stepmother is whispering to the pastor about the girl's abnormalities, telling him that she is perhaps insane. The pastor is respectful to the woman, but disbelieves her. The Accused rushes at her stepmother, scratching at the air in front of her. The woman accepts this as but another sign of the girl's insanity and threatens her. Then she and her husband beckon to the girl to come with them back to the house. The Accused gives them a quick look of appraisal, glances at the house, hesitates, and quickly, spasmodically, grabs at her mother's white shawl. Placidly she now goes to the pastor and takes his arm. They walk off together. For the first time in her life, the Accused has defied in action what she has always defied in her mind.

SCENE FOUR—A PRAYER MEETING: The lights go down; the house turns. Over the house, the green sky darkens ominously. But when the lights come up, we find ourselves at a prayer meeting. The pastor stands in the midst of his congregation. The Accused looks on like an out-sider: these happy people are like the lovers she saw dancing in front of her house, and she doubts that she can become one of them. The pastor per-ceives her thoughts, welcomes her, and the women of the church gather about the Accused and befriend her. One of the women kisses her and smiles. The Accused cannot believe her eyes. The congregation divides into two groups, dancing joyously to stimulated organ music. The Accused hesi-tates to participate, but no longer watches as if she were an outsider.

Suddenly the congregation leaves the scene. The Accused and her pastor are alone. The music becomes dispassionately sentimental. The Accused falls to the floor and curls up like a child: never since childhood has she known such kindness as this. She rises; the pastor goes to her and takes her hand. Still the girl is afraid. The Accused looks into his eyes and sees there none of the deception, none of the duplicity she fears. Now she submits wholly to the young man's tender feeling for her and, all doubt gone, allows him to give her hope in a triumphant dance. The music mounts steadily in volume; the two figures move faster, circling and leaping. Then, with a quick cut in the music, the melody becomes soft and yielding. The girl kneels against her lover. He lifts her in his arms, and she curls up against him. He releases her for a moment, and they stand together, side by side, as the other couples in the congregation return.

To fresh, vibrant music, the Accused dances among the other lovers in an ensemble dance strongly reminiscent of a country revival meeting. She is carried high off the ground by two boys and shakes hands with the girls. Knowing happiness, she now has the right to participate. Her joy is open and she moves with quick spontaneity.

Her stepmother enters. When the Accused sees her, her body stiffens, her face contorts in pain, as if her heart were slashed with a knife. She falls to the ground, hysterical in her agony. The pastor reaches out to help her, but the woman in black draws him aside. The Accused sees them whispering together and, losing all control, seems to become as mad as her stepmother imagines her to be. The music whirls insanely. The congregation closes in on her in a semicircle of slow motion. The Accused writhes on the ground, rises, and walks in a trance.

The stepmother and the pastor come to her. The pastor puts her mother's white shawl about her shoulders and politely says good-by. The girl turns to stare after the pastor. She holds out her hand to him in one last plea. He does not see her. The stage darkens. The church turns, to become the house again. The stepmother leads her to the door. Her last hope is gone.

SCENE FIVE—INSIDE THE HOUSE: When the lights come up, the stepmother has gone into the house. The Accused remains on the doorstep. From this position she watches the happy young couples of the town move before her. Changed entirely, she observes them from the private distance of her mind. Her face is a mask. Her father and stepmother sit rocking in the parlor. She can no longer envy the lovers, because the possibility of being like them has been destroyed. Now she moves like an automaton, as if her every step were predetermined. She walks directly to the chopping block. Two cheerful girls walk down the street. The girl does not know they are there. She touches the ax, then picks it up and turns back toward the house. She has no doubt about what she must do. When she enters the parlor, her father and stepmother jump up in terror. The Accused merely looks at them. As the scene blacks out, her free hand moves up to cover her face.

SCENE SIX—THE PRESENT AND THE PAST: A drop curtain falls, to enlighten us on the goriness of the crime. We see depicted here the parlor suspended in mid-air, its chairs overturned; on the floor of the room streams of blood meet to form a red flood.

The Accused enters. She has removed her dress; her petticoat is spattered with blood. Her mother appears. The Accused begins to act out the wish she imagines to be fulfilled by her terrible crime. The mother must approve of the double murder; it is for her that the Accused has killed.

Her mother embraces her, and the girl rests content in her arms. But then the mother notices the red stains. The girl, now again the small child of the ballet's first scene, tries to hide the stains with the hem of her skirt. The mother slaps her hand. She examines the stains and sees that her daughter is covered with blood. She slaps the girl's cheek and pushes her forward. The child's arms hang limp, her fingers flutter. The mother rocks the naughty child against her breast. She smiles a little as she upbraids the Accused and vanishes in the night.

SCENE SEVEN—THE HOME OF THE ACCUSED: The drop curtain rises and the house is seen again. In time, this scene follows immediately after Scene Five. No longer dark, the sky in back of the frame dwelling is now hideously and grossly red. There is no sound, yet the atmosphere is tense, expectant. Neighbors are running up and down the street, frantically trying to locate the source of the ghastly outcries they have heard.

The Accused can be seen emerging from the back hall under the stairs. The orchestra is still quiet. She tries to straighten up the parlor hastily, but stops when she sees that people are looking in the window at her. Then quickly, in a desperate rush, she dashes for the front door. When she appears on the doorstep, the orchestra crashes and blares. The girl runs into the crowd and circles the street. The orchestra continues to play fortissimo as the girl cries out to the world the horror of her home.

Meanwhile townspeople have entered the house. Two men bring forward the bloody ax and the mother's white shawl, laced now with blood. They confront the girl. Her hands quiver before her face. Moving as in a dream, she takes her mother's shawl and holds it to her lips.

The pastor makes his way through the crowd to the Accused. He holds her, lifts her gently as if to protect her. The girl's feet kick at the air in a spasm of desperation. Then she collapses at the pastor's feet.

SCENE EIGHT—THE GALLOWS: The house of the Accused disappears except for a piece of its framework, which forms the gallows we saw in the prologue. She stands with the pastor, awaiting her execution. The people of the town pass by and stare at her. She is not disturbed, for she is preoccupied with her own frantically rapid memories of her crime and what led up to it: the blissful childhood, the loving mother, the father destroyed in his weakness by the demon spinster, the love she has wanted to give all her life, and the love that must now die. She holds out her hand, grasping at her memories, kneels, and opens her arms. The pastor comforts her.

A mother and her small daughter, perhaps the Accused herself, come to see the condemned woman. Ironically, the child shakes her fists at the Accused. Contented couples pass and watch. The Accused lets her head rest briefly on the pastor's shoulder. There is not much time left. He kisses her and leaves her alone. The girl turns to the gallows and opens her arms, as if to welcome the hangman's noose. Her body twitches grotesquely; her neck breaks. The music finishes like thunder. The Accused has been hanged until she is dead.

NOTES: The day following its first performance, *Fall River Legend* was declared unanimously a hit. Louis Biancolli of the New York *World-Telegram* said that "in adroit weaving of story, dance and music," the ballet "shapes up as the ideal 'whodunit' on toes," while the *Herald Tribune*'s Walter Terry reported that "Ballet Theatre finds itself with a new hit on its hands." Francis Herridge wrote that it was "the best thing Agnes de Mille has done to date, and one of the finest ballets in the modern idiom."

The part of the Accused in *Fall River Legend* was designed originally for Nora Kaye, who, because of illness, was unable to dance its first performances. Diana Krupska and Alicia Alonso danced the part until her recovery. Diana Adams danced the mother, Muriel Bentley the stepmother, Peter Gladke the father, and John Kriza the pastor at the ballet's first performance.

FANCY FREE

Ballet in one act. Music by Leonard Bernstein. Choreography by Jerome Robbins. Scenery by Oliver Smith. Costumes by Kermit Love. First presented by Ballet Theatre at the Metropolitan Opera House, New York, April 18, 1944, with John Kriza, Harold Lang, and Jerome Robbins as the three *Sailors*; Muriel Bentley, Janet Reed, and Shirley Eckl as the three *Passers-by*.

This modern American ballet tells what happens to three sailors who go out on liberty in New York City. The time is the present: any hot summer night. The scene is a side street in Manhattan.

The music is quiet when the curtain rises. Outlined against the dark city night is the interior of a bar. The entrance to the bar, on the right, leads out onto a street corner. There a bright street lamp shines down on the sidewalk. Inside the bar there are no customers; the lone bartender lazily dries and polishes beer glasses. He begins to read a newspaper. In the background the myriad lights of distant skyscrapers penetrate the sultry night like stars.

Through the side windows of the bar we can make out three sailors walking toward the corner. The music blares out. They rush toward the corner, pivot on the lamppost, and begin to dance in the street in front of the bar. Dressed in clean summer whites, the sailors are out to make the most of the night. They preen a little, adjust their hats to jazzy angles, and strut along the pavement in anticipation of the good time that must naturally come their way. Their dance is like an improvised vaudeville act; it's clear that the three are friends and that they can kid each other and laugh about it. If they have their way, this is going to be an evening to beat all the rest. They try to outdo each other with brief trick dance steps and laugh. Two of them push the third high up in the air between them. Inside the bar the bartender smokes and reads his paper.

The rowdy music that accompanies the sailors' dance slows down and softens. The three men know from experience that simple determination isn't going to get them a good time. They straighten their jackets, readjust their hats, and wonder what to do next: which do they want first—women, drink, or music? One of the sailors leans against the lamppost to consider the problem seriously. One of his pals joins him. Before these two have made up their minds completely, the third sailor enters the bar. His friends race in after him.

The three sailors strut up to the bar with a special salty air for the bartender's benefit. They order three beers, clink their glasses together, down the drinks in unison, and slam the glasses back down on the bar. The bartender eyes them suspiciously: who's going to pay? The sailors look at each other as if such a thought had never entered their heads. Finally one of them is tricked into paying by the other two. As he puts down the money, he tries to shrug off the fact that he always ends up with the short end of the stick.

Now that they've had one drink, the sailors remember that they don't want to drink alone. They look around the empty bar with amused disgust, hitch up their pants, and head for the door. The music is moody, waiting for something to happen. The sailors are getting slightly tired of each other; they wonder if the evening is going to turn out to be a bust, after all. One of them pulls out a stick of gum. He starts to unwrap it, then remembers his friends and splits it with them. The three chew thoughtfully and, one by one, flick the pieces of gum wrapper out into the street to see which one can flick it farthest. The winner wonders what difference it makes.

At this point, just as the three are about to relax into boredom, they straighten up as if lightning had struck. The music breaks out into loud, rhythmic boogiewoogie, and a terrific-looking girl walks by. She wears a tight-fitting blouse and skirt, high patent leather shoes, and carries a red handbag. The girl knows she is being watched; she smiles and by her walk suggests all the things the sailors are imagining. The sailors are struck numb; standing close together, they move as one body—bending so far forward to watch the girl that they almost fall on their faces.

The girl pretends that she hasn't seen them, which sends the boys into action. Suddenly they are three very different individuals, each trying to interest the girl in his own special way. They imitate her walk, laugh at her, grab her purse and toss it around, and all but lie at her feet to get the girl to recognize their existence. The girl wants to be angry and tries to act as if she is, but the boys sense that she's just kidding. When she laughs in warm, friendly recognition, the three sailors smile back and wonder—who saw her first? A small fight breaks out. Two of the boys lift the girl high. She kicks free and stomps off impatiently. The battle has left one sailor lying in the street. He watches as his two friends follow the girl, then lazily picks himself up.

He smoothes out his uniform and starts to go back into the bar. Then, as in a dream, he bumps into a small, cute girl, younger than the first. He apologizes for his clumsiness, smiles winningly, looks her up and down adroitly, and introduces himself. The girl smiles back. The sailor looks over her shoulder to be sure his friends have disappeared and asks her into the bar for a drink. The girl consents.

Inside, the bartender is still reading. The sailor and his girl climb up on two stools and order drinks. He is feeling his way with the redhead, but decides on the old routine. The music stops as he gives her a dazzling, rapid display of What-I've-Been-Through. His hands circle the air and zoom down to attack imaginary ships, and his body vibrates to machine-gun fire as he describes the terrors of life at sea. When the girl takes this in and doesn't laugh at him, just watches, the boy decides that she's not only cute, she's adorable. He asks her to dance.

The orchestra plays a low blues number as they move together slowly. The *pas de deux* they dance is instinctively intimate, and the intimacy— their mutual liking and attraction—is so natural and unforced that formality and doubt would be out of place. This is a made-for-each-other dance that makes sense in its alternate casualness and conviction. He dances with her as he would with any girl, then holds her closely, and she responds warmly to this way of showing how special she is. When the dance is over, he bends down and kisses her softly. The girl smiles and wipes her lipstick off his face. They move together back to the bar.

The sailor picks the girl up and sits her on a stool. He has started to pay for the drinks when a roaring rattle of sound breaks the romantic spell and ushers in his two friends. The two gobs barge into the bar with the first girl and stop dead in their tracks when they see him with a date. He grabs his girl and pulls her toward the door to avoid the intruders. But the girl stops him. The girls are old friends, apparently, and begin to carry on together as girls will.

The boy sees that the situation is hopeless and goes to join his pals at a table. More drinks are ordered. The girls sit down. There are only four chairs, and one of the sailors is left standing. He tries to sit on the first girl's lap—she seems more experienced and tolerant—but she pushes him off. Two of the sailors dance with the girls, and the boy who found the redhead sits alone for a moment. Now he cuts in. The snare drum signals the quarrel that ensues: who's going to dance with whom? The situation is hopeless. One of the boys has got to clear out or the night will be ruined.

The three sailors finally get together and agree that they'll have a contest to see which one of them can dance best. The girls will be the judges of the two winners, and the third man will scram. Two of the sailors join the girls at the table, and one of the boys begins a solo.

His dance is rowdy and energetic as he tries to outdo all the steps he thinks his friends might try. The girls are delighted at his fresh and arrogant skill and begin to applaud as he finishes his number by jumping up on the bar with one leap. There he poses for an instant, then jumps down, grabs up a beer, and flourishes his glass. The other two sailors razz him as the girls clap their hands.

The next variation is danced by the cute girl's first partner. His dance is subtler, relying more on sinuous, flowing rhythm than boisterousness, more on false modesty than overt bragging. The girls respond to his quiet dance with a sigh, and his friends hold their noses. He lies on the floor with his legs in the air as his number ends. The last sailor tries to combine the two styles of his friends and succeeds brilliantly in a snaky, Latin dance at the end of which he jumps down from a bar stool to kneel on the floor before the girls.

The girls don't know which ones to choose! They argue about it; then the boys argue with them and start to fight among themselves. The competition that began when the first girl passed by on the street turns into anger and rage, and they begin to tear each other apart. The girls cringe against the bar, thinking at first that this can't be serious, but as the battle goes on in earnest, they decide to get out of there fast. The sailors dive behind the bar in a tussle and don't notice that the girls have walked out on them. When they pause and wake up to this fact, they look at each other frantically and dive for the door. Out on the street they can't find the girls. They look at each other with amused disgust, straighten out their uniforms, nurse their aches and pains, and relax again.

What are they to do now? Maybe another drink will help. They re-enter the bar, down a drink apiece, and again the same sailor pays. The friends head back for the street. They stand there under the lamppost, as they did before they first entered the bar at the beginning of the evening. They split another piece of gum three ways; they tear off the paper and flip it into the street.

The music sounds noisily, and a beautiful babe promenades across the street—terrific, you understand? As before, the three bodies slant in unison as they follow her every step and wiggle. The girl struts off down the street on the left. The sailors seem to recover from her fascination and remember the bruises of the battle royal the last girls got them involved in. Each watches the others carefully, to be sure that this feeling is unanimous. This is just a stall. They begin to idle away from each other, laughing the blonde off, when one sailor strikes off like a streak of lightning after the girl. His friends follow. The cycle is endless.

NOTES: *Fancy Free* was the first ballet by the distinguished American dancer and choreographer Jerome Robbins. It was also the first of his series of brilliant successes: *Interplay, Facsimile, The Guests, The Age of Anxiety, The Cage,* etc. Robbins conceived the idea of *Fancy Free* in 1942, two years after he joined Ballet Theatre as a dancer. Before then he had studied dancing intensively in many of its aspects, he had studied music, and had danced in musical comedies on Broadway (he appeared in the Ethel Merman show *Stars in Your Eyes,* 1938, with two other dancers who were to become famous: Nora Kaye and Alicia Alonso). During these years of preparation, he had also done his first choreography.

Robbins wrote the story of *Fancy Free* out on paper. He asked Leonard Bernstein to write a score for his story and devised the choreography gradually, while he danced on tour with Ballet Theatre throughout the country. For his dancers he chose four other unknowns in the company and himself. He invited the young designer Oliver Smith to design the set.

The morning after *Fancy Free*'s first performance, those who hadn't seen it were sorry they hadn't been at the Metropolitan Opera House. Edwin Denby reported in the *Herald Tribune* that *Fancy Free* "was so big a hit that the young participants all looked a little dazed as they took their bows. Besides being a smash hit, *Fancy Free* is a very remarkable comedy piece . . . Its pantomime and its dances are witty, exuberant and at every moment they feel natural . . . The whole number is as sound as a superb vaudeville turn; in ballet terminology, it is perfect American character ballet."

FANFARE

Classic ballet in one act. Music by Benjamin Britten. Choreography by Jerome Robbins. Lighting by Jean Rosenthal. First presented by the New York City Ballet at the City Center, New York, June 2, 1953, with a cast headed by Yvonne Mounsey, Todd Bolender, Frank Hobi, and Michael Maule.

Fanfare, which had its first performance on Coronation Night 1953, is a visualization of *The Young Person's Guide to the Orchestra*, a well-known work by the contemporary English composer Benjamin Britten. Britten's score consists of variations and a fugue on a theme by Henry Purcell. These variations and the final fugue illustrate, one by one, the different musical instruments, or group of instruments, that make up the modern symphony orchestra. The ballet is a set of dances arranged to these variations and fugue. A narrator stands at the side of the stage to introduce the ballet and the different instruments.

When the curtain rises, all the dancers who will later represent the different instruments of the orchestra are gathered together on stage under heraldic flags that depict ancient instruments. As Purcell's theme is played by the orchestra, the dancers imitate by noble gestures and attitudes the solemn dignity and nobility of the music. The dancers' costumes differentiate by color the four families of the symphony orchestra: the woodwinds are dressed in blue, the strings in orange, the brass in yellow, and the percussion in black. Each dancer's costume is embellished with a design that identifies the instrument portrayed. Each wears a crown.

After the opening theme has been stated, all the dancers exit. Now the narrator introduces the instruments. First, the woodwinds. The variation of piccolo and two flutes is charaterized by a *pas de trois*, danced by three girls. Next, the clarinets, who are represented by a *pas de deux* for a boy and a girl. A lone girl dances to the music of the oboe. She moves in slow, beautiful adagio to its music. Next, two boys dance comically to the variation for two bassoons.

The strings now take the stage. The first and second violins are represented by groups of girls. They are followed by a girl and a boy who dance to the music of the violas. Two girls depict the cellos, while a boy mimes and dances the difficulties of the double bass. Finally the harp, represented by a ballerina all in white, fills the eye with precise and flowing grace to tingling arpeggios.

Next the brass—horns, trumpets, tuba, and trombones—are depicted. Finally, the percussion—drums, cymbals, gongs, etc. The variation which these instruments play is represented by three boys who characterize by horseplay and wit the sudden booms, rattles, crashes, and slaps of the percussion instruments.

Now that all the instruments of the orchestra have been demonstrated, the narrator tells us: "We have taken the orchestra to pieces. It remains to put it back together again. We shall do this in the form of a fugue."

The first voice of the fugue is taken by the woodwinds, one by one; next come the different strings; then the brass; and, at the end, the percussion. The four great families of the orchestra mingle on stage, depicting by a massive dance the cumulative power of all the instruments. The original theme by Purcell is again sounded by the entire orchestra, and all the dancers accompany the music with triumphant, noble flourishes.

LA FILLE MAL GARDÉE
THE UNCHAPERONED DAUGHTER

> Ballet in three scenes. Music by Johann Wilhelm Hertel. Choreography and libretto by Jean Dauberval. First presented in the United States at the Park Theatre, New York, July 6, 1839. Revived by Ballet Theatre at the Center Theatre, New York, January 19, 1940. Choreography restaged by Bronislava Nijinska. Settings and costumes by Serge Soudeikine. Patricia Bowman, Yurek Shabelevsky, Edward Caton, and Alexis Kosloff were the principals.

Many people who go to the ballet and chance to come across a work that was originally presented more than a hundred and fifty years ago imagine that such a ballet must be sad—perhaps an antique tragedy. But *La Fille Mal Gardée* is a comedy. The earliest of all the ballets in the current repertory, its universally comical situations are no doubt responsible for its survival.

Soon after the music begins, a painted drop curtain depicts the principal characters of the ballet. On the left are Lisette and Colin, the two lovers. A rotund Cupid painted at the top of the scene directs a pointed arrow at the heroine. Lisette's mother, Madame Simone, dominates the scene, trying to watch her daughter and be pleasant to the suitor she has chosen for her.

The story contained in this picture gradually unfolds as the drop curtain rises. The ballet is set in a small provincial French town. The time is about two hundred years ago.

SCENE ONE — THE FARM OF MADAME SIMONE: Alongside the steep-roofed house of Madame Simone, a "rich farmerette," is the family barnyard. In back, a rushing stream cascades down a hill. Madame Simone sits on a bench at the left, whiling away the time of day. Two neighbors join her to gossip. She bustles off with them.

The music suggests the arrival of the heroine, and Lisette enters on the left. Dressed in a light-blue skirt with a red bodice, with blue ribbons in her hair, she is the picture of innocent, country prettiness. The day has just begun, and because she is supposed to be busy at one task or another, Lisette pretends to arrange several flowerpots on the bench. She bows to several of the village boys, bound for the fields with their scythes, as she waters the flowers. Colin, a good-looking young farmer, enters on the left, carrying a rake. He sits down on the bench, and Lisette, anxious to be surprised by his arrival, absent-mindedly waters his head. Colin jumps up, and he and Lisette immediately begin to dance together. Their dance reveals that the two have been attracted to each other for some time, that this is not their first rendezvous. Colin lifts Lisette boldly, yet gently.

The love duet is interrupted by Lisette's mother. Directly she approaches, the two lovers rush to hide behind the bench. Madame Simone discovers them, however, and chases Colin around the stage. Hastily he embraces Lisette and rushes off. Madame Simone, in a high temper, proceeds to lecture her daughter on her duty to make a proper marriage. Lisette protests that she is absolutely innocent of any flirtation, but her mother persists in her rage. The two neighbors come in to watch the scene. Lisette finally secures her mother's forgiveness by offering her, with a sweet smile, one of her own flowers.

Trumpets announce the arrival of four of Lisette's friends. They are followed by a group of villagers. The young people want Lisette to join them. Dutifully she asks her mother's permission and she begins to dance. Colin sneaks in at the back and conceals himself in the crowd. He runs out and takes Lisette's hand when her mother stalks off. The two dance a lively duet, surrounded by their friends. The music is gay and sparkling. The conviviality is short-lived, however, for Madame Simone returns, sees Colin, and sends him packing. She makes a point of her daughter's idleness by presenting scythes to her four friends.

Lisette attempts to console herself by dancing with her friends as they celebrate the harvesttime. She tries to leave with them when they go, but her mother pulls her back. Lisette herself is now in a temper. She stomps, shakes her fists pathetically, cries, and hides her face in her hands. Her mother takes her hands away and tries to make amends. Colin has entered quietly and stands in back of Madame Simone. That is consolation enough for Lisette. She waves to him. Her mother notes the gesture, but cannot find a reason for it. Colin does not conceal himself for long, however. The impetuous girl rushes to him. They embrace briefly before Madame Simone leaps at them to drag Lisette back toward the house.

She sits her daughter down on the bench. Lisette rises and brings out a butter churn. Her mother fills the churn with cream and orders her daughter to work. Lisette churns away, and her mother leaves the scene. Colin leaps in behind Lisette. He places his hands on hers and easily persuades her to stop her work. He sits down on the bench beside her; Lisette, suddenly embarrassed at being alone with her lover, rises and dances. She turns softly and slowly, beguiling Colin with her sweet motion. When she finishes her dance with a series of rapid turns, Colin throws out to her a long blue ribbon. Lisette catches it and, holding the flowing ribbon above their heads, the two dance together romantically. Lisette tosses the ribbon back to Colin, who fixes it halter-fashion around her shoulders, after which the girl performs her steps as if by his command. Lisette pirouettes into his arms, Colin ties the ribbon about her, and the girl poses against her lover. The two then leave the stage.

Thomas, a vinegrower, enters with his son, Alain. Come to see Madame Simone by appointment, the obese Thomas is decked out in a bright-green suit; he is determined to be formal and correct. His son, determined to be playful and completely oblivious to his surroundings, leaps about the stage trying to catch butterflies in a net. Thomas reprimands him and pulls him to a bench.

Madame Simone, dressed in her best purple, arrives to greet the guests. With ceremonious gestures, she and Thomas discuss the suitability of a marriage between their children. Madame Simone is readily persuaded of Alain's eligibility when Thomas dangles a bag of gold in her face. The woman approaches to examine the young man, ascertains that he is sound of limb if not of mind, and gives her approval. She drags Lisette out to meet her fiancé. Dutifully the girl has changed her clothes for the occasion, but she has no idea of its real meaning. Both parents push their children toward each other. Both children step back in horror as they realize the meaning of their parents' interview. Each tries to escape, but the parents hold them secure. The curtain falls as they both kneel, their faces turned away from each other. Lisette's white dress and pink ribbons are for the wrong man. Madame Simone stands over them in an attitude of supreme happiness. During the scene change, Thomas and Madame Simone, accompanied by the neighbors, drag the engaged couple off to the village notary to make the marriage settlement final.

SCENE TWO—THE VILLAGE GREEN: On the painted backdrop, wheat fields are seen in the distance. Sheaves of freshly cut wheat are propped up where the workers have left them. A windmill stands over the fields on a hill at the back. On the right is a great tree; two cows meditate near by. The workers of the village, colorfully dressed girls and their companions, pause for a general dance. Lisette and Alain are pushed into the scene by their parents. Despite all their complaining, the two are made to stand close together. They are able to separate only when Thomas asks Madame Simone to dance. The aged couple cavort grotesquely about the green; it has suddenly occurred to Madame Simone that she, too, might be quite a match, and she flirts with the vinegrower.

Meanwhile Colin has entered quietly on the right. He sees that his sweetheart has been promised to another and turns away. Madame Simone and Thomas race off to pursue their flirtation elsewhere, and some of Lisette's friends, noticing Colin's plight, encourage the girl to comfort the poor lad. Lisette touches his arm. By her soft, endearing gestures the girl convinces him that she herself has had nothing to do with the proposed match. Colin puts his arms about her, and their foreheads touch. He kneels, and the two begin an adagio to the melody of solo strings and an accompanying harp. The villagers sit on the ground to watch the lovers. Lisette leaves the scene after the dance is over, and Colin performs a bright, dazzling variation. Lisette returns for a winsome, engaging dance in which she lifts her skirt softly, with innocent coquetry. Her variation increases in momentum; at the end she turns brilliantly and cuts her movement off suddenly with a swift, pert pose.

Alain, who has been off chasing after butterflies, runs onto the scene, brandishing his net before him. He circles the stage in long, high leaps. Two of the girls try to engage his attention. The youth ignores their flattery, but the girls persist and dance on either side of him. Alain abandons them, jumping off into the wings in pursuit of his hobby.

Thunder is heard and the scene darkens; lightning flashes illumine the hurried dashing back and forth of the villagers. Lisette and Colin follow as their friends run for cover. Alain rushes in, trembling with fright at the lightning. He hides his head under a girl's skirts and pushes her off toward safety. The drop curtain falls.

SCENE THREE — MADAME SIMONE'S HOUSE: Lisette enters quickly to escape the storm. Her mother follows and bustles about the room. Lisette pours coffee for her, then sits at her feet as Madame Simone begins to work at her spinning wheel. Lisette tries to sneak away, but her mother orders her to read a book she gives her. Lisette looks at a page or two, then asks her mother the meaning of one of the words. Madame Simone is horrified: she has given her daughter the wrong book! A romantic novel, no less! The girl succeeds in crawling away a few feet until Madame Simone seizes her from behind and draws her back to her chair. She takes up her sewing again.

Colin opens the transom above the door and throws in a flower to Lisette. Lisette turns around and sees him. Immediately her mother senses her agitation and commands her to be still. Colin, by passionate signs, beseeches her to dance for him. The girl persuades her mother to play the tambourine so that she can practice her dancing. Lisette dances flirtatiously for Colin's benefit. The old woman tires of the tambourine and falls off to sleep. Lisette approaches her on tiptoe. As the girl takes her key, her mother wakens and beats the tambourine. Lisette continues her dance, and at its conclusion Madame Simone kisses her in reward.

Boys and girls of the village enter, bringing with them sheaves of wheat, which they stack against a table. Lisette would like to follow them off, but her mother commands her to take her turn at the spinning wheel. Lisette stamps her foot and throws herself down in the chair to sulk. Her mother leaves the room.

The orchestra repeats the melody to which she and Colin danced so happily, and Lisette imagines what it would be like to be married to the man of her own choice. She puts her hands on her heart and blows a kiss toward the door. She sees herself surrounded by Colin's children, whom she scolds; she rocks her arms as if they held a child.

To Lisette's embarrassment, Colin is there in the room watching her. The sheaves of wheat are thrown aside, and her lover sits smiling at her. She sits beside him for a moment, then jumps up as he proposes to her seriously. Colin pleads with her—after all, she has just imagined herself as his wife—but the girl in her embarrassment and confusion denies her love and shoves the boy toward the door. Colin begins to lose his temper at her stubbornness and is delighted to find her even more flustered when she finds that the door is locked!

Lisette runs to the chair and sees that she can keep up the pretense no longer. Colin kneels at her feet and places his head in her lap. The two trade their scarves as a pledge of their love. Madame Simone can be heard approaching. Lisette tries to hide Colin—under the little table, in a small chest. In desperation, she pushes him into the hayloft and slams the door shut just as her mother enters.

Lisette thinks she is safe but she has forgotten Colin's scarf. Madame Simone spots it instantly and fetches a large switch to beat the girl. Lisette runs, but the old woman catches up with her, spanks her soundly, and, as an additional penalty, locks her in the hayloft!

Visitors are heard outside. Madame Simone admits Thomas and Alain, the village notary and his secretary following in their wake. Villagers accompany them to witness the marriage contract. The notary buries his face in his registry, the parents rejoice, and the preoccupied Alain toys with the spinning wheel. Madame Simone presents him with the key to the hayloft and tells the youth where to find his bride. Alain unlocks the door. Lisette and Colin step out sheepishly, their clothes and hair covered with hay.

Madame Simone is scandalized. Before all the village, her daughter has ruined the family's reputation. Lisette begs her to understand. Colin joins

Lisette, and both lovers kneel before her. At first Madame Simone refuses to listen. Then she realizes that the notary can quite easily make another marriage contract and consents. Lisette kisses her joyfully. Colin kisses her. The two lovers kiss, and Madame Simone embraces them both.

NOTES: *La Fille Mal Gardée* is the oldest ballet in the contemporary repertory, with the possible exception of *The Whims of Cupid and the Ballet Master* (Jens Lolle-Vincenzo Galeotti), also 1786. The precise first performance date of *La Fille Mal Gardée* is uncertain. Galeotti's ballet has been in the repertory of the Royal Danish Ballet since its first performance, on October 31, 1786; its music and choreography remain the same, except for some recent revision by Harald Lander. In 1951 Richard Buckle described a performance in Copenhagen in *Ballet*: "In a formal garden with a temple on one side stands a small girl dressed as Cupid in a rose pink *tutu*. She is attended, fantastically, by priests in turbans and flowing robes. From the wings she beckons on in turn nine couples who execute dances in diverse styles. There are ancient Greeks, comic Quakers, Norwegian folk dances, grotesque blackamoors, rickety Louis XVI aristocrats and others. I find this *divertissement* quite charming with its mixture of classical, character and folk dances. Gerda Karstens is very funny as the gawky old Quakeress. Finally Cupid has them all blindfolded and pairs them off with the wrong partners. There is a mild scrimmage at the end, with portly negresses clasping blond young demigods and half the party in full flight from the other half. I guess this uproarious charade to be a modern concoction; then I find on the programme that it is *Les Caprices du Cupidon et du Maître de Ballet* by Vincenzo Galeotti, who was director of the Royal Danish Ballet in the eighteenth century." Harald Lander staged *Les Caprices* at the Paris Opéra on February 27, 1952.

The choreographer of *La Fille Mal Gardée*, Jean Bercher (1742–1806), known professionally as Dauberval, had studied with Noverre and had worked with the great French choreographer and with the great dancer Gardel at the Paris Opéra. Although comic ballets undoubtedly existed before *La Fille Mal Gardée*, none treated so realistic and worldly a subject; Dauberval has been called the father of comic ballet.

Very little of his choreography remains in current productions. The work has been extensively revised in different revivals, both in Europe and the United States. Auguste Bournonville, Mikhail Mordkin, and Bronislava Nijinska are a few of the choreographers who have staged new productions of the work.

Under the title *Useless Precautions*, *La Fille Mal Gardée* has been a fixture of the Imperial Russian and Soviet repertories for many years. Fanny Elssler, who danced it for her farewell performance in America (July 1, 1842), and Pavlova, Lydia Kyasht, Adeline Genée, Lucia Chase, Irina

Baronova, Janet Reed, and Nana Gollner are a few of the many dancers who have performed its leading role.

FILLING STATION

Ballet-document in one act. Music by Virgil Thomson. Choreography by Lew Christensen. Book by Lincoln Kirstein. Scenery and costumes by Paul Cadmus. First presented by Ballet Caravan at the Avery Memorial Theatre, Hartford, Connecticut, January 6, 1938, with Lew Christensen, Marie-Jeanne, Erick Hawkins, Michael Kidd, Todd Bolender, Eugene Loring, and Fred Danieli in the principal roles.

Filling Station is not only one of the first modern ballets on a familiar American subject, but one of the first ballets to employ American music, scenery and costumes by an American, and American dancers. It was the first ballet on an American subject commissioned by Lincoln Kirstein for his Ballet Caravan, a small American company founded in 1936 which, with the Balanchine-Kirstein American Ballet, was to be the precursor of the present New York City Ballet.

Filling Station is an attempt to discover an American hero, a hero equivalent to the heroes of classical European ballets. The makers of the ballet have chosen a filling station attendant as their hero. The fact that the ballet succeeded in its aim was recently demonstrated by the marked success of its revival, which clearly indicated that the popular American myth of 1938 was still viable fifteen years later.

After a robust overture, the curtain rises on the interior of Mac's filling station. It is night. A neon sign advertising gas is seen in reverse against the large plate-glass window on the left. In the rear, there is a door leading to the station rest rooms.

Mac, the station attendant, is whiling away the lonely hours of the night reading a tabloid. He puts down the paper and begins to dance. He moves about the stage with vigorous leaps and turns. His dance is interrupted by a motorist who comes into the station to ask for directions. The motorist is dressed like a golfer in a comic strip: he wears violently colored checkered knickers, straw hat, and smokes a cigar.

Mac tries to direct him to his destination by pointing out the route on a map. When the motorist fails to understand, Mac produces a huge enlargement of the map to set him right. Behind this map, two truck drivers, friends of Mac, sneak into the station while Mac gives the motorist final directions.

As soon as the motorist departs, the two truck drivers greet Mac and the three men dance an athletic *pas de trois* that features cart wheels and somersaults. Their good fellowship is cut short by the arrival of a state trooper, who accuses the truck drivers of speeding. The men deny this, and the state trooper leaves after warning them severely.

The motorist in knickers returns, this time with his family and his golf gear. His wife, a huge blonde in unbecoming slacks, towers over her husband and constantly berates him. Their daughter, a constantly whining child, is clearly in need of the rest room. While his wife and daughter disappear into the rear of the station, the motorist entertains Mac and the truck drivers by practicing golf. He is not happy for long, however. When wife and daughter return, they combine to make life so miserable for him that he happily leads them back to their car outside.

Now an intoxicated young couple drop by on their way home from a party at the local country club. The girl stumbles in first, followed by her escort. She is in no condition to dance, but insists on doing so. The boy supports her in adagio poses, holding the girl's almost limp body upright when she collapses in his arms.

As the couple finish this comic adagio, they are joined by Mac and the truck drivers. By this time, the girl wants to dance with everybody. All the men join her in a dance that is climaxed as she is tossed from one man to another and thrown high into the air. When the unhappy motorist, who has momentarily escaped from his wife and child, re-enters the station, the dance is at fever pitch. Noting the newcomer, the girl jumps into his arms just as his wife comes in after him.

The motorist tries to stay on the opposite side of the stage from his wife as all join in the "Big Apple." But the celebration is soon broken up. A gangster enters. He lines all the people up and instructs them to place all their jewelry and cash in a bag he snatches from the motorist's wife. Everyone conforms to his wish except Mac, who sneaks outside and turns out the lights.

Directly the lights go out, the stage is in confusion. Mac enters with a flashlight, and soon the stage is filled with the beams of flashlights carried by the others as they try to help Mac track down the gangster. Blinded by their lights, the gangster shoots.

When the lights come up, it can be seen that the girl from the country club is dead. All gather around her body. The state trooper enters and takes the gangster off to prison. The girl's body is lifted high and carried off in solemn procession. Just as the ballet seems about to end in a tragedy, the girl wakes from the dead and waves at Mac as her cortege moves out of the station. Mac saunters about for a moment, then returns to his newspaper.

NOTES: *Filling Station* was revived by the New York City Ballet on May 12, 1953, at the City Center, New York. Jacques d'Amboise, Janet Reed, and Michael Maule danced the principal roles. Reviewing this performance in the New York *Herald Tribune*, Walter Terry wrote:

"An old ballet and a brand-new star joined forces last evening at the City Center to provide the New York City Ballet with a presentation which may,

I think, be classified as a resounding hit. The ballet . . . was *Filling Station*, first produced by the Ballet Caravan (the present company's great-grand-parent in a direct line of ancestry) in 1938. The new star, only slightly older than *Filling Station* itself, was Jacques d'Amboise, just turned eighteen.

". . . *Filling Station* recalls the recent past (never as exciting as the long, long ago) and although American ballets of sturdier nature have since been created, it remains an unpretentious, lively, thoroughly entertaining and, I believe, lovable work.

"Virgil Thomson's infectious score, delightful to the ear and an invitation to dance, is based upon the popular rhythms (invigorated by some perennial folk memories) of the day. The scenery and costumes by Paul Cadmus suggest a time when comic strips tended to be comic and Lew Christensen's choreography, closely integrated with both sound and design, captures the buoyancy of the former one and the episodic speed inherent in cartoon strips.

"And what is *Filling Station* all about? Well, the hero is Mac, the strong and handsome attendant, and the visitors to his establishment include two truck drivers; a henpecked motorist, his buxom wife and their revolting child; a rich (and highly inebriated) young couple, a gangster and a state trooper. All of them involved in a very minor (but agreeably melodramatic) plot. Far more important, however, is the actual dancing and, if my memory has not failed, the New York City Ballet dances *Filling Station* better than it was ever danced before.

"It was a rousing performance all around, but heading the list was Mr. d'Amboise as Mac, a part which seemed to be tailor-made for his youthful exuberance and for his remarkable physical prowess. Muscular elasticity —a quality which usually disappears with maturity—was evident in the high and resilient leaps; jumps which found the body resting easily in air; leaping turns, apparently motivated by coiled springs, which described slow-motion arcs in space; rollovers, cartwheels, tumblings, rough-house. There were also slow and sustained pirouettes, impeccable entrechats and the disclosure of a young but beautifully schooled dance technique.

"But Mr. d'Amboise, although he had the leading role and generated the excitement attendant at the emergence of a junior star, did not steal the show. As the female inebriate, Janet Reed added another irresistible characterization to her long list of achievements in the theatre. The diminutive and ever-beautiful ballerina filled each action with delicious humor. Not a gesture evaded the touch of her perfect timing. Nothing was overdone, nothing left unfinished in a comedy portrayal as perfect as any I have ever seen in ballet.

"In supporting roles, Edward Bigelow and Robert Barnett were splendid as the tough truck drivers but there were also expert performances by Michael Maule, a joy as Miss Reed's intoxicated companion; by Walter Georgov and John Mandia, as the gangster and the state trooper, respectively, and by

Stanley Zompakos as the motorist, Shaun O'Brien (suitably padded here and there) as the wife, and Edith Brozak as the child.

"Thus did *Filling Station* enjoy a stirring revival. It . . . is something to see. It is also something to chuckle about and to cheer about and last evening's large audience did just that."

FIREBIRD

Dramatic ballet in three scenes. Music by Igor Stravinsky. Choreography by Michel Fokine. Scenery and costumes by Golovine and Bakst. First presented by Diaghilev's Ballets Russes at the Théâtre National de l'Opéra, Paris, June 25, 1910, with Tamara Karsavina as the *Firebird*, Michel Fokine as *Prince Ivan*, and Enrico Cecchetti as *Kastchei*. First presented in the United States by Diaghilev's Ballets Russes at the Century Theatre, New York, January 17, 1916, with Xenia Maclezova as the *Firebird*, Leonide Massine as *Prince Ivan*, and Enrico Cecchetti as *Kastchei*. Revived by the New York City Ballet at the City Center, New York, November 27, 1949. Choreography by George Balanchine. Scenery and costumes by Marc Chagall. Lighting by Jean Rosenthal. Maria Tallchief danced the *Firebird*; Francisco Moncion was *Prince Ivan*. The production of the New York City Ballet is described below.

The composer of *Firebird*, Igor Stravinsky, once said that Russian legends have as their heroes men who are "simple, naïve, sometimes even stupid, devoid of all malice, and it is they who are always victorious over characters that are clever, artful, complex, cruel and powerful." Prince Ivan in this ballet is such a hero: he is a simple hunter who stumbles into the eerie garden of an evil monster, there falls in love with a beautiful princess held captive by the ogre, and rescues her with a supernatural power granted him by a magical bird of fire.

SCENE ONE—A FOREST: As the music to the ballet begins, we have that first suggestion of the mystery and magic that will control Ivan's destiny. No sooner has the orchestra—with its low, throbbing strings and baleful trombones—given us a hint of darkness and foreboding, than the curtain rises to present us with an enormous painting of the ballet's heroine, the Firebird who will help the prince to free the world of one of its monstrous evils. The Firebird is depicted as bright, glorious, and triumphant—a fantastic creature, half bird, half woman. She has the face and arms of a charming young girl and a body of shimmering feathers that tapers off in orange-speckled flame. This colorful figure is painted against a background of amorphous, purple shapes. The music now suggests unimagined giants plodding across the earth and a fairyland peopled with primeval beings sadly singing an accompaniment.

Now the painted curtain rises. It is dark, and as the stage brightens slightly, we can see in the background trees so thickly crowded that the sun can scarcely penetrate. Here in the forest we are transported visually to the world of fantasy at which the music has hinted, and when the prince enters, his bow stretched tightly, ready to destroy any creature concealed in the thicket, we understand why he hunts with care. Ivan wears a costume more becoming to an untutored Russian peasant than to a royal prince, but this serves only to remind us that we are watching a story of a time before the primitive court of the czar was altered by European opulence.

Subdued, half-uttered cries come from behind the dark trees. Ivan looks about him, searching for the beasts that may lie waiting in the shadows, when a low, steady drum, followed by an answering horn, indicates that he is about to meet his prey. Suddenly the music whirs rapidly and brightly and from above a bright amber light races around and around the prince. Ivan, almost blinded, throws up his arms in astonishment and tries to avoid the shadow the light makes of his startled figure. He runs off, seeking the safe darkness. The music increases its speed, and on stage to its swift accompaniment dances the dazzling Firebird.

Her entrance is as strong and brilliant as the bright red she wears. As she crosses the stage in a series of swiftly executed leaps and poses, followed by that same amber light which announced her arrival, glints of light catch her figure in various attitudes to reveal the long red feather that rises high on her head. Her arms and shoulders are speckled with gold dust, and the shimmering red bodice reflects spangles of brilliance about her moving form. She dances frantically, in continuous movement, to music that mirrors her great joy in displaying vivid images of flight. Even here, in the secluded forest, the Firebird refuses to be earth-bound and seems to resist nature by performing dashing movements that whip the very air about her.

The prince emerges from the shadows to watch unseen. Wishing to capture this creature who moves so magnificently, he reacts with wonder as he discovers that this marvelous bird is also a ravishing woman. He follows her surreptitiously while the Firebird, unaware of the hunter who pursues her, darts about the stage climaxing her solo with rapid turns on point across the stage. This movement increases in momentum with the music, and just as her accelerating spin reaches its fullest force and the music its highest pitch, Ivan dashes forward and reaches out to catch the Firebird about the waist. Brought down to earth, she freezes at his touch, all movement ceasing. Slowly she backs away, in terror of the hunter, in modesty at sight of the man. She turns to escape, but Ivan, fascinated at her daring now that she is in his power, holds her secure. The Firebird, rigid with fear, her arms stiff across her body, falls back against him reluctantly, apparently resigned, but now her arms fly out and beat the air in a frantic effort to free herself.

Ivan will not release his prey, and the frightened Firebird, certain of death by his hand, pleads for mercy. The prince is moved to pity by this appeal for freedom and gently loosens his grasp. He holds out his arm, and the Firebird, in extended arabesque, falls across it, bending her head so that her headdress almost touches the floor at the prince's feet as she bows in tribute to his pity and courtesy.

Encouraged now by the prince's tenderness, the Firebird moves back to dance again. When she turns full circle, Ivan comes forward to support her. Moved by his compassionate strength, as Ivan is moved by her unclaimed love, the Firebird walks toward this man so strange to her. He holds her hand high, then she runs toward him, her body falling back full-length in mid-air. Ivan catches her swooping body and supports her again, as she repeats this movement of ultimate sacrifice and trust. Assured of his sympathy, the Firebird now dances with the prince.

Standing behind her, Ivan supports her arms with his own as the Firebird, standing on point, bends her knees to the floor, then rises to his embrace. Legs spread wide, she slides across the stage as Ivan holds her. The haunting melody of their *pas de deux* soars to its height as the Firebird is held motionless on point, her right leg extended in stillness. Then she falls back, and Ivan swings her around and around in great circles as her free arm flutters in flight. Reminded by this of her greater freedom in the air, the Firebird moves as if to leave the prince. He bows to her formally in homage, and in gratitude for his generosity in releasing her, the Firebird takes from her breast a brilliant red feather. She indicates to the prince that this feather is a magic charm: he need only wave it in the air and she will come to his aid, should he ever require it. Ivan, in respectful deference to the truly supernatural being he now understands the Firebird to be, thanks her and watches regretfully as she turns and leaps gloriously into the wings. The prince follows, transfixed as the music ends in enchanted serenity.

SCENE TWO—KASTCHEI'S GARDEN: While Ivan remains in the shadows, marveling at his encounter with the Firebird, we hear a gay melody from the orchestra. Ten young princesses run in, happily dancing to its tune. They wear long peasant dresses with little caps, and their innocent, carefree gambols make it impossible for us to believe that they are, in reality, captives of the monster Kastchei who rules over the forest. Two of the young girls carry scarves and, as the group dances with simple but elegant grace, these two playfully direct the dancing of the others. They are all dancing together when Prince Ivan startles them. Shocked at the intrusion of a stranger in their dangerous world, the princesses gather together and whisper excitedly. Ivan is amused at their fear and approaches them. From a respectful distance, in mock seriousness and formality, he beckons one of the maidens to come to him. The princesses are agitated by this request and wonder at Ivan's audacity. Ivan insists, and one of the girls at last leaves the group. Ivan bows to her, then whispers softly in her ear. The girl is shocked by what he says to her and runs back to tell her friends. The maidens confer, and then the most beautiful one of them all, in sweet and nervous modesty, steps forward to greet the prince.

The two bow formally and, linking hands, lead the group in a *khorovod* or Russian round dance, to the accompaniment of folklike themes. The chorus of girls become so entwined about their two leaders that it is impossible for the prince and the princess to remain long together. They close their arms about one another, but their partners come amusingly to break their embrace. The two lovers dance with their friends until the light begins to fade. A trumpet is heard in the distance, and the girls gather together quickly in fear. The princess then hastily bids Ivan farewell and runs off with her companions. Ivan stands alone, bewildered at their behavior, as the music takes on mysterious darkness and hints of things unseen.

Ivan stares into the dark thicket about him and is suddenly afraid, but before he can leave the threatening darkness that seems to close in on him, a sharp crash of sound comes from the orchestra and dozens of weird monsters leap with a single bound into the stage and surround him. Green, brown, and multicolored creatures with hideous features and maimed limbs cavort about Ivan to fierce, militant beats from the orchestra. The monsters—some masked with the heads of animals—divide into four groups and race backward and forward and sideways, each group trying to outdo the others in grotesque gestures of threat. One of the creatures is held upright, then thrown straight up into the air and caught by the others, only to be tossed up again. The music subsides, and all the creatures of this fantastic underworld fall on their faces as their master, Kastchei, enters menacingly. He is surrounded by the princess and her friends. Kastchei flourishes his dark cap at his creatures, and we glimpse his skeletonlike body. On his head he wears a spiked crown of burning gold. His fingernails, long as his hands, clutch at the air for victims to satisfy an insatiable appetite.

As Kastchei's slaves surround him in frantic attitudes of homage, Ivan moves to flee. But then he remembers the pledge of the Firebird, remembers that he need fear no danger, and brings out the magic feather. He runs, weaving in and out among the monsters, waving the charm in the air. The monsters try to close in on him. Kastchei stamps the earth in indignation and vows to kill the prince. To the theme to which they danced so playfully just a few moments before, the princesses encircle their evil lord and plead for mercy for Ivan. Kastchei dismisses them with curt disgust, but the prince, encouraged by the confusion he is causing among the monsters, races about with the brilliant red feather. The ogres step back, astounded at his fearlessness in the presence of the all-powerful Kastchei. Enormous snarls from the orchestra follow the prince as he provokes the demons to madness. Kastchei moves in to attack. Then a quick whir in the music proclaims the imminent arrival of the Firebird, come to Ivan's rescue.

The Firebird runs onto the scene with a magnificent leap, carrying over her head a naked golden sword. She hurriedly presents the sword to Ivan, then circles the stage in so rapid and fierce a spin that all the monsters are set to twirling with her. She exits quickly as Ivan falls upon Kastchei with the golden sword. The monster falls dead and Ivan, bathed now in the Fire-bird's brilliant light, holds the gleaming sword high in triumph as the music sounds his victory in a final crescendo.

The stage is dark. The prince stands alone among the fallen bodies of the monsters. The Firebird approaches. Harp strings are plucked gently. The prince finds the princess; he helps her rise. Both bow low before the beauti-ful Firebird, thanking her for saving their lives. The princess' friends rise and do obeisance before the magical bird, and the Firebird bows to them in re-turn.

Free now of mortals, the Firebird dances alone. The stage is completely dark save for the light that follows her. She rises on point, extends one leg straight out, and whips the air in daring turns. The Firebird now revives the fallen monsters. She gestures over them as the harp sounds swooping arpeg-gios and consigns them to an endless sleep. The orchestra plays softly a flowing lullably. The mysterious eerie forest of Ivan's adventure becomes serene as she sets all at peace with graceful, birdlike movement. Her mission over, the Firebird moves across the stage in a flowing dance, now turning, now stepping softly. Her feet tremble to release her body back into the air. Compelled to leave the earth, she moves away, her body thrown back. The last we see of her is her golden hand fluttering against the dark curtain at the side of the stage. The scene blacks out.

SCENE THREE—THE COURT OF PRINCE IVAN: The music begins a quiet, subdued statement of an ancient Russian folk song. The melody that seems simple at first is changed gradually into a majestic song of thanksgiving. The music mounts in dignity and volume as light slowly comes up to show us a blue-green drop curtain. On this curtain are repre-sented all those figures in fairyland who never will have any trouble in living happily ever after. Now that the music has asserted itself fully in praise and gratitude, we see two guards enter. They stand at attention in front of the curtain. The stage is fully lighted. Courtiers enter and bow to each other with each mighty chord from the orchestra, then join hands with the princesses who trip in to meet them. Now the drop curtain rises. Before another cur-tain of magical deep red, Ivan and his princess stand together. Pages enter with royal standards. A crimson carpet is pulled down the center of the stage, and onto it step Prince Ivan and his bride, in regal costume. All pay homage to the royal couple, and a page comes running out to present to the prince and princess a great wedding cake, aglow with hundreds of candles. The curtain falls as he kneels before them with his gift.

NOTES: *Firebird* was Igor Stravinsky's first ballet score, the first of many compositions with which he has enriched the musical repertory of our theatres. It was also Stravinsky's first score for Serge Diaghilev, whose Ballets Russes had brought Russian dance, painting, and music to Western Europe and revitalized all of those arts. Stravinsky's music, like the dancing of

Pavlova, Karsavina, and Nijinsky, the painting of Benois, Bakst, and Roerich, and the masterful choreography of Michel Fokine, contributed to that universal excellence of theatrical production so typical of Diaghilev's ballets.

Stravinsky was asked by Diaghilev to collaborate with Fokine on *Firebird* in St. Petersburg in 1909. The task of writing music for the new ballet had previously been assigned to someone else, to Liadov, Diaghilev's old music teacher. Liadov, however, procrastinated in finishing the work, and upon hearing a performance of Stravinsky's *Fantastic Scherzo* at a concert, Diaghilev decided to reassign the commission. He first invited Stravinsky to orchestrate several numbers for *Les Sylphides*, which Fokine was then mounting for the Ballets Russes, and then, with Liadov's consent, arranged for the young composer to write the score for *Firebird*.

Fokine worked out the choreography for *Firebird* as the music was completed, section by section. Stravinsky's score was finished on May 18, 1910, and the ballet's first performance took place less than two months later.

Stravinsky has described the ballet's production in his autobiography:

"Fokine elaborated the scenario, having worked at his choreography with burning devotion, the more so because he had fallen in love with the Russian fairy-story. The casting was not what I had intended. Pavlova, with her slim angular figure, had seemed to me infinitely better suited to the role of the fairy bird than Karsavina, with her gentle feminine charm, for whom I had intended the part of the captive princess. Though circumstances had decided otherwise than I had planned, I had no cause for complaint, since Karsavina's rendering of the bird's part was perfect, and that beautiful and gracious artiste had a brilliant success in it.

"The performance was warmly applauded by the Paris public. I am, of course, far from attributing this success solely to the score; it was equally due to the spectacle on the stage in the painter Golovine's magnificent setting, the brilliant interpretation by Diaghilev's artistes, and the talent of the choreographer. I must admit, however, that the choreography of this ballet always seemed to me to be complicated and over-burdened with plastic detail, so that the artistes felt, and still feel even now, great difficulty in coordinating their steps and gestures with the music, and this often led to an unpleasant discordance between the movements of the dance and the imperative demands which the measure of the music imposed.

"Although the evolution of the classical dance and its problems now seem much more real to me and touch me more closely than the distant aesthetics of Fokine, I still consider that I have a right to form and express the opinion that in the sphere of choreography I prefer, for example, the vigour of *Prince Igor*, with its clear-cut and positive lines, to the somewhat detached designs of *Firebird*."

Fokine's original *Firebird* has not been revived for some years. Its action differed in some details from my own version, which is based on Stravinsky's revised score. In Fokine's work, the entry of the Firebird precedes that of

Prince Ivan. Later the two dance together and Ivan releases the bird he has captured. The maidens, in the following sequence, play together underneath an apple tree. They shake the tree; the apples fall to the ground; the girls pick them up and toss them about. Toward the end of the ballet, when the Firebird has rescued Prince Ivan from the demons of Kastchei, the prince destroys the latter's evil soul by breaking a huge egg which contains the monster's evil power. The choreography in the New York City Ballet production is, of course, entirely different.

In addition to Fokine's first version of *Firebird*, Stravinsky's music has been choreographed by no less than thirteen choreographers.

Stravinsky revised his *Firebird* score in 1945 for the express use of the ballet orchestra—the smaller orchestra in the pit, as opposed to the large symphony concert orchestra. In redesigning the action, I sought to leave out those elements in Fokine's scenario (the egg containing Kastchei's soul, for example) that seemed to require a nonballetic explanation.

The Russian fairy tales upon which *Firebird* is based are actually Oriental in character, and it was this Oriental spirit that I sought to preserve in my rendering of the story.

Adolph Bolm revived *Firebird* in a new version for Ballet Theatre on October 24, 1945, at the Metropolitan Opera House, New York. Alicia Markova, Anton Dolin, Diana Adams, and John Taras were the principals. It was for this version that Marc Chagall designed the scenery and costumes that are used in the New York City Ballet production.

LES FORAINS
THE TRAVELING PLAYERS

Ballet in one act. Choreography by Roland Petit. Music by Henri Sauguet. Book by Boris Kochno. Scenery and costumes by Christian Bérard. First presented by Ballets des Champs-Elysées, Paris, March, 1945, with Roland Petit, Janine Charrat, and Ethery Pagava in principal roles. First presented in the United States by Les Ballets de Paris at the National Theatre, New York, October 8, 1950, with Polajenko, Belinda Wright, Danielle Darmance, Simone Mostovoy, Jack Claus, Gordon Hamilton, Elise Vallee, and Nina Bibikova.

The overture to *Les Forains* blares out with trumpets, drum rolls, and crashing cymbals—appropriate music for a parade, a vaudeville show, or a circus. The ballet that follows is something like all of these things. Although never familiar in America, bands of strolling players have entertained people in Europe for centuries, performing on street corners, on highways, and in remote villages, attracting such crowds as they could and living as their casual audiences rewarded them. *Les Forains* shows us what happens to one particular group of such players one night in a city street.

The stage is dark as the ballet begins. There is no decoration, only a plain backdrop. From the left, a young girl enters. She wears a simple costume, but carries a black-and-silver fan and dances across the stage oblivious of anyone who might be watching her. A troupe of poorly dressed young people trudge wearily onto the scene behind her, pulling along with them a battered wheelbarrow packed high with what seems to be a rolled-up tent. One man follows a little behind, supporting with his left arm a girl who sits on his shoulder. He appears to be the leader of the group. He lets the girl down, consults with the others, claps his hands, and the relaxed scene is transformed instantly into breathless activity.

The wheelbarrow is moved toward the back of the stage; several of the men begin to unpack it hurriedly while the other members of the troupe energetically practice their routines. They throw off their overcoats, and we see that they are wearing costumes. We see a clown and several acrobats; the rest are dancers. The boys support the girls as they warm up for performance; one of the acrobats cartwheels around the stage; while in the back a primitive stage is constructed of crude lumber and cloth. There is a white curtain across the stage proper; colored curtains conceal the wings. Several passers-by pause to watch. The company runs in back of the miniature stage, the lights are lowered, and our attention is fixed on the white curtain.

An intense green light is thrown against the curtain from behind, and we see the silhouettes of a man and a woman engaged in amorous dalliance. The light changes; a clown and a girl come out, bringing with them a chair; and there is acrobatic display. The girl does a running jump onto the chair, where the clown catches her and lifts her down. Next there appears a girl wearing a long white dress of gauze, with long, full sleeves. She dances slowly, to accentuate her movements with the airy movement of her costume. Then the clown enters again, this time to do his specialty, which consists of brisk acrobatics executed as clumsily and as amusingly as possible. Now the curtains part for the Siamese twins, two girls bound together in what appears to be one *tutu*. They step down from the stage and dance side by side, each indicating hopelessly the impossibility of ever dancing otherwise.

The magician who now takes his turn we recognize as the leader of the troupe. He is dressed formally now, in long black evening coat. He waves his wand, and the stage is filled with confetti and paper streamers. Then he approaches the stage, pulls the curtains aside, and brings to life a beautiful girl who lies there motionless in a glass case. The girl is under his power and obeys the magician, with the stiff movements of a mechanical doll. The magician now does his final trick: two live doves fly from his hands and circle the stage until they are retrieved by one of the men.

The whole company joins in for a finale. Each of the performers dances a short variation alone, then all participate in a final chorus, surrounding the magician, whose rapid spins in the air set an increasing tempo for the others to follow. The dance ends with everyone in the group cheerfully exhausted.

The small crowd that has been watching applauds lightly, and the magician passes his hat. But each member of the audience turns away as he approaches, and soon the players are left alone.

The youthful ebullience with which they had produced their show collapses almost at once; they are angry because they have received nothing for their entertainment and sad at their public's indifference. They take down the stage, pack up the cart again, and move off in the same melancholy manner with which they entered. The troupe seems to have forgotten the two white doves, which flutter against their cage as the light darkens. One of the girls comes back to find them, picks up the cage, and runs with it back to her friends.

THE FOUR TEMPERAMENTS

Classic ballet in five parts. Music by Paul Hindemith. Choreography by George Balanchine. Scenery and costumes by Kurt Seligmann. Lighting by Jean Rosenthal. First presented by Ballet Society at the Central High School of Needle Trades, New York, November 20, 1946, with Gisella Caccialanza, Tanaquil LeClercq, Mary Ellen Moylan, Elise Reiman, Beatrice Tompkins, Todd Bolender, Lew Christensen, Fred Danieli, William Dollar, José Martinez, and Francisco Moncion as the principal dancers.

Subtitled "A Dance Ballet without Plot," *The Four Temperaments* is an expression in dance and music of the ancient notion that the human organism is made up of four different humors, or temperaments. Each one of us possesses these four humors, but in different degrees, and it is from the dominance of one of them that the four physical and psychological types—melancholic, sanguinic, phlegmatic, and choleric—were derived. Greek medicine associated the four humors and temperaments with the four elements—earth, water, fire, and air—which to them composed the human body as well as the world.

Although the score is based on this idea of the four temperaments, neither the music nor the ballet itself make specific or literal interpretation of the idea. An understanding of the Greek and medieval notion of the temperaments was merely the point of departure for both composer and choreographer.

The ballet is in five parts that correspond to the divisions of the score. The first section, Theme, features three couples, who dance three *pas de deux* to different statements of the basic musical theme. The music is languidly paced at first; the strings carry the melody carefully, but effortlessly. The bright assertiveness of the piano interrupts this passage, and the music becomes syncopated, with a quick, tinkling brilliance. In the third statement the string orchestra and the piano combine to state the theme fully.

Melancholic, the first variation on the theme, begins sadly and slowly; a solo violin sings despondently against the piano's accompaniment. A dancer performs a helpless, despondent, and lonely variation. The tempo changes, and he is joined by two girls as the full orchestra plays with muted strings. Four mysterious girls stalk in fiercely, majestically, to the tune of a strong and vibrant march in which the piano joins percussively.

The second variation, Sanguinic, is bright and effusive in its waltz tempo. A ballerina and her partner dance with open gestures that are alternately sharp and flowing. A secondary group of four dancers accompanies them.

To the third variation, Phlegmatic, a dancer dances at first alone. His mood changes suddenly with the music. He is joined by four girls and with them dances a sequence of adroitly measured lightness to a gay, humorous melody.

After a brief variation by a ballerina who represents the choleric temperament, the entire ensemble returns to the stage for a recapitulation of their dances; this merges with the music for a finale characterized by high, extended lifts.

NOTES: *The Four Temperaments* has been in the repertory of the New York City Ballet since October 25, 1948, when Maria Tallchief, Tanaquil LeClercq, Herbert Bliss, and Todd Bolender danced the principal roles. Since the New York City Ballet's ninth New York season, in November 1952, the original costumes for *The Four Temperaments* have been abandoned in favor of practice costumes.

À LA FRANÇAIX

Ballet in five parts. Music by Jean Françaix (*Serenade for Small Orchestra*). Choreography by George Balanchine. Lighting by Jean Rosenthal. First presented by the New York City Ballet at the City Center, New York, September 11, 1951, with Maria Tallchief, André Eglevsky, Janet Reed, Frank Hobi, and Roy Tobias.

À *la Françaix* is a joke about love. The curtain rises after the first loud and playful chords of the music have been heard. A girl and two boys bounce onto the stage and dance together boisterously. All three are dressed in bright, informal clothes in the French fashion. The two boys flirt with the girl, and she doesn't know which to choose. Both of them kiss her hands frantically; still she can't make up her mind.

There enters on the right a tennis dandy, all in white, racket under his arm. He sees the girl, drops the racket, and approaches her. Immediately she is dazzled by his aggressiveness and loses all interest in her playmates.

The dandy dismisses the boys with rudely directed steps and dances alone with the girl.

The man is a conceited baboon, but the enchanted girl—small alongside his huge strength—is blind to any possible faults. He throws her high into the air and catches her. Their playfulness develops into a romance and they embrace. As the girl's face falls against his shoulder, the music changes to a slow, romantic melody and a *sylphide,* in full romantic costume, dances in on the left. The girl does not see her. The dandy gapes at the mysterious creature from another world and ignores the girl.

The sylph floats toward the couple, her arms undulating. Her face is a white mask, her eyes are cast down modestly. She flicks her hand in the girl's face. The dandy is hypnotized. He looks at the girl with so exaggerated an expression of distaste that she slinks away in terror.

The dandy follows the sylph as she circles the stage. She consents to dance with him. There is a short, flowing *pas de deux:* slow, billowing lifts, slow turns. Still the sylph does not change her expression. She circles her lover and beckons to him with undulating arm, then whispers in his ear softly. He watches, transfixed, as she drifts away from him into the night.

Alone now, the dandy dances a variation expressive of his joy in finding such a creature: clearly, there is nothing he cannot do. The music is bright and quick, as if the hero were whistling to himself. He leaves the stage, well satisfied with his new romantic adventure.

The girl returns with her two playmates. When they have renewed their friendship with jazzy dancing, the fickle dandy sneaks back to shoo the boys away again and have the girl to himself. The girl forgets his previous desertion and takes up with him happily. He tosses her about like a tennis ball and seems to be charmed afresh with playfulness. He kisses her and sets her on his shoulder.

The music changes again and the sylph comes back. The dandy stands motionless; his eyes light up. The poor girl on his shoulder, completely ignored, slips down and falls to the ground as he stares at his romantic love. Then, as he watches her, the sylph drops her costume and stands before him an ordinary girl in a red bathing suit! The dandy is shocked, but delighted, of course, and goes off with her.

The other girl's two companions return to comfort her, but now she has trouble being lighthearted. She ends up sitting on the ground; everything is lost. The music is about to run out. The dandy rushes back in and bows to her, asking for another dance!

GAÎTÉ PARISIENNE

Ballet in one act. Music by Jacques Offenbach. Choreography by Leonide Massine. Book by Comte Etienne de Beaumont. Scenery and costumes by Comte Etienne de Beaumont. First presented by the Ballet Russe de Monte Carlo at the Théâtre de Monte Carlo, April 5, 1938, with Nina Tarakanova as the *Glove Seller*, Eugenia Delarova as the *Flower Girl*, Jeannette Lauret as *La Lionne*, Leonide Massine as the *Peruvian*, Frederic Franklin as the *Baron*, and Igor Youskevitch as the *Officer*. First presented in the United States by the Ballet Russe de Monte Carlo at the Metropolitan Opera House, New York, October 12, 1938, with Alexandra Danilova as the *Glove Seller*; the other principals were the same as those who danced the *première* in Monte Carlo.

The trumpets and snare drum, which begin the overture to this ballet with loud and persistent good humor, proclaim a tale of the night life of old Paris, a story of romance, convivial dancing, and perpetual high spirits. The jubilant rhythm and sparkling melody of the music remind us of a time when love was brief and casual, but intense, of a time when the day began at nine o'clock in the evening.

The curtain rises on the most popular room of a fashionable restaurant in nineteenth-century Paris. High green draperies are looped back against brass pillars; brass chandeliers flood the room with light. Marble-topped tables and gold chairs stand at the back. Four waiters and our cleaning girls are preparing the *salon* for the evening's entertainment. The boys flick the tables and chairs with their towels and dance comically to amuse the girls. They run forward and sit at the front of the stage at the end of their act.

A girl with flowers in her hair enters gaily. She shakes hands with the waiters, who gather around her adoringly. This is the flower girl. She presents each boy with a bouquet. They reward her with a drink, and the flower girl joins them in a dance in which she toasts her admirers. One of the boys lifts her up to his shoulders and another kneels below her.

Three ladies of easy virtue—the *cocodettes*—enter with their escorts. The girls are dressed cheerfully in loud, candy-striped dresses; their companions wear black jackets and berets. The flower girl sets up her tray of flowers and leaves with the waiters. The *cocodettes* dance a lively mazurka with their partners. The waiters return to watch, but soon the company is distracted by the entry of the ballet's heroine, the beautiful glove seller. The men desert their partners and cluster around her. She carries a basket of gloves on her arm and tries to attend to her business, but the men insist that she dance with them. She is lifted high, then circles the stage as all stop to admire her. The glove seller is not as pert and flirtatious as the flower girl, yet her beauty is more striking.

Everyone is watching her when the gay Peruvian, just arrived in Paris, hustles in to a whistling tune. He has been so eager to get to the café and enjoy the proverbial night life that he has brought his bags with him. He scuttles about the stage in uncontrollable excitement at the possibilities of the evening, amusing the girls, who know that—though his pockets may be filled with gold—he is incapable of stopping long enough to spend it on any one of them: he will always pursue pleasure, but never enjoy it. Finally he drops his bags and goes over to the flower girl, who places a *boutonniere* in his white lapel. He wiggles with delight as the girls watch him. Only the glove seller does not notice him. The Peruvian is fascinated. He sneaks up on her and asks for a pair of gloves. The girl obliges and tries to fit him. The Peruvian dances even as he stands still.

The baron enters. A waiter takes his cape, and the flower girl, attracted by his handsome uniform, immediately goes over to him. The baron, however, has seen the glove seller; gently ignoring the other girl, he turns to her, introduces himself modestly, and asks her to dance. The glove seller responds graciously, and the guests retire as the two come forward and dance to a romantically rhythmic waltz. The couple move together not as if they had just met, but as if they were predestined to know one another; their dance is touching, in its quiet, flowing warmth.

In the background the jovial Peruvian entertains the *cocodettes*. With a flourish, he ceremoniously orders a bottle of champagne. He sips a glass, spits, and stamps his feet. The girls encourage him as he orders another bottle. He approves the new wine and offers it to the ladies. His flirtations are interrupted by the arrival of five soldiers and an officer, who strut into the café as if they expected all the girls to notice only them. The girls oblige them. The couples perform a martial dance at the conclusion of which the girls hang about the soldiers' necks in mock farewell as the soldiers salute them.

All are startled by the sudden entrance of La Lionne, the fashionable beauty of the day. She sweeps into the café in her red velvet dress and greets the group condescendingly; the girls are furious, the men anxious to please her. La Lionne's escort, the duke, is unable to make up his mind whether to be pleased or annoyed. Her companion, the lady in green, seeks an alliance among the men.

La Lionne makes eyes at the officer, who abandons his attempt to take up with the beautiful glove seller. The Peruvian returns. He douses himself liberally with perfume and approaches the glove seller. As he whispers in her ear, she plagues the baron by pretending to agree to the Peruvian's suggestion. The baron is furious with her. The duke is furious with La Lionne. Both fight with their rivals, and the guests, who seem to have been waiting for such an outbreak, take sides and join in the contest. The scene becomes riotous. It is too much for the Peruvian, who crawls under a table, his limbs quaking. The restaurant is cleared. The waiters return and see the Peruvian, who doesn't dare look up. They pound on the table, and the terrified playboy rushes off, carrying the table on his head.

The baron and the glove seller re-enter and, to a sumptuous waltz, dance together. Their mutual love now assured, the two dance in reunited harmony. No sooner have they finished than the café comes to life again. The dazzling cancan dancers enter with their dancing master, and all the guests regather to watch them display their high, bold kicks. The girls form in a line as the dancing master commands, one by one they fall to the floor in a split. The crowd is delighted and everyone joins in the boisterous dance, some taking the cancan girls for their partners. The Peruvian enters with his top hat. The girls circle him and rotate his hat about their slippers.

The whole cast is assembled on the stage for the finishing bars of the heated dance. All the girls are lifted high; their legs fall back in the air. The girls fan themselves briskly. The lights dim; wraps are brought. The girls take their partners' arms; the music becomes soft and mellifluous; and the couples glide away as if they were carried by quietly moving gondolas into the night—the baron with the glove seller, the flower girl with the duke, La Lionne with the officer. The glove seller, her hair covered with a black mantilla, waves farewell and falls back in the baron's arms. The Peruvian is left alone. The couples wave at him. He sulks.

GALA PERFORMANCE

Ballet in two parts. Choreography by Antony Tudor. Music by Serge Prokofiev. Scenery and costumes by Hugh Stevenson. First presented by the London Ballet at Toynbee Hall, London, December 5, 1938, with Maude Lloyd, Gerd Larsen, Peggy van Praagh, Hugh Laing, and Antony Tudor in principal roles. First presented in the United States by Ballet Theatre at the Majestic Theatre, New York, February 11, 1941. Scenery and costumes by Nicolas de Molas. The cast was headed by Nora Kaye, Nana Gollner, Karen Conrad, Hugh Laing, and Antony Tudor.

Gala Performance is a comedy, telling a joke about ballet and three different ballerinas. Today many of us are inclined to stay away from ballet because we think it's made up of silly mannerisms. *Gala Performance* shows us these mannerisms (exaggerates them in the style of its period) and makes us laugh. Three famous ballerinas—the Queen of the Dance (from Moscow), the Goddess of the Dance (from Milan), and the Daughter of Terpsichore (from Paris)—are performing on the same stage for the first time in their lives. In their attempts to outdo each other, the dancers invoke every trick of their trade: they not only compete in respect to their dancing, but resort to any ruse that will secure the most applause.

The time of this *Gala Performance* is about sixty years ago; the place is the Theatre Royal in London. The music is by Prokofiev: the first movement of the *Piano Concerto No. 3, in C* (for Part One) and the *Classical* Symphony (for Part Two).

PART ONE: The curtain rises on a backstage scene. The closed curtain of the Theatre Royal is the backdrop of the setting, and in the harsh light before the performance begins we watch the nervous, hurried preparations for an unprecedented program of ballet. Two *coryphées* come out through the wings and begin to warm up. Others join them. These girls are members of the Theatre Royal's *corps de ballet*, the chosen few who will have the honor of appearing with the three guest ballerinas. They are quite naturally frightened and wait apprehensively for the arrival of the great dancers. They practice dance steps, turn their backs to us, and pose in the direction of the audience behind the curtain. Other girls and a number of boys—attendant cavaliers to the ballerinas—come on stage.

A woman in black, the theatre dresser, enters and adjusts the costumes of the *coryphées*. Next comes the ballet master, who watches the *corps de ballet* as they quickly run through the steps they will dance when the curtain rises. All the company turn expectantly as the Russian ballerina approaches the stage. She walks commandingly. Everyone on stage is beneath her notice, and she accepts the homage of the company with marked indifference. Then, as she scrutinizes the *corps de ballet*, she notices that one of the *coryphées* is wearing a necklace. She motions to the girl, reprimands her, and orders her to remove it. She herself is loaded down with jewelry, to which she now directs her attention while the distraught girl dashes off, weeping.

The ballet master and the conductor hover about the ballerina. The conductor promises to heed her warning about the proper tempo, while the ballet master can only assure her that his *corps de ballet* will be impeccably unobtrusive. The Queen of the Dance makes final adjustments in her richly embroidered red dress, fixes the high feather in her hair, and turns toward the curtain to rehearse her bows. Her way of acknowledging applause seems to be more important than the dance that will apparently receive it, and the girls and boys are secretly amused at the number of kisses she expects to throw to her audience. She is watching out of the corner of her eye, however; she snaps her fingers at the *corps* and orders them to practice their routine.

This severe scene is interrupted by the arrival of the Daughter of Terpsichore, the sparkling French ballerina, who bounds onto the stage in a fluffy, delicate costume appropriate to her exuberance. She can hardly keep still long enough to be introduced to her Russian peer, who naturally scorns her, and has no time to be regal and domineering. But she has time to be demanding and takes the conductor aside to instruct him about the tempo *she* will require. Where the Russian ballerina will make her every wish a command, the scatterbrained French dancer imagines that everything will be all right because everyone loves her and wants to please her. We are suddenly thankful that this is a ballet and not a play, for the silly French ballerina must surely never stop talking.

But if we think that the Russian and French ballerinas are vain and absurd, we have not yet seen their peer in mannerism. The Italian ballerina, the famed Goddess of the Dance, now enters. She is dressed in dignified black and walks across the stage with slow, studied elegance; her steps are carefully measured: every time she puts a foot forward, it seems to hesitate, as if it were considering the worthiness of the floor she deigns to walk upon.

Automatically she holds out her hand to be kissed. The cavaliers, prompted by the ballet master, pay tribute to her. Now she orders the dresser to hold up a mirror so that she can make final adjustments to her coiffure and elaborate headdress. The dresser's attention wanders for a moment, and the Goddess of the Dance rewards her with a smack.

The ballet master huddles with the *corps de ballet*, giving them their final instructions. The stage lights come up; some of the dancers make a final rush to the rosin box so that their shoes will not slip on stage; others wish themselves luck by repeating private superstitious gestures; and one wonders how the performance will ever begin. But suddenly everyone is miraculously in place. The drop curtain rises, and the scene blacks out.

PART TWO — GALA PERFORMANCE : When the lights come up again, we are the audience at the Theatre Royal. Instead of the backstage picture, we now see an ornate setting, draped in orange and red, that might represent any regal hall. Eight *coryphées* are on stage. They wait tremulously for their cue and begin to dance. They are nervous, but not too nervous to try to ingratiate themselves with the audience: each tries to outleer the others with absurd chorine smiles.

Four cavaliers lead the Russian ballerina on stage. They bow and leave the stage. The ballerina comes forward slowly, almost to the footlights, and begins to dance when she has played upon the anticipation of the audience to establish what she doubtless imagines is a personal, lovable relation. In her dance she attempts to hit the audience between the eyes with the most elementary pirouettes, staring them down, *daring* them not to like her. And she wins our applause. When she leaps off into the wings, one of her cavaliers, invisible to the audience, catches her, and she poses in endless midflight. She accepts applause with no modesty whatsoever and finds it difficult to leave the stage for an instant while it continues.

Now the Italian ballerina comes on. She comes forward to the footlights, tantalizing us with possibilities, rises on point as if it were the supreme sacrifice, and nods curtly at the conductor. The dance she executes is an adagio, in which she eschews the assistance of her partner. No one can serve her great art but herself; the audience should be grateful to be watching her. She balances as long as possible in every pose and is coldly indifferent to gasps of amazement from the audience: to her, nothing is impossible. When her dance ends, she allows a cavalier to lift her off into the wings. As she returns for her curtain calls, she walks with the measured steps of her backstage entrance. After obligingly taking applause with the company and her cavaliers, she finally shoos them off so she can acknowledge her due alone.

The French ballerina now takes the stage and covers it with rapid leaps. She responds to applause by inflicting upon the audience an ingratiating and somewhat irritating charm.

The solos are over, and the three ballerinas appear together in the coda. They come out on stage and stand together and for a moment they are equals, but directly they begin to dance, competition is rampant. The French and Russian ballerinas try every means to attract the attention of the audience and thereby lose the contest, for the Italian "goddess" makes the audience love her by treating them as if they were idiots. She is surely in command of the whole situation and only at the final curtain does she give any sign of respecting any gift the audience might bestow on her. When the three ballerinas receive flowers, she manages to grab more bouquets than the other two. Not to be outdone, the French ballerina steps in front of the curtain to pick up more bouquets which the audience has thrown to her. But when the curtain rises again, the Italian still has the most flowers. The other two ballerinas look at her and then at us and smile and smile and smile.

GISELLE

Fantastic ballet in two acts. Music by Adolphe Adam. Choreography by Jules Perrot and Jean Coralli. Book by Vernoy de Saint-Georges, Théophile Gautier, and Jean Coralli. Scenery by Pierre Ciceri. Costumes by Paul Lormier. First presented at the Théâtre de l'Académie Royale de Musique, Paris, June 28, 1841, with Carlotta Grisi as *Giselle*, Lucien Petipa as *Albrecht*, Adèle Dumilâtre as *Myrtha, Queen of the Wilis*, and Jean Coralli as *Hilarion*. First presented in England at Her Majesty's Theatre, London, March 12, 1842, with Carlotta Grisi and Jules Perrot in the principal roles. First presented in Russia at the Bolshoi Theatre, St. Petersburg, December 30, 1842, with Elena Andreyanova as *Giselle*. First presented in Italy at the Teatro alla Scala, Milan, January 17, 1843, with choreography by A. Cortesi and music by N. Bajetti. First presented in the United States at the Howard Atheneum, Boston, January 1, 1846, with Mary Ann Lee and George Washington Smith in the leading roles.

Giselle is such an important and popular ballet that people who know something about dancing are always talking about it. They speak of Pavlova's Giselle, Karsavina's Giselle, Spessivtzeva's Giselle, Markova's Giselle, and those who are unfamiliar with ballet think it strange: it's as if the habitual theatregoer spent all of his time talking about *Hamlet*, without paying much attention to modern plays.

But there is good reason for the balletgoer to be preoccupied with *Giselle*. Like *Hamlet*, *Giselle* is a classic: it is not only important historically, it also happens to be good. It is just as popular today as when it was first performed, more than 110 years ago. People go to see *Giselle* and to see new ballerinas dance it for the same reason we go to see new interpretations of *Hamlet*: the work is such a good one that we always discover something in it we hadn't seen before, some variation in performance that brings out an aspect that seemed previously concealed; we learn something new.

There are many ballets important to history: the ballet in which the ballerina first discarded her heeled slipper, the ballet in which she first stood on the tips of her toes, and the ballet in which she jumped dangerously but effortlessly from a height of twenty feet to be caught in her lover's arms. But these ballets, with all their innovations, haven't come down to us; they are important only in a narrow academic sense. *Giselle* has come down to us, has been performed by one ballet company or another ever since its first performance, because it combines innovation with drama and dancing that make us forget all about history.

Giselle's innovation is its summing up of what we know as the Romantic ballet. To be romantic about something is to see what you are and to wish for something entirely different. This requires magic. The mysterious and supernatural powers that romantic poetry invoked to secure its ideal soon became natural to the theatre, where dancers attired in billowy white seemed part of the world and yet also above it. Marie Taglioni in the ballet *La Sylphide* (see page 379), popularized this fashion so completely that the sylph became ballet's symbol for romantic love—the girl who is so beautiful, so light, so pure that she is unattainable: touch her, and she vanishes.

Poets and novelists of the time were all interested in stories of the romantically supernatural, stories that told of lovely young girls whose love was never fulfilled because of intervening powers. One of these stories told of girls known as Wilis, who were engaged to be married yet died before their wedding days. In the evening they rose from their graves and danced alone in the moonlight. Their dancing was impassioned with their anger at death; but, dressed in their flowing bridal gowns and endowed with unearthly gifts of movement, their ghostly forms seemed never to touch the ground.

The Wilis were so beautiful that it was simple for them to attract young men into their midst. But they were as dangerous as they were irresistible. Their hearts had been broken with deceptive, ethereal charm; they danced with the young men who came only to trap them: their suitors were compelled to dance until they died.

This story of the Wilis seemed to be ideal for ballet: it made the story of *La Sylphide* look like merely the first step in the attainment of the romantic ideal. For the heroine of that ballet was purely a creature of the imagination, a figure in the hero's dream. We had admired her beauty and pitied her, but she was too illusory a character to make us feel deeply. What would accomplish this, what would make us care about such a character, would be to give her a basis in real life, to make her real and unreal at the same time—like the Wilis.

The poet, novelist, and critic Théophile Gautier read the story of the Wilis as it was related by Heinrich Heine, and thought it would make a good ballet and would be particularly fine for Carlotta Grisi. Gautier had seen Grisi's debut in Paris and had fallen in love with her. Under the tutelage of her husband, Jules Perrot, the great dancer and choreographer, she had become the potential rival of Marie Taglioni and Fanny Elssler.

However, the story of the ballet required considerable work before it was resolved. There was the problem of how the heroine would become a Wili, under what circumstances would she die? Gautier presented this difficulty to the popular librettist Vernoy de Saint-Georges. Within three days they had contrived a suitable story and the libretto had been accepted at the Paris Opéra. Within a week the score had been written and the ballet was in rehearsal. At its first performance, a few days later, *Giselle ou les Wilis* was proclaimed the triumphant successor to *La Sylphide* and the greatest ballet of its time. For the Giselle he created for her, Grisi owed Gautier her greatest triumph and Gautier's attachment later obliged the ballerina to leave Perrot.

ACT ONE—A VILLAGE ON THE RHINE: The first curtain is preceded by a brief overture. The contrast between the strong, virulent opening measures and the light romantic melody that follows gives us an indication of the pitiless fate that will govern this love story. When the curtain rises, we see a part of a wooden village on the Rhine. It is vintage time, and the people of the village are preparing to celebrate. Peasant couples cross the stage, talking to each other affectionately; a few girls enter alone, wave in greeting to their friends, link arms, and follow them off to the left, near the entrance to a cottage. This is the cottage of Giselle, the lovely village maiden who lives with her mother, Berthe. On the right we discern the entrance to another cottage.

The stage is empty for an instant. Trumpets sound a warning. Hilarion, a gamekeeper, enters. He is dressed somewhat rudely and his gestures are not refined, but he is a man of genuine feeling. Almost directly he walks over to the door of Giselle's cottage. He is in love. Hilarion is about to knock on the door when he hears someone approaching. He looks around hurriedly and hides behind Giselle's cottage to watch.

Two men enter. They are Albrecht, Duke of Silesia, a handsome young man who wears a royal cape over his peasant clothes, and his squire, Wilfrid. Albrecht, too, goes to Giselle's door. Hilarion, who watches the scene jealously, is interested in the cape and sword that Albrecht wears, for Hilarion, like Giselle, knows this young man only as Loys, a peasant. Albrecht stands before Giselle's cottage and holds his hands over his heart. He, too, is in love and has put on peasant disguise in order that his love may be returned. Wilfrid, his attendant, is not in favor of his master's love for Giselle and begs him to come away. Albrecht refuses. He gives his cape and sword to Wilfrid and dismisses him. Wilfrid conceals the cape and sword in the cottage on the right and reluctantly withdraws.

Albrecht, at the door of Giselle's cottage, listens, then knocks. The music anticipates. He runs and hides. Giselle emerges from the house. She is expecting Albrecht and runs out happily. She dances joyfully and beautifully, as if she wanted to be watched. But no one is there! She looks about, acts as if she were indifferent, and begins to dance again. Now she hears something. She stops and poses as she listens carefully. Albrecht is blowing kisses to her! But still he will not show himself. Giselle is annoyed at this teasing, stamps her foot impatiently, and prepares to go back into the house. At this point Albrecht steps out before her. Giselle frowns and pretends that she is not glad to see him. He nudges her shoulder, and she bows low before him, still unsmiling. She runs to the cottage door, lest her pretense break down. Albrecht stands before the door to prevent her escape, then reaches out and gently takes her wrist. Now she smiles, looking up at him with amused reproach.

The two lovers dance across the stage together and sit on a crude wooden bench at the right. Albrecht tries to sit close to Giselle, but she edges away every time he moves closer. Again she tries to go back into the house, and again Albrecht prevents her.

Suddenly Albrecht is completely serious. He expresses to Giselle his eternal love and vows that he will always be faithful to her. Giselle acts as if she did not take him at his word and, to prove this, she picks a flower and begins to pluck its petals in a game of he-loves-me-loves-me-not. Albrecht vigorously nods his head when the petals say he-loves-me, but the last petal she chooses to pick turns out to be loves-me-not. Giselle throws the flower to the ground and begins to cry. To comfort her, Albrecht picks up the flower again and declares that the last petal is really he-loves-me. Giselle is fully consoled and, linking her arm through Albrecht's, dances again with him.

The lovers are so absorbed in each other that they do not notice Hilarion, who has emerged from his hiding place. The gamekeeper boldly interrupts their rendezvous and separates them. Before they know what has happened, Hilarion is attacking Albrecht and warning him not to make love to Giselle. Giselle thinks that Hilarion is simply jealous and upbraids him for eavesdropping. Hilarion kneels before her and assures her that he alone truly loves her. Her anger mounting, Giselle dismisses Hilarion with rude laughter. The gamekeeper regards Albrecht with suspicion and hatred and, as he leaves the scene, shakes his fists at him.

Giselle is still shaken by this scene. Albrecht holds her in his arms and reassures her softly. They walk together. Village girls now enter, carrying huge baskets of grapes. They are all friends of Giselle's, and when they begin to dance, she joins them, dancing in their midst to a bright, melodious waltz. Albrecht watches Giselle from the bench near by. She soon runs over and asks him to join in. Boys join the girls as Albrecht and Giselle dance around the stage. The two lovers blow kisses to each other as the music accompanies their dance with a soft, hesitant theme that tinkles gently. The waltz ensemble ends as Albrecht holds Giselle on his knee.

Berthe, Giselle's mother, opens the cottage door and steps out. She does not wish to interfere with the festivities, but she is genuinely worried. Giselle playfully hides behind her friends, but her mother discovers her. She upbraids her daughter for dancing so much and reminds her that her heart will fail.

Berthe attempts to impress Giselle with the truth of what she says by warning her that if she dies, she will become one of the Wilis, one of those creatures doomed to dance forever, even in death.

Giselle's friends take Berthe's tale more seriously than her daughter does. She wishes to dance again and goes to Albrecht. Berthe, however, takes her by the hand, and together they go into the cottage. The door closes. The disappointed Albrecht wanders off, and the villagers disperse.

Now that the stage is empty, Hilarion, bent on vengeance approaches Giselle's cottage. He does not know how he can convince the girl that she is being deceived. A hunting horn sounds in the distance. Hilarion hears a hunting party come his way and seeks concealment in Albrecht's cottage.

Wilfrid, Albrecht's squire, is the first of the hunting party to enter. He looks about apprehensively, lest his master still be present. The prince of Courland and his daughter, Bathilde, follow with huntsmen and members of the court. The prince gestures to Wilfrid that they are in need of refreshment and rest and orders him to knock at Giselle's door.

Berthe responds to Wilfrid's knock. Seeing the prince and his daughter, she bows low before them and invites them to partake of whatever humble refreshment she can offer. She signals inside the house, and two girls bring out a table and stools, metal goblets, and a pitcher of wine.

Giselle steps out of the house and is astonished to see the royal party. She bows to Wilfrid, thinking him a prince. Wilfrid indicates the true prince; Giselle curtsies to him and his daughter and tries to assist in their entertainment. Bathilde is kind to the girl and indicates to her father, "How beautiful she is!" Wilfrid pours the wine, and the prince and Bathilde drink. While they sit at the table, Giselle kneels surreptitiously at Bathilde's feet and touches the hem of her long dress. Giselle has not seen such expensive fabric before and remarks its beauty when Bathilde looks down and sees her. Bathilde takes Giselle aside and asks her how she spends her day. "Weaving and spinning," Giselle replies. "But are these the things you like to do best?" Bathilde wonders. "No," Giselle indicates, "I like best to dance," and so saying dances several steps before Bathilde.

Giselle's mother disapproves and is about to reprimand her daughter, but the dance is quickly over. Bathilde wishes to express her admiration for the peasant girl by giving her a present. With the prince's consent, she takes off her necklace and, calling Giselle to her, places it about the girl's neck. Giselle, in rapture, kisses her hand and proudly shows the necklace to her mother.

The hunting party now accepts Giselle's invitation to rest within the cottage. Wilfrid remains without, ready to rouse the prince with the hunting horn should there be good cause for the hunt to continue. Wilfrid dismisses the huntsmen and follows after them.

Hilarion comes forth from Albrecht's cottage. He carries Albrecht's sword in his hand. He looks about quickly, sees no one, and gestures in triumph: now perhaps Giselle will believe him! He exits as the peasant girls and boys return to resume their dancing. They knock at Giselle's door and finally persuade her mother to allow her to join them. The girls and boys recline in a semicircle about Giselle, who dances a brilliant solo. Albrecht appears as the girls dance. He and Giselle join her friends, and as the dance ensemble ends, the lovers embrace.

The music crashes ominously. Hilarion runs out, tears the lovers apart, and tells Giselle what he has learned: "You might love this man, but he is an impostor." He rushes out, retrieves Albrecht's sword, and places it in Giselle's hand. Albrecht is motionless with horror. He knows that the game-keeper is right, but he knows that this is not the way for Giselle to learn the truth. She will never believe him again, never believe his love. Giselle seems to think Hilarion is lying; it does not occur to her that her lover has wronged her.

Wilfrid enters and attempts to protect his master. Hilarion persists in reminding Giselle that the sword is Albrecht's. She goes to Albrecht. With great faith she asks him if the gamekeeper is speaking the truth. Albrecht bows his head; he cannot speak. Then, looking up at Hilarion, who imagines that a duke cannot love as truly as a gamekeeper, seizes the sword and attacks him. Only Wilfrid prevents him from murdering the gamekeeper. The sword falls to the ground. Hilarion is glorying in his revenge so much that he does not notice what he has done to Giselle. He takes down the hunting horn and blows on it to summon the prince. Sobbing in her mother's arms, Giselle cannot yet believe what she has learned.

The prince and his daughter come out of the house with their party. The prince is surprised to see Albrecht in peasant's clothes; Bathilde goes to Albrecht and asks him what is wrong, why he is dressed like this? Giselle watches him closely. When he kneels before Bathilde and kisses her hand, Giselle tears herself from her mother's arms and accosts Bathilde. Albrecht tries to caution Bathilde, but before he can prevent it, she has pointed to the ring on her finger: she is engaged to Albrecht, Duke of Silesia.

Giselle, her heart broken, is so defenseless that her reason begins to disintegrate. Fiercely she tears the necklace Bathilde gave her from her neck and dashes it to the ground. She falls before her mother. Berthe comforts her as best she can and tries to quiet her and loosens her hair. Albrecht attempts to speak to her, to assure her of his love, but she will not listen. The girl is so stricken with grief, so helpless without the love she lived by, that all present, courtiers and peasants alike, pity her.

Giselle staggers to her feet. She moves about the stage slowly and pathetically, reliving her moments of happiness with Albrecht. With her reason gone, this is all she can think of. She picks up an imaginary flower and to herself plays another game of he-loves-me-loves-me-not. She circles the stage, and all the people stand back. Suddenly Giselle sees Albrecht's sword lying forgotten on the ground. She runs to it and, taking it up at the pointed end, holds it in front of her. Hypnotized by her madness, her friends do not move. Giselle bends low and drags the sword about with her, its handle rattling as she trails it around the stage at the feet of her friends. Then, before anyone can move, she raises the sword high and forces its point into her heart. Albrecht leaps across to her and seizes the sword.

The prince and Bathilde withdraw. Here they can only cause agony. Giselle, dying in her mother's arms, rises and goes to Albrecht. Her mind is now completely gone and she imagines that there has never been anything wrong, that he is her lover as before. She begins to dance with him, and again the soft, hesitant theme of romance that accompanied one of their happy dances together is repeated. Giselle awkwardly, falteringly, repeats the steps that she formerly danced with such grace. Then, in the midst of the dance, she is frightened. She runs to her mother, but falls to the ground before she can reach her embrace. Albrecht despairs as Berthe bends over her daughter. But Giselle asks for him. He comes to her and looks down into her eyes, which even now seek only his. He declares again his imperishable love. Giselle reaches up to touch his face in a gesture of forgiveness; then her hand falls. She is dead.

Albrecht rises and drags Hilarion to see what his jealousy has accomplished. As the gamekeeper weeps and kneels beside Giselle, Albrecht seizes the sword and again tries to kill him. Wilfrid again prevents him. Albrecht weeps beside Giselle. The dead girl lies before him, her arms crossed on her breast. The villagers turn their faces away to hide the grief they share.

ACT TWO — WITHIN A FOREST GLADE AT MIDNIGHT. In the second act we pass to a scene and a mood entirely different from that of Act One. Our first hint of this comes in the music. The strings sing softly against a rippling harp; all is quiet and ethereal. The curtain rises on a scene misty with the dewey night. The moon penetrates the thick trees occasionally; its light is reflected in a nearby lake, and in this dimness we discern Giselle's grave at the left. Her name is inscribed on a large cross that stands above the grassy mound. In the dark-blue sky, small shimmering lights appear.

Three huntsmen with a lantern enter to rest. They sit down near the lake. Hilarion joins them. Soon the men are disturbed by the eerie atmosphere of the place. They have heard tales that Wilis danced here and they fear the place is haunted. The lights in the sky are not constant, they appear to shimmer at will. Hilarion, aware that Giselle's grave is close by, becomes apprehensive. He approaches the grave. The men warn him to leave. Hilarion is reluctant, but joins his friends as they depart.

Across the back of the stage a veiled figure in a long white dress moves flowingly. She is Myrtha, queen of the Wilis. She enters, crosses the stage rapidly, and again appears at the back. At her second entry, she has removed her veil. She bows, poses in deep, still arabesque, and begins to dance.

Her movements are confident, controlled, beautiful, but they possess no warmth. The supernatural powers Myrtha possesses allow for nothing but perfection. She moves more rapidly now; the quickness of her dancing is brilliant and hard, like a diamond. She gathers two fern branches from the lakeside, throws them into the forest to dedicate the place to her awful purpose, and circles the stage in a brilliant display of virtuosity.

Now, with her wand, she calls forth the Wilis. Instantly obedient to her command, they appear on either side of the stage, their hands crossed over their breasts. Myrtha orders them to remove their white veils. They obey her and arrange themselves for a dance. Led by two attendants to the queen, the Wilis move with a perplexing, almost automatic, grace, as if they danced only at Myrtha's will. Myrtha dances among them, dances with relentless, abandoned force, as if she could not restrain herself, then orders the dancing to end. All the Wilis turn toward Giselle's grave, kneel, and bend low. A new creature is to be initiated.

Myrtha bends over the grave with a magical branch. The earth parts, and Giselle rises from the mound. She is dressed in white, veiled, her arms crossed over her breast. Instinctively, as if hypnotized, she responds to Myrtha's commands. She walks toward the queen and stands motionless as Myrtha removes her veil. Now Giselle opens her eyes. Following Myrtha's example, she begins to dance, imitating her movements exactly. Myrtha declares that she is now a member of the ghostly tribe and orders Giselle to dance alone. The girl suddenly seems to come to life and, turning around and around, rejoices in her liberation from the grave.

Surrounded by her sisters, Giselle dances as they, too, have danced at their first appearance from their graves—before the dreadful power of the queen dominated them completely. Giselle leaves the scene at the end of her dance, and Myrtha orders the Wilis to conceal themselves.

The stage is empty when Albrecht enters. He moves slowly, dejectedly. He has come to visit the grave of his beloved and is filled with memories of her tragic death. Wilfrid follows his master and attempts to dissuade him from reminding himself of Giselle. Albrecht dismisses him and kneels before Giselle's grave. As he thinks of her, Giselle appears. Albrecht cannot believe it; he looks again; she was not there, after all. He rises and looks about the scene. Now Giselle runs fleetingly in a swift diagonal before him. Albrecht catches her in his arms briefly, lifts her in mid-flight, and again she disappears. Albrecht's brief touch is like a glance; he thinks that he must be dreaming, yet prays that the dream is true.

As he kneels in prayer, Giselle re-enters and dances about him. He does not see her. Then Giselle walks up in back of him and lovingly touches his shoulder. Albrecht rises and watches her. Joyful that his prayer has been answered, he wishes to touch her. They begin to dance together, Giselle leading the way. Then suddenly she vanishes.

She returns, picks two white lilies, and, dancing in swift diagonals, throws the flowers back over her head. Albrecht, pursuing her closely, picks up the flowers and follows her into the forest as she exits.

Hilarion returns to the scene. No sooner has he done so than Wilis appear before him. He turns to escape them, but in every direction other winged creatures enter and surround him. Myrtha enters with her attendants to examine the captive. At her command, all the Wilis encircle Hilarion, then stand in a long diagonal line, reaching from the right front of the stage to the lakeside. Myrtha stands at the right, at the head of the line. Hilarion, now sure of her intent, begs her for mercy. The queen gestures grandly, "No." Hilarion rushes down the line, beseeching the Wilis to intervene for him. They all refuse. Myrtha declares that he must die. She points to the lake. Hilarion is turned around and around as he is thrust down the long line of Wilis. At the end, two Wilis seize him and cast him into the lake.

Myrtha, unrelenting and triumphant, crosses the stage in light, unremembering leaps and exits at the rear. Two by two, all the Wilis follow her, imitating her step precisely. When Myrtha leads them back on stage, Albrecht confronts the queen. He, too, asks that his life might be spared, and again the queen denies the request. Giselle pleads in his behalf, but her intervention serves only to increase Myrtha's anger. Giselle, determined to save Albrecht at all costs, gestures to him to take refuge beneath the cross at her grave. Myrtha quickly orders the Wilis to intercept Albrecht, but he succeeds in reaching the cross in spite of their efforts to ensnare him. Giselle stands before him in an attitude of protection, and the queen is helpless.

Determined that Albrecht shall die, and offended at this sudden curtailment of her power, the queen orders Giselle to descend from the cross and dance. The girl obeys her, dancing alone between the Wilis, who are arranged in lines down the sides of the stage.

At the conclusion of the dance, Albrecht leaves the protective cross, steps down, and the two lovers go down the lines of Wilis, pleading for their intercession. All obstinately refuse. Now Giselle and Albrecht begin a *pas de deux*. As Albrecht supports Giselle in the adagio, Wilis contrive to come between them and separate them. But the two are now so reunited, so reassured of their lasting love, that they escape these Wilis without even noticing them.

Myrtha commands Giselle to dance alone again. This is followed by a variation for Albrecht. Giselle rejoins him. He lifts her again and again, higher and higher, straight into the air, her phantomlike body seeming a part of the air. Giselle dances another solo. The queen of the Wilis knows that Giselle will never tire, that, like all Wilis, she has a passion for dancing. She knows also that Albrecht will wish to please Giselle and will dance with her. Albrecht will dance to his death.

Albrecht commences another variation. When he has finished, he pleads with the Wilis to make him dance no longer. They ignore his request and, in the midst of continuation of the dance, he falls exhausted to the ground. Giselle tries to help him up, but he cannot move. Giselle turns to the queen and dances to divert her. Finally Albrecht stirs as Giselle beckons to him. They resume their dance; Albrecht makes a new plea to Myrtha, and the dance is resumed as she again denies him. When Albrecht collapses and kneels on the ground, Giselle stands over him protectively. She humbly approaches Myrtha and when the queen obstinately rebuffs her, Giselle asks each of the Wilis to help her. They can do nothing; they are all in the queen's power.

Albrecht attempts to leave the scene, but the watchful Wilis prevent his escape and force him to dance again. He leaps again and again high into the air, then falls to the ground.

Dawn approaches. Four o'clock sounds in the distance. The Wilis must vanish, for with the coming of day, they are powerless. Giselle rejoices that Albrecht has been saved! The Wilis again bow at Giselle's grave, consigning her back to the earth. Giselle embraces Albrecht as she kneels beside him. She knows that this is farewell. The Wilis rush away into the coming dawn, followed by their queen. Albrecht succeeds in rising. Giselle, with mysterious longing, yearns to return to the earth. She goes to her grave. Albrecht follows her, but before he reaches the tomb, she has fallen back and been covered with earth. Albrecht despairs and falls to the ground where he first knelt beside the grave of his beloved.

NOTES: A week after the first performance of *Giselle*, the originator of the ballet, Théophile Gautier, wrote to Heinrich Heine, the German poet:

"My dear Heinrich Heine, when reviewing, a few weeks ago, your fine book, *De L'Allemagne*, I came across a charming passage—one has only to open the book at random—the place where you speak of elves in white dresses, whose hems are always damp, of nixes who display their little satin feet on the ceiling of the nuptial chamber; of snow-colored Wilis who waltz pitilessly, and of all those delicious apparitions you have encountered in the Harz mountains and on the banks of the Ilse, in a mist softened by German moonlight; and I involuntarily said to myself: 'Wouldn't this make a pretty ballet?'

"In a moment of enthusiasm, I even took a fine large sheet of white paper, and headed it in superb capitals: *Les Wilis*, a ballet. Then I laughed and threw the sheet aside without giving it any further thought, saying to myself that it was impossible to translate that misty and nocturnal poetry into terms of the theatre, that richly sinister phantasmagoria, all those effects of legend and ballet so little in keeping with our customs. In the evening, at the Opéra, my head still full of your idea, I met, at a turning of the wings, the witty man who knew how to introduce into a ballet, by adding to it much of his own wit, all the fairy caprice of *Le Diable Amoureux* of Cazotte, that great poet who invented Hoffmann in the middle of the eighteenth century. "I told him the tradition of the Wilis. Three days later, the ballet Giselle was accepted. At the end of the week, Adolphe Adam had improvised the music, the scenery was nearly ready, and the rehearsals were in full swing. You see, my dear Heinrich, we are not yet so incredulous and so prosaic as you think we appear. You said in a moment of ill-humor: 'How could a specter exist in Paris? Between midnight and one o'clock, which has ever been the hour assigned to ghosts, the most animated life still fills the streets. At this moment the Opéra resounds to a noisy finale. Joyous bands flow from the Variétés and the Gymnase; everyone laughs and jumps on the boulevards, and everyone runs to evening parties. How miserable a stray ghost would feel in that lively throng!' Well, I had only to take your pale and charming phantoms by their shadowy finger tips and present them, to ensure their receiving the most polite reception in the world. The director and public have not offered the least objection à la Voltaire. The Wilis have already received the right of citizenship in the scarcely fantastic rue Lapelletier. Some lines where you speak of them, placed at the head of the scenario, have served them as passports.

"Since the state of your health has prevented your being present at the first performance, I am going to attempt, if a French journalist is permitted to tell a fantastic story to a German poet, to explain to you how M. de Saint-Georges, while respecting the spirit of your legend, has made it acceptable and possible at the Opéra. To allow more freedom, the action takes place in a vague country, in Silesia, in Thuringia, even in one of the Bohemian sea-ports that Shakespeare loved; it suffices for it to be on the other side of the Rhine, in some mysterious corner of Germany. Do not ask more of the geography of the ballet, which cannot define the name of a town or country by means of gesture, which is its only tongue.

"Hillocks weighed down with russet vines, yellowish, warmed and sweetened by the autumn sun; those beautiful vines from which hang the amber-colored grapes which produce Rhine wine, form the background; at the summit of a grey and bare rock, so precipitous that the vine tendrils have been unable to climb it, stands, perched like an eagle's nest, one of those castles so common in Germany, with its battlemented walls, its pepper-box turrets, and its feudal weathercocks; it is the abode of Albrecht, the young Duke of Silesia. That thatched cottage to the left, cool, clean, coquettish, half buried among the leaves, is Giselle's cottage. The hut facing it is occupied by Loys. Who is Giselle? Giselle is Carlotta Grisi, a charming girl with blue eyes, a refined and artless smile, and an alert bearing; an Italian who tries to be taken for a German, just as Fanny, the German, tries to be taken for an Andalusian from Seville. Her position is the simplest in the world; she loves Loys and she loves dancing. As for Loys, played by Petipa [Lucien Petipa, younger brother of Marius Petipa, ballet master at the Imperial Russian Theatre, choreographer of The Sleeping Beauty, et al.], there are a hundred reasons for suspecting him. Just now, a handsome esquire, adorned with gold lace, speaks to him in a low voice, standing cap in hand and maintaining a submissive and respectful attitude. What! A servant of a great house, as the esquire appears to be, fails to lord it over the humble rustic to whom he speaks! Then, Loys *is not what he appears to be* (ballet style), but we shall see later.

"Giselle steps out of the cottage on the tip of her dainty foot. Her legs are awake already; her heart, too, sleeps no longer, for it is full morning. She has had a dream, an evil dream: a beautiful and noble lady in a gold dress, with a brilliant engagement ring on her finger, appeared to her while she slept and seemed about to be married to Loys, who himself was a great nobleman, a duke, a prince. Dreams are very strange sometimes! Loys does his best to reassure her, and Giselle, still somewhat uneasy, questions the marguerites. The little silver petals flee and scatter: 'He loves me, he loves me not!' 'Oh, dear! How unhappy I am, he loves me not!' Loys, who is well aware that a boy of twenty can make the daisies say whatever he chooses, repeats the test, which, this time, is favorable; and Giselle, charmed with the flowers' good augury, begins to leap about again, despite her mother, who scolds her and would rather see that agile foot turning the spinning wheel that stands in the window, and those pretty fingers questioning marguerites busied in gathering the already overripe grapes or carrying a vine-dresser's basket. But Giselle scarcely listens to the advice of her mother, whom she soothes with a little caress. The mother insists: 'Unhappy child! You will dance forever, you will become a Wili.' And the good woman, in an expressive pantomime, relates the terrible legend of the nocturnal dancers. Giselle pays no heed. What young girl of fifteen believes in a story with the moral that one should not dance? Loys and dancing, that is her conception of happiness. This, like every possible happiness, wounds unseen a jealous heart; the gamekeeper, Hilarion, is in love with Giselle, and his most ardent desire is to injure his rival, Loys. He has already been a witness of the scene where the esquire Wilfrid spoke respectfully to the peasant. He suspects some plot, staves in the window of the hut and climbs through it, hoping to find some incriminating evidence. But now trumpets resound; the Prince of Courland and his daughter, Bathilde, mounted on a white hackney, wearied from hunting, come to seek a little rest and coolness in Giselle's cottage. Loys prudently steals away. Giselle, with a timid and charming grace, hastens to set out on a table shining pewter goblets, milk, and some fruit, the best and most appetizing of everything in her homely larder. While the beautiful Bathilde lifts the goblet to her lips, Giselle approaches with catlike tread, and, in a rapture of artless admiration, ventures to touch the rich, soft material of which the lady's riding costume is composed. Bathilde, enchanted by Giselle's pleasant manners, places her gold chain round her neck and wishes to take the girl with her. Giselle thanks her effusively and replies that she wants nothing in the world but to dance and to be loved by Loys.

"The Prince of Courland and Bathilde withdraw into the hut to snatch a few moments' rest. The huntsmen disperse into the wood; a call on the prince's horn will warn them when it is time to return. The vine dressers return from the vineyards and arrange a festival of which Giselle is proclaimed the Queen and in which she takes the principal part. Joy is at its height when Hilarion appears carrying a ducal mantle, a sword, and a knightly order found in Loys's hut—all doubt is at an end. Loys is simply an impostor, a seducer who has been playing on Giselle's good faith; a duke cannot marry a humble peasant, not even in the choreographic world, in which one often sees kings marrying shepherdesses—such a marriage offers innumerable obstacles. Loys, or rather Duke Albrecht of Silesia, defends himself to the best of his ability, and declares that no great harm has been done, for Giselle will marry a duke instead of a peasant. She is pretty enough to become duchess and lady of the manor. 'But you are not free, you are betrothed to another,' asserts the gamekeeper; and seizing the horn left lying on the table, he blows it like a madman. The huntsmen run up. Bathilde and the Prince of Courland come out of the cottage and are amazed to see Duke Albrecht of Silesia in such a disguise. Giselle recognizes in Bathilde the beautiful lady of her dreams, she doubts her misfortune no longer; her heart swells, her head swims, her feet shake and jump; she repeats the measure she danced with her lover; but her strength is soon exhausted, she staggers, sways, seizes the fatal sword brought by Hilarion and would have fallen on its point if Albrecht had not turned it aside with the quickness born of despair. Alas, the precaution is in vain; the blow has struck home; her heart is pierced and Giselle dies, consoled at least by her lover's profound grief and Bathilde's tender pity.

"There, my dear Heine, that is the story invented by M. de Saint-Georges to bring about the pretty death we needed. I, who ignore theatrical effects and the demands of the stage, had thought of making the first act consist of a mimed version of Victor Hugo's delightful poem. One would have seen a beautiful ballroom belonging to some prince; the candles would have been lighted, flowers placed in vases, buffets loaded, but the guests would not yet have arrived; the Wilis would have shown themselves for a moment, attracted by the joy of dancing in a room glittering with crystal and gilding in the hope of adding to their number. The Queen of the Wilis would have touched the floor with her magic wand to fill the dancers' feet with an insatiable desire for contredanses, waltzes, galops, and mazurkas. The advent of the lords and ladies would have made them fly away like so many vague shadows. Giselle, having danced all the evening, excited by the magic floor and the desire to keep her lover from inviting other women to dance, would have been surprised by the cold dawn like the young Spaniard, and the pale Queen of the Wilis, invisible to all, would have laid her icy hand on her heart. But then we should not have had the lovely scene, so admirably played, which concludes the first act as it is; Giselle would have been less interesting, and the second act would have lost all its element of surprise.

"The second act is as nearly as possible an exact translation of the page I have taken the liberty of tearing from your book, and I hope that when you return from Cauterets, fully recovered, you will not find it too misinterpreted.

"The stage represents a forest on the banks of a pool; you see tall, pale trees, whose roots spring from the grass and the rushes; the water lily spreads its broad leaves on the surface of the placid water, which the moon silvers here and there with a trail of white spangles. Reeds with their brown velvet sheaths shiver and palpitate beneath the intermittent night breeze. The flowers open languorously and exhale a giddy perfume like those broad flowers of Java which madden whoever inhales their scent. I cannot say what burning and sensuous atmosphere flows about this humid and leafy obscurity. At the foot of a willow, asleep and concealed beneath the flowers, lies poor Giselle. From the marble cross which indicates her grave is suspended, still quite fresh, the garland of vine branches with which she had been crowned at the harvest festival.

"Some hunters come to find a suitable place of concealment; Hilarion frightens them by saying that it is a dangerous and sinister spot, haunted by the *Wilis*, cruel nocturnal dancers, no more forgiving than living women are to a tired waltzer. Midnight chimes in the distance; from the midst of the long grass and tufted reeds, will-o'-the-wisps dart forth in irregular and glittering flight and make the startled hunters flee.

"The reeds part and first we see a tiny twinkling star, next a chaplet of flowers, then two startled blue eyes set in an alabaster oval, and, last of all, the whole of that beautiful, slender, chaste, and graceful form known as Adèle Dumilâtre; she is the Queen of the *Wilis*. With her characteristic melancholy grace she frolics in the pale starlight, which glides over the water like a white mist, poises herself on flexible branches, leaps on the tips of the grass, like Virgil's Camilla, who walked on wheat without bending it, and, arming herself with a magic wand, she evokes the other *Wilis*, her subjects, who come forth with their moonlight veils from the tufted reeds, clusters of verdure, and calices of flowers to take part in the dance. She announces to them that they are to admit a new *Wili* that night. Indeed, Giselle's shade, stiff and pale in its transparent shroud, suddenly leaps from the ground at Myrtha's bidding (that is the Queen's name). The shroud falls and vanishes. Giselle, still benumbed from the icy damp of the dark abode she has left, makes a few tottering steps, looking fearfully at that tomb which bears her name. The *Wilis* take hold of her and lead her to the Queen, who herself crowns her with the magic garland of asphodel and verbena. At a touch of her wand, two little wings, as restless and quivering as those of Psyche, suddenly grow from the shoulders of the youthful shade who, for that matter, had no need of them. All at once, as though she wishes to make up for the time wasted in that narrow bed fashioned of six long planks and two short ones, to quote the poet of *Leonore,* she bounds and rebounds, in an intoxication of liberty and joy at no longer being weighed down by that thick coverlet of heavy earth, expressed in a sublime manner by Mme. Carlotta Grisi. The sound of footsteps is heard; the *Wilis* disperse and crouch behind the trees. The noise is made by some youthful peasants returning from a festival at a neighboring village. They provide excellent quarry. The *Wilis* come forth from their hiding place and try to entice them into the fatal circle; fortunately, the young men pay heed to the warnings of a wise graybeard who knows the legend of the *Wilis,* and finds it most unusual to encounter a bevy of young beings in low-necked muslin dresses with stars on their foreheads and mothlike wings on their shoulders. The *Wilis,* disappointed, pursue them eagerly; this pursuit leaves the stage unoccupied.

"Enter a young man, distracted, mad with sorrow, his eyes bathed in tears; it is Loys, or Albrecht, if you prefer it, who, escaping from his guardians' observation comes to visit the tomb of his well-beloved. Giselle cannot resist the sweet evocation of so true and profound a grief; she parts the branches and leans forward toward her kneeling lover, her charming features aglow with love. To attract his attention, she picks some flowers which she first carries to her lips and throws her kisses to him on roses. The apparition flutters coquettishly, followed by Albrecht. Like Galatea, she flies toward the reeds and willows. The transverse flight, the leaning branch, the sudden disappearance when Albrecht wishes to take her in his arms, are new and original effects which achieve complete illusion. But now the *Wilis* return. Giselle tries to hide Albrecht; she knows too well the doom that awaits him if he is encountered by the terrible nocturnal dancers. They have found another quarry. Hilarion is lost in the forest; a treacherous path brings him back to the place from which he had only just fled. The *Wilis* seize hold of him, pass him from hand to hand: when one waltzer is tired, her place is taken by another, and always the infernal dance draws nearer to the lake. Hilarion, breathless, spent, falls at the Queen's knees and begs for mercy. But there is no mercy; the pitiless phantom strikes him with a branch of rosemary and immediately his weary legs move convulsively. He rises and makes new efforts to escape; a dancing wall bars his passage, the *Wilis* make him giddy, push him on, and, as he leaves go of the cold hand of the last dancer, he stumbles and falls into the pool—Good night Hilarion! That will teach you not to meddle in other people's love affairs! May the fish in the lake eat your eyes!

"What is Hilarion but one partner for so many dancing women? Less than nothing. A *Wili,* with that wonderful woman's instinct for finding a waltzer, discovers Albrecht in his hiding place. What good fortune, and someone who is young, handsome and light-footed. 'Come, Giselle, prove your mettle, make him dance to death!' It is useless for Giselle to beg for mercy, the Queen refuses to listen; and threatens to give Albrecht to the less scrupulous *Wilis* in her band. Giselle draws her lover toward the tomb she has just left, signs to him to embrace the cross and not leave it whatever may befall. Myrtha resorts to an infernal feminine device. She forces Giselle, who, in her capacity of subject, must obey, to execute the most seductive and most graceful poses. At first, Giselle dances timidly and reluctantly; then she is carried away by her instinct as a woman and a *Wili*; she bounds lightly and dances with so seductive a grace, such overpowering fascination, that the imprudent Albrecht leaves the protecting cross and goes toward her with outstretched arms, his eyes burning with desire and love. The fatal madness takes hold of him, he pirouettes, bounds, follows Giselle in her most hazardous leaps; the frenzy to which he gives way reveals a secret desire to die with his mistress and to follow the beloved shade to her tomb; but four o'clock strikes, a pale streak shows on the edge of the horizon. Dawn has come and with it the sun bringing deliverance and salvation. Flee, visions of the night; vanish, pale phantoms! A celestial joy gleams in Giselle's eyes: her lover will not die, the hour has passed. The beautiful Myrtha re-enters her water lily. The *Wilis* fade away, melt into the ground and disappear. Giselle herself is drawn toward her tomb by an invisible power. Albrecht, distraught, clasps her in his arms, carries her, and, covering her with kisses, places her upon a flowered mound; but the earth will not relinquish its prey, the ground opens, the flowers bend over . . . The hunting horn resounds; Wilfrid anxiously seeks for his master. He walks a little in front of the Prince of Courland and Bathilde. However, the flowers cover Giselle, nothing can be seen but her little transparent hand . . . this too disappears, all is over!— never again will Albrecht and Giselle see each other in this world . . . The young man kneels by the mound, plucks a few flowers, and clasps them to his breast, then withdraws, his head resting on the shoulder of the beautiful Bathilde, who forgives and consoles him.

"There, my dear poet, that, more or less, is how M. de Saint-Georges and I have adapted your charming legend with the help of M. Coralli, who composed the *pas*, groups, and attitudes of exquisite novelty and elegance. For interpreters we chose the three graces of the Opéra: Mlles. Carlotta Grisi, Adèle Dumilâtre, and Forster. Carlotta danced with a perfection, lightness, boldness, and a chaste and refined seductiveness, which places her in the first rank, between Elssler and Taglioni; as for pantomime, she exceeded all expectations; not a single conventional gesture, not one false movement; she was nature and artlessness personified. True, she has Perrot the Aerial for husband and teacher. Petipa was graceful, passionate, and touching; it is a long while since a dancer has given us so much pleasure or been so well received.

"M. Adam's music is superior to the usual run of ballet music, it abounds in tunes and orchestral effects; it even includes a touching attention for lovers of difficult music, a very well-produced fugue. The second act solves the musical problem of graceful fantasy and is full of melody. As for the scenery, it is by Ciceri, who is unequaled for landscapes. The sunrise which marks the conclusion is wonderfully realistic . . . La Carlotta was recalled to the sound of the applause of the whole house.

"So, my dear Heine, your German *Wilis* have succeeded completely at the French Opéra."

Giselle continued to succeed, in London, St. Petersburg, Boston, and New York. Carlotta Grisi's great contemporaries, Marie Taglioni, Fanny Elssler, Lucile Grahn, and Fanny Cerito, danced the ballet throughout Europe; *Giselle* was as popular with these new interpreters as it had been at its first performance. And so it has been ever since.

Giselle was introduced to the United States by Mary Ann Lee, who is called by her biographer, Lillian Moore, "the first American dancer to attain nation-wide fame as an exponent of the classic ballet."* Mary Ann Lee had already danced in *La Sylphide* and other great European ballets throughout the United States, had studied with James Sylvain, Fanny Elssler's partner, and had become a very famous dancer indeed before she went to Paris and saw *Giselle*. In Paris she studied with Jean Coralli, who had choreographed the ballet with Perrot. She returned to New York, bringing with her the details of all the popular European ballets, the vehicles of Taglioni, Elssler, Grisi. The first American *Giselle* that she produced in Boston in 1846 was as popular there as it had been in Europe. The Boston *Courier*, on the occasion of her second appearance in the ballet, reported that "We think that we are not exceeding the boundary of truth when we aver that no ballet of action has ever been produced in Boston that could bear comparison with *Giselle*"; and in New York the *Herald* said of her performance in the ballet that "It is a pleasure to every well-organized mind to see talent and art obtain, at least in some degree, that which is the object of its painful toil and labors. . . . Miss Lee enacted Giselle with a beauty, charm, elegance and grace that cannot be described, and we will not attempt it."

In 1848, Fanny Elssler, who had been conquering America when *Giselle* was first produced in Paris, chose the ballet for her debut in St. Petersburg. In 1899, the Russian ballerina Preobrajenska danced Giselle; in 1903, Anna Pavlova first danced the role. In 1910 Diaghilev's Ballets Russes presented *Giselle* in Paris, with Tamara Karsavina and Vaslav Nijinsky. Alexandre Benois, who designed this production and was familiar with the ballet in Russia, has written of *Giselle*:

"What is the secret charm of this ballet? It is mainly due, one must confess, to its simplicity and clearness of plot, to the amazingly impetuous spontaneity with which the drama is developed. There is barely time to collect one's thoughts before the heroine, who but a moment ago charmed everybody with her vitality, is lying stiff and cold and dead at the feet of the lover who has deceived her.

"The second act is devoted to Giselle's life beyond the grave and serves

*In *Chronicles of the American Dance*, edited by Paul Magriel. Henry Holt and Company, 1948.

to make us feel her loss still more poignantly, just as we feel Euridice's second death even more keenly after Orpheus has succeeded in bringing her back to the earth. Something similar happens in *La Bayadère*, but the subject of that ballet is almost overshadowed by the extravagant display of Eastern luxury so alien to us Europeans. The 'middle-aged Europeanism' of *Giselle* is extremely problematic and one wonders whether Théophile Gautier didn't invent the 'Wilis' himself . . . Nevertheless the poetry is European, and it arouses a far deeper response in our hearts than the inventions born of inflamed Eastern imagination.

"One thing is certain—*Giselle* is deeply moving, and the magic of a true poet such as Gautier consists in making us accept without question any absurdities he may choose to offer us. It is strange, for instance, that a perfectly healthy young girl should become insane and die for the sole reason that she discovered her lover's betrayal. The Wilis themselves, who are supposed to be maidens punished after death for having danced too much on the earth, sound most unplausible. It seems extraordinary there should be so many of these sinful young girls—as if there had ever been an epidemic of dancing in that quiet little corner of Germany. But no one is inclined to criticize while under the spell of this strange idyl, especially in the second act, when the charming phantoms assemble in the graveyard . . .

"I must repeat that the outstanding place which *Giselle* occupies in the repertory of ballet is really due to its subject. It is in some respects an ideal ballet, for it is short . . . but comprehends nevertheless the whole gamut of human feelings. The subject is, within limits, both reasonable and unreasonable. A measure of fancy has been found and is so presented that it compels our belief. It is the same measure we find in our favorite fairy tales; they are beloved by us because they fulfill the same demands. Further, the choreographic story of *Giselle* has this advantage over many other ballet stories, that one of its chief elements is *the dance*. Thanks to this, *Giselle* remains something incomparable and inimitable. The number of similar subjects is very limited and they do not bear repetition. I am again tempted to compare it with *La Bayadère*, where the heroine is also a dancer and a professional dancer at that. The chief charm of Giselle's personality lies in the fact that she is a disinterested lover of the dance who indulges in it when inspired and cannot therefore fight against temptation. Her very love for Loys is aroused by his graceful dancing, whereas the amorous forester Hilarion has no chance of winning her heart because he dances like a bear, and the Wilis in the second act have no difficulty in exhausting the clumsy boor and then drowning him in the marshes.

"The reader may find it strange that I am relating so much about the heroine and saying nothing about the hero, whose role was greatly improved later on by Nijinsky. But the part of the *premier danseur* in this ballet is only auxiliary. It was Nijinsky's genius which was needed to bring it to the fore and thus interest the audience not only in Giselle herself, but also in her unfaithful lover, who is cruelly punished in the second part of the ballet. It was here that Nijinsky rivaled the ballerina. He made the grief of the repentant seducer profoundly pathetic; the scene where the Wilis, exalted by Hilarion's doom, try to dance him too to his death became genuinely terrifying."

During the same year that Karsavina and Nijinsky were dancing *Giselle* in Europe, Anna Pavlova and Mikhail Mordkin were dancing it in New York at the Metropolitan Opera House. Carl van Vechten wrote:

"To say that history repeated itself yesterday afternoon at the Metropolitan Opera House, when Pavlova and Mordkin reappeared with their own company, to give for the first time here a programme all by themselves, would be to express the case very mildly, indeed. It might almost be said that history was made on this occasion. It is doubtful if such dancing has ever been seen on the Metropolitan stage save when these two Russians were here last season, and it is certain that there never has been more enthusiasm let loose in the theatre on a Saturday afternoon than there was yesterday.

"The programme included two complete ballets and several *divertissements*, and from 2:30 to 5:30, with intermission now and then, Pavlova and Mordkin gave exhibitions of their highly finished and poetic art.

"The afternoon began with a performance of Adolphe Adam's ballet *Giselle*, which has never been given before on this stage and probably not often in New York. . . .

"The subject for the ballet was taken from Heinrich Heine's book about Germany. 'There exists a tradition of nocturnal dancers, known in the Slavic countries as the Wilis. The Wilis are betrothed girls who have died before their marriage. These poor creatures cannot remain tranquil in their tombs. In their hearts, which have stopped beating, in their dead feet, exists a love for dancing which they have not been able to satisfy during their lives. At midnight they rise and gather in troops, and unfortunate is the young man who encounters them. He is forced to dance with them until he falls dead.

" 'Garbed in their bridal robes, with crowns of orange blossoms on their heads and brilliant rings on their fingers, the Wilis dance in the moonlight like elves, their faces, although white as snow, are beautifully young. They smile with a joy so perfidious, they call you with so much seduction, their manner gives so many soft promises that these dead bacchantes are irresistible.'

"Théophile Gautier is said to have run across this passage one day and to have exclaimed involuntarily: 'What a subject for a ballet!' Whereupon he sat down and wrote across the top of a blank sheet of paper: '*Les Wilis, un ballet.*' However, he probably would have forgotten all about it if he had not encountered a composer at the Opéra that same evening. The result was that he and Saint-Georges collaborated on the book and Adam wrote the music. Coralli, the ballet master of the Opéra at that period, had enough to do with the book so that his name appears on the title page with the others. "This passage from Heine afterward attracted the eyes of other composers and librettists. The English composer Loder used the idea for his most successful opera, *The Night Dancers*, produced shortly after *Giselle*, and Puccini wrote his first opera, *Le Villi*, on the same theme.

"Carlotta Grisi danced the ballet and *Giselle* became the rage. Flowers, hats, gloves, dogs, and horses were named after her. The ballet was done almost immediately in England and America. But, strangely enough, it disappeared from the repertoire of the opera until it was revived in 1863 with Mlle. Mouravieva, herself a Russian from Moscow. She was described by one critic of the day as having plenty of technique but 'not an atom of poetry.'

"In Russia *Giselle* has always been popular, and Mrs. Newmarch says that it was Tchaikovsky's ideal ballet when he composed his *Lac des Cygnes*. In Paris the past season has seen a revival of it, again by Russians.

"The music is gently fragrant, a little faded here and there, but a pretty score, and one of Adam's best. Cuts were made freely. In fact, almost one-half of the music had been taken out, and this was probably for the best, as far as present-day audiences are concerned. There was one interpolation. In the first act a waltz from Glazunov's *Raymonda* was introduced, which was very much as if some conductor had performed *Also Sprach Zarathustra* somewhere in *Fra Diavolo*.

"Mlle. Pavlova yesterday revivified this honeyfied and sentimental score of Adam's, full of the sad, gray splendor of the time of Louis Philippe. Grisi is said to have been gently melancholy in it, but Pavlova was probably more than that. Her poetic conception of the betrothed girl's madness when she finds that her lover has deceived her, and her death, came very close to being tragic. It is almost impossible to describe the poetry of her dancing in the second act, where as one of the Wilis she engages in the wildest sort of measures under the forest trees."

Olga Spessivtzeva danced *Giselle* for her Paris debut in 1924. In 1932 she danced the ballet in England, with Anton Dolin.

It was not until 1934 that there was an all-English production of the ballet. On January 1, 1934, Alicia Markova danced her first *Giselle* at the Old Vic Theatre, London, with the Vic-Wells Ballet (now the Sadler's Wells Ballet). Margot Fonteyn first danced *Giselle* on January 19, 1937.

The Ballet Russe de Monte Carlo produced *Giselle* in 1938, with Markova and Tamara Toumanova alternating as Giselle and with Serge Lifar as Albrecht. This production was first presented in the United States at the Metropolitan Opera House, October 12, 1938, with Markova and Lifar.

Anton Dolin produced *Giselle* for the Ballet Theatre at the Center Theatre, New York, January 12, 1940. Annabelle Lyon and Patricia Bowman alternated in the part, with Dolin as Albrecht. This *Giselle* had scenery and costumes by Lucinda Ballard. During the seasons of 1941-44, 1945-46, and 1952-53, Alicia Markova danced Giselle with the Ballet Theatre. Edwin Denby wrote of Markova's performance in 1944:

"Alicia Markova in *Giselle* is Ballet Theatre's greatest glory . . . Miss Markova danced again with incomparable beauty of style—dazzlingly limpid, mysteriously tender.

"There is no other dancer whose movement is so perfectly centered, and who controls so exactly the full continuity of a motion from the center to the extremities. There is no other dancer whose waist and thighs are so quick to execute the first actions that lead to an arm gesture and to a step, or who diminishes the stress so precisely as it travels outward along the arms and legs. It is this that gives her dancing figure its incomparable clarity, its delicacy and its repose. It is this, too, that makes her dance rhythm so clear to the eye and so full of variety.

"This superlative dance intelligence makes her dance fascinating, both as pure motion and as motion to the music. The fragility of her figure, the dramatic conviction of her characterization give her dance another and equally strong expressivity. Her physical and intellectual concentration confer on her a mysterious remoteness and isolation, and this tragic dignity makes her express a tenderness extraordinarily touching and her qualities, of dancing, of mime, of presence, find a perfect use in the part of Giselle; the extraordinary effect Miss Markova creates in this part is obvious to the thousands who watch her, whether they are familiar with the ballet or not."

I staged a new version of *Giselle* for the Ballet Theatre, October 15, 1946, at the Broadway Theatre, New York, with Alicia Alonso and Igor Youskevitch in the principal roles. This production had scenery and costumes by Eugene Berman.

Alexandra Danilova danced *Giselle* for the first time on February 24, 1948, at the City Center, New York, in the Ballet Russe de Monte Carlo production staged by Frederic Franklin. Franklin danced the role of Albrecht for the first time on this occasion and Mary Ellen Moylan danced her first Myrtha, queen of the Wilis.

Other dancers associated with the part of Giselle are among the world's famous: Mia Slavenska, Nana Gollner, Lycette Darsonval, Yvette Chauviré, Galina Ulanova, Marina Semenova, Beryl Grey, Sally Gilmour, Nathalie Leslie (Krassovska), Nora Kaye, Moira Shearer, Mona Inglesby, and Rosella Hightower.

Vaslav Nijinsky, Mikhail Mordkin, Pierre Vladimiroff, Anatole Vilzak, Anatole Oboukoff, Anton Dolin, Igor Youskevitch, André Eglevsky, Serge Lifar, Robert Helpmann, Frederic Franklin, George Skibine, Alexis Rassine, John Gilpin, and Jean Babilée are among the many interpreters of the role of Albrecht.

Alexandra Danilova, Nora Kaye, Mary Ellen Moylan, and Marjorie Tallchief are among the dancers who have appeared in the role of Myrtha.

LA GLOIRE

Dramatic ballet in one act. Music by Ludwig van Beethoven. Choreography by Antony Tudor. Scenery by Gaston Longchamps. Costumes executed by Karinska. Lighting by Jean Rosenthal. First presented by the New York City Ballet at the City Center, New York, February 26, 1952, with a cast headed by Nora Kaye, Diana Adams, Francisco Moncion, and Hugh Laing.

Set on the stage and behind the scenes of a great state theatre, La Gloire shows us the private and public lives of a star performer: how they differ and how circumstances combine to make them the same. The star performer is a great actress and dancer whose fame is so unprecedented that it has become difficult for her and for her faithful public to distinguish between her performances on stage and her personal life: she is a *personality* and there is nothing personal about her. Her first great success, her first *gloire*, was many years ago and she is now the principal artist in a theatre where the management, the secondary artists, and the audience are willingly controlled by her presence.

Sarah Bernhardt's last play was called La Gloire, and it is the age of Bernhardt, the age of such other great European artists as Rachel, Réjane, and Anna Pavlova, that the ballet recalls. It is interesting also that the elaborate stage machinery of the French theatre, the backstage tricks that make sylphs seem to fly through the air and ghosts disappear, is called *gloire*. For the backstage machinations and intrigue come to control what happens on the stage: in La Gloire the heroine's performance is but a projection of the real life she lives behind the scenes. The music to the ballet consists of three overtures by Beethoven: *Egmont, Coriolan,* and *Leonore No. 3.* The time is sometime in the nineteenth century.

After a brief orchestral introduction, ominous and triumphant, the curtain rises on the huge stage of a state theatre. The stage which the audience in the theatre sees is on the left, separated from the backstage area by three wings, three golden strips of scenery. On the right is the stage dressing room of the star, furnished with a large mirror, a dressing table, and a lamp. A girl in gray stands on stage watching the star prepare for her performance. The star rehearses some of the gestures she will use in the scene she is about to act, and as she moves, the girl in gray imitates her. Like everyone else in the theatre, she worships the star, but she worships her so much that she wants to be like her, wants to learn from her, copy her, so that she, too, may someday have her *gloire*.

The star does not notice her. When she emerges from her dressing room, the girl runs to help her off with her cloak. The star is in Roman costume. She accepts the girl's servility as if it were her due and stands ready to go on stage. On the stage proper, two Roman handmaidens enter. The golden wings that have separated the two parts of the stage move to the right, and the backstage area vanishes. The star enters from behind the wings, and the scene begins.

The drama we watch is *The Rape of Lucretia*. Lucretia is the beautiful young wife of the Roman general Tarquinius Collatinus, whose absence at war disturbs her. One of her husband's friends, an officer named Sextus Tarquinius, enters to bring her news of her husband. Lucretia welcomes him and reads the message he has brought her. The unhappy news contained in the message causes her to faint, and Sextus Tarquinius catches her in his arms. The two handmaidens exit.

Sextus Tarquinius makes love to Lucretia as he comforts her. The music mounts to a fierce, rhythmic crescendo. He touches her body lasciviously. Lucretia gradually understands his purpose and resists with all the force of her body. But the Roman soldier bends her to his will and ravishes her. Lucretia, full of shame for her sin and detestation of her attacker, cannot bear to think of her loving husband. As Sextus Tarquinius contemplates miserably the satisfaction of his lust, Lucretia seizes his dagger. He grabs her arm and forces her to drop it. Lucretia's body is racked with grief and her shoulders shake with her sobbing. Sextus Tarquinius departs. Her handmaidens return. Before they can prevent her, she takes up the dagger and stabs herself to death.

The wings move back toward the center, and again the stage is divided. The star, no longer the hapless Lucretia, but the triumphant performer who has just acknowledged a fitting crescendo of applause, walks backstage from the wings. She carries a large bouquet of flowers and accepts calmly the attentions of her off-stage lover, the actor who has played Sextus Tarquinius. The girl in gray helps her on with her cloak. Another actor, who is to play the next scene with the star, comes on stage with six dancers. The star exits to dress.

With the first clipped chords of the *Coriolan* Overture, the girl in gray turns swiftly and poses in imitation of the star. The other performers watch her, a little amused, a little frightened that she should be doing this where the star might see her and disapprove. The star emerges from her dressing room and sees the girl imitating her. She stares at her in astonishment. It is time for her to go on, however, and she cannot make a scene. Her lover moves to help her with her costume. The star brushes him aside and allows the actor who is to play this next scene with her to assist her. Now she is dressed in a short white tunic and a long red cape, with a crown on her head. On stage, the principal actor of the next drama is dancing with the group of six girls. He is Hippolytus, the handsome son of Theseus, King of Athens. Theseus has recently taken to wife Phaedra. Hippolytus is playing with Artemis, goddess of the hunt, and her entourage.

The wings move back. The star, as Phaedra, enters. She goes to Hippolytus and tries to separate him from Artemis. The girls hide their faces in their hands, embarrassed at the queen's passion for her stepson. Phaedra persists, and now the drama of the first scene is reversed: Phaedra declares her love for Hippolytus and attempts to seduce him. Hippolytus resists. She entwines herself around him and when he still refuses her advances, Phaedra orders him to kill her. He refuses and leaves the stage, clutching the knife in his hand. Phaedra languishes. Now she rises and, with the return of the opening chords of the overture, turns swiftly and poses in the grand manner.

The wings again divide the stage in half. The star comes backstage to see the girl in gray practicing the scene she has just performed; her partner is the actor who has just played Hippolytus. The star cannot believe her eyes at first, but then wonders, "Why not? I am the greatest actress in the world: why shouldn't she imitate me: why not, indeed?" She sees that the girl is not playing the scene accurately and walks over to the couple. They are rehearsing the moment when Phaedra is trying to force Hippolytus to kill her. The star pushes the girl aside and again becomes Phaedra, showing the girl how the scene must be played. Then she orders the girl back and, taking the part of Hippolytus, runs through the scene again. As the star holds the knife over the girl, it occurs to us that she might indeed wish to kill her. The girl is grateful for this lesson, but stands motionless, unable to articulate her gratitude. She is embarrassed, knowing full well that the woman might at any moment cease to be kind and rail at her for her audacity in imagining that she might one day take her part on stage. The star looks at her, sees that her shoulders are hunched, and reaches out and corrects her as she sweeps off to her dressing room. The girl, alone, touchingly repeats the grand-mannered poses of her idol.

The star returns, watches her, and the two actresses repeat these poses together: the star with fierce contest, the girl in simple, youthful accuracy. The star is dressed now in a suit of somber black. She stares after the ingénue, as the accompanying music ends, and despises her. The scene blacks out.

When the lights come up again, we are watching the performance. On stage, in a spotlight, the star is Hamlet, dancing a tormented soliloquy. She throws herself to the ground in the agony of Hamlet's indecision and at length rises, triumphant, possessed by an idea that will catch the conscience of the king.

Ophelia enters and tries to comfort Hamlet. Hamlet at first welcomes her sympathy, then throws the girl to the ground. Ophelia leaves. Hamlet leaps and turns in a long diagonal across the stage. He is followed by the three players, whom Hamlet welcomes to the court. He asks them if they can play a certain scene and acts out for them a duplication of the murder of his father by his uncle, the king. The players learn the scene and exit to prepare for their performance.

Hamlet ushers in the king and queen and Ophelia. The players return. Hamlet rests his head idly in Ophelia's lap, then sits up to watch the play. The king admires the players until it becomes clear that what they are acting is not a play at all, but a scene that he so well remembers. As the figure in the play embraces the wife of the brother he has just murdered, the king rushes off. The queen goes to Hamlet.

At this point, the wings move back and we see the backstage area. There the girl in gray is imitating Hamlet's movements. The star looks off into the wings and stands transfixed by what she sees. Hamlet's agony becomes her own agony; she runs off the stage and hides in her dressing room. Her body trembles, she becomes hysterical. Is this the end? Has her art fallen off so much that a girl from the chorus can openly imitate her in the wings while she is performing? A distant trumpet calls. The star attempts to control herself and steps out of the dressing room.

Backstage, she notes that all the actors are embarrassed; they turn away and will not look her in the face. And looking out to the stage, she sees why. The girl in gray is dancing her part in *Phaedra*, in *her* costume. The star watches as she performs the scene perfectly. When the girl finishes and comes backstage, she is afraid to look at her idol. She bows her head. The star touches her hand softly in praise.

Now the star returns to the stage for the last scene of *Hamlet*. The king and queen and Laertes are on stage. The king presents swords to Laertes and Hamlet, and they fight over the death of Ophelia. The king gives a cup of poisoned wine to the queen and instructs her to offer it to Hamlet. Hamlet refuses it. The queen drinks it herself before the king can stop her. She dies. Laertes, who has been stabbed fatally, points accusingly to the king, and Hamlet, dying of wounds from Laertes' poisoned sword, gathers his strength and rushes upon the king. He kills the king with a fierce thrust. All about him are dead. He collapses and holds up the cup of poisoned wine. Hamlet, the character, dies as the star, who acts his part, symbolically perishes with him. This is her final *gloire*. The girl in gray emerges from the wings and stands over the star as she sinks slowly to the ground. The music ends on a final, determined note of triumph and glory.

GRADUATION BALL

Ballet in one act. Music by Johann Strauss. Choreography by David Lichine. Scenery and costumes by Alexandre Benois. Book by David Lichine. First presented by the Original Ballet Russe at the Theatre Royal, Sydney, Australia, February 28, 1940, with Tatiana Riabouchin-ska and David Lichine in the leading roles. First presented in the United States by the Original Ballet Russe at the Fifty-first Street Theatre, New York, November 6, 1940, with the same principals.

Graduation Ball is the story of a party. Young girls at a fashionable school in Vienna put on a gala entertainment to fete the graduates of a nearby military academy. The girls and boys meet, amuse themselves by performing a series of *divertissements*, discover a secret romance, and dance until the headmistress of the school ends the party. The music for the ballet—chosen, arranged, and orchestrated by Antal Dorati—is selected from the works of Johann Strauss.

The ballet is set in the high, formal drawing room of the girls' school. There the girls are excitedly preparing for the ball, which is clearly their one real social occasion of the year. The senior girls primp excessively and try out their newly acquired fashionable manners, while their more numerous juniors, in simple frocks and pinafores, laugh at their affectations. Soon they are all ready to receive their guests from the local military school. The head-mistress, an absurd and bustling busybody danced by a male dancer, rushes in and makes sure that her pupils look their very best.

Loud martial music announces the arrival of the cadets, who march in boldly to the staccato drums. Although the boys stand rigidly at attention when they halt, and face straight forward, their roving eyes size up their young hostesses in short order. The elderly general who leads the boys finally allows them to relax, and the young people are suddenly embarrassed: with all their pretense at worldly knowledge, they don't really know how to get the ball under way. The boys stay on one side of the room, the girls on the other, and there is a momentary stalemate.

The pompous old general has been immediately attracted to the head-mistress and escorts her off for a rendezvous. The young people are un-chaperoned and don't know quite what to do. A young girl, deciding to give the senior girls their comeuppance, leaves her friends and approaches the formation of boys. The cadets greet her with such loud heel-clicking and deference that the girl is terrified: she finds herself sitting smack in the middle of the floor.

The ball at last gets under way when the cadets elect a leader and order him to choose a partner and begin the first dance. Of course, he is more timid than his fellows and steps out of line only because of military dis-cipline. The girls feel so sorry for him that before he can really make a choice, a partner is dancing with him. With this example, the other cadets take partners and all dance.

The headmistress and her general return to supervise the entertainment they have so carefully rehearsed—first comes a *divertissement* by one of the cadet drummers, then a romantic Scottish *pas de deux* that recalls the spirit of such old ballets as *La Sylphide*. The young girl who tried to start the dance is enchanted by this dance of ethereal love and improvises an im-promptu dance of her own.

Next comes a dance-step competition in which the girls try to outdo each other in the number of *fouettés* they can execute, and there is a final *perpetuum mobile* in which all dance. The romance of the headmistress and the general has progressed during these entertainments, which they have hardly watched. The girls and boys leave the room seeking refreshments; the older people dance together and declare their love. They are in the midst of a passionate embrace when their students come back. The young people laugh and congratulate them, and the party hastens to a high-spirited conclusion. Despite their discovered romance, the headmistress and the general are compelled to end the dance. The cadets bid the girls a fond farewell and sadly take their leave. The lights dim.

The ballroom is now deserted. One of the cadets is seen trying to sneak back, to bid his girl a more private farewell. We are a little amused to see that this is the same cadet who was so hesitant about beginning the ball; no longer bashful, he is now bold. For a moment it appears that he'll be able to effect his rendezvous, but the headmistress darts out and shoos him off. He was only trying!

THE GUESTS

Classic ballet in one act. Music by Marc Blitzstein. Choreography by Jerome Robbins. Lighting by Jean Rosenthal. First presented by the New York City Ballet at the City Center, New York, January 20, 1949, with Maria Tallchief, Nicholas Magallanes, and Francisco Moncion in the principal roles.

This ballet concerns itself with prejudice: with "the patterns of adjustment and conflict between two groups, one larger than the other." What happens when these two groups meet and find themselves absolutely opposed? The ballet presents this problem socially, at what seems to be an ordinary party.

The curtain rises on a formal setting. High black columns in the back suggest a large ball. The host comes forward formally and prepares to welcome a group of guests. The guests enter in two distinct groups. At first it would seem that they are not distinct at all, for the boys and girls wear the same kind of clothes and move in the same way, but gradually we see that they never comingle, that the dances that now get under way are arranged in block patterns, and that the two separate groups instinctively avoid close contact. The host is not disturbed by the difference between the two. He leads the party on without nervousness, aware that the two groups have lived amicably side by side for a long time and cannot possibly achieve closer contact. Both sides of the party feel this almost naturally, the girls dancing only with partners from their group, gathering together and speaking together, but never paying attention to what the other side might be doing; they do not even acknowledge each other's existence beyond politely moving aside when they wish to pass each other. It is apparent, however, that the smaller group is more deferential to the larger.

The party proceeds. The host brings out masks and passes these favors out to members of the larger group of guests. Several masks are left over and put aside. The masked couples begin to dance, while the smaller group stands aside and watches. The dance has not proceeded long before we notice that the discarded masks have disappeared; two of the dancers are obviously wearing them. But the host does not note this breach of etiquette, and the dancing couples, unaware of true identities, continue to enjoy themselves.

One girl and boy in particular are strangely attracted to each other. They move together with a soft, relaxed ease as if they had been dancing together all their lives. The boy steps forward slightly and reaches out his hand, pointing the way to some distant happiness. The girl imitates this gesture. They stand facing each other; when their hands touch, the contact is electrically romantic. Yet their dance is not intimate; it is, rather, the dance of two people who are living a dream. There is no sudden passion, no questions need to be asked; the boy supports and lifts the girl tenderly, and she responds to this with soft grace.

The ensemble dance ends, and the host orders the guests to remove their masks. The guests discover that the boy and the girl who are so much in love belong to different groups; one of them has worn the mask in error! Chaos breaks out. The two groups drag the boy and the girl apart and make them dance separately. When the two groups pass, the boy and girl hold out their hands to each other longingly.

Finally they can bear the separation no longer. They defy convention and meet. The boy lifts the girl high and carries her away into the distance. The astonished guests look at each other in horror. The curtain falls.

NOTES: *The Guests* was the first ballet Jerome Robbins created for the New York City Ballet. He soon afterwards became Associate Artistic Director of the company and began to dance in its ballets. As a dancer, as a choreographer, and as Associate Artistic Director, Robbins has contributed immensely to the New York City company's reputation.

HAMLET

Dramatic ballet in one act. Music by Peter Ilyich Tchaikovsky. Choreography by Robert Helpmann. Scenery and costumes by Leslie Hurry. First presented by the Sadler's Wells Ballet at the New Theatre, London, May 19, 1942, with Robert Helpmann as *Hamlet* and Margot Fonteyn as *Ophelia*. First presented in the United States by the Sadler's Wells Ballet at the Metropolitan Opera House, New York, October 12, 1949, with the same principals.

This *Hamlet* is not an adaptation of Shakespeare's play for ballet; rather, it is a ballet version, a ballet interpretation of Shakespeare's subject. It does not follow the action of the play precisely, but rather recollects the plot of the play in its own drama. The ballet *Hamlet* is prefaced by these lines from the play:

> *For in that sleep of death, what dreams may come*
> *When we have shuffled off this mortal coil*
> *Must give us pause.*

These lines warn us to expect dreams, impressions, perhaps even flash backs of Hamlet's life and tragedy. The music for the ballet is Tchaikovsky's fantasy-overture *Hamlet*.

At the rise of the curtain we see a ghostly sight. A thin, bright shaft of light shines down on Hamlet's face. He is dead. Four pallbearers carry him slowly to his grave; the end of the play is the ballet's beginning. And still it is different, for the pallbearers are not the captains appointed by Fortinbras to bear Hamlet; they are hooded monks.

The monks bear Hamlet off, and the scene brightens. The scene is not literal, not so much a section of a Danish castle as a projection of Hamlet's imagination. It is ghastly and bloody and mad. A huge creature depicted on the backdrop rushes toward murder, a jagged knife poised in readiness. Over a portal at the left, a great detached hand holds a dagger casually, as if it were a cigarette. The scene is possessed with violence.

One by one, characters familiar to Hamlet appear—first the gravedigger. As we are remembering what he said to Hamlet and what Hamlet said to him, the Prince of Denmark himself enters. He watches the scene as we watch it; he is observing himself. Detached in death, he looks back over his life.

He does not like what he sees; his anticipation of vile deeds suffered and vile deeds done causes him to hide his face from view. Now he watches the gravedigger play with Yorick's skull, throwing it into the air, rolling it along the ground.

A crowing cock heralds the arrival of the ghost of Hamlet's father, who instructs Hamlet in the manner of his death: how he was murdered by his brother with the connivance of his queen. Hamlet's guesswork has proved true in a way he had not imagined, and the evil of the present king and Hamlet's mother, the queen, has new justification. Hamlet promises the ghost that he will seek revenge.

Old Polonius and Laertes appear, followed by the king and queen. The lusty king makes love to the queen while her son rages openly. But the king ignores him and turns his attention to Laertes, granting the youth permission to go to France. Polonius warns the king to beware of Hamlet. When the doddering chamberlain has promised him to spy on Hamlet, the king departs.

Hamlet watches his mother and approaches her. Mysteriously, Ophelia steps before the queen, and the two women are confused. Hamlet falls to the floor, moves his hands frantically in front of him as if to separate this double image, but still the two women shift before his eyes. When they leave the scene, Hamlet prays.

Now Laertes dances gaily with his sister, Ophelia. Soon they are interrupted by Polonius, who wishes his son a lengthy Godspeed. Laertes departs for France, and Polonius takes his daughter to Hamlet. He wishes to observe them and conceals himself as the prince courts his daughter sweetly and sincerely. But then Hamlet senses that something is rotten; he catches the king spying on him with Polonius and throws Ophelia to the ground.

Next Hamlet watches the play-within-a-play. All members of the court enter, and a page announces that the entertainment is about to begin. In the play, parts are taken not by professional actors but by the creatures of Hamlet's imagination: Ophelia is the player queen, the ghost of Hamlet's father is the player king. When the player king is to be murdered, both Hamlet and Claudius approach his sleeping figure. Both pour poison in his ear.

The king, again the spectator and no longer the murdering actor, is horrified at this re-enactment of his crime and goes to pray. Hamlet is about to seize this opportunity to kill his archenemy, but then rationalizes that it is the wrong occasion. But there is occasion for another death: Polonius is plotting with the queen; Hamlet stabs him.

Laertes returns to avenge his father's death and accuses the king. The queen points out the youth's error, and all turn to watch sadly the beautiful Ophelia, gone mad with grief at her father's death and her lover's inconstancy. Ophelia's madness spurs Laertes to seek out Hamlet.

Hamlet stands aside to watch a funeral procession. Ophelia is dead, and he would accompany her to her grave. But the pallbearers are not carrying Ophelia, his dead love; it is the queen they carry. Again Hamlet cannot distinguish the two in his affections. Laertes, who is marching in the procession, sees Hamlet and immediately attacks him. The prudent king pulls Laertes back and suggests to him another plot.

This plot is now set in motion. We watch another courtly scene, where all the principals are present. The king and Laertes are in concert, while Hamlet is apparently reconciled with his mother. Now the king offers Hamlet wine, which is poisoned. Hamlet will not accept it and turns away in wrath at such a social grace from such a man. The queen attempts to pacify her son by drinking a toast to him with the wine. The king, paralyzed with anxiety at her foolish act, draws her aside.

Laertes sneaks up on Hamlet and stabs him in the back. The wounded prince returns the thrust, and Laertes dies. Now Hamlet attacks the king. The queen watches, horrified, as her son kills her husband. Then she, too, dies.

The gravedigger returns, and the ballet has come full circle. Now that there is no need for him to live, now that revenge is done, Hamlet succumbs to his wounds. He falls to the ground. The monks come in, take up his body, and raise it high over their heads. The scene grows dark. Soon all we can see is Hamlet's face, ghostly white in the pin-point spotlight; his beginning is, after all, his end.

HARLEQUIN IN APRIL

Pantomime with *divertissements* in two acts, with prologue, entr'acte, and epilogue. Music by Richard Arnell. Choreography by John Cranko. Scenery and costumes by John Piper. First presented by the Sadler's Wells Theatre Ballet at the Sadler's Wells Theatre, London, May 8, 1951, with David Blair as *Harlequin*, Patricia Miller as *Columbine*, and Stanley Holden as *Pierrot*. First presented in the United States by the Sadler's Wells Theatre Ballet at the Eastman Theatre, Rochester, New York, October 25, 1951, with the same principals.

This dramatic ballet tells a modern story in terms of old characters. Here the old, typed characters—Harlequin, Columbine, and Pierrot—who have come down to us from Greek mythology and the *commedia dell' arte* and who figure in such ballets as *Carnaval*, are used to represent new notions while at the same time preserving much of their original symbolism. Here Harlequin is human aspiration reborn after fire and devastation. Harlequin returns to life among the flowers of April, earth-bound and self-sufficient creatures from whom he escapes. Columbine is Harlequin's love, the representation of the ideal he aspires to. Pierrot stands between the two; he is the perpetual fool, and we laugh at him until he interferes too much.

PROLOGUE: The curtain rises on an inside drop that depicts another, smaller stage hung with a tattered curtain. This interior theatre has not simply fallen into disrepair through age and use; it has been burned out and destroyed, and stands as a symbol of human wreckage where no human can flourish.

Pierrot, superhuman fool of the gods, ambles in carrying a bag. His face is painted white to match the loose white costume that hangs about his loose-jointed figure. He takes a sheet of music from the bag and opens his mouth to sing. When he discovers that he cannot sing, that he can make no sound, he hides his face behind the music. Now he tries again, a little more successfully, then puts the music back in his bag of tricks and exits. The lights grow dim.

ACT ONE—APRIL: When the lights come up, the drop curtain has disappeared and we are backstage in the interior theatre. Groups of girls dressed like plants lie about the stage. Pierrot enters with a watering can and goes about watering the plants. One of the groups begins to rise; the center group stirs. There is a fluttering of hands, and the plants in the center group huddle together closely, as if protecting something. Now the girls kneel, and Harlequin rises in their midst, born anew in the ashes of destruction. Naked to the waist, Harlequin wears a black mask across his eyes. He walks in and out among the flowers and plants, who celebrate his birth.

Pierrot takes from his bag a jacket for Harlequin. Harlequin puts on the coat and removes the mask. Now fully dressed in his traditional diamond-patched costume, Harlequin comes fully to life. A drum sounds loudly; he chases Pierrot off and dances, turning again and again to a persistent drum roll. The plants, which have remained lifeless, now rise and leave the scene. As the last plant moves off, Harlequin restrains her and the two dance a *pas de deux*. This is largely a dance of resistance, as the self-sufficient plant struggles to be free of this strange being who demands and requires her company. Harlequin tears the flowery mask from her face and for a moment she is just a young girl, but she reaches out trembling hands to retrieve the mask.

Harlequin kicks at the mask and throws it aside. The other plants begin to return; they find the mask and place it again on the face of the frightened girl, after which they form a line and leave the scene. Harlequin kisses the last girl, the girl he has danced with, and finds himself alone.

Harlequin is angry. He falls to the ground in his rage. Pierrot comes and tries to comfort him. Harlequin, armed now with a sword, watches astonished as a unicorn, traditional guardian of chastity, crosses the stage. Even now, Harlequin is aware that the unicorn will attempt to separate him from his ideal. He threatens the strange animal, but the proud unicorn stalks away. The drop curtain falls.

ENTR'ACTE: Pierrot comes out before the drop curtain and dances. Then he takes from his white bag a violin and a bow and plays the instrument. Like the song he tried to sing at the beginning of the ballet, Pierrot's violin concerto is not of high quality. Rather impatient with the unobliging violin, he kneels and plays it as if it were a cello. Then he thrusts it aside, returns it to the bag, and leaves the scene.

ACT TWO—THE SKY: The light is dim when the drop curtain rises again. Gradually the light rises. Now the interior backdrop is streaked with clouds. Harlequin, still carrying his sword, enters and watches the unicorn. Pierrot hides behind Harlequin, egging him on. The unicorn nods its head in assent to a command that Harlequin has made to it and returns, carrying on its back a lovely young girl—Columbine. Immediately in love, Harlequin kisses her. Pierrot pulls him away from the girl, and Columbine comes down from the unicorn's back. She seems to have some power over the creature, for at her order the unicorn goes to sleep.

Columbine goes directly to Harlequin and they dance. Harlequin pushes Pierrot away when he attempts teasingly to interfere. Columbine falls back in Harlequin's arm, and he buries his face in her breast. The two lovers fall to the ground and kiss. Columbine's arms reach up around Harlequin's head, and Pierrot rushes in to pull them apart. They are separated for a moment, but again Harlequin embraces the girl. He lifts her, and as he holds her aloft, her extended leg trembles. The lovers lie down again to fulfill their passion.

Pierrot, now fully alarmed, wakes the sleeping unicorn. The unicorn, militant and unfeeling, pulls Columbine from Harlequin's close embrace. Harlequin stabs at the unicorn, but the scene is filled with magical duplications of the unicorn and Harlequin is helpless against this multiple representation of chastity. Some of the unicorns claim Columbine as others stalk Harlequin down and stand over him. She is lifted onto the back of one of the unicorns, then lifted high into the air by the others. Harlequin climbs up on the strange creatures to reach her; at the pinnacle he is pushed off and falls to the ground.

Columbine disappears. Harlequin goes off in search of her as the unicorns leave the scene. Harlequin returns, with a rag-doll representation of Columbine in his arms. Pierrot bows to him, and Harlequin begins a wild, frantic dance that expresses his rage at his loss. He beats Pierrot, the interfering fool who has deprived him of the ideal, and chases him off.

To quiet, moving music, Harlequin holds the model of Columbine in his arms and kisses its hands. The plants return, gather about Harlequin, and enfold him. They place the black mask about his eyes and take off his jacket. The plants huddle over him closely, and as they kneel, he disappears in their midst.

EPILOGUE: Pierrot returns. He sees Harlequin's jacket lying on the ground and picks it up. For a moment he considers the loss of his friend, but not for long. He begins to try on the jacket. It is too small for him, he can get only one arm in, but so dressed he poses arrogantly, an absurd masquerade of Harlequin, while the real Harlequin sleeps.

NOTES: "Here is a work of fine imagination, poetic texture and sturdy choreographic substance for all its delicacy," wrote John Martin in the New York *Times* after the New York *première* of *Harlequin in April*. "The movement is quite free in style, full of invention and dramatic implications, and fascinating in its atmosphere . . . Pirmin Trecu is a superb Harlequin, Patricia Miller a lovely Columbine and Stanley Holden a beautifully stupid and meaningful Pierrot."

Harlequin in April was mounted by John Cranko for the Sadler's Wells Ballet on the occasion of the Festival of Britain.

THE HARVEST ACCORDING

Ballet in three parts. Music by Virgil Thomson. Choreography by Agnes de Mille. Scenery and costumes by Lemuel Ayres. Lighting by Peggy Clark. First presented by the Ballet Theatre at the Metropolitan Opera House, New York, October 1, 1952, with a cast headed by Gemze de Lappe, Ruth Ann Koesun, Jenny Workman, and Kelly Brown.

> *Life, life is the tillage*
> *And death is the harvest according.*
> —Walt Whitman

The Harvest According is a dance panorama of life as it is observed by a woman. The life cycle is divided into three parts, which present birth, games, and the harvest (war and home-coming). The locale and time of the ballet —New England in the Civil War—reflect only the American themes of the music and some of the dance patterns: they are not meant to exclude the work's application to any people at any time. The final scene is a revision of the choreographer's "Civil War Ballet" in the musical comedy *Bloomer Girl*.

PART ONE — BIRTH: The time is spring. Women depict the prelude to childbirth. The dancing displays apprehension, then agony, release, joy, and awareness of the miraculous. They celebrate birth in a square-dance ritual.

PART TWO — GAMES: Boys and girls of a seacoast town play games and reveal in their play something of the problems that face them as they become aware of the need for friends, bravery, and love.

PART THREE — THE HARVEST: The young people have grown up. The boys go off to war. The women mourn their absence. Some of the boys return. Their women welcome them.

THE HAUNTED BALLROOM

Dramatic ballet in three scenes. Music by Geoffrey Toye. Choreography by Ninette de Valois. Book by Geoffrey Toye. Scenery and costumes by Motley. First presented by the Vic-Wells Ballet at the Sadler's Wells Theatre, London, April 3, 1934, with a cast that included Robert Helpmann, Alicia Markova, and William Chappell. First presented in the United States by the Sadler's Well Theatre Ballet in Buffalo, New York, October 23, 1951, with David Poole in the principal role.

The drama of this ballet is based on its mysterious locale and the destiny that haunts the people who inhabit it. Set in the ancient ballroom of a Scottish castle, the ballet calls up those venerable but terrifying demons and ghosts which control the fate of a family. In two graphic scenes, *The Haunted Ballroom* displays the inscrutable power of these creatures and the helplessness of those who live in perpetual dread of their appearance.

The overture is low in volume, eerie and mysterious in mood. The music warns us of incipient danger—a danger that does not come suddenly, but quietly and patiently waits to pounce upon its helpless prey. There is a rush of sound from the harp, the orchestra plays a low, murmuring waltz, and the curtain rises.

The scene is dark, almost pitch-black. Slanting wings enclose a large, cavernous space. At the back, centered in the black wall, is an arched doorway. From the ceiling hangs a chandelier festooned with cobwebs. Long strips of rotting black cloth are draped from the chandelier to the corners of the room.

We are in an abandoned ballroom, a place seldom used by its owner. In the back, the door opens. Young Tregennis, son of the master of the house, enters. He is dressed in black velvet with a red sash about his waist. The youth looks about the room apprehensively, and we sense that even in some typical childish prank he would never choose to enter it alone. Three ladies in long, trailing evening dresses follow him into the musty ballroom. They flutter their large fans nervously and examine the ballroom with no little curiosity; it is clear that, during a ball that is being held elsewhere in the castle, they have asked the boy to show them this hidden room.

One by one, the ladies tap the boy on the shoulder with their fans, playfully commanding him to dance with them. As he moves about the dark ballroom with the ladies, the trains of their dresses drag along the floor and whirl the dust about their waltzing figures. But the youth is in no mood for dancing. He breaks away from the women and stands with his head in his hands. He seems to be aware of something the women cannot see and trembles like a small child.

The ladies still wish to be amused, however, and again tap him with their fans. The boy remains motionless. He knows that he should never have given in to their whim and, most of all, that he should not have come here himself. As the teasing women begin to lose all patience with their young host, his father is seen standing in the doorway.

The master of Tregennis is astonished to find the door open and shocked to find his guests in this part of the house. He observes his son standing in the corner. The youth cowers away from his father. He orders the boy to leave the room. The boy runs to his father, begging for forgiveness, but imperiously the father gestures him away. The boy flees.

Now the master of Tregennis turns and bows to the ladies. A waltz melody is heard. The master apologizes to his guests for his strange behavior and tells them the cause of his anxiety. He indicates to them that this is truly a haunted ballroom: his father died here and his father before him—indeed, all of his family have perished in this room. The ladies cover their faces with their fans to conceal their embarrassment and fear. Now that they understand, they bow to the master of Tregennis, take up their trains, and leave the room.

Alone, the man stands in the center of the haunted ballroom and stares into the dark corners. He is afraid and fascinated at the same time; he cannot move. The room darkens and a light shines upon him. He looks into the light, trying to control his fear, but his hand reaches out to ward off some unseen terror. The light has caused his frightened figure to be thrown against the back wall in immense silhouette. The curtain falls as he stands helpless in the sight of the fate he must someday meet.

During a brief interval, the orchestra recapitulates the happy dance theme to which the three ladies danced with young Tregennis. The harp interrupts this music to sound a warning, there is a muffled trumpet call, and the curtain rises again.

The ballroom is now almost completely dark. Gradually the lights come up, and we note that the door in the back wall is open. Into the room dances a strange figure dressed in somber black with a black mask. He plays upon a flute and then thrusts the flute into the air as if it were a sword. Ghostly creatures in white follow him and form a tableau. Their faces are veiled, their long white sleeves dangle from their arms to give their figures a disjointed, unearthly quality. Two veiled women, dressed similarly to two of the ladies who invaded the ballroom in the first scene, enter and dance at the command of the strange figure in black.

Just as we are wondering where the counterpart to the third lady might be, she enters and dances as the masked stranger plays upon his flute. The ghostly creatures collapse and form weird groupings that remain still throughout her demoniac dance. She is joined by the other two women, and all three move together until the strange player halts the dance suddenly: at his command, each ends her movement in an arabesque.

Now the strange player moves about the room, obviously preparing the scene for some portentous event. The master of Tregennis stumbles into the room. He wears a long white dressing gown, and a mysterious call seems to have demanded his return to the room. He observes his uninvited guests and rudely asks the strange player for an explanation. The master of Tregennis is told that a group of dancers have come to his ballroom and that they are eager to dance if he will be good enough to lead them.

The master apparently accepts this explanation, for he bows to the ghostly creatures. The music roars in violent crescendo. The master takes off his dressing gown to move more freely and enters into a violent dance. His strange guests surround him like flies, encouraging him to increase the tempo of his movements. The master is tired and wishes to stop, but is helpless to do so. Finally he collapses in the stranger's arms.

One of the ladies encourages him to renew his dance, and he moves with her about the room as figures cloaked in white robes weave in and out between them. The orchestra sounds the music of the dance fiercely and relentlessly. The master of Tregennis can move no more. He falls to the floor, dying. The lady is held poised above him. He reaches out and is caught up in the arms of the ghostly creatures. He struggles helplessly in their grasp. Weird women gather close about him; the music cries out with piercing pathos. He is carried aloft.

For a brief moment the master manages to free himself. He rushes away from his attackers, running to the front of the stage to cling to the proscenium. He knows now who they are and that he must soon be one of them. The time for his own death in the haunted ballroom has come, and he is powerless to resist.

A clock begins to clang. The ghosts who have made him one of themselves form a final tableau, and he dies. The curtain falls. The strange player in black emerges with three creatures in white and across the front of the stage, in step with the striking clock, they carry the body of the master of Tregennis to his forebears.

Once more the curtain rises on the ballroom. Two footmen enter by the door, carrying lanterns. A butler follows them, and the three men search the room for their master. When they discover his body, his son, dressed in a white dressing gown similar to his father's, stumbles into the room. He hastens to his father and turns away in grief and terror. The master of Tregennis, his lifeless arm dangling in the air, is carried out by his two footmen.

Three women, evidently members of his family, try to comfort the boy. He accepts their condolences, but then turns away from them. They know what he is thinking—that he will be next. They leave him alone. The light that shone upon his father makes of his startled figure a frightening silhouette against the dark wall of the ballroom; he clutches at his throat in terror and acknowledges his destiny.

HELEN OF TROY

Comic ballet in three scenes, with prologue. Music by Jacques Offenbach. Choreography by David Lichine. Book by David Lichine and Antal Dorati. Scenery and costumes by Marcel Vertès. First presented by Ballet Theatre in Detroit, Michigan, November 20, 1942, with a cast headed by Irina Baronova as *Helen*, André Eglevsky as *Paris*, Jerome Robbins as *Hermes*, and Simon Semenoff as *Menelaus*.

This ballet is a comic treatment of the legend of Helen of Troy: how the beautiful queen deserted her aging husband, Menelaus, and sailed away with

Paris to far-off Troy. The music, by Offenbach, was arranged and orchestrated by Antal Dorati.

PROLOGUE: After a jubilant, rousing overture, the curtain rises on a mountain scene. A drop curtain depicts rocks and trees. Half a dozen sheep kneel about the youthful Paris, who is sleeping. The shepherd rises, yawns, stretches, and begins to dance. A lamb joins him, and Paris holds her lovingly in his arms. Now all the sheep sit in a semicircle about Paris as he displays his youthful vigor. They applaud him when the dance is over.

Hermes, messenger of the gods, enters, idly chewing an apple. Three goddesses accompany him. The great Zeus, apparently, has a problem. Each one of these goddesses, Hera, Pallas Athena, and Aphrodite, has claimed a golden apple inscribed "To the fairest," and since only one of them can finally possess the apple, the ladies have been brought before Paris. Hermes tells him he will judge for Zeus which is the fairest.

Paris doesn't have much trouble making up his mind. Hera is the oldest and a little too grimly determined. Pallas Athena can't take her nose out of a book. Aphrodite, the goddess of love, promises Paris that he shall have the fairest of all women for his wife, and the shepherd immediately rewards her with the golden apple. The sheep circle about them, and Paris starts to leave with Aphrodite. But he has forgotten the lamb, who runs up and reminds Paris not to forget her. Paris takes her by the hand, and all exit. Hermes is left alone, still eating his apple. He reaches up and pulls down the curtain.

SCENE ONE—THE COURT AT SPARTA: Under the patronage of Aphrodite, Paris has come to Greece. We are at the palace of Menelaus. The aged king sits on his throne as the court entertains him. His beautiful wife, Helen, dances before him. Paris watches her closely. This must be the woman Aphrodite promised him! When her dance is over, Helen runs to the throne and kisses Menelaus, but it is clear that she has eyes only for the strange shepherd.

She dances again, this time with garlands. Paris comes forward and supports her in the dance. Menelaus is preoccupied with court business and only waves to her from time to time. All the men of the court seek to partner Helen, but she always chooses Paris. The two lovers approach Menelaus. Helen kisses her husband, and the jealous old man shoves Paris aside.

Courtly couples in white dance before the king and queen. Helen is bored. When the time comes for Menelaus to dance before his court, she ridicules him like all the rest. His absurd exhibition is cut short by a cramp. Paris is amused and comes forward to dance. The brilliant strength and graceful ease of his dance dazzle the court. He kneels to Helen.

There follows another courtly entertainment, in which Paris' pet lamb participates. Helen is now sitting at Menelaus' feet. The old man has dozed off. Hermes jumps into his lap, and the king embraces him. Helen is delighted at the success of this idiotic ruse and joins Paris for a *pas de deux* in which they acknowledge their love for each other. Paris lifts her high, to his shoulders, and carries her across the stage.

Menelaus is warned that his country is at war. He wakes up, pushes Hermes off his lap, and tries to recover his dignity. He straightens his crown and staggers blindly across the stage. His men drive on the stage in a chariot, and Menelaus, hastily decked out in battle dress, drives off to battle. All wave to him. Hermes sits on the royal throne of Sparta.

Paris caresses Helen. The members of the court form a great semicircle, and Helen, in their midst, dances. Now Hermes presents Helen with a duplicate to the key to her chamber. Helen gives it to Paris, who kneels before her. Helen's lady in waiting presents another duplicate to another adorer of her mistress, Orestes. Now that the stage is set for further complications, Hermes, back on the throne, gestures in comic triumph.

SCENE TWO—HELEN'S BEDCHAMBER: Before a drop curtain, the lady in waiting hastily provides Orestes with a dress similar to her own. Then she peeks behind the curtain. She takes Orestes by the hand, and the curtain rises. We are in Helen's private apartment. There is a screen on the left; the darkened room is dominated by a great canopied bed.

Helen enters, dressed in diaphanous white. The two maids help her prepare for bed and go behind the screen. Now Orestes declares himself. Discarding the attire of a lady in waiting, he assures Helen of his love, embraces her, and forces her to dance with him. Helen protests. Hermes wanders in, reading a book. When he sees what's going on, he wonders where the devil Paris is. He draws his arm back as if to strike Orestes, and the intruder, stricken by this godlike gesture, falls to the ground. Hermes pushes him out of the room.

Helen sprays herself liberally with perfume and is ready now for her true lover. Hermes unlocks the door, and Paris comes in. His pet lamb scurries behind the screen as he takes Helen in his arms. Hermes starts to knit. At first he pays no attention to the lovers, but when their mutual demonstrations become passionate, he rises and discreetly places the screen in front of them. The screen begins to vibrate.

And who should come in at this point but good old Menelaus, back from the wars. He carries a bouquet of roses for Helen. He assaults Hermes and tells him to get out. Then he observes the trembling screen. He rushes behind the screen. Paris runs out, followed by Helen, disguised in the lamb's coat. The poor lamb shivers in her underwear as Menelaus pursues Paris vainly, dashing hither and thither about the room. Paris and the pet lamb escape. Hermes blows a policeman's whistle to direct the busy traffic, stands behind Menelaus, and Helen pushes her deluded husband over his back. She stands over him as Hermes sits knitting on her bed. The drop curtain falls.

SCENE THREE—THE PORT: Menelaus emerges from his wife's boudoir and weeps despairingly. Ladies of the court join him, wring out his wet handkerchief, and try to cheer him up.

The drop curtain rises on a seaside scene. Ladies of the court gambol about the beach. A girl enters, leading a faun on a leash. The faun cavorts across the beach obligingly among the ladies and leaps off into the wings when they have had enough.

Courtiers come onto the scene, followed by Helen. She dances, surrounded by all the sheep in Paris' flock, who lift her to their shoulders. Menelaus puffs in and pleads with her.

Now Hermes sails up in a great barge of war. He takes out a Yo-yo and plays with it adroitly as Helen and Paris are confronted by Menelaus. The music laughs and chortles, and all the courtiers gather for a razzle-dazzle dance of farewell to the lovers. Menelaus is carried helplessly above the swirling crowd, and before he knows what has happened, Paris and Helen have climbed into the barge and set sail for distant Troy. All wish them Godspeed save Menelaus, who vainly tries to board the vessel.

L'HISTOIRE DU SOLDAT
THE SOLDIER'S STORY

Narrative ballet in five scenes; to be read, played, and danced. Music by Igor Stravinsky. Words by C. F. Ramuz. Choreography by Ludmilla Pitoev. First presented at Lausanne, Switzerland, September 28, 1918, with Gabriel Rossel, George Pitoev, and Ludmilla Pitoev in the principal roles. Scenery and costumes by René Auberjonois. First presented in the United States by the League of Composers at the Jolson (now Century) Theatre, March 25, 1928. Pantomime by Michio Ito. Scenery and costumes by Donald Oenslager. Tom Powers was the *Reader;* Blake Scott and Lilly Lubell were the principal characters.

L'Histoire du Soldat is a composition for eight instruments, a narrator, and dancers. The small orchestra and the narrator are on stage with the dancers, who perform in a separate central area. The story is taken from an old Russian fairy tale which tells of a soldier who gives up his violin, the instrument that "speaks like his own heart," to the devil.

SCENE ONE — A WOOD: Before the action begins, the narrator tells us that there is a soldier who is going home to his village on leave. He has walked all the way.

The scene reveals a wood, through which there runs a stream. The soldier enters. From his gear he takes out a holy medallion, a snapshot of his girl back home, and a violin, his favorite personal possession. He begins to play, sitting idly by the stream.

The devil comes to him, disguised as a harmless elderly man. He asks if he may buy the violin. The soldier, who knows that the instrument is really a poor one, cannot understand; he does not want to sell it anyhow.

The man insists, and the soldier finally agrees to trade his violin for a book the man tells him is of great value. The soldier is illiterate and does not know whether this is true, but the man's claim that the book will surely make him rich convinces him that the exchange is a good one. The man persuades him to teach him how to play the violin and to visit his home for several days.

SCENE TWO—THE VILLAGE: The narrator informs us that Joseph, the soldier, visited the devil and then resumed his homeward march. But when he got home, no one welcomed him. His girl had married someone else and had two children, and his mother was so frightened of him she would not come near him.

The action is renewed. The devil, disguised now as a cattle merchant, stands in the center of Joseph's native village. Joseph, outraged at his unpleasant homecoming, blames the barter of his violin for the mysterious book on the stranger. He attacks him with a sword. The devil, unmoved, commands him to become a civilian and to find the valuable book. As he takes out the book, the devil takes out his violin.

The narrator goes on to tell us how Joseph became a wealthy man by following the lessons of the devil's book. He is wealthy but miserable, able only to take money for additional orders for business.

SCENE THREE—JOSEPH'S OFFICE: Joseph is seen behind a great desk, reperusing the devil's book. A ragged old woman, the devil in disguise, enters and tries to sell him junk from her scavenger's bag. She lays before him his holy medallion, the photo of his girl, and his violin. He demands to know the price of the violin. The old creature tells him he'd better try to play the violin first: maybe it doesn't work well. Joseph takes up the instrument, but though he bows the strings frantically, no sound emerges. The hag has disappeared. Joseph destroys the violin and the book he received for it from the devil.

SCENE FOUR—A FOREIGN LAND—THE PALACE: The march that heralded the beginning of the soldier's story is heard again, and the narrator tells us that Joseph has tried to begin life anew. After destroying the book, he abandoned his wealth and went to a new country near by. There, in Joseph's new land, the king's daughter is dying of an unknown disease. The king has promised that the man who cures her shall marry her, and Joseph hopes to do this. Briefly the devil appears, this time as a gentleman in evening dress.

Joseph is seen sitting in a room at the palace, trying to determine what he should do by consulting a deck of playing cards. The cards augur well for him, but he is certain that he has not escaped Satan.

The narrator interrupts and tries to persuade Joseph to put up everything he has and gamble, all or nothing, with the devil. The soldier agrees and sits down to a game of cards with the devil. Although the devil wins each draw, he becomes strangely tired. Joseph forces him to drink, and he passes out in a stupor. Joseph seizes his violin and plays upon it the old, familiar music.

The narrator now tells us that Joseph will surely cure the ailing princess. Joseph is seen playing his violin before the princess, who lies back on a couch. She is revived by the music and rises to dance with him. Joseph embraces the princess.

Satan, all disguise thrown off, enters and demands the violin. Desperately, on all fours, the devil tries to snatch the instrument. Joseph begins to play upon it. The devil dances to this music until he collapses. The princess and Joseph drag him away.

They return to talk of their love. The devil, from outside, vows vengeance. He indicates that if Joseph remains in the princess' kingdom, he will survive, but that if he goes beyond the borders of the land, he will again be Satan's victim.

Again the narrator intervenes. He tells us how the princess, wishing to know more about her beloved, persuades him to take her on a visit to his native village. He realizes that this trip outside the kingdom will be fatal, but he cannot resist her demand.

SCENE FIVE — THE VILLAGE : In this scene, the soldier's old village and the border of his new home are both seen. When Joseph crosses the border of the princess' kingdom, the devil attacks. The devil now plays upon the violin. The princess calls to Joseph, but he cannot answer. He is now the devil's perpetual slave.

ILLUMINATIONS

> Dramatic ballet in one act. Music by Benjamin Britten. Words from Arthur Rimbaud. Choreography by Frederick Ashton. Scenery and costumes by Cecil Beaton. Lighting by Jean Rosenthal. Soprano soloist, Angelene Collins. First presented by the New York City Ballet at the City Center, New York, March 2, 1950, with a cast headed by Nicholas Magallanes as the *Poet*, Tanaquil LeClercq as *Sacred Love*, Melissa Hayden as *Profane Love*, and Robert Barnett as the *Dandy*.

A sequence of danced pictures or charades, *Illuminations* was inspired by prose poems written in 1871–72 by the French symbolist poet Rimbaud and by certain incidents in the short, violent life of the poet. Rimbaud lived to be thirty-seven, but he wrote no poetry we know of after he was nineteen. What he wrote before then is contained principally in two works, of which *Les Illuminations* was the first.

The title of this book and its meaning relate not only to the poems, but to the poet. For it was Rimbaud's special idea that the poet should be a seer, a visionary, one who arrived at a new, fresh illumination through the disordering of the senses, one who participated fully in darkness in order to see the light. His poems recollect the process by which this light is discovered, and in them we see sudden flashes of light illuminating the darkness the poems enclose. Throughout the ballet, selections from *Les Illuminations* are sung in French.

FANFARE: The music begins with loud, strident cries from the strings. The curtain rises. About the stage, reclining in various postures, are mysterious white figures. All of them are asleep. In the center, in waistcoat, high white collar, and striped pants, lies the poet. The soloist sings:

"J'ai seul la clef de cette parade sauvage."

The poet rises, falls back, rises again, and wakes, wakes the sleepers, turning their drowsy bodies. Now he puts on a hat and encourages the strange people to dance. The soloist sings portions of these impressions of the poet:

"Ce sont des villes! C'est un peuple pour qui se sont montés ces Alleghanys et ces Libans de rêve! Des chalets de cristal et de bois se meuvent sur des rails et des poulies invisibles. Les vieux cratères ceints de colosses et de palmiers de cuivre rugissent mélodieusement dans les feux. Des fêtes amoureuses sonnent sur les canaux pendus derrière les chalets. La chasse des carillons crie dans les gorges. Des corporations de chanteurs géants accourent dans des vêtements et des oriflammes éclatants comme la lumière des cimes. Sur les plates-formes, au milieu des gouffres, les Rolands sonnent leur bravoure. Sur les passerelles de l'abîme et les toits des auberges, l'ardeur du ciel pavoise les mâts. L'écroulement des apothéoses rejoint les champs des hauteurs où les centauresses séraphiques évoluent parmi les avalanches. Au-dessus du niveau des plus hautes crêtes, une mer troublée par la naissance éternelle de Vénus, chargée de flottes orphéoniques, et de la rumeur des perles et des conques précieuses, la mer s'assombrit parfois avec des éclats mortels. Sur les versants, des moissons de fleurs grandes comme nos armes et nos coupes mugissent. Des cortèges de Mabs en robes rousses, opalines, montent des ravines. Là-haut, les pieds dans la cascade et les ronces, les cerfs tettent Diane. Les Bacchantes des banlieues sanglotent et la lune brûle et hurle. Vénus entre dans les cavernes des forgerons et des ermites. Des groupes de beffrois chantent les idées des peuples. Des châteaux bâtis en os sort la musique inconnue. Toutes les légendes évoluent et les élans se ruent dans les bourgs. Le paradis des orages s'effondre. Les sauvages dansent sans cesse la Fête de la Nuit. Et, une heure, je suis descendu dans le mouvement d'un boulevard de Bagdad où des compagnies ont chanté la joie du travail nouveau, sous une brise épaisse, circulant sans pouvoir éluder les fabuleux fantômes des monts où l'on a dû se retrouver."

Now the people leave the stage and the poet is alone. The music is quiet and expectant. The poet throws gold stardust into the air to the song:

"J'ai tendu des cordes de clocher à clocher; des guirlandes de fenêtre à fenêtre; des chaînes d'or d'étoile à étoile, et je danse."

Stars glow brightly on the backdrop as the poet seems to string pearls between the distant steeples.

Two women come to the poet. One is all in stark white—even her face is a white mask; the other, also in white, wears her clothes loosely, voluptuously. The pure white figure, Sacred Love, leaves the poet alone with her opposite. Profane Love and the poet join in a ferociously passionate dance to a new song:

> "Gracieux fils de Pan! Autour de ton front couronné de fleurettes et de baies, tes yeux, des boules précieuses, remuent. Tachées de lie brune, tes joues se creusent. Tes crocs luisent. Ta poitrine ressemble à une cithare, des tintements circulent dans tes bras blonds."

As the lovers embrace, they look up and see a parade enter, led by a drummer and a trumpeter. There follow two acolytes, a bishop, and a royal couple whose long trains are held out behind them. The parade moves to the center, and the royal pair are crowned king and queen by the bishop. They kneel together. The poet watches this procession and ceremony as if he couldn't believe it. The soloist sings:

> "Un beau matin, chez un peuple fort doux, un homme et une femme superbes criaient sur la place publique: 'Mes amis, je veux qu'elle soit reine!' 'Je veux être reine!' Elle riait et tremblait. Il parlait aux amis de révélation, d'épreuve terminée. Ils se pâmaient l'un contre l'autre.
> "En effet, ils furent rois toute une matinée, où les tentures carminées se relevèrent sur les maisons, et tout l'après-midi, où ils s'avancèrent du côté des jardins de palmes."

Finally the poet can bear it no longer. When the procession begins to leave the scene, he rushes upon it, throwing himself on the king's back. He knocks off the crowns of the royal pair and sends the whole parade packing. Alone, he takes up the king's crown and puts it on his head. Profane Love enters and throws herself at his feet. The poet ignores her. The girl grovels in the dirt for a moment, then reaches out her hands and tries to crawl up to his shoulders. The poet repulses her and begins to walk away, and the girl, refusing to give up her hold on him, is dragged along behind him. The poet, now enraged, strikes her in the face. She leaves the stage, promising vengeance. The poet lies at the front of the stage.

The scene darkens. Two spotlights show us the figure of Sacred Love, who enters with four men. The song is renewed as the poet lies dreaming:

> "Devant une neige, un Etre de beauté de haute taille. Des sifflements de mort et des cercles de musique sourde font monter, s'élargir et trembler comme un spectre ce corps adoré; des blessures écarlates et noires éclatent dans les chairs superbes.—Les couleurs propres de la vie se foncent, dansent, et se dégagent autour de la vision, sur le chantier.—Et les frissons s'élèvent et grondent, et la saveur forcenée de ces effets se chargeant avec les sifflements mortels et les rauques musiques que le monde, loin derrière nous, lance sur notre mère de

beauté,—elle recule, elle se dresse. Oh! nos os sont revêtus, d'un nouveau corps amoureux.

"O la face cendrée, l'écusson de crin, les bras de cristal! le canon sur lequel je dois m'abattre à travers la mêlée des arbres et de l'air léger!"

Supported by the four men, Sacred Love is turned around and around in graceful poses, lifted high above the stage, and carried across it as the men form a chariot beneath her. As the dream subsides, she is lifted off in a long, quiet rush toward the wings.

The poet rises. He tosses his crown away. The curious crowd that peopled the stage in the first scene now fills the stage. Its members grab the poet, toss him about, turn him upside down and attack him, to the words:

"Des drôles très solides. Plusieurs ont exploité vos mondes. Sans besoins, et peu pressés de mettre en oeuvre leurs brillantes facultés et leur expérience de vos consciences. Quels hommes mûrs! Des yeux hébétés à la façon de la nuit d'été, rouges et noirs, tricolorés, d'acier piqué d'étoiles d'or; des facies déformés, plombés, blêmis, incendiés; des enrouements folâtres! La démarche cruelle des oripeaux!—Il y a quelques jeunes,—comment regarderaient-ils Chérubin?—pourvus de voix effrayantes et de quelques resources dangereuses. On les envoie prendre du dos en ville, affublés d'un *luxe* dégoûtant.

"O le plus violent Paradis de la grimace enragée! Pas de comparaison avec vos Fakirs et les autres bouffonneries scéniques. Dans des costumes improvisés, avec le goût du mauvais rêve, ils jouent des complaintes, des tragédies de malandrins et de demi-dieux spirituels comme l'histoire ou les religions ne l'ont jamais été. Chinois, Hottentots, Bohêmiens, niais, hyènes, Molochs, vieilles démences, démons sinistres, ils mêlent les tours populaires, maternels, avec les poses et les tendresses bestiales. Ils interpreteraient des pièces nouvelles et des chansons 'bonnes filles.' Maîtres jongleurs, ils transforment le lieu et les personnes et usent de la comédie magnétique. Les yeux flambent, le sang chante, les os s'élargissent, les larmes et des filets rouges ruissellent. Leur raillerie ou leur terreur dure une minute, ou des mois entiers.

"J'ai seul la clef de cette parade sauvage."

The strange creatures chase the poet and surround him. Hidden for a moment in their midst, he is then lifted high above them. Profane Love enters to watch the scene with pleasure. Back in the distance we see the figure of Sacred Love soaring across the landscape. The poet is helpless and beckons to Profane Love for help. She laughs and orders one of the men to shoot the poet.

A man draws a pistol, aims it, and fires. The poet is wounded in his wrist, just as the real poet, Rimbaud, was wounded by his sometime mentor and guide, the poet Verlaine.

Profane Love, now wishing to be forgiven, falls at the poet's feet. He does not even look down at her. He grasps his wounded arm and steps over her body. Blood spills from the wound. The poet turns and slowly moves backward toward the transparent backdrop, where Sacred Love can still be seen in flight. The poet steps through the backdrop, the front of the stage darkens, all the curious people collapse again in sleep, and we see the hero walking alone beneath a blazing sun.

NOTES: The work of the chief choreographer of the Sadler's Wells Ballet, Frederick Ashton, *Illuminations* was the first ballet commissioned by the New York City Ballet of a foreign artist. Its success led to an exchange. In April 1950 *Ballet Imperial* (Tchaikovsky-Balanchine-Berman) was staged for the Sadler's Wells Ballet. Two years later Ashton returned to New York to create another ballet for the New York company, *Picnic at Tintagel*.

In reviewing its first performance, John Martin of the New York *Times* found *Illuminations* "a work of rare and delicate poetic beauty, a ravishingly romantic ballet," while Walter Terry of the *Herald Tribune* said of the principal dancers: "Nicholas Magallanes . . . was in every way perfect. His characterization, subtly, yet richly drawn, was notable for its emotional hues, for beauty and strength of style and motion . . . Melissa Hayden also gave a tremendous performance as the figure of Profane Love. It was wild, pagan and free in character and Miss Hayden danced it for all it was worth. Tanaquil LeClercq in the paler role of Sacred Love and elsewhere in the ballet danced beautifully, as did the other members of the large cast . . ."

INTERPLAY

Ballet in four movements. Music by Morton Gould (*American Concertette*). Choreography by Jerome Robbins. First presented by Billy Rose, in *Concert Varieties*, at the Ziegfeld Theatre, New York, June 1, 1945, with a cast headed by John Kriza, Janet Reed, and Jerome Robbins. First presented by Ballet Theatre at the Metropolitan Opera House, New York, October 17, 1945, with settings by Oliver Smith and costumes by Irene Sharaff; Janet Reed, John Kriza, and Harold Lang headed the cast of dancers.

Interplay is an American ballet for eight dancers: four boys and four girls. It has no subject matter and no locale; but directly the dancing and music begin, it is apparent that it could only be an American work. The setting is simple: a plain colored backdrop and wings of differently colored cloth. The costumes are informal. So is the music. Loud and brassy at the beginning, the score is overtly raucous and playful.

FIRST MOVEMENT—FREE PLAY: A boy dances out onto the stage. He is followed by three companions. He dances alone for a few seconds, showing off. The others join him. The boys take turns jumping over each other's backs and horsing around. They all end up lying on the floor with their legs in the air.

A girl enters. The boys sit and marvel at her. Three other girls follow, and now the boys are moved to action. They get up, take partners, and the four couples, one after the other, execute a number of turns in a quick, graceful, athletic fashion. The lead boy runs through, under the arms of the dancers, and takes them to the front of the stage. There are no footlights, and the modern jive motions of the couples are silhouetted against the backdrop.

Now the couples move back and form a wide circle. The boys toss the girls around, and the music becomes quieter as the dancers stand in a straight line. The dancers seem to be playing a game that they all understand. There is some competition among the couples in the execution of conventional pirouettes and arabesques, but the game isn't really that serious. They are all having a jazzy good time. They all clap hands, the boys roll the girls over their backs, and the first dance ends with the four boys sitting on the floor; their girls stand in back, holding their hands.

SECOND MOVEMENT — HORSEPLAY: After a brief pause, the music resumes. Though still modern in its rhythm, the melody now has a buoyant lightness. A few of the couples sit lazily on the stage; the others stand apart. One of the boys begins to dance alone. His solo is quietly comic, like the music, and amusingly impertinent in its imitation of some conventional movements in classic ballet. The dance increases in pace. The boy circles the stage, spins rapidly in the air, and finishes his solo. He kneels and opens his arms to two of the girls.

THIRD MOVEMENT — BYPLAY: The lights dim, and the piano begins a slow, sentimental blues. All the couples stretch and rearrange themselves about the stage. The lead boy and lead girl commence a *pas de deux*. Their dance is openly romantic, but has no particular intensity Love is a game, too, they seem to say. The boy lifts the girl high over his head as she maintains an open position, pushes her forward across the floor on her toes as if she were a toy cart, then holds her close. The girl wraps herself around the boy, then both sit down on the floor and hold hands, like two children sitting on the beach.

FOURTH MOVEMENT — TEAM PLAY: The light brightens; the music returns to a fast, vigorous tempo. Now the dance becomes a contest. Two of the boys choose sides, and the two sides go into huddles to decide on tactics. They line up opposite each other. All turn cart wheels, then soloists from the two sides try to outdo each other in complicated movements. The boys vie with one another to see who can do the most turns in the air without stopping. Two girls, one from each side, begin to turn around and around on point as the game comes to a heated close. All the boys and girls run back and turn about the stage in a circle. The girls dash forward to the footlights. The boys sprint after them. With the last crash of the music, the boys take a running fall on the floor and slide under the girls' legs. Black-out.

NOTES: *Interplay* has been a steady hit with ballet audiences, here in America, in Europe, and in South America, ever since its first performance by Ballet Theatre. At that time, Edwin Denby wrote in the New York *Herald Tribune* that *Interplay* "is of serious interest both for being young Robbins' second work and for being, of all ballets by American-trained choreographers, the most expertly streamlined in dance design . . . Robbins alone of our native choreographers has grasped at one stroke that the basis of ballet logic is a view of time and space as a closed entity. The time of a ballet is that specified by the musical architecture of its score and the space is the stage area as a static whole. The architectural frames of reference, so to speak, give to the mazes of a ballet its coherent and cumulative distinctness. And the formal distinctness in spacing and timing *Interplay* has in action are of serious ballet quality . . ."

Interplay is in the repertory of both Ballet Theatre and the New York City Ballet. The latter staged it on December 23, 1952, at the City Center, New York, in a production designed by Irene Sharaff and lighted by Jean Rosenthal. Janet Reed, Todd Bolender, Michael Maule, and Jacques d'Amboise were the principals.

LE JEUNE HOMME ET LA MORT
THE YOUNG MAN AND DEATH

> Dramatic ballet by Jean Cocteau. Music by Johann Sebastian Bach. Choreography by Roland Petit. Scenery and Costumes by Georges Wakhevitch. First presented by Ballets des Champs-Elysées at the Théâtre des Champs-Elysées, Paris, June 25, 1946, with Jean Babilée and Nathalie Philippart in the title roles. First presented in the United States by Ballet Theatre at the Metropolitan Opera House, New York, April 9, 1951, with the same cast.

This modern fable of love pictures the plight of a young man whose passion for a girl is requited only in death. The boy is the typical young romantic Parisian painter, thinking and dreaming only of the girl who does not love him: of the girl who never comes, but for whom he constantly waits. The ballet is performed to an orchestration of Bach's *Passacaglia and Fugue in C minor.*

The orchestra states the music's dominant theme deeply and softly. The curtain rises. The scene is a corner of a Paris garret. Dirty walls on both sides converge at the rear. In the center, a high stanchion supports a rafter.

A rope hangs down from the rafter, tied in a noose at the end. Alongside it stands an iron stove. There is a door at the left. The stark furnishings of the room—a bare table, a stool, half a dozen old wooden chairs—are illumined by the harsh light of a bare electric bulb shaded with newspapers. Against the right wall stands a cot, partially covered with a red silk cloth. A young man in paint-covered overalls lies sprawled back on the cot, smoking slowly, languidly, apparently relaxed. His body tightens, becomes tense. He looks at his watch, sits up. His eyes watch the door as he mashes out the cigarette; his feet move restlessly. The boy rises and moves toward the door, where he poses adroitly and turns swiftly in the air to indicate his increasing anxiety. When he has examined his watch again, he turns away angrily and throws himself on the cot.

The door opens slowly. A dark girl in a yellow dress and black gloves stands there in the doorway. Her feet vibrate against the floor arrogantly as she watches the boy across the room. There is a brief moment of recognition, and he runs across the room to leap to her side. He attempts to embrace the girl; she is reluctant, cold in his grasp. They begin to dance together around the room. The boy is indifferent to anything but the girl. They move rapidly and roughly, banging chairs aside. The girl dances with fierce stiffness, like a violent mechanical doll.

The girl pushes the boy away and sits down on a chair and crosses her legs. He stands in back of her, declaring his love for her with generous, open gestures. The girl ignores him. The boy tries to force her to dance with him again. The girl joins him for a moment, but it is apparent that he is not content merely to dance. The girl turns stiff in his embrace and pushes him to the floor. She dances over to the table. He jumps onto the table and crouches for an instant above her. The girl shoves him to the floor and sits nonchalantly against the table, watching him writhe on the floor.

The boy reaches out for a chair, pulls himself up, and sits with his back to the girl. She lights a cigarette. The smoke drifts over to him. He points his leg out toward her and rises, hypnotized. He moves toward her like a toy soldier, his movements imitating the quality of the girl's gestures. He stands close, his face against hers. The girl blows smoke in his face. The boy angrily knocks the cigarette out of her hand and stamps on it. Now the girl moves around the table, and he cannot seem to catch her. He decides on a more careful approach.

The girl sits in a chair, absolutely oblivious to him, as if she were at a cocktail party and he was only one of the many people who were quite naturally looking only at her. The boy takes a chair and walks it over beside her. He steps up on the chair, and the girl moves away. He chases after her and dances with bold, desperate leaps in the air, pleading for her love. The girl does not notice. He turns rapidly and comes close to her. The girl slaps him off fiercely, and he falls away in the slow motion of agony. Now he moves about the room frantically—back to the corner and to his love again.

Kneeling behind her, he embraces her legs. The girl wrenches herself free and pushes him away. The boy falls against the table.

He has lost control of his will and only wishes to be close to her. He lies on the floor and reaches out to caress her. She kicks him in the face savagely. His body reacts in agonizing, painful slow motion as his face falls against the floor and his feet describe a high arc in the air. Twice more he attempts to touch her, and twice more she kicks him away.

The boy rises and chases the girl back to the corner of the room. The music approaches a crescendo. They meet and move forward. The music softens. Suddenly the girl responds to the boy's embrace. She caresses his face softly; he is motionless in her gentle arms, oblivious to the violence they threaten. She leads him to a chair. The boy moves in a dream. He sits down, his head falls forward, and the girl raises his arm high in a wide arc of slow movement. She moves away. The boy seems to be asleep; his arm hangs pendulously over the back of the chair.

The girl moves a high stool to the foot of the post in the center of the room, steps up on it, and adjusts the noose that hangs from the rafter. Carefully she sets the noose swinging. Then she moves back to the boy. Her cold hands touch his neck. The boy wakens, startled. She twists his head around toward the noose. As he lifts his arms in terror, the girl pushes him backward. The chair clatters to the floor. The boy's foot trembles. The girl runs through the door, triumphant.

The boy leaps after her, but she has vanished. He takes a chair, swings it wide, and throws it against the wall. He jumps upon the table and turns briskly in his anger and fear, then falls, helpless. He rises. He is standing beside the table, and his line of sight crosses the swinging noose. He drags the table with him as he moves forward stiffly. His body arches back as he holds the table, and he topples to the floor. He rises, leaps boldly and assertively to regain his courage, and moves stiffly toward the noose. He grabs the stool and backs away, circling the post. His frantic, nervous shadow is seen reflected against both converging walls. Slowly, inevitably, he sets the stool down firmly at the foot of the post. He climbs up, fixes the noose about his neck, and pushes the stool away with his feet. The stage darkens. Two crossing beams of light are focused on his hanging body. His leg trembles spasmodically as he dies.

Mysteriously, the walls of the garret fall back and the night sky line of Paris is seen in the distance. The room is illumined by the light of the city. A woman wearing the white mask of death enters on the left from over the rooftops. Her arm points forward. As if by her command, the boy's body stirs. He releases the noose and slides down the post to stand beside her. The strange figure removes her mask and places it on the boy's face. Her own face is revealed as the face of the girl he loved. The girl points forward, and the boy moves magically through the wall before her. As the curtain falls, the two are seen moving against the rooftops of the dark sky line.

NOTES: *Le Jeune Homme et la Mort* was fully prepared and rehearsed before the music was chosen. At the first rehearsals the dancers worked to the rhythm of jazz recordings. Later a piano accompanied them with accented rhythms. After the dress rehearsal, the necessary seventeen-minute score was discovered: the dancers were told that they would dance the following night to the accompaniment of an orchestration of Bach's *Passacaglia and Fugue in C minor*.

This ballet has been the principal success of its two stars, Jean Babilée and Nathalie Philippart, who have danced it in Europe and throughout the United States. Anatole Chujoy, reviewing the first New York performance in *Dance News*, noted that the plot of the ballet "offers Babilée and Philippart an excellent chance to do some of the most charged and exciting acting-dancing seen here for a long while. If one may judge from one ballet, Jean Babilée ranks technically with the greatest male dancers of our generation. He has wonderful elevation, excellent turns, a good extension, great control over his body—especially remarkable in his sustained movements, extraordinary balance, and a tremendous reserve of power . . . His superior acting . . . is expressive in every detail . . ."

JEUX
GAMES

Ballet in one act. Music by Claude Debussy. Choreography by Vaslav Nijinsky. Book by Vaslav Nijinsky. Scenery and costumes by Léon Bakst. First presented by Diaghilev's Ballets Russes at the Théâtre des Champs-Elysées, Paris, May 15, 1913, with Tamara Karsavina, Vaslav Nijinsky, and Ludmilla Shollar. First presented in the United States by Ballet Theatre at the Center Theatre, New York, April 23, 1950, in a new choreographic version by William Dollar, with Nora Kaye, Igor Youskevitch, and Norma Vance. Scenery and costumes by David Ffolkes.

For his second ballet, the famous dancer Vaslav Nijinsky chose a modern subject. Today, when we are accustomed to ballets about garden parties (*Lilac Garden*) and sailors on liberty (*Fancy Free*), the new ballet without a modern subject is a rarity, but in 1913 the opposite was the case. Nijinsky was the first choreographer to create a ballet related to the modern world. His subject is love as it is revealed in a tennis game.

The curtain rises on a formal garden of a large estate. The sky is dark-blue; it is almost night. A tennis ball bounces onto the stage, and after it comes a young man leaping in pursuit. He is dressed in tennis clothes and carries a tennis racket, but is clearly somewhat bored with the game. He searches halfheartedly for the ball and welcomes the distraction of two girls who enter the garden. With the approach of night they, too, have left off a game of tennis.

The boy begins to flirt with the girls, at first casually, then more seriously. He dances with them playfully, as if he were continuing with each of them a game of tennis. After he has partnered the two girls singly, he dances with both of them together. He lies down on the grass between them and then, rising, touches their faces tenderly.

Now the boy does not know which girl to choose. He wants both; both are beautiful. The girls long for him to make a choice, but at the same time know how unhappy such a choice will make one of them.

Another tennis ball bounces in from the nearby court. The boy leaps to retrieve it, and the girls follow him as he abandons the game of love for tennis.

NOTES: *Jeux* was the second ballet created by Vaslav Nijinsky (his first had been *The Afternoon of a Faun*, 1912). It was revoluntionary in its modern subject matter and in its treatment of that subject; and it was also new in its music, which was, like that of the *Faun*, by Debussy. *Jeux* was never revived by Nijinsky. Contemporary efforts to recapture its original intention have not yet achieved success. Carl van Vechten once wrote that he remembered *Jeux* for the glissando with which Debussy's music begins "as the tennis ball bounces across the stage, followed by Nijinsky, who bounds across the broad stage of the Théâtre des Champs-Elysées in Paris in two leaps. These leaps are triumphs of dexterity, grace of motion, and thrill. They have given rise to the rumor that Nijinksy's element is the air."

JINX

Ballet in one act. Choreography by Lew Christensen. Music by Benjamin Britten (*Variations on a Theme by Frank Bridge*). Scenery by James Stewart Morcom. Costumes by Felipe Fiocca. First presented by Dance Players at the National Theatre, New York, April 24, 1942, with Janet Reed, Lew Christensen, and Conrad Linden in principal roles. Revised and presented by the New York City Ballet at the City Center, New York, November 24, 1949, with Janet Reed, Francisco Moncion, and Herbert Bliss in leading roles.

Jinx is a dramatic ballet about superstition, in particular a superstition that comes to dominate the lives of performers in a small circus troupe. The setting for the ballet is simple. Two white poles on either side of the stage reach up toward the center of an invisible tent. The back curtains are drawn aside slightly for an entrance to the circus ring. Gaily colored performing boxes stand in a pile on the left, and in the center of the stage, on top of one of these boxes, stands a young girl dressed in pink. Sitting at her feet is a young bareback rider who obviously admires her. He takes the girl's hands and turns her in arabesque slowly, as if they were performing before a quiet but attentive imaginary audience. He lifts her down, and the two change places. From above, he supports the girl as she continues her modest display. Then he pulls her up to him, and they embrace warmly but gently. They sit together for a moment, and the boy goes off.

A clown enters on the right and watches the girl. She does not notice his presence, but it is apparent that he, too, admires her. He dances for a moment, assuming attitudes that make him appear grimly sad, rather than pathetic. The girl gets up to leave, the clown approaches her, and she accidentally runs into him. He catches her before she can fall and holds her in his arms, but only for an instant, for the girl breaks away in terror at this intimacy and runs off. Two men, the ringmaster of the troupe and one of the wire walkers, have come in quietly and observed this scene with interest.

Three girls enter as these men turn and leave the ring. Two of the girls are bareback riders and they go through a rehearsal of their act. The grotesque clown joins the wire walker and the boy whom we saw first on the stage, and the three men turn cart wheels in a vigorous athletic routine. In the middle of one of their tricks, the clown bumps into the boy and he falls. The wire walker helps him up and looks long and suspiciously at the clown. From this point on, the clown is Jinx to the whole troupe.

The ringmaster runs in, and, at a flourish of his whip, the company goes into an ensemble dance. They all exit, and through the entrance to the ring walk three girls in long capes. Their backs are to the audience. One by one, they turn and perform brief specialty numbers. The first girl drops her cape, to be revealed as the Tattooed Lady; the second is the muscled Strong Lady; and the third girl, the Bearded Lady, conceals her face as long as possible with a large orange ostrich feather. They dance together briefly, put their capes back on as if they were great ladies, and walk off in a stately fashion.

Next the bareback riders put on their act. The ringmaster stands in the center, and around and around him the two girls and the boy ride their imaginary horses. They finish and bow. Now Jinx is rolled in on a wheelbarrow, where he sits smelling a bouquet of rotten flowers and vegetables. The wire walker presents parasols to his two female partners, and in a straight line across the stage each does a turn on an imaginary wire. The lovely young girl in pink displays her skill first. Jinx climbs up on the boxes to watch her performance more closely. The girl is nervous at his nearness, but finds reassurance in the presence of the boy she loves, who stands at the other end of the wire. Jinx cannot take his eyes off her; after each of the wire walkers has done a turn and the three have begun their finale, his attention grows intense. Suddenly the girl slips and begins to fall. She is caught in the nick of time, and Jinx rushes to comfort her. He touches her, and the frightened girl jerks away from him. The bareback rider takes up the ring-master's whip and chases Jinx out of the ring.

Now the entire troupe is thrown into confusion and terror. Jinx runs in. The boy is cracking the whip close behind him. They run around the group at top speed until Jinx stumbles and falls. The boy brings his whip down on him, lashing the clown over and over again to rhythmic chords from the orchestra. The troupe steps back and turns away in horror as the clown curls up in agony, straightens out, and, with a final spasmodic tremble, dies. The Bearded Lady comes to him and grieves for him in a slow dance that reveals her pathetic attachment. The Tattooed Lady and the Strong Lady try to comfort her, but she is inconsolable. The boy brings in the wheel-barrow, and when Jinx is placed on it, the troupe forms a procession. They march slowly behind the body, bowing their heads rhythmically. When they have placed the body high up on the boxes, the Bearded Lady collapses and all bow their heads.

The music now becomes ghostly. The company senses that something is wrong and turns to look at the body. It is not there. They separate the boxes and take them down, but Jinx has disappeared. As they gesticulate in astonishment, Jinx enters from the other side of the stage, where they cannot see him. He walks stealthily to pick up the forgotten whip and cracks it at the feet of the boy. Everyone turns and steps back in fright. Jinx follows them and, cracking the whip in the center of the ring, forces them to dance around him. He urges them to dance faster and faster, and gradually the whole troupe collapses from exhaustion. Jinx then revives them with a beseeching gesture, and all leave the stage but the boy and the girl. The boy holds the girl up and lifts her high over his head, but she cannot stand by herself. She stands on point for a moment, but falls forward over his sup-porting arm in an attitude of complete and pathetic helplessness. The boy himself loses his strength and dies. Jinx takes the girl's hands to claim her, but at his touch she, too, expires, falling across her lover's body. The rest of the circus troupe has come in and looks on this scene with dread. The clown turns and stares at them intently without moving. A jinx is something you cannot kill, he seems to say, and the curtain falls slowly.

JOB

Masque for dancing in eight scenes. Music by Ralph Vaughan Wil-liams. Choreography by Ninette de Valois. Book by Geoffrey Keynes. Scenery and costumes by Gwendolen Raverat. Wigs and masks by Hedley Briggs. First presented by Camargo Society at the Cambridge Theatre, London, July 5, 1931, with Anton Dolin as *Satan* and Stanley Judson as *Elihu*. First presented in the United States by the Sadler's

Wells Ballet at the Metropolitan Opera House, New York, November 2, 1949, with scenery and costumes by John Piper. Robert Helpmann was *Satan* and Alexis Rassine was *Elihu*.

The subtitle of this ballet, *Being Blake's Vision of the Book of Job*, tells us that this "masque for dancing" is based on the *Illustrations to the Book of Job* that William Blake published in 1825. The ballet's book is based directly on Blake's twenty-one engravings, as is its music; and the choreography, in its groupings and tableaux, aims at a projection of Blake's imagination into the theatre.

SCENE ONE: Before a decorative back cloth Job sits with his family in a group on the right. With him are his wife, his seven sons, and three daughters. Job is content, materially prosperous, with no complaint in the world. He and his wife watch as his children—first the boys, then the girls, then all together—perform a light pastoral dance which symbolizes in its ordered balance and harmony the respect and love that bind the family together.

Night begins to fall. The family gathers about Job, and he gives thanks on this day for his earthly blessings. His children pray with him. There is no servility in their attitude toward their father. Prayer is natural to them as it is to him. Job and his wife bid the children good night, and the parents are left alone. They sleep.

Satan enters. His spirit hovers over Job and his wife, and their sleep is disturbed. Satan invokes evil dreams for this good man and his wife, appealing to heaven that Job's faith be tested. As Satan makes his appeal, heaven is depicted before us by a broad, high flight of steps at the top of which sits the Godhead, Job's spiritual self. The children of God dance before the Godhead, moving between him and Satan, who rests below. The Godhead gestures toward Satan, to include him in his family, but Satan will not be one of them. He proposes to Job's spiritual self that Job's material self be tested by temptation. The Godhead consents, and Satan, satisfied, leaves the scene, which darkens as the children of God pay homage to their king.

SCENE TWO: When the lights come up, the scene again is heaven. Satan is alone, standing before the throne of the Godhead. Delighted with the opportunity to tempt the faithful Job, he commences a triumphant dance, demoniac in its impudent power, frightening in its strength. His dance over, he leaps to the throne. His leg coils beneath him and he looks out over the scene gloatingly. We think of Milton's lines:

High on a Throne of Royal State, which far
Outshon the wealth of Ormus and of Ind,
Or where the gorgeous East with richest hand
Showrs on her Kings Barbaric Pearl and Gold,
Satan exalted sat . . .

The children of Job enter, observe Satan in his exaltation, and gather together in a group, anticipating the trouble to come.

SCENE THREE: We return to the first scene, but now we see Job's family as Satan would wish us to see it. Job's sons and their wives and his daughters are wining and dining in an evil bacchanal, yielding to temptations of the flesh. Satan descends from the throne he has usurped and kills the children of Job.

SCENE FOUR: Now we see enacted the terrible dreams that Satan causes Job and his wife to experience in their sleep. Visions of war, pestilence, and famine appear to torment the God-fearing pair.

SCENE FIVE: Satan's worst is yet to come. Three messengers come to Job and dance before him. They inform him of the death of his children and the loss of all his material goods. Satan enters briefly to warn Job of his end and disappears. Three Comforters, insidious creatures of Satan, replace their leader and attempt to insinuate themselves into Job's confidence. They pretend at first to be sympathetic, to grieve with him over his loss, then they rail at him. Job cannot contain his grief and cannot understand that these things can be visited upon him. He rebels, as if crying out, "Let the day perish wherein I was born." He appeals to heaven, but when heaven opens before him, he sees Satan on the throne. Dark angels are gathered about Satan.

SCENE SIX: A handsome young man, Elihu, pure and beautiful in his simple holiness, appears to Job and in a dance indicates to the old man his error in accusing God of injustice. Job comes to see that he has done wrong and comprehends his sin of complacent materialism. Elihu is kind to him. Again Job appeals to heaven, and this time he sees the Godhead on the throne, surrounded by angels.

SCENE SEVEN: Satan reappears before the throne of the Godhead, claiming that Job has failed the test and demanding the fruits of his victory over him. The Godhead orders Satan to come to him. As he draws near to the throne, Satan kneels and kisses his flowing robe. The Godhead will not endure this absurd flattery. He extends his arm, and Satan rises to fall back, full-length, down the great flight of steps tumbling into darkness.

SCENE EIGHT: Again, as in Scene One, Job and his family rest together, but this time—in realization of spiritual, rather than material, wealth—Job blesses his wife and his children with new meaning.

JONES BEACH

Ballet in four parts. Music by Jurriaan Andriessen. Choreography by George Balanchine and Jerome Robbins. Lighting by Jean Rosenthal. First presented by the New York City Ballet at the City Center, New York, March 9, 1950, with a cast headed by Maria Tallchief, Tanaquil

LeClercq, Melissa Hayden, Beatrice Tompkins, Yvonne Mounsey, Nicholas Magallanes, Herbert Bliss, Jerome Robbins, William Dollar, Todd Bolender, and Roy Tobias.

Although this ballet has no specific plot, its four movements picture in a general way the different interludes in a typical summer's day at New York's most famous beach. It is Sunday. Dozens of girls and boys lie about the beach in bright bathing suits lazily sunning themselves. Some of them get up and play. They dance. One of the boys tries to flirt with one of the girls. He chases her; she runs off. Soon the girl comes back. The boy pretends not to notice her. This time she chases him. The whole group joins in a vigorous athletic ensemble. They run off.

A boy enters, carrying a girl whom he has rescued from the deep water close in his arms. The girl's body is limp; her head falls forward on her knees. When the boy moves her, we see that she is unaware of his touch. He moves her patiently, unhurriedly, in his arms. Gradually the girl revives. She shakes the boy's hand in gratitude. Then she pretends to collapse. She falls limply into the boy's arms. He carries her out.

Three boys enter. They frolic about the beach, then lie down to rest in the sun. They are plagued by mosquitoes—seven small girls who leap over them in sharp, pointing attitudes. The boys try to slap them away, but the mosquitoes are only encouraged by this resistance and persist in biting them. The boys give up and leave the scene, followed by the triumphant insects.

A group of bathers enter. Couples group themselves about invisible fires, cook hot dogs, smear them with mustard, and eat them in rolls. One of the boys introduces his girl to another boy. The two lift her high, and the girl, her body curved in a swan dive, is carried rapidly across the stage. Other girls are carried similarly, and the stage is filled with figures simulating diving and swimming. The tempo of the music changes, and the entire ensemble joins in a furiously rapid dance to pounding drums.

KHADRA

Ballet in one act. Music by Jean Sibelius. Choreography by Celia Franca. Scenery and costumes by Honor Frost. First presented by the Sadler's Wells Theatre Ballet at the Sadler's Wells Theatre, London, May 27, 1946, with Sheilah O'Reilly as *Khadra* and Anne Heaton and Leo Kersley as the *Lovers*. First presented in the United States by the Sadler's Wells Theatre Ballet at the Portland Auditorium, Portland, Oregon, with Sheilah O'Reilly in the title role and Svetlana Beriosova and Michael Hogan as the *Lovers*.

Khadra is a ballet without a plot, a ballet of impressions based on Persian miniatures. Khadra is a young girl who has had little experience with life. In the ballet, she emerges from her isolation and is confronted for the first time with the colorful beauties of life in the outside world. The ballet is set to the suite *Belshazzar's Feast* by Sibelius.

The curtain rises on a scene of splendid and varied color. A great transparent screen stretches across the back, behind which we can discern a magical landscape. On the right is a decorative high platform, with a long ramp leading up to it on the left and steps descending from it on the right.

Khadra, a lovely young girl dressed in orange, is mysteriously drawn to this scene. She herself is a child of the East, but the beauty of this scene astonishes her. The folk who people the scene dazzle her still more. The richness of their costumes and their natural beauty are completely unfamiliar to her, and she finds only in a lady carding wool any resemblance to her ordinary life.

Sitting on the platform above the multitude are two lovers in white. As three girls dance a *pas de trois*, the girl in white descends. Her lover follows her, and they dance a *pas de deux* to slow Oriental music. Their attitude toward each other is formal, yet sweet, and their gestures are considerate, with measured affection. They kneel together on the right.

Two musicians enter and go to the top of the platform. The man in white dances a brief variation as the colorful folk leap around him. His lady rejoins him; he lifts her high over his head and sets her down gently. The music quietens and the scene grows dark.

A bright spotlight shines on Khadra, and she dances. Two Oriental processions enter to dazzle her further. The girl in white is seen walking up the ramp in the back, toward the platform. There she is lifted off into the arms of men who await her below. Khadra is held high above a tableau of all the romantic figures.

The man in white appears on the ramp. He gestures to his love below, and she holds out her arms to him longingly. He comes down the steps on the right, joins her, and they dance briefly together.

Now all the dancers join hands and form a semicircle about the enchanted Khadra. They rise, circle her, move faster and faster. The circle is broken, and the man in white ascends to the platform. His lady and Khadra join him there, and the young girl looks down to see all the people below kneeling to her and the lovers. She bows to them in gratitude, and the curtain falls.

LADY OF THE CAMELLIAS

Dramatic ballet in four scenes. Music by Giuseppe Verdi. Choreography by Antony Tudor. Scenery and costumes by Cecil Beaton. Lighting by Jean Rosenthal. First presented by the New York City Ballet at the City Center, New York, February 28, 1951, with Diana Adams,

Hugh Laing, Vida Brown, Brooks Jackson, and John Earle in the principal roles.

Paris in 1848 is the setting of this romantic ballet. Based on the novel of the same name by Alexandre Dumas, *fils*, it pictures in one act the tragic passion of a woman of the world for a man younger than herself, and the fabulous society that allows her love to be misunderstood. Marguerite Gautier, the Lady of the Camellias, romantically exposes this world as her love flourishes and dies.

SCENE ONE—PARTY ''CHEZ PRUDENCE'': Low, threatening music, interrupted by blasts foreshadowing fatal doom, is played by the orchestra before the curtain rises. As the scene is revealed, the orchestra changes to a soft, mellifluous dance melody and we see five couples dancing leisurely, but happily, in an ornately decorated room. Two high French windows on each side are draped with heavy red brocade; in the back, three windows look out on to a balcony. A high white ceiling, embellished with designs, hangs over the dark-green walls. The people in the room, in their rich velvet gowns and uniforms, dance formally. Their hostess is Prudence, a woman whose ebullient good spirits are momentarily suppressed by the formality of her party.

Marguerite Gautier enters with Monsieur le Comte de N—. The dance stops, and everyone moves forward to greet them. Marguerite is dressed in white; camellias cover her dress at the breast; there is a camellia in her hair. She is a woman aware of her own beauty, but one who displays it innocently, like a child. She acknowledges the greetings of the women. The count, who follows her closely, is obviously an unwilling guest, and Marguerite is ill at ease lest he embarrass her. These are her friends. She pats the count's cheek. He turns with her as she greets Prudence fondly. He bows to the woman somewhat coldly. Marguerite leaves him and dances briefly with the men, all of whom are eager for her favor.

Armand Duval enters quietly on the right. Before greeting Prudence, he watches the group. His eyes become fixed on Marguerite, dancing blithely from partner to partner. He moves toward her as the count leaves the room, followed by four of the ladies. Prudence steps between Armand and Marguerite and introduces them. She smiles archly, as if she had planned that the couple should meet. Armand is motionless—he has never seen anyone more lovely; Marguerite looks at him with considered appraisal. She has never seen the strange dark young man before and wonders who he can be. She begins to dance alone before him. Several couples re-enter the room.

Marguerite's dance but verifies her charm to Armand. He had not known that one woman could seem so worldly and appear so young. Suddenly the music of her dance pauses; the strings are plucked warningly. Marguerite stands close to Armand and her movement falters. She coughs;

she looks at her hand. The body that had seemed vibrant and strong in movement relaxes against her will; we see that she is ravaged by tuberculosis, a disease for which there is (in 1848) no cure. Armand senses her trouble and approaches to comfort her, but Prudence compels him to leave the room with the other guests. She exits too.

Marguerite has gained control over herself. Armand returns, running to hold her as she comes out of a rapid turn. He holds her softly, and she falls forward over his arms, close to the floor, still exhausted from her attack. She rises and bows to Armand, thanking him for his compassion. He kneels before her. She kisses his hand. Now the two begin to dance together to a deep, flowing melody. Their dance is slow, Armand assisting almost every one of Marguerite's movements. She discovers in his eyes more than pity. She leans against him contentedly. The music becomes abruptly brisk. Prudence runs in and breaks them apart, warning Marguerite. She takes Armand aside. The count enters and goes directly to Marguerite. The six couples dance. The count bows to Prudence, as if he were doing her a favor, and takes his mistress off.

Armand turns in despair: he has no sooner found his love than he is abandoned. Marguerite hurries back into the room. She runs over to him, spins happily, and the two rush out into the night. The orchestra sounds a crescendo of fulfillment. Prudence and her guests stare after them, astonished and still. Gradually each of the guests turns to his partner, and the couples circle off into the wings as the great French windows are pulled back to make way for their dance. The lights go out.

SCENE TWO — IN THE COUNTRY — TWO MONTHS LATER: Light comes up slowly. All the windows have disappeared; light penetrates through the ceiling; dark trees are visible at the back and on both sides. Marguerite and Armand enter, hand in hand, on the left. Now Marguerite wears a cool white summer dress; one camellia is pinned to the bodice. They dance a love duet. She rests at Armand's feet, he points off into the distance, their hands join, they embrace. They dance youthfully and joyfully. Armand pushes Marguerite away from him unseriously, lifts her, and kisses her hand. The dance becomes ecstatic as the lovers reveal their passion in movement.

The music sounds a warning. Marguerite sees that a stranger is approaching. Armand's back is turned. She pretends that she is cold and sends him for her cape: she suspects that she knows who the stranger is. He comes up to her, and Marguerite bows before her lover's father. She is humble before him, innocent, in love, and eager to please. Monsieur Duval, however, is insensitive to everything but his son's welfare; he is aware of Marguerite's reputation. He stands between her and the absent Armand and shakes his head at his son's situation. Marguerite tries to plead with him, but he rebuffs her, holding his hand out to push her away from him and his son. She turns daringly in defiant hope. He threatens again, and Marguerite gives up. She bows to him, her hand on her heart, and he leaves. Marguerite, remembering that Armand will soon return, hurries off. He comes in with her cape, looks about, misses her, and turns around and around slowly as he waits. Black-out.

SCENE THREE—PARIS—SEVERAL MONTHS LATER: We see a room much like the first, but more resplendent. It is a public room, with a gaming table at the back. The scene is lighted first by four candelabra, which are carried in by the guests. Prudence is among them. The five couples of the first scene dance until Prudence, weary of the idle pleasure, motions them all toward the gaming table. Armand enters and stands near them. Marguerite comes in on the other side, escorted by the count. The count looks across at Armand as if he knew everything about him; he looks down at Marguerite, trusting her. They greet Prudence.

Now dressed in black, her camellias coldly white against her flesh, Marguerite is visibly ill. She moves over to the table with the count, terrified at Armand's audacity in returning to her after she has disavowed her love for him and moved by the possibility that he might not have believed her. She turns away from the table to join Armand; the count gestures for her to return to his side. She goes obediently. The count becomes preoccupied with his cards, Prudence moves close to him, and Marguerite comes up to Armand. He turns away from her; she turns him back. As they dance together slowly, Marguerite seems to persuade Armand of her sincerity; by the quality of their motion, we are reminded of their happiness in the second scene.

Marguerite moves to rejoin the count at the table. A muffled drum beats, and Armand seizes her, and they dance with heated passion. The count looks at them, then looks back at his cards. Then he walks over to Marguerite quickly, carrying in his hands a diamond necklace. Marguerite and Armand stand away; the count puts the necklace about her throat. At its cold touch, Marguerite trembles.

The count challenges Armand to a duel at cards. All but Marguerite go to the table. Cards are dealt out to her two lovers. Armand wins and demands payment. The count angrily presents him with a handful of bank notes, turns his back, and walks out. Armand goes over to Marguerite. She reaches out expectantly. Armand thrusts the count's money into her hand in payment for her love. Marguerite faints. He holds her fiercely, kisses the diamonds at her throat, and abandons her to her friends. They take up the candelabra and help Marguerite to the door as the lights go out.

SCENE FOUR—MARGUERITE'S BEDROOM: A large bed covered with red velvet dominates this bare room. Marguerite, dressed in a clinging, flowing nightdress, walks slowly across the room on point. She stops, poses helplessly, and falls at the foot of the bed. She rises and limps to the windows at the back, comes forward, kneels, and looks out the window on the right.

Armand enters. She approaches him hesitantly, her arms moving out loosely in inarticulate welcome. He takes her hands, and she rests her head on his shoulder. Armand grasps her body tightly then and lifts her up. Marguerite wilts in his arms and seems unable to stand; her body grotesquely reflects her approaching death. Armand kneels before her as she rises and attempts to walk. Marguerite uses her lover's extended arm for support and guide. She reaches the foot of the bed. Armand holds her hands. Marguerite rises high, falls back face downward, dead. Armand moves away from the bed in terror and grief, controls himself, moves back, turns her over gently to see her face, and looks upon her. The curtain falls.

NOTES: *Lady of the Camellias* was the first work created by Antony Tudor for the New York City Ballet. John Martin of the New York *Times* called it "far and away the most substantial creation Mr. Tudor has given us in years," while Lillian Moore reported in *The Dancing Times* that "Tudor has long been an acknowledged master of the narrative ballet, and his *Lady of the Camellias* confirms this reputation. The lyrical quality of movement so typical of his work is perfectly adapted to the romantic theme . . ."

The music by Verdi, selected by the choreographer for this work, was drawn from the less familiar works of that composer. The scenery and costumes by Cecil Beaton were first used for a ballet treatment of *Camille* by the Original Ballet Russe in 1946.

LILAC GARDEN

Dramatic ballet in one act. Music by Ernest Chausson. Choreography by Antony Tudor. Setting and costumes by Hugh Stevenson. First presented by the Rambert Ballet Club at the Mercury Theatre, London, January 26, 1936. Maude Lloyd, Hugh Laing, Peggy van Praagh, and Antony Tudor were the principals. First presented in the United States by Ballet Theatre at the Center Theatre, New York, January 15, 1940, with Viola Essen, Hugh Laing, Karen Conrad, and Antony Tudor in the principal roles.

This ballet is a tragedy of manners. It portrays the problem of a young woman who is about to marry a man she does not love. The time is the latter part of the Victorian era. It does not occur to the girl that her marriage can be put off: that she can escape from its "convenience." *Lilac Garden* depicts her mute acceptance in the kind of world where confession of any difficulty would be impossible. The drama of the ballet arises from a social situation that seems to demand confession and release.

The name of the girl is Caroline. She is giving a party for all of her friends and relations before the wedding. The scene is a lilac garden; the time is evening. The music is Chausson's *Poème*, for violin and orchestra.

When the curtain rises, Caroline and the man she must marry are standing together in the center of the garden. Giant shrubs of lilac surround the small open space. The light is misty. The girl wears a long white dress and white flowers in her hair. Her fiancé wears a formal suit with a long, formal coat reaching to his knees. There is a boutonniere in his buttonhole. They are a handsome couple, but each is preoccupied; they seem to have nothing to say to each other, no gestures to make. The man looks off to the left as if he were searching for someone. On the right, Caroline's lover enters. As she sees the man she really loves, the girl motions him away. The dark young man in uniform turns away. Caroline takes her fiancé's arm and they walk off, side by side. She glances back over her shoulder as they disappear. Another guest arrives at the party, a woman in a slate-blue dress. This is the former mistress of Caroline's husband-to-be. Other women come onto the scene. Caroline re-enters. She greets the newcomer. She does not know that this woman loves her fiancé. Now Caroline is alone. She moves backward toward the right. Her lover emerges; she falls back against him. He slips his arms under hers, and the two begin to dance. Their steps are so in harmony that it is apparent they have danced together many times before. Now the occasion is different. Caroline nervously looks to left and right whenever they pause in motion.

The woman in blue, her back turned, moves ominously across the back of the garden. The boy kisses Caroline's hand. The girl draws her hand back quickly; the woman in blue turns around. Caroline nervously introduces her two guests. Her hand moves to her lips; perhaps she should have kept them apart. The three dance forward together. As soon as she dares, Caroline draws her lover aside, and they dance away. Two men leap onto the stage and exit with the woman in blue.

Caroline re-enters, alone. She dances plaintively to the threnody of the violin's romantic theme. She holds her hand to her forehead in a gesture of hopelessness. As a group of her guests disturb her solitude, the girl moves her hand slightly, pretending that she is smoothing her hair. The melody mounts in intensity. The guests leave as two of the girls are lifted high by their escorts. Caroline pirouettes desperately toward the other side of the garden. Her lover appears while she turns frantically, and he catches her in his arms. He lifts her high above him, then the two kneel together. Then Caroline is afraid, suddenly, and hurries off.

Three couples and a girl come into the garden. Caroline's lover takes the girl for a partner, and the couples separate and bow, preparatory to a formal dance. Caroline disturbs the pattern by entering swiftly and dancing down the line between the couples. She moves off to the right.

The woman in blue joins the couples. She is searching for Caroline's fiancé, her former lover. By common instinct, the other women turn away and leave the garden. The woman bows to Caroline's lover. He turns away and follows the other men off. One man is attracted to the woman and remains until it is apparent that she will not notice him.

ing glory, Horace Armistead has provided a setting that actually participates in the drama by its subtly authoritative establishment of the mood and the mores of the action."

Alicia Markova, Nora Kaye, Diana Adams, and Alicia Alonso have all danced the part of Caroline. Maria Tallchief danced the part of the other woman in guest appearances with Ballet Theatre in 1949. Tanaquil LeClercq and Yvonne Mounsey have danced it in the New York City Ballet revival. Hugh Laing and Antony Tudor resumed their customary roles in first performances of this revival; Tudor's role has been taken since by Brooks Jackson.

MADEMOISELLE FIFI

Comic ballet in one act. Music by Theodore Eduard Dufare Lajart, arranged by Samuel Grossman. Choreography by Zachary Solov. Scenery by Peter Larkin. Costumes by Helene Pons. First presented by the Slavenska-Franklin Ballet at John Hancock Hall, Boston, Massachusetts, October 13, 1952, with Alexandra Danilova, Roland Vazquez, and Marvin Krauter.

Mademoiselle Fifi is a "capsule French farce" that displays the familiar romantic triangle of this form of entertainment. The time is the 1890s; the place, Paris. The scene is a dressing room.

The occupant of the dressing room is a great star, a tightrope-walker champion, a dancer, a great beauty. She has been the toast of the town and is accustomed to everyone's being in love with her. She likes everyone to be in love with her.

Mademoiselle Fifi's current love is a handsome young man, who adores her passionately. The boy's father, however, learning of his son's liaison with the entertainer, is determined to break it up.

He calls in Fifi. She is delighted to see him; she is delightful to him. Soon the father has lost all thought of upbraiding her for ruining his son. He is in love with Fifi himself!

MADROÑOS

Ballet in one act. Music orchestrated by Ivan Boutnikoff from works by Moskowski, Yradier, and others. Costumes by Castillo of Elizabeth Arden. First presented by the Ballet Russe de Monte Carlo at the City Center, New York, March 22, 1947, with a cast headed by Nathalie Krassovska, Frederic Franklin, and Leon Danielian.

This ballet has no theme beyond its Spanish genre of dancing. Its title is derived from the pompons on the girls' costumes. There are five tableaux. There is no scenery.

A trumpet blares forth, and twelve girls in splendid Spanish costumes dance with their castanets. They form various geometrical figures in small groups, moving to a staccato rhythm. A dashing cavalier enters at the rear and strides forward for the second tableau. His costume is white; shiny black epaulets grace his shoulders; pink ribbons encircle his calves. The girls move toward him. Two of them lift him high, and he beats his legs in the air. Black-out.

The lights come up slowly to the melody of a violin. Girls lie about the stage lazily. They gradually rise. Two men, grotesque in their deformities, stand at the rear. The ballerina, La Niña del Oro, enters in a dress of red velvet draped with black lace and a white mantilla about her black hair. The two men lift her. She is taken off and returns to pose on the shoulder of one of the men. The lights go down as she is poised high. Now the ballerina dances with the cavalier, who carries her off into the wings. He returns alone, to stomp with simulated impetuosity, and waves his handkerchief in the air. He smells its perfume, is enamored of himself, and departs.

Six men—Los Bastoñeras—enter, carrying sticks which they click together in the air. They are joined by the twelve girls, who sound their castanets. The finale begins. The cavalier enters, executes brilliant leaps and beats, and kneels before the ballerina. They dance together, as three of the girls in the back swing back and forth on sticks held by the men.

The ballerina and her partner leave the stage, and the two old men perform a quasi-comic dance before the group. When the principal dancers return, they are carried by the group. They dance together briskly when they are released, the entire ensemble joins in, and the ballet finishes.

METAMORPHOSES

Ballet in four parts. Music by Paul Hindemith. Choreography by George Balanchine. Costumes by Karinska. Lighting by Jean Rosenthal. First presented by the New York City Ballet at the City Center, New York, November 25, 1952, with Tanaquil LeClercq, Todd Bolender, and Nicholas Magallanes in principal roles.

Metamorphoses is a musical ballet with costumes and settings that change from one part of the ballet to the next. The costumes do not represent any particular type of people, or even a particular type of animal. They are merely intended, like the movement of each part, to symbolize the metamorphoses of the different parts of the score. The ballet has nothing to do with Kafka's short story "Metamorphosis."

Hindemith's *Symphonic Metamorphosis on Themes of Carl Maria von Weber*, the ballet's score, uses and changes original themes from Weber's *Piano Music for Four Hands* in the first, third, and fourth movements. The principal theme of the third movement Weber took from an authentic Chinese melody found in Rousseau's *Musical Dictionary*.

The first part of the ballet, "Allegro," is danced by the ensemble. The second part, "Scherzo," is danced by the ensemble, led by two principals, a girl and her partner. The third, "Andantino," is a *pas de deux* for the girl and another partner. The finale, "March," is a dance for the ensemble, led by the girl and her first partner.

THE MIRACULOUS MANDARIN

> Ballet in one act. Music by Béla Bartók. Choreography by Todd Bo-
> lender. Libretto after Melchior Lengyel. Scenery and costumes by Alvin
> Colt. Lighting by Jean Rosenthal. First presented by the New York
> City Ballet at the City Center, New York, September 6, 1951, with
> Melissa Hayden as the *Woman*, Hugh Laing as the *Mandarin*, and a
> cast that included Beatrice Tompkins, Frank Hobi, and Roy Tobias.

This is a modern melodrama. It is a story of the city streets, a story of the slums, set to a score that reflects the violence of people who live in dark alleys: footpads, procurers, and prostitutes.

The scene of the ballet is "any city street, anywhere in the world." The time is now. The city street is in semidarkness as the curtain rises. Five men stand about on stage, absolutely still. They look directly out into the audience. Their eyes are filled with contempt and derision; their menacing attitudes are so striking that we scarcely notice their tattered clothes and filthy faces.

On the left there are high, steep flights of steps which converge to form a high platform that dominates the empty street area. The steps, the platform, and the city street are all the color of fresh blood. The background is dark.

One of the dead-end kids begins to snap his fingers in rhythm to the music. The others are restless for activity, and soon there is a fight among them, simply for the sake of violence. The fight breaks up as the men look toward the top of the steps and see the woman. She sits high above the street on the great platform in a ragged costume bespattered with blood. The men scatter. The woman stands, stretches her arms, then lies down to stretch her legs in the air. Her movements are lazy, bored, voluptuous only to herself. The men re-enter. The woman rails at them, then comes down the steps to stand among them. They are all angry with her. She spits at them in defiance.

Just as we are beginning to wonder what relation this woman has to the mob, we find out. One of the men sees a stranger coming down the street. Everyone hides but the woman. The man—small, bent, and tottering—walks on the scene. He sees the woman, is immediately attracted, and circles back toward her to seize her body. The woman thrusts him away; the man falls to the ground. She dances over him, then helps him up. He reaches out for her in uncontrolled lust. Four of the men close in on him silently. They rob him and kill him.

The woman is alone. She hangs on the bars of the huge platform in despair and loathing for what she has done and slides slowly to the ground. Then, defiant again toward her partners and the world, she dances alone, hideously justifying her trade with grotesque gestures. Her dance is interrupted by the entrance of a dark young man. Despite herself, the woman is attracted to him, as he is to her. Together they dance a slow *pas de deux* that presages no violence.

One of the men watches secretively. He calls the others. The woman sees that they will kill her lover and tries to prevent the murder. She fails. As they carry him off, she returns to the full height of the platform and hides her face in her hands. Now a blind girl enters, holding out her hands to feel her way about the street. The woman comes down to jeer at her. The blind girl approaches, and the woman spits at her. The blind girl persists in following her. She seems to know instinctively what the woman is up to and continues to follow her with admonishing hands stretched out before her. The stage darkens.

There is a huge clap of sound, and, at the full height of the platform, a handsomely dressed mandarin looks down at the woman. The stage is bathed in red light. Still watching her, he comes down the long flight of steps. He holds his hands out, inviting her to dance. The woman ignores him, but gradually she is persuaded. She is repelled by the mandarin's insinuating attentions. She hits him in the face. At this signal, the men, who have been watching the scene from the platform, leap into the street. The mandarin tries to escape, but the men surround him. They beat him, stab him, and yet he does not die. His hands reach out and touch the woman. She kicks him away. One of the men seizes him about the throat. His body relaxes completely, and as he seems to die, the men and the girl sit and meditate over this man, who was so difficult to kill. The arms of the mandarin move again. The men, now desperate, secure a rope and hang him from the platform. The mandarin's body sways back and forth; his hands reach out in supplication toward the woman. The men stand back in astonishment and fear. The girl orders them to cut him down. They do so and scatter into the night. She takes the mandarin in her arms and responds to his desire. He dies. His body lies across her lap; her mouth moves in a perpetual moan.

A MIRROR FOR WITCHES

Dramatic ballet in five scenes with prologue. Music by Denis Aplvor
Ivor. Choreography by Andrée Howard. Book by Andrée Howard.
Scenery by Norman Adams. Costumes by Andrée Howard. First pre-
sented by the Sadler's Wells Ballet at the Royal Opera House, Covent
Garden, London, March 4, 1952, with Anne Heaton as *Doll*, Leslie
Edwards as *Bilby*, Julia Farron as *Hannah*, Philip Chatfield as *Titus*,
and John Hart as *Stranger* among the principals.

This dramatic ballet about witchcraft in New England, and its effect on the
people who lived at the time when it was much believed in, is based on
the novel *A Mirror For Witches* by the American historical novelist Esther
Forbes. The English choreographer Andrée Howard was interested in creating a ballet on this novel when she first read it in 1928 and was finally able
to make use of the theme in her first ballet for the Sadler's Wells Company.

PROLOGUE — BRITTANY : The principal action of the ballet,
which takes place in New England, is preceded by a prologue laid in Brittany. Even before the curtain rises, we sense in the music the irrational terror
and cruelty that we are soon faced with in the burning of three alleged
witches. The clergy has made its decision, and these unfortunate creatures
are to suffer "purification by fire." The women are tied to upright ladders;
the fires are about to be laid at their feet, when suddenly, in the midst of
these frightful preparations, there is a moment of pathos. A young girl is
assisted by the townspeople that she may say good-by to her mother, who is
to be one of the victims. The farewell over, the villagers resume their contempt for the witches, the fires are lighted, and the sky is red. An American
sea captain, Bilby by name, comforts the daughter of the witch.

SCENE ONE — SALEM : The benevolent sea captain takes the
abandoned girl, Doll, into his household. Doll accompanies Bilby and
Hannah, his wife, to their new home in Massachusetts. The curtain rises
on an open area, with Bilby's house on the left and a church on the right.
Doll has grown into a young woman, and it is apparent that Hannah is
jealous of Bilby's affection for her. Two young girls, twin sisters of a young
neighbor, Titus, enter and watch the townspeople dance. Soon Titus enters.
He and Doll are alone. Titus is in love with the girl, but his affection only
reminds Doll, in a flash back to her childhood, that her mother was a witch.
In this flash back Doll, as a child, watches her mother make a bargain with
a man dressed in green. Whether this flash back is accurate, or whether it is
the result of the investigations of the clergy that pronounced sentence on her
mother, we are not sure. The flash back over, we observe Bilby encouraging
the romance of Doll and Titus. But Doll repulses Titus as they dance to-

gether. Bilby tries to effect a reconciliation, but Doll refuses. Bilby persists, and Doll curses him. The old man clutches at his heart and falls. Now Hannah, Bilby's wife, vows vengeance on Doll. Bilby's last words are that the girl is not responsible for his death. Doll flees into the night.

SCENE TWO—THE FOREST: In the forest where Doll hides herself, she grieves over Bilby's death and blames herself. She prays, but finds no release in prayer. Finally she invokes the devil, who arrives in the form of a handsome man dressed in green. After dancing with Doll, this man seduces her. As she lies on the ground with her demon lover, fantastic creatures from hell parade around them, glorying in the triumph of their master.

SCENE THREE—SALEM: Hannah and Doll and Titus and his twin sisters are together again, but beneath their relations a growing tension exists. Titus still loves Doll and would help her, but the girl refuses his help. Hannah sits quietly, determined that Doll will not go unpunished for Bilby's death. Soon she finds a way to punish her. Doll makes two toys for the twin sisters, crudely fashioned dolls made of straw. The two girls, while playing with the dolls, fall to the ground with convulsions. Hannah pronounced Doll a witch. The townspeople are alerted, and Doll attempts to escape. The curtain falls as she is carried away by the constabulary.

SCENE FOUR—THE COURT: Now Doll is faced with her accuser and with those villagers who can give evidence against her. Hannah, standing over Doll in triumph, swears that she is a witch. Titus speaks next. Because of his love for Doll he attempts to protect her, but the evidence of his stricken twin sisters will not aid him. Doll cries out that she is innocent, but the court has no mercy and she is condemned to be burned.

SCENE FIVE—THE PRISON: In prison Doll tries to secure help. She still believes herself innocent and pathetically asks for aid. But the only source of help who will answer her is the stranger in green, who magically appears before her. He embraces her, and in his arms, as the sky again glows with the fierce red fire that marked her mother's death, Doll dies.

MOTHER GOOSE SUITE

Classic ballet in five scenes. Music by Maurice Ravel. Choreography by Todd Bolender. First presented by the American Concert Ballet at the Central High School of Needle Trades Auditorium, New York, October, 1943, with a cast headed by Mary Jane Shea and Francisco Moncion. Revised and presented by the New York City Ballet at the City Center, New York, November 1, 1948, with Marie-Jeanne, Francisco Moncion, Todd Bolender, and Beatrice Tompkins in the principal roles.

This ballet is based on Ravel's score *Ma Mère l'Oye*, rather than on the "Mother Goose" fairy tales of Perrault that inspired Ravel to compose his well-known suite. The choreographer has devised a fantasy in which an older woman dreams of her adventures as a young girl. Her dreams are presented by groups of dancers, who portray in mime and movement certain flash backs of her youth, while the woman herself watches from the side lines. The parts of Ravel's suite are played in the following order: "Pavanne," "Enchanted Garden," "Hop o' My Thumb," "Enchanted Princess," "Beauty and the Beast."

The stage is dimly lighted as the curtain rises. A girl stands in a soft blue spotlight. She bows slowly, as if waking from some romantic reverie, and circles the stage on her points. Clouds drift by, enclosing the girl in her dream. The music is quiet and illusive. A strange woman enters in a stiff, long dress. Her face is veiled; she carries a fan. She does not see the girl at first, but turns to look at her lingeringly. The strange woman crosses over to the small theatre box at the side of the stage. She sits carefully under a small crystal chandelier. As she looks out to the stage, the clouds return to perpetuate the dream she watches.

The young girl, the spectator's second self, stands alone in the center of the stage. Four girls in red join her and support her as she poses in arabesque. The girls weave in and out under her extended arms. They bow to her, and she returns their greetings.

The music of the "Enchanted Garden" begins to build to a sumptuous, flowing climax. Four other girls enter, then four boys, who partner the girls alternately in a continuous dance in which they surround the young girl. She chases them, imitates the girls to attract the attention of the boys, and stands sad and helpless as the couples seem unaware of her existence. The girl goes over to the spectator and gestures questioningly: what is she to do? The spectator has no answer. Now desperate, the girl goes to each couple and asks to be recognized. The music pulsates. To its rhythms, the boys lift their partners high and carry them off over the girl's head. The girl stands with bent head. All is quiet again.

Hop o' My Thumb enters. This character is derived from the fairy-tale hero who dropped bread crumbs as he went away from home, imagining that they would lead him back. Here in the ballet, he is accompanied by the bird who ate his crumbs and caused him to lose his way. The bird-girl drapes her long blond hair over the boy's head, ensnaring him. The boy is undisturbed.

The young girl watches, astonished. The bird leaves the boy. He looks after her longingly, then begins to dance with the young girl. They kneel together and look at each other's hands, reading their fortunes. In the background, the bird can be seen crossing the stage in open flight. The boy and girl stare at each other, then rise to stand in front of the spectator. The girl stands motionless as the clouds flow in, envelop the boy, and carry him back to his true love. The girl leaves the stage.

Four girls in red, with long green gloves, enter with a Chinese prince who is dressed in brilliant gold. The orchestra plays a tinkling, Oriental tune, and the prince dances blithely. The young girl re-enters. Momentarily she is blinded by the strange, foreign spectacle. The prince approaches her deferentially and takes her hand, but she refuses to believe that a real prince has appeared to her. The prince takes her hands from her eyes, and now the girl dances with him gaily. He lifts her high, and the two dance before the group. Just as the girl has begun to enjoy herself thoroughly, the magical prince and his escort hop off into the wings.

A young man with the hideous and frightening head of a lion comes in. Before she knows what she is doing, the girl leaps to his shoulder; he lets her down softly. The beast looks into her eyes; the girl is terrified and backs away. The beast falls to the floor and, as the music moans and groans his agony, he mimes his misery and ugliness. Still frightened, the girl approaches the spectator. What can she do with the pathetic creature? The spectator presents her with a magic ring.

The girl runs about the stage rapidly, then puts her hand gently on the beast's shoulder. They dance. Clouds drift in and surround the beast. When they have passed by, he has become a handsome youth. He holds the beautiful girl softly and possessively. The spectator rises and leaves her box. The girl's fairy godmother intervenes and stands over the couple. The boy kneels, holding out his arms. The girl falls against him. He lifts her and carries her out. The spectator exits slowly, openly rejecting her own dream. The clouds drift by. The spell of the dream is still with her.

NOTES: *Mother Goose Suite* is the first ballet by the contemporary dancer Todd Bolender, a leading soloist of the New York City Ballet since it was founded in 1948. Reviewing a performance of the ballet in 1950, Walter Terry wrote: "*Mother Goose Suite* is a haunting reverie, a woman's dream of the half-forgotten but wholly-sensed adventures of her childhood. Here symbolized in dance, are the memories of space and clouds and of a vast world; of the first searchings for friendship and love; of youthful romance and of the passing anguish, the resultant joy of mature love. This dance is fragile, even evanescent in quality, but its very intangibles give it a hypnotic beauty and rare power. As the young girl—the figure of the spectator's dream —Janet Reed was utterly lovely in a part which made full use of her lightness of motion, her delicacy of gesture, her girlishness and her masterful command of the dramatic values of dance." The principal role in *Mother Goose Suite* has also been danced by Nora Kaye.

NAPOLI

Romantic ballet in three acts. Music by E. Helsted, Gade, and Paulli. Choreography and book by Auguste Bournonville. Scenery by Christensen. First presented by the Royal Danish Ballet at the Theatre Royal, Copenhagen, March 29, 1842.

Napoli is the great ballet by Auguste Bournonville, the dancer, choreographer, and ballet master of the Royal Danish Ballet for many years and the founder of its famous continuous tradition of training and performance. Since 1829, when Bournonville mounted his first ballet in Copenhagen, ballets by him have been danced by the Royal Danish Ballet more than four thousand times. *Napoli*, the finest of them, is but a year younger than *Giselle*; but unlike *Giselle*, *Napoli* has not been changed by succeeding generations of choreographers, dancers, and musicians: it is still danced in Copenhagen today as it was more than one hundred and ten years ago.

ACT ONE—NAPLES, BY THE BAY OF SANTA LUCIA —EVENING: Three boys are in love with the beautiful Teresina, the daughter of a watchful widow. Teresina loves only one, a fisherman, Gennaro. Her two suitors—Giacomo, who sells macaroni in the town, and Peppo, who sells lemonade—try to persuade her mother that Teresina will be better off married to one of them. Teresina, the mother indicates, will make up her own mind. Teresina ignores her suitors as she waits for Gennaro, who is returning to port with all the other fishermen of the town.

Soon the fishermen return. Gennaro embraces Teresina, and her mother reluctantly consents to their marriage. A monk, Fra Ambrosio, enters and asks the fishermen and the assembled townsfolk for alms. Gennaro and Teresina both contribute. Teresina's suitors, Giacomo and Peppo, still persist in bothering her and her mother; they try to make the girl jealous as Gennaro jokes with a girl who has come to buy fish from him. But when Gennaro places an engagement ring on her finger, Teresina is convinced that her happiness lies only with him.

The two lovers go out into the bay in order to be alone. After they have been gone for some time, thunder and lightning fill the air. A violent storm breaks over the Bay of Santa Lucia. Gennaro, out in the bay, rows frantically, trying to reach shore. His fellow fishermen go to help him, and he is rescued. But Teresina has been swept overboard by the giant waves, and no one can find her. Gennaro curses his destiny. The girl's mother accuses him of drowning Teresina, and all the people of the town abandon him.

Gennaro is alone. He is about to despair, but then he prays beneath a likeness of the Madonna. Fra Ambrosio comes to him and, giving him an image of the Madonna to carry with him for protection from harm, tells Gennaro not to give up hope: he must take a boat and go out to sea and there find his love. Gennaro goes to find a boat. Fra Ambrosio kneels in prayer.

ACT TWO—CAPRI—A BLUE GROTTO: In Act Two, the scene changes to an entirely different world. Here, in a blue grotto, we are in the abode of Golfo, a powerful sea sprite who rules over the sea around and about him. Two of Golfo's naiads approach the grotto in the great sea shell they use for a boat. They bring to their master Teresina, whom they have rescued. Teresina still holds the guitar she was playing to Gennaro in the fishing boat before the storm broke over Naples.

Teresina asks Golfo to return her to her home, but the sea sprite is fascinated by the girl's beauty and wishes to keep her by him. Over her head he pours the magical water of the grotto, and the girl becomes a naiad; she forgets entirely that she was ever a mortal.

All of Golfo's naiads and Tritons forgather and celebrate the initiation of the newcomer. Golfo himself makes love to her, but Teresina repulses his advances.

Gennaro's boat enters the grotto. Golfo signals his slaves to disappear: he, alone, will deal with the intruder. Gennaro beaches the boat and looks about him. He sees Teresina's guitar. He knows now that she is alive! Golfo tries to induce him to leave the grotto by causing fire to engulf the grotto, but Gennaro refuses to go. He asks for Teresina, and finally the other naiads bring the girl to him.

Of course, since she is no longer a human being, the girl does not recognize her lover. Gennaro tries to bring back her memory by speaking of their life together in Naples and by playing upon her guitar, but still the girl is unmoved. Gennaro is about to give up, when he remembers the image of the Virgin which Fra Ambrosio gave him. He beseeches the Madonna that Teresina's memory may be restored. Slowly Teresina recognizes him. She remembers their love, and the two lovers embrace.

Golfo, enraged at the reconciliation of the lovers, contrives to kidnap Teresina. But the girl will not leave Gennaro. The Tritons and naiads cannot separate them. Teresina realizes, though, that they will never be able to return home unless Golfo's rage is calmed. She holds up the image of the Madonna and commands Golfo and his sea creatures to bow to the Queen of Heaven. Golfo and his Tritons and naiads submit, and the two lovers set sail for Naples in a boat weighed down with gifts.

ACT THREE — MONTE VIRGINES, NEAR NAPLES: The people of the city are gathered together on a religious pilgrimage outside Naples, when Teresina appears with her mother. The people are astonished. Gennaro arrives, and Teresina informs her friends that her lover rescued her. But her friends, who believed her dead, find that such a claim is too mysterious: perhaps witches are at work. Teresina's mother separates her from Gennaro.

Gennaro rails at Teresina's mother for believing such nonsense. The people flee in fear of witchcraft. Only Fra Ambrosio can set them right. He is sent for, blesses Gennaro, and tells the crowd how Teresina was rescued through the power of the Virgin.

Everyone believes the monk instantly, and all gather about Teresina and Gennaro. They dance to celebrate the reunion of the lovers, and Teresina and Gennaro are lifted into a cart, in which their friends draw them toward their home, marriage, and a happy life together.

NIGHT SHADOW

Ballet in one act. Music by Vittorio Rieti, after Bellini. Choreography by George Balanchine. Book by Vittorio Rieti. Scenery and costumes by Dorothea Tanning. First presented by the Ballet Russe de Monte Carlo at the City Center, New York, February 27, 1946, with Alexandra Danilova as the *Sleepwalker*, Nicholas Magallanes as the *Poet*, Maria Tallchief as the *Coquette*, and Michel Katcharoff as the *Host*.

This dramatic ballet was suggested by the opera *La Sonnambula* (*The Sleepwalker*) by Vincenzo Bellini. *Night Shadow* has a dark, romantic mood appropriate to the suppressed and clandestine loves that dominate the story. The time is long ago, a time of rigid conventions that the romantic spirit aimed to destroy.

The ballet begins with a masked ball in the garden of a great house. The host, an elderly man, welcomes his guests, who bow to him deferentially. Near the host stands the coquette, a beautiful young girl, who tosses her head quickly and seems to have a decided hold on his affections. Her controlled vivacity appears slightly out of place in this gathering. All join in a general dance led by the host and his partner.

The poet enters. He is a handsome young man, renowned for his work, and all the guests turn to look at him. There is a pause in all movement, and the atmosphere is expectant. Finally, reluctantly and carefully, the host introduces the poet to his mistress.

All the guests have arrived, and the host orders the entertainment to begin. The couples stand aside and watch two peasant couples in a pastoral dance, a Moorish dance by two blackamoors, followed by a harlequin, who performs an amusing, grotesque solo. The guests applaud the entertainers and gradually move out of the garden to go to supper.

The coquette and the poet watch as the others depart. Both remain on the scene. They approach each other and dance a *pas de deux* that shows us the mutual attraction they feel. The poet is somewhat passive as the willful coquette claims him. Their love duet is cut short by the return of the party. The host goes immediately to the coquette and claims her attention. He is angry. The guests sense an embarrassing tension and turn away. The coquette smiles at the host, reassures him, and takes his arm. They follow the guests and leave the poet alone.

As he is bemoaning his misfortune, he sees what appears to be a ghost coming toward him slowly. The figure is all in white and carries a tall lighted candle in one hand. As it comes closer, the poet sees before him a beautiful woman walking in her sleep. Her long black hair hangs about her shoulders, her face is composed in sleep, and she moves as in a dream, rapidly but softly, dancing across the garden on point, never descending to the ground.

The poet is instantly enamored of this strange, lovely creature, who seems to be a part of his own dream, and he approaches her. But the woman does not waken. The poet dances around her, lies before her on the ground, encircles her, begging her to waken and respond to his love. The woman does not notice him and walks alone in her own dream, stepping over his recumbent body as if he were merely a stone. She begins to drift away, out of the garden. The poet, now desperate, follows.

The coquette returns at this point for a quick rendezvous and sees her lover following the woman in white. She is furious. The host returns to the garden with his guests. The coquette takes him aside and whispers to him. The host looks up, startled and enraged. The coquette leaves him and joins the other guests in a formal ensemble dance. During the dance, we watch the host, dagger in hand, leave the garden unobserved.

When the guests have applauded a final *divertissement*, the poet runs into the garden. He staggers in pain and clutches at his heart. Blood streams through his fingers. The couples stand back, horrified. The coquette watches him and does not move. The poet falls to the ground and dies. The guests stare at the beautiful woman in white, who moves, still in her sleep, across the garden. They follow her. She is the wife of the host.

NOTES: Bellini's *La Sonnambula* (1831) merely provided the subject matter for the ballet *Night Shadow* and not its plot. The opera tells the story of a romance between a farmer and a miller's daughter who is addicted to walking in her sleep. The score for the ballet is an arrangement of music from *La Sonnambula* and *I Puritani*, by the same composer.

Created for Danilova, the principal role in *Night Shadow* has been danced by Nathalie Krassovska, Ethery Pagava, and, more recently and with marked success, by Marjorie Tallchief. The ballet was staged for the Marquis de Cuevas' Grand Ballet two years after its American *première* and had its first performance by this company in London on August 26, 1948, with Ethery Pagava as the sleepwalker, George Skibine as the poet, and Marjorie Tallchief as the coquette. The Grand Ballet has performed *Night Shadow* in Europe, on its foreign tours, and in New York.

Soon after the ballet was first presented, the American critic Edwin Denby wrote, in *Looking at the Dance*: "Mysterious in the interaction of its elements; the vapid ballroom dances; the winsome exhibition numbers that have a perverse and cruel undertone; the elaborate, encircling artifices of the coquette's *pas de deux*; the directness and space of the sleepwalking scene . . . The progress of the piece is 'romantic'—it is disconcerting, absurd and disproportionate; but its effect when it is over is powerful and exact. It gives you a sense—as Poe does—of losing your bearings, the feeling of an elastic sort of time and a heaving floor. As a friend of mine remarked, 'When it's over, you don't know what hit you.' "

LES NOCES
THE WEDDING

Cantata with dances. Music and words by Igor Stravinsky. Choreography by Bronislava Nijinska. Scenery and costumes by Nathalie Gontcharova. First presented by Diaghilev's Ballets Russes at the Théâtre Gaîté-Lyrique, Paris, June 14, 1923, with Felia Dubrovska as the *Bride*. First presented in the United States by the League of American Composers at the Metropolitan Opera House, New York, April 25, 1929, with scenery and costumes by Serge Soudeikine and choreography by Elizaveta Anderson-Ivantzova.

Stravinsky's dramatic cantata *Les Noces* depicts the ancient Russian peasant marriage ritual. Singers on the stage sing words which the dancers accompany with meaningful movement.

SCENE ONE—BENEDICTION OF THE BRIDE—THE TRESSES: The voice of the bride is heard chanting before the rise of the curtain. The scene is the interior of a peasant home in old Russia. The bride stands in the center of the stage, surrounded by her mother and her friends. Her friends help to calm the grief she feels at leaving her home, her fear of life with a man who seems to her now a stranger, and her hatred of the person who has arranged the match. The women tell her that her husband's father will accept her in their home and that her life will be much as it has been, that she must go through with everything for her own parents. At the bride's request, the women comb and bind her hair. They tell her that the birds outside the house are singing happily. Can't she be happy, too? They ask God to bless her marriage.

SCENE TWO—BENEDICTION OF THE BRIDEGROOM —THE BRIDEGROOM'S HOUSE: The bridegroom's father and friends help him to prepare for his wedding. His hair, too, is combed and anointed. All wish him good luck. The parents of both the bride and the bridegroom lament the loss of their children, who are no longer children. The friends of the families congratulate the parents.

SCENE THREE—THE BRIDE'S DEPARTURE—THE WEDDING: The bride is prepared to go forth from her house to meet the bridegroom at the church. Her friends tell her she is a princess this day. At the church, the bridegroom kisses the cross. The best man declares his friend is present to greet his bride. The guests pay tribute to the bridegroom's love for his parents. The bride enters, and the wedding ceremony takes place. As the couples leave, all congratulate them. Their parents lament.

SCENE FOUR—THE WEDDING FEAST: At the wedding feast, the father of the bride presents her to the assembled guests. Men in the company inform her of the household duties she must perform. The bridegroom is informed of his responsibilities to his wife. Everyone drinks and is joyous.

An older married couple is selected, from among the guests, to warm the marriage bed. There is a toast to the young couple, after which they are conducted to the door of their room. The older couple returns to the feast.

The guests gather about the parents of the bride and the bridegroom as they sit beside the door to their children's room. The bridegroom sings of his love for his wife.

NOTES: *Les Noces* was first performed in the United States in concert form, at Aeolian Hall, New York, in February 1926, under the auspices of the International Composers Guild.

Leopold Stokowski conducted the first United States performance of the complete cantata with dances. Marc Blitzstein, Aaron Copland, Louis Gruenberg, and Frederick Jacobi were the four pianists on this occasion.

Bronislava Nijinska's staging of *Les Noces* was first presented in the United States by the Ballet Russe de Monte Carlo in 1936, with Irina Baronova and Yurek Shabelevsky in the principal roles.

THE NUTCRACKER

Classic ballet in two acts, three scenes. Music by Peter Ilyich Tchaikovsky. Choreography by Lev Ivanov. Book by Lev Ivanov. Scenery by M. I. Botcharov. First presented at the Maryinsky Theatre, St. Petersburg, December 17, 1892, with Antonietta dell-Era as the *Sugarplum Fairy* and Paul Gerdt as the *Prince*. First presented in Western Europe by the Sadler's Wells Ballet at the Sadler's Wells Theatre, London, January 30, 1934, with Alicia Markova and Harold Turner. This production was staged by Nicholas Sergeyev, after the choreography of Lev Ivanov. Scenery and costumes by Hedley Briggs. *The Nutcracker* was first presented in the United States by the Ballet Russe de Monte Carlo at the Fifty-first Street Theatre, New York, October 17, 1940, with Alicia Markova and André Eglevsky. Scenery and costumes by Alexandre Benois.

The music to this ballet—Tchaikovsky's third and last ballet score—is so familiar in various "suite" arrangements that few people ever think of the original ballet from which the "suites" are taken. One reason why the fame of the music is greater than the fame of the ballet is that *The Nutcracker* has never been presented in its entirety in the United States. Some people have imagined, therefore, that the score is superior to the dancing. Actually they have no way of knowing, for *The Nutcracker* has never been properly presented in complete form outside of Russia.

The Nutcracker is a Christmas ballet and one of dancing's most beautiful gifts, not only for children, but for all those who appreciate magic in the theatre. The story of the ballet is based on "The Nutcracker and the King of Mice," a tale by E. T. A. Hoffmann, the great German storyteller whose work also inspired the ballet *Coppélia*. Although its action centers around Christmas, *The Nutcracker*, like *The Sleeping Beauty* and other ballets based on fantastic stories, has a perennial, year-round enchantment.

The three scenes of the ballet are arranged in two acts. In the first act, we are in the real world and begin a journey to a magical kingdom.

The overture to the ballet is bright and delicate. Pizzicato strings and tinkling triangles create a light, intimate atmosphere that almost seems to make a fairy story possible. Because the ballet begins not in fairyland, but in an ordinary house, and because its heroine is at first an ordinary little girl, the music in the first part of *The Nutcracker* is not grandiose and regal, as is the music in *The Sleeping Beauty*; true to the story, the music is on a miniature scale, quiet and modest, anticipating the grander events to come.

ACT ONE, SCENE ONE—THE CHRISTMAS PARTY: When the curtain rises, we find ourselves in the living room of a pleasant European home. The time is Christmas Eve, about 1850. This is the home of a city official, the president of the local council. He and his family live comfortably, and the living room is decorated unostentatiously in the fashion of the time. The room is dominated by a large, lighted Christmas tree. The president and his wife stand near the door, where they welcome guests to their annual Christmas party. The party is a family affair, for close friends and relatives, but most of all it is a party for the children, who rollick about the room excitedly.

Clara and Fritz, the two children of the house, have been joined by their friends and cousins. All the children are dressed in their best clothes—the girls in white dresses, the boys in smart velvet jackets and long trousers. They are all busy guessing at the contents of the prettily wrapped packages that lie under the tree. They are a little too preoccupied with Christmas to be altogether aware of their elders, and their parents watch delightedly as they play. The music, which has been soft and warm in keeping with the intimacy of the family party, now anticipates the importance the gathering has for the children and strikes up a bright march, the horns and trumpets and clarinets sounding the delicate but curtly rhythmic theme.

The children come forward, take partners, and dance to the march, parading around the room before their parents. It is past nine o'clock by the large clock in the room when the march is over, and that is the usual time for the children to go to bed. The parents tell them, however, that because this is Christmas Eve, they can stay up until ten and continue their play. The orchestra plays a flowing waltz.

A new guest arrives—an old man with white hair and a black patch over one eye. This is Drosselmeyer, an old family friend who is also Clara's godfather. The president and his wife greet Drosselmeyer affectionately and draw him into the room. When Clara and Fritz see that the kindly gentleman has brought presents for them, they jump up and down with excitement. Drosselmeyer gives Clara a beautiful doll and Fritz a handsome toy soldier. The two children show their gifts to their friends and hardly want to go to bed when their parents warn them that it is ten o'clock. Clara has had such a wonderful time that she doesn't want the party to end; she begins to cry.

Old Drosselmeyer sympathizes with his godchild and, to make things easier for her, gives her another present. The gift is a nutcracker made in the shape of a handsome soldier. Clara immediately forgets about having to go to bed and dances around the room with her new present. The orchestra plays a light, tripping tune in which a rattle, representing the nutcracker, sounds an accompaniment to the lilting strings. Clara's brother, Fritz, teases his sister about her affection for her new present and tries to snatch it away from her. He chases the girl around the room and finally, as the orchestra cuts the dancing melody short with a loud crescendo, grabs the nutcracker away from her. Clara stamps her foot and demands that Fritz return her present, but he holds it tightly when she tries to pull it out of his hands. Angry at his sister, Fritz throws the nutcracker across the room. The little girl runs to retrieve it and finds that her new toy has been broken.

Her parents try to console her. All the children are tired and upset and are clearly in need of sleep. The president and his wife now take hands and lead their friends in the "Grandfather Dance," a traditional formal dance with music based on an old German folk song. Reluctantly the children go off to bed. They kiss their parents, take a last, lingering look at the Christmas tree, and move toward the stairs. Drosselmeyer and the other guests take their leave. The president and his wife take a last look about the room, and the lights are put out. Only the Christmas tree shines in the darkness.

It is midnight. The stage is empty for some moments, then we see Clara, in her white nightgown, peeping out from behind the tree. She comes slowly into the room, being careful not to make any noise. She is walking directly over to the couch to retrieve the nutcracker, when she hears strange noises. The girl has never been alone in the living room in the dark like this and is thoroughly frightened. Suppose there are mice! Clara shudders and looks over at the Christmas tree for comfort. There *are* mice—a whole army of them! Under the tree they are staging a pitched battle with a company of minute toy soldiers. And who should be leading the soldiers against the mice but the nutcracker! Clara is a little less frightened and watches the battle with interest, trusting the nutcracker to lead his troops to victory. The nutcracker attacks the king of the mice bravely, brandishing his sword at the scampering creature. When his victory seems uncertain, Clara, now a real participant, can bear it no longer: she takes her shoe off and throws it at the mouse's head. The king of the mice falls dead, and the defeated mice scamper away in the darkness.

There is a crash of music. The nutcracker stands before Clara and bows, thanking her for saving his life. As he straightens up, Clara sees that he is no longer a toy, but a young, handsome prince. Clara is charmed by his politeness and deference, and when the prince indicates that he must reward her for rescuing him, Clara nods her assent. The prince takes her by the hand and leads her away into the darkness.

ACT ONE, SCENE TWO — THE JOURNEY: When the lights come up again, snow is falling. The ground is covered with whiteness, and great trees are incrusted with ice. In the background a magical boat glides onto the scene, bringing Clara and her prince to this strange forest. The prince orders the boat to stop, gives Clara his hand, and invites her to step ashore. The music is a mellifluous waltz that sounds merrily in the crisp, wintry air. The King and Queen of Snow come forward to greet the visitors. Now Clara discovers that she is in a forest of sweets—that all the whiteness is sugar, all the ice is rock candy! The royal pair that rule over this forest dance for Clara, as living snowflakes flurry around them to the lovely waltz. The music grows louder and faster and finishes with a whirling flourish on the harp. Clara and the prince go back to their royal barge and continue their journey to the heart of the kingdom. As the nutcracker has changed, so has Clara. She is no longer just the nice young daughter of the president of the council; she is a lovely young princess who looks up at the prince with shining eyes.

ACT TWO — THE KINGDOM OF SWEETS: The boat sails on. Clara and her prince do not set foot on land until they arrive at the royal palace of the Kingdom of Sweets. Now the flowing melody of their journey is climaxed by surging strings. Cymbals crash, then all quietens; accompanied by the harp, the celesta tinkles a gentle melody, heralding the arrival of the Sugarplum Fairy. In a splendid, formal throne room, Clara and the nutcracker are welcomed by the court. The Sugarplum Fairy, who is dressed in a spun-candy pink dress, steps forward to greet them. She wears a brilliant crown, symbolic of her supreme power in the candy kingdom, yet she is kind to the newcomers and listens attentively as the nutcracker prince describes in gesture his battle with the mouse king and how Clara secured victory for his side. In tribute to Clara, the Sugarplum Fairy leads her to a small throne on a dais decorated with candy, and the court members ready themselves to entertain the girl with the specialties of the kingdom. The nutcracker stands by her side.

First, to a sharp Spanish dance sounded first by a trumpet, a member of the court performs a "Chocolate Dance." She moves like a mechanical doll who has just been wound up and delights the new princess with her skill. Next comes a quiet, mysterious Arabian dance, a reminder to Clara of the aroma of special Eastern coffee.

In sharp contrast to the flowing Arab melody, a piercing tune is sounded on a flute. To the accompaniment of muttering bassoons and low pizzicato strings, a bearded Chinaman comes forth, representing tea from the Orient. His head bobs up and down to the rhythm of the music and, like animated dolls whose energy will never run down, he and a diminutive Chinese partner make Clara laugh with sudden high leaps and strange gestures.

A merry *divertissement*, the piping dance of the *mirlitons* (reed pipes) follows the Chinese dance. The *trepak*, a strong, whirlwind Russian folk dance, brings to a close the series of short entertainments devised for Clara's pleasure. Soft woodwinds, runs on the harp, and a brief harp cadenza begin the famous "Waltz of the Flowers," which is danced by the crystalline candy flowers.

Now, just as Clara is certain that she has seen everything beautiful in the world, the Sugarplum Fairy and her prince dance a *pas de deux* and give the little girl a royal display of sparkling and sustained grace. Soft, flowing runs on the harp herald the arrival of the fairy and her cavalier. The prince leads the ballerina nobly and tenderly to the center of the stage. He supports her as she extends her pointed toe straight before her; then the fairy puts her hand on the prince's shoulder and stands in *attitude*. A majestic romantic melody emerges beneath the sound of the harp. The ballerina turns in swift pirouettes and falls backward, as her partner holds her about the waist. The prince is quiet and attentive, assuming a secondary role as the ballerina displays her beauty demurely and modestly.

The romantic adagio now brightens with the music, and the Sugarplum Fairy executes quick, precise movements. She travels to the left and right in open arabesques, supported by her partner. Her dance is now dazzling, and the prince proudly assists her virtuosity. The ballerina holds his hand and again extends her leg. The prince releases her, and the Sugarplum Fairy, her arms raised and curved about her head, balances for an instant. The magic moment over, she falls back and the prince catches her in his arms.

Beginning again slowly, the dance of the ballerina reaches a final climax to the crashing command of the music. At the end she falls back and lies in repose across the prince's knee.

The prince now dances a variation. Little Clara claps her hands as he leaps through the air and covers the stage with strong, virtuoso movements. The Sugarplum Fairy returns. Pizzicato strings introduce a melody on the tinkling celesta, the instrument that marked the first appearance of the fairy as she welcomed the visitors to her kingdom. The dance is piquant, sharp, and delicate. The ballerina hops forward on her toes, her light movements fulfilling the sweet gaiety of the music, then pauses in breath-taking susained poses. The tempo quickens, the violins whirl, and the music seems to compel the racing and flourishing finish to the dance.

The orchestra now strikes up a sonorous, climactic waltz. All the couriers join the Sugarplum Fairy and her prince and, dancing to its lovely, flowing strain, pay final tribute to Clara. The girl looks up at the nutcracker prince to thank him for bringing her to this wonderful place. When all the people at the court bow to Clara, as she sits on her miniature throne, she appears to be a real princess, indeed, and it seems unlikely that this dream she has had about her favorite Christmas toy will ever end.

NOTES: The choreography of *The Nutcracker* was originally projected by Marius Petipa, who became ill and assigned the ballet to his assistant, Ivanov. Petipa had collaborated closely with Tchaikovsky on the score of *The Nutcracker*, the ballet, giving him specific instructions for every sequence in the ballet. The composer finished his score in the summer of 1891.

The grand *pas de deux* from the last scene of *The Nutcracker* is often performed as a *divertissement* on ballet programs. The principal ballerinas and *premier danseurs* of ballet companies in the United States and in England are associated with this *pas de deux* and with the principal roles in various productions of the ballet.

The Sadler's Well Ballet revived *The Nutcracker* on January 8, 1937, at the Sadler's Wells Theatre, London. Nicholas Sergeyev again reproduced the Ivanov choreography. Scenery and costumes were by Mstislav Dobouinsky. Margot Fonteyn and Robert Helpmann danced the principal roles. The most recent revival of the ballet is that of the Sadler's Wells Theatre Ballet (September 11, 1951), with revision of Ivanov's choreography by Frederick Ashton. This production has scenery and costumes by Cecil Beaton. Svetlana Beriosova, Elaine Fifield, David Blair, and Robert Lunnon danced the first performance. This production was first presented in the United States by the Sadler's Wells Theatre Ballet at the Buffalo Theatre, Buffalo, New York, October 23, 1951, with Elaine Fifield and David Blair in the principal roles. *The Nutcracker* has never been produced outside Russia in a manner approaching its original form (see the Notes on Dance, Dancers, and Choreography, page 523, for details of the Russian production). The most recent productions of the ballet have been mounted by the Slavenska-Franklin Ballet in the United States and by the Festival Ballet in England.

At Christmastime, 1944, Edwin Denby wrote of *The Nutcracker* in the New York *Herald Tribune*:

"Thinking of Christmas, I remembered the Christmas tree conspicuously on stage and the Christmas party in the first scene of *The Nutcracker*, the venerable fairy tale ballet that Petipa's collaborator Ivanov set long ago to Tchaikovsky's lovely score. Has the action anything to do with Christmas? What is its nonsense plot really about and how does *The Nutcracker* create its mild and beneficent spell? This serene old vehicle complete with all the

1890 ballet conventions—pantomime scene, ballroom dance, grand *pas de deux, divertissement* and *ballabile*, all of them strung in a row on a story nobody pays attention to—still works as a theatre piece. It does even in such a form as the Monte Carlo's three-scene version, which though cut, patched and mauled by years of hard wear, keeps the formal continuity of the original three acts. At the Monte Carlo most of the young dancers show no manners in the pantomime part and they may do their stint in the dance scenes as if they were reciting 'Thanatopsis.' But the great Danilova as the Sugar-Plum Fairy (especially with Youskevitch as partner) has a radiant and tender presence that lets you see the heart of the ballet and convinces you of its expressive power. Through her performance the choreographic intentions of the work emerge once more. If you are curious about choreography, you find that the dance logic of *The Nutcracker* is solid and that the nonsense plot— its idea content—has a rational structure too. The intentions of *The Nutcracker*, when you do catch on, are humane and sensible, and its 1890 formal method is highly intelligent.

"What is the method? This is what happens on the stage. The long first scene is a clear pantomime story. The dance is plain, realistic, with embellishments, it does not lead to leaps; it is all *terre à terre*. The second and third scenes, in contrast to the first, tell hardly any story; instead they are dancing that clearly looks like dancing, with steps in patterns, leaps and lifts, dancing with 'elevation.' The two dance scenes are made up of successive dance numbers, each with a beginning and an ending, each a set piece, all of them together arranged in a suite ending with an ensemble finale.

"The suite method in ballet, as in opera, does not have the urgency of the continuous, symphonic method. The suite ballet does not try so hard to get somewhere. The emotional tone is stable, it changes en bloc from number to number. The series of emotions that constitute the whole work are grouped in clear rubrics, the imagination dwells on one at a time and then proceeds satisfied to the next. The momentary detail is seen in relation to the number it appears in; when the number is finished one has a complete image, and the detail loses its insistency. There is a sense of repose in action, a control of the emotion that is both modest and noble. In short, the set piece structure is not at all a foolish device.

"*The Nutcracker* is not foolish in form, nor is it foolish either in its literal content. It is a fairy-tale ballet and certainly looks like nonsense. But nowadays with psychoanalysis practically a household remedy, grownups take the nonsense of fairy tales more seriously than children. We call them narratives in free association and solve them like cross-word puzzles. *The Nutcracker* is an easy one—the title gives it away. The story begins on Christmas Eve in an upper-class home, the *locus classicus* of ambivalent anxiety. An elderly bachelor with one eye gives a pre-adolescent girl a male nutcracker (the symbols and inversion couldn't be more harrowing). Her young brother tears it away from her by force and breaks it. But she takes it up from the floor and nurses it; she loves it. She dreams that the nutcracker turns almost into a boy. Then she dreams of a deep forest in winter with restless girl-snowflakes and a handsome young man who keeps lifting up a young lady (and who is this lady but the little heroine's own dream image?). And after that she dreams she is watching a lot of dancing Chinamen and Russians and oddly dressed people—all of them somehow 'sweet'; and at last the previous young man and the previous young lady turn up again, too. They furnish a brilliant climax, and that leads to a happy dazzle for everything and everybody everywhere at once."

L'OEUF À LA COQUE
THE SOFT-BOILED EGG

Ballet in one act. Choreography by Roland Petit. Music by Maurice Thiriet. Scenery and costumes by Stanislas Lepri. First presented by Ballets des Champs-Elysées, Paris, in 1948. First presented in the United States by Les Ballets de Paris, at the Wintergarden, New York, October 6, 1949, with Colette Marchand and Serge Perrault in the leading roles.

"The scene is Hell, in the shape of a vast and weird kitchen. The characters are demons in the form of white-coated chefs, and chickens are being prepared for the roasting oven." So runs the brief program note that introduces a rollicking fantasy rich in surprises.

Three busy chefs are mopping a gigantic black stove as the curtain rises. In the back a chimney reaches high up into the rafters of the great kitchen, and hanging against the walls are pots and pans large enough to prepare meals for a regiment. Chicken crates are piled up on the right. On top of them sits a girl in white tights with a ruffle of chicken feathers at her waist. She is resigned to her fate in the boiling pot and ignores the excited chefs. Two cooks parade into the kitchen, led by the head chef. They go over to the crates, push the chicken off the top, and unload three more girls. The chefs are delighted with their beautiful chickens and close in on the frightened creatures like demons, pulling at their scanty feathers, sticking them with long kitchen forks, and smacking their lips in anticipation of the splendid meal they will make. The poor chickens shiver and shake under this torment and see they are helpless to resist. At a signal from the head chef, they are shooed into the oven. They crawl in rapidly, but as the last chicken goes into the oven, she lays an egg—an egg the size of a football.

The chefs slam the oven door shut and examine the curious object. They shake it, throw it up to the rafters, after quick consultation toss it to each other, and at last agree to boil it. They drop it in a steaming caldron. Then the chefs begin to dance about the kitchen in celebration of the fare they will serve up to themselves. Their dance does not last long, for in the caldron something unpredicted seems to be happening. The chefs all gather around, listening to the strange noises that come from the pot. The egg has hatched! They start back, shocked, as a long black feather begins to emerge. When they see that this feather is the headdress of a stunning, beautiful woman who slowly rises from the caldron, the chefs all fall flat on their backs in incredulous surprise. The woman is tall and slender, with lovely long legs. Her tail is feathered! She poses, hand on hip, when she has stepped out of the caldron, and the two chefs run forward to help her off the stove.

This magical feathered creature steps down, brazenly walks about the kitchen, and accepts the cooks' admiration in her stride. Clearly, she will grant no favors. The devilish chefs are unable to touch their own delectable dish. They remember hopefully the chickens roasting in the oven. The door is flung open, and the four hens jump out, freshly browned for the table. But the cooks are indifferent to the smaller fowl and turn again to take in the charms of the bird who has beat them at their own game. The head chef finally secures permission to dance with her. She sits high on his shoulder, waving her arms, and then the two dance a daring display of acrobatics. Their dance ends as the long-legged bird, hands around her partner's neck, is swung around and around with ever increasing velocity.

ORPHEUS

Ballet in three scenes. Music by Igor Stravinsky. Choreography by George Balanchine. Scenery and costumes by Isamu Noguchi. Lighting by Jean Rosenthal. First presented by Ballet Society at the New York City Center, New York, April 28, 1948, with Nicholas Magallanes as *Orpheus*, Maria Tallchief as *Eurydice*, Francisco Moncion as the *Dark Angel*, Beatrice Tompkins as the *Leader of the Furies*, Tanaquil Le-Clercq as the *Leader of the Bacchantes*, and Herbert Bliss as *Apollo*.

This ballet is a contemporary treatment of the ancient myth of Orpheus, the Greek musician who descended into Hades in search of his dead wife, Eurydice. With his music, Orpheus charms the God of the Dead into returning Eurydice to him. He promises not to look at her until they have reached the earth again. Eurydice, unknowing, persuades Orpheus to break this promise, thereby bringing about her irrevocable death. The ballet tells this story and its aftermath as simply as possible with its music, its dramatic action, and its dancing.

SCENE ONE—THE GRAVE OF EURYDICE: The first notes of the orchestra remind us that Orpheus' instrument was the lyre. A harp sounds descending scales in a slow, mournful rhythm accompanied by quiet strings. Eurydice is dead, and Orpheus cannot console himself with his own song. The curtain rises. Orpheus stands alone beside Eurydice's grave with his back turned. His arms hang limp, his lyre is discarded at his feet, and his head is bowed to the intensely blue sky that would pierce his sorrow with brightness. Three friends enter on the left, cross over to the grave, and place upon it relics of Eurydice. Orpheus does not notice them; he remains motionless when they place their hands on his shoulder to console him. He ignores their departure. The music ceases its slow lamentation, and Orpheus wakens from his grief. He takes up his lyre and begins a dance that expresses physical grief as well as mental anguish. He raises the lyre high above him in supplication, then holds the instrument in one hand as he dances. The song of the lyre is inadequate to his bereavement; yet the lyre is the only possession Orpheus has left, and in his dance he tries to make the instrument a partner to his woe. This effort fails, and Orpheus places the harp on Eurydice's grave, where he beseeches it to speak for her. Then he falls in despair at the grave and reaches out to pluck the lyre's strings. At this sound, a satyr and four wood sprites leap out from behind rocks in the background and attempt to distract Orpheus. Orpheus rises to meet these creatures who have been moved by his song and he darts in and out among them for a moment, but soon leaves them, to dance alone with his lyre. His misery is unabated and his pathetic figure seems to demand the sympathy of the gods he invokes to aid him. Again he stands beside Eurydice's grave with downcast eyes.

Now the prayers of Orpheus are answered. In the back, against the vivid blue sky, appears a strange, dark figure whose body is enveloped in black coils. The Angel of Death poses briefly, then moves forward toward the grieving poet. He approaches softly, so as not to disturb Orpheus in his reverie, and touches him. Orpheus stands immobile. The Angel of Death frees himself of the black coil that represents his power in Hades, raises Orpheus' arms high, and entwines the coil between his outstretched hands. As he wraps the coil about the silent musician, the Angel of Death by his intimate presence endows Orpheus with the power to accompany him on the long journey across the River Styx to Eurydice. The angel stands away from Orpheus and dances triumphantly for a moment, then prepares for the trip into Hades. He frees Orpheus of the bonds of death, then places over the minstrel's eyes a golden mask which must not be removed until the journey is over. Then he picks up the lyre, slips his arm through it, and beckons to Orpheus. Orpheus moves toward him hesitatingly; pliantly he stretches out his hand to grasp the angel's upturned palm. The open, widespread fingers of the angel close about his hand with the strength of steel. A trumpet sounds. The angel moves the lyre down his arm to rest on their clasped hands and begins to lead Orpheus on the downward journey. The music is slow and spacious as the two figures move toward the front of the stage. From above, a flowing white gauze falls in slow motion, and in front of this curtain the Angel of Death leads the blinded Orpheus on the tortuous journey. The progress in their descent into Hades is marked by bright objects that can be seen moving upward in back of the transparent curtain. The passage becomes difficult as the two figures cross the stage toward the left, and as they disappear, the angel, exhausted, pulls Orpheus over the ground. When they have gone, mysterious figures in back of the gauze push the curtain forward with a movement similar to the helpless beating of wings against a cage.

SCENE TWO—HADES: The gauze curtain rises swiftly, and crouched about the stage in fearful attitudes are the Furies, creatures of Hell who would destroy those who enter the Land of the Dead unlawfully. Bright cones of light from above illuminate their hideous and fantastic attire. The leader of the Furies proceeds to direct them harshly in a rapid, rhythmic dance. Orpheus and the angel enter on the left. The leader of the Furies turns and points at them menacingly, followed by her weird creatures. But the angel and Orpheus stand motionless. The Furies finish their dance, and their leader directs them to gather in a group. Tortured souls who have remained in the background now stir with great effort. They carry heavy burdens of rock on their shoulders and bend painfully under the strain. They set boulders down behind the group of Furies, as if to protect themselves, and all turn toward the two interlopers.

The Angel of Death moves away from Orpheus, slips the lyre from his arm, and, standing in back of the minstrel, places the lyre for Orpheus to play. But Orpheus does not understand—he cannot see—and the angel moves his hands so that they touch the strings of the harp. The angel plucks the strings, and now Orpheus comprehends and begins to play. His music is accompanied closely by two oboes and the orchestra. The lovely, soft melody of his lyre enchants the Furies, who are lulled to silence and rest. Yet Orpheus is still reluctant to play the harp as he once did, before Eurydice died, and the angel continues to exact the music from him. He knows that only by his great music will Orpheus persuade the ruler of Hades to release Eurydice. The two figures dance to the beautiful song, the angel constantly encouraging Orpheus to prolong the melody. The burdened, tortured souls move closer to hear more perfectly, and the music reflects their agony, which Orpheus' song has temporarily relieved.

But now the song is over. Orpheus bows stiffly in obeisance toward the back. In the dark recesses of the stage a strange shape begins to turn toward him. This is Pluto, God of the Underworld. Standing before him, her hands resting on his shoulders, is Eurydice. Orpheus does not move. Although he cannot see, he senses her presence and waits for Pluto's answer to his prayer. Eurydice moves forward, haltingly at first, with a slight limping motion, then more freely as her dance becomes syncopated. She turns to Pluto and beseeches him to come forward. Eurydice's arms move constantly to express her desire for freedom, and Pluto moves toward her. The Furies take Orpheus by the hand and bring him to Eurydice. Pluto joins their hands, and for a moment the two stand motionless before the god as Orpheus pledges not to look at his wife until they have ascended to earth. A blue stalactite descends from on high to symbolize the reunion, and the Dark Angel comes forward to lead Orpheus and Eurydice back to earth. He takes Orpheus by the hand, and all the inhabitants of the underworld circle the three figures, who move with hands joined to the front of the stage. The gauze curtain falls behind them, and the Dark Angel proceeds ahead, holding out Orpheus' lyre as a guide to the couple.

Orpheus and Eurydice dance together to a sumptuous melody as their journey begins. At first Eurydice merely follows Orpheus, imitating his steps as he leads the way. But the ascent is difficult, and their dance becomes for a short time a kind of portrayal of the hardships they undergo in passing unseen obstacles. Orpheus is blind, and when Eurydice is not holding him by the hand, she is lost to him. Eurydice puts herself in his way constantly: she longs increasingly for Orpheus to see her. Her longing is infinitely tender and appealing because of the warmth of the love in her own eyes; she therefore seems to tempt Orpheus to tear the mask from his face not so that he can see her, but so that she can see him as she remembers him. She wishes to help him as they proceed along the way, but the one way in which she cannot help him is by showing her love for him. Eurydice is tormented momentarily by the fact that, although they are really together once again, they are actually remote to each other: Orpheus, because he cannot see; Eurydice, because she cannot be seen by the man she loves.

The tempo and the theme of the dance change briefly as Eurydice moves away and dances before the blind Orpheus a gay and pleasant measure. She holds in her hands an invisible pipe, and plays upon it in celebration of their reunion. Orpheus catches the mood of her dance and joins her in it. Both are attempting to suppress the impassioned longings they feel so deeply. But Orpheus becomes even more intently aware of his lack of sight as Eurydice beguilingly dances out of his reach, and the principal theme of their *pas de deux* returns, this time prefaced with a short musical warning from the harp. On the extreme left, the arm of the Dark Angel still holds out the guiding lyre, and the two lovers turn to follow it. They start out as before, Orpheus leading and Eurydice duplicating his movements, but now Eurydice moves close to him in intimate contact. Orpheus tries to hold her, but she slides down to the floor, where his arms reach out desperately to find her. The melody mounts to a brief crescendo. Now that he cannot touch Eurydice, Orpheus abandons all patience and takes his head in his hands. Eurydice stands beside him, her face close to his, and he tears the mask from his eyes. There is absolute silence. Instantly she falls against him and dies. At first too stunned to move, Orpheus stretches out his arms, eager to touch her and to feel her touch. Invisible creatures of Hades push forward the gauze curtain to make good their promise and slip

Eurydice away. Orpheus kneels alone, his open arms clasping the empty air. Now that he has lost Eurydice until he himself shall die, Orpheus is afraid. Horns sound in terrifying judgment upon his fatal error. He remembers that the Angel of Death is still with him, just ahead, and he turns, half crawling, half running, to grasp his lyre. But just before his fingers reach the lyre, it disappears. Powerless now in the Land of the Dead, Orpheus knows that he is powerless, too, on earth; he crawls off in search of his lyre.

The gauze curtain rises rapidly when Orpheus has left the stage. Here again on earth the sky is still blue, but now it is bathed also in blood-colored lights. There is a small hillock in the background. At the crash of a drum, there comes in from the left a tall Thracian woman with long red hair. This is the leader of the bacchantes, pleasure-seeking women who have not known love. She stalks the scene as if seeking desirable prey, moving with quick thrusts of legs and arms, looking to the right and left. She is soon followed by eight bacchantes, all with brilliant yellow hair. Orpheus enters carrying his mask. Immediately the bacchantes surround him. Their leader seems to demand his favor. Orpheus repulses her, indignant that she should try to sully his grief. The woman smiles her contempt and tries to take the mask from him. He runs, but the bacchantes are all around him. The leader embraces Orpheus savagely with her long arms, and the two fall to the ground. They roll over and over, and Orpheus frees himself, but the bacchante rises in triumph, holding his mask. Her face contorted with demoniac delight, she throws the mask out of sight. Orpheus cannot escape. The entire orchestra imitates his terror and the ferocity of the bacchantes with frenzied, rhythmic fortissimos. The bacchantes move in for the final attack. They push Orpheus back toward the hillock. He does not resist. They push him again. His head is bowed, his body listless. The bacchantes raise his arms, and for a brief moment they seem open in supplication. The leader stalks in on Orpheus and cuts off his right arm, then his left. He raises his head; she decapitates him. The body of Orpheus lies behind the hillock, torn to pieces. The bacchantes exit, strutting proudly, unregretfully.

SCENE THREE—APOTHEOSIS: The stage is empty. Gradually the red disappears from the blue sky and the earth is bright once more. Again we hear the harp play the theme that opened the ballet, but now the accompaniment is different: this seems but a mere imitation of Orpheus' music. Apollo comes in slowly and approaches the grave of Orpheus. He kneels beside it and takes from behind the hillock a golden mask of the minstrel's face. Apollo holds the mask high, invoking the spirit of Orpheus as the God of Song, then holds it gently with his arm, as Orpheus held his lyre. The harp sounds as Apollo plucks the air before the mask, but the music—accompanied as it is by two horns—makes us all the more aware of the death of Orpheus and of Apollo's inability to call forth his music alone. Finally Apollo sets down the mask and stands poised over the grave of Orpheus. Slowly he moves his arm upward, and from the grave rises the lyre of Orpheus entwined in a long garland of flowers. The lyre rises higher and higher, carrying with it for the ages the tenderness and power of his song.

NOTES: The *Orpheus* that I produced in collaboration with Stravinsky in 1948 was my second treatment of this story. The first was in 1936, when my dances to Gluck's opera *Orpheus and Eurydice* were performed on the stage of the Metropolitan Opera House while the singers performed their parts in the orchestra pit. Lincoln Kirstein, who planned that production with me, has written about it in his book *Blast at Ballet:*

"After considerable study and discussion of the legend of Orpheus and Eurydice, we decided to present what was most living for our epoch in the Orphic myth. We saw it as the eternal domestic tragedy of an artist and his wife, with Love himself a male angelic embodiment, with real feather wings and real muscles for flying, not a girl androgyne, which was the tradition of the Paris Opéra. Balanchine also had suggested that the singer who sang the role of Orpheus while Lew Christensen danced, should not have a woman's voice, in the Franco-Italian tradition of the *castrati*, but instead a tenor. This replacement had long been achieved in the Russian Theatres. Instead, the Metropolitan permitted the dancer to be a male (which even Paris still refuses), but insisted his voice should remain female.

"We saw Hell as a concentration-camp with flying military slave-drivers lashing forced labor; the Elysian Fields as an ether dream, a desiccated bone-dry limbo of suspended animation, and Paradise as the eternity we know from a Planetarium arrayed on the astronomical patterns of contemporary celestial science. The movement was danced and mimed in some of Balanchine's most accomplished erotic patterns, touching and electric encounters, and noble plastic groups. Attic vase drawings, themselves, and not polite dancing-school scarf dances, in his love-knots and amorous garlands had really come to life. Pavel Tchelitchev's scenery and costumes, which in tonality and atmosphere recalled Massacio, Piero della Francesca, and our everyday work-clothes, clad pseudo-Eleusinian mysteries equal in dignity and grandeur to Gluck's superb score."

Lincoln Kirstein goes on to note that this production of *Orpheus*, far ahead of its time, was a complete failure with the press and the Metropolitan audiences.

In 1947, when Kirstein and I agreed that Ballet Society should commission a new ballet from Stravinsky, the composer consented to the project. He asked for suggestions, and I told him that I would like to do a new, modern *Orpheus*. It seemed to me that the Orpheus myth, with its powerful portrayal of the poet-musician's destiny and of his love, was particularly appropriate for ballet, and particularly a ballet with music by Stravinsky. It also seemed to me that the Orpheus myth was familiar to most people, that people would like to see it danced.

Stravinsky agreed. We conferred on a plan for the ballet, Stravinsky taking notes on the time each part would take. He then wrote the music, in Hollywood, in about eight months. Stravinsky watched rehearsals of the ballet in New York and actively collaborated in the production.

Noguchi, the designer, and Jean Rosenthal, who lighted the work, collaborated closely, too. Of course, there have been many treatments of the Orpheus story, in opera and in ballet. But I had in mind no particular period of time for the setting of the ballet or for the costumes. The time of the ballet seemed to me the period of the Greek earth legends, the time of sand and snakes. Noguchi marvelously created settings that conveyed this idea of open, deserted spaciousness, with skies blue and red for the scenes on earth and with a seemingly impenetrable darkness for the scene in hell. Jean Rosenthal's lighting of these settings was masterful, as is all her work. The settings appear actually to represent neither earth nor Hades, but the areas of existence between them, the places, perhaps, where myths are never mortal. Noguchi, in designing the costumes, thought of the heavy rope entwining the Dark Angel that I worked into the choreography.

PAS DE QUATRE

Divertissement. Music by Cesare Pugni. Choreography by Jules Perrot. First presented at His Majesty's Theatre, London, July 12, 1845, with Marie Taglioni, Carlotta Grisi, Fanny Cerito, and Lucile Grahn.

This short ballet is probably the most famous *divertissement* in the history of dance. It displayed in one work four of the greatest ballerinas of its time, bringing these talents together for several memorable performances that have excited the curiosity of dance lovers for more than a hundred years. At this distance, it is impossible for us to tell exactly what *Pas de Quatre* looked like as a ballet, but information about what it resembled, and the unprecedented occasion it undoubtedly was, has come down to us in lithographs and reviews. If the greatest ballerinas of the United States, France, England, and the U.S.S.R. were to appear together in a ballet today, we should have some approximation of the excitement caused by the original *Pas de Quatre.* If such a *Pas de Quatre* seems impossible in 1953, we must remember that it also seemed impossible in 1845.

Among all artists there is bound to be competition, and in the 1840s it seemed unlikely that any four of the great ballerinas would consent to dance on the same stage. Marie Taglioni had been acknowledged the finest dancer in the world when she created the title role in *La Sylphide* in 1832, and even thirteen years after her first famous role, she was still considered supreme in the realm of the romantic ballet that she had helped to create. But with the coming of the romantic era, there were also other ballerinas who danced in similar ballets: exceptional among these dancers were Fanny

Cerito, who was acclaimed in the early 1840s, Carlotta Grisi, who danced in 1841 the first performance of *Giselle*, and the Danish ballerina Lucile Grahn, who had successfully danced Taglioni's role in *La Sylphide*. The fact that each ballerina had danced *Giselle* (Taglioni, Cerito, and Grahn undertook Grisi's original role in 1843) gives us an indication of their rivalry. There was, in short, so much natural jealousy between these four—and each faction of the public showed so great an amount of enthusiasm for its chosen goddess among them—that it appeared unlikely that the ballerinas would expose themselves to any common venture.

The man who thought otherwise and acted with persistence until he achieved his goal was the enterprising manager of His Majesty's Theatre in London, Benjamin Lumley. "The government of a great state was but a trifle compared to the government of such subjects as those whom I was *supposed* to be able to command," he recollected almost twenty years after the event. "These were subjects who considered themselves far above mortal control, or, more properly speaking, each was a queen in her own right—alone, absolute, supreme."

Lumley was encouraged to assemble the four ballerinas by a success he had brought off in 1843, when Fanny Cerito danced at his theatre in a *pas de deux* with Fanny Elssler, the fifth great ballerina of this period. Why Elssler was not invited to participate in Lumley's assembly of ballerinas in 1845 is perhaps partially explained by this earlier triumph, but not altogether so. For Elssler's fame equaled, if it did not actually exceed, Taglioni's. No doubt that is exactly the point. Taglioni's superiority was unquestioned throughout Europe until Elssler made her debut at the Paris Opéra in 1834. From this point on, the rivalry between the two was bitter. Elssler taunted Taglioni and her admirers by threatening to dance *La Sylphide*, which no other dancer yet dared to do. When Elssler essayed Taglioni's famous role in this ballet in 1838, open war broke out, and seven years later it must have been clear even to Benjamin Lumley that between these rivals there could never be peace. Théophile Gautier, who was to become the originator of *Giselle*, the friend and critical sponsor of Carlotta Grisi, wrote in 1837 that Fanny Elssler's dancing had a special quality that distinguished her from all other dancers and proceeded to make his point clear in a fashion that must have made the rivalry between the newcomer and the "Sylphide" intense: ". . . it is not the aerial and virginal grace of Taglioni, it is something more human, more appealing to the senses. Mademoiselle Taglioni is a Christian dancer, if one may make use of such an expression in regard to an art proscribed by the Catholic faith: she flies like a spirit in the midst of transparent clouds of white muslin with which she loves to surround herself, she resembles a happy angel who scarcely bends the petals of celestial flowers with the tips of her pink toes. Fanny is a quite pagan dancer; she reminds one of the muse Terpsichore, tambourine in hand, her tunic, exposing her thigh, caught up with a golden clasp; when she bends freely from the hips, throwing back her swooning, voluptuous arms, we seem to see one of those beautiful figures from Herculaneum or Pompeii which stand out in white relief against a black background . . ."

And Elssler was not praised only in Europe. She came to the United States in 1840 for a three-month tour and did not return to Europe for two years—two years during which she became the toast of the nation. She was welcomed by President Martin Van Buren, escorted by his son, entertained by Congress, carried on the shoulders of adoring crowds, and so universally acclaimed that she could declare, with accuracy, that "never was an artiste more completely seated in public sympathy." In nineteenth-century America she anticipated the exclusive success enjoyed by Anna Pavlova seventy years later.

But Benjamin Lumley also had grounds for being discouraged. His predecessor at His Majesty's Theatre had announced, but had been unable to present, Taglioni, Cerito, and Elssler in a special performance. Circumstances, too, contrived against him. He had chosen Jules Perrot, the former partner of Taglioni and the choreographer who had collaborated on *Giselle*, to arrange the dances for the *Pas de Quatre*, and everyone was ready to begin —except one of the ballerinas. Carlotta Grisi, Perrot's wife, seemed unable to fulfill her engagement on time. She was dancing in Paris; how was she to get to London for rehearsals? Lumley tells us how: "A vessel was chartered . . . to waft the sylph at a moment's notice across the Channel; a special train was engaged and ready at Dover; relays of horses were in waiting to aid the flight of the *danseuse*, all the way from Paris to Calais."

When Grisi arrived, Perrot began to work on the most difficult assignment a ballet master ever had. He had not only to invent an ensemble that the four ballerinas would perform together, he had also to devise individual dances that would display ideally the particular artistry of each performer without distracting from the excellence of her sisters. In Lumley's words, "no one was to outshine the others—unless in their own individual belief." Perrot had worked closely on other projects with each of the four dancers previously and knew their temperaments; as the finest *danseur* of his time and a choreographer of equal fame, he also knew his job.

He seemed to succeed. The ballerinas were content with what they were to dance together and pleased with their variations; the costumes were ready, the theatre sold out. And then came the problem of who was to dance first —or, rather, last, for the final variation in every ballet, as in regal processions, according to Lumley, is performed by the superior artist. Cerito, Grisi, and Grahn agreed that Taglioni, because of her unprecedented fame, should occupy this place of honor. But as to the penultimate variation, the ladies disagreed: who was to be closest to Taglioni? Cerito and Grisi vied for the position and quarreled on stage. Finally Grisi lost her temper, called Cerito "a little chit," and the two ballerinas vowed they would never appear together.

Perrot, in despair, told the bad news to the manager. Lumley recalled what the choreographer said: "*Mon Dieu!* Cerito won't begin before Carlotta, nor Carlotta before Cerito, and there isn't anything that will make them change their minds: we're finished!" And Lumley also recalled what he replied: "The solution is easy . . . In this dilemma there is one point on which I am sure the ladies will be frank. Let the oldest take her unquestionable right to the envied position."

Perrot returned to the stage to try this ruse. When he told the two ballerinas the manager's decision, everything suddenly changed: they "tittered, laughed, drew back, and were now as much disinclined to accept the right of position as they had been eager to claim it." The trick worked! Taglioni was at this time forty-one, Cerito was twenty-eight, and Grisi twenty-six: the reverse order was thus established, with Grahn, who was twenty-four, leading with the first variation. Lumley says that "the *grand pas de quatre* was finally performed on the same night before a delighted audience, who little knew how nearly they had been deprived of their expected treat."

What this audience saw was recorded by several critics, and approximations of the performance have been given us in modern representations of this *divertissement*. When the curtain went up, the four ballerinas appeared before a romantic background. They entered in a line, holding hands; each was dressed in billowing muslin and each wore in her hair a crown of white flowers, except Cerito, who wore flowers in the knot at the back of her head. The ballerinas smiled, walked to the footlights, and bowed. The audience could not believe it. One member of the audience did not want to believe it and threw down from the gallery a shower of placards that declared Cerito the peer of all dancers in the world. The audience was embarrassed and frightened of the possible consequences, but then someone laughed, the dancers smiled, and the music began.

The *Pas de Quatre* commenced in soft stillness as the four ballerinas moved toward the backdrop and arranged themselves in charming tableaux about Taglioni, who looked down upon her sisters with an expression of sincere sweetness. Even the slightest display of jealousy was impossible now, for each artist was thoroughly aware that the ballet would surely fail if any of them failed to be as perfect as Perrot imagined they were and that they would be responsible. And so they knelt about Taglioni, opened their arms to her in a gesture of affection and respect, and smiled as innocently as she did. They changed their position, and the graceful Taglioni seemed to fall back in their welcoming arms.

The actual dancing began with a short variation by Grahn to quick, lively music. This was followed by a *pas de deux* by Cerito and Grisi, which came to an end as Taglioni crossed the stage in high, light leaps that seemed to make her a part of the air. This introduction was merely a hint as to what was to follow in the four virtuoso variations. Grahn came first, dancing quickly, lightly, turning and hopping on point, moving about the stage with the controlled vigor of shining youth. Next, as the music changed, Carlotta Grisi stepped forward and danced with a sharp but airy vibrancy, a solo that summed up in a few short minutes her great fame.

Taglioni and Grahn, the oldest and the youngest, now danced together to a brief romantic measure. Cerito was posed gracefully on stage with them, apparently waiting for them to finish their duet. Suddenly she cut this dainty and quiet sequence short, darting forward like an arrow released from the taut bow and describing a long, swift diagonal of accelerated turns. She finished her variation in a display of still, balanced poses contrasted with unparalleled verve and speed.

Taglioni, as the last of these great dancers, had the most difficult variation of all: she had to show the audience that what they had rejoiced in so far could be climaxed. And this she did, not by dancing in any fashion novel to her, but in a manner that epitomized her reputation: she moved with supreme lightness and she moved effortlessly, dazzling the audience with controlled poses even in mid-flight. And she moved with unquestioned authority, with the highest knowledge of her great gift and of her own faithful obedience to it, pausing in perfect balance with the grace and refinement of the mature artist.

Now, at the end, the three other ballerinas joined her. They all danced together, each trying to outdo the others in a final display of virtuosity. Then, as if they all understood that competition was in vain, they arranged themselves again in the tender tableaux with which they had begun. Taglioni raised her arms over her head and looked down upon the other three, who gathered about her quietly and looked toward the audience with pensive, beguiling smiles, as if they had never moved.

NOTES: And what was the critical opinion of this *Pas de Quatre?* *The Times* of London called it "the greatest Terpsichorean exhibition that ever was known in Europe. . . . Never was such a *pas* before. The excitement which a competition so extraordinary produced in the artists roused them to a pitch of energy which would have been impossible under other circumstances, and hence everyone did her utmost, the whole performance being a complete inspiration . . . The whole long *pas* was danced to a running sound of applause, which, after each variation, swelled to a perfect hurricane. . . . Bouquets flew from every point, an immense profusion, as each *danseuse* came forward, so that they had to curtsy literally in the midst of a shower of floral gifts. Cerito's wreaths and nosegays were more than she could hold in both her arms. . . . The front of the stage was almost covered with flower leaves."

The critic of the *Illustrated London News* reported: "No description can render the exquisite, the almost ethereal, grace of movement and attitude of these great dancers, and those who have witnessed the scene may boast of having once, at least, seen the perfection of the art of dancing. . . ."

The best accounts of three of the four ballerinas are given by their contemporary Théophile Gautier. Gautier did not review the *Pas de Quatre*, but he speaks here of Taglioni the year before the London *divertissement*: "Mademoiselle Taglioni is not a dancer, she is the embodiment of dancing. . . . Fortunate woman! Always the same elegant and slender form, the same calm, intelligent and modest features; not a single feather has fallen from her wing; not a hair has silvered beneath her chaplet of flowers! As the curtain rose, she was greeted with thunders of applause. What airiness! What rhythmic movements! What noble gestures! What poetic attitudes and, above all, what a sweet melancholy! What lack of restraint, yet how chaste!"

Gautier speaks of Cerito two years after the *Pas de Quatre*: "Fanny Cerito's principal qualities are grace of pose, unusual attitudes, quickness of movement, and the rapidity with which she covers ground; she bounds and rebounds with an admirable ease and elasticity; there is a charming grace about her whole body. . . . She radiates a sense of happiness, brilliance, and smiling ease which know neither labor nor weariness. . . ."

Of Carlotta Grisi, Gautier had this to say at the time of her debut at the Paris Opéra (1841): "She is possessed of a strength, lightness, suppleness and originality which at once place her between Elssler and Taglioni." Two years later he was to write that "Grisi's dancing has a quite special style; it does not resemble the dancing of either Taglioni or Elssler; each one of her poses, each one of her movements, is stamped with the seal of originality."

Pas de Quatre with its original cast was performed only four times (July 12, 15, 17, and 19, 1845). Queen Victoria and the Prince Consort attended the third performance. Three of the original cast—Taglioni, Cerito, and Grisi—danced in a revival of the *divertissement* that was performed twice in Lumley's theatre: on July 17 and 19, 1847. Carolina Rosati replaced Lucile Grahn in these performances. Rosati at this time was only twenty years old; fifteen years later, in Russia, she was to dance the leading role in *The Daughter of Pharaoh* (Pugni), the first great success of the ballet master Marius Petipa.

A year after the first performance of the original *Pas de Quatre*, Taglioni, Grahn, and Cerito danced together at Lumley's theatre in a ballet called *The Judgment of Paris* (Pugni-Perrot). The ballerinas danced the parts of three goddesses in this *divertissement*, which was hailed almost as loudly as *Pas de Quatre*. *The Judgment of Paris* was Marie Taglioni's last new ballet.

Marie Taglioni retired soon after she danced the revival of *Pas de Quatre* and died impoverished in Marseilles, France, in 1884, at the age of eighty. Fanny Cerito, at the time of her appearance in London, had yet to achieve her fullest fame and in the 1840s and 1850s secured for herself additional triumphs. She died in 1909 at the age of ninety-two. Carlotta Grisi had new successes after the famous *divertissement,* creating the title role in *Paquita* (Mazilier-Deldevez) in 1846 and dancing at the Imperial Theatre in St. Petersburg. She was seventy-eight when she died in 1899. Lucile Grahn, the youngest of the *Pas de Quatre* ballerinas, had danced in Russia before she came to London for Lumley's *divertissement.* Trained in her native Denmark by the great Danish ballet master Auguste Bournonville, Grahn made her debut at the Royal Theatre, Cophenhagen, in 1835. In this theatre Grahn danced a version of *La Sylphide* created for her by Bournonville (1836). This production of the famous ballet has been in the repertory of the Royal Danish Ballet ever since it was first performed. Grahn died in 1907 at the age of eighty-six.

Perrot's *Pas de Quatre* was reconstructed in England in 1936 by Keith Lester, with the assistance of C. W. Beaumont, and presented by the Markova-Dolin company with the original music. This revival was staged for Ballet Theatre on the occasion of its first visit to London in 1946. Another version of the *Pas de Quatre*, by Anton Dolin, was first presented by Ballet Theatre at the Majestic Theatre, New York, on February 16, 1941. This version was presented by the Ballet Russe de Monte Carlo at the Metropolitan Opera House in 1948 and by the Festival Ballet in London in 1951. Following is a list of notable productions of the *Pas de Quatre* and their casts:

Production	Taglioni	Cerito	Grisi	Grahn
Ballet Theatre, 1941	Alicia Markova	Annabelle Lyon	Nora Kaye	Irina Baronova
Ballet Russe de Monte Carlo, September 18, 1948	Alicia Markova	Alexandra Danilova	Mia Slavenska	Nathalie Krassovska
Festival Ballet, June 4, 1951	Alicia Markova	Alexandra Danilova	Nathalie Krassovska	Tatiana Riabouchinska

In 1943 Edwin Denby wrote of a production of *Pas de Quatre:* "Miss Markova takes the part of the greatest of the four, Marie Taglioni—Marie *pleine de grâces,* as she was called—who was a sallow little lady full of wrinkles, celebrated not only for her serene flight through the empty air, but also for the 'decent voluptuousness' of her expression. Watching Miss Markova's performance one feels that not even the eminently respectable British queen could have found any fault with the female modesty of such a look as hers. And that 'refined' look is Miss Markova's joke on Victorian propriety, and a little too on the vanity of exhibiting technique just for its own sake.

"Her expression is a parody, but the leap itself is no parody of a leap. It is the real, incredibly difficult thing. Taglioni's leap couldn't have been any better."

LES PATINEURS
THE SKATERS

Ballet in one act. Music by Giacomo Meyerbeer. Choreography by Frederick Ashton. Scenery and costumes by William Chappell. First presented by the Vic-Wells Ballet at the Sadler's Wells Theatre, London, February 16, 1937, with a cast headed by Margot Fonteyn, Robert Helpmann, and Harold Turner. First presented in the United States by Ballet Theatre at the Broadway Theatre, New York, October 2, 1946. Scenery and costumes by Cecil Beaton. Nora Kaye, Hugh Laing, and John Kriza danced the leading roles.

Some people watch ice skating and say how like dancing it is. *Les Patineurs* shows us how dancing, among other things, can imitate ice skating. The ballet has no story; it simply organizes what any of us might see at a skating rink into a series of nine *divertissements*. The music, arranged by Constant Lambert, is based on selections from Meyerbeer's operas *L'Etoile du Nord* and *Le Prophète*. The Ballet Theatre production is described here.

The music is whistling, thumping holiday fare. The scene is any secluded skating pond, the time, night. Snowy branches of barren trees hang over the pond; brightly colored paper lanterns light up the forest. Four couples skate across the scene. Two pretty girls follow them, slipping and turning on the ice. One of the boys in the skating party falls; his girl brushes him off, and they exit. A boy in bright green rushes in and treats us to a quick, dazzling display of virtuosity and skates off as though he'd done nothing at all.

The harp signals a romantic melody, and two lovers enter. The boy carries the girl high on his shoulder, sets her down, and she turns close to the ground. The couple are dressed in white and seem at home in the snow-laden scene. They circle the stage, the boy lifting the girl softly to the right and left. For a moment they separate; then they rejoin, and the boy spins the girl around and around. They skate away, hand in hand.

Eight couples—the girls in bright red and the boys in yellow and blue—fill the skating area. Two girls take over the pond and dance brightly to a tinkling tune. The lovers join the eight couples and dance with them a gay ensemble. The boy in green circles the stage, then leaves. Now the ensemble moves with a slower grace. The boy in green now shows off among them, and all watch him. When he is finished, they turn to watch four girls who are skating apart from the crowd; then all skate off in a circling line.

The boy in green and the two girls who danced the first *divertissement* perform a *pas de trois*. Soon they are followed by two other girls, who do an incredible number of fast, accelerated *fouettés*. The boy in green hails the others in the party to come back, and everyone promenades. Snow begins to fall. The girls resume their *fouettés*, whirling away faster than ever as the exhilarating music comes to a climax. The boy in green is challenged by their skill to turn faster than ever and he is spinning like a top when the curtain falls.

PETROUCHKA

Ballet burlesque in one act, four scenes. Music by Igor Stravinsky. Choreography by Michel Fokine. Book by Stravinsky and Alexandre Benois. Scenery and costumes by Benois. First presented by Diaghilev's Ballets Russes at the Théâtre du Châtelet, Paris, June 13, 1911, with Vaslav Nijinsky as *Petrouchka*, Tamara Karsavina as the *Ballerina*, Alexandre Orlov as the *Moor*, and Enrico Cecchetti as the *Charlatan*. First presented in the United States by Diaghilev's Ballets Russes at the Century Theatre, New York, January 25, 1916, with Leonide Massine, Lydia Lopokova, and Adolph Bolm in the principal roles.

Petrouchka tells the story of a puppet with a human heart, a creature of straw who comes to life only to be disbelieved. Characters similar to Petrouchka, half comic, half tragic, have been common to popular theatrical tradition in Europe for hundreds of years—characters such as Pierrot and Puck, clowns no one will ever take seriously, funny men who are always unlucky but who somehow manage to have in the end more wisdom than anybody else; funny men such as Charlie Chaplin's tramp. *Petrouchka* is ballet's representation of this universal character, of what the creators of the ballet knew in their youth as the "Russian Punch and Judy Show." At first the puppet is happy to be a mere automaton. Then he falls in love with a beautiful dancer and tries to win her, though all the world seems against him. He loses her, dies, and everyone laughs. He wins by returning for the last laugh himself.

SCENE ONE—THE SHROVETIDE FAIR: The first scene of the ballet is set in a great public square in old St. Petersburg. The year is 1830; the season, winter—the last week before Lent, when all the populace gather together for final feasting and celebration. Even before the curtain rises, the orchestra tells us it is carnival time, as the cheerful blatancy of the music swells and varies to bring up images of a surging festival, where everyone is determined to have a good time in his own way. Peasants, gypsies, soldiers, and well-dressed folk, all in holiday attire, mingle in the snow-covered square. Fair booths decorated with bright bunting and flags surround an open area, and in the back stands the largest booth of all. It has blue curtains drawn across it like a stage. Above the booth, in Russian, are the words "Living Theatre." Behind it are the spires of government buildings topped with flags. The crowd tries to keep warm by moving constantly; its members stamp and throw their arms around their chests as they talk to each other; some buy hot tea at a booth with a large, steaming samovar. But the cold weather serves only to intensify their good spirits. Everyone seems to be happy and carefree in the pursuit of a traditional pleasure all can share. The open, undisguised merriment of the music whirls with the circling crowd and its quick-changing rhythms accentuate the variety of noises that refuse to blend into one tune—the loud, comradely greetings, the laughter, the shrieking of persistent barkers, the vigorous dancing of three enthusiastic peasants.

The crowd hears a barrel organ grinding away in the distance, but its small sound is almost immediately drowned out by the hubbub in the square. The organ-grinder enters, playing a street song, and the people stand aside to watch his approach. With him comes a girl who carries a little rug under her arm and a triangle. She spreads the rug over the snow, strikes the triangle in a steady beat to secure everyone's attention, and begins to dance to a gay tune. Her dance is clearly designed to show the crowd how rapidly she can turn on one point without stopping; and as people begin to be impressed by her virtuosity, the organist shows off too, by grinding out the song with one hand and duplicating it on a cornet he holds with the other. When he finishes, he begins to play again his rather mournful street song, while on the other side of the stage a rival team of entertainers has appeared to attract the crowd away. There another dancer begins to turn to the tune of a hurdy-gurdy, and a new group forms about the girl and her accompanist. The organist and his partner glance over at the newcomers and speed up the tempo of their act. The two dancers and the two instruments compete openly: each of the girls imitates the other's movements, and the crowd watches first one and then the other as if they were looking at a tennis match. Finally the girls have spent all their energy and the contest is over. Both end their dances in identical positions; the spectators applaud, reward both couples, and everyone is delighted.

The square is now packed with people, who mill about greeting one another and conversing as the orchestra renews the raucous overture. Rowdy peasants come in and dance an animated Russian folk dance to the amusement of some of the crowd. The scene is now feverish with liveliness and hearty good spirits, and the music reaches a high volume to duplicate this enthusiasm. Two drummers step out from behind the blue-curtained stage at the rear and walk forward. The crowd stands back. The drums roll commandingly; everyone looks toward the stage; a loud chord from the orchestra is cut off sharply. A man with a high-peaked hat pokes his head through the curtains. This is the Charlatan, the showman in charge of the "Living Theatre." Everyone is silent as they watch him. He is a showman who entertains by magic, and when he steps out from behind the curtains, no one is quite certain what he will do. His long black robe decorated with mysterious signs, his white face, and his menacing gestures attract the crowd strangely. He takes out a flute. The orchestra sounds a few weird bars suggestive of incipient evil. Then the Charlatan surprises us by playing on his instrument not an Oriental incantation, but a pleasant melody, beseeching in its repetitions. This is his magic song, the music that will bring to life the unseen show behind the closed curtains. The crowd waits, fascinated. The Charlatan gives a sudden imperious signal. The curtains fly back. We see a stage separated into three small compartments. In each compartment rests a motionless puppet, staring out at the audience with blank expression. The three figures are supported by high armrests. In the center is the prima Ballerina, with perfect, Dresden-china features and pink cheeks. She poses rigidly, waiting to be wound up. On the left is the Moor, with white eyes and a white mouth set in a coal-black face. He wears a turban, a bright blouse with a sash about his waist, and trousers of gold brocade. On the right, completely relaxed, is Petrouchka. His face is a white mask, his body is limp, like that of a rag doll. His costume has no conventional design: the loose-fitting trousers that hang down over black boots, the blouse ruffled at the neck, the haphazard cap— all make his figure absurd. While the ballerina and the Moor hold themselves erect, Petrouchka's head lolls to the side. Of the three, he is the least eager to move or to be moved. Lifeless as he is, Petrouchka therefore seems to be more natural. The ballerina and the Moor are posed tensely, ready to spring into activity, but Petrouchka's attitude suggests that perhaps he is tired of being a puppet.

The three puppets remain still as the Charlatan finishes his invocation to his magical gods. The ensuing music is low and mysterious. The Charlatan cuts it short by sounding his flute three times, whereupon Petrouchka, the ballerina, and the Moor instantly wake up and move their feet to the sharp and lively rhythms of a Russian dance. The puppets still stand, and their feet move so fast on and off the floor that their bodies seem suspended. They have come to life so spontaneously, and their feet mark each accent of the dance with such energetic unison, that it is difficult to believe they were inert but a moment before. The music becomes more demanding in its tempo, but the puppets follow the dance perfectly, as if they were toy soldiers obeying the beat of a snare drum. Now they abandon their armrests and step down. The crowd gives them room, and, to the great pleasure of the spectators, the puppets act out a dumb show almost as mechanically as they danced. Both the Moor and Petrouchka are enamored of the ballerina. The Moor flirts with her, and the ballerina seems to favor him, upon which Petrouchka, in a jealous rage, attacks his rival. The Charlatan signals for the drama to stop, and the three puppets involuntarily return to their dance routine. The stage grows darker, and the crowd begins to wander off. The Charlatan makes another signal, and the puppets immediately cease all movement and become rigid and still. The curtain falls.

SCENE TWO—PETROUCHKA'S ROOM: Now we are taken behind the scenes, into the private lives of the puppets. Petrouchka's room is a barren cell. The peaks of icy high mountains are painted all along the walls, near to the floor, while up above, near the ceiling, is a border of puffy white clouds. The room has been decorated, the set implies, for a character not altogether of this world. On the right wall hangs a large portrait of the Charlatan. A door on the left is embellished with satanic figures carrying pitchforks. Petrouchka is suddenly tossed into the room through this door by the Charlatan. The door slams shut. Petrouchka makes a feeble effort to pick himself up, but wonders whether it is worth it. His wooden gestures indicate that everything is hopeless. Here he is in prison again, with nothing to look at but a picture of his master. A piano takes up a despondent theme that embodies Petrouchka's despair, while the rest of the orchestra tries to drown it out. He moves about the room helplessly, he tries to open the door, he pounds on the walls, hoping that someone will release him. Then, all alone, he rages against the world that ignores him. As trumpets blare a loud fanfare, Petrouchka turns to the portrait of the Charlatan and shakes his fists in challenge to the evil magician who limits his life to public performances.

As if to prove that he is worthy of a better fate, Petrouchka then does a little dance in which he imitates human expression of feeling. The piano accompanies him. His arms are stiff, but when he holds them close to his heart and then opens them in a gesture of hope, we see that the puppet understands more than the dumb-show version of love. He is a marionette who might become human, but cannot because of the Charlatan who made him. His hatred of the Charlatan is his hatred of his inarticulate self, that part of his dual nature that can but pathetically copy the human gestures for the human emotion his other nature feels so intensely. He arouses our pity because we see that his rage against the world is also his rage at himself. His clumsy wooden limbs try in vain to express their freedom, and his white face is a mask of sorrow.

But Petrouchka's whole attitude changes when he turns to see that the ballerina has entered his prison. Now the music is gay and lighthearted and Petrouchka jumps about joyfully. The ballerina, who stands motionless on point, registers shock at this inelegant expression of pleasure. She makes the appropriate formal gestures of delicate disapproval and turns to go. Petrouchka is beside himself with anxiety and proceeds to increase the ballerina's distaste by leaping higher to attract her attention. Clearly, the ballerina has had enough of the uncontrollable puppet. She turns and leaves.

Once again Petrouchka is in despair and again, to the accompaniment of the piano and the overpowering orchestra that represents the world he fights against, he gives himself up to his grief. The Charlatan will always think him a mere puppet; the ballerina will never regard him as anything but an idiotic buffoon. He flings his exhausted body about the room, bangs against the walls, finally succeeds in tearing open a large hole in the right wall, and collapses when he sees that it leads nowhere.

SCENE THREE — THE MOOR'S ROOM: The Moor, too, has been imprisoned by the showman, but his abode is ornately decorated and sumptuously furnished. Everything is splashed with color. A large couch, covered with the skin of a tiger and backed with cushions, is on the left. Tall, bushy palm trees are painted on the walls. Serpents and ferocious beasts depicted in bright colors peer out into the room through thick jungle foliage. On the right is a door ornamented with a snake rampant. On the couch lies the Moor. He is playing idly with a coconut. The music is slow, almost lazy, as the Moor amuses his indolence by tossing the coconut and catching it. Unlike Petrouchka, the Moor is satisfied with his abode and appears happy whiling away the time of day like the caged beast contentedly resigned to an imitation jungle. He is also unlike the clown in his inhumanity: he is all puppet. He is soon bored with his simple pastime and tries to vary it with complications: by grasping his toy with his feet and letting it fall, by catching it in many ways. But this is not sufficient for the Moor's entertainment. He grows angry with the coconut. He shakes it, as an animal would shake the head of a helpless victim. He hears something inside, but he cannot break the coconut. He pulls out his scimitar, places the coconut on the floor at his feet. The music crashes with his effort to break the coconut in two, but it is hard as a rock. The Moor is astonished. He stares at the mysterious object that can withstand his mighty blow and decides that it must be magical. He kneels then, bows and worships his plaything as he would worship a god.

The door moves aside, and a roll on a drum signals the entrance of the ballerina. She dances in, horn held to her lips, and steps gaily about the room, the beat of the drum accompanying the tune she plays. The Moor forgets his fetish and watches her with great pleasure, a pleasure which the music expresses with brief cries. The ballerina is charmed by this simple response, so different from the open approval of Petrouchka, and obliges the Moor by dancing a waltz. He is delighted beyond mere approval by this performance and insists upon dancing too. His motions are primitive alongside her elegant steps, but he nevertheless tries to make his crude dance fit the rhythm of the ballerina's waltz. He fails miserably and persists in his own private rhythm as the orchestra imitates the chaos of their duet by opposing different melodies. The Moor is now infatuated with the dainty ballerina and demonstrates his affection by pulling her toward the couch. The ballerina pretends to be aghast at this behavior, but secretly she is charmed also and scarcely resists when the Moor holds her on his lap. Their amorous dalliance is interrupted, however, by strange noises from outside. One of Petrouchka's melodies is proclaimed on the trumpet, and the clown thrusts his arm in at the door in an effort to wedge himself into the room. He has imagined the plight of the ballerina and has come to her aid! The couple jump guiltily as he forces his way in; they spring apart. The jealous Petrouchka berates the Moor for his behavior and approaches him menacingly as the music resounds his rage. The Moor recovers from the surprise of Petrouchka's sudden appearance and replies with animal grunts. Then he draws his scimitar and begins to chase the clown around the room. The ballerina faints on the couch, the Moor closes in on Petrouchka, whose end seems certain until he makes a quick dash for the door and escapes. The Moor is about to pursue the interloper, when he remembers the ballerina. He drops his sword, goes back over to the couch, and pulls the ballerina back onto his lap. The curtain falls as his head bobs up and down in savage satisfaction. The private lives of the three puppets have turned out to be almost identical to the dumb show they acted before the public: Petrouchka always loses.

SCENE FOUR—GRAND CARNIVAL: The Shrovetide Fair, the outside world, has gone on while we watched the inner drama backstage, and the music now takes us back to the festivities. Very little time has elapsed, for the stage is not yet dark and the celebrating crowd is by no means ready to go home. The puppet theatre in the back is dark and silent. Stimulated by their continuous refreshment, the peasants are all laughing and whipping themselves up to a final high pitch of excitement. A group of nursemaids emerge from the multitude, line up, and start a traditional dance to a Russian folk song that is exhilarating in its open melody; the crowd sways to the rhythm of the dance. The nursemaids' round is interrupted by deep, plodding notes from the orchestra, which herald the arrival of a trained bear. The bear swaggers clumsily onto the scene, led by his trainer, who laughs at the fears of the spectators and directs the bear in a few simple tricks. Then follows the dance of the coachmen, whose performance outrivals all the others in color and vigor. The theme to which the nursemaids danced is heard again, and the nurses join the coachmen. The couples seem to exhaust themselves in joyous abandon, but gain fresh strength with each step. Garishly dressed masqueraders—a demon, various animals—scurry about in the square trying to frighten people, but almost everyone is involved in the dance, in watching it at first, then imitating it while standing still, then participating fully, so that the stage gradually becomes a mass of whirling color. The frenzied beat of the music, and its increasingly raucous volume, intoxicates the dancers, and—as night descends on the scene and snow begins to fall—their movements in this picture frame of old Russia surge with a final expression of carnival fervor.

The enthusiasm of the revelers has not allowed them to notice that in the back, within the puppet theatre, there are signs of activity behind the drawn curtains. They all turn, as they hear strange noises inside the theatre, and wait expectantly. Petrouchka comes running out, the music sounds his fanfare, and we see that he is trying to escape from the Moor, who dashes out after him. The crowd is struck dumb by this apparently spontaneous life in the puppets and looks on, fascinated, as the clown tries to avoid the blows of the Moor's scimitar. The Moor's animal strength overpowers Petrouchka. The clown is cornered. He covers his head with his arms, shaking with fright. The Moor, with one blow of his sword, strikes him down. Petrouchka doubles up in pain. The music reflects his agony and his great effort to remain alive, but his legs stretch out, his whole body quivers spasmodically, and he is dead.

His death has been so realistic that the people who surround his body cannot believe that he is a mere puppet; a crime seems to have been committed. Someone calls a policeman, who observes the dead clown and hauls out the Charlatan to give an account of the strange goings on. The Charlatan is much amused at his suspicions and picks up the body to show everyone they are mistaken. Petrouchka is now a limp rag doll, a creature who could never have been anything but lifeless. The policeman is satisfied, people shake their heads, the crowd begins to leave slowly. The charlatan remains alone, holding the puppet, and the stage is almost completely dark. He turns to re-enter the theatre—perhaps to put the errant clown back in his cell—when Petrouchka's fanfare blares out loudly to stop him in his tracks. He looks up: on the top of the theatre the ghost of Petrouchka shakes his fist at the Charlatan—and at everyone else who will not believe he is real.

NOTES: The idea of *Petrouchka* was first of all a musical idea. Stravinsky had finished *Firebird* and was about to begin work on his next project for Diaghilev—*The Rite of Spring*—when he interrupted his plans to compose a purely nonballetic piece. He wanted to write a piece for piano and orchestra in which the piano would seem to be attacked by the mass of instruments. It would fight back, flourish a bit, but then the large orchestra would win out.

Stravinsky began to think of this composition as a contest between a puppet, represented by the piano, and the orchestra. After he had finished it, he tried to find an idea that would express the image that had been in his mind as he composed. He found it in a word, *Petrouchka*, "the immortal and unhappy hero of every fair."

He conveyed his idea to Diaghilev, who, upon hearing the music, decided to produce a ballet on this theme as soon as possible. The painter and designer Alexandre Benois collaborated with the musician and the impresario on the story, which Michel Fokine choreographed for Nijinsky, Karsavina, Orlov, and Cecchetti.

Although it is perhaps the most famous ballet in the modern repertory, *Petrouchka* has seldom been revived with sufficient competence to remind us that its first production was a very great one indeed. Stravinsky has written in his *Autobiography*: "I should like . . . to pay heartfelt homage to Vaslav Nijinsky's unsurpassed rendering of the role of Petrouchka. The perfection with which he became the very incarnation of this character was all the more remarkable because the purely saltatory work in which he excelled was in this case dominated by dramatic action, music and gesture. The beauty of the ballet was greatly enhanced by the richness of the artistic setting which Benois had created for it. My faithful interpreter Karsavina swore to me that she would never relinquish her part as the dancer, which she adored. But it was a pity that the movements of the crowd had been neglected. I mean that they were left to the arbitrary improvisation of the performers instead of being choreographically regulated in accordance with the clearly defined exigencies of the music. I regret it all the more because the *danses d'ensemble* of the coachmen, nurses and mummers, and the solo dances, must be regarded as Fokine's finest creations."

Carl van Vechten describes Nijinsky's Petrouchka in this way: "He is a puppet and—remarkable touch—a puppet with a soul. His performance in this ballet is, perhaps, his most wonderful achievement. He suggests only the puppet in action; his facial expression never changes; yet the pathos is greater, more keenly carried over the footlights, than one would imagine possible under any conditions. I have seen Fokine in the same role, and although he gives you all the gestures the result is not the same. It is genius that Nijinsky puts into his interpretation of the part. Who can ever forget Nijinsky as Petrouchka when thrown by his master into his queer black box, mad with love for the dancer, who, in turn, prefers the Moor puppet, rushing about waving his pathetically stiff arms in the air, and finally beating his way with his clenched fists through the paper window to curse the stars? It is a more poignant expression of grief than most Romeos can give us."

One modern production of *Petrouchka* seems to have remained very close to the original—that of the Royal Danish Ballet. Fokine revived the ballet in Copenhagen in 1925. The painstaking care with which older members of the Danish company teach the younger dancers, and ensure the accuracy of a choreographer's original step and idea, has kept this production intact. P. W. Manchester, in the fifth volume of his work, *Chrysalis*, has written that, in Denmark, "Fokine plainly spent much time on every movement of the two crowd scenes, which unfortunately he failed to do in the original production, which is why so much has been lost down the years. In Copenhagen we therefore see *Petrouchka* given as the master would have wished it, most faithfully remembered and adhered to, with a crowd made up of people everyone of which knows exactly what he or she should be doing every second. . . . The present leading male soloist, Borge Ralov, is the Petrouchka and certainly the leading exponent of the present day . . . . If anyone has felt of recent years that *Petrouchka* is either an outmoded masterpiece or must always have been overrated, let him wait until he has seen what the Royal Danish Ballet has to show before making a final decision."

PICNIC AT TINTAGEL

Dramatic ballet in three scenes. Music by Arnold Bax. Choreography by Frederick Ashton. Scenery and costumes by Cecil Beaton. Costumes executed by Helene Pons. Lighting by Jean Rosenthal. First presented by the New York City Ballet at the City Center, New York, February 28, 1952, with Francisco Moncion as the *Husband* (*King Mark*),

Diana Adams as the *Wife* (*Iseult*), Jacques d'Amboise as her *Lover*
(*Tristram*), and Robert Barnett as the *Caretaker* (*Merlin*).

Today, on the west coast of England, stands "wild Tintagel by the Cornish
seas," a rocky promontory reaching out into the water. Here we find the
ruins of an ancient castle celebrated by poets and chroniclers for centuries
as the stronghold of King Arthur and his Knights of the Round Table. One
of King Arthur's trusted knights was Tristram, who brought the beautiful
Irish maid Iseult to Cornwall to be the wife of his uncle, King Mark. The
love story of Tristram and Iseult has inspired writers from the time of
Geoffrey of Monmouth to the times of Tennyson, Swinburne, Wagner,
Hardy, Edwin Arlington Robinson, and Jean Cocteau.

This modern ballet recalls the story of Tristram and Iseult in a setting
that is centuries later. The time is 1916, the year Sir Arnold Bax composed
The Garden of Fand, the ballet's score. The place is Tintagel.

SCENE ONE: The curtain rises as the music begins. The melody
is soft and magical, weaving in sound a mysterious spell. The scene is dominated by arches of gray, slatelike stone, the ruins of the castle where the
romance of Tristram and Iseult took place almost a thousand years ago. A
man is on stage. He is the caretaker. Dressed in green tweeds with a cap, he
moves about the scene as if only he understood it, as if he shared some secret
with the ancient castle that tourists could not understand.

Tourists enter on the right. They are a motoring party, dressed in the
long dusters of the time. We see a man, his wife, and another man. Two
other men follow behind. The husband looks about and goes over to the
caretaker. As soon as he turns his back, the second man goes to the wife and
takes her hand in his. She glances nervously at the other two men in their
party, who are watching them, and cautions him to be discreet. The husband
comes to take his wife on a tour of the castle, and they exit. As they leave,
the wife waves to the second man, who walks off in the opposite direction.

The woman's maid enters, followed by her master's chauffeur and footman, who carry picnic baskets. A cloth is laid on the ground, the baskets
are opened, goblets and a bottle of wine are set out, and the servants leave.
The second man enters and asks the caretaker if he has seen the woman.
He leaves. Now the woman inquires after the man and goes off in search
of him.

The caretaker, alone, looks about quickly and takes up the bottle of
wine. He opens the bottle, reaches into his pocket, gestures magically over
the bottle, and then replaces it on the picnic cloth. All the picnickers return.
The maid pours wine for her mistress and the second man, who stand
together as the others sit on the ground. The two lovers look in each other's
eyes, make a toast, and drink. As the glasses touch their lips, a trumpet is
heard and the music bursts into thunderous sound. The party is alarmed,
and all leave the stage.

SCENE TWO: The chauffeur and footman, magically transformed into two heralds, rush in bearing the flag of King Mark. The caretaker turns around and around in the center of the stage as the scene, almost at his command, is magically transformed. The ruins disappear, and in their place, rising from the ground, stands a colonnade that graced a room in King Mark's castle. The caretaker's wish has come true: the man and the woman have drunk the magic potion, to become Tristram and Iseult, and again he is Merlin, the magician, who can stand aside and watch the workings of his mysterious art.

Merlin leaves the scene, and King Mark enters with Iseult and Tristram. Except for their costumes, they are the same as before: two men in love with the same woman. King Mark knights Tristram with his sword, and Tristram kisses the hand of his king. Then, for a brief moment, Tristram is alone with Iseult. The lovers snatch at the opportunity to be together. They are unaware that one of King Mark's knights watches them from the colonnade in the rear. Tristram lifts Iseult lovingly in his arms. Brangaene, Iseult's maid, rushes in and separates the lovers. She warns them to be careful, that the king approaches.

King Mark enters, and Brangaene dances with Tristram so that the king will suspect nothing. Two knights propose a hunt to the king. Mark assents and asks Tristram if he will join them. Tristram, anxious to be alone with Iseult, pleads some excuse. The two knights watch this and whisper together. Iseult observes their suspicions and separates the two talkers. Now Iseult herself whispers to Brangaene how delighted she is that she and Tristram can be alone at last.

King Mark thinks it strange that Tristram will not accompany them, but leaves the scene for the hunt. His knights and heralds follow. Iseult, alone, seeks Tristram, running in and out among the arches of the colonnade. She is unaware that one of the king's knights has entered surreptitiously and concealed himself behind one of the columns to watch her. The music is quiet, expectant.

Tristram enters, and the two lovers run together from opposite sides of the stage. The orchestra commences a restrained, almost suppressed, romantic melody that gains gradually in intensity. Tristram kneels, and Iseult falls back over his shoulder. They kneel together. The spying knight moves to watch them more closely. As the melody gathers to a soaring crescendo, Tristram lifts Iseult straight into the air.

The lights dim and the music quietens. The lovers are almost motionless, content merely to be alone together, but their passion returns. To the call of a flute, Iseult entwines her body about Tristram, and the two fall to the ground in a close embrace.

The quiet of the music is broken by a sudden, shocking fortissimo. The false knight rushes out. Tristram attacks him. Brangaene, much alarmed, goes to her mistress. A herald enters with two crossed swords, and the flags of King Mark return. Mark, who has been forewarned, enters and points accusingly to Tristram. Iseult goes to her husband to plead with him, but he brushes her aside. The two knights suggest to the king that he engage Tristram in a duel. Tristram accepts the challenge, and the two men take swords from the herald and begin to fight. As she tries frantically to separate the duelers, Iseult is stabbed. The heralds holding the flags of the king let them fall to the ground. King Mark renews his attack upon Tristram and wounds him fatally. As he falls, Tristram grasps the arm of the king and sinks slowly down. King Mark moves over to stand over Iseult's body.

SCENE THREE: The lights dim. Merlin returns, and the principals in the ancient tragedy disappear. Darkness envelops the scene briefly. When light returns, the castle has vanished and in its place we see again the ruins—dark fingers of stone against the sky. The wife and her lover stand together in their motoring coats, as we left them, about to drink the magic wine. They still look into each other's eyes, and for an instant we feel that they will never cease being Tristram and Iseult. But the husband steps in. He pushes his friend away. His wife's lover stands there, not understanding, holding out his glass: what has he done, he wonders?

The caretaker comes forward, and the stage darkens about him. Alone now in the castle, he holds up the crossed, gleaming swords of Tristram's mortal combat for Iseult. The curtain falls as the music that began the ballet returns us to the twentieth century, suggesting also that, at Merlin's command, the cycle might begin all over again.

NOTES: Frederick Ashton's first ballet for the New York City Ballet, *Illuminations*, had been such a success in 1950 that the American company immediately asked the distinguished English choreographer to return to the United States and mount a second work. Ashton's obligations as principal choreographer of the Sadler's Wells Ballet made it impossible for him to do this until two years later. In the meantime, however, he had agreed with the directors of the New York City Ballet on a subject: a modern treatment of the legend of Tristram and Iseult. Ashton and Cecil Beaton, who was to design the work, traveled to Tintagel, in Cornwall, England, where they observed the ruins of the ancient castle associated for centuries with the love story of Tristram and Iseult.

Ashton wished to use as a score for his new ballet *Iseult at Tintagel* (1915), by Sir Arnold Bax, Master of the Queen's Musick. The score, however, was found to be too short for his needs, and consultation with the composer suggested alternative music—Bax's *The Garden of Fand* (1916), which had had its first performance in the United States, by the Chicago Symphony Orchestra under Frederick Stock. Ashton adopted this score, cast the ballet, and in a very short space of time staged his new work.

Walter Terry reported in the New York *Herald Tribune* that "*Picnic at Tintagel*—musically, pictorially, choreographically, dramatically," was a "theatre piece of which the New York City Ballet may be justly proud . . . Not only has Mr. Ashton used well the dramatic urgency of time but he has also choreographed with craftsmanlike shrewdness and considerable artistry . . . The love duet itself is a work of great beauty. . . ." On the occasion of the New York City Ballet's first presentation of *Picnic at Tintagel* in Europe, at the Edinburgh Festival in August 1952, the New York *Times* reported that the ballet "was swift, exciting and dramatic, and is likely to occupy a permanent place in British ballet."

THE PIED PIPER

Ballet in two parts. Music by Aaron Copland. Choreography by Jerome Robbins. Lighting by Jean Rosenthal. First presented by the New York City Ballet at the City Center, New York, December 4, 1951, with a cast headed by Diana Adams and Nicholas Magallanes, Jillana, Roy Tobias, Janet Reed and Todd Bolender, Melissa Hayden and Herbert Bliss, and Tanaquil LeClercq and Jerome Robbins.

The Pied Piper is a dance ballet set to Copland's *Concerto for Clarinet and String Orchestra*; its title has nothing to do with the famous Pied Piper of Hamlin and refers instead to the clarinet soloist. Copland's score (1948) was not written with a ballet in mind, but *The Pied Piper* derives its inspiration directly from the music, so that we are always being reminded visually of what we are listening to.

Many people imagine that ballets without stories, ballets that are based simply on music—and music which was not composed for ballet in the first place—are a dull prospect. Of course, it is natural for all of us to like stories; but with a little careful listening and watching, it is just as natural for us to be entertained by a visual spectacle based on a musical narrative. After all, we begin to like stories first because we hear them, listen to them, before we learn how to read. If we listen to music in the same way, we find ourselves just as entertained: we don't have to know how to read it. *The Pied Piper* is another ballet that proves how much fun we can have if we recognize this.

Before the music begins, the curtain rises. The stage is dark, and as our eyes try to see what is there, we can barely discern a man walking out from the side toward the center. He is wearing a plain business suit and carrying a clarinet. He looks around him at the bare stage, where there is no scenery —only ladders left propped up against the back wall by stagehands, and a few idle, unpainted flats standing at the left. He looks up, where a little light filters down to illuminate the plain back wall and the radiators that cling to it. He plays a few testing scales on the clarinet and ambles across the stage to the right-hand corner. There he finds a music stand, a lamp, and a high stool. He turns the music stand so that it faces the stage, adjusts the lamp, opens the music, and sits down. Harp strings are plucked softly. Low strings reflect their chords, and the piper begins to play.

The clarinet melody is slow, quiet, sounding lonely and lyrical on the empty stage. Slowly two great doors in the back wall begin to open, and a bright slash of light widens and fans out from the doorway, making an aisle of light across the stage. Two dancers, a girl and a boy, stand silhouetted in the doorway. They are listening to the mysterious music, which seems to come from nowhere. Attracted by its sweet melancholy, they walk forward, holding hands. Both of them wear rehearsal clothes. The door closes behind them. They bow their heads as they stand facing the soloist, then their bodies fall back into a dance that responds irresistibly to the plaintive romance of the music.

The boy supports the girl in low turns and high, soft lifts. The *pas de deux* is tender and yearning, the pace slow, the steps wide, open, and reaching. The dancers pause as a spotlight at the front of the stage throws their shadows against the back wall, then move over to the right, seeking refuge at the source of the music. Another girl enters on the left with a boy. They watch their shadows on the wall. The first couple cross the stage and the boy lifts the girl high over his head as the strings piercingly sound the climax of the melody. Now they join the other two for a moment. All bow low to their shadows on the back wall. A group of dancers wander in and, with the intruding couple, watch as the lovers finish their dance. In the slow rhythm of the dance and the music, lights come up and fade one by one to make the whole stage picture balance in the romantic mood. Lights at the back, against the wall, and on the sides shine directly onto the stage, making a carpet of yellow light. The scene grows dark again, and the boy lifts the girl off into the wings toward the disappearing yellow light.

The dancers who have been standing quietly, watching the love duet, look at the soloist. The stage is now lighted, and we see that all the dancers wear rehearsal clothes—shirts and sweaters and tights of varied colors. The piper begins a cadenza as the romantic music fades behind, and gradually the dancers gather together to listen. Others straggle on, see the group, and listen too. This is music that seems to be asking a question, in quick, lively, darting phrases. The atmosphere is expectant. Instinctively the boys and girls are attracted by the piper's song, and their bodies, almost uncontrollably, begin to answer its phrases. A blond girl's hand shakes to the music, and she holds it out at the end of her arm as if it didn't belong to her. The hand creeps around to the back of her neck, and soon her whole body is miming the music.

The solo ends after a swift climbing scale; the music is curtly and demandingly rhythmic. A redhead seems to go crazy with the insistence of the piper's call. Mysteriously she finds herself climbing on a boy's shoulders. Another boy begins to chase her. Other boys crowd in, there is a scuffle— the boys fighting, but not touching, pointing their fingers like guns.

Drawn to the scene by the light, driving melody, another couple enter. They join the redhead and her partner. The boys and girls separate into two groups and follow their leaders. When a final lead couple is seen to emerge, the boy chases the girl in mock seriousness, turns, and she chases him. Now the whole group is dancing, responding to the music with spontaneous and spasmodic jerkings and jivings as it becomes brisker and hysterically care-free. In different groups, they run back and forth, crisscrossing the stage. Then, suddenly, all the dancers are flat on the floor. Their bodies remain quiet for a minute, but then the music drives at them again with sharp, shrieking calls and they bounce on the floor. Their arms reach up into the air, then their legs. The redhead tries to control her dancing legs by pressing down on the top of her head, as if to put a lid on the vitality created by the music, but her whole body begins to vibrate. The others rise automatically to the music's call, and the stage is a mass of hurried, comic twitchings to the loud beat of the music.

Now the song of the clarinet above the music attracts the dancers like a magnet, and they gather round the piper. But his music drives them back across the stage. Grouped closely together on the side, they reach up their hands to the clarinet's high, piercing song and bow down low when the piper sounds a low note. This low note begins a fast ascending scale and propels them again into motion, and in one movement all the dancers dash across the stage toward the piper. They fall at his feet in a wave, and the music explodes on a final high note.

NOTES: Reviewing *The Pied Piper* in *The New Yorker*, Douglas Watt called it a "brilliant and contagious dance work . . . The whole production made it seem as if Walt Disney had finally succeeded in creating people."

The music for *The Pied Piper*, Copland's *Clarinet Concerto*, was commissioned by Benny Goodman and first played by him.

This ballet enjoyed great popularity during the New York City Ballet's five-month tour of Europe in 1952. Europeans found it typical of the best in contemporary American ballet.

PILLAR OF FIRE

Ballet in one act. Music by Arnold Schoenberg. Choreography and book by Antony Tudor. Scenery and costumes by Jo Mielziner. First presented by Ballet Theatre at the Metropolitan Opera House, New York, April 8, 1942, with Nora Kaye as *Hagar*, Hugh Laing as the *Young Man from the House Opposite*, Lucia Chase as the *Eldest Sister*, Annabelle Lyon as the *Youngest Sister*, and Antony Tudor as the *Friend*.

This ballet tells a story to a piece of music that was inspired by a story. Schoenberg's *Verklärte Nacht* (*Transfigured Night*) is based on a nineteenth-century German poem called *Weib und die Welt* (*Woman and the World*), which had a theme daring for its time. In the poem there are two characters, a man and a woman who walk together in a cold, moonlit wood. They are lovers. First the woman addresses the man. She tells him that she has sinned, that she is going to have a child that is not his. All this happened, she tells her lover, before she was sure of his affection, at a time when she was desperate for any kind of security. She has learned since that sensuality is no security at all and that her new love for him is the blessing she really sought. The man replies that she must not feel guilty, that their mutual love is so great that even her child will be unblemished, that it will be in reality his child. He says that, as the light of the moon embraces the dark night, her love for him will transfigure the child, just as his love for her has transformed him. There is no need for forgiveness: they have love.

Such is the story of *Pillar of Fire*; but because it is a ballet, it takes this story and presents it dramatically, introducing additional characters, giving us a picture of the community in which such an event can take place, motivating the principal characters and their actions as completely as possible. The time is about 1900. The place is any town. The curtain rises to a low throbbing of strings. We see a wide street, lined with houses, under a darkening sky. The street narrows and vanishes in the distance. In the foreground, on the right, stands a high, narrow house, its woodwork embellished with Victorian scrolls. On the front steps a girl sits, brooding. She is plainly, almost severely, dressed; her long dark hair is braided about her head. She sits absolutely erect, her whole body seeming to delight in an intense placidity that is belied only by the clenched fists in her lap. This is Hagar, who lives in this house with two sisters.

The music is dark, heavy, oppressive; yet within this gloom, the principal melody cries out yearningly. Hagar watches the townspeople pass by in the twilight. Young people walk in the street, young people in love, and we sense immediately that Hagar has never been like them. Spinsters walk down the street with exaggerated daintiness, and Hagar turns away in disgust. She herself is not a young girl, but already she is frightened: she cannot be like the beautiful young girls in love, and the spinsters suggest the only alternative. She smooths back her hair, and we see that she is not unattractive.

Her two sisters emerge from the house. One is older, prim, and straitlaced; the other is young, a blond girl with long curls, soon to become a woman. The contrast between these two is apparently the same as the difference Hagar has noted in the passers-by. The younger sister is obviously spoiled, and when the older sister seems to reprimand Hagar for sitting apart from them, the young girl pokes fun at her. A young man comes across the street to their door. Hagar is delighted to see him. He is her only friend, and she is in love with him. Now she is no longer moody, but she hesitates to display her true feelings before her family. She knows them too well. The friend observes this and, being a very polite, conventional young man, is pleasant to her sisters.

The sisters, in turn, are more than civil to him. They are thoroughly aware that he has come to the house mainly to see Hagar, but the one—older, strong, possessive—and the other—young, demanding, accustomed to having anything she wants—soon draw his attention to themselves while Hagar watches. The young sister sidles up to him, flirting with cunning innocence. The friend observes her manner, is charmed by her blond youth, and ignores Hagar. The spinster is delighted at this sudden success of her favorite and asks the friend into the house. He goes in, and Hagar again is alone. It occurs to no one that she would enjoy going with them.

Hagar's despair turns to anger and hatred. It is not enough that her sister has dominated her family; she must also dominate all those who come in contact with it. The girl sees her last hope of freedom gone: her friend is hopelessly ensnared. And so she tries to forget her hope that he will respond to her love. The house across the street aids her forgetfulness. Lights come up inside the house, and Hagar sees through the walls all she has imagined must take place within it. For this is a place where love is celebrated all night long, where bold, unpolite men come to meet their women.

Shadows of lovers embracing are thrown against the walls of the house, and Hagar reaches out in open longing. She is taken aback when a man comes out of the house and glares at her. He walks jauntily, confidently, putting himself on display a little. She pretends to be embarrassed when he looks at her boldly and openly. Under any other circumstances this man would seem absurd to her, but now he embodies all the longings that Hagar cannot satisfy in a normal way, and she is attracted to him and the mysterious life in the house across the street. The man gives her a final look and goes back inside.

Now Hagar's young sister returns with the friend. The friend observes Hagar and has no understanding of her dilemma. Instead of questioning her, instead of helping her, it is much easier for him to succumb to the designs of the younger girl. Now more a woman than a child, the girl curls herself around his affections with the sinuousness of a cat. Hagar sees that her older sister has succeeded in making of the younger a frightening, pretty projection of her own willful selfishness and turns away in horror at the contrast between the girl's innocent beauty and inner evil. Should she warn the friend? How can she? He would laugh and not believe her. And so she watches as the girl takes her friend's arm and goes off with him for a stroll in the moonlight.

As they disappear, Hagar is frantic. She despises not only her sisters, but the man who will be duped by them. She contorts her body obscenely to express the depth of her disgust. Feeling now completely severed from all

she might hold dear, she turns instinctively toward the mysterious house
The man who watched her in the street sees that she is still alone and leaves
the house to join her.

Hagar welcomes him, and the two dance together. The girl loses all
sense of modesty and decorum and for the first time in her life gives open
expression of her feelings. The man encourages her passion. When Hagar
leaps across the stage, he seizes her in mid-air, cutting short her flight of
freedom, directing her warmth only to himself. He takes her by the hand
and leads her to the house. Now eager to learn its secrets, Hagar enters
ecstatically.

When she leaves the house a little later, she is alone. The conventions
she renounced to discover love renew their hold on her to expose her act as
sin, and she is filled with remorse. Now she has nothing, for she has rapidly
learned the inadequacy of the kind of life led by the bold young man.

Her older sister enters and sees the guilt on Hagar's face. Neighbors
passing by seem to know of her guilt, and Hagar, bitterly ashamed, seeks
some friendly response from the crowd. She is shunned by everyone, even by
the sordid people who frequent the house she has just left. These lovers-in-
experience look at her in contempt while the youthful lovers-in-innocence
scarcely see her.

The younger sister and the friend return from their walk. While the
older sister mingles with a group of spinsters, confirming the shame Hagar
has brought on the family, the young girl cavorts with new playmates from
the house across the street. She is delighted to discover how nice they are

The tormented Hagar can turn to no one. Obediently, like a child, she
goes with her sisters toward the house. The two women say good night to
her friend, as if to apologize for her behavior. The scene blacks out.

The street and the houses have vanished when the scene is lit again
The three sisters find themselves outcasts from society because of Hagar's
indiscretion. Secretly her two sisters are delighted at her defection; but they
are angry at what it has cost them and they repudiate her. The friend comes
to her with his sympathy and help, but Hagar cannot bear to confront him
with her evil. She seeks recognition instead from the townspeople, from the
loose women, from men like her seducer. All are aghast at her downfall and
will not help. Finally, in desperation, she reaches out pathetically to the
seducer himself. He looks at her as if he'd never seen her.

Seeing her final despair, the friend returns. Hagar twists away to flee
but now the young man will not let her go. He holds her strongly, yet
tenderly, tells her that she has forgotten his love and that he is there to stand
by her and welcome her as his own. The girl is overwhelmed with his loving
kindness and dances with him a *pas de deux* that is not only passionate, but
tender. Hagar now possesses the permanent love that she despaired of finding. The lovers disappear for a moment, then we see them again, walking
away in the distance, their hands clasped, their shoulders touching. They

move slowly away out of sight in a deep green forest to the singing romantic music.

NOTES: *Pillar of Fire* at its *première* received twenty-six curtain calls. Edwin Denby called it the "first large, completely serious and poetic work ever created by Ballet Theatre on its own initiative." It is generally agreed to be the finest work of Antony Tudor. Tudor came to the United States and to the Ballet Theatre from England at the suggestion of Agnes de Mille. De Mille had worked with Tudor at Marie Rambert's school in London, when he was first beginning to choreograph, and had been inspired by the first production of his ballet *Lilac Garden*. For Ballet Theatre, which he joined at its beginning, Tudor revived *Lilac Garden, Judgment of Paris, Dark Elegies,* and *Gala Performance,* all of which he had created in England. *Pillar of Fire* was his first new work in America.

Antony Tudor prefers to work slowly in creating his ballets. Many months before rehearsals began for *Pillar of Fire,* he played the music through for the dancers and talked to them, telling them the story, describing the town where it took place, and the characters, in historical and psychological detail. Key movements symbolic of crucial moments in the ballet were then worked out, after which the pattern was filled in with the movements appropriate to the characters and their situation at these points.

Writing soon after the work's first performance, Edwin Denby described the quality of these movements:

"In point of dance style, *Pillar of Fire* is a work of originality and precision. The devices used are dramatic ones: Brief phrases urgently interrupted—they re-emerge and do amplify; gesture that tends in or braces itself against a direction, an imperative direction in which the dance is driving, urgently into an imminent future. It is the thrill of needing, not the delight of having. And the need is so intense, so unrelieved, it is unbelievable in any but a private faith.

"Or looking at the style statically as a complex of devices, you see how it employs three separate techniques of body carriage, of body tension. The ballet technique—firm, with gesture flowing controlled, with taut leaps and high lifts; a kind of modern-school technique—flexible, with impulsive gesture explosive as jitterbugging, loose low leaps, low lifts; and third, a technique of the body as in everyday life, modest, unstraining, as if at ease. . . . The technical devices don't have the effect of tricks, the effect of them isn't that of professional symbols of style or pattern or meaning. While you watch the dance, the eye sees everything plain. If Tudor uses a grand *jeté,* with high carriage and legs spread taut in the air, the carriage, the taut legs don't tickle you as a gadget would, they are a direct act. . . . In other words, at every moment you see the dancer as a person, as a man or woman dancing; not as an unhappily defective instrument of a choreographer's flights of fancy."

Pillar of Fire made a dramatic ballerina of its American star, Nora Kaye. On the opening night of *Pillar of Fire*, Nora Kaye danced in the *corps de ballet* of *Swan Lake*, the first ballet on the program. After the ovation that followed *Pillar of Fire*, she was elevated to stardom. Since 1942 Nora Kaye has carried still further her great gift for dramatic dancing, creating roles that demand fine acting as well as dancing in new ballets especially created for her by Ballet Theatre and the New York City Ballet. She has also danced the heroines of the great classical ballets, *Swan Lake* and *Giselle*.

Other dancers who appeared in the first performance of *Pillar of Fire* have become famous: John Kriza and Maria Karnilova were among the lovers-in-innocence; Jerome Robbins and Rosella Hightower danced two of the lovers-in-experience.

PINEAPPLE POLL

Comic ballet in three scenes. Music by Sir Arthur Sullivan, arranged by Charles Mackerras. Choreography by John Cranko. Scenery and costumes by Osbert Lancaster. First presented by the Sadler's Wells Theatre Ballet at the Sadler's Wells Theatre, London, March 13, 1951, with Elaine Fifield as *Pineapple Poll*, David Blair as *Captain Belaye*, and David Poole as *Jasper*. First presented in the United States by the Sadler's Wells Theatre Ballet at the Buffalo Theatre, Buffalo, New York, October 23, 1951, with Maryon Lane as *Pineapple Poll* and David Blair and David Poole in their original roles.

Pineapple Poll is a Gilbert and Sullivan ballet, based on one of the *Bab Ballads* of Gilbert and on a selection of Sullivan's music from the famous operettas that he wrote with Gilbert's collaboration. Like *H. M. S. Pinafore* and *The Pirates of Penzance*, *Pineapple Poll* is typically and charmingly British. It is the first ballet to exploit the universal fame of the Royal Navy and, like our own native ballets *Rodeo* and *Fancy Free*, gives us a story that is both happy and sentimental.

The story of the ballet takes its cue from Gilbert's ballad the *Bumboat Woman's Story*. (A bumboat is a boat carrying provisions, vegetables, trinkets, and so forth, to ships at anchor.) This ballad tells the history of the bumboat woman, Pineapple Poll, who joyfully recalls her past by saying:

My cheeks were mellow and soft, and my eyes were large and sweet,
Poll Pineapple's eyes were the standing toast of the Royal fleet!

A bumboat woman was I, and I faithfully served the ships
With apples and cakes, and fowls and beer, and half-penny dips,
And beef for the general mess, where the officers dine at nights,
And fine fresh peppermint drops for the rollicking midshipmites.

SCENE ONE—PORTSMOUTH—A PUBLIC SQUARE:
Poll's history in the ballet begins one day in spring in a public square at
Portsmouth, the great port in South England. Painted statues of the god
and goddess of the sea stand on either side of the stage, framing the scene.
The buildings—shops and naval supply stores—are clean and brightly
painted. In the distance, over the shoulder of the statue of an admiral that
stands in the background, we see the pointed roofs of warehouses and masts
of anchored ships. On the right stands a pub, the Steam Packet. Jasper,
potboy at the pub, is busy polishing the window that advertises wines and
spirits.

Jasper turns and watches longingly as two pretty girls come into the
square, dancing with a sailor. The sailor is dressed in a typical British sea-
man's uniform of the late nineteenth century; the girls wear colorful summer
dresses. Two other tars enter the Steam Packet; a crowd of girls come in
with a group of sailors, take partners, and dance. Two girls who are left
without partners go to the door of the pub and knock. Two sailors come out
to join them, and the waltzing couples pause for refreshment. The sailors
call Jasper to bring them pots of beer, and the potboy runs frantically back
and forth from the pub to the street with tankard after tankard. Finally he,
too, is in need of refreshment and downs two mugs of beer before he reaches
the sailors. The hearty tars toss him about, and he retreats to the door of
the Steam Packet to watch them renew their dance. The vigorous dance ends
with all the girls sitting on their partners' knees.

The music is bright and merry, a triangle tinkles, and Pineapple Poll
dances into the square. She is dressed in a candy-striped dress and wears
green ribbons in her red hair. She carries on her head a basket filled with
flowers and trinkets, and soon all the sailors are surrounding her. Poll sells
most of her wares and begins to dance. From the door of the pub, Jasper
waves to her. She does not acknowledge his greeting, and he places his hand
over his heart, signifying his love for her. He, too, would like to buy a trinket
from Pineapple Poll and goes through all his pockets, one by one, searching
for the one coin he knows he possesses. He finds a piece of silver and
approaches Poll hopefully, but she treats him like any other customer and
when he gives her the flower he has purchased, she throws it on the ground.
Poll, however, consents to dance with him briefly, and Jasper holds her in
his arms until he sees that his love is not requited; he returns to the pub.

The girls and the sailors promenade about the square, and Poll, without
a partner, picks up the flower Jasper gave her and for a moment reconsiders.
Then she tosses it away again and circles the stage. She and all the girls stop
their dancing at this point and watch breathlessly the entrance of Captain
Belaye:

Of all the kind commanders who anchor in Portsmouth Bay,
By far the sweetest of all was kind Lieutenant Belaye.

Lieutenant Belaye commanded the gunboat, Hot Cross Bun,
She was seven and seventy feet in length, and she carried a gun.

The tars salute their captain while the girls begin to swoon. Captain Belaye, dark and handsome, wears a blue jacket, white duck trousers, and an officer's cap at a natty angle. Belaye jauntily inspects his crew, who automatically line up before him. He straightens one of the sailor's neckerchiefs and tries to act as if he were oblivious to the admiring glances of the girls. Casually he touches Poll's cheek, and she steps back in a romantic daze.

The orchestra sounds a drum roll, and Belaye begins to dance. His merry, rapid dance depicts the routine of life at sea: he peers through an imaginary long glass, climbs imaginary ropes, and orders his crew about. The crew, who stand in back of him during this solo, throw their hats in the air at a final dazzling display of virtuosity by their commander. The girls rush to surround him. The tars take their swooning partners out of the square, lest they begin to devote all of their time to the side-whiskered captain. Poll is the last reluctant girl to leave the scene and whirls out of sight, dizzy with love for the captain.

Belaye is alone for a moment, but soon he is joined by a pretty overdressed young lady and her chaperone. This is Blanche, the girl he wants to marry, accompanied by her aunt, Mrs. Dimple. Blanche is all decked out in red, white, and blue and clearly is in love with her fiancé's navy. Mrs. Dimple, in black, wears a high feathered hat and brandishes an umbrella, which gets in the way every time the captain tries to speak to her or to Blanche. He and Blanche snatch a few moments together; he embraces her, and the music is romantic. But Mrs. Dimple is on the job again; the music mimics her busybody authority as she scolds the two lovers. They begin to dance together, but Mrs. Dimple good-humoredly interferes again and in the process drops her umbrella and shawl over and over again. When she turns away to look about the square, Belaye kisses Blanche; upon the return of the crowd, he escorts her and Mrs. Dimple to another part of the town.

Poll observes his departure disconsolately, and all the girls follow her example in a slow ensemble dance that is listless and despondent. The sailors try to cheer the girls up, but the girls will have none of them. The tars are a little angry now and play tug of war with their sometime sweethearts. When they end up flat on their backs, they vow vengeance on their handsome captain.

Good Captain Belaye dances back in at this point, and again the girls are in a daze. The sailors rage as the girls reach out to touch him and blow him kisses frantically. Belaye reprimands them as if they, too, were members of his crew, but the sailors are still jealous and threaten him. He dances in their midst and is tossed about by the men, as the girls continue flirting. Belaye dances gaily down through a line of adoring girls, who kneel and try to touch him as he passes, and the curtain falls.

SCENE TWO — THE QUAYSIDE : Night has fallen. A drop curtain places us on a dock that stretches out into Portsmouth Harbor. *H. M. S. Hot Cross Bun* is seen at the right. Above the ship's anchor chain a nude figurehead winks amusingly. Across the water a lighthouse stands at the end of a long seaside quay, where the Lord Nelson Tavern and the customhouse face us. Captain Belaye strides across the scene and mounts the gangway, shaking his head at the impertinent lasses of Portsmouth town.

Pineapple Poll follows him. She knows that the *Hot Cross Bun* has been ordered back to sea and is sad that she will not see Belaye for some time. Then, on the right, at the foot of the gangway, she discovers a discarded sailor's uniform. Suddenly her face brightens and she rushes off into the wings.

Liberty has expired for the crew of the *Hot Cross Bun*, and in slow single file the sailors make their way across the dock to their ship. When they have disappeared up the gangway, Poll returns. She now wears white sailor's pants and her mood has changed completely:

And I went to Lieutenant Belaye (and he never suspected me!)
And I entered myself as a chap as wanted to go to sea.

Poll is delighted at the ruse, whirls happily, puts on the blue jacket, takes the ribbons out of her hair, and adjusts the sailor hat at a jaunty angle. Now she is ready for sea. She steps up the gangway with salty determination.

The music now sounds a pathetic strain, and Jasper arrives on the scene. He is looking for Poll and has come to the dock as a last resort. He cannot find her and, as he looks down at the water, he fears the worst. Suppose she has thrown herself into the sea, all for the love of Captain Belaye! Jasper doesn't quite believe it, but soon he finds it impossible to believe anything else: there on the dock is Poll's hair ribbon and there are her discarded clothes. Jasper shakes his fist at the *Hot Cross Bun* and weeps for his lost love. He knows she is dead. He holds Poll's dress against his shoulder, as if she were still dancing with him, and caresses the dress. Slowly he walks away.

SCENE THREE — ON BOARD THE H. M. S. HOT CROSS BUN : The curtain rises, the music brightens, and we find ourselves on the afterdeck of Captain Belaye's ship. In the back, under the poop deck, is the captain's cabin. The white ensign of the Royal Navy flies free in the wind. Belaye is at the helm. The crew lines up at quarters on deck, and Captain Belaye leaves the helm to put them through their paces. He dances before them, long glass in hand. The crew watch respectfully, all that is except the sailor Pineapple Poll, who adores her captain so much that she can barely keep in line. At Belaye's command, Poll spreads her arms wide and the rest of the crew, in a close line, turn around her, like an anchor chain winding around a capstan.

Although the crew seem to be exhausted and Poll is plainly seasick, Belaye has other tasks for them to do and orders them to aim one of the ship's guns at a target he spies in the distance. The crew haul out a cannon, set it in place, load it, and stand ready. Belaye walks over to fire the gun and is astonished to see his crew hold their hands to their ears and run to the starboard side. The cannon is delayed in firing, and when it finally explodes, Pineapple Poll falls back in a dead faint. The other sailors don't know what to do, and Belaye tries to revive this supersensitive member of his crew. He is holding Poll in his arms when she recovers, and this is sufficient to send her into another swoon.

At this point Belaye sees that the *Hot Cross Bun* has reached its destination: Portsmouth again! He takes a ring out of his pocket and smiles. He all but drops Poll, runs across the deck, and leaps over the side to the dock. Poll is left alone for a moment and assumes that all the crew will go ashore. But then she observes that the men are behaving in a curious fashion, very unlike the seafaring type, and a number of curious incidents come back to her:

> We sailed that afternoon at the mystic hour of one,—
> Remarkably nice young men were the crew of the Hot Cross Bun.
> I'm sorry to say that I've heard that sailors sometimes swear,
> But I never yet heard a Bun say anything wrong, I declare.

> When Jack Tars meet, they meet with a "Messmate, ho! What Cheer?"
> But here, on the Hot Cross Bun, it was "How do you do, my dear?"
> When Jack Tars growl, I believe they growl with a big big D—
> But the strongest oath on the Hot Cross Bun was a mild "Dear me!"

One sailor, striding across the deck with affected saltiness, stops to primp girlishly at the porthole of the captain's cabin. No wonder, Poll says to herself, that:

> Belaye would admit that his men were no great use to him,
> "But then," we would say, "there is little to do on a gunboat trim.
> I can hand, and reef, and steer, and fire my big gun too—
> And it is such a treat to sail with a gentle well-bred crew."

Poll begins to wonder where Captain Belaye has gone and picks up his long glass to train it on the town. One of the crew points out that she's looking through the wrong end and grabs the instrument to have a look himself. Captain Belaye leaps back aboard, and they are delighted at his return until they see that he is not alone. He lifts over the side his new bride, Blanche, and Mrs. Dimple.

When the sailors see Blanche in her wedding dress, they fall over in a mass faint. All but Poll, that is, who is so angry that she goes to the captain and claims him for her own. Blanche will not believe her, and Poll takes off her hat and jacket to prove that she has been intimate with Belaye on the ship. Belaye cannot believe his eyes. No one can believe their eyes when all the sailors tear off their false beards and turn out to be girls, too!

Blanche now hates her new husband and will not listen when he tries to explain that he is surprised by all this. She is threatening to leave him when the real "Jack Tars," the real crew of the *Hot Cross Bun,* climb over the bulwarks to berate their captain for sailing away with their girls. Attacked from all sides, Belaye can do nothing. Some of the girls swoon and fall over the helm. But the sailors will have no more nonsense. They grab the girls, throw them on the deck, and stand over them triumphantly. Belaye leaves with his Blanche and her aunt.

The girls seem delighted at this reconciliation and rock contentedly back and forth in their sailors' arms. Now Jasper enters with Poll and they dance together happily. Poll is joyful that at least one man can be constant in his affections! Captain Belaye and his new wife have now settled their argument and they enter with Mrs. Dimple. Belaye is in full-dress uniform —gold epaulets and cocked hat. Mrs. Dimple carries his regular jacket and cap; she goes and presents them to Jasper. The potboy puts both of them on. Poll kisses him, admires his appearance, and they leave the scene to the sailors.

The crew of the *Hot Cross Bun* dance a vigorous, rowdy number and then hail the return of Jasper. Poll joins Jasper; he lifts her high in his arms, then releases her, and Poll dazzles the assembled crowd with rapid, whipping turns on point. Belaye and Blanche return; Poll circles the stage swiftly and then rejoins Jasper. The crew and their girls stand aside as Jasper and Belaye, arm in arm, lead the procession of principals. When these two come to the front of the stage, they separate and stretch between them a large Union Jack, which they drape about Mrs. Dimple's shoulders. She kneels between the two happy couples, umbrella in one hand, trident in the other. Some of the sailors move forward and lift her high over the deck. They begin to turn her as the other sailors and their girls circle them, and the curtain falls as Mrs. Dimple, ruling Britannia with all her might, smiles down upon all the happy lovers.

NOTES: After its first performance in London, Clive Barnes in *Dance and Dancers* reported that *"Pineapple Poll* is funny, bright, and best of all exhilarating." *The Dancing Times* of London found the new ballet "A brilliant example of the work that John Cranko is doing as the Sadler's Wells Theatre Ballet choreographer . . . Like Dame Ninette de Valois before him, Cranko has taken well-known English literary and musical scores and completely transformed them in dance and gestures . . ."

PRINCE IGOR

Ballet in one act. Music by Alexander Borodin. Choreography by Michel Fokine. Scenery and costumes by Nicholas Roerich. First presented by Diaghilev's Ballets Russes at the Théâtre du Châtelet, Paris,

May 18, 1909, with Adolph Bolm, Sophie Fedorova, and Helen Smirnova in the principal parts. First presented in the United States by Diaghilev at the Century Theatre, New York, January 18, 1916, with Bolm, Lubov Tchernicheva, and Sophie Pfanz.

Set to the music of the "Polovtsian Dances" from the second act of Borodin's opera *Prince Igor*, this is purely a dance ballet, without any connection with the plot of the opera. When it was first performed with full chorus and orchestra, the ballet served to introduce to Western Europe the unimagined color of Russian music and dancing combined in a striking single work.

The scene, when the curtain rises, is suffused in the violet light of the approaching dawn. The light of two campfires is thrown against two great tents made of animal skins. Gathered about the fires, the men and women of the Polovtsy tribe sleep soundly. In the distance, around other campfires, other members of the tribe are curled in sleep. A lone warrior stands on watch.

One of the sleeping girls begins to stir. She raises her arm, rises, and stretches. As soon as she is fully awake, she goes from group to group, gradually waking the whole tribe. The somnolent music becomes expectant in its rhythm, as the drowsy villagers prepare for their daily tasks. The sun rises, and the people's dark garments take on their vivid natural colors.

The girl moves forward, turns rapidly, and begins to dance to the music. Other girls join her dance; in the back a group of youths accompany them. The young warlike villagers are unable to contain the vigor which sleep has stored up within them; they seek to release their energy. The girls sit on the ground as one of the boys comes forward and dances with keen strength, spinning swiftly to the pulsating rhythm of the music. The girls surround him, gyrating with brilliant turns. As the youth concludes his dance, the girls fall at his feet.

A great warrior, the leader of the tribe, moves forward, brandishing a brilliant sword. A dozen girls appear, as if at his silent command, and dance softly. Their primitive costumes are embellished with flowing gauze, which follows their movements in dancing waves. A girl in white, with long braided hair, is among them. The music mounts in intensity; the girls sit on the ground and a brave warrior leaps over their heads. He dances fiercely, called by some distant battle call. The girls dance in a group, as a formation of warriors circle their leader. The warrior slides forward, brandishing his weapon, and the entire ensemble forms a warlike tableau to the insistent demand of the music.

The men gather in the center of the stage and dance around and around to the demanding tempo. The girls enclose them in a wide circle of whirling movement. Suddenly the music hesitates. The two groups cross the scene quietly, then the men move up behind the girls and lift them high. The youths slap their thighs in their enthusiasm for battle and they race back and forth across the stage.

Six of the Polovtsy girls come to the front and dance with an energy that emulates the warriors' strength. They are joined by the girls dressed in gauze, who reassert the femininity of their sex. But the warlike dancers take over again, stomping the ground with their feet and clapping their hands to the beat of the music. The finest warrior of them all comes forward and, as the entire tribe beats out the rhythm of his dance, the brave Polovtsian dances a whirling climax to the ballet. He comes forward to the footlights and continues his dance, turning like a persistent top. The whole tribe gathers behind him and turns with him. The scene is alive with whirling movement as the curtain falls.

PRODIGAL SON

Ballet in three scenes. Music by Serge Prokofiev. Choreography by George Balanchine. Scenery and costumes by Georges Rouault. First presented by Diaghilev's Ballets Russes at the Théâtre Sarah Bernhardt, Paris, May 21, 1929, with Serge Lifar in the title role, Felia Dubrovska as the *Siren*, Michael Fedorov as the *Father*, and Leon Woicikowski and Anton Dolin as *Servants to the Prodigal Son*. Revived by the New York City Ballet at the City Center, New York, February 23, 1950, with Jerome Robbins as the *Prodigal Son*, Maria Tallchief as the *Siren*, Michael Arshansky as the *Father*, and Herbert Bliss and Frank Hobi as *Servants to the Prodigal Son*. Lighting by Jean Rosenthal.

The story of the prodigal son is told first in the Bible: ". . . A certain man had two sons. And the younger of them said to his father, Father give me the portion of goods that falleth to me. And he divided unto them his living. And not many days after the younger son gathered all together, and took his journey into a far country, and there wasted his substance with riotous living. And when he had spent all, there arose a mighty famine in that land; and he began to be in want . . . And he would fain have filled his belly with the husks that the swine did eat: and no man gave unto him. And when he came to himself he said, How many hired servants of my father's have bread enough to spare, and I perish with hunger! I will arise and go to my father, and will say unto him, Father, I have sinned against heaven and before thee, and am no more worthy to be called thy son: make me as one of thy servants. And he arose and came unto his father. But when he was yet a great way off, his father saw him, and had compassion, and ran, and fell on his neck, and kissed him. And the son said unto him, Father I have sinned against heaven, and in thy sight, and am no more worthy to be called thy son. But the father said to his servants, Bring forth the best robe, and put it on him; and put a ring on his hand, and shoes on his feet:

And bring hither the fatted calf, and kill it; and let us eat, and be merry:
For this my son was dead, and is alive again; he was lost, and is found . . ."
(St. Luke, 15:11-24)

This ballet tells the parable dramatically, with certain necessary omissions from and additions to the original story, but with the central theme preserved.

SCENE ONE — HOME: The curtain rises almost immediately after the orchestra has played the first few bars of a strong, high-spirited theme. The scene is opulently colored. A painted backdrop depicts the distant view and imaginative sky line of the ancient Near East. A bright yellow sun hangs in a rich blue sky over a port with a lighthouse watching over the sea. At the right, in the back, is the opening to a tent; on the left, toward the front, stands a low picket fence with a small gate. Two boys, friends to the prodigal son, are busy about the scene, hurriedly arranging a store of large wine jugs as if they are preparing for a long journey. The prodigal son emerges from the tent, followed by two sisters. He is dressed in a short blue tunic and an open vest. His sisters, dressed in long, flowing garments, try to engage his attention, but the carefree youth ignores them to greet his friends. He picks up one of the wine jugs and throws it to one of them playfully. The music becomes terse in tempo, and the prodigal son dances vigorously in response to its pounding rhythm. With robust gaiety he seems to act out for his friends the adventures in store for them away from home and to reveal, at the same time, an innocent, headstrong spirit that urges him to seek those adventures. His sisters are frightened at his strong determination to leave home so selfishly and watch apprehensively. The prodigal son leaps about the stage with boundless energy, oblivious to their care. His dance stops in an open gesture when he looks up, to find himself face to face with his father, who has come out of the tent. He is embarrassed for an instant and steps back.

As a new, poignant melody begins, the father beckons to his children. They come and sit before him, the son unwillingly, but obediently. The son's attention wanders, and the father patiently turns his head back to the family circle. He holds up his arms over his children and looks upward in humble prayer. He touches their heads softly. The son turns away in protest at the ritual, but his father persists gently. When the son twists his body away, the father takes the boy's hand and places it on his sisters' hands.

The tension between the son and the father increases; the son turns away in disgust, leaps up, and flaunts his indifference in his father's face. The father rises and stands motionless and unprotesting in his grief, as his son dances in defiance before him. The son's temper is so high and his eagerness to leave home so intense that his sisters watch in terror and sadness. His dance is closely similar to his first dance, but here he is emboldened by anger. He ignores his family, beckons to his two friends, and points toward the open highway. They gather together their gear and run off through the gate, closing it hastily behind them. In a final gesture of rebellion, the son turns rapidly in the air before his father, dashes across the stage, and jumps high over the fence after his companions. The sisters stand close to their father in sympathy, but the old man walks forward slowly, raises his hand in unacknowledged farewell, and stands for a moment watching. Then he motions his daughters to the tent and follows them into their home. The scene blacks out.

SCENE TWO — IN A FAR COUNTRY: The backdrop has been changed when the lights come up again. Still heavily colored, it now depicts an open tent furnished with a festive table. The small, symbolic fence that figured in the first scene stands as it was, on the left. A loud, crashing march heralds the arrival of a group of revelers, who enter on the left in a close line. They wear short tunics and white tights. All of them are bald. The manner in which they cross the stage to the raucous music is grotesque. As they separate, the beautiful, jubilant melody that will dominate the scene receives its first statement from the orchestra. They go over to the fence, turn it upside down, and we see that the prop is also a long black table. The table is moved back. The revelers form in short lines before it and hop across invisible lines toward each other, playing some fantastic game. Four of them lie down on the stage and spread their legs to form a star. One of the revelers lies across the middle of the star as the others move forward and rotate the pattern their companions have made. Their frolic is renewed until the prodigal son enters on the right with his two friends.

The revelers cease their play and gather in a close group on the other side of the stage; they are just as frightened as the intruders. The prodigal son doesn't see them at first. Then he approaches carefully, urging his friends to follow. They refuse, and he abandons his fears, to greet the strangers with open cordiality. He tries to shake hands with one of them, then with another, but all the revelers pull their hands back. He doesn't understand. They touch his rich clothes covetously and come closer. He hesitates and moves away apprehensively, but his friends force him back and he remembers the wine they have brought with them. He tells his companions to give the revelers drink, and immediately the situation changes. The revelers form a parade behind him, and the prodigal son is carried on the shoulders of his two friends. Everyone is now his friend. He is lifted up and, from above, shakes hands with all of his new companions. They throw him from side to side in jovial welcome. Then he dances between his two fellows as everyone watches admiringly. He grasps their hands elatedly, and all the revelers rush to shake his hand. The whole group dances boldly and vigorously with the prodigal son. He jumps over the table as the dance ends, and all gather about him.

The siren comes in, dancing on point slowly and seductively to a tune of Oriental character. She wears a tight red tunic about her slim body, a high headdress, and from her shoulders there trails a crimson cape of velvet. The men watch her intently; the prodigal son is dazzled by her strange beauty and the confidence with which she fascinates. She turns slowly, wrapping the cape around the upper part of her body, then unwinds the garment. She handles the cape as if it were a part of her own body—an animate object obedient to her will. When the cape is fully extended behind her, the siren steps back over it, pulls it up between her legs, and winds it around them. Holding the cape with one arm, she dances proudly. She seems oblivious to the fact that she is being watched; this dance seems to please her more than it could please anyone else. She drops the cape and falls to her knees in an attitude of conventional despair. Then she rises, proud and assertive, to turn intricately on point. She throws the cape behind her, falls back on her arms, and, moving slowly on her hands and points, drags it across the floor slowly. Then she kneels low and pulls the cape up over her head, covering her body completely.

The prodigal son, now helplessly attracted, moves from behind the table and pulls the cape away. The siren rises on point, unsurprised. He tosses the garment aside as she turns to look at him. The prodigal son becomes now as obedient to her desire as the castoff raiment. He stands transfixed as the siren dances before him. She turns with strong, sinuous grace and holds out her arms in a gesture of approval and welcome. She approaches him closely; the prodigal son places his hands on her waist; they move backward in response to her lead. The siren pushes him back against the table. The revelers gather about them, and the siren is thrown back high above the table, into the waiting arms of her accomplices. She sits in triumph over the suppliant prodigal son, who lies on the table beneath her.

The siren is lifted down and sits facing the prodigal son. His eyes look down. His two friends begin a dance to amuse the group. Relieved by this distraction, the prodigal son watches with the others, but glances at the siren when her eyes leave his face. The siren touches his hand and moves her fingers up his arm to caress the golden medallion that hangs about his throat. He looks her full in the face.

His friends finish their dance, kneel before the table, and everyone applauds. The siren and the prodigal son come forward, watching each other intimately. They stand apart. It is as if he were imitating her movements. The siren falls back in his arms. She repulses his caress and entwines her arms back around his neck, and the two dance forward. They pause, and he puts his head between her legs, rises, and the siren sits proudly on his shoulders. Then she slides down his back. She stand on point before him and coils her leg about him, holding him fast, as he turns her. She releases him, and he pulls her over his back; the siren's hands reach out for her feet so that her body forms a hoop about him. Her body snakes about him completely, and slowly she slides to the floor. He steps out of the coil, rolls the siren upright, and holds her under her arms. Her knees rest on his feet as he moves across the stage. Now the prodigal son becomes bold and caresses the siren openly. He sits at her feet, his knees drawn up. She approaches him and sits on his head while resting her feet firmly on his knees. Now she rises straight up, arrogant in her voluptuousness and power. She steps away, and the prodigal son lies supine. She lies back across his body; their legs tangle. Now powerless, the prodigal son lies entwined in the siren's grasp. She gestures in insidious exultation.

The music pounds and shrieks fiercely. The prodigal's two friends pull the couple apart. Their companions are now reveling in drunkenness and force the prodigal son to join them. They drag his exhausted body about the stage while the siren watches from the table. He seeks her help, but the profligates carry her above the table and she pours wine down his throat as he slides down the table beneath her. They lift him high and carry the siren under him. Both are held by the waist as their bodies fall back hideously. They embrace frantically, are finally released, and two drunkards crawl under their legs. The prodigal staggers from group to group in his intoxication and falls against the table, where he cannot distinguish one of his companions from another. The siren watches him expectantly. He rushes up on the table, but the revelers tilt it up high under him and he slides down it, all his strength spent. The siren places her pointed toe on his chest in triumph.

The table now stands up on end. The revelers conceal themselves behind it. The prodigal is shoved back against the table, where he rests helpless. Hands reach out from either side and move down his body. The friends rush out from behind, turn him upside down, shake him, and collect his gold greedily. They stand aside as the siren is carried out. She stands upright on a man's shoulders, her arms akimbo. She gets down and gathers up all the remaining gold. Now the thieves rob the prodigal of all his outer garments, even his shoes. He is still unaware of what they have done to him, and the debauchers celebrate by crawling over and under each other, like eels. The siren yanks off the prodigal's gold medallion, kisses it, and exits. Her companions leave the scene, running across the stage, back to back, like many-legged insects.

The prodigal son wakens slowly from his stupor. He slides down the table to the ground and falls on his face. He pulls himself back up, gripping the table with agonized effort. He looks down at his hands, then at his body. He remembers and holds his head in disbelief. Stretching his hand up plaintively in despair, he acknowledges the betrayal of his friends and his own self-betrayal. He falls to the ground, sees water, crawls to it, drinks, and curls up like a child. He rises, looks behind him at the scene of his debauchery, and struggles off on his knees.

The profligates return, bringing their loot with them. The siren follows. The table is now turned upside down to form the gate and fence. The siren's companions run to the fence, arrange themselves within it, and the siren joins them. One of the men lifts high the end of her crimson cape, others begin a rowing motion, and the table becomes a ship, the siren's cape its sail, and her arched body its figurehead. Her companions blow their trumpets, and the scene blacks out.

SCENE THREE — HOME : The stage is set as it was for the first scene. The prodigal son, covered now with a thin and tattered black cloak, crawls across the stage, supporting his exhausted body with a staff. The music is dark, almost funeral-like in its persistent beat. The traveler's progress is slow and, to him, endless, for he has no idea where he is. He looks about hopelessly. Suddenly he sees the gate to his home. He staggers toward it, reaches out his hand, touches it, and collapses with the effort.

His sisters emerge from the tent. One of them sees him and calls to the other. Together they go to him and open the gate to lead him in lovingly. The piercing melody of the music reflects their great joy. They stand on either side of their kneeling brother as their father comes out. They are so happy that they do not move. The father remains near the door of his home. The son slowly and hesitatingly raises his head and looks up at his father. He beseeches him with outstretched arms. The father does not move. The son twists away toward the fence, but he has no sooner moved than his father raises his hand to keep him. He turns back toward his home, bows his head to the ground, and stretches his arms out behind in self-denial. With head still bowed, he crawls toward his father slowly, wretchedly. He falls full length just as he nears him, reaches out to drag himself forward by grasping his father's feet. He pulls himself up, clinging to his father's arms. The father reaches out to gather him close in forgiveness, love, and protection and, holding him like a child, he covers his son with his cloak.

NOTES: *Prodigal Son* was suggested to Serge Diaghilev by Boris Kochno. The story seemed to him clear and understandable, unlike the many complicated plots people sometimes think appropriate for ballet, and it was an immortal story which everyone knew. It seemed relatively simple to portray the roles of father and son: no one could mistake their identity, and on stage their relationship could be immediately projected to the audience.

The story of the prodigal son in the Bible includes also the story of the older son who stays home and is faithful to his father and the land. But since this aspect of the story was not interesting for the dance and couldn't fail to take up a great deal of time, with no dramatic interest, we wisely omitted it from the idea of the ballet.

The choreography of *Prodigal Son* was assigned to me. What I did was at first not liked by the critics. People found fault with the music, too, because it did not express a religious, Biblical quality. They did not understand that this was a Russian version of the story and that it was designed for the theatre. In designing the choreography, I had in mind the Byzantine icons that are so familiar to all Russians. The siren, for example, I did not think of as a French courtesan, which some people apparently would have preferred; I conceived her as cool, strict, calculating.

The end of the ballet was inspired by a story of Pushkin's, "The Stationmaster." In this story Pushkin described a wayside station at which travelers rested and changed horses. The walls of the waiting room were covered with lithographs of the story of the prodigal son. The last print showed the boy returning home on his knees.

The wonderful setting and costumes that Georges Rouault designed for the ballet materialized in an interesting way. Rouault is, of course, a painter and knew little about stagecraft, but he seemed to enjoy the whole experience of doing scenery for the ballet. Diaghilev, however, was unable to get any designs from him. He begged Rouault to finish them. Finally, only a short time before the *première*, Diaghilev locked Rouault into a room at the Hôtel de Paris, sent in his meals, and told him to get to work. Rouault did hundreds of sketches, but no costume designs. Diaghilev and Vera Arturovna Stravinsky got to work and hurriedly put the costumes together on the basis of Rouault's sketches.

Prokofiev was unhappy about the ballet because he wanted it to be more realistic; when wine was used, he wanted it to be real wine. Diaghilev did not agree, and the two men quarreled. Prokofiev's score to this ballet seems to me his best.

The use of the fencelike structure in the ballet as a boat happened at the first performance. The ballet was produced very hurriedly, and a few hours before the *première* there was still this one point with music and no movement. In desperation, I told the dancers to get into the structure and use it as a boat. I planned to change this the next night, but it worked out well and the audience liked it very much.

Prodigal Son has been danced by Jerome Robbins, Francisco Moncion, and Hugh Laing in the revival I staged for the New York City Ballet. Each of these dancers brings a special quality to his portrayal of the title role and each has been praised for his performances.

THE PROSPECT BEFORE US

Dramatic ballet in seven scenes. Music by William Boyce. Choreography by Ninette de Valois. Scenery and costumes by Roger Furse. First presented by the Sadler's Wells Ballet at the Sadler's Wells Theatre, London, July 4, 1940, with Pamela May, Mary Honer, Margaret Dale, Frederick Ashton, Robert Helpmann, and John Hart among the principals. First presented in the United States by the Sadler's Wells Theatre Ballet at the Pabst Theatre, Milwaukee, Wisconsin, November 3, 1951, with Svetlana Beriosova, Pirmin Trecu,

Stanley Holden, Pauline Harrop, and Michael Hogan among the principals.

The Prospect before Us, or *Pity the Poor Dancers,* is a comedy based on eighteenth-century English art, music, and theatrical history. The art is that of the colorful caricaturist Thomas Rowlandson (1756–1827), one of whose drawings, entitled *The Prospect before Us,* gives the ballet its name; the music is an arrangement by Constant Lambert of selections from the works of the English composer William Boyce (1710–79); and the history is taken from an incident related in John Eber's *History of the King's Theatre.*

The King's Theatre and its rival, the Pantheon, were popular London theatres of the time. Rowlandson's engraving shows us the stage of the Pantheon, where the celebrated French dancers Mademoiselle Théodore and Monsieur Didelot are dancing a ballet before an enthusiastic audience. But there were also enthusiastic audiences at the King's Theatre. The ballet *The Prospect before Us* tells us the story of these two theatres—the intense rivalry of their managers, the resorting to any means to achieve success, the fierce competition for guest artists, and the pitiable condition of dancers who did not know from one day to the next on which stage they would appear.

SCENE ONE—THE STAGE OF THE KING'S THEATRE, 1789 : After the orchestra has played a brief, charming overture, the curtain rises on a ballet rehearsal backstage at the King's Theatre. Five ladies of the ballet await the direction of Monsieur Noverre, the great ballet master, who stands on the right studying a choreographic chart. Madame Noverre sits in the background, knitting. Monsieur Didelot, the *premier danseur,* paces up and down, wondering when the devil Noverre will get on with the show. Mademoiselle Théodore, the *première danseuse,* wanders in. She sits down on the stage and blithely tries on one pair of dancing slippers after another while her fellow performers fret. Finally she finds a pair that suits her, and the rehearsal resumes. Monsieur Noverre pulls Monsieur Didelot into the rehearsal, and this *premier danseur* automatically supports Mademoiselle Théodore in a series of poses. He is not the least bit interested in dancing with her, and when he lifts her indifferently, the girl begins to complain. Didelot rages back at her.

Mr. Taylor, the manager of the King's Theatre, enters with a party of guests. The manager of the Pantheon Theatre, Mr. O'Reilly, wanders in to see what his chief competitor is up to. He trips over some of the dancers and watches the rehearsal with broken, humble envy. When the great Vestris is given a chance to rehearse his variation, he is so disdainful of these spectators that he merely indicates with his fingers the difficult steps he will dazzle them with in actual performance.

The visitors parade off the stage, and the rehearsal ends. When Mr. Taylor returns, Monsieur Noverre and his wife attack him with a demand for more money. As the three squabble over a contract, Mr. O'Reilly tries vainly to find out how much money Taylor is giving them. Finally Taylor accedes to Noverre's demands and he and his rival are alone.

Mr. Taylor and Mr. O'Reilly sit down on chairs at the back of the stage. Poor O'Reilly sits wrapped in thought as Taylor regales him with stories of the dancers, the unprecedented success they will have, and the money he will rake in. He brings out a bottle and offers his friend a drink. O'Reilly hardly notices his glass and drinks almost automatically as he sits sulking, thinking that all this might be his. But suddenly O'Reilly leaps up from his chair, claps his friend on the back, and is all expansive good humor. Taylor is bewildered by this change of mood, but listens patiently as O'Reilly gabbles about the beauty of the dancers and congratulates him on his good fortune. Soon O'Reilly staggers off and Mr. Taylor sits alone, wondering what on earth could have happened to change his rival's mood so quickly.

SCENE TWO — THE BURNING OF THE KING'S THEATRE: Mr. Taylor finds out the answer to his rival's strange behavior soon enough. It is June 17, 1789. A drop curtain depicting the burning of his theatre falls on the previous scene. Mr. Taylor ambles by, not noticing that anything is wrong. O'Reilly enters and calls his attention to a blazing wreckage. Taylor despairs. The dancers come into the street to watch the fire, and O'Reilly instantly directs them toward his theatre, the Pantheon, where new, profitable jobs await them. Mr. Taylor tries to get between his rival and his dancers, but O'Reilly steps over his back to welcome Monsieur Noverre and his wife and take them on to his theatre.

SCENE THREE — A LONDON STREET: Four kids in ragged clothes run into a street in the poor section of the city. A half-dressed harridan looks down from the window of a nearby house as they play aimlessly, tumbling and dancing and clapping hands. They hear a parade approaching and sit down, their backs to the footlights, as a strange procession enters. A horn player and drummer announce the arrival of a party of poor, impoverished dancers, who enter carrying a model of the Pantheon Theatre. Mr. O'Reilly is evidently not paying them very well, for written across the model of his theatre is the legend "Pray Remember the Poor Dancers."

SCENE FOUR — THE STAGE OF THE PANTHEON THEATRE: Mr. O'Reilly's opening night has come, and he sits watching the first performance of the ballet in a stage box on the left. Mr. Taylor observes his rival's success from the opposite box on the right. Dancers enter and, before a conventional pastoral backdrop, enact a *divertissement* with some semblance of plot. Mr. Taylor is anxiously looking for empty seats in the house and does not give his full attention to the ballet. Mr. O'Reilly is delighted with the dancing and when Monsieur Didelot wanders about the stage, anxiously looking for his love, does not in the least hesitate to direct him toward the right girl.

A girl in the *corps de ballet* stands in front of poor Mr. Taylor, obstructing his view of the stage. When another girl prevents Mr. O'Reilly from watching the stage, he flirts with her openly and outrageously, and all but pulls her into the box with him. Soon Mr. O'Reilly gets so carried away by the wonder and beauty of this performance in his own theatre that he, too, must become a part of the *divertissement*. He steps out of his box onto the stage and stumbles about awkwardly among the dancers. He is gradually enveloped by the *corps de ballet* and becomes, at the end of the ballet, a grotesque and embarrassed figure of the final tableau. The curtain falls as O'Reilly poses thus in triumph and Taylor, in his box, despairs at his rival's success.

SCENE FIVE — THE STAGE OF THE NEW KING'S THEATRE: Some time has passed: it is now 1790. Mr. Taylor has secured funds and has rebuilt the King's Theatre. The curtain rises on the stage of the new theatre, its equipment refurbished to duplicate the first scene of the ballet. The stage is dark. Four men stand near the footlights, disputing. Their shadows are thrown up against the back wall of the stage, making a comic enlargement of their obviously petty argument. One of the men is Mr. Taylor; the others are his lawyers, who prance about daintily examining a contract as they pursue their legal dialectic. The problem is: can Mr. Taylor, with his New King's Theatre, oblige Monsieur Noverre and his dancers to return, or has Mr. O'Reilly of the Pantheon a legal right to their continued services? O'Reilly observes the dispute.

The lawyers decide in favor of O'Reilly, who oddly enough is impatient with his advantage. He has grown tired of the whims, tempers, and persistent demands of the great choreographer and wishes to be rid of dancers forever.

SCENE SIX — THE BURNING OF THE PANTHEON: Hardly has Mr. O'Reilly had a chance to return to his theatre with his problem than the Pantheon catches on fire, and, as in Scene Two, we are treated to the pyrotechnical drop curtain. Mr. O'Reilly dances a jig of delight before his flaming theatre and sees himself happily released from the uncertainties of the world of ballet. He is so delighted with the fire that he turns around and warms his pants near its flames.

His dancers, the girls first, flee the burning wreckage. They flee with obvious pleasure: perhaps they, abetted by the dauntless Mr. O'Reilly, have had a hand in the holocaust! Mr. Taylor welcomes them with open arms. Monsieur Noverre and his wife are the last to accept their former manager's greetings and to accompany him back to the New King's Theatre. Mr. O'Reilly, his troubles now but a heap of ashes, looks upon the smoking scene with the uncontrolled relish a stepfather might feel in seeing off to school a thankless child. He will pay for it, in the end, but now he is happy.

SCENE SEVEN — THE STAGE OF THE NEW KING'S THEATRE: Back at Mr. Taylor's new theatre, Monsieur Noverre is again rehearsing his dancers on their home stage. Monsieur Vestris uses the back of one of the chairs for a bar and warms up for his solo, while the ballet master and his wife hover busily over the *corps de ballet*.

Mr. Taylor enters, followed by the inevitable parade of lawyers. Now that the Pantheon has burned down, there is no problem: the French artistes can return to the King's Theatre without fear of suit from Mr. O'Reilly. Mr. Taylor shakes hands with the lawyers one by one, and they dance about him joyfully.

In the midst of this celebration, Mr. O'Reilly stumbles in. He has lost his wig and his coat, and his stockings flap about his ankles: he is very drunk. Whether he is drunk because he is happy or drunk because he is sad, we cannot at first determine, but it soon appears that he has had second thoughts: again he is jealous of Mr. Taylor, who always seems to have all the luck, what with his faithful dancers, his friends to lend him money, and his brand-new theatre.

As soon as he sees the dancers, he begins to imitate them, ruthlessly and absurdly, burlesquing both the ladies and the gentlemen in their artificial poses. When they reprimand him, he apes their movements even more outrageously. Finally O'Reilly collapses on the floor, where he sits with affected dignity. Monsieur Noverre cannot quite believe that he can be so intoxicated. The rank odor of spirits that the besotted manager breathes upon him causes the dancing master almost to swoon. The dancers are aghast at this scandalous interruption to their rehearsal and exit in a huff, followed by Monsieur Noverre and his wife. O'Reilly hoots at them, and as Madame Noverre passes, he grabs hold of her skirt and almost pulls her to the floor.

Mr. Taylor sees nothing for it but to give his unfortunate friend more to drink: it would be useless to *stop* him from drinking. The two sit side by side, as they did at the end of Scene One, Mr. Taylor happy and triumphant, bragging of his good fortune, whispering stories about the dancers, and clapping poor Mr. O'Reilly on the back again and again to display his bumptious good nature. After all, business is business, he seems to say, one must not cast out one's rivals. And business is business, also, to Mr. O'Reilly, who all of a sudden, drunk as he is, comes to. He slaps *Taylor* on the back and staggers about the stage, almost falling into the orchestra, wholly possessed with a new and brilliant idea. He clutches his rival's bottle of whisky in his arms and, zigzagging, nearly tripping, he stumbles off into the wings. Mr. Taylor, left alone, recalls that O'Reilly was similarly jubilant some while back, when, just as now, he had no right to be. Drunk as O'Reilly is, could he be plotting another ruse? Could he? After all, there is a limit to the number of new King's Theatres. The curtain falls.

PULCINELLA

Dramatic ballet in one act. Music by Igor Stravinsky, based on scores by Giambattista Pergolesi. Choreography by Leonide Massine. Scenery and costumes by Pablo Picasso. First presented by Diaghilev's Ballets Russes at the Théâtre National de l'Opéra, Paris, May 15, 1920, with Leonide Massine as *Pulcinella*, Tamara Karsavina as *Pimpinella*, Vera Nemtchinova as *Rosetta*, Lubov Tchernicheva as *Prudenza*, Stanislas Idzikowski as *Caviello*, Nicholas Zverev as *Florindo*, Enrico Cecchetti as *Il Dottore*. First presented in the United States by the New York Music Guild in Chicago, 1933, with choreography by Laurent Novikoff.

Stravinsky's score for *Pulcinella* is based on music by the great Neapolitan, Giambattista Pergolesi. The story of the ballet is based on an early eighteenth-century Italian manuscript found in Naples, and its principal characters are taken from the *commedia dell' arte*, the popular Italian masked comedy, which beginning in the sixteenth century captured the imagination of all of Europe with its universal types: the pathetic Pierrot, the heartless and flirtatious Columbine, the deathless Pulcinella (Punch, to the English-speaking world), and others. The ballet tells a new variation of Pulcinella's immortality.

A narrow street in Naples is the scene. A volcano can be seen in the distance, over the bay at the end of the street. The end house to the left is that of Tartaglia, whose daughter, Rosetta, is beloved by the youth Caviello. The end house to the right is that of *Il Dottore* (the doctor), whose daughter, Prudenza, is beloved by Florindo.

At the beginning of the ballet Caviello and Florindo enter to watch the houses of their sweethearts. Soon Prudenza and Rosetta look out of their windows. They smile at their suitors, seemingly encouraging them, then pour water out over their heads. The doctor, meanwhile, has discovered the presence of the boys and drives them away.

Pulcinella enters—the familiar figure with a long, pendulous red nose. He dances in the street to the tune of a small violin he plays. His dance and his music attract the girls. Prudenza, who clearly adores him, tries to embrace him. Pulcinella chases her back into her house. Rosetta appears, properly chaperoned by her father, Tartaglia. She tells him that she is in love with Pulcinella and must marry him. Tartaglia upbraids her for loving the ugly little man, but Rosetta ignores him. She tries to interest Pulcinella, who is as indifferent to her as he was to Prudenza. She dances before him. Enchanted, Pulcinella kisses her and takes her for a partner in a dance.

Pimpinella, Pulcinella's wife, discovers the two dancing together. The husband protests that he is innocent, that he still loves only her; Pimpinella is at length convinced of it, and the couple dance.

Meanwhile the two suitors, Caviello and Florindo, have been watching the street. They have seen that Pulcinella is the favorite of both Rosetta and Prudenza, and they are furious with jealousy. Their rage is still more inflamed when it becomes obvious that Pulcinella dares to reject the advances of the girls.

They attack Pulcinella, both jumping on him at once. Pimpinella screams for help, and both Rosetta and Prudenza rush out to help. The boys flee, and poor Pulcinella, left in the hands of three women, all eager to assist him, is almost torn in two by their fierce sympathy.

Summoned by their fathers, the two girls return to their homes. Pulcinella dances with his wife.

Florindo and Caviello have been waiting for this moment. They re-enter the street, disguised in black cloaks, carrying swords. Just as they run for him, Pulcinella sees them. He crosses himself hurriedly and pushes his wife into their house. Before he can enter too, he is caught by the two boys. Florindo strikes him dead with his sword. The murderers leave. Pulcinella gets up as if nothing had happened to him. He turns down the street and disappears.

The stage is empty for a moment. Then an astonishing thing happens. Four little Pulcinellas enter, carrying on their shoulders a fifth Pulcinella, apparently dead. They lay the corpse down in the street and dance.

Tartaglia and the doctor come out with their daughters, to see what has happened. The two girls, horrified to see their Pulcinella lying thus in the street, helplessly hover over his body. The doctor examines Pulcinella and declares him dead.

A magician joins them and assures the girls that he can bring Pulcinella back to life. The four little Pulcinellas and the two girls anxiously await the result of his mysterious incantations. The two fathers stand aside, disbelieving. After pommeling Pulcinella's body thoroughly, the magician commands him to live again. Pulcinella gets up, and the onlookers rejoice. The two girls swear to him that he is their only love.

Their fathers, however, remain unconvinced, even by appearances. To prove these skeptics wrong, the magician takes off his long cloak and wig: *he* is the real Pulcinella! His friend, Fourbo, has been the body.

Fourbo and Pulcinella trick the two fathers into retreating into their homes. Pimpinella comes into the street and, seeing two Pulcinellas, runs away in horror. Fourbo, still alias Pulcinella, brings her back.

Now everyone tries to get into the act. Caviello and Florindo enter, wearing Pulcinella disguises, to renew their romances with Rosetta and Prudenza. The girls accept them. Pimpinella, Rosetta, and Prudenza are dancing with three fake Pulcinellas. The real Pulcinella intervenes and kicks each of his imitators. While his friend Fourbo seeks safety in the magician's costume, Pulcinella unmasks the other two impostors before their girls.

The doctor and Tartaglia, still astonished by the goings on, are persuaded by Fourbo, the magician, to permit their daughters to marry Florindo and Caviello. The fathers agree. Pulcinella dances joyfully with Pimpinella, and the magician declares that they and the other two couples are man and wife.

THE RAKE'S PROGRESS

Dramatic ballet in six scenes. Music by Gavin Gordon. Choreography by Ninette de Valois. Book by Gavin Gordon. Scenery and costumes by Rex Whistler. First presented by the Sadler's Wells Ballet at the Sadler's Wells Theatre, London, May 20, 1935, with Walter Gore as the *Rake* and Alicia Markova as the *Betrayed Girl*. First presented in the United States by the Sadler's Wells Ballet at the Metropolitan Opera House, New York, October 12, 1949, with Harold Turner as the *Rake* and Margot Fonteyn as the *Betrayed Girl*.

This ballet is based on the series of paintings of the same name by the great English satirist William Hogarth. Hogarth showed in this famous work the gradual corruption of an adventurous youth who suddenly found himself endowed with unlimited money. The scenery and costumes, the characters—their situation and their dancing—are a vivid reproduction of eighteenth-century London, its people, and their habits as Hogarth saw them. The music is in appropriate eighteenth-century style.

SCENE ONE: The curtain rises on a drop curtain that depicts a street in eighteenth-century London. Georgian houses, public buildings, and a church line both sides of a cobblestone street that extends into the distance. When this curtain rises, we find ourselves in the elegant apartment of the rake. There are doors left and right, and across the back there is a large window. The rake is a youth who has recently come into a fortune, and this morning all the merchants, hangers-on, and toughs who hope to profit by his good luck are paying their daily call. He is still in his night clothes, but this doesn't prevent a tailor from measuring a new coat for him. The rake seems to enjoy this attention, however, and is hardly disturbed when his jockey informs him that his horse won an important race the day before. Now a fencing master takes over and beseeches the rake to practice at his art. The rake obliges him briefly, then practices the horn under the direction of a musician.

The rake begins to dress, and all come to his assistance when needed. When he is fully dressed, he turns to his dancing master. The dancing master takes out a violin and, as he plays on the instrument, shows the rake fancy steps. The rake is not very agile, despite his youth; the truth is that he is not accustomed yet to the gestures of the youthful rich.

The dancing lesson is interrupted by an altercation at the door. There a determined old woman is arguing familiarly with the maid. She forces the maid, her daughter, into the room and follows after. The old harridan upbraids the rake for seducing her daughter and threatens blackmail. The pretty girl obviously does not approve of this procedure and is embarrassed when the rake gives her mother money. They leave the scene, and the dancing lesson continues. The drop curtain falls as the rake succeeds in affecting the manner, if not the skill, of the dance his teacher has set him.

SCENE TWO: Three ladies of the town, apparently on their way to a party, parade the street in front of the drop curtain. The rake's maid and her mother pass them. When the curtain rises, we find ourselves in a bedchamber. The room is hardly private, however, for the two women sitting at a table on the right are clearly of loose character. They are drinking and gossiping together. Three other winsome bawds are exchanging jokes in the center of the room; they guffaw lustily at the slightest innuendo. In the back, on the left, in a curtained alcove, is an unmade bed. A lush painting of Venus and Mars in a gilt frame hangs on the back wall, giving the room an air of hopeful respectability.

Soon a friend of the rake's swaggers into the room, followed by the rake himself. Rake he is determined to be: he is drunk and delighted with himself. The girls take immediate advantage of him and his friend, treating them as if they were the only attractive men in the world.

The guests are treated to *divertissements* by a professional dancer, who does an eighteenth-century version of the strip tease by removing her stockings, and a female ballad singer, who creaks out a song. This song delights the drunken rake, who throws his arm about the ballad singer and insists upon joining her. The music goes to his head, unfortunately, and he begins to pass out.

He is revived, however, as the girls begin to dance. Soon everyone in the room is dancing, whirling and whirling about in a manner that reflects the rake's intoxication. The rake expresses his admiration for this display by throwing coins about the room. One of the rowdy girls scurries about trying to pick up all the money, while the others devote themselves to affected gaiety to amuse the rake. The curtain falls, leaving the rest of the bawdy scene to our imagination.

SCENE THREE: Before the drop curtain, three creditors lie in wait to accost the rake. He strolls in haughtily. They present their bills, which are long overdue, and demand payment. Evidently the rake has run through his inheritance rather rapidly, for he is not in the least condescending: he is afraid. The pretty maid whom we met in the first scene comes into the street. As we might have expected, from her annoyance with her demanding mother, she does not despise her seducer. On the contrary, she observes him with some sympathy and intercedes in his quarrel with the creditors. The poor serving maid tells the men that she will pay the bills! The rake appears to be unimpressed by this expression of love, but the creditors are pleased with her promise; they exit. The rake goes on down the street, immediately forgetting the trouble he has had. The girl does a dance that expresses her love for the rake and the impossibility of its fulfillment.

SCENE FOUR: The rake has seriously come down in the world, for this time the curtain rises on a low gambling dive. The rake, no longer dressed in finery, enters and joins three burly-looking characters in a game of cards. Cleaned out in the higher-class gaming rooms and brothels, he imagines that he can easily regain his losses among such ignorant folk. His fellow players are cleverer than he thinks, however, and luck seems to be against him. He begins to lose steadily. He clings to his few coins as if they were the last moments of a happy life. It is not difficult for us to imagine that the betrayed girl, the lovely chambermaid he has spurned, would have a great deal of pity for him. The poor devil cannot bear to lose: he loses not only his money, but his connection with reality, as he hopes that this last bet will bring back all the opulence of his former life—the tailors and jewelers and race-track touts indebted to *him* again, much wine, many women, and endless song. Simultaneously he sees that if he loses, he will enjoy none of these things: that leaves, for him, poor fellow, nothing. The last wager is made, the last card is turned up, the tables are turned; he is wiped out! Less rake than pauper, the unfortunate fellow collapses.

SCENE FIVE: Before the curtain, the betrayed girl dances alone, hoping that the Rake, who has now been put in the debtor's prison, will be released and come back to her.

SCENE SIX: When the curtain comes up again the scene, like the rake's progress, has gone from bad to worse: we are in a madhouse, a dark place and damp, where therapy consists of filthy isolation. The more dangerous lunatics can be seen behind iron grilles, posing as kings and cardinals. Creatures less preoccupied sit in an open area. One of these men entertains himself and his fellow madmen by a grotesque dance with a rope, which outlines in the air the images that haunt him.

The outside door clangs open, and the rake is thrown into the cell. The men watch the new inmate while he tries, as they did, to escape. When he falls to the floor exhausted, they display their individual manias for his benefit. While the rake looks at them, we think for a moment that he is not really mad, that there has been some mistake: an eighteenth-century solution to a down-and-outer's problem, some gross misjudgment. But we are wrong. The rake rises and dances like a demon.

The girl he has betrayed comes to visit him and tries pathetically to make him remember her, but now this man's only thought is to escape from her, to escape from everyone, to get out. He attacks the door again, and again he falls to the floor. The lovely girl attempts to mend his agony by sweet and loving gestures that might give him some hope. Her thoughtfulness and devotion are contrasted vividly with the fashionable world that her lover has left, when some well-dressed ladies enter the asylum and observe the inmates for entertainment and diversion.

The rake becomes hysterical, catatonic, and thrashes about the floor uncontrollably. He dies in the midst of his paroxysms. The betrayed girl holds him close in her arms, weeping that her love might have saved him, weeping that he did not understand the path of self-destruction.

LES RENDEZVOUS

Ballet *divertissement* in one act. Music by François Auber, arranged by Constant Lambert. Choreography by Frederick Ashton. Scenery and costumes by William Chappell. First presented by the Sadler's Wells Ballet at the Sadler's Wells Theatre, London, December 5, 1933, with a cast headed by Alicia Markova, Stanislas Idzikowski, Pearl Argyle, Ninette de Valois, and Robert Helpmann. First presented in the United States by the Sadler's Wells Theatre Ballet at the Northrop Auditorium, Minneapolis, Minnesota, November 7, 1951, with Elaine Fifield and Pirmin Trecu in the principal roles.

Les Rendezvous is a dance entertainment set to music from Auber's *L'Enfant Prodigue*. In a private park, young couples promenade and dance to give appropriate expression to youthful sentiments that take hold of their ebullient spirits. There is no plot.

The curtain rises on a bright, sunny scene. A high white fence of wrought iron stands out against a light-green back cloth. The gate to the park, in the center, is open. The orchestra plays music that is light and charming, music suggestive of the good nature we always feel when we watch boys and girls show their happiness by dancing together. Trumpets sound a fanfare and the ballet begins.

Young couples out for a stroll dance into the park one by one from the corners of the stage. They are all dressed in white; the girls wear pink ribbons in their hair and pink sashes, and the boys wear belts of light blue. The young people move back and forth across the park. Finally there are six couples. They stand on either side of the gate, and a seventh couple enters. They pass down the line formed by their friends, greet them effusively, and then, more formally, shake hands.

Now the couples divide into different groups and fill the stage with shifting, quick movement. The boys dance alone briefly, then leave the stage to a couple who dance a short *pas de deux*. The boy lifts the girl off into the wings; the music is rapid and joyful, the lift is long and slow, and there is an effect of joyfulness mixed with romance. Other boys enter and lift their partners more rapidly, more in direct imitation of the music. Six girls surround the romantic couple when they return, and the introduction to the ballet finishes as the boy again lifts the girl into the wings.

Four girls dance a bright *pas de quatre*. They are joined by their partners and leave the stage as the boy of the lead couple enters and dances a bold leaping-and-turning variation to brilliant, flourishing music. The boy gestures toward the gate, his girl rejoins him there, and they leave the stage together. The other couples have returned and form three tableaux about the stage. The boy, reaching out to his partner who kneels below, comes back, leading his girl forward, and the two of them dance a slow, romantic duet. Four of the boys lift the girl to their shoulders as the adagio ends. There she poses gracefully, as the girls gather about her raised figure, hold hands, and enclose her with a circle of arabesques.

The music becomes saucy and bouncing. A girl bounds on stage with two partners, turning from the arms of one boy into the arms of the other. The two boys lift her high into the air, release her, and their steps quicken to the hastening music. The *pas de trois* finishes as all three kneel.

Next the lead girl dances alone. She leaps onto the scene, turns dizzily, delighting us with her deft, swift movement. She is very pretty, apparently in love, and enjoys showing off a little. Boys emerge from the wings one by one and bow to the girl, in tribute to her beauty and her masterful dance. She bows gratefully in return and leaves the stage on the left.

Rhythmic handclaps are heard off-stage. Six boys run into the park to dance in unison a strong, buoyant ensemble, dazzling with its long, high leaps, mutiple turns, and the quick, steady certainty with which they finish their brilliant sequence of movement. A trumpet fanfare announces the arrival of six girls, who join their partners for a brief dance before the reappearance of the ballerina, who whirls about the stage. The *corps de ballet* returns and forms a background for another virtuoso variation by the ballerina's partner, who places his hands on his shoulders and spins like a top.

Four girls approach the boy and blindfold him. He plays their game for a moment, then turns in their midst and rushes off as the ballerina enters on the right to hop backward on point in a long diagonal. All the couples are now on stage. They bow to each other and bid their partners a fond farewell. One by one, they leave the park through the gate. When the ballerina disappears into the wings, her partner leaps after her in a high trajectory. Four girls, who remain in the park, pose amusingly, as if the fun has just begun.

REVENGE

Dramatic ballet in four scenes with prologue. Music by Giuseppe Verdi. Choreography by Ruth Page. Book by Ruth Page with the collaboration of Nicolas Remisov. Scenery and costumes by Antoine Clavé. First presented by Les Ballets des Champs-Elysées at the Théâtre de l'Empire, Paris, October 17, 1951, with Sonia Arova as *Azucena*, Vladimir Skouratoff as *Manrico*, Jacqueline Moreau as *Leonora*, and Gérard Ohn as the *Count di Luna*.

Like the ballet *Carmen*, *Revenge* is also based on a great popular opera—Verdi's *Il Trovatore*. The ballet is faithful to the opera's theme of passionate revenge and condenses into a comparatively short space of time the principal elements of the musical drama. The time is the sixteenth century. The place is Spain.

PROLOGUE—THE COURTYARD OF THE CASTLE OF THE COUNT DI LUNA: The elderly Count di Luna has two infant sons, of whom he is very proud. One day an old gypsy woman is discovered hovering over the cradle of one of these boys. The child's nurse, suspecting sorcery, sounds the alarm, and the old count's servants capture the gypsy. The hag pleads that she meant no harm, that she was only interested in reading the child's fortune. She is driven out of the castle, but when the child becomes ill, she is brought back. At the count's order, she is burned at the stake for sorcery. His child recovers.

The old gypsy's young daughter, Azucena, dances in despair as the flames of her mother's burning light the distant sky. Gentlemen of the count's household stand on the steps of the courtyard watching the fire with indifference. Azucena vows to avenge her mother's horrible death. She steals the count's other son and flees into the night.

SCENE ONE—THE CASTLE: Twenty years have passed. The old Count di Luna is dead. On his deathbed he urged his remaining son never to abandon search for his brother. Unknown to the new count, his brother still survives as Manrico, whom Azucena has brought up as her own son.

Both the Count di Luna and Manrico are in love with the beautiful Leonora, lady in waiting to the queen. Leonora favors Manrico, and the count, enraged that the girl should prefer a ragged gypsy to a nobleman, is determined to separate them. Leonora escapes with Manrico to a gypsy camp.

SCENE TWO—THE GYPSY MOVEMENT: The Count di Luna traces the two lovers and comes in person to the gypsy camp. There he challenges Manrico to a duel. The young gypsy, warned by a premonition, reluctantly consents to this contest, and the two brothers, completely ignorant of their relationship, begin to fight. Manrico gains the upper hand and might easily slay the count. The premonition returns, and he stays his hand. Azucena regrets that her ward has not killed the count; after twenty years, she can still think only of revenge.

The count, enraged by jealousy and Manrico's contempt, is determined to force his love on Leonora. He sends her to prison with Manrico.

SCENE THREE—IN FRONT OF THE PRISON: The two lovers endure torture in prison by the count's order. Leonora, in desperation, promises that she will marry the count if he will set Manrico free.

SCENE FOUR—THE BETROTHAL: The marriage ceremony

has been arranged. Manrico, who does not know that she has arranged for his release, accuses Leonora of faithlessness. But Leonora, unwilling to marry the count, has taken poison and urges Manrico to seek his freedom. Manrico discovers what she has done and weeps as she dies in his arms.

The Count di Luna orders Manrico's execution. The youth bids farewell to his foster mother, who despairs that her revenge means such a sacrifice. But when Manrico is dead, she weeps no more. She turns to the Count di Luna in fierce triumph. Glorying in her revenge, she holds out to him the locket that hung about the neck of his brother twenty years before. To the count's horror at this secret, Azucena responds with demoniac exultation: she has had her revenge at last.

RODEO

Ballet in two scenes. Music by Aaron Copland. Choreography and book by Agnes de Mille. Scenery by Oliver Smith. Costumes by Kermit Love. First presented by the Ballet Russe de Monte Carlo at the Metropolitan Opera House, New York, October 16, 1942, with a cast headed by Agnes de Mille as the *Cowgirl*, Frederic Franklin as the *Champion Roper*, and Casimir Kokitch as the *Head Wrangler*. Revived by Ballet Theatre at Rhine-am-Main Air Force, Frankfort, Germany, August 14, 1950.

Rodeo, subtitled "The Courting at Burnt Ranch," is a love story of the American Southwest. The problem it deals with is perennial: how an American girl, with the odds seemingly all against her, sets out to get herself a man. The girl in this case is a cowgirl, a tomboy whose desperate efforts to become one of the ranch's cowhands create a problem for the cowboys and make her the laughingstock of womankind.

SCENE ONE: The corral of Burnt Ranch. The ballet's brief overture begins with a crash of cymbals and continues with a rowdy, rhythmic melody reminiscent of the wild west. The music becomes quiet, and the curtain rises on the corral of Burnt Ranch. The time is Saturday afternoon, the time of the weekly rodeo, about the turn of the century. Against an orange-red sky whose intense heat seems to bear down on the scene, a high wooden fence encloses the parched, dusty ground of the corral. Half a dozen lazy cowhands stand about, idling away the time. Among them stands the cowgirl, self-assertive in a bright red shirt, brown hat tilted back over her head, and brown pants and boots. Long pigtails hang down her back. One of the cowhands holds his hand up to shield his eyes from the glaring sun and looks out into the distance. Another cowboy rides in, twirling his arm over his head in a lassoing motion. The cowgirl hitches up her pants, as if to prepare for the rodeo that is about to begin. The cowboys tell her that she can't come along and ride off rapidly. Not to be outdone so easily, the cowgirl decides to follow them and rushes off to the right, roping the air with a fast-turning arm.

Three cowhands ride on vigorously. Six of their fellows join them, and all dance wildly, imitating in their movements the jolts and tricks of the rodeo. The music is fierce and a challenge to the dancers. The cowgirl re-enters and tries to join one of the groups. The cowgirl secretly hankers after the head wrangler, and watches him anxiously. He and the others motion to her to go away—she isn't wanted. The girl is used to this kind of treatment, however, and stays put, trying to compete in the rodeo. She disgraces herself, and the head wrangler is about to lose all patience with her.

But suddenly the corral is transfigured by the arrival of girls in city clothes—Eastern friends of the rancher's daughter, who have come out with her to get a taste of ranch life. The cowboys slap their thighs in enthusiastic welcome; the girls wave to them with their handkerchiefs and giggle among themselves in feigned bashfulness. The cowgirl is both contemptuous and envious of their finery; she is visibly disgusted by their silly flirting.

The champion roper steps out to show off his skill before the girls. When the head wrangler steps over to them politely and takes off his hat to the rancher's daughter, the cowgirl can bear it no longer and rides off in a jealous fit of petulance. Four women from the ranch come out to watch the rodeo. They are entertained until the cowgirl rides in on what appears to be a bucking bronco. All the women raise their hands in despair at this foolish show-off. The cowgirl falls. The Eastern girls rush over to her and can't control their laughter: never in *their* born days has a *girl* done anything like that. The cowgirl is furious. She gets up and thumbs her nose at the women. Soon, alone with the cowboys, the girl sees that she's made a fool of herself all around; the women may laugh at her, but the men are worse: their silence makes her despair. She tries to regain her old familiarity with them. They ignore her and stare into the distance. The head wrangler jerks his thumb toward the house, telling her to leave the corral. He is the one man in the world the girl respects; smothering her tears, she obeys him.

The rodeo is over. The girls wave at the champion roper as he leaps away. The scene darkens, the music softens, the womenfolk cross the stage, moving slowly, bravely, yet wistfully, and there is created an impression of what home is like after a tiring, busy day. The cowboys cross the stage behind the women, and when the girls step backward, hesitating in their homeward march, the men move forward to them, place their arms about their waists, and move forward again with them.

The couples disappear. The cowgirl re-enters and tries to attract the head wrangler's attention. But it's as if she weren't even there: he goes to the rancher's daughter, who stands demure in her long blue dress with ribbons in her hair, lifts her softly, and takes her off into the night.

The cowgirl dances for a moment alone, trying to shake off what she knows has happened to her. She isn't any good as a woman and she's a miserable failure as a cowhand. The head wrangler returns. He doesn't understand what's wrong with this strange girl. A cowboy calls to him, and he leaves before the girl can tell him. The womenfolk try to call the girl home; she ignores them. The champion roper crosses the back of the corral, snapping his fingers in private anticipation of the Saturday night dance at the ranch house. He disappears. The cowgirl falls to the ground, all alone now with her problem. The stage blacks out around her.

A bright blue drop curtain, decorated with galloping wild horses, falls in front of the scene. Four couples rush out and begin a square dance. A caller shouts out directions to the dancers, and the couples respond by moving quickly into more intricate patterns as he commands. Soon they are out of breath, but turning still more rapidly and now shouting as they run around and around in a circle, faster and faster. They run off into the wings.

SCENE TWO: The ranch house. The curtain rises on the ranch house. The cowgirl is sitting alone on a bench at the left, watching three cowboys dance a jig to a jazzy piano accompaniment. One of the cowboys is the champion roper, dressed now in his Saturday-night best—violet shirt, a loud vest of cowhide, and striped yellow pants. He jumps high into the air and clicks his heels together repeatedly. The cowgirl, still dressed in the dusty clothes of the corral, feels out of place, though she is making an obvious effort to enjoy herself. The boys finish their jig. Three couples come in and dance about the room, oblivious to whether anyone is watching them. Two of the couples waltz into the parlor as the remaining pair quarrel: the boy kisses the girl, and she rushes out.

The boy despairs of women and sits down beside the cowgirl. She tries to comfort him, man to man. But another girl has come in looking for a partner. She sees the boy alone, lifts her dress flirtatiously, and runs out. He chases after her. The cowgirl can see no hope for such an idiot. The champion roper strides back in and notices the lonely girl. He doesn't know what the matter is; but since this is Saturday night and dancing time, he can see only one cure. He tells her to get up and dance. The cowgirl says she doesn't know how to dance. Well, first, he tells her, you'd better look a little cleaner. He tries to fix her face up and smacks the dust off her bottom.

Just as the girl is beginning to forget about the head wrangler, he comes in and goes over to the rancher's daughter. The cowgirl forgets all about the champion roper. He loses patience with her; after all, he's just as interested in other girls as she is in the head wrangler: he was only trying to make her have a good time. When the champion roper walks out on her, the girl begins to cry. She looks at the romantic dancing couple and falls to the floor in tears.

Gradually the room fills with people. The bench is moved back, and everybody gets ready for a community dance. The girls line up on one side, the boys on the other. Bravely, the girl decides to try again and hopefully stands in line with the girls. The boys approach and take their partners; the cowgirl is left standing alone! The music becomes sweet and lyrical; the couples form a circle; the boys lift the girls tenderly high above them; the girl turns away.

The champion roper dances in, jumping high in the air, clicking his heels together, breaking the romantic spell. When he finishes this bit of exhibitionism, he comes over and leans on the girl's shoulder. She stifles a sob. The other couples leave the scene. The roper puts his hand under her chin and tells her to cheer up, to try to dance with him again. He opens his arms wide, the girl smiles, hitches up her belt, comes close to him, and everything is all right for a few seconds while they dance.

Everything is spoiled, however, by the head wrangler and the rancher's daughter, who come back and remind the cowgirl of her real love. The roper catches her watching them; before he can do anything about it, she has run away. The roper sees a girl walking alone and pursues her into the wings.

All the cowboys and their girls dance now, filling the scene with violent color and vigorous movement. The couples clap their hands joyously in rhythm to the music. They stop dancing all at once and stare, as the cowgirl comes in, dressed from head to foot in bright red. The girls are shocked by this lack of taste; the boys are eager to find out what it means.

The champion roper goes to her, hitches up his pants, and asks her to dance. Even in her new dress the girl hitches up her clothes, too. They dance. The violins saw away at a square-dance theme, and the moving couples form a circle around them.

The cowgirl finds herself standing between the head wrangler and the roper. Both want to dance with her. The wrangler has forgotten the rancher's daughter long enough to notice the cowgirl. The roper and the wrangler throw the girl back and forth between them. She tries to escape, but the wrangler grabs her and tries to kiss her. The roper steps in and says, "No! She's my girl!" He takes her face in his hands and kisses her hard. He kisses her again, harder. Both of them wake up: they've both been wrong all along and didn't know what was happening. The head wrangler rejoins the rancher's daughter, and the whole group dances happily. As the curtain falls, the girls step into stirrups formed by the boys' hands and stand poised high over their heads. The cowgirl and the roper look into each other's eyes.

NOTES: In her autobiography, *Dance to the Piper*, Agnes de Mille has described the first performance of *Rodeo*:

"If it is possible for a life to change at one given moment, if it is possible for all movement, growth and accumulated power to become apparent at one single point, then my hour struck at 9:40, October 16, 1942. Chewing gum, squinting under a Texas hat, I turned to face what I had been preparing for the whole of my life.

"This was not a great performance; we gave better later. Neither was it a great ballet. The style, as I always feared, did break. But it was the first of its kind, and the moment was quick with birth.

"There was applause on my first exit. An unexpected bonus. There was applause or response on every phrase. Did the audience laugh on count eight as I had promised in July in California? They laughed, not just female titters, but real laughing with sound of men's voices, and the laugh turned into handclapping. This happened again and again. The dancers were elated but not surprised. I had promised them laughs. The pantomime was spaced to accommodate them.

"There were mishaps. At one point, Kokitch grew confused with his new costumes and failed to make an entrance, leaving me to improvise a love scene, without partner, alone, and exposed for sixty-four bars of music on the Met stage. Lines were crooked. Some of the girls clapped off beat. It didn't seem to matter.

"The pace of the performance rushed us like a wind. The audience were roused and urging us on. Great exchanges of excitement and force and gaiety were taking place all around. The dancers rushed and whirled, grabbing the right person, because the right person was there, though unrecognizable in an unexpected dress and hair-do. And throughout the pace which was too quick for me, beyond my understanding, faster than could be savored or appreciated, was Freddie's arm, Freddie's strong back, propelling, pushing, carrying, and Freddie's feet like bullets on the wood. It was beyond endurance. It was beyond help. It was slipping away too fast, too fast. Also my collar was too tight.

" 'Freddie,' I said at the back of the stage, 'I'm fainting. Loosen my collar.'

" 'No time duckie. Here we go.'

"And as though we were blown out of the mouth of a gun, he propelled me to the footlights. We separated. Bob, bob. All the trumpets and horns threw their shafts between us. We hung on the brink. The music tore open. We rushed. We clashed. We were lifted. And all the girls had faces like stars with their hair dropping over the boys' shoulders. The great curtain fell. There was dust in my nostrils from the dusty lining of the curtain. It was over. It was done. And I had made so many foolish mistakes. So many hasty things gone wrong. Once more I had been incapable of the perfect effort. 'Oh, Freddie,' I said gasping, 'what a stinking, lousy performance. We must rehearse like demons tomorrow.'

"I looked at him wistfully but we were walking forward and we were all holding hands and bowing. A large bunch of American corn was put in my arms tied with red, white and blue ribbons. More flowers came, more flowers. The Russians did things this way. They also clapped and called out. Hadn't I stood grinding my teeth at the back of the house for years while they cheered bogus nonsense? We bowed and bowed. At the eighth bow, I looked into the pit. The fiddlers were beating their bows on their instruments. The others were standing up yelling. No one gets the union boys to do this easily. I looked at Freddie in amazement. 'Freddie,' I said, 'this is not a claque. This is not Libidins's contriving.'

" 'Darling, darling,' said Freddie, kissing me, 'this is an ovation. This is the real thing. Take it.' He pushed me forward, and all the company backed away to the edge of the stage and stood there clapping.

"We had twenty-two curtain calls.

"The grips and members of the company helped me carry my flowers to the dressing room. They filled half the floor space. The doorman could not hold my friends in check.

"In the hall between dressing rooms, I met Massine. He bowed formally, and then apparently thought he must say something. He stared at me with his binocular eyes. 'You have done a characteristic ballet.' I struggled to follow this. 'And in Europe I think it will have success.' We bowed.

"Mary Meyer sat at my dressing table crying and crying. 'I can't stop,' she said, mopping her nose. 'It isn't that this is the most wonderful ballet I've ever seen. I've seen better. It's just that I can't stand you making a success after all these years.'

" 'Aren't you proud of her?' said friends to Mother. And Annie drew herself up to her shoulders and looking at them steadily with her penetrating blue eyes answered, 'I've always been proud of her. Always. When no one hired her. I'll go home now and start the coffee.'

"And in the lobby Billy Rose was marching up and down shouting. 'But where has she been? Why haven't we known about her? How could we have overlooked this talent?'

"And Terry Helburn was phoning in a wire to Western Union: WE THINK YOUR WORK IS ENCHANTING. COME TALK TO US MONDAY.

"I did some phoning of my own. I called Officer-Candidate School at the Aberdeen Proving Grounds and spoke to a soldier. 'It is a success. It has made a furore.'

" 'Oh,' he said, 'that does not surprise me. I knew it would.'

"He knew it would! He'd known me six months and seen nothing of my work at all. He took this evening for granted. Well so, miraculously, did my mother. But she had waited, fourteen years, had sewn costumes, sold bonds, nagged at her friends to attend her girl's concerts, run errands, done without all luxuries, and hoped, and hoped, and hoped, steadily and without default in the face of reason and proof unlimited that her efforts would meet with no success. She was home now, serving coffee and chocolate cake and salad to all and sundry. This time the doors were wide open. Anyone could walk in."

Rodeo has been in the repertory of the Ballet Theatre since August 14, 1950, when it was first danced by this company at Rhine-am-Main Air Force, Frankfort, Germany, with Allyn McLerie, John Kriza, and James

Mitchell in the leading roles. Jenny Workman, John Kriza, and Kelly Brown have danced the ballet with great success throughout the United States and Europe.

ROMEO AND JULIET

Narrative ballet in one act, based on the play by Shakespeare. Music by Frederick Delius. Choreography by Antony Tudor. Scenery and costumes by Eugene Berman. First presented by Ballet Theatre at the Metropolitan Opera House, New York, April 6, 1943, with Alicia Markova as *Juliet*, Hugh Laing as *Romeo*, Nicolas Orloff as *Mercutio*, Antony Tudor as *Tybalt*, and Jerome Robbins as *Benvolio*.

This dramatic ballet compresses into one vivid act the tragic love story of Romeo and Juliet. Within a single-unit setting representing the ordered golden beauty of the Italy of the Renaissance, the narrative proceeds without scenic interruption; and what might be spoken of as "scenes," in an ordinary dramatic spectacle, move together and coalesce with a flow that suggests the inevitability of the tragedy itself.

The score for the ballet is an arrangement by Antal Dorati of selected works by Delius: *Over the Hills and Far Away, The Walk to the Paradise Garden, Eventyr,* and *Brigg Fair.*

PROLOGUE: The curtain rises immediately on a drop curtain depicting the entrance to a palace in Verona. There are two great arches to the left and right, and in the center, cut out of the curtain, is a draped entry. A spotlight centers on this doorway, and Romeo steps out cautiously. He looks behind him, and Rosaline, a beautiful girl, follows him. Romeo takes her hand and attempts to embrace her. Rosaline warns him that he is too hasty, and Romeo follows her impatiently within.

Now members of the opposing families of Montague and Capulet dance onto the scene and challenge each other. The two leaders of the factions, Mercutio and Tybalt, are eager for a contest, and the two groups commence dueling. But the heads of the two houses at variance with each other enter with their wives and order their kinsmen to desist. The men reluctantly abandon their fighting and bow to the peers. It is apparent that their battle will be renewed at the first opportunity. Romeo and his friend Mercutio remain behind when the others have left. Only the entrance of the fair Rosaline persuades them that they have better business elsewhere.

BALL AT THE HOUSE OF THE CAPULETS: The drop curtain rises on a wide, open area of red marble enclosed by a decorative colonnade. Couples in richly embroidered costumes are dancing in elegant, courtly fashion. The music softens, and Juliet enters on the right. She lingers slightly, hesitating to step into the ballroom, for she knows what awaits her. She greets her parents warmly, yet formally. Capulet turns to introduce her to a young nobleman, Paris, but Juliet seeks instead the company of her cousin Tybalt. The understanding Tybalt consoles her, but also reminds her of her duty and leads her to Paris. The assembled company begin to dance again, and Juliet accepts Paris as her partner.

Romeo enters on the right. He looks directly at Juliet. Juliet, her back to Paris for a moment, glances back at him. As Paris bends down to kiss her hand, Juliet looks across the room toward Romeo. The dance continues, and Romeo chooses a partner to join the ball. The two couples dance on opposite sides of the room. The set pattern of the dance separates them, and Juliet and Romeo despair of meeting. Soon the entire company circles the hall and the dance ends. The guests proceed to move toward the rear for refreshment, and Romeo and Juliet are alone.

Romeo falls at her feet and declares the overpowering love he has felt since he saw her. He rises, their faces touch, and they kiss. Then, formal again, the two bow to each other and begin to dance together a delicate, flowing measure. When the dance is over, they realize that they must separate and both say their farewells. But as they turn to go, they move together again and kneel.

Mercutio and Tybalt emerge from the banquet hall. Juliet's nurse urges her away, lest there be trouble. Tybalt warns Romeo and turns to Juliet questioningly, and all depart.

ROMEO WOOS JULIET IN THE CAPULET ORCHARD: The lights dim. White drapes are drawn across the back colonnade. Four torchbearers enter on the right, followed by Romeo and Mercutio. Romeo is preoccupied and will not listen to his friend's appreciation of the beauty of the evening. Mercutio grows impatient and tells his friend that the romance he contemplates is out of the question. The music builds in intensity, and Romeo refuses to heed Mercutio's advice. Mercutio leaps to the back of one of the torchbearers and urges Romeo to follow them to a tavern. Romeo pretends to go, then conceals himself. The others return to look for him, but soon follow after Mercutio.

Two couples enter. Romeo holds his arm across his face, lest he be recognized. The couples disappear, and Romeo dances alone. Above the colonnade at the rear, Juliet looks down into the orchard and sees her lover. She is enchanted and rests her head sweetly on the balcony railing, wondering when he will look up and see her. Romeo glances up and blows kisses to her. She returns the kisses, but warns him away. Just as he hides behind a pillar on the right, Juliet's nurse comes into the garden. No sooner has she departed than Tybalt and Paris stroll by. When they are alone again, Romeo holds out his arms to Juliet and from above she gestures to him yearningly. Romeo gestures defiance of their families and proposes marriage. Juliet consents.

BETROTHAL OF ROMEO AND JULIET BY THE FRIAR:
Drapes are drawn across the colonnade, and Friar Lawrence stands in his
cell. Romeo enters. He is impatient and afraid and paces the floor. There is
a sound at the door, and Romeo rushes to see who it is. Friar Lawrence pulls
him back warningly. Romeo's back is turned as Juliet runs into the room. He
turns to her, and the two kneel before the friar, who blesses them. Juliet
rises, turns rapidly, and falls low in Romeo's arms. Then she rushes off into
the night, promising him that her nurse will bring him a message.

STREET SCENE: The curtains are drawn back, the friar disappears, and the open area becomes the street. It is still night. A cripple and
a blind man enter, followed by the gay Mercutio and a friend. Romeo enters,
followed by Juliet and her nurse. The nurse beckons Juliet away. The concern of the lovers is contrasted with the friction between their families, for
Tybalt has entered and threatened Mercutio in earnest. The two fight,
their kinsmen join the battle, and the music is ominous, like the sound of an
approaching storm. Mercutio is stabbed by Tybalt and dies in Romeo's arms.

Romeo recovers from his grief and attacks Tybalt. He leaps to his back,
forces him down, and stabs him to death. Now there is no hope of recon-
ciling the two families. Romeo does not know what to do. Friar Lawrence
enters and takes the dagger from him. Finally the youth is persuaded that
he must flee for his life.

Juliet and her nurse enter the square and see what has happened. Juliet
weeps for Tybalt, but then, suddenly desperate, instructs the nurse to run to
Romeo and reassure him.

ROMEO'S FAREWELL TO JULIET: The scene is Juliet's
bedroom. Day is breaking. Juliet rises first and dances joyfully, with a sweet,
youthful happiness, as Romeo watches her from the bed. She returns to him,
he lifts her, and they embrace. Romeo prepares to leave. He must escape
from Verona. They will meet elsewhere. Juliet weeps because of her happiness and its quick ending. They kiss. Romeo departs, and Juliet falls back
on the bed, still weeping.

PREPARATIONS FOR THE WEDDING OF JULIET TO
PARIS: Some time passes, and handmaidens to Juliet enter with her
nurse to prepare her for the marriage her parents have insisted upon. They
waken Juliet. Instantly she sits up and looks off into the direction that
Romeo took when he left her. She cannot believe that this day she must
marry another man. The nurse holds her in her arms and tries to comfort
her. Juliet rises and protests to her father that she cannot marry Paris.
Capulet refuses to listen to her or to his wife, who tries to intercede for Juliet.

Then, to the accompaniment of a melody almost unbearable in its
sweetness and pathos, Juliet's four handmaidens form a tableau beside her.
They hold before her a wedding dress of gold, and Juliet slips her arms into it
as if the cloth were on fire.

When she is dressed, she weeps softly in her father's arms. Her father blesses her and places on her head a shining crown. She is presented with a bouquet of white flowers. Friar Lawrence enters, and Juliet falls into his arms. When they are unobserved, the friar gives her a vial containing a secret drug and instructs her to drink it without delay: all may yet be well.

Juliet walks away, drinks the contents of the vial, whirls frantically, and swoons. Her family gathers about her. Six women bear slowly across the stage a great cloth trimmed in somber black.

PROCESSION TO THE TOMB: Two of Juliet's attendants head her funeral procession. Juliet lies on a bier carried high by her black-cloaked kinsmen. Her father and mother follow behind. When the procession has passed, the women holding up the cloth of mourning disappear to reveal another scene.

SCENE IN THE VAULT OF THE CAPULETS: We are in Juliet's tomb. She lies immobile on her bier, her hands pressed together at her breast. Romeo enters. He imagines that his beloved is dead and drinks a vial of poison. He falls at the foot of the bier.

Juliet gradually revives from the drug she has taken. She rises. Romeo sees her, pulls himself up with difficulty, reaches out for her, and—when Juliet comes to him—lifts her with his remaining strength. He falls. Juliet understands what has happened. She spins around and around frantically. Romeo rises again and lifts her in his arms. He holds her for a moment, then collapses across her bier. He dies. Juliet looks down upon him. She takes out his dagger, waits for a moment, and—rising suddenly on point, as if to meet the happiness only death can bring her—stabs herself in the heart. She falls across her lover's body and, with her last gesture, touches his face.

NOTES: Reviewing a performance of *Romeo and Juliet* in 1945 in the New York *Herald Tribune*, Edwin Denby described Alicia Markova's performance: "Miss Markova's delicacy in lightness, in rapidity; the quickness in the thighs, the arrowy flexibility of the instep; her responsiveness in the torso, the poise of the arms, the sweetness of the wrists, the grace of neck and head; all this is extraordinary. But her dancing is based on a rarer virtue. It is the quiet which she moves in, an instinct for the melody of movement as it deploys and subsides in the silence of time, that is the most refined of rhythmic delights. The sense of serenity in animation she creates is as touching as that of a Mozart melody.

"And like Mozart, too, if you will, she is a completely objective artist. Who Markova is, nobody knows. What you see on the stage is the piece she performs, the character she acts. She shows you, as only the greatest of actresses do, a completely fascinating impersonation, completely fascinating because you recognize a heroine of the imagination who knows all about vanity and love and authority and death. You watch her discover them.

"Markova's Juliet is a miracle of acting. Every nuance of pantomime is poignantly clear and every moment is a different aspect of the cumulative tragedy. Her shy loveliness in the balcony scene, her moment watching Romeo die—but one would like to enumerate them all minute by minute. And the restraint of them all, the slow-motion continuum from which they each arise as dance gestures and which flows so steadily through the whole hour-long ballet, are wonders to have seen."

The role of Juliet has also been danced by Nora Kaye and Alicia Alonso, while Igor Youskevitch and John Kriza have also taken the part of Romeo.

LE SACRE DU PRINTEMPS
THE RITE OF SPRING

Ballet in two parts. Music by Igor Stravinsky. Choreography by Vaslav Nijinsky. Book by Igor Stravinsky and Nicholas Roerich. Scenery and costumes by Nicholas Roerich. First presented by Diaghilev's Ballets Russes at the Théâtre des Champs-Elysées, Paris, May 29, 1913, with Marie Piltz as the *Chosen One*. Rechoreographed by Leonide Massine and presented by Diaghilev's Ballets Russes at the Théâtre des Champs-Elysées, 1920, with Lydia Sokolova as the *Chosen One*. First presented in the United States, with new choreography by Massine, at the Academy of Music, Philadelphia, April 11, 1930, under the auspices of the League of Composers. Martha Graham danced the leading role in the first American presentation.

Subtitled "A Picture of Ancient Russia," this ballet returns us to a time when pagan rites dominated the lives of the Russian tribes. Every year spring was consecrated by a human sacrifice; only then could the success of the season be assured, only then would the prehistoric people place their trust in the fertility of the land.

Le Sacre du Printemps has been performed only a few times as a ballet, though it has been choreographed five separate times—once by Nijinsky, twice by Massine, by Romanov in 1932, and by Milloss in 1941. Soon after the ballet's *première*, when the music was performed as a concert piece, *Le Sacre* began its career as a permanent part of the symphonic repertory. The music was performed in the United States for the first time by the Philadelphia Orchestra under Leopold Stokowski, on March 3, 1922.

The program that his music suggested to the composer is divided into two tableaux, which are embodied in the ballet.

FIRST TABLEAU—ADORATION OF THE EARTH: A musical prelude recalls man's first relations with the world about him. The curtain rises. In a wasteland scene dominated by great masses of stone, young girls and boys sit in separate groups. They do not move, they wait and watch, as if expecting some sign from the stone shafts they revere. The girls rise, as if drawn by the abundance of nature to which the music calls their attention. A wise man stands among the dancers; the girls rush around and around him. Now he moves toward the sacred mound of the enclosure. The girls follow and bow before him. The opening phrase of the ballet—the quiet, plaintive cry of man against all-powerful nature—is repeated.

The strings sound strong, persistent chords that rouse the young men. To the virile beat of the music, they begin to dance, their movements accelerating at its demand, their feet stamping, stamping the earth. The girls join in the dance, the music becomes joyous, and the adolescents abandon themselves to the swift, exuberant rhythms of the orchestra.

This music changes sharply. A new, penetrating melody shrieks warningly and disturbs the young people. The happiness of the boys and girls shifts abruptly to fierce savagery. They split into different groups; the boys face the girls and move toward them. The boys seem bent on attack, but at the last minute they hesitate; they move back and forth in an almost helpless effort, ignorant of their own true intent. The rhythmic crescendos give place to the soft trilling of flutes. Now the boys break their formation, and each carries a girl away.

Four boys remain on the scene. They choose four girls, lift them up on their backs, and dance slowly, bending low under the weight of their burdens in imitation of the plodding chords of the music. This "Round Dance of Spring" gradually increases in volume, and all the adolescents participate. All the dancers step back as the trilling flutes repeat their love call.

Drums herald the beginning of a contest between two rival tribes. Groups of men from each tribe engage in vigorous games. In the midst of their activity, the wise man, represented in the orchestra by a portentous melody on the tuba, tries to interrupt the games. The stronger theme of the games at first drowns out the wise man's theme, then recedes. The men turn to the wise man. There is a brief, taut silence, then all the men fall to the ground and worship the earth.

The drum rolls loudly, and all rise to dance, as if they had felt the pulse of the earth and been renewed by its power. The dance grows frenzied in its intensity. The curtain falls.

SECOND TABLEAU—THE SACRIFICE: Night is about to fall as this second scene begins; the setting sun has turned the sky scarlet. The girls sit near the wise man at a fire. One of these girls must be chosen by the others to make the sacrifice to the earth: this girl must dance herself to death. The music is calm; the figures on stage are quiet and they are unafraid. The girls regret what they have to do, but they are resigned to it with a kind of physical tiredness that the music reflects. They do not feel that they are victimized by Nature, but rather that they must obey what they believe to be its rules.

Soon the girls rise and move in the patterns of the "Dance of the

Mysterious Circles." Their movements are trancelike, as if they themselves were not to make their dreadful decision. Their inspiration arrives, and they rush to the periphery of the scene; the chosen one stands alone in the center of the stage.

Now begins the dance that glorifies the victim. The chosen one remains motionless as the girls and men of the tribe whirl around her. All are transfixed at her power. They invoke the spirit of their ancestors, terrified anew by the force of Nature. Marking the relentless, sharp rhythms of the music with their feet, their dance reaches an ultimate expression of uncontrolled glory in sacrifice.

All the tribe members retire to watch the chosen one. The orchestra sounds strong, militant chords, trumpets blare harshly, cutting the air. The dance of the chosen one begins. The brutal savagery of the demanding music compels her to imitate it. Brief moments of comparative quiet, which seem at first to be periods of rest and release, are in reality more deadly because of the thrashing force that follows them. The girl is now wholly a part of the music, part of the earth. Hypnotized by her movements, the tribe joins in the violent dance. The chosen one begins to lose her strength, but—forced on by the convulsive violence of the music—is endowed with a new, superhuman compulsion. When it seems that Nature can demand no more, the girl is pushed into a fresh frenzy. Then she falls. She is dead.

The men of the tribe catch her up in their arms and hold her high over their heads before the sacred mound. The people of the tribe rush around her, holding up their arms. At the last slapping crescendo of the music, they fall to the earth.

SCÈNES DE BALLET

Classic ballet in one act. Music by Igor Stravinsky. Choreography by Anton Dolin. First presented by Billy Rose at the Ziegfeld Theatre, New York, December 7, 1944, as part of the revue The Seven Lively Arts. Alicia Markova and Anton Dolin danced the leading roles. Presented by the Sadler's Wells Ballet at the Royal Opera House, Covent Garden, London, February 11, 1948, in a new version with choreography by Frederick Ashton and scenery and costumes by André Beaurepaire. Margot Fonteyn and Michael Somes were the principal dancers.

Stravinsky wrote the music to this ballet after the forms of the classical dance, and the work consequently has no literary meaning or plot. In the composer's words, "The parts follow each other as in a sonata or in a symphony in contrasts or similarities."

The pattern of the ballet follows the divisions of the score. Scènes de Ballet is danced by two soloists and a corps de ballet of four boys and twelve girls. Stravinsky specified different dances for the eleven parts of his score.

The brief opening fanfare heralds an introduction by the *corps de ballet*, "Moderato." Now the ballerina dances a variation to bright, quick rhythms. After a brief pantomime section, "Lento," the *pas de deux* begins. In the Sadler's Wells production, the ballerina in the adagio is supported by five men. As they support her in pirouettes at one point, she keeps turning and another partner steps in to support her. A variation for the *danseur* "Risoluto," is followed by a variation for the ballerina. During her dance, her partner kneels before her and holds his hand to his heart; the four boys recline about him. There is another brief pantomime "Andantino," a final dance by the *corps de ballet*, "Con moto," and an apotheosis. Here the music gradually mounts in grandeur; the ballerina and her partner stand together in the center of the stage, and about them the *corps de ballet* are arranged in their original tableau.

SCHEHERAZADE

Dramatic ballet in one act. Music by Nikolai Rimsky-Korsakov. Choreography by Michel Fokine. Book by Alexandre Benois. Scenery and costumes by Léon Bakst. First presented by Diaghilev's Ballets Russes at the Théâtre National de l'Opéra, Paris, June 4, 1910, with Ida Rubinstein as *Zobeide*, Vaslav Nijinsky as the *Favorite Slave*, and Enrico Cecchetti as the *Chief Eunuch*. First presented in the United States by Gertrude Hoffman's Saison Russe at the Winter Garden, New York, June 14, 1911.

Color is the dominant element in this lavish ballet, color as brilliant and resplendent as the Eastern sun—color in music and dancing, in lush *décor*, and in the burning passions that consume the principal characters in the story. Those who are familiar with Rimsky-Korsakov's music, which the ballet uses, know that it is an orchestral suite—program music appropriate to a series of stories told by the beautiful Scheherazade to fascinate her husband. The makers of the ballet chose to abandon the composer's musical scheme and to fashion a dance drama out of the first story in the *Arabian Nights*, a drama that would embody all the mystery, passion, and violence that all these tales contained.

The first movement of the suite, the section known as "The Sea and Sinbad's Ship," is played by the orchestra before the curtain rises. Its music insinuates an Oriental atmosphere, prognosticating the voluptuous adventure the ballet relates and intimating the excitement and deadly risks attendant upon it. The second movement begins; the curtain rises.

The scene is the great hall of an Oriental palace. Rich hangings of purple and green and orange are looped from the ceiling, creating an impression of abundant wealth that spends itself on every conceivable extravagance.

On the left a purple stairway carpeted with golden cloth leads to the upper reaches of the palace. In the back there are three small blue doors decorated with silver stars. The king, Shahriar, sits upon his royal cushion. He ignores the members of his court as he turns constantly to caress Zobeide, his favorite concubine and leader of his harem.

The scene is relaxed and luxurious, the music languid. Eight girls of the harem recline lazily on multicolored cushions. Shahriar evidently wishes not to be distracted from his dalliance as he rests in the cool, open room. But his brother, Shah Zeman, who sits beside him, endeavors to engage his attention. Shahriar's chief eunuch, an obese, conniving caricature of a man, waddles before him, unctuously suggesting entertainment. Shahriar grants him permission by his silence, and the chief eunuch claps his hands. Three girls dressed in gold run out, bow to their master, and sit down together to perform a preface to their specialty. Shahriar holds Zobeide in his arms and does not notice them. The girls rise and dance sinuously. No one is amused.

The chief eunuch and several attendants assist Shahriar to rise. He is a tall man, whose costume is covered with jewels; a high gold collar surrounds his proud bearded face. His brother looks with hatred upon Zobeide, who stands beside her lord and master, her supple, yielding body scarcely disguised in transparent gauze and myriad ropes of pearls. She pleads with Shahriar for a favor. He refuses and points off into the distance. He commands a hunt in the forest. Zobeide is enraged: she has been embarrassed before the entire harem. She stalks away and flops down on a cushion, to look on with sulking defiance.

Shah Zeman, suspicious of Zobeide's fidelity to his brother, seizes upon the sudden tension between the two lovers and whispers his fears to the king. Shahriar listens. Although he is annoyed by her behavior, he disbelieves the gossip about his favorite. Shah Zeman persists, and briefly the king is a willing listener. Zobeide turns away contemptuously. The king calls over several of his attendants and gives them secret instructions. They bow and retreat.

All the girls save Zobeide rise from their cushions to bid their lord farewell and to wish him luck on the hunt. Four of the girls circle him. He protests lightly, but when four others surround him, he bends down to kiss two of the concubines. The girls dress him for the hunt. Shahriar looks over at Zobeide, enraged by her rage and by her power over him.

The chief eunuch brings in silver halberds. The trumpeting music heralds the start of the expedition. Shahriar attempts to persuade Zobeide that she has no cause for her anger. The sullen concubine resists his explanation at first, then fondly bids him farewell. All the girls kneel and hold up their hands beseechingly as Shahriar walks past them with his entourage toward the waiting expedition. Several girls wave to him. The chief eunuch exits with his master.

Now free from care and eager to enjoy their own pleasure, the harem women gather together and whisper excitedly, like schoolgirls. The light dims. They run to the back of the room and peer through the keyholes of the locked doors. They consult again and exit, bringing with them chests of jewels. One of the girls pulls in the chief eunuch, who protests helplessly. The girls surround him and, by the movement of their bodies, try to secure a favor. The eunuch refuses. All the girls circle about him, but the adamant eunuch shoos them off. One of the girls steals the big ring of keys he carries at his waist. He chases her and takes them back. The girls kneel about him, and the eunuch's resistance begins to disappear. Shall he, or shall he not? The girls see that he requires a bribe and dangle dazzling necklaces before him. The eunuch consents.

He walks to the doors at the back and unlocks one of them. Three Negro slaves dash out, like quick stallions, to their waiting lovers and throw them down upon the cushions. The second door is unlocked; three other couples are reunited in heated, reclining embraces. It is as if the girls, each momentarily out of favor with the king, are rejoicing openly in their contempt for his fickle affection as they welcome the eager advances of their secret lovers. The slaves, who so seldom gain admittance to the harem, cover their bodies with frantic kisses.

Zobeide pleads with the chief eunuch to open the third door. He turns away. Zobeide stamps and insists. The eunuch demands payment. She takes up a necklace, throws it at his feet, and now, consumed by her desire, drags him impatiently toward the door. She stands beside it in a voluptuous pose, slithering like a cat. The door opens. The favorite slave sneaks out with wary delight. He sees Zobeide; she stands breathless, her head thrown back, as he touches her body intimately. The chief eunuch exits.

The girls of the harem and their lovers abandon themselves to riotous dancing. Servant boys enter. Zobeide and the favorite writhe together on the cushions. The favorite slave springs up, and everyone watches as he throws himself into a vigorous dance. Now the entire group moves about the stage in whirling circles. The music whips their natural excitement into a frenzy of pleasure. The favorite slave holds the group fascinated with his bold leaps and assertive passion. The room becomes a whirling mass of climactic, flashing color. Zobeide and her lover are lost to each other on the king's divan. At its height, Shahriar rushes in, his scimitar raised threateningly. The hunt was but a ruse designed by his brother to expose the unfaithfulness of Zobeide.

The group rushes away from him like a receding wave. The king's men stand poised, with their swords ready to strike them down. Zobeide and the slave are so involved in their ecstasy that at first they do not notice. The slave springs up as he sees the king; Zobeide gropes back toward the corner of the stairs and tries to press her body into the wall. The slave dashes across the stage. Shah Zeman cuts him down in mid-flight, and the slave falls. His legs rear up into the air, his body refusing to die. The shah strikes again, and the slave expires. The king's soldiers chase the slaves and the concubines, killing them mercilessly at his command. The eunuch is stabbed to death. Zobeide pleads with the king for her life as his men close in on her with their scimitars. He orders them aside and the repentant woman kisses his hand. The king pulls his hand away. Zobeide reminds him of his devotion to her and her faithfulness to him. For a moment Shahriar believes her and is fascinated again by her loveliness. He embraces her and kisses her. As he raises his eyes, his brother kicks viciously at the body of Zobeide's secret lover and reminds him of her betrayal. He pushes her away. He hesitates. He does not wish to kill the woman he loves, despite her infidelity, for her repentance appears so genuine, but his kingly honor demands that a price be paid for his abused pride. He stands irresolute. His cohorts move toward Zobeide. Before they reach her, she pulls out a dagger and stabs herself in the belly. Her body doubles up over her arm. She is dead. The men drop their swords. Shahriar raises his arms in despair and weeps over her. His pride seems as nothing compared to his lost love.

NOTES: *Scheherazade*, the work that popularly identified the "new Russian Ballet" in the early days of Diaghilev's Ballets Russes, has managed to be in the active repertory of one company or another ever since. Its initial fame is understandable when we recall that its subject matter was new to its first audiences and when we remember its principal dancers. Tamara Karsavina soon took over the role of Zobeide, while Nijinsky continued in the part of the favorite slave. Carl van Vechten wrote that "Karsavina's *Zobeide* is a suggestive picture of languorous lust, and Nijinsky, as the principal slave, alternates between surprising leaps into the air and the most lascivious gestures; like some animal, he paws the reclining Sultana." The librettist of the ballet, Alexandre Benois, wrote that Ida Rubinstein was "absolutely inimitable . . . in her proud, cunning and unrestrained passion" and that Nijinsky as the favorite slave was "half-cat, half-snake, fiendishly agile, feminine and yet wholly terrifying."

What has happened to *Scheherazade* since, is best reflected in a review by Edwin Denby in the New York *Herald Tribune*: "Seen on a ballet program today, *Scheherazade* . . . is an illustrious warhorse foundering in dishonor. Not that there isn't some kind of life left in the old girl. The bundling and the clinches are still fine for laughs and whistles and cries of 'Take it off' . . . A great many people register sex all over the stage with an earnestness that is disarming rather than embarrassing. But one wonders what *Scheherazade* looked like when it scandalized our parents or when Parisians swooned at the lushness of it in 1910. In the 1910 photographs the slave girls look soft and abandoned. Nijinsky bounded about them like a panther in thrilling spasms that grew to a paroxysm of death at the climax. Bakst the great decorator—the Berman of his day—dazzled the public by the sensual shock of the brilliant decor. And the 'slavic harmonies' of Rimsky's score dunked the orgy on the stage in a bath of gold.

"Nowadays the small orchestra, the clumsily executed decor, the earnest but overworked dancers can't create any sense of abandon. The trouble is that there is no dance form, nothing for them to do as dancers. There is only miming and hubbub, and that doesn't keep for thirty years. A dance ballet can keep fresh because of its form, because arms and legs stay arms and legs; but when the dancers have to pretend to be something they aren't, a ballet disintegrates into a charade."

The first production of *Scheherazade* in the United States was not rehearsed by Fokine and not authorized by him. It remained for Diaghilev's Ballets Russes to present the first authentic version in this country, in January 1916, at the Century Theatre, New York. Nijinsky danced *Scheherazade* with Diaghilev's company for the first time in the United States on April 15, 1916, at the Metropolitan Opera House. His part has been danced since by such dancers as André Eglevsky, Frederic Franklin, Leonide Massine, and Yurek Shabelevsky. The part of Zobeide has been danced by many ballerinas, among them, Alexandra Danilova, Mia Slavenska, and Lubov Tchernicheva.

SCHUMANN CONCERTO

Ballet in three movements. Choreographic concerto by Bronislava Nijinska. Music by Robert Schumann (*Piano Concerto in A minor*). Scenery and costumes by Stewart Chaney. First presented by Ballet Theatre at the Metropolitan Opera House, New York, September 27, 1951, with a cast headed by Alicia Alonso and Igor Youskevitch.

The romantic mood of Schumann's music is the inspiration for this abstract ballet. Two central figures represent the romantic center of the ballet, and above this couple a *corps de ballet* of boys and girls dance as a background. The setting is romantic, too. Three gray stone arches draped with red cloth frame a backdrop that depicts a high, desolate cliff.

FIRST MOVEMENT—ALLEGRO AFFETTUOSO: When the curtain rises, after a long musical introduction, we see on stage the ballerina, who stands in an attitude of wistfulness. She is dressed all in white, in full romantic costume. To the right is her lover, who holds out his arms to her longingly. The couple and the small group of girls who stand to either side of them begin to dance. What they dance has no plot in any usual sense; they exit and re-enter, not continuing a pattern they have started, but simply dancing along with the dynamics of the music. The piano in the concerto represents no one in particular. When the music becomes vigorous, groups of boys cross the stage in high leaps. The *premier danseur* dances with one of these groups and exits. The ballerina now performs a variation. Her partner returns to watch as she circles the stage with rapid turns. They leave the stage to the *corps de ballet* briefly. The music becomes quiet; six of the girls form a tableau. The ballerina rejoins them, still turning, to the accompaniment of soft trills of the piano. Three of the boys lift her high, carry her around the stage and off into the wings. She and her partner return, as the last chords of the first movement begin, and join the *corps de ballet* to dance its final measures.

SECOND MOVEMENT—INTERMEZZO: The light dims. Eight girls in rust-color skirts covered with black net join other girls dressed in softly tinted dresses to form a backdrop for a *pas de deux* between the ballerina and her partner. Alternately, with the rhythm of the music, the *premier danseur* supports the ballerina in swift pirouettes that stop sharply with the music's hesitation and high lifts that end, again, with pirouettes. As the dance progresses, the ballerina turns more and more rapidly; her white dress seems to be in a perpetual whirl about her moving figure.

THIRD MOVEMENT—ALLEGRO VIVACE: The scene brightens, and a new backdrop reveals in the distance ancient ruins, overrun with moss and weeds and grass. A luminous yellow sun in a cloudless sky shines down on the nostalgic vista. The ballerina and her partner return. Three boys go to the front of the stage and recline to watch the ballerina dance. Soon they rise and, with a second group of men, stand at either side of the stage as the ballerina moves across it. She leaves the scene now to her partner, who dances brilliantly down a diagonal formed by the male *corps de ballet*. All the girls come back and re-form a tableau, as the two principals dominate the scene. The ballerina encircles her lover with accelerated turns; he spins in the air, as the music reaches a crescendo of joyousness, and carries her off into the wings. The different units of the *corps de ballet* fill the stage with movement until the principals join in for the finale. The curtain falls as the ballerina is lifted high above the group. Her lover stands facing us with outstretched arms.

SCOTCH SYMPHONY

Classic ballet in three parts. Music by Felix Mendelssohn. Choreography by George Balanchine. Scenery by Horace Armistead. Costumes by Karinska and David Ffolkes. Lighting by Jean Rosenthal. First presented by the New York City Ballet at the City Center, New York, November 11, 1952, with Maria Tallchief, André Eglevsky, Patricia Wilde, Frank Hobi, and Michael Maule in the principal roles.

When the New York City Ballet appeared at the Edinburgh Festival in August 1952, I had my first opportunity to see the great massed demonstration of parade units from the Scottish regiments in the famous nocturnal Military

Tattoo. I greatly enjoyed this spectacle, as I also enjoyed seeing Scotland as a whole. It occurred to me that when my company returned to New York, we might do a Scottish ballet. Scotland, after all, was the scene of the first great romantic ballet, La Sylphide, and a new ballet might well recollect this fact as it also remounted dances in the Scottish manner. Mendelssohn, too, had written his Scotch Symphony, and this music seemed to me appropriate for the idea I had in mind.

Back in New York, we decided to do the ballet Scotch Symphony almost immediately, omitting the first movement of Mendelssohn's score, which is not appropriate for dance.

In the first movement of the ballet there are general dances by the ensemble, all in appropriate Scottish costume: there is a pas de trois by a girl and two boys, and there are solo passages for the girl.

The second movement is an adagio for a ballerina and her partner that represents, without a story, the general mood and atmosphere of the romantic ballet as epitomized in such ballets as La Sylphide.

The third movement is again an ensemble, in which the ballerina and her partner participate with pas de deux and variation, joining the soloists and corps de ballet in a finale.

SERENADE

Classic ballet in four parts. Music by Peter Ilyich Tchaikovsky. Choreography by George Balanchine. Costumes by Jean Lurcat. First presented by students of the School of American Ballet at the estate of Felix M. Warburg, White Plains, New York, June 9, 1934. Presented by the producing company of the School of American Ballet at the Avery Memorial Theatre, Hartford, Connecticut, December 6, 1934, with Kathryn Mullowney, Heidi Vosseler, and Charles Laskey in the principal roles.

Named after its music—Tchaikovsky's Serenade in C major for String Orchestra—Serenade tells its story musically and choreographically, without any extraneous narrative. Because Tchaikovsky's score, though it was not composed for the ballet, has in its danceable four movements different qualities suggestive of different emotions and human situations, parts of the ballet seem to have a story: the apparently "pure" dance takes on a kind of plot. But this plot, inherent in the score, contains many stories—it is many things to many listeners to the music, and many things to many people who see the ballet.

Most people would agree that a nonprogrammatic piece of music doesn't have to have a story to be a pleasure: we enjoy symphonies by Tchaikovsky and Mozart just as much as we enjoy a symphony with a story, such as

Beethoven's *Pastorale*. *Serenade* is programmatic only insofar as its music is programmatic.

To tell a story about something is simply a very human way of saying that we understand it. Making a ballet is a choreographer's way of showing how he understands a piece of music, not in words, not in narrative form (unless he has in mind a particular story), but in dancing.

The four movements of Tchaikovsky's score are danced in the following order, without interruption: (1) Piece in the Form of a Sonatina: *Andante non troppo, Allegro*; (2) Waltz; (3) Tema Russo: *Andante, Allegro con spirito*; (4) Elegy. Twenty-eight dancers in blue costumes dance the ballet before a blue background.

FIRST MOVEMENT: The orchestra plays the strong and spacious opening chords of the brief Andante section and repeats them deeply before the curtain rises. When we see the stage, a group of girls stand in a tableau of crossing lines. It is night. The shadowed light that shines upon them is soft. They are motionless at first, then respond to the music as the light brightens and the new melodious Allegro is heard.

The girls dance in small groups, forming patterns on the stage. One girl dances alone, turning, posing, leaping among the others. Others seem to imitate her originality, but then all are whirling faster and faster in a wide circle together. Suddenly, quickly, each girl stands motionless in the same tableau that opened the ballet, and the familiar chords of the introductory Andante are repeated.

One girl comes in late. She finds her place in the group and stands with the other girls. A boy enters at the back of the stage. As he walks forward toward the girl, her friends leave the stage.

SECOND MOVEMENT: A waltz begins as the boy reaches the girl. They begin to dance together, the girl moving away from him, then rejoining him. When her friends re-enter, the girl dances joyously among them; then she and her partner lead them in a dance, the boy lifting the ballerina high in front of the group. The waltz slowly and softly ends, and the group walks off to the tempo of its concluding rhythms.

THIRD MOVEMENT (the fourth movement in the original suite): Five girls remain on stage. They sit together on the stage as the music is quiet, turning toward each other in gentle movements. They rise and, at the first sound of the brilliant Russian melody, respond immediately and dance with open gaiety. A boy rushes on and meets a girl; they dance together; and when the ensemble runs off, as the music finishes, we see that the girl has fallen to the floor, her head buried in her arms. She is alone.

FOURTH MOVEMENT: Another girl brings a boy to her. This girl walks behind the boy, guiding him forward: it is as if she moved him, as if he saw only what she wished. When they reach the fallen girl, the boy helps her to rise and now dances with the two of them. He remains with them, dancing with one of them alone, then both together, until there comes a time when he must choose. The girl who possessed him first, the girl who brought him to the other, claims him irrevocably and he leaves with her. The forsaken heroine collapses, revives briefly, and then is lost. Three boys lift her straight up above their shoulders. Her body arches back slowly as they carry her forward in a quiet procession; her arms open wide.

NOTES: *Serenade* was my first ballet in the United States. Soon after my arrival in America, Lincoln Kirstein, Edward M. M. Warburg, and I opened the School of American Ballet in New York. As part of the school curriculum, I started an evening ballet class in stage technique, to give students some idea of how dancing on stage differs from classwork. *Serenade* evolved from the lessons I gave.

It seemed to me that the best way to make students aware of stage technique was to give them something new to dance, something they had never seen before. I chose Tchaikovsky's *Serenade* to work with. The class contained, the first night, seventeen girls and no boys. The problem was, how to arrange this odd number of girls so that they would look interesting. I placed them on diagonal lines and decided that the hands should move first to give the girls practice.

That was how *Serenade* began. The next class contained only nine girls; the third, six. I choreographed to the music with the pupils I happened to have at a particular time. Boys began to attend the class and they were worked into the pattern. One day, when all the girls rushed off the floor area we were using as a stage, one of the girls fell and began to cry. I told the pianist to keep on playing and kept this bit in the dance. Another day, one of the girls was late for class, so I left that in too.

Later, when we staged *Serenade*, everything was revised. The girls who couldn't dance well were left out of the more difficult parts; I elaborated on the small accidental bits I had included in class and made the whole more dramatic, more theatrical, synchronizing it to the music with additional movement, but always using the little things that ordinarily might be overlooked.

I've gone into a little detail here about *Serenade* because many people think there is a concealed story in the ballet. There is not. There are, simply, dancers in motion to a beautiful piece of music. The only story is the music's story, a serenade, a dance, if you like, in the light of the moon.

Serenade has seen a number of different productions. It was produced by the American Ballet, the company made up of our dancers at the School of American Ballet, in its first season, at the Adelphi Theatre, New York, March 1–15, 1935. It was staged for the Ballet Russe de Monte Carlo, October 17, 1940, at the Metropolitan Opera House, with costumes by Lurcat and a cast headed by Marie-Jeanne, Igor Youskevitch, and Frederic Franklin. In 1941 *Serenade* was mounted for the South American tour of the

American Ballet Caravan in a new production with costumes by Alvin Colt. In 1947 it was staged for the ballet of the Paris Opéra. On October 18, 1948, *Serenade* became part of the permanent repertory of the New York City Ballet. This production has costumes by Karinska.

The leading role in *Serenade* was first danced by a group of soloists, rather than by one principal dancer. In a number of productions, however, I arranged it for one dancer. But when the New York City Ballet was to make its first appearance in London, at the Royal Opera House, Covent Garden, in the summer of 1950, it seemed appropriate to introduce the company by introducing its principal dancers and the leading role was again divided and danced by our leading soloists. Diana Adams, Ruthanna Boris, Alexandra Danilova, Melissa Hayden, Marie-Jeanne, Tanaquil LeClercq, Yvonne Mounsey, Mary Ellen Moylan, Janet Reed, Maria Tallchief, and Patricia Wilde are among the dancers who have appeared in leading roles in *Serenade* in various productions. Herbert Bliss, Leon Danielian, Frederic Franklin, Frank Hobi, Nicholas Magallanes, and Igor Youskevitch are among those who have danced the leading male roles.

SLAUGHTER ON TENTH AVENUE

Dramatic ballet within a musical revue. Music by Richard Rodgers. Choreography by George Balanchine. Scenery by Jo Mielziner. Costumes by Irene Sharaff. First presented by Dwight Deere Wiman in the musical revue *On Your Toes* (Richard Rodgers-George Abbott-Lorenz Hart) at the Imperial Theatre, New York, April 11, 1936, with Ray Bolger, Tamara Geva, and George Church as the principal dancers.

The ballet *Slaughter on Tenth Avenue* was not a separate dance number in the great musical comedy *On Your Toes*, but a ballet that was part of the story. This story, a take-off on Russian ballet, had for its central theme a question very appropriate for its time: how could an American upstart hope to make good in a famous Russian ballet company?

Junior (Ray Bolger) was the American. Almost overnight he found himself a member of this famous Russian company when he successfully substituted for a dancer who had fallen ill. But young Junior didn't like the ballets the company danced. Sergei Alexandrovitch (Monty Woolley), the company's impresario, preferred ballets in the lush, pseudo-Russian, romantic style.

Junior thought he knew how to remedy this situation. He himself came from a vaudeville family, he knew a lot about music, and he tried to induce the company to accept an idea for a new kind of ballet. The ballerina (Tamara Geva) was all in favor of the idea, but the pompous Russian *premier danseur* (Demetrios Vilan) was jealous of Junior's talent and immediately began to plot against him. Only the enthusiasm of the company's rich patroness permitted Junior to proceed with his plan.

Rehearsals for the new ballet began. It was called *Slaughter on Tenth Avenue* and told a modern story of love and death. Junior himself was to dance the hero, a hoofer who one night visits a low dive on New York's West Side. Here he meets the strip-teaser (Tamara Geva), dances with her, and the two fall in love. But the girl is married to the big boss (George Church), who has been watching his wife dance so warmly with one of the customers. He breaks up the dance, fights with the hoofer, and pulls a knife on him. Accidentally he stabs the girl. She dies. The hoofer attacks the big boss and kills him. He dances around the body.

We learn that the ballet will end with the hoofer's suicide. He has killed the murderer, but is himself a murderer. The girl is dead; he has nothing to live for.

The day of the *première* of the new ballet approaches. Already *Slaughter* is popular with the company. But the *premier danseur* is determined that it shall fail and that Junior shall leave the company. To ensure his ends, he hires a group of gangsters, men very similar to the tough guys standing around the bar in the Tenth Avenue joint depicted in the ballet. The *danseur* gives these men tickets for a box near the stage for the opening night of the ballet, instructs them to eliminate Junior, and tells them how they can do it without being caught. At the end of *Slaughter on Tenth Avenue*, Junior is supposed to shoot himself. If they shoot him from the box, the ballet will end as planned, the curtain will fall, and no one will have any idea who committed the crime.

The gangsters agree. On the night of the *première*, they sit in a box in the theatre overlooking the stage. *Slaughter on Tenth Avenue* begins. We watch the action, are moved by the lyrical *pas de deux* danced by the hoofer and the girl, then see her murdered. As she dies in her lover's arms, the ballerina who is playing the girl speaks to Junior. She warns him of the plot against his life, which she overheard just before the rise of the curtain. She tells him that the gangsters will not dare to kill him if at the end of the ballet he keeps on dancing: he must change the ending and not shoot himself! The ballerina has called the police; they are sure to arrive in a matter of minutes.

When the big boss has been dispatched, Junior begins his dance of despair around the dead man's body. Then he improvises, dancing so artfully a frantic dance of death that the audience is unaware of any change. He moves faster and faster, incredibly spinning with ever greater energy, when his last strength seems to be spent. As he almost collapses on the stage from exhaustion, the police arrive. They arrest the frightened gangsters and the *premier danseur* amid tremendous applause for the new ballet. *Slaughter on Tenth Avenue* is a hit. Junior is the dancer of the hour. His success assured, the upstart hoofer marries the American girl he has loved all along and lives happily ever afterward.

NOTES: *On Your Toes* was the first musical I choreographed in the United States. Working with Lorenz Hart, Richard Rodgers, and George Abbott on this show made my job a pleasure from the start. The team of Rodgers and Hart represented for me, as it did for so many Americans, superb entertainment in the musical theatre. These men devised over the years a seemingly endless series of revues that were melodically and lyrically filled with great wit, touching humor, and eminent theatricality. After *On Your Toes*, it was my privilege to work with them on three other revues. *On Your Toes* was also my first association with the fine artist and comedian Ray Bolger, whose dancing throughout the show, and in *Slaughter*, will scarcely be forgotten by those who saw it.

Richard Rodgers' music to *Slaughter on Tenth Avenue* is dramatic and lyrical, immensely danceable. The listener will easily discern this. The score is an eloquent reminder of a great evening of entertainment in the theatre.

THE SLEEPING BEAUTY

Classic ballet in three acts, with prologue. Music by Peter Ilyich Tchaikovsky. Choreography by Marius Petipa. Book by Marius Petipa and Ivan Vsevolojsky, after tales by Charles Perrault. Scenery and costumes by Ivan Vsevolojsky. First presented at the Maryinsky Theatre, St. Petersburg, Russia, January 15, 1890, with Carlotta Brianza as the *Princess Aurora*, Paul Gerdt as the *Prince*, Marie Petipa as the *Lilac Fairy*, Enrico Cecchetti as *Carabosse*, Varvara Nikitina as the *Enchanted Princess*, and Enrico Cecchetti as the *Bluebird*. First presented in Western Europe by Diaghilev's Ballets Russes at the Alhambra Theatre, London, November 2, 1921. Staged by Nicholas Sergeyev after the choreography of Marius Petipa. Additional choreography by Bronislava Nijinska. Orchestration of Prelude to Act Three and the Princess Aurora's variation in Act Three by Igor Stravinsky. Scenery and costumes by Léon Bakst. The cast included Olga Spessivtzeva as the *Princess Aurora*, Pierre Vladimiroff as the *Prince*, Lydia Lopokova as the *Lilac Fairy*, Carlotta Brianza as *Carabosse*, Felia Dubrovska, Lydia Sokolova, Bronislava Nijinska, Lubov Egorova, and Vera Nemtchinova as the *Fairies*, Ludmilla Shollar as the *White Cat*, Lydia Lopokova as the *Enchanted Princess*, and Stanislas Idzikowski as the *Bluebird*. Revived by the Sadler's Wells Ballet at the Sadler's Wells Theatre, London, February 2, 1939, in a new production staged by Nicholas Sergeyev after choreography by Marius Petipa. Scenery and costumes by Nadia Benois. The cast included Margot Fonteyn as the *Princess Aurora*, Robert Helpmann as the *Prince*, June Brae as the *Lilac Fairy*, and Mary Honer and Harold Turner as the *Bluebirds*. Revived by the Sadler's Wells Ballet in a new production under the supervision of Nicholas Sergeyev at the Royal Opera House, Covent

Garden, February 20, 1946. Additional choreography by Frederick Ashton and Ninette de Valois. Scenery and costumes by Oliver Messel. Margot Fonteyn as the *Princess Aurora*, Robert Helpmann as the *Prince*, Beryl Grey as the *Lilac Fairy*, and Pamela May and Alexis Rassine as the *Bluebirds* headed the cast. First presented in the United States by the Sadler's Wells Ballet at the Metropolitan Opera House, New York, October 9, 1949, with Margot Fonteyn and Robert Helpmann, Beryl Grey, Moira Shearer, and Alexis Rassine. Catherine Little-field, Director of the Philadelphia Ballet, produced a complete version of *The Sleeping Beauty* with her own choreography at the Academy of Music, Philadelphia, February 12, 1937. This version was later pro-duced at the Lewisohn Stadium, New York, July 29 and 30, 1937.

The crashing, commanding chords of the brief overture to *The Sleeping Beauty* herald the special magic of the fairy tale the ballet relates, a fairy tale that is rich and formal in presentation, but warm and intimate in effect. Tchaikovsky and Petipa have so fashioned Perrault's story of the sleeping princess ("*La Belle au Bois Dormant*," from *Mother Goose*), for the theatre, that notions of reality are suspended in favor of belief in characters who can live forever, in a curse of black magic that can put a forest to sleep for a hundred years, and in a beneficent fairy whose magic can rescue all goodness from evil. The time is unimportant, as is the place. The nameless mythical kingdom of the mythical King Florestan XXIV becomes the scene of our imagination.

The intensity of the music demands the attention, focusing it, as it were, on the splendor of the opening scene. The overture to *The Sleeping Beauty* also contains in miniature the story it introduces. Concealed within the opening regal chords is a theme that represents the fairy Carabosse, the evil fairy who will cast a spell upon the ballet's heroine and her family. This music is quickly interrupted by the melodious harp, which introduces a soft, slow, magical, compassionate theme—the melody of the Lilac Fairy, whose beauty and goodness will triumph over the evil fairy's challenge.

Now the music changes to a march tempo, quietly at first, then more assertively. The melody swells. The curtain rises.

PROLOGUE—THE CHRISTENING: The hall of King Flo-restan's palace is high-ceilinged. Great arches of stone cross the back of the stage; through them can be discerned the foliage of the garden. Drapery of resplendent color and ornament warms the spaciousness of the scene. On the right, on a small platform, stands the canopied cradle of the Princess Aurora, guarded by two nurses on each side. Two heralds stand at the back. Almost immediately the king's master of ceremonies, Cattalabutte, enters in elaborate full dress. With great flourish, he busies himself seeing that all is ready for the ceremony. Satisfied, he comes forward, gives a page his stick of office, and scans the list of guests who have been invited to attend the christening of the princess.

Twelve ladies in waiting enter the chamber. They circle the stage and ceremoniously ask Cattalabutte if they may see the child. He consents and leads them over to the cradle, where they hover over the princess. Cattalabutte directs a page to notify the king that all the preparations have been made and nervously unrolls the guest list again to check his memory. The ladies retire from the cradle and stand to one side. A fanfare sounds in the distance; it grows louder; three pages enter. To the blaring of trumpets, the king and queen approach. They pause for a moment under the silk canopy that is held high above them by Negroes dressed in gold and survey the scene. Then their attendants drop their trains. The queen goes to the cradle. She kisses the princess and greets the ladies in waiting, who bow to her. She joins the king, who stands in conference with Cattalabutte. After a brief consultation with their servant, the two monarchs mount the steps to their thrones.

An arpeggio on the harp announces the arrival of the fairy godmothers of the princess. The royal fairies are preceded by their pages, who enter two by two and bow to their sovereigns. Five of the fairies enter in a group: the Fairy of the Crystal Fountain, the Fairy of the Enchanted Garden, the Fairy of the Woodland Glades, the Fairy of the Songbirds, and the Fairy of the Golden Vine. Eight maids of honor attend them. Last of all comes the Fairy of the Lilac, accompanied by six cavaliers, one for each of the fairies. The cavaliers carry, on plush cushions, the gifts the fairies have chosen for their godchild. The Lilac Fairy leads the group forward. The fairies bow low to the king and queen, who welcome them cordially, and arrange themselves about the royal cradle to bless the princess. They bow again to the king and queen and leave the scene.

The maids of honor come forward in two lines and, to the syncopated rhythm of a new melody, they dance in linear patterns. They are joined by the cavaliers, who leap boldly in the air. The fairies return, and all dance together briefly. The queen thanks the Lilac Fairy for the dance and asks the group to continue. The Lilac Fairy bows.

A new tender theme is heard, accompanied by runs on the harp. The fairies and their partners arrange themselves in five moving circles, the Lilac Fairy in the center. Two of the girls in the back are lifted to their partners' shoulders and turned around and around so that they appear to be swimming high in the air. The fairies come forward to the footlights. One by one, the fairies pirouette rapidly and pose in attitude supported by their cavaliers. The maids of honor lie at their feet in respectful obeisance.

The tableau is broken; the music subsides, then regains in volume; in a hushed pause, the royal nurses bring the small princess to the center of the stage. There is a magical rushing run on the harp, and the Lilac Fairy is lifted high above the princess. She blesses the babe with her wand. The *pas de six* is over. The harp plays for a moment, the tempo changes, and the fairies leave the stage while the maids of honor dance a new sprightly measure in unison.

Now each of the fairies returns to perform a variation before the assembled court. These variations are very short; they have no literal significance, and the attributes of the different fairies cannot be read into them; but the different music and different dances that Tchaikovsky and Petipa devised for the six fairies gives each of the variations an individual, distinctive character. First is the Fairy of the Crystal Fountain. She enters and waits for her music to begin. Its movement is slow and leisurely; its melody, calm. The fairy dances forward and moves back and forth across the stage on her points, her body in graceful repose. As her feet mark the retarded rhythm of her music, her head and arms depict the quiet sweetness of the melody. She kneels to the king and queen as her variation ends and leaves the stage.

The Fairy of the Enchanted Garden emerges to dance with quick steps to a brighter tempo—music which carries her into swift pirouettes that accelerate as she moves across the stage. For the Fairy of the Woodland Glades, the music is characterized by a soft, tempered pizzicato. This fairy's skill in quiet, slow movement is revealed in the daring figure that highlights her dance: she dances forward on one foot, her other foot extended before her. With subdued brilliance her extended foot moves back, and the girl stands poised for a breathless moment in arabesque. This figure is repeated as she continues to move forward. Then her dance becomes luminous and light, with rapid dancing on point. She ends her variation standing on point, with open arms, one leg raised pertly before her.

In a flashing yellow costume, the Fairy of the Songbirds dances now to a hurried, tinkling melody, her arms moving ecstatically in simulated flight, her bright head turning to the shimmering elevation of the rhythm. She is followed by the Fairy of the Golden Vine, whose dance is characterized by the curt, staccato movement of her head and the quick pointing of the index fingers of both her hands—the so-called "Finger Variation." The tempo of the music increases sharply, and the brilliant fairy whirls to a quick, sudden stop.

The Lilac Fairy comes forward. She stands toward the back of the stage. The orchestra begins a sumptuously melodic waltz, and the Lilac Fairy accompanies its flowing line with extended, open movements in which her raised point traces small circles in the air. Then she turns in arabesque; she pauses briefly each time her body is seen in profile. In the rapid complexity of its movement and in the fullness of the magnificent waltz, the variation of the Lilac Fairy sums up in splendid grandeur the dances of all the other fairies.

Now the cavaliers dance. The maids of honor join them with light, precise movements. The fairies reassemble at the front of the stage. Their cavaliers hold them in attitude. The fairies' gifts are presented to the king and queen. The queen leaves the throne and delightedly examines the presents. There is a deep, rumbling sound, like an earthquake, off stage. Some of the courtiers imagine it to be only thunder, but the king is apprehensive. The queen trembles for the safety of her child, and the master of ceremonies cowers. A page rushes in and gestures helplessly to the king, pointing off to the left. The king understands suddenly and rushes over to Cattalabutte and demands to see the invitation list. He scans it rapidly, then dashes the scroll to the floor in a gigantic rage. Cattalabutte's fate is averted momentarily by the frightening appearance of two great rats, who emerge from the left and dance a few insidious steps. They run back out. Before the court has recovered, they return with other rats, pulling along behind them an enormous black coach. Standing majestically in the coach is the fairy Carabosse, the hunchbacked godmother of the Princess Aurora, whom the forgetful Cattalabutte has neglected to invite to the christening. She grasps at the air in her fury; her black chariot circles the stage, sweeping all the courtiers aside.

Assisted by her four rodent attendants, Carabosse steps down. The music gives a low warning. Her face is a hideous blue-white mask covered with moles and magical, shining spangles. Her long black dress is tattered and dusty, yet she wears it as if it were ermine. Carabosse hobbles forward on her stick and inquires fiercely of the king, by gesture, "Why was I forgotten? Do you realize what this will mean to the fate of your child?" Already, the king is afraid. He points to Cattalabutte as the real culprit. Carabosse approaches the cowardly master of ceremonies, who kneels at her feet. He throws up his hands, begging for mercy and to protect himself, but Carabosse reaches out her talonlike fingers and tears off his wig, which she throws at the hungry rats. Now, deprived of all his dignity, the courtier attempts to escape.

Carabosse raises her stick and, with a quick thrust in the small of his back, sends him flying. She caresses the rats, who form a small square about her as she dances blithely. She gestures to the royal couple, pointing to the cradle: "Your daughter will grow up . . . She will grow up to be a beautiful princess . . . the most beautiful princess of them all; and then"— Carabosse brings down her stick loudly; the music thunders—"and then . . . she will die! . . . She will prick her finger, no one will prevent it, and she will be a beautiful dead princess!" The wicked fairy cackles with glee as the king tries to comfort the distraught queen. He motions Carabosse imperiously away, but the evil fairy persists in laughing at his discomfort. She whips her great black cape through the air to the sound of the harp.

The Lilac Fairy steps out. Carabosse tries to approach the cradle to repeat her curse. The Lilac Fairy holds up her magic wand in quiet defiance; Carabosse stumbles back. All the other fairies gather around her to guard the cradle. She threatens them with her stick, but the good fairies stand placidly impervious. The hideous, servile rats surround the grotesque Carabosse, and she dances a final, frantic jig, at the end of which she holds up her hand in triumph. She climbs back into her carriage; as she stands under its high roof of black plumes, shaking her fists at the whole court, the obedient rats draw the black chariot off. The thunder subsides.

The queen weeps in the king's arms. He cannot comfort her. The Lilac Fairy comes to them. The lovely melody that identifies this good fairy fills the hall. She gestures toward the cradle and gives them this message in pantomime: "Your daughter, the princess, will grow up to be beautiful, and it is true that she will prick her finger and seem to die . . . but in reality she will only go to sleep . . . she will sleep for a hundred years, and all the court with her . . . but one day a prince, as handsome as she is beautiful, will come to the princess . . . she will wake at his kiss, and all will live happily ever after."

The king and queen bow to the Lilac Fairy and thank her. The release from the evil curse of Carabosse causes the court to be joyful. All the fairies bow to the king and queen, and then the entire assembly turns toward the cradle of the Princess Aurora. The queen stands over her daughter; the ladies in waiting and the maids of honor kneel in homage, and the fairies stand in attitudes of infinite protectiveness. The curtain falls.

ACT ONE — THE SPELL: The scene is the garden of the palace. A colonnade of huge columns, topped by ancient statues, sweeps in a curve about a high fountain toward the right to support a great arch of stone over the back of the garden. Thrones for the king and queen are arranged at the right. On the left, a flight of wide stone steps leads up toward the palace. Peasants idle in the distance. Ladies in waiting and their cavaliers walk about the garden, marveling at its beauty and anticipating the day's festival. For today is the Princess Aurora's sixteenth birthday, and the king has decreed a celebration in her honor. The king has also invited the court and kingdom to entertain four foreign visitors: princes from England, India, Italy, and Spain, who have come long distances to meet the young princess and pay court to her.

Three old hags in black, their dark hoods concealing their faces, stoop together over spindles. As they sew, they keep looking about cautiously. Cattalabutte enters. He has aged somewhat in the sixteen years that have passed, but still flourishes his cape and stick at every opportunity. The old women dance away from him. Cattalabutte regards them suspiciously. They try to escape, but the master of ceremonies catches them. He takes the spindles from them forcibly and stands over them threateningly. The women cower at his feet as Cattalabutte reminds them that for sixteen years, ever since the curse of the wicked fairy Carabosse, the king has ordered that no spindles be brought within a mile of the Princess Aurora. He is interrupted by the arrival of the king and queen, who are followed by the four princes. The old women scurry into a corner.

The king greets Cattalabutte and wonders what his courtier holds concealed in the hand behind his back. Reluctantly Cattalabutte holds out the dread spindles. The king is shocked and furious. Cattalabutte points to the weird women; the king commands them to come forward. He tells them that they must hang for this offense; how otherwise can he protect his daughter from the spell of Carabosse? The women kneel at his feet and plead for forgiveness. The king is adamant. To a sudden crescendo of surging, pulsating music, the queen steps forward and asks the king to relent. After all, this is Aurora's birthday and the women are truly sorry. The king smiles and consents.

The king and queen mount their thrones, carrying fresh garlands. A group of peasant girls enters. They bow deeply to their lord. The courtiers gather on the steps, and the four princes stand to one side as the girls commence to dance to a flowing waltz. The girls weave in and out under the garlands and arrange themselves in circles that travel around the stage in opposite directions. Cattalabutte thanks them when the waltz is over, and they bow to the monarchs.

Four musicians enter, carrying golden instruments, followed by eight girls—friends of the princess. The four foreign princes stand ready to greet the guest of honor. The music is expectant. The four princes look toward the back of the garden and peer down the colonnade, hoping for a glimpse of the princess. Softly the music hesitates. In the distance, under the arch, we see a beautiful girl in a pink dress embellished with silver. She poses for an instant and disappears like an apparition. Then, brilliantly, to a burst of music, she is on stage, dancing joyfully with the sweet, innocent exuberance of youth. The four princes approach her. The princess goes to her mother, who embraces her warmly, then to the king, who kisses her on the forehead. The king then introduces her to the foreign princes, who bow low to her. She responds gently. The harp plays a rushing cadenza; all the other instruments are silent, waiting; there is a brief hush, a momentary interval of preparation like the soprano's measured intake of breath before a great aria commences. The "Rose Adagio" begins.

The four princes move to the front of the stage in a line. One by one, the princes support the Princess Aurora as she dances softly and openly her preparatory steps. Then she steps back; standing on point in attitude, she greets the first prince. Holding her right hand, he turns her in attitude, as she maintains the graceful pose. When she has come full circle, the prince releases her hand; both hands are raised to form a crown above her head for a moment of balance; then the second cavalier steps forward to hold her right hand. This design is repeated. Finally, as the last prince releases her, the princess extends her body in arabesque and holds this position with breath-taking equilibrium.

One of her suitors now supports Aurora, who modestly displays her dancing skill without conveying the least impression that she is unlike any other young girl who is beautiful and happens to be dancing. Sweetly holding her hands to her cheek, the princess leans forward. She is lifted high in the air. When she is released, she dances alone in a small circle, her arms invoking the melody of the music, her strong points tracing its rhythms.

Each of the enamored princes now presents Aurora with a freshly picked rose. The theme is played softly by the oboe. One prince supports her as the others come forward, one by one, with their gifts. The princess pirouettes swiftly as she accepts each of the flowers. Then, charmingly, she leaves her suitors and presents their flowers to the queen. She moves to the back of the stage and dances forward. Armed with fresh roses, the princes kneel at her feet. As she pirouettes past them, the princes hold out their flowers; the princess pauses in her turning to receive each rose. She holds the flowers to her breast for a moment, then tosses them in the air as her dance continues.

The music approaches its fullest, final expression. One of the princes holds her hand as the princess stands again on point in attitude. He releases her, and she sustains her pose as if it were effortless. Then, moving only her arm, she takes the hand of the second prince, to prepare briefly for a second, longer balance. Her modest confidence in balance increases as the adagio comes to a conclusion. When the fourth prince releases her, she stands in what seems perpetually perfect balance until the final chord breaks the enchantment. She runs off into the garden.

The eight friends of the Princess Aurora dance to a tinkling, blithe melody. Soon the princess returns. The four princes beseech her to dance again. She turns to her mother, who encourages her with a smile, and the princess begins a *pas seul*. After posing in attitude and arabesque, she goes to the corner of the garden. She dances forward on point in a diagonal line with slow precision. Step by step, she bends her right knee and brings her right leg up so that it touches gently the back of her supporting leg. The diagonal completed, she dances backward toward the corner in a series of pirouettes, each of which ends in secure, perfect position. The princess circles the garden, with brilliant, accelerating spins, and leaves the stage.

When friends commence to dance, the princess comes back. She dances toward the front with high, broad leaps in which she kicks her front foot forward—a movement that gives her dance a new urgency. She circles the stage again, this time with open, free turns rapidly executed. The tempo of the music builds with her speed, with her joy in dancing.

On the right, in the corner, half concealed by the crowd, an old woman in black emerges. She watches the happy princess and, when Aurora circles near her, holds out a present to the princess. Aurora, barely stopping, takes it and dances on, delighted with the strange, new object. The gift is a spindle! The king rises in terror and warns the court. Everyone attempts to stop Aurora's dance and take the spindle from her. But the innocent, impetuous girl is so charmed by the spindle that she cannot cease to play with it. Suddenly, she pricks her finger. Instantly, she falls to the ground.

The king and queen rush to her. The angry monarch orders the court to find the criminal who presented the princess with the fatal spindle. The princess herself has no idea of what has happened. She stirs, looks into her father's disturbed face, and shakes her head slowly, as if to say, "Don't worry, nothing is wrong." Similarly she comforts her distraught mother. To prove that everything is all right, the anxious girl rises and begins to dance again. She moves rapidly, the music accelerates ominously, and there is a clap of thunder. The princess falls into her father's arms. The cymbals clash in evil triumph, and the old woman in black steps out. She throws aside her cape: she is the fairy Carabosse, come back to court to fulfill her prophecy. She cackles with delight. The princess seems to die. Armed courtiers chase the evil fairy as she runs into the garden.

A trumpet sounds, then the harp, and the melody of the Lilac Fairy is heard. She enters with her wand and comforts the king and queen, telling them that the princess, as she foretold, is not really dead, she is merely asleep, and this is the beginning of the spell that will last a hundred years. The king and queen thank the Lilac Fairy and bow humbly. Courtiers take up the princess and carry her slowly up the steps to the palace. The Lilac Fairy ascends the stairs; the last members of the court disappear. She holds out her wand, casting a spell over the kingdom.

The stage grows dark; the garden fades in the distance. From the ground, enormous shrubs, great branches of foliage rise magically and seem to entwine the garden and the palace, smothering them in sleep. In a small point of light, the Lilac Fairy can be seen dancing softly, waving her magic wand, as the palace and its people, obedient to her command, go to sleep for a hundred years.

ACT TWO — THE VISION: A brief orchestral introduction features the sound of hunting horns, and when the curtain rises on a wooded glen, we are prepared for the entry of the royal hunting party. The scene is the forest of King Florestan XXIV, a part of the forest remote from the sleeping palace; the time, one hundred years later. The setting sun glows in the distance over rocky hills that enclose a still stream. As the hunting party comes upon the scene, it is apparent that the style of dress has changed considerably. Duchesses and dukes, marchionesses and marquesses stride about the wood in their colorful riding habits. Gallison, tutor to Prince Florimund, the leader of the hunt, totters onto the stage exhausted. Prince Florimund follows. Dressed in red riding habit, with high red boots and a feathered hat, the prince bows to his guests. A countess approaches him and makes a suggestion. The prince responds lazily and motions her away gently. The persistent countess does not acknowledge the rebuff, however. She has in mind a game of blindman's buff and persuades the tutor to bind his eyes. The old man obliges her and chases after the royal couples, who egg him on by whipping their riding crops at his feet. He stumbles around, becomes dizzy, and takes the hand of what he imagines to be a beautiful lady. He is somewhat staggered as he takes the handkerchief from his eyes and finds himself embracing a peer.

The game has not amused the guests sufficiently and they turn to other entertainment. Reluctantly the prince yields to the countess' persuasion and takes her as his partner in a stately mazurka. Peasants enter the wood at the conclusion of the dance and perform a farandole, a round dance in which the boys and girls join hands and curve about the stage in a continuous serpentine line. Every member of the hunting party is diverted by the farandole except the prince, who is moody and preoccupied. The hunting horns sound again. Attendants bring in spears for the hunt, and the lords and ladies prepare to leave. But the prince has suddenly changed his mind and urges his guests to leave without him. He will remain in the forest for a little while and rejoin them later. The countess is visibly upset at her inability to attract the prince away; she attempts to change his mind; the prince dismisses her.

Now alone in the glen, the prince walks about. Night falls; the setting sun becomes the new moon. He stares out over the lake, hoping that the beautiful scene will settle his gloom. He turns away dejectedly and walks forward. Just as he turns his back, the theme of the Lilac Fairy is heard and a magical boat floats onto the lake from the right. Its gossamer sail hangs from a silver mast; motioning the boat forward is the Lilac Fairy, who stands with upraised wand in the great sea shell that forms the boat's hull. The boat stops at her command, and the fairy steps down to earth. Still preoccupied with his own thoughts, the prince does not see her. As he moves back toward the lake, he is astonished by her presence. He bows deeply.

The Lilac Fairy then begins to instruct the prince in the cause of his woe. In a palace not far from this forest, she tells him, sleeps a beautiful princess, a princess so lovely that his mind must have envisaged her all his life. This princess has been asleep for a hundred years, yet she is only sixteen. She will sleep forever unless she is kissed by a prince who loves her.

The prince is enchanted, but somewhat skeptical, and impatiently asks the Lilac Fairy to let him see the princess. The fairy consents to show him a vision of the Princess Aurora. She points her wand to the left, and concealed within a dark tree trunk we see a misty vision of the princess. The specter disappears as quickly as it came. The prince demands to see more of her; already he is enamored of Aurora. The Lilac Fairy now allows the vision of the princess to enter in person.

The princess comes in on the right. Still the beautiful young girl of the first act, her movements are now soft and romantic. A haunting melody begins, dominated by the cellos, lending the scene a dark, mysterious atmosphere. The prince lifts Aurora high off the ground and, when he lets her down, attempts to embrace her. Fairies who have followed the princess pull him away from her, and he watches as she dances alone. The fairies form a circular tableau in the center of the scene. The princess moves about this circle, momentarily disappearing from the prince's sight. He pursues her softly, patiently, yet never catches up to her. Finally he holds her for a brief moment in his arms. The vision relaxes against him for an instant and then leaves him, like a phantom. He beseeches the Lilac Fairy to call her back again.

The sixteen nymphs dance for a short interval, and suddenly the princess returns to their midst. The flowing music becomes strongly rhythmical. Standing in the center of the stage, she dances quickly, with staccatolike urgency, a brilliant variation that excites the prince's love for her. He holds out his arms and she vanishes.

The nymphs fill the scene again with their dancing, and the princess makes a final, spinning, illusory appearance. The prince asks the Lilac Fairy, "Where has she gone? Where can I find her again?" The Lilac Fairy calms his curiosity and tells him that to find the princess, they must sail across the lake to her father's palace, where the princess lies asleep. She motions for him to follow, and the curtain falls as the Lilac Fairy's magical boat disappears in the midst of the lake.

ACT THREE, SCENE ONE—THE AWAKENING: The orchestra plays a long overture, the composition that was designed originally to accompany the journey of the Lilac Fairy and the prince toward the palace, a slowly paced interlude during which the fairy's magic barge passed slowly across the lake, surrounded by a panorama of dense forest and splendid vistas of the enchanted palace.

When the curtain rises, the Lilac Fairy and the prince have already disembarked. The fairy leads the prince across the stage from the right. He follows several paces behind her, looking about him cautiously, both amazed and delighted at the sleeping forest. Only shadows can be distinguished in the background. The two walk off at the left and reappear almost immediately behind a gauze curtain. Light emerges from behind; the palace can be seen, rising high on the summit in the distance. On the ground, two guards, frozen in an attitude of perpetual slumber, sleep away their watch. The prince stares at them, unbelieving. The Lilac Fairy leads him off; the light is extinguished, only to come up again in a moment in a high-vaulted chamber—the boudoir of the Princess Aurora. The Lilac Fairy enters first, holding her wand before her. She enters through a maze of great columns entangled with cobwebs, beckoning to the prince to follow. In the half-darkness, on the left, a silken bed canopied with royal drapes dominates the apartment. Guards stand in a line, motionless, sleeping against their upright spears.

The prince enters, marveling at the oppression of the sleeping rooms and the splendor they still contain. He glances incredulously at the sleeping guards. The Lilac Fairy motions him forward to the bed. In the dim light, he sees the sleeping princess. He hesitates, not wishing to disturb her sleeping beauty. The Lilac Fairy waves her wand, and he steps forward toward the bed. Curled in an attitude of peaceful contentment, the princess lies in deep slumber, her head on an ancient, dusty pillow. The prince bends down toward her face; the Lilac Fairy gestures with her wand; he kisses her softly. The music mounts to a vivid crescendo. The princess stirs, wakens, and rises slowly as the prince gathers her in his arms.

The light flashes out, and miraculously the giant spiders who hover over the chamber rise and vanish; the cobwebs are disentangled from the great pillars and gradually fall away. The light comes up slowly, royal pages stand against the high columns, and we see before us the great hall of King Florestan's palace.

ACT THREE, SCENE TWO — THE WEDDING: The lofty columns of stone support high-vaulting arches. In the distance, great, sweeping staircases climb up to the farther reaches of the castle. The thrones of the king and queen stand at the right.

With pomp and ceremony, as if he had not been disturbed by more than a night's sleep, the courtier Cattalabutte enters with all his old-time flourish. He struts about the hall as if he himself were responsible for the festivities that are about to follow.

The king and his queen enter regally. Cattalabutte bows to them and escorts them to the dais. Courtiers and ladies in waiting with their escorts dance in and promenade about the hall to the virile rhythms of a polonaise. Six other ladies enter. As the dance theme is repeated quietly, the special guests who have been invited to attend the wedding of Princess Aurora and Prince Florimund dance in to pay their respects to the parents of the bride.

These royal guests are perennial fairy tale characters. First comes the White Cat, held high on a pillow which her escorts carry on their shoulders. She paws the air plaintively and washes her face. Behind her comes Puss in Boots, who watches her possessively while waving his hat in greeting. Bluebeard and his wife, Goldilocks and her prince, Beauty and the Beast, and Florestan, the crown prince of the kingdom, and his two sisters follow behind. Last of all come the enchanted princess and the bluebird. Now, led by the Lilac Fairy, all six of the Princess Aurora's fairy godmothers enter in all their glory.

All the courtiers and guests arrange themselves in a great circle about the hall. Prince Florestan, Aurora's brother, and their two sisters step out and stand at the back of the stage toward the right. A lovely, lilting waltz begins; to its enchanting melody, the three dance a *pas de trois*. When the waltz ends, each of the two girls dances a short variation to music that is light and sparkling in its tinkling sound. Prince Florestan rejoins them, and all three leap off into the wings.

The next *divertissement* features the White Cat and Puss in Boots. This oboe mimes their mewing as Puss in Boots tries to ensnare the winsome cat in a love trap. The White Cat pretends to resist Puss's caresses, but actually she is delighted. Finally Puss can contain himself no longer and puts an end to the flirtation by carrying his ladylove off.

The Enchanted Princess enters with the Bluebird. Both flutter their arms in light, airy motions of flight and commence a *pas de deux*, perhaps the most dazzling dance duet of the entire ballet. The Bluebird, in his variation, seems to be suspended in soaring flight.

Another *divertissement* enacts the tale of Little Red Ridinghood. Four pages bring small trees onto the stage. Red Ridinghood walks lightly through the wood, treading as softly as possible, glancing behind her at every turn. The wolf enters with a bold leap and conceals himself behind one of the trees. The girl passes; he steps out in front of her. Red Ridinghood tries to pretend that he is just another passer-by, like herself, and, holding her basket close, proceeds on her way. The wolf is fooled only for a moment: quickly he throws her over his shoulder and runs off.

Now the moment for which all the court has been waiting finally arrives. Princess Aurora and Prince Florimund enter. A spotlight brightens the brilliant white the bride wears for her wedding day, and all the lords and ladies bow. The royal couple come forward and begin to dance. Their *pas de deux* is gracious and formal. The Princess Aurora reveals, in her mastery of movement and balance, a maturity and perfection for which the "Rose Adagio" was but a youthful rehearsal. Still charming, the youthful princess is now about to be married, and her radiant poise reflects the lesson her love has taught. Prince Florimund supports his bride gallantly, lifting her effortlessly, holding her confidently—by each of his gestures and motions drawing the court's attention to her loveliness. As the *pas de deux* concludes, its tender music ascends to a pitch of everlasting joy. The princess turns with incredible speed on point and dives toward the floor. The prince catches her falling figure and holds her in the daring pose.

A final *divertissement* is offered by the Three Ivans, who perform a virile, stomping Russian dance for the bride and groom. The court is now at the height of good humor, and when the Princess Aurora returns to dance briefly alone, everyone is suddenly saddened by the fact that soon she will go away with her prince. But everyone watches closely this last dance of their princess; the entire assembly is infected by her happiness. Now the whole court—all the fairies, all the nobles, all the fairy tale figures—joins the bride and groom in a spirited mazurka, at the end of which the guests form a circle about the prince and princess who, standing in close embrace, become, in reality, a part of that fairy tale world that brought them together. Everyone kneels to them.

NOTES: Alexandre Benois describes the first Russian production of *The Sleeping Beauty* in his *Reminiscences of the Russian Ballet*:

"The production of *La Belle au Bois Dormant* was a most significant turning point in the history of the Theatre because it put an end to the

Maria Tallchief in *Swan Lake*, New York City Ballet.

ABOVE: Margot Fonteyn and Robert Helpmann rehearse *The Sleeping Beauty* (Act III) at the Royal Opera House, Covent Garden.
OPPOSITE ABOVE: *Orpheus:* Maria Tallchief and Nicholas Magallanes, New York City Ballet. OPPOSITE BELOW: *Firebird:* Maria Tallchief and Francisco Moncion in the New York City Ballet production.

LEFT: *Sylvia* (Act III): Margot Fonteyn and Michael Somes. Sadler's Wells Ballet. BELOW: Margot Fonteyn and Michael Somes in *Swan Lake* (Act II). Sadler's Wells Ballet.

©Felix Fonteyn

Roger Wood

Tanaquil LeClercq and Francisco Moncion in *Afternoon of a Faun*
(Debussy-Robbins-Rosenthal), New York City Ballet.

LEFT: Tanaquil LeClercq i[n]
La Valse, New York City B[allet.]
BELOW: *Card Game:* Janet
Reed and Todd Bolender
in the New York City Balle[t]
production.

Walter E. Owen

Walter E. Owen

Igor Youskevitch.

LEFT: André Eglevsky. BELOW: Moira Shearer in *Cinderella*, Sadler's Wells Ballet.

Fred Fehl

©*Baron-Pix*

back-water slackness that had prevailed on the stage of the Maryinsky Theatre since the departure of Zucchi.

"Interest in the ballet, which had been somehow declining, was suddenly regenerated with fresh vigour and has never lessened since. It can be said with confidence that, had this production not proved to be such an outstanding success, the whole history of the ballet in general—not only that of the Russian ballet—would have been totally different. The *Ballets Russes* themselves would never have seen the light of day had not the *Belle au Bois Dormant* awakened in a group of Russian youths a fiery enthusiasm that developed into a kind of frenzy. It is a curious fact that Diaghilev had not at that time arrived in St. Petersburg. When he came, he did not at first share our enthusiasm, possibly because he was not as fully prepared as we were for artistic appreciation; but later on he also became infected. By contrast, Dima Filosofov was, after me, the most enthusiastic admirer of *La Belle au Bois Dormant*. He actually 'went quite mad over it.' This was all the more wonderful as Dima was, on the whole, of a very reserved nature, inclined to analyze and be sceptical about most things—often, in consequence, considered 'hard' by those who did not know him well. He raved about the new ballet and when Seriozha arrived to spend the summer with his cousin, he must doubtless have heard endless descriptions of the winter season that had been such an eventful one for Dima.

"There can be no doubt that the chief reason for the success of the ballet *La Belle au Bois Dormant* lies in Tchaikovsky's music, which the composer considered his *chef-d'oeuvre*. The music really possesses so strong a power of suggestion that those who give themselves up to it are completely transported from reality into the magic world of fairy tale. Marius Petipa, himself inspired by the music, achieved in the composition of the dances a height of perfection hitherto unsurpassed by him. It is enough to recall the *variations* of the fairies in the prologue, the *grand pas de deux* in the third scene and, the greatest masterpiece of all, the dance of the Blue Bird and the Enchanted Princess. But what innumerable other gems of choreographic art are scattered by Petipa throughout *La Belle au Bois Dormant!* The *grande valse* in the second act, all the fairy-tale dances, the *mazurka*, the *sarabande!* The ballet-master was no less inspired when he created the mimed scenes which abound in *La Belle au Bois Dormant*—all so expressive and in such perfect taste. What other scene of fairy-tale grotesque can stand comparison with the arrival of the wicked fairy Carabosse and her horrible attendants? How enchanting is the reproduction of the most poetical pictures of Watteau and Lancret in the scene of the hunt in the forest! How delightful is the arrival of Prince Charming at the enchanted castle, what perfect style and solemnity in the final act—later to become one of Diaghilev's greatest successes under the title of *Le Mariage d'Aurore!*

"In the enumeration of all these successes I must not forget to add that never before had the St. Petersburg ballet stage possessed so perfect and harmonious a company of artistes as were at the disposal of Vsevolojsky and Petipa at the time of the creation of *La Belle au Bois Dormant*. It is true that the prima ballerina of the ballet—Carlotta Brianza—could in no way be compared with Zucchi, but she was nevertheless attractive, very graceful, very accomplished, technically, and had at the same time an extremely agreeable personality. Her dancing was faultless and she succeeded in conveying all the waywardness with which Tchaikovsky has characterized the heroine. Gerdt, who was the Prince Charming, was ideal, for he gave the absolute illusion of a genuine prince—in fact, he seemed to be Louis XIV in person. Those who did not see this miracle for themselves can hardly imagine how perfectly suited this fine artist was to the role, how obvious were the traditions that he had inherited from Johannsen and Petipa, traditions which went back to the days when the youthful *Roi Soleil* himself would deign to appear on the stage as a ballet dancer.

"In the last act Gerdt performed a short *variation*. Although perfectly simple and lasting less than a minute, it aroused such enthusiasm in the public that even people who knew nothing of the history of the *Grand Siècle* seemed, during the dance, to achieve a clear vision of the distant past. An incomparable Master of Ceremonies was my favorite artist Stukolkin, the creator of the roles of Ivan the Simpleton and Coppélius. In this case Vsevolojsky's wide experience of court life was a great help and enabled the artist to parody it very subtly. In his Cattalabutte, Stukolkin impersonated the very type of the absurdly zealous, conceited and servile courtier. There was no exaggeration or malice, but good-natured humor, behind which one felt the typical smile of Ivan Alexandrovitch himself—a great but good natured joker.

"Among the best dancers in the ballet—from the point of view of dancing, in fact, the very best—was Enrico Cecchetti, the Italian who had recently been engaged by the Imperial Theatres. The Russian School had had no part in his education, but he had fortunately preserved enough of the excellent Italian traditions which had, in their time, so strongly influenced the elder Vestris of the French ballet, and, through the influence of French ballet-master, had reached the Russian ballet too. Cecchetti's ardent southern temperament was perhaps a trifle out of tune with the severe *bon ton* of the Imperial stage—as had also been Zucchi's. Now and again there would burst forth from Enrico something of Truffaldino and Pulcinella. But in the present case, in the role of the terrifying yet comical witch, Carabosse, those traits were only an asset, as they helped to make him all the more alive and convincing. And how wonderful it was when, in the last act, the same artist, who had just been so ingenuous a grotesque, suddenly appeared in the beautiful dance of the Blue Bird as partner to the charming Nikitina. Here he amazed and enchanted the Russian public with his extraordinary softness and grace, performing intricate *entrechats* and *pirouettes* as yet inaccessible to Russian artists, who had not even been taught to attempt them.

"*La Belle au Bois Dormant* was first presented to the St. Petersburg public on the 15th of January, 1890. It has never since then been taken off the repertoire and remains to this day the highest achievement of the Russian Ballet. Let who likes say that this ballet cannot be considered purely Russian because the subject is a fairy tale of Perrault, because the music is written by Tchaikovsky, whose work many Western judges refuse to pass as characteristically Russian, because it was produced by the *marseillais* Petipa, because the two principal roles were created by the Italians, Brianza and Cecchetti. In spite of all this, the ballet of *La Belle au Bois Dormant* is a typical production of Russian or rather St. Petersburg culture. Nowhere else in the world could this fairy tale have been produced on the stage as it was in those days in the Maryinsky Theatre. To make this achievement possible, the coincidence of various factors in the mode of life of the country was essential: the aristocratic spirit, untouched by any democratic deviations, which reigned in Russia under the sceptre of Alexander III; the unique atmosphere of the St. Petersburg Theatre School and the traditions that had been formed in consequence; and finally a rejuvenation of these traditions so that, on this occasion, shaking off the dust of routine, they should appear in all the freshness of something newly born.

"Chief credit for this triumph of resuscitated traditions belong to Vsevolojsky. Although the costumes invented by him could be criticized for their rather helpless amateurishness, he was the person responsible for *creating this masterpiece*, for he made the production of the ballet his own personal work. It was he who, by entering into all the details, became the link as well as the head of the whole production—a feature indispensable in the creation of a *Gesamtkunstwerk*. This resulted in a coherence and polish hitherto unseen. Vsevolojsky had exceptional tact and never forced his ideas on anyone, striving to convince by persuasion, and, as Ivan Alexandrovitch was a great charmer by nature, he found it very easy to convince. Thanks to his aristocratic politeness, he always managed to get what he wanted from people without using the authority to which he was entitled.

"It was Vsevolojsky's idea to contrast two different epochs, divided by a hundred years. According to his version, Aurora falls asleep in the middle of the sixteenth century and wakes up in the days of the youthful Louis XIV. This 'bridge' joining two centuries, gives the ballet a special poetical charm. The idea was executed by Vsevolojsky with remarkable tact in the style of the days of Perrault himself. The more distant epoch was presented in a somewhat fantastic transformation; the period contemporary to Perrault was realistically historical. Tchaikovsky was enchanted with the problem and followed the programme with all his heart, and this is why the music of the first part is lyrical and free in character while that of the second half is more classical in style. But even the second part, though formally imitative of the style of Lully and Couperin, bears the stamp of Tchaikovsky's creative invention."

The great choreographer and ballet master of the Imperial Theatre, Marius Petipa, collaborated closely with Tchaikovsky on the score for *The Sleeping Beauty*, defining the nature and length of the music at every point. Describing the climax of Act One, Petipa specified for Tchaikovsky: "Suddenly Aurora notices the old woman who beats on her knitting needles a 2/4 measure. Gradually she changes to a very melodious waltz in 3/4, but then, suddenly, a rest. Aurora pricks her finger. Screams, pain. Blood streams —give eight measures in 4/4, wide. She begins to dance—dizziness . . . Complete horror—this is not a dance any longer. It is frenzy. As if bitten by a tarantula she keeps turning and then falls unexpectedly, out of breath. This must last from 24 to 32 measures. At the end there should be a tremolo of a few measures, as if shouts of pain and sobs: 'Father, Mother!' And later, when everybody notices the old woman, she throws off her clothes. For this moment it is necessary that a chromatic scale sound in the entire orchestra."[*]

Such directions are required by every composer who is seriously interested in writing music for a new ballet. In the ideal ballet—and *The Sleeping Beauty* is an excellent example—the musician and the choreographer collaborate.

Tchaikovsky thought *The Sleeping Beauty* his finest ballet score. He and the choreographer were disappointed at the reaction of the Russian court to a dress rehearsal of the ballet given two nights before its first public performance. The Czar remarked to the composer that the ballet was "very nice." Tchaikovsky died before his work became, with *Swan Lake,* the most popular works in the Russian repertory.

When Serge Diaghilev decided to revive *The Sleeping Beauty* in 1921, all of his collaborators in the Ballets Russes—Stravinsky, Bakst, and others who had fresh memories of the Russian production—were particularly happy about it. The revival that they produced under Diaghilev's direction was unrivaled in its opulence and in its dancers. Spessivtzeva, Lubov Egorova, Lydia Lopokova, and Vera Trefilova alternated in dancing the role of the Princess Aurora. Bronislava Nijinska alternated with Lopokova in the role of the Lilac Fairy. Carlotta Brianza, who had been, in 1890, the first Princess Aurora, portrayed the wicked fairy, Carabosse. On January 5, 1922, Enrico Cecchetti danced his original role of Carabosse on the occasion of his fiftieth anniversary as a leading dancer.

The Diaghilev revival of *The Sleeping Beauty,* however, was a failure with the public, which supported it for a run of only three months. Through the programs of Diaghilev's Ballets Russes, the ballet audiences of 1921 were accustomed to three different ballets an evening: not one evening-long ballet. After the failure of *The Sleeping Beauty,* Diaghilev's ballet returned to the production of the shorter, modern works. Only twenty-five years later, with

[*]*Marius Petipa* by Yury Slonimsky. Translated from the Russian by Anatole Chujoy. *Dance Index*, Vol. VI, No. 5–6, May–June, 1947.

the great success of the Sadler's Wells revival of *The Sleeping Beauty* at Covent Garden, did the ballet audience catch up to the value of Diaghilev's original idea.

To accommodate the ballet to his audience, Diaghilev compressed a series of *divertissements* from *The Sleeping Beauty* into one act of dancing: *Aurora's Wedding* (1922). This work was the final ballet at the last program of the Ballets Russes, at Covent Garden, July 26, 1929. Alexandra Danilova danced the Princess Aurora on that occasion and Alicia Markova and Anton Dolin appeared as the Bluebirds.

Excerpts from *The Sleeping Beauty* had been performed as *divertissements* in Europe and the United States before Diaghilev's revival of the complete ballet, however. Nijinsky and Mathilde Kchessinska danced the *grand pas de deux* from the last act with the Ballets Russes in London in 1911. In 1916 Anna Pavlova danced excerpts from the ballet with Alexandre Volinine at the Hippodrome in New York.

Aurora's Wedding, also called *Princess Aurora*, was first presented in the United States by the De Basil Ballet Russe (1935) and by the Ballet Theatre (1941). Different choreographers have remounted and rearranged the Petipa dances in various productions by these companies. In the more recent production of the Ballet Theatre, all of the company's principal soloists have appeared in *Princess Aurora*.

In the Sadler's Wells production, Beryl Grey, Moira Shearer, Violetta Elvin, Nadia Nerina, and Rosemary Lindsay have alternated in the role of the Princess Aurora with Margot Fonteyn. When *The Sleeping Beauty* was revived at Covent Garden on January 9, 1952, two new variations had been included: one a dance for the princess in the "Vision Scene," arranged by Frederick Ashton; the other a solo for the prince, arranged by Ninette de Valois.

John Martin reviewed in the New York *Times* the first performance of the Sadler's Wells *Sleeping Beauty*:

"The American debut of the Sadler's Wells Ballet from Covent Garden, London, at the Metropolitan Opera House . . . was an occasion in every sense of the word, complete with national anthems, a list of distinguished patrons and flag-draped boxes in which were seated British Ambassador Sir Oliver Franks, Mayor O'Dwyer, Consul General Sir Francis Evans and Lady Evans, Trygve Lie, Sir Alexander Cadogan and other notables from the United Nations. As a matter of fact, almost everybody in the auditorium bore a label of some kind in the arts or public affairs.

"What occurred on the stage was worthy of no less, for the Sadler's Wells Ballet, one of the leading organizations of its kind in the world, is subsidized by the British Government and must, in spite of itself, provide something of an example for the rest of us in the matter of ballet producing.

"Such an ensemble performance as was shown to us last night in *The Sleeping Beauty* could not conceivably be achieved except by a company which works together all the year around with financial and artistic security and a set of high ideals about what it is doing. It is with a great feeling of comfortableness that one relaxes before an aggregation of dancers so sure of themselves technically, so impeccably rehearsed and so unified in approach.

"But the admirable policy of having no stars can go only so far; when a star of the first magnitude appears before our eyes, it makes no earthly difference how she is billed. Margot Fonteyn is unmistakably such a star, a ballerina among ballerinas. London has known this for some time, Europe has found it out and last night she definitely conquered another continent.

"She is young and lovely to look at, has a technical equipment so strong that she seems to ignore it altogether, moves not only with ease but with an active pleasure in movement, and is just about as enchanting a dancer as has come along in a score of years. What she did with the by no means unfamiliar title role of this old ballet was artistically beautiful and theatrically exciting. Indeed, it is possible to say that we have never seen the famous 'Rose Adagio' really danced before. It is pleasant to know that we shall be seeing considerably more of Miss Fonteyn . . ."

SONG OF THE NIGHTINGALE

Dramatic ballet in two scenes. Music by Igor Stravinsky. Choreography by Leonide Massine. Scenery and costumes by Henri Matisse. First presented by Diaghilev's Ballets Russes, February 2, 1920, Paris. Revived by Diaghilev's Ballets Russes, 1925, with choreography by George Balanchine and with Alicia Markova in the principal role.

This work, based on the story of "The Nightingale" by Hans Christian Andersen, is both an opera and a ballet; it has also been arranged by the composer as a symphonic poem. First performed as an opera, the score was revised to exclude voices for ballet performance. The opera consisted of three acts. In the ballet the first act was omitted, but it is necessary to mention its contents here.

The scene of Act One is the home of the nightingale, a wood in China, near the palace of the emperor. A fisherman glides his boat across a lake. He sings to himself. As his boat goes into the distance, we hear the magical song of the nightingale. At the emperor's order, the imperial chamberlain and his followers come to the wood to hear the nightingale. As they seek its voice, they mistake other sounds for the song of the bird. They are led to the nightingale by a humble scullery maid. The courtiers are disappointed in the bird's ordinary appearance, but delighted at its song. The nightingale accepts their invitation to sing at court.

SCENE ONE—THE IMPERIAL PALACE: When preparations have been made for his arrival, the Emperor of China enters his court.

The nightingale is brought before him. The bird waits until the emperor signals her to begin her song, then commences.

The emperor is so enchanted with the song that he tells the bird she may have anything she wants. The bird replies that she has moved the emperor to tears and that is all the favor she requires.

Now the noble ladies, noting the high favor in which the lowly nightingale is held by their emperor, try to imitate her song. They fail miserably.

A gift arrives from the Emperor of Japan: a mechanical nightingale, beautifully wrought in gold and set with gems. The song of the toy bird delights the emperor and his court, and they forget the presence of the real nightingale. When the emperor tires of the toy and turns to ask the bird to sing again, she has disappeared. The angry monarch thereupon banishes the bird from his kingdom and makes the toy bird principal songster at his court.

SCENE TWO — THE EMPEROR'S BEDCHAMBER: The mechanical nightingale stands by the emperor's bedside. The emperor is dying. Death stands ready to welcome the monarch, and courtiers prematurely prepare the way for his successor. Spirits taunt the emperor with a list of his good deeds and wrongdoings. He cannot bear their chatter and calls for music. He begins to expire.

The song of the nightingale is heard. The return of this beautiful music delights the emperor, and Death is so struck by the wonderful song of the nightingale that he asks the bird to continue to sing.

The bird consents if Death will permit the emperor to live. Death makes this bargain and vanishes as the nightingale again takes up her song.

The emperor recovers completely and again offers to do any favor the bird wishes. The nightingale replies that his tears are her best reward and that she will sing to him every night until the rise of the sun.

Officials of the court, come to continue the deathwatch, enter the bedchamber. They are astonished to find the emperor standing in all his majesty, ready to receive them.

NOTES: *Le Rossignol* (*The Nightingale*) was originally composed as an opera in three acts, which Serge Diaghilev presented for the first time at the Paris Opéra, May 26, 1914, under the direction of Pierre Monteux. Alexandre Benois designed the scenery and costumes. This work was first presented in the United States at the Metropolitan Opera House, New York, on March 6, 1926, with Marion Talley in the principal role.

Stravinsky revised his score for symphonic performances, eliminating the first act of the original. He was persuaded by Diaghilev that this new arrangement of his music might be suitable for ballet, and, now called *Le Chant du Rossignol*, the work was presented, with the choreography by Leonide Massine.

A new ballet to this music was my first assignment for Diaghilev's

Ballets Russes, soon after I joined the company. I chose for the leading role in the ballet the young artist Alicia Markova, who had just joined Diaghilev's company, when she was only fourteen years old. We saw Markova dance in London, in 1924, at the studio of Serafima Asafieva, where she was a brilliant student. Diaghilev engaged her—the youngest dancer ever to belong to his company—immediately after seeing her dance.

LE SPECTRE DE LA ROSE

Ballet in one act. Music by Carl Maria von Weber. Choreography by Michel Fokine. Book by J. L. Vaudoyer. Scenery and costumes by Léon Bakst. First presented by Diaghilev's Ballets Russes at the Théâtre de Monte Carlo, Monte Carlo, April 19, 1911, with Vaslav Nijinsky and Tamara Karsavina. First presented in the United States by Diaghilev's Ballets Russes at the Metropolitan Opera House, New York, April 3, 1916, with Alexander Gavrilov and Lydia Lopokova.

This is a ballet danced by two people, a romantic *pas de deux*. The ballet has a simple story, but the story is so slight that we must refer to the actual dancing for an impression of the ballet. Its first performances convinced audiences that it was possible for two dancers, alone on a stage, to create a story and at the same time to create a mood in which that story could become real, like a lyric poem.

Le Spectre de la Rose is based on a poem, a poem by the nineteenth-century French poet and novelist and great critic of the ballet Théophile Gautier. Just as Gautier adapted the work of another poet, Heinrich Heine, to produce the romantic classic *Giselle*, so his own creative work gave to another age the inspiration for another romantic ballet. In Gautier's poem *The Rose-Ghost*, a rose addresses the girl who wore it to a ball. The rose is grateful for having danced with her all evening, grateful even for death on her breast, and tells the maiden that his ghost will continue to dance, at her bedside, all night long, to express his love.

The ballet *Le Spectre de la Rose* has a real setting but, as in *Giselle*, it is a dream that comes to life within this setting that creates its romanticism. The music is Carl Maria von Weber's *Invitation to the Dance*, as orchestrated by Hector Berlioz.

The curtain rises on a young girl's boudoir. The room is formal, high, and cool, with immense windows that look on to a garden. There is a bed on the right and on the left a small dressing table. The colors are blue and white, and as we look at the walls and the furniture and see the moon through the French windows, we imagine that the girl who lives here is demure and innocent. The room is uncluttered, plain in spite of its elegance; it makes you interested in the life it contains. The young girl enters. She is dressed formally, in a long white gown. She takes off the cape she wears about her shoulders, unties her bonnet, and we notice that she holds in her hand a red rose. She refuses to relinquish it as she moves about the room, turning slowly, dancing with an invisible partner, remembering the excitement of her first ball. She has come back from the dance to her familiar surroundings and finds the room a little old-fashioned; it has not changed as she imagines she has changed. She is in love. She presses her lover's rose against her cheek and sits down in a white chair near one of the windows. Half-asleep from fatigue, she still wishes to relive her first encounter with romance. But sleep soon overtakes her. Her hand falls from her face, and the red rose slips from her fingers to the floor.

There is almost no sound for a moment, and then suddenly, buoyantly, the orchestra plays at full volume a quick, intoxicating waltz. As this rush of sound fills the room, through the open window the spirit of the rose leaps in a high, smooth trajectory to stand poised behind the girl's chair. He dances alone as the girl sleeps, moving about the room effortlessly, seeming to touch the floor almost against his will, dancing with the lightness of the rose petals that adorn his body.

He touches the girl, and now—awake in her dream—she dances with him. When the two dance together to the soaring waltz, the young girl moves with the grace of the spirit she has invoked; as they glide and leap about the room, their dance is absolutely continuous, never-ending, unbroken in its flow of movement into movement; the only thing that can stop it is the music. The girl is inspired by her partner as naturally as she held the rose to her cheek and—with his strong, but tender, aid—she becomes not simply a beautiful young girl in love with love, but a part of the romantic night.

The dream cannot last. The waltz melody fades. The girl goes to her chair and sits as before, her arm limp at her side, pointing to the rose on the floor. The spirit of the rose hovers gently over her head in farewell and in a continuous movement rushes toward the window. He disappears into the oncoming dawn at the high point of a leap that seems never-ending.

The light of the sun disturbs the girl. She moves in her sleep, then wakens lazily, rubbing her eyes, not yet aware of where she is. She is still thinking of the spirit of the rose and looks for her mysterious partner. He is not there! She sees she is alone in her own room and that she must have been dreaming. Then she sees the rose on the floor at her feet. She picks it up gently and holds it against her breast, content that the dream is still with her.

NOTES: The fame of *Le Spectre de la Rose* is best explained by an account of the original production. Carl van Vechten described a 1916 performance in his book *Interpreters*:

"Nijinsky danced for the first time in New York on the afternoon of April 12, 1916, at the Metropolitan Opera House. The pieces in which he appeared on that day were *Le Spectre de la Rose* and *Petrouchka*. Some of us feared that eighteen months in a detention camp would have stamped their mark on the dancer. As a matter of fact his connection with the Russian Ballet had been severed in 1913, a year before the war began. I can say for myself that I was probably a good deal more nervous than Nijinsky on the occasion of his first appearance in America. It would have been a cruel disappointment to me to discover that his art had deteriorated during the intervening years since I had last seen him. My fears were soon dissipated. A few seconds after he, as the Rose Ghost, had bounded through the window, it was evident that he was in possession of all his powers; nay, more, that he had added to the refinement and polish of his style. I had called Nijinsky's dancing perfection in years gone by, because it so far surpassed that of his nearest rival; now he had surpassed himself. True artists, indeed, have a habit of accomplishing this feat. I may call to your attention the careers of Olive Fremstad, Yvette Guilbert, and Marie Tempest. Later I learned that this first impression might be relied on. Nijinsky, in sooth, has now no rivals upon the stage. One can only compare him with himself.

"The Weber-Gautier dance-poem, from the very beginning until the end, when he leaps out of the girl's chamber into the night, affords this great actor-dancer one of his most grateful opportunities. It is in this very part, perhaps, which requires almost unceasing exertion for nearly twelve minutes that Nijinsky's powers of co-ordination, mental, imaginative, muscular, are best displayed. His dancing is accomplished in that flowing line, without a break between poses and gestures, which is the despair of all novices and almost all other virtuosi. After a particularly difficult leap or toss of the legs or arms, it is a marvel to observe how, without an instant's pause to regain his poise, he rhythmically glides into the succeeding gesture. His dancing has the unbroken quality of music, the balance of great painting, the meaning of fine literature, and the emotion inherent in all these arts. There is something of transmutation in his performances; he becomes an alembic, transforming movement into a finely wrought and beautiful work of art. The dancing of Nijinsky is first an imaginative triumph, and the spectator, perhaps, should not be interested in further dissection of it, but a more intimate observer must realize that behind this the effect produced depends on his supreme command of his muscles. It is not alone the final informing and magnetized imaginative quality that most other dancers lack; it is also just this muscular co-ordination. Observe Gavrilow in the piece under discussion, in which he gives a good imitation of Nijinsky's general style, and you will see that he is unable to maintain this rhythmic continuity.

"Nijinsky's achievements become all the more remarkable when one remembers that he is working with an imperfect physical medium. Away from the scene he is an insignificant figure, short and ineffective in appearance. Aside from the pert expression of his eyes, he is like a dozen other young Russians. Put him unintroduced into a drawing room with Jacques Copeau, Orchidée, Doris Keane, Bill Haywood, the Baroness de Meyer,

Paulet Thévenaz, the Marchesa Casati, Marcel Duchamp, Cathleen Nesbitt, H. G. Wells, Anna Pavlova, Rudyard Chennevière, Vladimir Rebikow, Henrie Waste and Isadora Duncan and he probably would pass entirely unnoticed. On the stage it may be observed that the muscles of his legs are overdeveloped and his ankles are too large; that is, if you are in the mood for picking flaws, which most of us are not in the presence of Nijinsky in action. Here, however, stricture halts confounded; his head is set on his shoulders in a manner to give satisfaction to a great sculptor, and his torso, with its slender waistline, is quite beautiful. On the stage, Nijinsky makes of himself what he will. He can look tall or short, magnificent or ugly, fascinating or repulsive. Like all great interpretative artists, he remoulds himself for his public appearances. It is under the electric light in front of the painted canvas that he becomes a personality, and that personality is governed only by the scenario of the ballet he is representing."

A STREETCAR NAMED DESIRE

Dramatic ballet in one act. Music by Alex North, orchestrated by Rayburn Wright. Choreography by Valerie Bettis. Costumes by Saul Bolasni. First presented by the Slavenska-Franklin Ballet at Her Majesty's Theatre, Montreal, Canada, October 9, 1952, with Mia Slavenska as *Blanche*, Frederic Franklin as *Stanley*, and Lois Ellyn as *Stella*. First presented in New York at the Century Theatre, December 8, 1952, with the same principals.

This modern dramatic ballet is based on the play by Tennessee Williams. It tells the story of the play, and the movie that was based on the play, with slight alteration. The place is the same, the characters are the same, and their behavior is the same. The scene is a dingy apartment in New Orleans, the home of Stanley Kowalski and his wife, Stella. On the left, a flight of iron stairs leads to an apartment above. The front of the stage represents the street.

Down this street comes Blanche du Bois. She is a stranger to the city. She is seeking the home of her sister, Stella. She finds the apartment and looks about, as if this were not quite what she had expected. Blanche is finicky; her gentility is offended. Stella enters. The sisters embrace.

Their happy time together is interrupted by the arrival of Stanley, Stella's husband. He, too, is not quite what Blanche had expected. Stanley senses this distaste immediately, and the struggle of the ballet has begun.

Stanley has so sympathy with Blanche's fulsome gentility, her affected manners. He does not care that she has seen her young husband die or about her recollections of the lost family plantation. He is only interested in money, in how the plantation came to be lost and why his wife has had no share in the profits from any sale of family property. Blanche's neuroses give him a pain.

Stanley sees that her presence endangers his happy marriage. He antagonizes his sister-in-law, breaks into her suitcase, reads the letters of her dead husband. Blanche, torn with self-pity and hatred, begins to despair.

She seeks comfort in the company of Mitch, one of Stanley's "nice" friends. One night, when Stanley, Mitch, and their friends are playing poker in the apartment, Blanche foolishly interferes in the game. There is a drunken brawl, and Blanche is left alone when Stanley takes his wife to bed.

Blanche's comfort in Mitch does not last long. Stanley discovers that, far from being lily-white and genteel, she has for many years been giving men her favors. Stanley informs Mitch of Blanche's past, and their relation is broken off.

Blanche can now resort only to the resources of her inner world: the world of the old family plantation, fine dresses, and an ideal love. Visions of the past pass before her, and she retreats into those visions.

While Stella is in the hospital having a baby, Stanley comes home one night to discover Blanche parading about the apartment in her old finery. She appears to be terrified of him and attempts to flee through endless doors that fill the scene—the doors of her past. Stanley catches her and attacks her.

Blanche now has no relation to reality. Reality, as she has had to face it, as she has seen it in her sister's home, has caused her to reject everything but her private world of dreams.

A man comes and takes her away to an asylum. The happy marriage of Stella and Stanley is renewed.

NOTES: Louis Biancolli, reviewing this ballet in the New York *World-Telegram and Sun,* wrote:

"The ballet is masterly in every respect. The inner world of Blanche du Bois' twisted fancy is visualized and given life in a way that the spoken word could never duplicate, and the tragic division of her mind is carried out in a sustained splendor of symbolism.

"Those who remember the play and the film need no reminder of Blanche du Bois' helpless shifts from fantasy to reality, and back again to that haunted realm of memories that claims her for good in the end.

"Miss Slavenska was incredible in the power of characterization she gave the troubled heroine—the moments of calm, courtly prudery suddenly offset by seizures of savage desire, the spiritual poise shattered by the frenzies of physical abandon.

"How beautifully—and pitifully—the deranged girl groped through a row of open doors for fleeting figures of a taunting past. I had the feeling last night that only ballet could express the inexpressible lurking in the corners and crevices of Mr. Williams' play. Even the brutal attack—the crux of the drama—caught new overtones of tragedy in this eerie pantomime of lust.

"Frederic Franklin never danced the way he did last night. The dancer had become an artist, the athlete, an actor. The role of Stanley suited him perfectly, offering the frank brutishness of the character in terms of a lunging ferocity of grace and a brooding undercurrent of menace."

SWAN LAKE

Dramatic ballet in four acts. Music by Peter Ilyich Tchaikovsky. Book by V. P. Begitchev and Vasily Geltzer. First presented, with choreography by Julius Reisinger, at the Bolshoi Theatre, Moscow, March 4, 1877, with Pauline Karpakova in the leading role. This incomplete and unsuccessful production was superseded by a new choreographic version by Lev Ivanov and Marius Petipa, which was presented for the first time in a complete, four-act production at the Maryinsky Theatre, St. Petersburg, February 8, 1895, with Pierina Legnani in the double role of Odette-Odile. Act Two of this version was presented for the first time at the Maryinsky Theatre, St. Petersburg, February 29, 1894, with Legnani as Odette. Scenery by Botcharov and Levogt. First presented in Western Europe in complete form in Prague, Czechoslovakia, June 27, 1907, with choreography by Achille Viscusi. First presented in the United States at the Metropolitan Opera House, New York, December 20, 1911, with Catherine Geltzer as Odette-Odile, Mikhail Mordkin as Prince Siegfried, and Alexandre Volinine as Benno. This production was staged by Mordkin after the Petipa-Ivanov choreography. Scenery by James Fox. First presented in England in complete form by the Sadler's Wells Ballet at the Sadler's Wells Theatre, London, November 29, 1934, with the Petipa-Ivanov choreography reproduced by Nicholas Sergeyev; Alicia Markova as Odette-Odile, Robert Helpmann as Prince Siegfried. Scenery and costumes by Hugh Stevenson. Revived by the Sadler's Wells Ballet in a revised version September 7, 1943, with Margot Fonteyn and Robert Helpmann in the principal roles and with scenery and costumes by Leslie Hurry. Fonteyn first appeared as Odette on December 16, 1935, and as Odette-Odile in the first Sadler's Wells production, November 15, 1937. The Sadler's Wells revival of 1943 has been extensively revised in new productions of 1948 and 1952, all with scenery by Leslie Hurry. This production was first presented in the United States at the Metropolitan Opera House, New York, October 20, 1949. The San Francisco Ballet, in 1940, presented a complete Swan Lake with new choreography by William Christensen.

Musically, and as a dance drama, Swan Lake is undoubtedly the most popular of all classical ballets. It is possible to see at least a major portion of the complete Swan Lake—the famous second act—danced by almost every ballet company in the world. And the ballet is a favorite of ballerinas as well as audiences. All leading dancers want to dance Swan Lake at least once in their careers, and all audiences want to see them dance it. To succeed in Swan Lake is to become overnight a ballerina. Petipa and Ivanov are to the dancer what Shakespeare is to the actor: if you can succeed in their choreography parts, there is a suggestion that you can succeed at anything.

Why is it that *Swan Lake* has been so consistently popular with both audiences and dancers for so long a time? What about its chief rivals in the classical repertory—*Giselle, The Sleeping Beauty,* and *Coppélia*—why are they not as popular? If we set aside practical considerations (unlike *Swan Lake,* these other ballets cannot successfully be shortened into one-act versions; the part does not provide the spirit of the whole), we find the answer in *Swan Lake's* romantic and tragic story and the music that accompanies its unfolding.

The heroines of these other classics all have some relation to the real world—they are peasant girls or princesses. Strange things may happen to them, but they live within determined conventions. The heroine of *Swan Lake* has another story. She is a princess of the night; she is all magic, a creature of the imagination.

On one level, her story is a girl-meets-boy story: girl meets boy, girl loses boy, girl gets boy, and then both are lost. What prevents this from being silly is the character of the girl. She is Queen of the Swans, a beautiful bird, except for the brief time—between midnight and dawn—when the mysterious sorcerer, Von Rotbart, allows her to become a beautiful woman. In the world of sky and water she is at home, but in the real world, where romance is possible, she seems to be irretrievably lost. The great love she comes to have for a worldly prince is doomed at its start; she has no control over her destiny.

The Swan Queen is the opposite of the Firebird, the bird triumphant; she is immediately pathetic, a creature whose initial fear and consuming love interest us immediately. The dignity and courage and authority she possesses as Queen of the Swans become, in the ballet, the dignity of the woman in love. Humanly speaking, even in this magical world she inhabits, she is never unreal or absurd to us, because we see that love does not shatter her dignity; rather, it ennobles her beauty and explains her universal appeal.

ACT ONE—THE GARDEN OF PRINCE SIEGFRIED'S CASTLE: Before the curtain rises, an overture warns us of the impending tragedy of the story. After the woodwinds have introduced the principal romantic theme, and the strings have taken it up, there is a faltering: a soft, gradually building questioning by the strings. And the answer comes in boldly asserted warnings by the crashing of cymbals and resounding trumpet calls. But soon, over these crescendos, the romantic theme returns at full, conquering volume. It quietens, and the curtain rises.

This is Prince Siegfried's twenty-first birthday, and the young prince is celebrating the occasion in the garden of his ancestral palace. Young people from the surrounding estates have come to pay tribute to him. Benno, friend to the prince, is talking to a group of twelve young men. Wolfgang, the prince's old tutor, comes in merrily and is almost immediately attracted to the bottles of wine that stand on a table at the right. The atmosphere is one of anticipation, and as the trumpets blare the climax of a spirited march, the host enters. The handsome prince is not haughty; neither is he familiar. He is delighted to see his friends, thanks them as they congratulate him, claps his old tutor on the back affectionately, and prepares to enjoy the festivities that have been arranged in his honor.

First there is a *pas de trois*, danced by two girls and a boy. (Since the Diaghilev company's second-act version of 1911, this *pas de trois* has often been performed as a *divertissement* in Act Two. Sometimes it is danced by Benno and two cygnets, sometimes by a first huntsman and two swan princesses, as in the production by the Sadler's Wells Theatre Ballet. Where the *pas de trois* is not interpolated in Act Two, the music for the variation of the *danseur* is almost invariably used for a variation by Benno.) For the dance of the two girls and a boy, the music is lightly melodic and flowing. Now each dances alone: the first girl performs to blithe, tripping music that increases in speed; the boy, to strongly accented rhythms that mark the precision of his *entrechats* and turns in the air; and the second girl, to a light, almost joking theme. Climactic music accompanies the final display of virtuosity that all three perform.

While most of the assembled guests have been watching the dance, the old tutor has been privately celebrating the prince's coming of age by drinking as much wine as possible. Just as everyone begins to enjoy the party, the conviviality is disturbed by the entrance of the princess mother and her four ladies in waiting. Siegfried goes to his mother and escorts her into the garden. She observes his friends with considerable disdain; there is an effort to hide the wine bottles, and poor old Wolfgang finds himself in obvious disfavor. The princess mother indicates to her son that his coming of age is hardly the occasion for levity. He responds to this opinion dutifully, but with apparent resistance. Siegfried is further disturbed when his mother points out to him that he must soon choose a wife. Her suggestion is in the nature of a command, and Siegfried turns stubbornly away. Tomorrow night, his mother reminds him, his birthday will be celebrated formally at a court ball, and there, from among the loveliest ladies of the land, he must select his future wife. Siegfried sees that argument is impossible; as he kisses his mother's hand and leads her out of the garden, he seems to bend to her will.

Wolfgang gestures his pleasure at the departure of the dominating princess mother. He attempts to restore the spirit of the happy occasion by claiming that, old as he is, he can dance better than any of the younger men. Everyone laughs at him, but Wolfgang is not to be outdone. He approaches one of the village maidens, who giggles as he takes her by the hand and begins to dance. The melody to which he partners her is subdued and charmingly sentimental, sweetly echoing the joys of youth. Soon Wolfgang is having such a good time that he tries to surpass himself by whirling his partner around and around. In the process he becomes dizzy and falls to the ground, taking his partner with him.

Now Prince Siegfried is convinced that the only thing to do is to enjoy himself to the utmost: tomorrow, after all, is another day. The prince signals that the celebration should continue. Wine is poured for all the guests, and village couples dance a vigorous polka that completely restores to the gathering its natural spirit of gaiety. Still Siegfried broods; the celebration has failed to dispel his apprehension in regard to the morrow.

Night begins to fall. Benno knows that Siegfried must be distracted for the remainder of the evening. He hears the sound of fluttering wings overhead, looks up, and sees in the sky beautiful wild swans in full flight. Against the sound of harp and strings, the oboe sounds softly the theme of these enchanted birds. Benno suggests that the prince form a hunting party and go in search of the swans. Siegfried consents; crossbows are brought, and flaming torches are provided to light the way through the woods. The village girls circle the stage and exit. Wolfgang alone is unwilling to accompany the hunting party. As the full orchestra takes up the mysterious and doomful theme that heralded the swans, Wolfgang tells Siegfried that he is too old, that he will remain in the garden. The young men bid him good-by and rush off into the night. The curtain falls as the old tutor stands alone in the center of the empty garden, his bottle his only friend.

ACT TWO — A LAKESIDE : While the curtain is lowered, the music continues to develop the theme of strange foreboding. Then all is quiet for a moment. As the music resumes, the curtain rises on a forest scene; a great lake, its shining surface undisturbed by the wind, shimmers in the moonlight. The music begins again. The hunting party enters, led by Benno. All carry crossbows. The men look above them through the trees, searching for the swans; they are astonished to see that the swans have settled on the lake and, within a few feet of them, are placidly gliding by. Leading the group of swans is a beautiful white bird, apparently their queen. The diamonds in her crown reflect spangles of light over the dark water.

A flourish from the orchestra heralds the arrival of the prince. The hunting party bows to him. Benno hastens to point out to Siegfried that the swans can be seen close by. The prince directs the men to hasten along the lakeside ahead of the swans; he is about to follow them off, when he sees something in the distance that gives him pause. He stops, close by the lakeside, then retreats hurriedly across the glade to conceal himself. He has seen something so strange and extraordinary that he must observe it closely in secret.

No sooner has Siegfried hidden himself than the most beautiful woman he has ever seen enters the quiet glade. He cannot believe his eyes, for the girl appears to be both swan and woman. Her lovely face is enclosed by swan feathers, which cling closely against her hair. Her pure white dress is embellished with soft, downy swan feathers, and on her head rests the crown of the Queen of the Swans. The young woman thinks she is alone. She poses in arabesque, then remains almost motionless, softly bending her cheek down against her shoulder in a gesture reminiscent of a swan smoothing its feathers. The music informs us of the pathos of this gesture, and Siegfried is so enchanted by the magical creature that he enters the glade. He moves quietly, lest he disturb her.

The girl is terrified, her whole body trembles, her arms press against her breast in an attitude of almost helpless self-protection; she backs away from the prince, moving frantically on points that drive desperately against the ground. Her arms seek the air for freedom, for escape. The prince, already in love, begs her not to fly away. The girl looks at him and gestures that she is afraid. Siegfried wonders why. She points to his crossbow and draws her arm back as if to let fly an arrow, then holds her arm over her face, cowering with fear. The prince indicates that he will never shoot her; he will protect her. The girl bows to him in gratitude.

The prince now asks her who she is, why she is here? The girl's hands enclose the crown on her head: she is Odette, Queen of the Swans. The prince salutes her and says that he will honor her, but how is it that she is the Swan Queen? The Swan Queen asks for his patience and points to the lake. The lake, she indicates, was made by her mother's tears. Her mother wept because an evil sorcerer, Von Rotbart, made her daughter into the Swan Queen. And swan she must always be, except between midnight and dawn, unless a man should love her, marry her, and never love another. Then she will be saved and be a swan no longer.

Siegfried holds his hands to his heart and says that he loves her, that he will marry her and never love another. He swears his faithfulness. Now angry at the fate of his love, he demands to know where this Von Rotbart hides himself. Just at this point, the magician appears at the lakeside. His owl-like face is a hideous mask; he reaches out his claws, beckoning Odette to return to him. [In one-act versions of Swan Lake, this lengthy mime passage is often shortened and the music is used to accompany a dance in which the prince, his bow set aside, follows the dancing Swan Queen, lifts her as they circle the stage, embraces her, and supports her gently in poses until she breaks away from him at the entrance of Von Rotbart.] Von Rotbart points menacingly at Siegfried. Odette moves between them, begging Von Rotbart for mercy. Trumpets sound in blaring, warning crescendo. The prince seizes his bow, kneels, and aims it at the magician. Odette beseeches him to stop and runs diagonally across the stage toward Siegfried. She touches his stretched bow and stands over it and her lover in extended arabesque. Von Rotbart disappears. Siegfried rises and embraces Odette. The music quietens. The prince puts his arm about the girl, and they go toward the forest.

The prince tells the girl that she must come the next evening to the court ball. He has just come of age and must marry and at the ball he will choose her as his bride. Odette replies that she cannot come to the ball until she is married—until Von Rotbart no longer has power over her—otherwise the magician will expose her and their romance will perish. She knows, she tells Siegfried, that Von Rotbart will stop at nothing to keep her in his power, that he will contrive artfully to make Siegfried break his promise to her, and that should he do so, should he be faithless, Von Rotbart will cause her own death. Siegfried again swears his faithfulness.

When the lovers have left the glade, Odette's charges, all the swans who, like herself, assume human form only between the hours of midnight and dawn, dance in from the lakeside. They form a single serpentine line that moves toward the front, then face the audience in a triangular grouping.

Soon Benno, the prince's friend, comes upon the dancing swans. They encircle him, rushing past him with their fluttering arms. Benno, unaware of the mystery of these creatures, thinks only of the hunt. The swans cower in fear and rush together in a close group by the lakeside. Benno hails the rest of the hunting party. The huntsmen marvel at his discovery and aim their crossbows at the swans. Suddenly the music crashes warningly; Siegfried runs in and behind him comes Odette. The Swan Queen stands before the group of trembling swans and stretches out her arms to protect them; the huntsmen must kill her first. As Odette begs the men for mercy, Siegfried orders them to lower their bows and to respect the magical birds. When the huntsmen have learned that, like Odette, the swans are really unfortunate girls in the hands of an evil magician, they remove their caps and bow in apology to the swan maidens.

Siegfried and Odette again vanish into the forest, the huntsmen leave the scene, and the swan maidens come forward in three columns to dance. They dance to a charming waltz; their ensemble is dominated by two swan maidens who emerge from the group to dance in unison between lines formed by their friends. When the dance is over, the swans gather together in picturesque groupings to form a final tableau.

Now the swan maidens gather at either side of the stage. Siegfried enters with Benno. The harp sounds a series of arpeggios. The prince searches for Odette among the swans. He does not find her. The huntsmen return and stand among the swan maidens. Siegfried stands with his friend in the center of the glade. At the back, behind them, Odette enters softly. She touches Benno's shoulder, poses for a brief second in arabesque, then comes forward. It is as if she had not seen the prince. The harp is plucked gently. Odette rises on point, then sinks slowly to the ground. She rests on her left knee, her right leg stretched before her. She bends down low, her arms reach forward like enclosing wings, and to the quiet rhythm of the music her body stirs expectantly. Siegfried comes forward, reaches down to her hands, and raises her. The solo violin begins quietly the wistfully romantic theme of the adagio. Odette pirouettes with slow, romantic adroit-ness in his arms. Now her love supports her as she bends low in a deep arabesque. Each of the huntsmen, observing the beauty of this love duet, now stands between two swan maidens, his arms about their waists.

Odette moves to Benno, and the prince admires her loveliness as his friend holds her in arabesque. The beautiful Swan Queen returns to her lover, moves in supported attitude, then rests for a moment against his breast. She moves now slightly away, rises on point, takes Siegfried's hand, and then—raising her right leg straight before her—removes her hand from his; for a fraction of a second, as she lifts both arms up, the idyllic nature of this dance is luminously clear: the relation of Odette and Siegfried is one of complete sweetness and absolute trust. Odette falls back, and Benno catches her gently in his arms as her right leg closes against her left. Benno lifts her up, she returns to the prince, nestles against his shoulder as he embraces her softly, and the movement is repeated a second time. Siegfried puts his arms about Odette at its conclusion and leads her toward the lakeside. The swan maidens turn in arabesque, to the gently hopping rhythm of the woodwinds, and cross the stage before the lovers. As the solo violin resumes, Odette and the prince run forward quietly between the swan maidens. Siegfried lifts Odette high in his arms to the violin's music; he lifts her again, and then she pirouettes in his arms. He continues to lift her effortlessly to the demand of the theme; she turns to his encircling arms, then moves away on point with a gesture of obeisance and love.

Now a number of the swan maidens are arranged in a diagonal line across the stage. The huntsmen, standing in back, lift some of the girls to their shoulders. The prince moves back. Odette goes to him, and Siegfried opens his arms to her. She turns away then and, hopping softly, moves in arabesque down the line formed by her charges. Siegfried follows her adoringly and, taking her about the waist, lifts her at arm's length high above his head. He lifts her again, releases her, and, as she reaches the end of the diagonal, lifts her to carry her to the right side of the stage. The violin repeats the theme of the first lifts of the adagio, and this time, to the melody, Odette executes supported arabesques followed swiftly by pirouettes that she terminates with an open pointing of her leg to the left. These movements are repeated with the music.

The swan maidens are now grouped on the left. After the final pirouette, Siegfried stands close behind Odette. She leans back softly against him and balances. The prince opens his arms as Odette opens hers and gently he moves her arms close to her body, as if he were quieting her frightened wings. Siegfried moves slightly from side to side, gently rocking his love. Odette rushes away, seemingly compelled to resist the embrace, and balances in arabesque, both arms encircling her head. From behind, the prince takes her arms, moves them back close to her body, and Odette leans back against him, now confessing the power of her love for him.

The adagio nears its end. Siegfried turns the Swan Queen slowly as she stands on point, her right foot trembling in *petits battements*. She turns a final series of slow pirouettes in his arms and then is held by the prince; both arms over her head, her left leg extended to the side. Siegfried holds her thus, then releases her; she balances for an instant and then, holding her pose, falls to the side; at the last breathless moment she is caught in the arms of her lover's friend. The adagio is over. The two lovers and Benno leave the stage.

Four cygnets appear and dance with bright, youthful precision a *pas de quatre* that is accompanied by lightly bouncing music of great charm. This is followed by a dance for two swan princesses. Here the music is openly joyous, uninhibited in its bounding, youthful expression of happiness in new-found love.

Just as this dance ends, we notice that dawn is approaching. Odette returns and dances a variation that is at first modestly lyrical; her arms stretch back and her neck arches backward as she balances in arabesques, and we feel that to this beautiful woman such a pose is the most beautiful and natural thing in the world. The music increases in momentum, and the variation finishes with a dazzling diagonal of rapid pirouettes across the stage.

The swan maidens are alerted by the coming light and prepare to return to the lake. Odette, in their midst, comes forward and—from the front of the stage toward the back—executes to the driving rhythm of the rapid music a series of quick, desperate movements that reflect her fear at her departure from her lover. Siegfried beseeches her to stay, but she cannot. Benno kneels before her. Now impelled to become again the Swan Queen, she rushes toward Benno and stands in full flight on his extended knee. Siegfried reaches out for her, lifts her down gently. The swan maidens have responded already to the return of the mysterious music that presaged the first appearance of the magical creatures: Odette and Siegfried are alone. Von Rotbart appears by the lakeside, beckoning Odette to come to him. She is helpless and must obey. She holds out her arms yearningly toward Siegfried, but her feet carry her back toward the lake. Her body trembles with helplessness, and she glides farther and farther away from him, to disappear in the new dawn. Siegfried reaches out toward her, unable to console himself by her promise to return.

The huntsmen enter the glade. Benno comforts the prince, and then, at the sound of wings overhead, all look up to see the swans in full flight, led by their queen. The curtain falls.

ACT THREE—THE GREAT HALL OF PRINCE SIEG-FRIED'S CASTLE: The time is the following evening. The ball that the princess mother has arranged in honor of her son is about to take place. After a long and regal musical introduction, the curtain rises on the hall of the palace. There is a roll of drums, and a march begins. Here in the great hall, the royal thrones are placed on a dais to the right; on the left, with a short flight of steps leading down to the ballroom, is the formal entrance. Across the back, stretching into the distance, is a long, curved colonnade.

A flourish of music marks the entrance of two royal pages. The prince and his mother enter the room. The assembled guests bow to them as they proceed to the dais. The princess mother turns to speak to her son. Siegfried looks out over the ballroom with a blank stare; he is thinking of his meeting with Odette and his vow to be faithful to her. His mother, jealous of his preoccupation, addresses him somewhat in the manner of Gertrude upbraiding Hamlet: "Are you ill? You must pay attention to our guests; they are beginning to remark your strange behavior." The prince throws off his thoughts and assures his mother that he will not fail in his obligations.

Ambassadors from foreign lands, attired in colorful native costume, have come to pay tribute to the prince on his coming of age. A trumpet sounds a flourish, and a herald announces the arrival of six beautiful girls invited by the princess mother as prospective brides for her son. The girls are attired identically in stunning evening dresses and each carries a large feathered fan. The princess mother nods to them, and they begin to dance before the prince to the strains of a courtly waltz.

Siegfried pretends to watch them, but actually he thinks only of the lakeside glade and his meeting with Odette. His mother taps him on the arm and warns him that he must dance with his guests. The prince descends from the dais and dances briefly with each of the would-be brides. He dances automatically, with no interest, holding the girls casually about the waist and scarcely looking at his partners. The girls are dismayed at his indifference, but cannot display their displeasure too markedly lest their hostess be disappointed in them. Siegfried returns to the dais and again sinks into melancholy.

The princess mother rises and approaches the prospective brides. She thanks them for the lovely waltz and congratulates them on their beauty. Now she turns to the prince, asking him to confirm her opinion. Siegfried gestures that the girls are very pretty, indeed, but he does not wish to marry any of them. He loves another. He bows coldly to the girls. As his mother upbraids him, the music is interrupted suddenly.

Again the trumpet sounds a flourish. All the guests turn to watch the door. A herald hastens to inform the princess mother that a strange couple has arrived. He does not know who they are, but avows that the woman is a creature of rare beauty. Siegfried looks expectantly toward the door. His mother orders that the guests be admitted. There is a crash of cymbals, the room darkens mysteriously, and the music hurries warningly into a repetition of the theme that marked the fate of the Swan Queen.

The light returns, and a tall bearded knight enters with his daughter. As the knight introduces himself and his daughter, Odile, to the princess mother, Siegfried—excited almost beyond control—stares at the beautiful girl.

Although dressed in somber black, she is the image of his beloved Odette. [Although not originally designed for the same dancer, Odile for many years has been danced by the same ballerina who performs the role of Odette; Odette-Odile has become the most famous dual role in ballet.] Odile returns his stare with a steady glance of cold, but passionate, interest. In the distance, framed by an arch of the colonnade, Odette is seen holding out her hands to Siegfried. The prince is so enchanted by the girl he supposes to be the Swan Queen that he does not notice Odette's warning. The vision of the Swan Queen fades. Siegfried takes Odile by the hand. Now he foresees that the ball will be a happy occasion after all! He escorts Odile into the palace garden. Odile's father watches their departure with interest. Unknown to the prince, he is in reality not a knight at all, but Von Rotbart, the evil magician, who has transformed himself and his conniving daughter in order that Siegfried will be deceived and break his promise to Odette never to love another. Convinced that his trickery will doom Odette and Siegfried, Von Rotbart turns to the princess mother with a gracious smile. She is charmed by his flattery and—hopeful that her son will marry a lady of rank, as Odile appears to be—invites Von Rotbart to sit beside her on the dais.

Now the guests from foreign lands, who have come to honor the prince on his birthday, come forward to dance. First, two Spanish couples dance a quick and supple *divertissement* to the sound of music reminiscent of the melodies and rhythm of Spain. Next five Hungarian couples line up and, to the slow, anticipating measures of the music, commence a *czardas* that gathers in speed to end in a whirling finish. A vigorous Polish mazurka danced by eight couples concludes this series of *divertissements*. Von Rotbart indicates his appreciation of this entertainment to the princess mother and then suggests that his daughter, Odile, is the most beautiful dancer at the ball. Just as the princess mother is about to wonder where her son has taken Odile, Prince Siegfried appears with the stunning girl. Von Rotbart leaves the dais and tells Odile that the time has come for her to dance before the princess mother and Prince Siegfried. The orchestra sounds a rhythmic flourish, and the *pas de deux* between Odile and the prince begins. [When it is performed as a separate *divertissement*, this dance is known as the "Black Swan," or "Magic Swan," *pas de deux*. As a *divertissement*, the *pas de deux* necessarily lacks the dramatic impact it possesses as a part of the complete *Swan Lake*.]

This dance dramatically displays the cunning of Odile and the infatuation of the prince. In opposition to the adagio of Act Two, it has another kind of grace: it is full of pride and arrogance, rather than tenderness; it has the cold, dazzling light of a bright diamond. As Odile goes to Siegfried, Von Rotbart stands on the right, watching with guile and satisfaction. The prince welcomes his new love with joy: now his mother and the whole court will see how wonderful she is. Odile pirouettes across the ballroom floor, then turns rapidly in Siegfried's arms. Von Rotbart calls to her, and she goes obediently to her father, standing in arabesque with her hand on his shoulder. Von Rotbart whispers in her ear. Odile looks back at the prince and nods. She has grown confident with the success of her disguise and, when she returns to the prince, is determined to display her power over him with even more breath-taking skill. Siegfried supports her adoringly as she bends low in arabesque, but then Odile lets go his hand to stand alone, poised, balanced, splendidly self-sufficient. She goes back to Von Rotbart, and this time the impetuous prince follows her. After receiving more instructions from her father, she rejoins her lover, who supports her with glowing pride in bold and confident movements. For a moment the two are separated. They promenade across the ballroom floor, Odile walking with masterful authority and steely confidence, and meet in the center of the stage to resume the dance. Suddenly Odette again appears in the distant colonnade. Von Rotbart immediately notes her presence and signals to Odile, who steps between Siegfried and the vision. Odette extends her clasped hands to Siegfried, despairing of her fate if he abandons her. The enchanted Siegfried has no idea that she is there; the cunning Odile smiles at him—a cold, even smile in which he can discern nothing but warmth for his passion. The vision of Odette persists, and Odile becomes angry at this interference. She runs to Siegfried and places her hands over his eyes. Siegfried is so infatuated that he regards this gesture as flirtatious and fails to see that Odette, all hopes gone, has vanished, weeping, in the distance.

The *pas de deux* continues. Odile, now the winning seductress, carries her conceit still farther, and the innocent prince is utterly in her hands. The dance ends as the prince kneels before Odile and the proud, evil girl stands over him in high, conquering arabesque. With the final note of the music, she gives a curt, triumphant toss of her head.

The prince now dances a variation expressive of his great joy in rediscovering the girl he supposes to be Odette. Odile follows with a quick final dance designed to whip Siegfried's passion still further, and she succeeds in this brilliantly. Her variation contains a dazzling circling of the stage with small, swift turns, a series of quick, close movements performed in a straight line from the front of the stage to the back, and finally a series of thirty-two *fouettés*. These relentless, whipping turns sum up her power over the prince and, with disdainful joy, seem to lash at his passion. Helplessly bewitched, he rejoins his enchantress for a brief final dance.

Siegfried then approaches Von Rotbart and asks for Odile's hand in marriage. Von Rotbart immediately consents. Siegfried announces his decision to his mother, and Odile bows before the princess mother. Von Rotbart, still unsatisfied, addresses the prince further: he asks Siegfried to swear an oath of fidelity to Odile, asks him to promise that he will never love another. Siegfried's love for Odile is so great that he is offended by this request, and then, too, he knows that he has heard those words before. Why should they be asked again, he wonders. He looks at Odile, and his fate hangs in the balance. The music hesitates. He takes the oath. At that moment there is a crash of thunder. The ballroom darkens. The theme of the abandoned Odette screams above the orchestra. Quick flashes of light show the frightened courtiers fleeing the ballroom, the distraught princess mother, and Von Rotbart and Odile standing before the prince in a final triumph of self-revelation. Their hideous, cruel laughter Siegfried cannot bear, and he turns to see in the distance the pathetic figure of Odette, reaching out to him helplessly, her body racked with sobs. He falls to the floor in an agony of guilt.

ACT FOUR—THE LAKESIDE: The swan maidens have gathered by the side of the lake. They are sad and wistful at the fate of their queen. Their grief is reflected in the still tableaux they form with a group of small black swans who have joined them and in the dance the little swans do with their elders to soft, tender music. They yearn for the return of Odette. When she appears, weeping, they try to comfort her, but she tells them they do wrong to give her false hope. "I have been betrayed and I must die: the magician has won."

The music cries out with her grief, and she runs toward the lake. Two swan princesses intercept her and urge her to wait. They remind her that Siegfried is only human, that he could not have known the power of sorcery and thus could have had no suspicion of Von Rotbart's design. "You must wait," they advise her, "and hear the prince." "No," she gestures, "I have lost him and could not bear it."

Some of the swans hear Siegfried in the distance, calling for Odette, and tell her that he approaches. The Swan Queen orders a group of little swans to stand before her so that the prince will not discover her. Siegfried rushes into the clearing and frantically searches for Odette among the swans. Desperate, he asks the swans if they have seen her; he is about to abandon hope when the swans that surround Odette bend down and he sees her standing among them. He runs to her and takes her in his arms, asking for her forgiveness, swearing his infinite love. They go into the forest, and the swan maidens continue their dancing. When the lovers return, Odette has forgiven her lover, but she tells him—with tears streaming down her smiling face—it is no use, for what is her forgiveness alongside her death, which now must surely follow. "Von Rotbart is relentless. My life was forfeit if I should be betrayed. Only in death am I released from his power."

Now Odette dances to music that is tenderly beautiful. She moves softly in a long diagonal enclosed by the swans and, at the moment of her imminent death, expresses her undying love for the prince. Von Rotbart, enraged at Odette's delay, hovers over the scene disguised as a monstrous owl. He vows vengeance on her and all the swans. The swan maidens tremble as Siegfried defies Von Rotbart, who is momentarily overpowered by the strength of the prince's love for Odette.

The lovers embrace as Von Rotbart disappears. Odette then reminds the prince that only in death will she be released from Von Rotbart, only in death will she be free to love him forever. Her gestures are dramatic and sure as she tells him this, and suddenly she rushes across the stage in a swift diagonal to the shore's edge and throws herself into the lake as the music reaches a surging climax. Siegfried is motionless for a moment and stands helpless among the grieving swan maidens. Then, knowing that life without Odette will be nothing, he declares that he will follow her. He runs down the same diagonal that Odette took to the lakeside and drowns himself.

Siegfried's sacrifice of his love that Odette might not be destroyed by the evil magician has caused Von Rotbart's downfall. Again the malevolent owl-like creature appears, but only briefly. He lingers among the distraught swan maidens only long enough to see that love has triumphed in the end. He dies.

The stage darkens. The music softens. The swan maidens form two diagonal lines at the right, and as the light of day gradually rises in a soft glow, we see their figures bent low to the ground in grief at the loss of their queen and in gratitude for their own liberation from the evil sorcerer. Then, on the waters of the lake, a gleaming jeweled bark glides into view, its ornaments brilliant in the morning sun. Odette and Siegfried, clasped in each other's arms, move in the magical bark to a new and perpetually happy life. The swan maidens raise their heads, and their arms move softly, like ripples on the water, in quiet farewell to their queen.

NOTES: In 1949 John Martin reviewed the first presentation in the United States of the Sadler's Wells production in the New York *Times:*

> Heretofore we have seen countless performances of the second act under the title of "Swan Lake," at least one production of the third act under the title of "The Magic Swan," as well as the *pas de trois* from the first act; but as the Sadler's Wells production gives it to us, it is not just an assemblage of bits and pieces selected for their virtuoso aspects but a unified work of art, realized with loving care and an amazingly rich and intuitive sense of its style and its values. The venerable Nicolai Sergeieff [Sergeyev] is credited with the production, for he perhaps alone has a record of the original choreography of Ivanov and Petipa, but the artistic directors of the organization must share generously in the credit, for the many beautiful aspects of the production in addition to the choreography.
>
> Tchaikovsky and this unnamed scenarist created the ballet a good fifty years after the great Gothic revival of the last century, but that is still its dominant spirit and the present version has built upon it superbly. Leslie Hurry's story-book settings and lovely costumes (especially those of the second act); Constant Lambert's tender evocations from the score, and the tone of sweet sadness which underlies all the dramatic action are pure examples of romanticism. It is true that there are also marked elements of the much later Nineties with their fireworks and irrelevancies, but they have been seen for what they are and blended into the general unity of style with fine taste and artistry.

The performance itself is as exquisite as the production, and Margot Fonteyn is, of course, its bright and shining star. But never for a moment does she treat it as a star role; both as the enchanted swan queen and the wicked magician's daughter, she is always an integral figure in an artistic whole. Here is no ballerina's holiday.

Michael Somes makes an ideal prince, in appearance, bearing and dramatic deportment. Alexis Rassine, Margaret Dale and, particularly, Nadia Nerina dance the *pas de trois* delightfully. Pamela May and Gillian Lynne and the incomparable *corps de ballet* make sheer magic of the swan maiden scenes.

March 4, 1952, was the seventy-fifth anniversary of the first performance of *Swan Lake*. In observance of this occasion, Anatole Chujoy wrote the following authoritative article in the April 1952 issue of his informative and popular publication, *Dance News*:

Troubled less than it is in our days, a civilized world would have rested from its labors on March 4 to celebrate an important occasion in the history of ballet and music, the diamond jubilee of *Swan Lake*, the greatest romantic-classic ballet of all times.

Swan Lake, as it were, stands at the highest point of the curve which represents the history of the source of all ballet as we know it today—the romantic-classic era which began with *Giselle* in 1841 and ended with *Les Sylphides* in 1909—the greatest period the classic dance has ever known. *Swan Lake* is often accepted as a strictly classic ballet; actually it is much more a romantic ballet. In conception, content, structure and emotion it is much closer to *Giselle*, for example, than to *The Sleeping Beauty*. In fact, it owes some of its choreographic invention to *Giselle*.

Swan Lake, which has been variously called the greatest ballet of all times and an old war horse, was first presented on March 4, 1877, at the Moscow Imperial Bolshoi Theatre.

Two years earlier, in the spring of 1875, the Director of the Bolshoi Theatre, V. P. Begitchev, commissioned Tchaikovsky to compose a score for a ballet then called *The Lake of the Swan*, based on a libretto written by the director himself, who was also a playwright of sorts, in collaboration with Vasily Geltzer (the future father of Catherine Geltzer, subsequently the famous prima ballerina of the Moscow Theatre [and the first to dance the complete *Swan Lake* in the United States]).

Tchaikovsky hoped to create in *Swan Lake* a score that the Bolshoi Theatre would accept with the same regard as orchestras accepted his symphonic works. This hope was not realized. The choreographer assigned to the ballet was Julius Reisinger, a hack ballet master who possessed neither the talent nor the taste to choreograph a work to the music of a major composer.

The ballerina, Pauline Karpakova, was a run-of-the-mill dancer past her bloom, who insisted upon interpolating sure-fire 'numbers' from other ballets in her repertoire to replace some of Tchaikovsky's music which she could not appreciate, understand or even count. The premiere of the ballet was to be a testimonial gala in her honor and she was not going to take any chances.

When the premiere of *Swan Lake* took place it was a disappoint-ment to everybody, especially to its composer. Herman Laroche, a well-known music critic, composer and friend of Tchaikovsky, wrote about the premiere as follows:

'If during the creation of the ballet he [Tchaikovsky] had pictured fairy-tale splendor and brilliance he must have felt a bitter disappoint-ment when he saw the work of the ballet master on the stage. I must say that I had never seen a poorer presentation on the stage of the Bolshoi Theatre.

'The costumes, decor and machines did not hide in the least the emptiness of the dances. Not a single balletomane got out of it even five minutes of pleasure. The greater, however, was the joy of the melomane. From the very first measures of the introduction one felt the hand of a true master; a few pages later we knew already that the master was in excellent humor, that he was fully at the height of his genius.'

It cannot be said that *Swan Lake* was a total failure. It had a moderate success with the spectators and it remained on the stage until 1883 during which time it was given thirty-three performances.

According to another contemporary of Tchaikovsky, N. Kashkin:

'It [*Swan Lake*] was kept in the repertoire until the scenery was worn to shreds. The music also suffered a great deal. The substitution of the original numbers with others was practised to an even greater extent, and toward the end almost a third of the music of *Swan Lake* had been substituted with that from other ballets, usually from the most mediocre ones.'

When the scenery finally gave out the directorate of the Bolshoi Theatre took *Swan Lake* off the repertoire, and the ballet was not revived until January 1901, when Alexander Gorsky, a talented chore-ographer not sufficiently appreciated by his contemporaries and almost entirely neglected by historians, staged a new version of it.

The version of *Swan Lake* which came down to our generation dates back to the St. Petersburg production choreographed by Lev Ivanov and Marius Petipa and first presented at the Maryinsky Theatre on January 17, 1895, more than a year after the death of Tchaikovsky.

The production of *Swan Lake* at the Maryinsky came about in a rather unorthodox manner. The initiative for it stemmed from Ivanov, not from Petipa, as is generally supposed.

After Tchaikovsky died of cholera on November 6, 1893, there was a general upsurge of interest in his work. His operas were being revived by Imperial and private opera houses, his orchestral composi-tions, even those which earlier had not been successful, were being played by symphonic organizations all over Russia.

On March 1, 1894, an evening honoring the memory of Tchaikov-sky was given at the Maryinsky Theatre. The program included several excerpts from the composer's operas and what is now called Act 2 of *Swan Lake*, independently staged for the occasion by Lev Ivanov, Marius Petipa's assistant who carried the unpretentious title of second ballet master and *regisseur*, the same Ivanov who had staged in 1892 Tchaikovsky's *The Nutcracker*.

The role of Odette, the Swan Queen, was taken by Pierina Legnani, the great Italian ballerina, who had made her debut at the Maryinsky the year before in the ballet *Cinderella*, in which she introduced to St. Petersburg balletomanes her famous thirty-two *fouettés*. The short ballet caught the imagination of the audience.

Petipa saw the performance and decided to profit by its success. He ordered a repetition of the performance at a gala evening and on that occasion placed his name alongside Ivanov's (and ahead of it) as choreographer. The second performance had an even greater success and Petipa decided to revive the whole ballet.

Richard Drigo, the composer of the ballets *Talisman, The Magic Flute* and others, who was then conductor of the Maryinsky, was commissioned by Petipa to clean up the Moscow score. Drigo, on the whole, did a conscientious job, but found it necessary for some reason to eliminate several numbers from the ballet and substitute for them a few of Tchaikovsky's short 'salon pieces,' among them Op. 72 Nos. 11, 12, and 15, as well as one number in Act 3 by an anonymous composer (Drigo himself, perhaps).

Outside Russia there has often been speculation about what choreographer staged which part of the ballet. Indeed on several occasions the entire ballet, through sheer negligence, has been credited to Petipa, which is not only historically incorrect but also a great injustice to Ivanov. It has been established beyond any doubt that Petipa staged Act 1 (called Act 1, Scene 1 in the original St. Petersburg version) and most of Act 3 (called Act 2 in the original version). Ivanov staged Act 2, which constitutes the familiar one-act version (called Act 1, Scene 2 in the original version), and Act 4 (called Act 3 in the original version).

Unlike the Moscow opening, eighteen years before, the St. Petersburg premiere on January 17, 1895, was a huge success. The occasion was also a testimonial gala for Pierina Legnani, who danced the double role of *Odette-Odile* and could not restrain herself from injecting her thirty-two *fouettés* from *Cinderella*, this time as the coda of her *pas de deux* in the ballroom scene (Act 3).

The two acts of *Swan Lake* which Lev Ivanov was permitted to stage were a great achievement for the choreographer and the culmination of his long but frustrated career at the Maryinsky, too little of which is known to the outside world.

In staging the two acts Ivanov went contrary to the basic artistic direction in ballet during the second half of the 19th century, which aimed to demonstrate the technical proficiency of the dancer and the spectacular solution of complicated technological choreographic problems. Ivanov built Acts 2 and 4 on musical principles, thus breaking a strong and generally accepted tradition. An excellent example of this is the adagio in Act 2.

In Petipa's ballets the adagio usually unfolds against the background of a picturesque backdrop or an immobile group of dancers who do not take part in the action. Ivanov's composition of the adagio in Act 2 is a duet with an active ensemble which accentuates and participates in the dance of the two principals. It is motivated entirely by the construction of the music, which was inspired, according to memoirs of Tchaikovsky's friends, by the vocal duet in his opera *Ondine*, the score for which he had destroyed before the opera was ever produced.

This may sound less than revolutionary now, but in 1894 it was quite a step forward, so much so, in fact, that no choreographer dared to take a similar step until Michel Fokine, at the very height of his avant-garde Fronde'ism, utilized Ivanov's idea in *Les Sylphides* in 1909. Fokine also made use of some of Ivanov's choreography in *The Dying Swan* which he staged for Anna Pavlova in 1905.

But Ivanov did more than just violate the canonical principles of the construction of the adagio by subordinating it to the problems of the musical themes. His two acts of *Swan Lake* very effectively dethroned the ballerina as the alpha and omega and, one might say, the *raison d'être* of the ballet. For some forty years Petipa constructed his ballets *ad majoram ballerinae gloriam*. The ballerina was all that mattered and everyone and everything else was on the third plane. No so in *Swan Lake*. Here Ivanov treated the ballerina only as one of the protagonists. Here she either participates in the dances together with other dancers or alternates with them, or, if she performs a solo passage, the other dancers echo or accompany her. But no one leaves the stage for her variation, no one freezes into the painted backdrop.

The adagio in Act 2 is a remarkable example of Ivanov's choreography, a testimonial to his choreographic and musical genius, but it is not the only example. One has but to think of the witty and compositionally perfect *pas de quatre* of the cygnets, the man's variation, and especially the entire last act to realize the great talent of Ivanov that was never allowed to achieve full bloom because of Petipa's dictatorial position in the Imperial Theatre.

An appreciation of Lev Ivanov in English and an analysis of his work on *Swan Lake* and *The Nutcracker* is still to be done, and this writer hopes to do it before very long. It can be said here, however, that Ivanov's two acts of *Swan Lake* have been an inspiration to many contemporary choreographers whose origin was in pre-revolutionary Russia. If one man can be considered the precursor of modern ballet, especially in the musical approach to choreography, that man was Lev Ivanov.

Since its St. Petersburg premiere *Swan Lake* has never left the stage. The greatest ballerinas of pre-revolutionary Russia, among them Mathilde Kchessinska, Olga Preobrajenska, Anna Pavlova, Tamara Karsavina and Olga Spessivtzeva, have vied for the privilege of dancing it.

The current production of *Swan Lake* in Russia is based on the Ivanov-Petipa version, revived by Agrippina Vaganova in 1935. It is being given both in Moscow and Leningrad and is unquestionably the most popular ballet of the repertoire of both state theatres. It is also the ballet always presented on gala occasions and it is safe to say that every American and Western-European diplomat and dignitary visiting Moscow has seen it.

In Western Europe the full-length *Swan Lake* is only being given by the two British companies, the Sadler's Wells Ballet and the International Ballet. Both productions are based on the St. Petersburg version and both were staged by Nicholas Sergeyev, a former *regisseur* of the Maryinsky Theatre.

The familiar one-act version of *Swan Lake* dates back to the Diaghilev Ballets Russes, which presented the ballet first in two acts [November 30, 1911, at the Royal Opera House, Covent Garden, London, with Mathilde Kchessinska, *prima ballerina assoluta* of the Imperial Theatre and Vaslav Nijinsky. Mischa Elman played the solo violin passages for these performances.] and later in one act (ca. 1925). With the exception of the small French groups, nearly all professional contemporary ballet companies in America and Western Europe have a one-act version in their repertoire, based more or less on the Ivanov choreography.

The latest company to add *Swan Lake* to its repertoire is the New York City Ballet, which premiered it on November 20, 1951, with Maria Tallchief and André Eglevsky. The choreography is by George Balanchine and is probably closest to Ivanov's conception of the ballet, whether the actual steps are exactly those used by Ivanov or not.

In its Act Two form, *Swan Lake* is most familiar to the American audience in productions by the Ballet Russe de Monte Carlo, the Ballet Theatre, the New York City Ballet, and the Sadler's Wells Theatre Ballet. The Ballet Russe version was first performed in the United States in 1934 by Alexandra Danilova and David Lichine. The Ballet Theatre production was staged by Anton Dolin.

The Sadler's Wells Theatre Ballet version of Act Two was produced by Nicholas Sergeyev after the original choreography, with *décor* and costumes by Hugh Stevenson. It was first performed in the United States at the Masonic Temple, Detroit, Michigan, October 29, 1951, with Svetlana Beriosova as Odette.

My own version of Act Two of *Swan Lake* was first presented by the New York City Ballet at the City Center, New York, November 20, 1951, with Maria Tallchief, André Eglevsky, Patricia Wilde, Yvonne Mounsey, and Frank Hobi as principals. Scenery and costumes were by Cecil Beaton; costumes were executed by Karinska; and lighting was by Jean Rosenthal. In this production only the central *adagio* and the *pas de quatre* of the cygnets remain of Ivanov's original; the rest of the choreography is new. I hope eventually to produce Acts Three and Four of this ballet, omitting Act One, which consists mostly of pantomime.

The principal roles in *Swan Lake* have been performed by leading dancers in almost every ballet company throughout the Western world.

A new production of *Swan Lake*, with new scenery and costumes by Leslie Hurry, was presented by the Sadler's Wells Ballet at the Royal Opera House, Covent Garden, London, December 18, 1952. Beryl Grey and John Field danced the principal roles. Among the choreographic changes introduced in this production are, in Act One: a *pas de six* (by Frederick Ashton) to music of the waltz used formerly as a prelude to Act Three, and a revised version of the final peasant dance; in Act Three: a revised version of the dance by the six prospective brides and a Neopolitan *pas de deux*. Changes in entrances and in exits of some characters and in groupings of the *corps de ballet* were also made. This production was directed by Ninette de Valois. It was first presented in the United States, September 11, 1953, at the Metropolitan Opera House, New York, with Margot Fonteyn and Michael Somes in the leading roles.

LA SYLPHIDE

Ballet in two acts. Music by Jean Schneitzhoeffer. Choreography by
Philippe Taglioni. Book by Adolphe Nourrit. Scenery by Pierre Ciceri.
Costumes by Eugène Lami. First presented at the Théâtre de
l'Académie Royale de Musique, Paris, March 12, 1832, with Marie
Taglioni as La Sylphide and Mazilier as James. Marie Taglioni danced
the title role when the ballet was introduced to London (1832), St.
Petersburg (1837), and Milan (1841). A version of La Sylphide was
presented in the United States for the first time on April 15, 1835,
with Mademoiselle Céleste in the leading role. It was subsequently
danced in the United States by the same ballerina; by Augusta Maywood (1838); Amélie Galster (1839), sister-in-law of Marie Taglioni;
and by Fanny Elssler (1840). In 1836 La Sylphide was presented by
the Royal Danish Ballet in a version by Auguste Bournonville with
music by Herman Lovenskjold. Lucile Grahn danced the Sylphide in
the first performance of this version, which has been in the active
repertory of the Royal Danish Ballet ever since. Taglioni's La Sylphide
was revived in 1946 by the Ballets des Champs-Élysées, Paris, with
choreography by Victor Gsovsky, scenery by Serebriakov, and costumes
by Christian Bérard. Nina Vyroubova and Roland Petit danced the
principal roles. This revival was first presented in London on June 4,
1947.

Like most nineteenth-century ballets that have long since passed out of the
active repertory, La Sylphide would seem to be a mere curiosity. It is seldom, if ever, seen any more; never is it seen in its original condition. But
La Sylphide must interest the modern audience because of its story, what we
know of its dancing, and because of the ballerina who danced it. Marie
Taglioni is the first great dancer we know anything about. She and the men
who made La Sylphide her most famous part created a revolution in the art
of theatrical dancing that we are still witnessing every time we go the ballet. It is to them that we owe ballet stories that are at once real and fantastic, dancers who rise above the floor into the air, ballet scenery that is
naturalistic, then ethereal, costumes of flowing white, pink tights and satin
shoes—all the things, in fact, that began what we know now as the
Romantic ballet.

ACT ONE: The story of La Sylphide is a romance of old Scotland. The scene is the living room of a Scottish farmhouse. The time is 1830.
The room is large and high. On the left a fire blazes in a great fireplace; a
huge stone mantel rises from it to the rafters. The mantel is hung with
trophies of the hunt—colorful stuffed birds, powder horns, and flintlocks.
A staircase runs up the back of the room to the upper story, and a bright
plaid decorates the banister. Near the first landing of the stairs is a high,

peaked window through whose diamond-shaped translucent glass we can discern the break of day.

This is the wedding day of James Reuben, the young Scots peasant who lives in this house with his mother. The bridegroom sleeps restlessly in a high wing chair drawn close to the fire. He is dressed for his wedding: kilts, cap with high feather. His dark head stirs against the back of the chair; he is dreaming. His dream is with us in the room, and we understand his restlessness. For kneeling on the floor at his feet, her long white dress against the bridegroom's bright tartan, is the diaphanous, winged sylphide, who glances with quiet happiness about the room and seems with her penetrating gaze to look into the eyes of her dreaming lover.

Gurn, another young peasant, rests in a corner against the fireplace. In his deep sleep, Gurn is not disturbed by the realization of his friend's dream; he himself dreams of Effie, James's bride-to-be, and the love he will lose this day.

The sylphide rises effortlessly and circles about the chair. She looks down upon the sleeping James with wistful longing, moving around the room with a lightness and grace that make her wings more than a part of her costume. James turns his head as she dances about him; he is still asleep, but in his dream he watches every gesture she makes. Creature that she is from another world, the sylphide now seems a part of this room. Her smile is the considered smile of possession; she is both beautiful and serious, and her face tells us that her love is great enough to endure beyond James's dream. Should James respond to her love, we feel that this dream might become permanent.

James stirs in his sleep. He wakens suddenly and beholds the sylphide before him. He reaches out for her desperately. Frightened now by reality, the sylphide eludes his grasp. She rushes toward the fireplace. She disappears like the smoke from the dying embers. James moves his hand to his forehead in disbelief at the apparition: was she really there, after all? He becomes frantic and unable to understand the mystery and decides to question Gurn. He shakes his friend awake rudely. Did he see the beautiful vision? How long have we slept? Gurn is a little embarrassed at his own dream and is about to tell James yes, he saw the beautiful girl, but he sees that his friend is not talking about Effie, the bride, but about someone quite different. He wonders at his friend.

James is angry at Gurn for allowing himself to sleep so soundly. He is still trying to piece together the fragments of his dream when he hears his mother approach. She comes in from another room with Effie. Reminded by his bride's presence that he has scarcely thought of her, James is embarrassed. Gurn greets the bride first. The beautiful young lass smiles at him. Gurn can hardly control himself, he is so moved by her loveliness; meekly he presents her with a rare bird he killed yesterday while hunting. Effie accepts the gift, but turns to her fiancé. Why, she wonders, is he preoccupied? Has he no greeting for her? James shakes off his dream and kisses her fondly. They embrace. Effie cannot see James's face as he stares over her shoulder into the fireplace. His mother and Gurn watch him curiously.

Again James kisses his bride. Amused by his own formality, he kisses her hand and tells her that this is the day he has long awaited. Effie sees that he is sincere and his old self again. She is therefore a little annoyed when Gurn steps in, takes her hand and tries to kiss it too. She shakes her finger at him, and James, seeing that he has a rival in his friend, jokes with him about it. Gurn, however, is in no mood for jokes and walks away to nurture his private dream.

James's mother embraces her son and Effie. The lovers kneel before her; she blesses them and hopes for their eternal happiness. Effie and James look into each other's eyes; in her sight, he has forgotten his dream.

Now the music brightens and becomes festive with the arrival of Effie's bridesmaids. The young peasant girls, dressed in brilliant plaids, surround the lovers and wish them well. Gurn approaches. The girls giggle at his discomfiture: after all, he might choose one of them instead of Effie, who is already spoken for. The unhappy Gurn pleads with them to intercede for him; can't anything be done, he wonders, before it is too late? The girls put him off and bring out the wedding gifts they have for Effie: bunches of freshly picked flowers, decorative cloths, and simple jewelry. The bride is delighted with the presents, tries on the jewelry, and drapes the new material over her shoulder.

She and her friends do not notice James as he walks away from them and stares into the fire. Gurn watches him suspiciously. What can be wrong with his friend? James turns his head to look at the precise spot where he last saw the sylphide. He catches his breath and jumps back, startled. Someone is there! He reaches out his arms hopefully, and out of the dark corner steps not his sylphide, but a frightening figure: Old Madge, the village sorceress. The girls are pleased and run over to her. Old Madge stumbles forward, bent low over her crude walking stick. Her ragged clothes are filthy; her stringy gray hair hangs loose about her white, ghostly face. She cackles hideously and walks straight over to James and looks up into his face. His fear turns to anger. He orders her away. Madge cowers pathetically, and the girls are shocked at James's behavior.

The bridegroom stalks away. The girls persuade Madge to tell their fortunes. Effie is the first to hold out her hand. She asks the sorceress if her marriage will be a happy one? Effie does not really have any doubts; it is, after all, the conventional question. Old Madge nods her head and grins, "Yes, you will be happy in marriage." Emboldened by this answer, Effie asks another question: does James love her? James looks over at the group. The witch says "No," smiling the same toothless smile as she shakes her head. James will tolerate this no longer. Old Madge cackles ominously. He picks up a broom and drives the hag from the room.

Effie, reassured by James's indignation, tells him that she never doubted his love and that Old Madge is a proverbial liar. James believes her and is comforted. As long as Effie is with him and he can look into her eyes, he, too, has no doubt.

His mother comes to take Effie away. It is time for her to dress for the wedding. Mother Reuben laughs at her son when he doesn't want to let Effie go. She takes the girl by the hand and leads her and her bridesmaids up the stairs. Effie glances back at James, who smiles at her reassuringly.

But now, alone in the room, James has his doubts. He cannot get his dream out of his mind, though rationally he knows it is nonsense. Effie is his real love and so she will remain. But will the dream recur? What would he do if it did? Could such a vision really exist? As he asks himself these tormenting questions, he feels a draft. He turns around, and there—standing in the window—is the sylphide! She is leaning against the window frame; her hands are clasped before her; her expression is one of sweet sadness; and her eyes look down, refusing to meet James's glance. James goes to the window and asks her why she is so sad. Before she vanished so mysteriously, the sylphide was blithe and happy; what can be troubling so beautiful a girl? The sylphide replies that she loves someone who does not love her. James turns as if to move away, but the sylphide continues. He must know, she says, that she loves him. She is the one who brought him the beautiful dream; she is the one who will always watch over him and keep him from harm. Gurn, who has been sulking in a dark corner near the fireplace, emerges from the shadows to watch closely.

James reminds the sylphide that he is to be married this very day. The sylphide knows. Tears fall upon her cheeks. She murmurs that there can be no more beauty in her life: she must die. She starts to leave. James can suppress his secret no longer. He kneels before her and tells her that since she disappeared from his sight he has not been able to forget her for a single moment; he has tried, for he owed it to his love for his fiancée, but he could not: he has loved her as she loves him.

The sylphide dances about the room. James is enraptured to see his dream become real and to find the creature even more graceful in life. She moves toward the window, beckoning James to follow her. He does not move. She whispers softly into his ear. The unhappy bridegroom looks toward the stairs and hangs back. The sylphide watches him and sees the source of his anxiety. Lightly, without seeming to have the least idea of what it is, she takes up the plaid Effie has left behind on the chair, puts it around her shoulders, and poses demurely with downcast eyes as the bride. James can resist her no longer. When the sylphide kneels at his feet, he draws her to him and kisses her.

Gurn is now convinced of his friend's faithlessness and dashes up the stairs to Effie. James and the sylphide are frightened. Excited voices approach. Quickly the sylphide cuddles up in a corner of the huge chair. James throws the plaid over her just as Gurn and Effie, in her bridal gown, rush down the stairs. Her friends follow. Gurn accuses James of having kissed another woman in this room. But where is she? James asks him; he laughs and swears he has been quite alone. Effie and Gurn see no one, but Gurn notes the plaid that covers the chair. James trembles. Gurn pulls the plaid away, and underneath is . . . nothing! The sylphide has vanished! James is as surprised as his friend, but immediately reassures Effie, who now berates Gurn for allowing his jealousy to govern his sense of truth. The girls ridicule Gurn mercilessly, and he slinks out of the room.

James's mother enters with the wedding guests—her friends as well as the friends of the happy couple. Refreshments are served, toasts are made, the bagpipes tune up, and soon everyone is either dancing or talking volubly. Everyone, that is, except James. As all the other young men of the village surround the bride, James stands apart, reminded anew of the sylphide. Effie breaks away from her admirers and reminds the bridegroom that he has not asked her to dance. James is shocked at his forgetfulness, and the two begin to dance. The other guests stand back and watch them. The couple dance together happily until the formal pattern of the peasant dance forces them to separate for a moment. At this point the sylphide returns. She is seen only by James, and the other guests are astonished—when James rejoins Effie—to see him turn his head away from his bride. The *pas de deux* becomes a *pas de trois*: every movement of Effie's is imitated and elevated by the sprightly sylphide. The guests join Effie and James in a general dance, while the sylphide runs hither and yon, now visible, now concealed by the turning couples.

James tries not to lose sight of her and whirls Effie around and around as he frantically pursues the sylphide. Effie is so happy she doesn't notice his anxiety. The sylphide continually eludes him, and James can no longer see her. The dance stops, and some of the guests surround James and inquire about his strange behavior.

They are put off, however, by the beginning of the wedding ceremony. The guests stand in formal groups about the fireplace, where James and Effie stand with his mother. The ritual begins. The couple start to exchange wedding rings. James takes off his own ring and holds it at Effie's finger tip. He moves to slip it on her finger, when the sylphide darts out from nowhere and takes the ring from his hand. The guests gasp at the sudden disappearance of the ring. James turns away from his bride. The sylphide whispers to him that she will die if he marries anyone else. James is so appalled at this possibility that he now sees his course: he must prevent such a tragedy. The sylphide beckons to him and stands there in the room by the window before his wedding guests; the bridegroom vanishes.

Effie dissolves in tears. No one can understand how or why James has abandoned her thus. Gurn rushes in and announces that he has just seen the bridegroom running across the moor with another woman. Effie will not believe it. Gurn tries to comfort her, assuring her that she can be certain of his love. Mother Reuben and all the guests gather about the troubled bride. Effie sits down in the chair by the fire. The plaid is placed around her shoulders, her wedding veil is removed. Gurn kneels beside her.

ACT TWO: Eerie music suggestive of an unnatural world marks the beginning of this second scene, which will unravel the mystery of the magical sylphide and confront the romantic James with his destiny. When the curtain rises, it is still night. On the left, a small fire throws grotesque shadows against the walls of a small, dark cave. The surrounding forest is impenetrably black. The witch, Old Madge, emerges from the cave and stands over the fire. Hovering over the flames, she invokes her demons, beseeching them to obey her commands. With her crooked walking stick, she draws a magic circle about the fire, then hurries into the shadows of the cavern. She returns with her sisters in witchcraft: hunchbacked, cackling hags who gather about the circle. The hideous women hang a huge black caldron over the fire and dance around and around it. Suddenly Old Madge orders silence and, walking up to stand over the caldron, she points her finger downward in unquestioning command. The other witches are silenced by this gesture and wait expectantly for some result. Old Madge orders them to dance again; as they circle the fire, smoke and steam and blue flame arise from the caldron, illuminating the forest for a few flashing moments. The conflagration in the caldron simmers down, and the old women crowd around to see what remains inside. With an imperious sweep of her arm, Old Madge tells them to stand back. The sun is about to rise, and they must hasten their work. Madge takes her stick and pokes it into the caldron; when she pulls it out, we see on the end of the stick, like a banner, a lovely shimmering scarf. The old women grab at it, but Madge holds it to her breast; only she is aware of the power of this beautiful scarf. She orders her sisters away, and all the witches disappear into the cave.

In the distance, the sun rises brightly over the fields of heather and we see a clearing in a thickly wooded glade. The green trees hang down over the scene, almost obscuring the witches' cave. Dew covers the ground as the morning mist settles on the earth.

On the right, James enters the forest. No longer dressed like a typical Scots peasant, James wears a costume befitting the bridegroom of his sylphide: white tights and a plaid vest. He carries a bird nest in his hand. Carefully he examines the colorful eggs and replaces them. He looks about the forest for his love, but she is not to be found. As he begins to approach the cave, he discovers the sylphide standing by his side. He is astonished at the suddenness of her appearance and asks her where she has been hiding. The lovely girl smiles back at him so beautifully that James leaves off his questioning. As if to show him how she appeared so swiftly and silently, she dances about the forest like a magical sprite; the tips of her toes seem to require only the air to support them in flight. James is bewitched anew by her charm and becomes apprehensive when the sylph darts in and out behind the trees. He holds out the bird's nest and tells her he has brought her a gift. The sylph shrinks back; and we see suddenly that she is not frightened because James has probably harmed the eggs in the nest, but because the living birds who fly about the forest are moved by a power quite different from the mysterious force that makes her a sylphide as well as a woman. The sylphide is afraid of the nest. Scrupulously she takes it between her hands and runs to place it high on an overhanging branch. James smiles warmly at what he believes to be her tenderness; lightly the sylphide moves her finger tips over her diaphanous white gown.

James draws her to his side. The sylphide places her head on his shoulder for a moment, and James moves to take her face in his hands. Before he can do so, the sylphide has danced away toward the back. James observes her as she calls forth a band of sylphs, who pay homage to her and to him. The sylphs surround the happy lovers, and James would dance with his bride; but every time he turns to take her in his arms, she is mysteriously gone and before him stands another sylphide. This happens repeatedly, and James becomes frantic in his search. Then, just as if nothing had happened, the sylphide is at his side again, looking up into his eyes. James is satisfied, but again the vision disappears: all the sylphs seem to fly away in the blazing light of the sun.

Alone, James considers that he has made a mistake. Yesterday, in his mother's house, the sylphide was always appearing and vanishing mysteriously, but that he could understand—for there he alone shared her secret; but here in the forest with her, with no one to see, why should she wish to escape *him?* She had sworn that she loved him and would love him eternally, and yet she would be loved only from afar. Was his love an illusion, he wondered?

On the left, close to where he last saw his beloved, the branches rustle. James is startled to see Old Madge come out of her cave. In his present state of mind, he greets her like an old friend. He remembers his rudeness of yesterday and hastens to apologize. Old Madge tells him not to mind, she understands the momentary follies of youth—but why is he here in the forest? What has happened?

James tells her briefly that he has run away with his true love, the most beautiful girl in the world. Why then does he look so dejected, Madge inquires? "Because," James tells her, "the sylphide is never with me: I search for her, and she is not to be found; I reach out to touch her beside me, and she eludes my embrace."

Madge offers to help him with her occult powers. James, willing to try any device to still the sylphide's flight, beseeches the witch to ease his state of mind and secure his permanent happiness. Old Madge holds out the bright magic scarf and offers it to James. She instructs him to place this scarf about the sylphide's shoulders, and then the sylphide will never fly again:

her light, transparent wings will fall to the ground and flutter no more; she will be his, on earth.

James is delighted with this magic and kneels before the witch in gratitude. Old Madge's eyes gleam with triumph as she looks down upon him. Then she hurries away into the dark cavern as she sees the sylphide approaching. James runs to his bride and embraces her. She responds warmly to his affection and seems to be charmed by the gift he offers her. James places the scarf about her shoulders. As the cloth touches her flesh, the sylphide clutches at her heart in a spasm of agonizing pain. Her wings fall to the ground. She stumbles forward. James, struck dumb by this outcome, tries to hold her in his arms and comfort her. The dying sylphide looks at him in horror and pushes him away. Slowly her body relaxes, and she lies dead before him, like a leaf fallen from a tree.

As James kneels beside her, weeping, the mirthful cackle of Old Madge ricochets against the dark walls of her hidden cavern. The sylphide's winged sisters emerge from the trees above. They do not comfort the despairing hero, but take the sylphide tenderly in their arms. As they lift her from the ground, they themselves are lifted up; the branches of the trees overhead move back, and high into the clear sky the winged creatures carry their dead queen.

James is inconsolable in his grief. The softness of the music that has carried his ideal love away forever is interrupted by the shrill, open sound of joyous bagpipes, reminding him of his home and the happiness he might have found there. Across the forest, in the distance, we see a wedding procession moving over the moor. Gurn and Effie, arm in arm, lead the happy party, and the curtain falls as the faraway church bells sound their welcome.

LES SYLPHIDES

Classic ballet in one act. Music by Frédéric Chopin. Choreography by Michel Fokine. Scenery and costumes by Alexandre Benois. First presented by Diaghilev's Ballets Russes at the Théâtre du Châtelet, Paris, June 2, 1909, with Anna Pavlova, Tamara Karsavina, Maria Baldina, and Vaslav Nijinsky as the principal dancers. Fokine's first arrangement of this ballet was presented on March 21, 1908, in St. Petersburg, under the title *Chopiniana*. The dancers were members of the Imperial Ballet; Pavlova and Oboukoff danced a classical *pas de deux* to the "Waltz," which was the only part of the original production without a realistic setting or suggestion of plot. The second production, given by Fokine's students, April 6, 1908, was wholly classical; like the first "Waltz," it had no plot, and the musical structure was altered. Preobrajenska, Pavlova, Karsavina, Nijinsky, and Bekeffy were the principal dancers. This second version was costumed in the long white ballet dress made popular by Marie Taglioni in *La Sylphide*. The title of this famous ballet of Taglioni's was Diaghilev's inspiration for the new name he applied to *Chopiniana* when it was first presented in Western Europe in substantially the same form as its second production. First presented in the United States in its authorized version by Diaghilev's Ballets Russes at the Century Theatre, New York, January 20, 1916, with a cast that included Lydia Lopokova, Lubov Tchernicheva, Xenia Maclezova, and Adolph Bolm. An unauthorized version, not credited to the choreographer and not supervised by him, was presented in the United States by Gertrude Hoffman's Saison des Ballets Russes on June 14, 1911, at the Wintergarden, New York, with Maria Baldina, Lydia Lopokova, and Alexandre Volinine as the principal dancers.

No one knows exactly when the first *ballet blanc*, or white ballet, was first performed. It is probable that this kind of ballet, which involved a new conception of dance based on ethereal atmosphere, soft music, and diaphanous white costumes, was first performed before *La Sylphide*; but it was *La Sylphide*, and the dancing of its ballerina, Marie Taglioni, that made the *ballet blanc* famous. *Les Sylphides*, its twentieth-century namesake, has carried this fame into our time more than any other ballet.

For the *ballet blanc* did not remain popular. Théophile Gautier, who first used the phrase, was complaining in 1844 that since *La Sylphide* the Paris stage was so dominated by white gauze, by tulle and tarlatan, that the "shades became mists of snow in transparent skirts" and "white almost the only color in use."

And so the misty white ballets gradually passed out of fashion. The ballets that replaced them for half a century were more concerned with dancing than with mood—more devoted to elaborate, regal stage spectacle, and the development within this frame of the classic dance, than to simple stories of fantasy and ethereal romance.

Les Sylphides restored the *ballet blanc*, now embellished with the developed classic dance; but it did so without a story. Here, instead of characters with definite personalities and a narrative, we have simply dancers in long white dresses and a *danseur* in white-and-black velvet, whose movements to music invoke the romantic imagination to a story of its own. It is the music, and the care with which the classic dance embodies it, that tells us the story of these magical creatures who dance in the light of the moon.

The overture, Prelude, Opus 28, No. 7, to the ballet is quiet and contemplative. The curtain rises on a secluded wood near an ancient ruin, where lovely girls in white are grouped about the scene in a still, charming tableau. The light is bluish-white, soft, and misty. As the Nocturne, Opus 32, No. 2, commences, some of the girls begin to dance to the light, airy melody. They are joined by the principal dancers, who stand in a cluster at the rear.

Now a girl dances a variation to a gentle but joyous waltz, music suggestive of beautiful and controlled happiness.

The next dance, like the Mazurka, Opus 33, No. 3, that accompanies it, is not as soft; it is bolder, more open and free, but still restrained in its exuberance as the ballerina bounds diagonally across the stage in *grand jetés*, over and over again.

A variation to another Mazurka, Opus 67, No. 3, is danced by the *danseur* after the girls have formed a decorative tableau about the stage.

When the overture is repeated, the sylphs form picturesque groups, the girls kneeling about central figures. The *danseuse* who now enters comes softly, pauses, and seems to listen to a distant call. She moves among the groups adroitly and sweetly, but completely removed from them in her rapt attention to what she might hear.

The Waltz, Opus 64, No. 2, commences, and the *danseur* lifts the ballerina across the stage from the wings. She appears to be so light that it must require no effort to hold her. She is released, and the *pas de deux* begins. Throughout this dance, as the music increases in momentum, the girl responds with unhesitating swiftness and flight to the inspiration of the music and the night: she abandons herself to the air.

The stage is empty for a moment, there is no music; then, to the final buoyant Waltz, Opus 18, No. 1, the dancers return, move diagonally across the stage, mingle, brush past each other, and fill the stage with movement like the swift fluttering of butterfly wings. The principal dancers join them for short solos; and at the final chords, there is a swift, silent rush and all are standing still, in the same tableau in which we first saw them.

NOTES: *Les Sylphides* is associated with many famous dancers. Fokine staged his work for the Royal Danish Ballet on October 21, 1925 (in a revised version), for René Blum's Ballet Russe de Monte Carlo in 1936, and for Ballet Theatre in 1940. The ballet has been in the repertory of the Sadler's Wells Ballet since March 9, 1932 (with Markova and Dolin) and of the Sadler's Wells Theatre Ballet since April 22, 1946. All the principal dancers who have been associated with these ballet companies have danced principal roles in *Les Sylphides*.

In the first Diaghilev production in Paris, the first solo, Waltz, was danced by Karsavina; the second, Mazurka, by Anna Pavlova; the third, Mazurka, by Nijinsky; the Prelude, by Maria Baldina; the *pas de deux*, Waltz, by Pavlova and Nijinsky; and the final Waltz, by all the soloists and the *corps de ballet*. Vaslav Nijinsky danced *Les Sylphides* in the United States on April 14, 1916, at the Metropolitan Opera House.

The music for Fokine's first arrangement of the ballet that was later to become *Les Sylphides* was orchestrated by Glazunov. Music for the second version was orchestrated by Keller and Glazunov. Music for the Diaghilev production was orchestrated by Stravinsky (his first Diaghilev commission), Tcherepnine, Glazunov, and Liadov. Later orchestrations include those of Vittorio Rieti and Lucien Caillet.

Alexandre Benois, who designed the scenery and costumes for the

Diaghilev production, designed a revival of *Les Sylphides* by the Sadler's Wells Ballet, December 26, 1939, when Margot Fonteyn and Robert Helpmann danced the principal roles. Ballet Theatre's scenery for *Les Sylphides* is by Eugene Dunkel, after Jean Corot.

In his book, *Reminiscences of the Russian Ballet,* Alexandre Benois records his impressions of the Diaghilev production of *Les Sylphides:*

"In *Sylphides* too we interpreted an epoch common to the whole of Europe, the epoch of 'Romanticism.' And again we passed the test—in spite of our highly dangerous plan of translating Chopin's dreamy music into dance and transforming his pianoforte compositions by elaborate orchestration.

"If the original idea of 'expressing Chopin on the stage' belonged to Isadora Duncan, Fokine accomplished a very successful and significant variation of that principle by illustrating this typically 1830 music with a ballet *à la Taglioni,* instead of a classic Greek dance. Our first-class composers Liadov, Glazunov and Tcherepnine had not wished (or had been unable) to preserve Chopin's mood, and in solving the problems of orchestrating piano pieces they stamped them, too obviously, with their own style. They made their orchestral version too complicated and modern, lacking simplicity and airiness. Perhaps it would have been more in harmony to have kept to the piano, increasing its effectiveness here and there by a delicate accompaniment of flutes, violins and bassoons. The sounds should be softened, wrapped, so to speak, in a haze, in order to convey the impression given on the stage— the languid vision of spirits of dead maidens, dancing their dreamy dances among the moonlit ruins and mausoleums.

"This was the atmosphere that my decor was calculated to evoke and it was enhanced by Fokine's dances, wonderfully performed by our artistes. This atmosphere became especially tender and convincing when Pavlova (who had arrived for that performance) and Nijinsky appeared together on the stage. Their 'dance-duet' with its high, noiseless, soaring flights, full of a tender delicate grace, conveyed the impression of a strange romance 'beyond the grave,' the hopeless love of bodiless spirits, who knew neither fiery embraces nor the sweetness of kisses, for whom all passion is replaced by sad caresses and soft, tremulous flitting . . .

"I was not very pleased with the costume I had composed for Nijinsky. It seemed to me to be a trifle comic when I saw it on the stage. It consisted of a black velvet jacket, a collar *à l'enfant,* a light tie, long curls and white legs. And yet, his slightly caricatured appearance made the artist more like a figure from some old beaded *réticule* or painted lamp shade. It was just such 'funny improbable troubadours' who formed the dreams of our own grandmothers, the creators of the embroidered *réticules* and painted lamp shades. In Chopin's music, through the sad tears of a tormented soul, there appears sometimes the strange and yet infinitely touching image of the pale youth who is danced to his death by the spirits of the cemetery . . ."

SYLVIA

> Ballet in three acts and four scenes. Music by Léo Delibes. Choreography by Louis Mérante. Book by Jules Barbier and the Baron de Reinach. Scenery by Chéret, Rubé, and Chaperon. Costumes by Lacoste. First presented at the Théâtre de l'Opéra, Paris, June 14, 1876, with Rita Sangalli as *Sylvia* and Louis Mérante as *Amyntas*. Revived at the Paris Opéra, by Léo Staats, December 19, 1919, with Carlotta Zambelli; by Serge Lifar, February 12, 1941, with Lycette Darsonval; by Albert Aveline, 1946. First presented in Russia at the Maryinsky Theatre, St. Petersburg, December 15, 1901, with Olga Preobrajenska in the title role. First presented in England in a one-act version, produced by C. Wilhelm, at the Empire Theatre, London, May 18, 1911, with Lydia Kyasht as *Sylvia*.

Until recently, *Sylvia, or The Nymph of Diana,* was more familiar to the English-speaking world for its music than for its dancing. Its original choreography survives only at the Paris Opéra, where the production has long been one of the glories of France. To the rest of the world, selections from the ballet's score, selections such as the often-played *Valse Lente* and *Pizzicato Polka,* have been the principal reminders of the ballet's existence. These selections, as a matter of fact, are so familiar to us that we sometimes forget that they are part of a score for a three-act ballet and that this particular score was extraordinary for its time, as it remains for ours. The American critic Carl van Vechten reminded us some years ago that before Delibes composed his ballets, "music for dancing, for the most part, consisted of tinkle-tinkle melodies with marked rhythm." Before *Sylvia* and *Coppélia,* Delibes' first great ballets, ballet music was universally subservient to the dancer: it had no drama to it and merely accompanied the steps of a dance with embellishing sound. Delibes changed all that, fusing drama with lyric melody, to become the father of modern ballet music, the inspiration of Tchaikovsky in his own ballet scores, and the precursor of Igor Stravinsky.

The story of Delibes' ballet *Sylvia* is a return to mythology. Sylvia, nymph of Diana, chaste goddess of the hunt, is loved by a mortal, Amyntas, the shepherd. The gods contrive against the romance until, with godlike privilege, they change their minds and the nymph and the mortal are united forever.

ACT ONE — A SACRED GROVE : The orchestra plays an Olympian prelude before the curtain rises. In this regal-sounding music—with its majestic trumpet calls suggestive of a royal hunt and its alternate light, open, joyous melody—we have a brief musical picture of the ballet's story.

The curtain rises on a grove sacred to the goddess Diana. Dominating the scene is a statue of Eros, the child god of love, armed with his bow and arrows. It is night. Magical creatures of the wood, fauns and dryads, cavort about by the light of the moon. The fauns flirt playfully with the dryads and finally succeed in ensnaring the creatures with garlands of flowers. But the sylvan lovers soon pause in their flirtations. A stranger is approaching! They conceal themselves to watch in secret.

Amyntas, the shepherd, enters the grove. He thought he had heard singing and dancing and looks about suspiciously. He sees nothing and cannot understand. Some nights ago he looked into this place and saw dancing a lovely nymph, the most beautiful girl he had ever beheld. Perhaps he was dreaming, but no—there is a soft horn call and soft, rustling, tripping music, as if a mysterious, unfelt wind had disturbed all the leaves of the forest.

Amyntas hides and observes the scene as his beautiful nymph, Sylvia, comes into the wood with her followers. They dance in honor of the chase, the pursuit of their patron goddess. Their innocent joy in the hunt seems to be curiously out of place as they dance before the statue of Eros, who would surely think them unnatural creatures to be so satisfied. Soon the girls tire and rest.

Now it happens they are observed by another. Orion, giant hunter of the forest, loves Sylvia in secret and wishes to abduct her. He is disturbed when some of the nymphs find the shepherd's crook and cloak lying on the ground and is immediately jealous. Sylvia orders her nymphs to seek out the intruder in the sacred grove, and Amyntas is brought before her. Enraged that a man has cast his eyes upon her and intent above all on preserving her purity, Sylvia determines that he must die. She draws her bow, though the young man is obviously in love with her. The love that he feels, Sylvia decides, he himself is not responsible for: it is some mischief of Eros. She therefore aims her bow at the statue.

Amyntas, shocked at this offense to the god who has inspired his love for her, runs across the wood and stands before the statue of Eros to protect it. But Sylvia has drawn her bow: her arrow sinks into the shepherd's breast, and he falls to the ground. Now the statue comes to life and Eros retaliates by aiming his arrow at Sylvia's heart. The girl collapses, clutching at her heart. Her nymphs gather about her, fearing that she is dead, but Sylvia holds out the arrow of Eros and says that she has not been hurt, it is nothing. She departs from the forest as day begins to dawn.

Villagers enter the forest and pay tribute to Eros. They do not notice the body of Amyntas. As soon as they depart, Orion enters in search of Sylvia. When he discovers the dead shepherd, he rejoices that he now has no rival and makes a new plan: he will capture Sylvia with a golden chain. Orion is observed by a straggling peasant, who remains on the scene in hiding to see what will happen.

Sylvia returns to the forest. Orion hides. The girl, remorseful at the death of the shepherd, hovers over his body. We wonder at her change of heart and then recall that she brushed off Eros' arrow too lightly. Orion takes advantage of her lack of vigilance, throws the chain of gold about her, lifts the struggling nymph into his arms, and runs toward the inner darkness of the forest.

A peasant who has seen all this is unable to help Sylvia. He runs to tell the other peasants that Amyntas is dead. His friends try to revive Amyntas, but the shepherd does not stir. An old magician comes forward and presses a rose to the shepherd's lips, and he returns to life. When he discovers, however, that Sylvia has disappeared, he wishes himself dead again. The sorcerer comforts him and tells him that perhaps Sylvia loves him; perhaps the arrow of Eros really touched her heart. Amyntas is then told of Sylvia's capture by the hunter Orion. He instantly prepares to save her; before departing, he bows to the statue of Eros. The statue again comes to life: Eros points the way to Orion's hiding place, and Amyntas sets out to rescue his beloved.

ACT TWO — THE CAVE OF ORION: Orion watches as his captive wakens. As soon as she opens her eyes and sees her abductor, Sylvia attempts to escape from him. But the weapons of the hunt have been taken from her, and she has no defense. She is impervious to his declarations of love, and the repulsed Orion grows angry. Sylvia placates him with wine, which the hunter has never tasted before. His servants willingly prepare it at their master's suggestion.

At first the wine merely increases Orion's passion, and the nymph dances before him to encourage him to drink more. He does so, but—tiring of the dance—seizes Sylvia in his arms. She easily eludes him, and the intoxicated giant falls to the ground.

Still she cannot escape. Orion has blocked the entrance to the cave with a huge boulder. The girl prays to Eros. The god appears to her, takes her by the hand, and leads her into the forest. There he turns around and, with an impatient godlike gesture, causes Orion, his grotto, and his servants to vanish into the earth.

The sound of a hunting horn causes her to rush to the nymphs she has abandoned, but Eros reminds her of Amyntas, who more than anyone grieves over her disappearance.

ACT THREE, SCENE ONE — A WOODED LANDSCAPE ON THE SEACOAST: Amyntas is still unaware of Sylvia's rescue; he enters lonely and dejected soon after the curtain rises on a celebration in honor of the god Bacchus. The sea stretches into the distance behind the trees; at the left is the sacred temple of Diana. Bacchantes dance and present grapes to the god of wine.

A ship is seen approaching the shore. A pirate captains this ship and as it reaches shore, he interrupts the festival and attempts to interest the natives in the purchase of slave girls. In reality, this pirate is Eros, who wishes to return Sylvia to Amyntas. Eros urges the veiled slave girls to surround the shepherd, but the moody Amyntas takes interest in only one of the girls, who seems to him strangely familiar. The girl dances before the youth to a pizzicato melody. He is completely delighted with her and when she removes her veil, he is overcome with happiness. He clasps Sylvia in his arms.

Orion bursts in on the scene. Eros has not been able to suppress the hunter, and Sylvia, knowing the giant's power, rushes into the temple of her patron goddess. Amyntas prepares to engage Orion in combat, but Orion runs past him to force the doors of the temple.

ACT THREE, SCENE TWO—THE TEMPLE OF DIANA: A distant roar that grows louder and louder reminds us of the anger of the gods. Lightning flashes. Within her temple, Diana, her bow drawn tight, stands over Sylvia, who kneels before her protectress. Orion dashes toward Sylvia. Diana releases her bow, and the evil hunter is pierced through the heart.

The angry goddess, who divines the real reason for Sylvia's fears, asks her how it has happened that she is in love. Sylvia confesses that Eros wounded her with one of his darts. Upon this declaration, Eros removes his disguise. Diana threatens him, but the god of love reminds her that once upon a time even she was grateful for his gift of love: the one time Diana was moved by his power and kissed the sleeping Endymion by the light of the moon.

The embarrassed goddess, confronted by her one fault, forgives Sylvia for breaking her vow never to love. She rises to her high seat in her temple with Eros. All her handmaidens bow low to the god and goddess, and the village peasants stand amazed as Amyntas and Sylvia—having received the blessing of Olympus—are transfigured by their love.

NOTES: *Sylvia* was revived in the original three-act version by the Sadler's Wells Ballet, at the Royal Opera House, Covent Garden, London 1952, in a new version with choreography by Frederick Ashton, and with Margot Fonteyn, Michael Somes, and Alexander Grant in the leading roles.

SYMPHONIC VARIATIONS

Classic ballet in one act. Music by César Franck. Choreography by Frederick Ashton. Scenery and costumes by Sophie Fedorovitch. First presented by the Sadler's Wells Ballet at the Royal Opera House, Covent Garden, London, April 24, 1946, with Margot Fonteyn, Pamela May, Moira Shearer, Michael Somes, Henry Danton, and Brian Shaw. First presented in the United States by the Sadler's Wells Ballet at the Metropolitan Opera House, New York, October 12, 1949.

This classic dance ballet is arranged to Franck's *Symphonic Variations* for piano and orchestra. There is no story, only a mood created by the setting and costumes, the music, and the dancers' response to it.

When the curtain rises, six dancers are on stage. Three girls stand forward in a line parallel to the front of the stage. In the back, turned away from us, are three boys. The backdrop is of abstract design: curved and slanting black lines on a light-green cloth.

The orchestra begins. The dancers do not move: they stand quietly in youthful meditation on the music. Directly the piano begins, the girls commence to dance. As if activated only by the instrument, they pause as the orchestra takes up the theme. A variation on the theme is stated, and one of the boys comes forward. He takes turns dancing with the three girls, then remains still as they dance about him. Now he holds the girls, one by one, as they whirl in his arms.

The girls rest as the two other boys join the leading male soloist in a line similar to that which was formed at the beginning by the three girls. The three dance—the two boys on the outside miming in motion the part of the orchestra, while the soloist, in the center, takes the part of the piano. The boys dance now to the girls, who respond to their statement of a theme. Two of the girls dance alone, then with one of the boys. They retire; another boy takes the center of the stage and dances a variation.

The principal ballerina now comes forward and, while the boys in the background dance quietly, she moves with sweet splendor to the music of the piano. The male soloist joins her, and they dance a *pas de deux*.

After this romantic sequence, all six dancers move together. Now they are not so much separate individuals responding to the music, as one group animated by the same theme. The boys and girls divide, come together in couples, and make swift, open patterns about the stage while the music rushes toward its conclusion. Their swift ebullience is broken at the end, as the dancers resume the meditative poses with which the ballet began.

1952, in a new version with choreography by Frederick Ashton, and with Margot Fonteyn, Michael Somes, and Alexander Grant in the leading roles.

SYMPHONIE CONCERTANTE

> Classic ballet in three movements. Music by Wolfgang Amadeus Mozart. Choreography by George Balanchine. Scenery and costumes by James Stewart Morcom. Lighting by Jean Rosenthal. First presented by Ballet Society at the City Center, New York, November 12, 1947, with Maria Tallchief, Tanaquil LeClercq, and Todd Bolender in the principal roles.

Set to Mozart's *Sinfonia Concertante in E-flat major, for Violin and Viola* (K.364), this ballet follows closely the design of the music. It has no story. Its gold backdrop represents the formal classical frame into which both music and dancing fit. The three parts correspond to the three movements of the score. There are two ballerinas, corresponding to the solo instruments, a *danseur*, a group of six secondary soloists, and a *corps de ballet* of sixteen dancers.

FIRST MOVEMENT—ALLEGRO MAESTOSO: The curtain rises and the stage is empty. The music begins, allegro maestoso. After the opening chords, eight dancers emerge from either side of the stage, dancing to the light, quick rhythm of the music. They arrange themselves in a pattern that encloses the front part of the stage. The six soloists enter and dance in a close line. Now they move to the back and dance forward in rapid, crossing diagonals.

The introductory passage is over. Quietly the solo instruments are heard. All the dancers move to the sides of the stage, and slowly the ballerinas enter at the back. They meet in the center of the stage and dance together. Then, as the violin alone is heard against the orchestra, one of the ballerinas dances briefly alone. The other ballerina succeeds her as the viola returns with the same melody. The two dancers follow the turns of the solo instruments throughout the ballet, dancing together and alternately. They do not represent the instruments in any literal sense; their dances are simply accompanied by the instruments. The ballerinas leave the stage when the violin and viola are silent, returning when the instruments are heard again. Three girls enter with each of the ballerinas in turn and support them in brief, extended poses, after which the two dance together.

The opening section of the first movement is now repeated. The *corps de ballet* kneels, and the two ballerinas enter as they did at the beginning. The violin, which took priority over the viola, now takes a secondary position. The ballerinas dance closely together, almost touching, as the two instruments intertwine the melody. One of the ballerinas supports the other as the violin plays in the background against the dominant viola. Then both pirouette off while the *corps de ballet* accompanies the final orchestral bars. All kneel on the last chord.

SECOND MOVEMENT—ANDANTE: The six soloists remain on stage as the *corps* exits. The second movement begins, and the girls dance forward slowly. They separate and retire as the two ballerinas enter with the *danseur*, who supports each of the girls in turn to the music. When the principal theme of the movement is stated by the orchestra, the six soloists cross the stage with measured pace. The *danseur* leads the ballerinas to the back, the soloists dance, then the ballerinas move forward again to dance to the intricate alternation of violin and viola. The movement ends as softly as it began. As the three principals exit, the six soloists enclose them in a moving semicircle.

THIRD MOVEMENT—PRESTO: To the high-spirited, joyous finale, the two ballerinas and their partner take turns in dancing alone and in the brief duets and trios. The *corps de ballet* forms a moving background to their movements. Each of the principals circles the stage brilliantly. The dancing becomes brisk with the clipped, delightful cheerfulness of the music. The girls flick their wrists elegantly as the movement draws to its conclusion, then dance together with the principals, who kneel before the group as the ballet ends.

NOTES: This ballet is a good example of how dancing might aid appreciation of the music. Mozart's *Sinfonia Concertante* is long and difficult; to the inexperienced listener it might be boring; perhaps only the musician likes it immediately. The ballet, on the other hand, fills the time measured by the music with movement and seems to shorten the length of the music. What seemed dull at a first *hearing*, is not so dull when the ballet is first *seen*.

It is interesting that although Mozart wrote no music for ballet, of all composers his music is most adaptable for ballet, of all composers his music is the most danceable. Children who hear Mozart's music without knowing what it is, instinctively wish to dance to it. They appreciate its true quality better than their elders, who are often too impressed by Mozart's greatness to listen to his work with unaffected ears.

SYMPHONY IN C

Classic ballet in four movements. Music by Georges Bizet. Choreography by George Balanchine. First presented under the title *Le Palais de Cristal* by the Paris Opéra Ballet at the Opéra, July 28, 1947, with Lycette Darsonval, Tamara Toumanova, Micheline Bardin, Madeleine Lafon, Alexandre Kaliujny, Roger Ritz, Michel Renault, and Max Bozzoni as principals. Scenery and costumes by Léonor Fini. First presented in the United States by Ballet Society at the City Center, New York, March 22, 1948, with Maria Tallchief, Tanaquil LeClercq, Beatrice Tompkins, Elise Reiman, Nicholas Magallanes, Francisco Moncion, Herbert Bliss, and Lew Christensen in the principal roles. Staged by the Royal Danish Ballet at the Royal Theatre, Copenhagen, October 4, 1952, with Margrethe Schanne, Mona Vangsaa, Inge Sand, Kirstin Ralov, Frank Schaufuss, Borge Ralov, Erik Bruhn, and Stanley Williams.

Symphony in C is not based on a story, but on the music to which it is danced. Bizet's symphony is in four movements; each of these movements develops different themes, different melodies. Correspondingly, in the ballet, there is a different dance scheme and development for each of these four movements. Each movement has its own characteristic ballerina, *premier danseur*, and *corps de ballet*. Toward the end of the ballet, when the different groups have danced their special parts of the symphony, all the groups combine with their ballerinas for a kind of dance summing up of all that has gone before. There is no scenery, only a blue background; the dancers are dressed in classical ballet costumes.

FIRST MOVEMENT—ALLEGRO VIVO: The curtain rises before the music begins. Two small groups of girls begin to dance with the opening chord. As the orchestra plays the first theme and repeats it, the two groups dance in opposition, first dancing all together, then alternately following the movements of two leaders.

The ballerina appears as the second theme is announced by the oboe and strings. She dances forward in crisp, open movements to the rhythm of the melody, turning gracefully as she poses and balancing for a moment as she waits for the theme to begin anew. Her dance now becomes brisk and flourishing. She pirouettes swiftly as the two soloists join her, balances again briefly, and leaves the stage.

After the orchestra has given an intimation of the first theme and horns have played a short transition, two boys enter to support the soloists. The ballerina returns with her partner. She dances around the stage, retires to the rear, and, as the first theme of the movement returns, leads the ensemble. On the last clipped chord she stands supported in a quick, graceful pose.

SECOND MOVEMENT—ADAGIO: The corps de ballet moves slowly to the introductory passage. A second ballerina enters with her partner as the soft central theme of the movement is sounded by the oboe. She is lifted low off the floor and moves as if in slow motion, then is lifted high, her legs describing sweeping arcs in the air. Her partner supports her in long, slow lifts and held poses while the corps de ballet gathers about her. As the movement ends, the ballerina falls back in her partner's arms.

THIRD MOVEMENT—ALLEGRO VIVACE: Here the music is spirited and lively. Six girls, in a third corps de ballet, dance forward; two couples join them to leap across the stage; and, finally, a third ballerina and her partner enter to circle the stage in broad leaps. They dance together briefly, turning rapidly in the air together, and rush off into the wings. Soon they return, repeat their dance, and lead the corps de ballet to the bright, ebullient music. At one point the boy lifts the ballerina off the floor and drops her, pushing her forward, so that she seems to bounce to the music. The entire group joins in the final measures, the corps de ballet kneeling as the ballerina is held in a graceful pose at the last chord.

FOURTH MOVEMENT—ALLEGRO VIVACE: In the final movement, the principals of the first three movements join with a fourth ballerina and her partner in an exhilarating display of virtuosity that becomes at times a contest. The fourth ballerina and her accompanying group dance first. They are followed by the ballerina of the first movement and her corps de ballet. The ballerina of the Adagio movement appears next, then the ballerina of the third movement.

The thirty-two girls who have made up the four *corps de ballet* now line the stage at the sides and across the back. All four ballerinas dance in their midst, each executing the same brilliant steps. Their partners enter for their turn, while secondary soloists dance behind them. At the close, all forty-eight dancers—soloists and *corps de ballet*—join the principals in a brilliant finale. As the last chord of the music sounds, the ballerinas turn quickly and fall back over their partners' arms as the secondary soloists are lifted high behind them in a climactic tableau.

NOTES: *Symphony in C* was originally mounted for the Paris Opéra during my visit there as guest choreographer in 1947. For the Opéra, I staged revivals of three ballets: *Apollo*, *Le Baiser de la Fée*, and *Serenade*, and although the two latter ballets had never been seen in Paris before, at the end of my engagement I wished to stage a new work especially for the principal dancers of the Opéra.

It seemed fitting to select for this new work music by a French composer. I accordingly chose the little-known *Symphony in C major* written by the French master Bizet when he was only seventeen years old. Composition of the ballet was completed in about two weeks.

The ballet was staged for Ballet Society in New York the following spring. When this company became the New York City Ballet seven months later, *Symphony in C* was the concluding ballet on the first program. The ballet has been a part of the permanent repertory of the New York City Ballet ever since.

In September 1952, after the conclusion of the New York City Ballet's first European tour, I traveled to Copenhagen, Denmark, to select the dancers and begin rehearsals for a production of *Symphony in C* by the Royal Danish Ballet. Vida Brown, my assistant, remained in Denmark to rehearse the ballet completely and to see it through the final stages of production.

THEME AND VARIATIONS

Classic ballet. Music by Peter Ilyich Tchaikovsky. Choreography by George Balanchine. Scenery and costumes by Woodman Thompson. First presented by Ballet Theatre at the City Center, New York, November 26, 1947, with Alicia Alonso and Igor Youskevitch in the leading roles.

In addition to his ballet scores, Tchaikovsky composed a great deal of music ideal for dancing. This was perhaps natural for a man who had discovered in ballet a genuine inspiration. Between the time of his first ballet, *Swan Lake* (1877), and his second, *The Sleeping Beauty* (1890), Tchaikovsky wrote four orchestral suites. They were not composed for dancing, yet to listen to them is to think immediately of dancing. They remind us that it is a pity that the composer was not, during this period, a favorite of his contemporary choreographers.

In 1933 I arranged the ballet *Mozartiana* to the fourth of these orchestral suites. *Theme and Variations* is arranged to the final movement of the *Suite No. 3, in G*. This is a dance ballet; like *Ballet Imperial*, it evokes that great period in classical dancing when Russian ballet flourished with the aid of Tchaikovsky's music.

When the curtain rises, we see that the setting is formal: the scene is a great ballroom with huge, towering pillars decorated with vines, luxurious red draperies, and crystal chandeliers containing thousands of candles. A formal garden can be seen in the background. There is a *corps de ballet* of twelve girls arranged in two groups about the ballerina and the *premier danseur*. The girls are dressed in muted colors; the ballerina is in white with a coronol of white flowers. The *premier danseur* wears a blue costume and a blue beret embellished with a white plume.

The music begins, and the ballerina points her toe, dancing softly as the violins play the principal theme. Her steps are simple and graceful, like the melody, and with her feet she seems to point to the quiet charm of the music. Her partner similarly introduces the music and leaves the stage with the ballerina. The twelve girls move forward lightly. They dance a brief ensemble as the theme is repeated on insistent plucked strings to the accompaniment of flutes and clarinets.

Now the tempo increases. The ballerina returns and, surrounded by the *corps de ballet*, begins to display her virtuosity, whirling quickly and brightly in *fouettés* to a restatement of the theme which the strings treat like a *perpetuum mobile*.

The woodwinds announce the theme in a slower tempo; the *corps de ballet* of twelve girls divides into three close groups and describe shifting, flowing lines on the stage. The music becomes assertive again in the fourth variation. The full orchestra plays the theme with a flourish, and the *premier danseur* performs a graceful, yet animated, dance.

When the soloist has left the stage, the orchestra snaps the *corps de ballet* into movement with a sudden chord and plays a fast fugue to which the girls dance their first brilliant ensemble. Just as suddenly, the variation ends. The *premier danseur* now dances alone, describing diagonals across the stage with long, bold leaps. The music is staccato, the strings whirring in tarantella fashion to strong, persistent chords.

The seventh variation is a subdued and noble treatment of the theme. Four girls gather softly, hold hands, and move slowly on point. The ballerina enters. The girls cluster about her in a close semicircle. The English horn varies the theme, and the girls support the ballerina as she executes beautiful adagio movements.

The music trippingly accelerates. The ballerina separates herself from the *corps* and dances vigorously and joyously to the demanding rhythm, her pose changing with quick elegance to the beat of the music, her *pointes* stabbing at the floor in response to the sharp attack of the orchestra. She turns rapidly across the stage and pauses.

The *premier danseur* joins her. A solo violin sounds the melody, and a *pas de deux* begins. Its beginning is softly playful; but as a new variation sweeps the orchestra into a piercing, flowing melody, the dancing is noble and tender. To this theme of open joy and romance the ballerina, supported by her partner, executes slowly and perfectly movements—simple, yet also difficult—that display her full beauty.

When the two principals leave the stage, a drum roll sounds, followed by a bright fanfare on the horns. Eight boys enter with a flourish. The *corps de ballet* joins them, with the two principal dancers, as the orchestra announces with blaring pomp a regal polonaise. There are swift variations by the two principals—the ballerina accompanied by the girls; the *premier danseur*, by the boys—and rapid regroupings and shiftings of partners in the ensemble as the final variation increases in liveliness. The two principals, hand in hand, lead the dancers about the ballroom in a sweeping circle. There is vigorous dancing to the final crashes of music, and then, at the last chord, a tableau in which the ballerina is lifted high to her partner's shoulder while all her court salutes her.

NOTES: The principal *danseur* in *Theme and Variations* has been danced only by Igor Youskevitch. The part of the ballerina has been danced by Diana Adams, Nora Kaye, Mary Ellen Moylan, Maria Tallchief, and Melissa Hayden, in addition to Alicia Alonso. The ballet has been performed by Ballet Theatre on its European and South American tours and on its annual tours of the United States.

THE THIEF WHO LOVED A GHOST

An entertainment. Music by Carl Maria von Weber, arranged by Hershy Kay. Choreography by Herbert Ross and John Ward. Scenery and costumes by John Ward. First presented at the Y.M.H.A., New York, October 14, 1950. Presented by Ballet Theatre at the Metropolitan Opera House, New York, April 11, 1951, with a cast that included John Kriza, Ruth Ann Koesun, Ilona Murai, and Lucia Chase.

The originators of this work properly call it an "entertainment," rather than a ballet. As its title suggests, *The Thief Who Loved a Ghost* is a story ballet. The plot, which is rather tricky, moves so rapidly that we are continually asking what has happened right in the midst of a further complication, and some knowledge of the story is necessary if we are to follow it at all.

The entertainment begins with a loud, crashing overture. The curtain rises, and there is a drop curtain that gives us the name of the piece. Suddenly all is quiet. Lights come up in back of the curtain, and we find ourselves looking into the windows of a house. The curtains are drawn, and we can make out only silhouettes, but we can see plainly that a large party is going on; dancing couples waltz by.

The thief enters on the right. He walks carefully like a trained footpad and watches the window of the house with interest. He leaves the stage. In a window of the house we see the shadows of a man and woman talking together. An arm reaches out from nowhere and grabs the woman's necklace from her throat. She screams! We hear a shrill police whistle, and, mounted on shining bicycles, policemen race across the stage to the scene of the robbery.

A detective comes in and with his flashlight searches for the thief. The music is soft and spooky. He goes up to the window and peers into the house. Just then the thief sneaks in. Someone spots him, he runs off the stage, and the idle policemen climb on the bicycles and pursue him.

Now the scene shifts. We find ourselves in a run-down, old-fashioned house inhabited by two former ballerinas. There are cobwebs everywhere, a ramshackle piano, a broken-down gramophone. One of the ballerinas, dressed in black, sits on a trunk filled with momentos of her past glories. She is as grotesque as the house she lives in and she dances absurdly to prove that she is still capable of exciting some kind of attention. The other ballerina, who is more modest, if less sane, makes her entrance holding a pair of curtains before her face.

With this strange couple lives a beautiful young girl. She comes into the room, dressed in baby blue with a pink ribbon in her hair, and prepares for a dancing lesson. The woman in white peeps through the curtains she carries, and the woman in black fights her. There is a serious question, apparently, about who is to give the girl the lesson. The woman in white tries to prove that she is the more talented teacher by giving us a display of her specialty. The lights go down, and she begins to dance with the draperies, swirling them about her body and making diaphanous figures in the air, something in the manner of Loie Fuller's famous moth dance (circa 1901). A spotlight shifts its color rapidly as it shines on the dancer, and her veils become wings, multicolored wings that seem to carry her off her feet. Finally she swoops down like a bat, kneels, and the dance is over.

The girl kisses her, the hag in black kisses her, and everyone is happy. The girl is alone for a moment, but soon the woman in black is back in the room instructing her on the dance. She takes the girl about the waist and dances her around the room as if she were her handsome cavalier. The ex-ballerina is so enchanted with her pupil's progress that she opens her treasure trunk and drags out blue gauze draperies to present to her.

The room is empty. The music sounds a warning. The creature in black sneaks back in to take a drink out of a dusty decanter. The thief steps into the room. He starts to flee when he sees the woman, but she grabs him, forces him to dance with her, and offers him a drink. To her, he is just a handsome young man who happens to be down-and-out at the moment, and she is delighted to have his company. More simply, he is the first man fool enough to enter her house.

The thief soon has enough of her fulsome attention and leaves the room through a curtained doorway. His hostess runs off to get the girl and brings her in. The backdrop rises, and the exterior of the house can be seen. The girl climbs a tree and looks into the room where the thief is hiding. He sits in a chair, fast asleep. The girl goes to him, drapes the blue gauze about him, and wakes him up. It is still dark, and he is sure he is seeing a ghost. He touches the girl.

But the girl is a docile ghost. He follows her, clutching the stolen necklace in his hand. When he enters the dance studio, he drops the necklace in the trunk and begins a dance with the girl. She is very small and light beside him, and he lifts her high, so that her veils flutter in the air over his head. At the end of the romantic duet, the girl rushes to the trunk to retrieve the necklace. The thief heads her off, throws open the trunk, and puts the string of diamonds about her neck. The girl runs off and he follows her.

The backdrop falls into place again; and without the night sky, the room is almost completely dark. The black witch enters carrying a candle. The girl, lost in a romantic daze, joins her. The woman demands the necklace. She is frantic to touch the diamonds and persists so much that the outraged girl finally throw sthe necklace on the floor and leaves her. The woman takes all of her old costume jewelry out of the trunk and puts it on. The mad woman in white returns, still carrying her draperies.

The detective comes in and inquires of the woman in black if she has seen a thief. She flirts with him. The police enter and search the house. Nothing can be found. Everyone leaves, and the thief and the girl are seen dancing alone to a violin solo. The woman in white watches them from between her draperies. Suddenly the thief can no longer believe that his love is a ghost; he takes off her gauze headdress. At this point the police find him. The thief runs. The woman in white helps him make a getaway on one of the bicycles. The girl jumps on the bike with him, and they race off, presumably to live happily ever after. The tardy police give up the chase and leave the two mad women alone. The woman in black goes to the gramophone, reaches into the loud-speaker, and pulls out the necklace. She is not as mad as we might think.

THE THREE-CORNERED HAT

Dramatic ballet in one act. Music by Manuel de Falla. Choreography by Leonide Massine. Book by Martinez Sierra. Scenery and costumes by Pablo Picasso. First presented by Diaghilev's Ballets Russes at the Alhambra Theatre, London, July 22, 1919, with Leonide Massine as the *Miller*, Tamara Karsavina as the *Miller's Wife*, Leon Woicikowski as the *Corregidor*, and Stanislas Idzikowski as the *Dandy*. First presented in the United States by the Ballet Russe de Monte Carlo at the St. James Theatre, New York, March 9, 1934, with Leon Woicikowski as the *Miller* and Tamara Toumanova as the *Miller's Wife*.

The Three-Cornered Hat tells a love story of Spain with humor and warmth. The scene is a small Spanish village. The Spanish tone of the ballet is established immediately by the music, by cries of *"Olé! Olé! Olé! Olé!"* from behind the curtain, and by the sound of rhythmic castanets, dancing feet, and hand clapping.

The curtain rises on the village scene. The village miller stands before his house, whistling to a black bird who sits in a cage. The bird will not sing as he wishes it to. The miller's wife comes out of the house and teases her husband. He chases her and they embrace.

The couple go to the well to draw water. While the miller is busy at the well, a dandy passes by and blows kisses to his wife, who responds flirtatiously. The miller looks up and sees this exchange and chases the dandy off. He is not angry with his wife. He is delighted that other men find her as beautiful as he does. They are very much in love.

Now the governor of the province, the corregidor, enters with an escort. A doddering old fool, he looks absurd in his finery among the simple folk of the village. He wears a three-cornered hat, symbol of his class and position. Almost immediately the corregidor eyes the miller's wife and decides that she must be his. The miller's wife is polite to him, but no more. He passes on. Noting that his wife is getting all the attention, the miller decides he'd better give another girl some favor. He playfully flirts with one of the lovely girls of the village. Now that both husband and wife have cause to be jealous, they are amused at each other and embrace.

The miller goes into the house. His wife, remaining outside, dances a brilliant *fandango*. The corregidor has come back and secretly watches her. Soon he approaches her and tries to make advances. The woman eludes him cleverly and flees. The old man, however, pursues her.

The miller has watched this scene from inside the house and runs out to help his wife. The corregidor can run no more and falls to the ground, exhausted. The miller and his wife pick him up, dust him off, and try to act as if it were all an accident, but the corregidor, furious with them, suggests that this is only the beginning of what they may expect of him. The husband and wife dance together.

Evening falls. The village folk come to the miller's house to join in a festival with the happy couple. The miller gives them wine and then dances alone a *farruca*, which everyone applauds. The villagers hear the approach of marching soldiers. The escorts of the corregidor enter. The men arrest the miller and take him off. Abandoned by her friends, the miller's wife is alone.

But not for long. The corregidor is back again, seeking her favor now with real determination. The miller's wife throws him to the ground as he clumsily holds her. He rises with difficulty and pursues her to the village bridge, which crosses a running stream. On the bridge, the corregidor again attempts to embrace the girl. In the process of pushing him away, the miller's wife pushes him off the bridge into the stream. She laughs at him, but helps the corregidor out of the water. But the old fool takes up the chase again. The miller's wife takes a gun from the house and, threatening the corregidor with buckshot, flees over the bridge away from the village.

The corregidor stands in front of the miller's house, alone, his clothes still dripping from the dunking he got in the stream. He takes off his outer garments and his three-cornered hat, lays them out to dry, and goes into the house to sleep.

Dawn comes. The miller has escaped the corregidor's henchmen and returns home. In front of his house he sees the corregidor's clothes and the three-cornered hat! Then he observes the corregidor himself, walking around in one of his own nightshirts! The miller decides there's only one thing to do. He will pursue the corregidor's wife, who is also young and beautiful! On the walls of his house he draws a caricature of the corregidor and leaves.

Now the poor corregidor is attacked by his own soldiers, who don't recognize him in the miller's nightshirt. He curses them, and the village folk come to see what the trouble is. The miller and his wife, who have found each other outside the town, come in. Their friends are told what the corregidor has tried to do, and in anger all the people rise up against the governor and his cohorts. The intruders are routed, and all dance triumphantly, led by the miller and his wife. A dummy representing the defeated corregidor is thrown higher and higher into the air by the crowd.

NOTES: Although Leon Woicikowski first danced the miller at the American *première* of *The Three-Cornered Hat*, Leonide Massine later danced the role in the United States. The ballet was revived by Massine for Ballet Theatre in 1943 and for the Sadler's Wells Ballet in 1947.

TIL EULENSPIEGEL

Ballet by Jean Babilée. Music by Richard Strauss. Choreography by Jean Babilée. Scenery and costumes by Tom Keogh. First presented by Les Ballets des Champs-Elysées, November 9, 1949, at the Théâtre des Champs-Elysées, Paris, with Jean Babilée in the title role. First presented in the United States by Ballet Theatre at the Metropolitan Opera House, New York, September 25, 1951, with a cast headed by Jean Babilée and Ruth Ann Koesun. Costumes by Helene Pons.

Richard Strauss's score *Til Eulenspiegel's Merry Pranks* was not composed to be danced, but the fact that the music has a plot and relates incidents in the life of one of the most popular figures in European folklore has made it naturally attractive to choreographers. Til Eulenspiegel is the perennial prankster who never seems to get his comeuppance. Although he may hurt people when he tricks them, he really has no harmful intentions; he is a maker of fun motivated by his own innocent pleasure and not by cunning. Such a man sooner or later runs into trouble with the law, for much as we may admire his artfulness and daring, the law will be more impressed with the number of his misdemeanors.

This ballet shows us the roguery of Til—his inability to conform to convention and his contempt for the law. Here his pranks are so good-humored that even the law is inclined to forgive him.

The curtain rises as the music begins. The scene is an improvised impression of an ancient market place. Against a mottled gray background, five colorful booths are arranged in a semicircle. The light is dim; spotlights shine down on the brightly colored awnings over the booths. A girl enters. She is small, has long blond hair, and wears a flowing dress. She dances across the market place to the soft opening bars of the music and disappears.

Two by two, a group of ragamuffin merchants march out to stand behind their booths and wait for customers. As soon as they are all stationed at their jobs, they look in unison from right to left. A quiet, impudent theme is heard in the orchestra, and the men sense that something is going on behind their backs. They are right. Til Eulenspiegel dances in. His face is chalk-white beneath his orange hair, but this does not disguise his expression of impudence. His dance is spontaneously graceful and grotesque at the same time; we imagine already that anything he does will be funny.

As he runs about the market place, Til almost collides with a young girl. Immediately he begins to make up to her. He kneels before her, begging for a mere glance. The girl, dressed in formal medieval costume, will have none of his impertinence and repulses him. This only encourages Til, who encircles her in a tumbling dance that infuriates the girl. When he sees that she does not like him, Til makes fun of her behind her back. The merchants are delighted. The girl orders him away. The exuberant Til complies and jumps up backward to sit on one of the booths. There he watches the girl with what seems to be an innocent eye. But the cymbals crash, the music bursts into a loud ruckus. At a sudden signal from Til, all the merchants jump out from behind their booths. They grab the girl and toss her in the air. She crawls off, disheveled, on all fours—no longer a charming young lady: Til's magic has turned her into a witch.

Til and the merchants go back to their booths. A courtly theme is heard, and a gentleman enters with his lady. Til is very amused at their formal ways and laughs at the flowing feather in the gentleman's cap. They try not to notice him, but Til forces himself between them and tries to engage the lady's attention. He jumps up and down in his excitement to please her. He pleads with her to notice him and to send her escort away so that they may dance together alone. The lady, however, is shocked by this behavior. Unfortunately her escort cannot assist her, for just as he flirts with the lady, Til is also trying to humiliate the gentleman. He runs out and returns quickly, dressed in a hat filled with variously colored long-flowing feathers. When he bows to the lady, these absurd feathers reach to the floor. She now thinks him ridiculous as well as rude and will never respond to his advances. Til must have his good-humored revenge. He throws down his hat with a flourish at the lady's feet and challenges her lover to a duel. The lady is aghast as the two men assume dueling stances before her. The merchants applaud the combat. The two duelists rush each other, turn each other upside down in a cart wheel of movement, and roll over and over together, their bodies joined in a tumbling hoop. The gentleman has clearly had enough by this time and, seizing his lady by the hand, dashes off.

No sooner have they departed than a group of ragged hunchbacks come into the market place, begging for alms. The lights dim, Til runs out, and the merchants hide behind their booths. Now Til is back again, but dressed in a long black cape and a high-peaked hat. He, too, is a hunchback all of a sudden; he joins the pilgrimage of the stricken men. The men accept him as their equal in misery and marvel when by a quick miracle he is cured: the hump on his back has vanished! They congratulate him on his cure and, to ensure a cure for themselves, do what Til anticipated: they give him all their money and walk out of the square, certain that this tribute to one of their former fellows will hasten their own recovery. The wealthy Til rids himself of cap and cloak and counts his fortune.

His girl, Nell, the blonde who appeared at the beginning of the ballet, comes into the square. In the soft light, she and Til dance together. Now completely happy, he swings her around and around in the air. A distant trumpet call is heard; Til cups his hand to his ear for a moment to listen, but then continues with the dance. He and Nell rush off into the night together.

The trumpet theme grows in the orchestra. Til runs back in and circles the stage in leaps timed to its open, joyous melody. The merchants jump out from behind their booths, tear down the awnings, and—using the awning poles for lances—surround him in a mock military drill. Til, in the center, jumps up and down in glee. The merchants form a parade and rush around the stage. At the theme's fullest crescendo, Til leaps onto their backs and rides high above them in triumph.

But the theme is cut short sharply. There is a menacing drum roll, the theme of the gallows, and ominous, plodding music changes Til's ebullience into fear. Six soldiers dash in and rush him. Til runs for one of the booths, but the soldiers jump up after him. Til escapes between their legs and hides underneath. Til's impudent theme, sounded by the clarinet, laughs at the loud, heavy theme of the law. The soldiers gang up on him again; again he escapes and the music ridicules them. Finally they grab him and hold him securely after a long tussle.

One of the soldiers runs off. He returns with a judge and a hangman. Til's legs run in the air as he is held motionless; he wraps his legs around one of the soldiers in his fright. The judge flourishes a scroll and begins to read the indictment against Til for all his crimes. The criminal is led forward, his head bowed. A soldier kneels down to form the chopping block, and Til is placed across it. The hangman aims the ax. The sonorous theme of authority is sounded firmly; Til's merry theme reaches a high shriek of terror and disintegrates as it descends the scale. There is a moment of silence. Still the ax is posed above Til, but the executioner does not move. Nell enters on the right. The judge, the executioner, the soldiers—all turn to look at her. They pardon Til because of the reality of his love for her and imagine that with Nell he will lead a less prankish life. His head still on the block, Til anxiously feels the back of his neck. He looks up carefully. When he sees that they don't intend to execute him, after all, he rushes over to Nell and kneels to her in gratitude. He touches her hands then, and they dance briefly.

Now that everything is back to normal, now that he still has his neck and his Nell, Til reverts instantly to his old ways: he runs over, assaults the judge, and berates him for treating him like a common criminal! Before the judge can retaliate, Til has run off after Nell.

NOTES: Reviewing the first American performance of *Til Eulenspiegel* in the New York *Herald Tribune*, Walter Terry wrote:

> Possible choreographic treatments of the theme are numberless. Some would wish a theatre piece to stress the social implications of the character with respect to medieval mores; others might desire Til's inherent brutality to be accented; still others might request ribaldry or period color or bouncy humor. Any, all and still others constitute valid approaches to a theatrical treatment of Til. Mr. Babilée has elected to touch upon several of these possibilities and he has come up with a handsome and engaging ballet. His is a balletic survey of Til, his character, his pranks and his era.

In his ballet, Mr. Babilée has shown us Til the Knave, Til the Impostor, Til the Clown and, briefly, Til the Near-Punished, and the incidents selected to tell his tale include the transforming of a lady into a witch, the inciting of a duel, stealing from pilgrims and his rescue from judgment by Nell, the one girl he loves. The scene is a market place, splashed brightly with colors we have come to associate with medieval art and peopled with those who are rough and ready, those who are savoring the elegance of gentility, those who are cruel, those who are forlorn.

Against this background and amidst this throng, Til Eulenspiegel accomplishes his rogueries. Mr. Babilée has kept his ballet active but uncluttered. Pictorial values are many, choreographic sequences are logical and dramatic and freshness of movement invention gives the ballet vitality, wit and point. It is a highly refreshing dance creation and, I believe, an important addition to Ballet Theatre's expansive repertory.

As Til, Mr. Babilée performed wonderfully, showing us still another, and unexpected, facet of his dance genius. He has given us the somber, violent figure in 'Le Jeune Homme et la Mort,' the lyrical and remote Cupid in 'L'Amour et Son Amour' and a virtuosic 'Bluebird.' Here his gift for comedy reveals himself as a superb humorist, using gesture, dance and acting to create the bold lines of caricature and the penetrating lines of characterization.

Babilée's *Til Eulenspiegel* was the second ballet based on Richard Strauss's famous score. The first was by Vaslav Nijinsky, whose last ballet it was. Nijinsky's *Til* was presented for the first time by Diaghilev's Ballets Russes at the Manhattan Opera House, New York, October 23, 1916. The scenery and costumes were by Robert Edmond Jones. Carl van Vechten wrote of this performance:

> *Til Eulenspiegel* is the only new ballet the Russians have produced in America. In selecting this work and in his arrangement of the action Nijinsky was moved, no doubt, by consideration for the limitations of the company as it existed. The scenery and costumes by Robert E. Jones, New York, were decidedly diverting—the best work this talented young man has done, I think. Over a deep, spreading background of ultramarine, the crazy turrets of medieval castles leaned dizzily to and fro. The costumes were exaggerations of the exaggerated fashions of the Middle Ages. Mr. Jones added feet of stature to the already elongated peaked headdresses of the period. The trains of the velvet robes, which might have extended three yards, were allowed to trail the full depth of the Manhattan Opera House stage. The colors were oranges, reds, greens, and blues, those indeed of Bakst's *Scheherazade,* but so differently disposed that they made an entirely dissimilar impression. The effect reminded one spectator of a Spanish omelet.
>
> In arranging the scenario, Nijinsky followed in almost every detail Wilhelm Klatte's description of the meaning of the music, which is printed in programme books whenever the tone-poem is performed, without Strauss' authority, but sometimes with his sanction. Nijinsky was quite justified in altering the end of the work, which hangs the rogue-hero, into another practical joke. His version of this episode

fits the music and, in the original *Til Eulenspiegel*, Til is not hanged, but dies in bed. The keynote of Nijinsky's interpretation was gaiety. He is as utterly picaresque as the work itself; he reincarnated the spirit of Gil Blas; indeed, a new quality crept into stage expression through this characterization. Margaret Wycherly, one of the most active admirers of the dancer, told me after the first performance that she felt that he had for the first time leaped into the hearts of the great American public, whose appreciation of his subtler art as expressed in *Narcisse*, *Petrouchka*, and even *Scheherazade*, had been more moderate. There were those who protested that this was not the Til of the German legends, but any actor who attempts to give form to a folk or historical character, or even a character derived from fiction is forced to run counter to many an observer's preconceived ideas.

TIRESIAS

Dramatic ballet in three scenes. Music by Constant Lambert. Choreography by Frederick Ashton. Book by Constant Lambert. Scenery and costumes by Isabel Lambert. First presented by the Sadler's Wells Ballet at the Royal Opera House, Covent Garden, London, July 9, 1951, with Margot Fonteyn and Michael Somes as *Tiresias*.

This dramatic ballet tells the story of Tiresias, the ancient soothsayer who figures so prominently in the classical Greek drama and epic poetry. Tiresias was a blind soothsayer, a blind *seer*, a man to whom blindness was a kind of power, enabling him to see through the darkness that surrounded so many characters in Greek mythology. There are many stories about how he became blind and how he acquired his power of prophecy. The ballet relates one of these stories.

SCENE ONE — THE ISLAND OF CRETE: The scene is laid in the sunny island of Crete, in the eastern Mediterranean. After the rise of a decorative drop curtain, we find ourselves in a tremendous gymnasium, where warriors and young Cretan girls test their strength and skill in ancient sports. Tiresias, young prince of Crete, joins the athletes and shows them how to execute the difficult feats they are trying to achieve. The warriors, carrying shields and long spears, gather about Tiresias after he has shown the people that he is their natural peer. The warriors cross their spears and lift the triumphant Tiresias aloft.

A young girl enters and informs Tiresias that the priestesses of the land have decided to reward him for his prowess. He is presented with a magic wand and finds himself alone on the scene with his new-found power. Two snakes slither into the gymnasium. Before he realizes what he has done, Tiresias approaches to kill them; he strikes the female serpent dead. As the snake dies, Tiresias' sex changes: he is no longer the handsome young Cretan prince, but a beautiful young girl.

SCENE TWO—IN THE MOUNTAINS: Tiresias, the girl, is alone in a pastoral scene. Rural folk enter and try to distract her, but she is not moved by them. Soon she is attracted to a young man. He responds to her beauty, and the shepherds and shepherdesses pay tribute to their love. Again the young girl of the first scene presents Tiresias with the wand of the priestesses. Again two snakes appear. This time Tiresias kills the male and, as the curtain falls, becomes a man.

SCENE THREE—A PALACE: In their Olympian palace the all-powerful Zeus and his wife, Hera, are arguing about which is happier in love: man or woman? Hera claims that man's is the better lot, whereas Zeus takes woman's part. Neither one of the royal pair will give in to the other, and they call upon Tiresias to give an answer. Tiresias is now an old man. He approaches the god and goddess, who stand at the rear on high platforms above their court. They demand that he settle their dispute.

Tiresias answers that a woman has more pleasure in love. As Zeus rejoices in this decision, Hera angrily strikes the old man blind. He falls and struggles about the stage helplessly on his hands and feet. Zeus compensates for his wife's cruelty by endowing Tiresias with the power of prophecy. Again he is presented with a magic wand, which he uses as a staff to guide him on his way.

TYL ULENSPIEGEL

Dramatic ballet in two scenes. Music by Richard Strauss. Choreography by George Balanchine. Scenery and costumes by Esteban Frances. Lighting by Jean Rosenthal. First presented by the New York City Ballet at the City Center, New York, November 14, 1951, with Jerome Robbins as *Tyl*, Brooks Jackson as *Philip II*, and Frank Hobi and Beatrice Tompkins as the *Duke* and *Duchess of Alba*.

"Two babes are born—the one in Spain, the Infante Philip; the other in Flanders, the son of Claes, who shall later be called Ulenspiegel. Philip will grow up an executioner, being engendered by Charles V, the destroyer of the country. Ulenspiegel will be a great master of jolly words and youthful pranks but goodhearted withal, having had for father, Claes the valiant laborer, who knows how to earn his bread bravely, honestly and simply . . . Ulenspiegel, ever young and deathless, will roam the world, settling nowhere. He will be peasant, noble, painter, sculptor—all in one. And throughout the world he will go praising all good and lovely things and flouting loudly all stupidities."

This prediction, at the beginning of Charles de Coster's nineteenth-century epic, *The Glorious Adventures of Tyl Ulenspiegel*, contains in small the plot of this mime-spectacle. Tyl is not here the general mythic figure; he is specifically Flemish—the liberator of his country from the Spanish invaders led by King Philip II's henchman, the Duke of Alba. The careers of Philip, king of blood, and Tyl, king of the people, run parallel throughout the ballet, as they do in De Coster's novel; whenever they meet, there is a contest. The ballet *Tyl Ulenspiegel* begins in their youth.

SCENE ONE: A long drum roll, which gradually increases in volume, sounds a prologue to Strauss's score. The thundering drum presages a storm at sea. The curtain rises on a warm, dark room. On the right, a candle flickers in a tall candelabrum. In the center, across the room, is a long table draped in black and gold and emblazoned with the arms of Death. The top of the table is checkered, like a chessboard, and standing at the head of the table is a fleet of ship models—caravels, frigates, and sloops. Tyl Ulenspiegel, as a child, stands at the foot of the table, clutching a loaf of bread. He looks up at the beautiful ships of black and gold and marvels at them. Prince Philip, as a child, all in black, sneaks out from behind the ships and stares down the table at Tyl. He challenges the peasant by pushing one of the ships forward on the chessboard. Tyl moves forward his loaf of bread. Philip counters by challenging him with a larger ship, but Tyl persists and pushes the bread toward the center of the table. Philip moves out his greatest man-of-war. Now the two boys stand close. Quickly Philip grabs the loaf of bread and tries to make off with it. Tyl holds the bread secure, and the two begin to fight. They chase each other around the table and disappear for a moment. The drum roll ends.

Strauss's music begins, and Tyl and Philip, now grown to manhood, stand up behind the table. Tyl stretches, as if awakening from a long sleep. But the two immediately begin to fight again, as they did when they were children. Tyl holds the same loaf of bread, and Philip, armed with a sword, tries to capture it. Tyl eludes him. Now, re-acting their childish chess game in earnest, Philip attacks Tyl. Tyl cleverly dodges the king's sword and ensnares him in a fishing net. Philip drops the weapon and runs away. The orchestra sounds a solemn chord as the scene blacks out. A drop curtain falls.

Playful woodwinds sound the hero's theme, and Tyl comes out before the curtain. He scratches his head, smacks invisible lice, and smells the air, amused at his own filth. Then he turns rapidly and curls up on the ground, as if to go to sleep. He rises instantly when two figures bring out a huge magical mirror with no glass. Tyl puts on a hideous birdlike mask and terrifies himself by looking in the mirror. He stands on the mirror as it slides off into the wings.

SCENE TWO—FLANDERS: The drop curtain rises on sixteenth-century Flanders. The scene represents imaginatively any Flemish city of the period. In front of the backdrop runs the high street, which crosses over a small bridge at center. The backdrop is crowded with symbolism in the style of Hieronymus Bosch: high over the buildings of the city sits an owl, the symbol of heresy associated with Tyl Ulenspiegel. The colors are not brilliant, but soft and shaded yellows and browns—earth colors. Tyl is seen standing on the bridge. He looks down on the stage and sees a group of peasants begging in the street. He is hidden from view for a moment and re-emerges on stage in the guise of Death, his face masked in a hideous skull, his body draped in a sheet. He carries a long, sharp spear and steps carefully. The peasants don't seem to see him as he moves among them, stabbing them all, one by one. But suddenly cymbals crash, and they look up and see that they are being pursued by Death. Frantically, to a rattling crescendo, they rush out in terror, leaving all their belongings behind. Tyl scoops them all up, then throws them into his white cloak and runs off to the left.

The music grows quiet; gradually the peasants return to look for their things. They are all maimed—some with hunched backs, others with twisted or missing limbs—and grope their way about the stage pathetically. The Duke and Duchess of Alba, accompanied by their court, enter on the right as the orchestra plays a courtly theme. They hold their heads high above their stiff white collars; the black-and-gold of their splendid dresses contrasts strangely with the plainness of their surroundings. Four Spanish soldiers follow them and push the crowd back with their spears. The ducal party bows low as King Philip enters. He crosses the street and stands at the left, where all come to do obeisance before him.

A solo violin plaintively marks Tyl's return. He comes into the street disguised as a monk. He wiggles his finger at the Duchess of Alba, calling her to him. She approaches deferentially, but carefully. Tyl orders her to confess. The duchess hesitates for an instant, then leans over and whispers in his ear. Tyl's face lights up with amusement, then with lusty delight. He dismisses the duchess with a stern admonishment. As he turns to her, two soldiers drag a woman in bonds across the street. She is a heretic, on her way to be tortured. Tyl stands over her to bless her and, in the process, cuts her bonds. The woman runs off to the right before the soldiers notice. Pandemonium breaks out. Tyl helps out by pointing to the left, and the soldiers pursue their prey.

Tyl is lost in the crowd for a few seconds as Philip and his court make ready to depart. He drops his monk's disguise and runs into the street as a hideous, bent hag. He begs alms of the Duchess of Alba. The duchess looks about to be sure that none of the court will see her. Tyl grabs her lasciviously and covers his face with kisses. The duke turns to see what is happening and attacks Tyl. Tyl rolls a barrel toward him; the duke loses his balance and his dignity and ends up kicking wildly, with his head in the barrel, as Tyl renews his embrace with the duchess. Finally Tyl releases the duke, who flees with his wife. Tyl throws the barrel and his beggar's mask after them.

The stage darkens. Two by two, the Spanish soldiers return, seeking heretics in the night. They proceed stealthily, walking almost on tiptoe to soft, surreptitious music, holding their spears ready for attack. Tyl, dressed now in a long black cloak, his face disguised in a mask, brings his glassless mirror out to the center of the street. Soon Tyl has the soldiers jumping through the mirror at the same time and knocking each other down. Their spears clatter to the street. In the shadows, a crowd gathers on the bridge. They pelt the soldiers with the flaming fagots of the Inquisition. Tyl climbs up on the bridge to encourage the crowd. The frightened Spaniards flee. Tyl comes down to the street and dances a sprightly measure, happy at this momentary victory over the invaders. Nell, his wife, comes onto the scene and watches him lovingly. Tyl tears off the grotesque mask, goes to her, and puts his head in her lap. The scene blacks out.

Strauss's music has come full circle, and the first theme is heard again. King Philip and his court promenade in the street and stand in a group at the left. A line of soldiers protects them from the mob. Tyl's theme is heard on the horns. The knave, now bearded, rushes in disguised as a painter, palette and brush in hand. He observes the royal tableau before him thoughtfully. Philip and his court preen themselves. Tyl rushes over to the group, redisposing the court about the king. Now Philip rests his foot on the back of a nobleman and is surrounded by upturned faces. Tyl instructs all the court to bow to the king. As the Duchess of Alba bends over to bow, Tyl looks up the back of her dress, snickers, and kicks her royally. The duchess turns on him. But Tyl cannot understand what she is talking about. He gestures helplessly to the members of the court, all of whom, one by one, look at their king.

Tyl rushes over to an imaginary wall and rapidly paints the group as he sees it. The king becomes impatient and demands to see the artist's work. Tyl allows them to break their pose and all gather about him. He unveils his painting. All are astonished to see—nothing! The music sounds a crescendo of whirring, blaring triumph for Tyl. Tyl runs off laughing, pursued closely by the king's soldiers.

The street darkens. The soldiers stand in an implacable line across the front of the stage, their long spears crossed before them. Tyl enters, and the people of the city rush up and reach their hands out to touch him through the barricade of soldiers. Horns and woodwinds play Tyl's theme and quietly mock the Spaniards. In the back, high over the city, great red flames of the Inquisition reach to the sky, engulfing all of Flanders. High over the ramparts of the city, an owl, symbol of Tyl's immortal life and wisdom, stands implacable—refusing to be consumed in the raging Spanish fire. A crowd gathers on the bridge. Suddenly Tyl is alone with the Duke of Alba and two of his men, who attack him with swords. Tyl draws his own sword and beats them all off, fighting fiercely and cleverly, duping the enemy one by one with his lithe tricks. The music mounts in volume. The fire over the city is snuffed out. Now Tyl urges the frightened people to come into the street and dances joyously. Men on the bridge attempt to raise the orange flag of Flanders. Cymbals crash and the music is victorious for an instant, but the men lose courage as they hear the sound of Spanish drums, proclaiming th burning of another heretic. Three inquisitors, in peaked black cloaks, thei faces hidden, come into the street with Philip and his court. Tyl Ulenspiege is the heretic! The inquisitors begin to pronounce sentence. Tyl's body be comes loose and disjointed, as if he had been hanged. He collapses as the music sounds low, frightening chords. He seems to die and lies down. Then he pulls over him an enormous skeleton; its bones are stark white from fire and Tyl drags it over his body. Now he rises and dances with the skeleton As he passes King Philip, he waves the bones of Flanders in his face. The king dies. Then Tyl throws the skeleton to the inquisitors. The inquisitor: lift their hoods, and we see that in reality they are rats. They attack the skeleton voraciously, gnawing away at the charred bones of the people.

The Flemings watch silently as King Philip is carried out, high over their heads, on a black catafalque. The king's courtiers move alongside hi: body, carrying back to Spain the small ships with sails of gold, the models o: his Invincible Armada.

No longer threatened now by the Spanish, Tyl relaxes. He yawns stretches, and curls up in the middle of the street. Then his body straightens and he dies. Four girls bring out a plot of grass, place it over him, and mark his grave with a wooden cross. Nell comes to weep at her husband's grave. All the people stand with bowed heads.

Tyl moves in his grave and pokes his head out to look at his weeping wife. He throws the grass off as if it were a blanket, rises, and embraces Nell Ulenspiegel, the spirit of Flanders, can sleep—but never dies. The lovers go off together as the people rejoice. The flag of Flanders at last flies free.

NOTES: Walter Terry described Jerome Robbins' performance in Tyl Ulenspiegel in the New York Herald Tribune:

> At the present, New York audiences are especially fortunate in having Mr. Robbins back as a dancer (as well as choreographer) with the New York City Ballet at the City Center. Furthermore, he has a great new role in which his dance genius can be experienced afresh. In George Balanchine's 'Tyl Ulenspiegel,' Mr. Robbins has a triumphal procession all his own as he unfolds, in dance terms, the biography of a legendary prankster-hero.
>
> In the latest balletic version of 'Tyl,' the rascal is shown as the liberator of Flanders from the Spanish invaders. Here, as Milton might describe it, his 'quips and cranks and wanton wiles' are directed against the enemy. By trickery, he rescues the sentenced; through valorous bravado, he duels for his cause; with wit, he makes a mockery of the would-be conquerors; he is everywhere at once, pricking pomp, creating chaos, having fun.
>
> And as Tyl, Mr. Robbins is fabulous. With a vulgar gesture or a mischievous glance, he can bring hilarity and, conversely, with a sag of the shoulders, he can rouse a tear for the weary and lonesome Tyl. Through the artistry of a great dancer, a myth has been humanized and, while Mr. Robbins is dancing, Tyl lives again.

Obviously, the dancer could not have worked this theatrical magic alone and unaided. . . . the Richard Strauss score gives stimulus and form to dance rhythm and mood and episode and the glorious scenery and costumes of Esteban Frances complement both choreography and music.

UNDERTOW

Ballet in one act with prologue and epilogue. Choreography by Antony Tudor. Music by William Schuman. Libretto by Antony Tudor, after a suggestion by John van Druten. Scenery and costumes by Raymond Breinin. First presented by Ballet Theatre at the Metropolitan Opera House, New York, April 10, 1945, with a cast headed by Hugh Laing as the *Transgressor*, Alicia Alonso as *Ate*, Diana Adams as *Cybele*, Nana Gollner as *Medusa*, Shirley Eckl as *Volupia*, Patricia Barker as *Aganippe*, and Lucia Chase as *Polyhymnia*.

Modern ballets are continually enlarging the subject matter of the dance. It might seem strange to us now, but not until 1936—when Antony Tudor produced *Lilac Garden*—did we ever see on the ballet-stage people who looked and acted somewhat like ourselves, in a dramatic ballet. The women in *Lilac Garden* wore long party dresses, not romantic *tutus;* the men were anxious lovers, not mechanical cavaliers. And the characters in the ballet were caught up in a dramatic situation that was dominated by their inner feelings.

Undertow represents another effort to extend the dramatic dance. It attempts to show us why a young man, called the transgressor, commits murder. It shows us where he was born, the people he grew up with, and the people who influenced his life. All the characters in the ballet, except the hero, have names derived from mythology. They are thus not particular personalities, but universal characters recognizable in the life of every man. The time is the present.

PROLOGUE — BIRTH AND INFANCY: The light is dim. We make out Cybele, great mother of gods, in labor. She gives birth to a son, who creeps out from between her limbs and cries. The mother is revolted by the sight of her son and the agony she has suffered. She abandons him and seeks a lover—Pollux, the immortal youth who is born anew each day. Her son instinctively despises his mother and nurtures his grief. Even as a child, the transgressor discovers in the world no love.

THE CITY — ADOLESCENCE AND MANHOOD: The scene is a street in the slums of a huge city. We sense immediately the irony of the splendid statues that dominate the nearby square: great winged horses fly away from a place the inhabitants can never leave. Their life is so miserable that they cannot entertain the notion of accustoming themselves to anything else. A woman, made up hideously, stands pouting, waiting for someone to notice her. She is Volupia, here a bedraggled personification of sensual pleasure.

The transgressor, now a youth, enters with a pretty young girl. Her name is Aganippe and she is innocent inspiration. They appear to be having a good time together until the boy notices the streetwalker. He is fascinated by her and observes her with open curiosity. His girl abandons him. Volupia looks at the boy contemptuously and smartens up for a man who now struts onto the scene. He goes directly to her and follows, as she knowingly leads the way.

A rowdy bunch of boys race into the street. What seems to be playfulness on their part is genuinely mean and cruel. They are aware of nothing else in the world but the nuisance they may cause. The hero observes them. On the surface he has no reaction; underneath we suspect that he despises his life and is compelled to watch these people only because he seeks an explanation of their grossness.

Volupia, her first mission over, comes back looking for another man. An old man makes furtive advances toward her. He is so timid that the woman turns on him and ridicules him. He leaves the scene.

The youth's companion, Aganippe, comes back into the street. She is accompanied by another girl, Nemesis, with whom she is playing a private game. The man who has just recently finished his rendezvous with Volupia is attracted by Aganippe's beauty and innocence. He tries to strike up a conversation with her. The transgressor turns on him in a rage, orders him to leave the girl alone, and chases him off.

Polyhymnia, the muse of sacred music, enters as an overcheerful, pious busybody who is deluded into thinking she can change the lives of the people in this slum with the right word. She is recruiting an audience for a prayer meeting and invites all the passers-by to come. Several people join her: among them, Pollux, still the handsome youth, who is now courting the modest Pudicitia, and Ate, the hideous creature who would lead all men into evil. Ate's body is demure and innocent, her face and gestures grotesquely obscene. She accompanies the religious woman only out of malice and soon leaves.

Ate approaches the transgressor, but he is immune to her invitations and she seeks the company of Aganippe's discouraged admirer. In vivid contrast to this sordid couple, a bride and groom, Hymen and Hera, enter and—in a gay and tender dance—suggest to the young hero the true power of love. The transgressor watches them enviously, then disbelieves in their happiness to conceal his own misery.

Three lewd drunken women cavort about the scene noisily, braying and bawling Polyhymnia's call to prayer. Ate comes back to seek more mischief with the gang of dead-end kids. The transgressor and Aganippe watch her. She runs off with the gang, and the two innocents look at the ground in disgust. When Ate re-enters, this time alone, the youth goes directly to her and accosts her. He puts his hands around her neck and threatens to choke her to death. Aganippe flees. The transgressor proceeds to kill Ate, but stops, frightened, when the girl Nemesis comes in, guiding home one of the besotted women. Ate takes advantage of the youth's hesitation to elude him.

Still another kind of woman comes on the scene to disturb the hero. Medusa, true to her name, seems to be attractive, but her beauty is empowered to turn men to stone. She is so different, and yet so like the streetwalker and Ate, that the transgressor watches her with interest. She tries to take up with Pollux, but this youth has sense enough to repulse her. Medusa looks toward the transgressor: she must have someone. He is about to join her, when Polyhymnia begins to lead a revival meeting in the middle of the street. The youth participates in the meeting, hoping to escape. Medusa perceives this ruse and sends Polyhymnia and her crowd packing.

Now the transgressor is alone with a woman for the first time in his life. He is tense, expectant. The woman appears to control the youth as he responds to her advances. But gradually his true feelings become plain and we see that in reality he has control of the woman. Finally he can no longer conceal the hatred he has felt for women all his life. He becomes violent, and Medusa is afraid. The transgressor laughs. It is too late. He throws her to the ground, embraces her as she at first desired, and in the act, seizes her throat and chokes her viciously to death. The full orchestra is unleashed in a thundering, violent crescendo. The scene blacks out.

EPILOGUE — GUILT: The hero is alone on the scene. In the back, the misty panorama of the city and the winged horses of the square gradually rise into the sky, as if the very scene of the crime would flee from the criminal. The transgressor moves as if recovering from a hideous nightmare, the dream that has been his life. Yet in remembering the end of the dream, he sees that he has destroyed his life. He wonders what else he could have done, what other ending such a dream could have had. He finds no answer. But perhaps no one knows what he has done! Perhaps he can escape!

Curious people come into the street to watch him. He ignores them. Surely, in every way, he is better than they. Then Aganippe comes in, playing with a balloon. She stops and stares at him. The transgressor recalls their early friendship, smiles at her, and walks toward her. But the girl knows. She points at him, and everyone watches as her forgotten balloon rises in the sky. His guilt reaffirmed by the one person in the world he respects, the hero walks away to meet his end.

LA VALSE

Ballet in two parts. Music by Maurice Ravel. Choreography by George Balanchine. Costumes by Karinska. Lighting by Jean Rosenthal. First presented by the New York City Ballet at the City Center, New York, February 20, 1951, with Tanaquil LeClercq, Nicholas Magallanes, and Francisco Moncion in the principal roles.

Ravel called his composition *La Valse* a "choreographic poem." It was composed to be danced, "a sort of apotheosis of the Viennese waltz . . . the mad whirl of some fantastic and fateful carrousel." The ballet follows in outline the theatrical scheme Ravel imagined for his music: "At first the scene is dimmed by a kind of swirling mist, through which one discerns, vaguely and intermittently, the waltzing couples. Little by little the vapors disperse, the illumination grows brighter, revealing an immense ballroom filled with dancers . . ." Prior to this scene, the ballet makes use of another composition of Ravel's, *Valses Nobles et Sentimentales*, a group of eight short waltzes that introduces the ballroom scene and its principal dancers.

PART ONE — VALSES NOBLES ET SENTIMENTALES: The first waltz serves as the overture. Percussion instruments underline the liveliness of the animated waltz rhythm. The curtain rises, and the second waltz begins.

Three girls stand before a blue net curtain in formal dress. They hold their white-gloved hands in a light, mannered pose. The music is soft and beguiling. The girls bow low and begin to dance, at first somewhat wistfully, then coyly, but always their movements are as formal as their long white gloves, which seem to accent every one of their gestures. Underneath their slate-colored costumes their full skirts are brilliant red, and as they separate and move more freely, the whirling dresses color their dance. Far behind the blue net curtain, in the obscure distance, hangs a cluster of dimly lighted chandeliers. The girls exit modestly, their white-gloved arms before their faces.

A handsome couple, holding hands, dance out gaily to the tinkling tune of the third waltz. Their lighthearted duet is marked by quick, sprightly steps. They dance together closely and separate only as they exit at opposite sides of the stage.

The next waltz is more open in its melody, and to its rapid rhythms another couple dance boldly and freely. They run past each other in high, joyful leaps. The fifth waltz begins with subdued, romantic contrast. The girl who dances it moves gracefully and deliberately. Her partner kisses her hand and kneels. The music becomes blithe, and the ballerina dances before the boy with close, lighthearted steps. The boy marvels at her beauty and reaches out to claim her. This girl dances alone to the sixth waltz, after which her partner rejoins her.

As this couple exit toward the right, they are met by two girls. The couple pause, then the ballerina leaves the stage and a third girl takes her place. These are the same three girls who danced the first waltz. The seventh waltz begins. They claim the boy, covering him with their arms. One girl breaks away to dance, then another. The boy joins them, lifts them high as the music races its tempestuous theme. The four stand together, and one of the girls falls back in the boy's arms. He kneels as the girls run off. The music hesitates in its momentum, and the girls and boys of the earlier waltzes rush in and out, over and about him. He rises, turns swiftly, and the three girls confront him. He dances with them again as the waltz theme returns, then leaps off into the wings.

The stage is empty as the sinuous, final waltz commences. A girl in white emerges. She steps forward, opening her arms slowly; her body recoils slightly as she moves forward. She walks over to the right; her arms mime the flow of the expectant music. A boy enters at the back. They do not see each other. They exchange positions, then each bends backward and recognizes the other. They approach, touch hands warily, and with formal, sophisticated movements of her arms, the ballerina gives her partner her hand. They separate, pass, and come together back-to-back in the center of the stage, where they turn together, their arms entwined. Now they separate again and repeat their introduction. The boy lifts the ballerina slowly; her white dress flows with the final measures of the waltz. He lifts her off into the wings.

PART TWO—LA VALSE: The lights dim, the blue net curtain is raised, the distant chandeliers brighten, the music to *La Valse* begins. The music throbs low and mysteriously; light catch-phrases from a waltz hover over a deep, foreboding background of sound. A spotlight picks up a boy, who runs onto the stage in search of a girl he cannot find. He looks for her helplessly in the dark ballroom. Another boy enters with his dancing partner. They appear to be lost. Suddenly, on the opposite side of the stage, the spotlight shines on three girls, whose white-gloved arms are held up before their faces like masks. The boy chooses one of the girls and starts to dance with her, but the girl falls back strangely in his arms as they move in a circle. They exit. Another couple moves across the scene hurriedly, and three girls and three boys run on and off seeking their partners. All the dancers seem to be waiting for the waltz to emerge through the weird music that holds it in abeyance. The waltz rhythm pulsates; a sparkling rush of sound from the harp heralds its full waltz melody. The ballroom brightens; eight couples fill the stage.

They dance joyously in a large circle; the color of the girls' skirts contrasts vividly with the black walls of the room. As the couples swirl past, we see that the chandeliers are hung with crepe. The black cloth hangs low into the room. The couples change partners in the center of the circle and continue their tempestuous dance. A loud fanfare in rapid waltz rhythm announces the arrival of two new groups of dancers, who cross the stage diagonally as the others stand back. Two couples dance before the group, then the boys gather in the center of the circle, where they choose partners. Now there are two girls for each boy.

The ballerina of the fifth waltz enters with her partner, and the fierce, pounding waltz abates to a soft, mellifluous volume and tempo as they dance softly. The boy exits; the ballerina dances with a group of girls as the couples stand and watch. The cymbals clash, the momentum increases, and the ballerina in white enters. She leaps toward the front, all the dancers gathering on each side of the stage to form wide, opening doors of movement to heighten the speed of her dazzling entry. The dancers move toward the center of the room, where one of the girls is lifted high above them all; the group circles about her. In back, the black crepe swirls as the dancers pass.

The ballerina in white dances happily with her partner; the waltz is quiet again. The couples stand aside and converse and do not notice them. Their dance is slow at first; the ballerina's movements are retarded and she seeks to move more freely as the waltz attempts to resume its previous intensity. But the music hesitates overlong; it unwinds with a snap of sound like a spring that has been wound up too tightly. Disintegrating patterns of waltz melody and tempo struggle helplessly against the orchestra. The once brilliant theme sounds with the pathetic intensity of a hurdy-gurdy. The girl turns with despairing speed to her partner's arms. A staccato trumpet heralds a pause; the weird, warning first bars of La Valse cause all to stand aside. They all look toward the back.

A figure in black emerges beneath the funereal chandeliers. His head is bowed as he walks forward slowly. About his neck hangs a heavy black medal on a black chain. The girls kneel before him; their partners turn their faces away. The ballerina in white turns away in terror. The black specter is followed by a page, who holds in his arms a mirror and a black gown. The music whirls frantically in anticipation.

The girl in white staggers toward the man unwillingly, as if hypnotized by his presence; she goes to him recognizing her own fears of his fatal attraction. He presents her with a splendid necklace and holds the mirror before her. He waits anxiously for her reaction. The girl turns away in horror: the mirror is cracked black glass. Her horror turns to fascination as the waltz attempts to penetrate the mystery of sound and sight. It races suddenly to a desperate loud statement, falters away again. The man offers the girl a pair of long black gloves. He holds them open, and she slides her arms into them as the music sounds a booming, relentless crescendo. Presented now with a black gown, the girl slips into it delightedly and covers her white costume. The stranger rewards her finally with a black bouquet. He kisses her hand, takes her about the waist, and begins to turn her about the room.

The crescendo has now receded, and the waltz attempts again to come to life. The girl is moved faster and faster by her partner as the waltz resumes its momentum. She throws down her bouquet and begins to fall limp in his arms. He turns her faster; she cannot break away. The waltz reaches the peak of driving, irrevocable rhythm; crashes of its beauty tear the air. The girl falls back, then rises to the close embrace of the grotesque black figure. She dies. The specter disappears. Her lover drags her off.

The couples return to their dancing, now rushing about the cold, dark ballroom in frantic pursuit of the pleasure the music will no longer allow them. The exhausted waltz is now heard only in a climactic struggle of instruments. The boy enters in the back, carrying the dead girl in his arms. The boys lift her away from him to their shoulders. Her head falls back, her arms hang loose. Her lover attempts to embrace her, but she is lifted high above him. All of the dancers close in. The girl's body is turned around and around. About the circling center, the group races in a fateful, fantastic carrousel.

NOTES: Anatole Chujoy reviewed the first performance of *La Valse* in *Dance News:*

". . . In *La Valse*, . . . Balanchine has chosen a different style. If we still want labels, neo-romantic would suit nicely. Balanchine's *Cotillon*, to Chabrier's music, was more or less in that style.

"*La Valse* does not have the definite scenario of a *Giselle* or the romantic (i.e. amorous) mood of a *Les Sylphides*, but it is permeated with the spirit of the romantic period of the 30's of the past century and still more with the sense of futility which pervaded Europe some thirty years ago, when Ravel wrote the music, and which, justifiably or not, makes itself felt at the present time.

" 'We are dancing on the edge of a volcano,' Ravel quoted Comte de Salvandy in his notes to *La Valse*, and this short statement is the underlying motif of both the music and the choreography. In a way, then, *La Valse* can be classed with Jerome Robbins' *Age of Anxiety* as a comment on our times and all times of insecurity and change.

"Structurally, Balanchine has used seven of the eight *Valses Nobles et Sentimentales* as an approach to his main theme, expressed in *La Valse* proper, and to establish the various figures who later take part in the denouement of his theme. The first of the eight waltzes is employed as an overture.

"Choreographically, each of the seven waltzes is different in mood and style, all of them are integral parts of a mounting feeling of restlessness, at some times hidden, at others apparent, but never obviously justified until they culminate in a grand ball with all the couples 'dancing on the edge of a volcano.' Death finally enters in the form of a man dressed all in black (Francisco Moncion), who presents black jewels to a dancer all in white (Tanaquil LeClercq), dresses her in black, and dances her to death. . . .

"*La Valse* is an ensemble ballet in the best sense of this classification. For excellent individual performances and more wonderful teamwork and discipline credit goes to the entire company and particularly to Vida Brown, Edwina Fontaine, Jillana, Patricia Wilde, Frank Hobi, Yvonne Mounsey, Michael Maule, Diana Adams, Herbert Bliss, Nicholas Magallanes and, of course, to the already mentioned LeClercq and Moncion.

"The orchestra directed by Leon Barzin never played better.

"The imaginative and talented Karinska designed elegant and beauti-

ful costumes. No program credit was given for the effective stage set. Jean
Rosenthal deserves special mention for her inspired lighting of the ballet.

"The New York City Ballet has scored another momentous success."

A WEDDING BOUQUET

Comic ballet in one act. Music by Lord Berners. Choreography by
Frederick Ashton. Words by Gertrude Stein. Scenery and costumes by
Lord Berners. First presented by the Vic-Wells Ballet at the Sadler's
Wells Theatre, London, April 27, 1937, with Mary Honer as the
Bride, Robert Helpmann as the Bridegroom, Margot Fonteyn as Julia,
June Brae as Josephine, Julia Farron as Pépé, and Ninette de Valois as
Webster. First presented in the United States by the Sadler's Wells
Ballet at the Metropolitan Opera House, New York, October 25, 1949,
with Margaret Dale as the Bride, Robert Helpmann as the Bridegroom,
Moira Shearer as Julia, June Brae as Josephine, Pauline Clayden as
Pépé, and Palma Nye as Webster.

When A Wedding Bouquet was first presented, one critic called it a ballet
bouffe. That is exactly what it is: a comic work that achieves some of its fun-
niest farce by exposing the absurdity of great dignity and seriousness. Its
subject, a wedding in a provincial French town near the turn of the century,
presents a set of conventions that must not be upset; and at the cost of many
laughs, all the conventions are observed. They are observed in the determined, apparently senseless fashion with which people in René Clair
movies observe their conventions: everything seems to combine against them,
but in the end everything is all right. It is possible to watch A Wedding
Bouquet and see it as a continental comic equivalent to the Edwardian
pathos of such a ballet as Lilac Garden. Gertrude Stein's commentary on the
action is spoken during the ballet by an observing orator.

The curtain rises on the garden of a farmhouse near Bellay. There is a
long table set out for the wedding feast, and the ballet begins as people
scurry about preparing the refreshments. Webster, the maid, is certain that
things will not be ready by the time the bride and groom arrive. On the
right, sitting apart from the scene, is the orator. He pours himself a glass of
champagne.

As the guests begin to arrive, the orator speaks over the music to tell us
about some of them. In addition to the peasant girls and boys and the usual
gate crashers, there are Josephine ("She may be wearing a gown newly
washed and pressed") and her two friends, Paul ("Pleasant, vivacious, and
quarrelsome") and John ("An elder brother who regrets the illness of his
father"). There is the aggressive young lady Violet ("Violet, oh will you

ask him to marry you?"), who eagerly pursues a young man named Ernest ("May be the victim of himself"). Ernest eagerly repulses Violet's advances.

Now Julia enters. The orator tells us that she "Is known as forlorn," and forlorn she certainly is. She can hardly walk, she is so dejected. Apparently the trouble is that the fickle bridegroom of the day has abandoned her. Tagging along behind Julia is her dog, a Mexican terrier called Pépé ("Little dogs resemble little girls"). Julia directs all her affections to Pépé, and Pépé switches her tail like a little girl honored with a lollipop. One of the men tries to cheer Julia up, but Pépé protects her mistress. It appears that Josephine is terribly sorry for Julia. She tries to comfort her like a true friend, and Julia sulks with lunatic pleasure.

The bridal party approaches. First, the bride ("Charming! Charming! Charming!"). The bridesmaids dance together under her bridal veil. The bridegroom is clearly harassed. ("They all speak as if they expected him not to be charming.") As if the silly wedding weren't enough, he must now deal with the guests ("They incline to oblige only when they stare") and with Julia. The sight of this demented past indiscretion of his makes the bridegroom despair. Patiently he poses with the bridal party for a photograph of the wedding group. Then he tries to act as if nothing had happened.

Julia won't let him. She hangs on him like a cat. She won't give him up! The guests titter and chatter among themselves, guessing at the bridegroom's situation. Pépé tries to distract the bride, who begins to be suspicious. The bridegroom tries to push Julia off, and she throws herself at his feet. The bride despairs.

Now Josephine, too, is crying in her beer. She is so upset, because Julia is upset, that she drinks far too much. She starts to make the inevitable scene and is asked to leave. The groom, alone with Julia and all the other girls he's been intimate with, dances a bright tango. When he observes all these demanding women, he is lighthearted: marriage has set him free at last! Apparently his new bride sees how lucky she is.

Night begins to fall and the guests start to leave ("Thank you. Thank you."). The bridegroom goes to his bride, and the unhappy Julia is left alone. She still has Pépé, however. The dog tries to comfort her as Julia stupidly stares off into space.

NOTES: Margaret Lloyd, the dance critic of the *Christian Science Monitor*, reviewing *A Wedding Bouquet*, found the ballet ". . . a delicious concoction of Gertrude Stein's nonsense verse, Lord Berners' witty music, costumes, and scenery, and Mr. Ashton's witty choreography. It is all *non sequitur* yet somehow sequential, making a vague sort of sense concerning a provincial wedding in France. The backdrop, in the form of an enlarged, old-fashioned photograph, sets the locale, two long refreshment tables indicate the reception, the straw sailors of the men and sweeping skirts of the women point the period, while the dancers suggest among other things that the marriage is one of convenience.

"As in the play, 'Yes Is for a Very Young Man,' Miss Stein's repetitious word patterns are strongly rhythmic, and, as wittily read by Robert Irving over a loud-speaker, they accentuate the tempo and mood of the comedy. It is danced in the vein, i.e., wittily, by the entire cast . . ."

Part Two

HOW TO ENJOY BALLET

It is strange that many people think ballet is a difficult thing to enjoy. Ballet isn't any harder to enjoy than a novel, a play, or a poem—it's as simple to like as a baseball game.

Yet imagine a person who goes to a baseball game for the first time. He hasn't played the game, he doesn't know the rules, and he gets confused trying to watch everything at once. He feels out of place and annoyed because he isn't sure why everyone else is so excited.

If he had played baseball himself, he wouldn't have this problem. But he doesn't have to play to enjoy. Once he knows what it's all about, once he understands why the players run and slide and leap and catch as they do, he begins to appreciate the game. He becomes familiar with its elements, he enjoys it. The same thing is true of ballet.

Dancing is very popular here in America. Most of us learn to dance when we are young. And I don't mean ballet dancing. We hear music just about everywhere we go; we have a response to its rhythm and melody and want to express this response in a natural way, so we begin to dance. Ballet dancing is an entirely different thing from ballroom dancing, the dancing most familiar to us, though that, too, requires skill. Ballet also began in the ballroom, in the courts of Italy and France, but over the years it has been elevated to the stage and has become an art. This art is based on something natural to us, response to music, but it expresses this response in a specific, formalized way. Over the past four hundred years, dancers and ballet masters have built up a grammar of movement, a synthesis of what is anatomically possible and pleasing. This is the basic vocabulary of the dancer and the people who make ballets. They have to learn it like a language, from the elementary forms and words. The choreographer chooses certain elements he wants from ballet's extensive vocabulary, makes some new ones, and arranges all these in a new pattern to a meter he derives from music. But we don't have to understand this language in detail to enjoy ballet, any more than we have to know about the pigments of the painter or the complex meters of the poet.

Ballet takes our natural impulse to move, to make signs, to make ourselves as attractive and graceful as possible, and turns it into something new, something entirely different. Perhaps what we see the first time we go to the ballet we don't like at all. Dancers in strange costumes do nothing but move to a piece of music we're unfamiliar with; people who represent characters in an ancient Greek myth, for example, dance a story we don't remember much about; or characters in a modern story-ballet behave quite differently from the people next door. We come away saying that ballet's unnatural.

This is exactly true: ballet is unnatural, it has nothing to do with our daily lives in an immediate sense. What ballet does is to take movements we're all familiar with—running and jumping, turning and balancing, lifting and holding—and mold attitudes that underlie these actions into a spectacle that entertains. The melodies we hear in music are very different from the natural noises we hear in the everyday world: the slamming of doors, running brooks, the sound of wind in the trees. Melody is artificial, it is made by man. Ballet is artificial in this same sense: its roots are in everyday life, but it is created by artists. What ballet takes from life it transforms.

Broadway at Times Square, for example, is certainly a kind of spectacle, but it doesn't always entertain. It depends on how good we are at seeing. A talented choreographer can see superbly: he can watch this same scene and, by showing us special patterns of movement and behavior, entertain us with a character ballet, make us laugh or make us sad. He makes order out of what seems to us crowded and chaotic, makes what is fleeting and transitory permanently interesting.

The choreographer can do this in a number of ways: in ballets with stories, in ballets that aim to create a certain mood, or simply in dance ballets, where the music provides the plot the dancers move to. I think it's important to understand these distinctions.

Story ballets are entirely different from the stories we read in books: or they should be. In a story depicted on the ballet stage, we *see* what happens, it can't be explained. The plot is simple, the characters easily identifiable, and what happens to them is luminously clear.

What I've called "mood" ballets don't necessarily tell any kind of story; usually, as in *Cotillon* and *La Valse*, they are ballets in which an outside force, like destiny, seems to control the movement of the dancers.

In dance ballets there is no story, no outside force, only the music. The choreographer works with the music he has chosen much as the poet works with his meters. Most ballets, indeed, are like dramatic or lyric poems: they are created in relation to music and sometimes set within a fable or story. In ballet, the clumsy becomes graceful, the hesitant, inarticulate thought is expressed in direct, eloquent gesture, and nothing appears impossible: love can triumph over everything. In many great ballets, love does.

If you say that all this is fantasy, all imagination, you are right. Some people try to persuade us that poetry and painting and music and dancing are like what we see and do every day. In order to convince us that art is interesting, they tell us that the rumble of drums and the loud crash of cymbals in a piece of music represents Fate, for example, or that a certain portrait painter has depicted a girl's coloring just as it was in real life.

These people, well intentioned as they often are, actually put a stumbling block in our path. They make art easy in the wrong way. If we're told a great deal about a moment of history represented in a painting, for instance, and learn the background of the historical event, our appreciation is severely limited. Our appreciation is intellectual, based on something besides the picture. We could much more profitably spend our time just *looking* at the picture.

Some works of art can be appreciated intellectually, but not many good ones. To enjoy the good ones, we must have an openness of mind in addition to information or their beauty will forever escape us. First of all, we must suspend our prejudices.

As adults, we are well informed about certain things and we have definite ideas on many subjects. But in a sense we are all prejudiced. The older most of us get, the more we have to unlearn in order to learn something new. For instance, many of us were introduced in school to only certain types of music, only certain forms of poetry, and only particular schools of painting. As a result we have a tendency to resist anything new, as well as innovations in something we have become fond of. Children don't have this problem. You can play a Bach suite or a Mozart serenade to a child, and she may very well dance to it. It doesn't occur to her that these composers are old and "classical" or dull and cold or different from what she hears over the radio. She realizes instinctively that the exciting thing about all the arts is that they don't confirm what we already know, so much as they inform us of something new. They contain, in words, in music, in movement, new visions of the world.

Just as a child has her ears open, she keeps her eyes open if you take her to the ballet. Don't be afraid that she will be bored—with no trouble at all she'll become part of the magical world ballet is portraying and she'll not resist its impact. She is not afraid of being afraid (she even enjoys it a little when a wicked fairy appears), she is capable of being moved by love, by the attitudes people have toward one another on the stage. She will sense instantly that a boy partnering a girl well is gentle, respectful, eager for the girl to be as beautiful as possible and that a boy who is a bit of a show-off is not right in his part. She is apt to know, in short, much more than we do.

In order to place ourselves in her position and learn what she knows instinctively, we must go to the ballet with an open mind. If we go often, if we learn gradually that we can't see everything on the stage at once, if we learn to identify dancers and see different dancers in the same part, we'll establish a familiarity with the art and begin to enjoy it. There's no sense in being like the man who says he doesn't know anything about dancing, but he knows what he likes. By saying this, he cheats himself, protects his prejudices from exposure, nurses his own stubbornness. He's not only unwilling to learn anything, he would be embarrassed to learn anything.

Where ballet is concerned, learning by doing is impossible for most of us. We can learn, however, by seeing and by listening; we can learn nothing if we don't go see the ballet, and our appreciation of it will be severely limited if we do not have an awareness of the music that is played there. For ballet is not dancing alone: it is a composite of music and dancing. The relation of dancing to music is not a literal one. It is not a matter of plotless interpretation, a note-by-note, bar-by-bar rhythmic picture of music. On the contrary, it is a complement to the music, something added that is in the mood and spirit of the music as a choreographer sees it. We all have certain emotions when we hear a piece of music. So does a choreographer. He expresses and orders his emotions by placing people on the stage in a particular fashion and arranging their movements so that they have a certain quality: they may be sad, for example, though there isn't always a story to give them a reason for this. The music is sometimes the story. If the choreographer has chosen his music well, we will appreciate the complement the dance makes to its sound: the music will be, as it were, the floor on which the dancer moves. It will not be an excuse for the imposition of literary ideas foreign to music.

But frequently a too sensitive awareness of music can be a disadvantage to the inexperienced balletgoer. Some music lovers are very stubborn, they know what they like, they hold certain things sacred and won't even entertain the notion that they might enrich their musical experience. Their ears are open to only a few pieces, or they think dance "violates" the pieces they love. It may be difficult in such cases to expect a music lover to keep both ears *and* eyes open. I know an intelligent young lady, for example, who walked out on a performance of *The Sleeping Beauty* because she didn't like Tchaikovsky; and a young man who said he loved Bach so much that he could not watch *Concerto Barocco*. Both these people missed a chance, I think, to see in ballet things that might have changed their minds. Love of music can be so intense with some of us that it is acutely private and we resent any intrusion on that privacy.

Ballet in many cases can show us how to appreciate music. The structure of a symphony, how a piece of music is put together, may be something we have no interest in now, but continual attendance at the ballet will cause us to think differently. Dancing is always pointing to music, showing it, making it visually interesting. If our eyes are entertained, we begin to listen in a new way.

Reading about the ballet can be of help to the balletgoer. The numerous story-ballets with complicated plots are not always intelligible when we see them the first time, and it is advisable to know what happens. After our appreciation has matured somewhat, we will find other books—histories and criticism—interesting. Some two or three books of criticism on dancing, such as Noverre's *Letters* and Gautier's ballet reviews, are among the finest works of art appreciation.

But until we have *seen*, no amount of reading will help us. There is no short cut to seeing. *What* you see is not important. Good ballet can be seen frequently throughout the United States. Ballet companies may not visit your community with any regularity, but many of the large cities have their own permanent ballet organizations. Nor does it matter which you see. You cannot tell who is or who is not a good dancer if you don't know anything about the subject, and it is absurd to let anyone tell you. He may very well be wrong, and you'll miss a great deal, perhaps never go back to the ballet because you thought he was right. Much antagonism toward ballet is often created by someone who tells us that so-and-so is the world's greatest dancer in such-and-such a ballet. The inexperienced balletgoer sees the ballerina, doesn't like her, and never goes again.

Certain people don't like "cold" dancers. They use this word as if it meant something bad, something negative. The strange thing is that this quality of "coldness," which some regard negatively, often achieves positive results. I think you will find that people who say they prefer "hot," fiery dancers tend to create their own image of what they want to see, instead of watching the stage and seeing that the dance has its own quality—which might be cool and clear as crystal or, like a diamond seen in different lights, first cold, then hot.

What is it, then, that we should appreciate about a dancer? What things should we watch for the first time we go?

You will often hear people talk about the technical accuracies of dancers. They will say, "It's not important how many *fouettés* a girl can do, it's important that her supporting foot remain in place" and "Male dancers must always point their toes while doing *entrechats*." These things are quite true, there are many other such things, many finer points of technique, and we learn them as we watch, but all these criticisms are only part of a general appearance and manner that we must watch for first.

We should be ready, too, to enjoy the artist who perhaps has not yet achieved great success. We may discover later on that we saw the first of many dances that made her eventually a ballerina. That will be exciting. However, the good dancer will not in performance remind us of this kind of success. Watching her dancing over the years, we will see and appreciate the movement, the victory she appears to achieve in executing effortlessly a particular step or gesture at a specific time in a specific place. Her dancing will refract and amplify and make spacious, as music does, the emotion a particular dance intends. She is not someone we are in love with, or someone we should like to love, though some of her dancing reminds us of the happiness, the understanding, the playfulness and tenderness love has.

Only the professional dancer can analyze a performance and tell us that a certain dancer missed something. Dancers are not automatons. Every performance is different. Dancers must adjust themselves at almost every performance to a new pair of shoes, just as the tennis champion adjusts his hand to a new racket and the violinist adjusts to a new bow. Moreover, the condition of the stage floor is crucial to all dancers. No dancer dances well on a stage with a bad floor. If you have been to ballet performances where famous ballerinas seemed to be holding something back, where all the members of the *corps de ballet* danced hesitantly, refusing to commit themselves wholly to the dance, it was probably because they were risking their professional lives on the floor they were dancing on. The ideal stage for dancing is unfinished pine, smoothed over: it is not glossy linoleum or highly polished hardwood or the shiny plastic distances we see in the movies, or wood laid over cement or linoleum. When the nineteenth-century French critic Gautier remarked that an Italian dancer's feet were "like two steel arrows rebounding from a marble pavement," he was able to make the simile because she was dancing on a wooden stage. The dancer feels most secure when she knows that her ballet slippers are in real contact with the floor when she wants them to be; when she can feel the friction of the floor as she turns in pirouettes; when she can descend from a jump without fear of sliding.

Some stages, too, are precariously raked, or pitched: the back of the stage is higher than the front. The designers of such stages had more consideration for the audience's ability to see than for the perfection of the performance that entertains the audience. The degree of rake differs from stage to stage in old theatres, and it is naturally extremely hard for dancers to adjust their balance to them. These are not excuses; they are the conditions under which every dancer works, and no dancer should be punished for them. In one recital a pianist plays millions of notes; if you aren't a pianist yourself, you won't know the ones he missed. The great pianist Anton Rubinstein once said that if he'd been paid a penny for every note he missed, he'd be a very rich man.

Ballet is now so advanced in the United States that very seldom do we see incompetence on the stage. Bad dancers appear less and less. Our dancers are professionals. Like professional ball players, they must possess a technique. Usually their technique is so great that however tired they are (and tired they often are, with eight performances a week), their exhaustion is invisible to the audience. Only the professional can see it.

The audience must watch technique as part of a performance, not as a separate thing. The stage illusion and the atmosphere created by the dancing are destroyed if you sit in your seat and count turns or stop-watch changes of position. We take it for granted that flowers are beautiful; we don't have to take them apart to see this. We take them as they are. The taking apart is the job of the botanist, just as the technical analysis of a performance is the job of the professional dancer.

Great technical ability is only part of being a great dancer. At first we might find ourselves applauding a feat that seems astonishing, and six months later, when we've seen dozens of dancers do the same thing with an equal amount of facility, we might applaud less. We have to see to know better. We have to compare. But what we will all like at the beginning and what will make us want to go again soon is a dancer who interests us in an extremely simple way: we will remember afterward what her dance looked like. We will remember the girl, but only because of the dance she showed us. No doubt she was attractive, but she didn't play on that and make us think of it. No doubt she did some steps that seemed incredibly hard, but she didn't stress this, she didn't try to hit us between the eyes with her skill as if to say, "Look! *This* is good." Instead, the big moments of the dance came with the same lack of effort and stress as the small ones. She will quietly and effortlessly seem to conquer the stage space in which she moves to the time of the music.

Where the dancing of dramatic roles is concerned, we must beware of standard images. Some people think that the heroine in *Swan Lake* must always be very slender, short, have black hair parted in the middle, and dance like a bird, with lyrical feeling. Actually, what they mean by lyricism is often lethargy. I have seen dozens of Swan Queens. Some of them looked like birds, others did not, and all gave fine performances. Great ballets were not devised for one type of dancer. Sometimes I hear people say, "But so-and-so wasn't like Pavlova." They forget that if Pavlova and other great dancers of the more distant past were here today, they would not be so sentimental. They were professionals. They would appreciate the greater technical difficulties of modern classical choreography and admire our dancers with an affectionate, professional understanding. If they were dancing today, they know, they would be trying to do the same things our dancers do.

Seeing great classical ballets of the past is like seeing great plays: we are so familiar with *Hamlet* and *Romeo and Juliet,* know the lines so well that we think we can say them with more understanding than any actor. We may see these plays many times and come away disappointed, but one day we experience an extraordinary thing. We hear an actor say the words that are so familiar to us, and suddenly they are no longer private quotations to us. The play becomes new and moving. The same thing happens at the ballet.

Like all the arts, ballet is many things to many people. It is high-brow and something to make fun of to some people because they are afraid to understand it. Others have no wish to understand it and go to the ballet merely to show off their clothes, to see their friends or to make new ones. Still others seek the fashionable and go to the theatre because a particular dance or dancer has been praised extravagantly. Finally, there are those who enjoy the ballet with no pretension at all. They are able to do this because they understand what ballet is as a particular form of entertainment, because they are not frightened by other people telling them that ballet is "important" and "significant." Ballet is important and significant, but first of all it is a pleasure.

When we first start going to the ballet, it is no more significant or important than most of the other things we enjoy watching. It may become significant later, after we have enjoyed it and been entertained by it, after it has become important to us in a personal way. But at first we should simply watch it, as we watch our friends swimming or ice-skating, or playing baseball or tennis.

Music, we all know, is an aural perception: reading notes is not sufficient, we must hear them. Ballet is a visual art, like painting or architecture. But unlike painting or architecture, ballet is a visual spectacle that moves: it is not static. We can always see famous paintings by going to museums or famous buildings. Ballet, by comparison, is transitory. We no sooner take in a particular movement in a ballet than it has become another movement. The movements accumulate rapidly, and if we don't watch carefully, we are lost. We must train ourselves to see.

I think we must do this for the same reason and in the same way that we train ourselves to enjoy any of the other arts. To read a book—and we all have experience with this—is not necessarily to understand it. Similarly, to listen is not always to *hear*, and to look not always to *see*. Often, when we want to say that we understand something, we say that we "see" it. Ballet, with application and attention, can be seen and not merely watched.

We go to the theatre to see ballet and watch dancers—people like ourselves, with bodies and heads and arms and legs, running and jumping and lifting to a piece of music. We ask ourselves, why should they do this? The answer is that ballet displays the most beautiful movement of which the human body is capable. The human body, of course, has its limitations. We can bend it and stretch it and lift it, but only to a certain degree. We can, however, decrease the body's limitations with practice. After we have learned to walk, we can run; after we have lifted light objects, we are able to lift heavy ones. The dancer's concern is to fulfill the maximum of what the body can do in a beautiful way.

But the skill of dancers is useless unless it is displayed in a certain form. No one would enjoy watching a group of dancers jump about the stage aimlessly, no matter how well they jumped. Ballet asks the body to move in time. Ballet uses music to indicate time.

Not only in its movement and transitory nature, then, is ballet different from other visual arts. It is two things at once: a composition, a unification of music and dancing. We must hear and see at the same time. This process is something like reading a poem or watching a movie. A poem says something to us, but it speaks in a certain rhythm, a certain time scheme, a certain music. In a movie, the continuous pictures the camera shows us are controlled in sequence and length by what the script specifies. Music is ballet's timekeeper.

To show dancers moving with ideal strength and grace requires beautiful people. Few dancers are beautiful when they begin to study, but when they dance well, they become beautiful. Beautiful dancers are easily associated with ideal characters in stories, with kings and queens and princesses, with love, victory over evil, and death. Many ballets have stories with such heroes and heroines. But sometimes there is no literal story at all in ballet, no narrative. Just as people in real life make different gestures and stand in different positions when they are in different moods, so do dancers in a ballet. A *pas de deux*, for example, is simply a dance for two people, a man and a woman; and even when it is performed on a bare stage with no surrounding story, a *pas de deux* is always a kind of romance. The man is tender and admiring as he lifts the woman and supports her in order to display her beauty, while she, in her reliance on his strength and assurance, admires him in return. This quality in the *pas de deux* may not be apparent to the newcomer to ballet, but the more often this kind of dance is seen, the clearer become its romance and tenderness.

Program music is very easy for most of us to understand. When a composer tells us that his symphony is about a thunderstorm, we immediately have something to compare it with. Some ballets are like program music. These ballets require program notes to tell us what the ballet is really about. Some things, of course, are impossible to represent clearly on stage without the spoken word, but the central idea of every dramatic ballet is clear the first time we see it.

Many ballets are like symphonies that only have identifying numbers. A *pas de deux* or a dance ballet may have to be seen a number of times before we begin to enjoy it. Then passages we were able to like at the beginning become connected with other passages we appreciate later; we soon retain in our minds all the different passages and detect their connections.

Here are a few final suggestions which I hope will enhance your enjoyment of this great art. All ballets are accompanied by music, but because it is hard to listen to music and watch dancers at the same time, play the music over before you go to the ballet or listen to it on records. (See "Annotated Selection of Ballet Recordings," page 559.) This is particularly important, naturally, in ballets that do not have conventional stories, where the ballet is based on the music.

Many ballets have plots. There are stories taken from fairy tales (*The Sleeping Beauty*), from ancient myths (*Orpheus*), from the Bible (*Prodigal Son*), from poems (*Illuminations*), and from stories devised especially for particular ballets. Not all of these stories are simple, and brief program notes are often insufficient. As I have said, ideally the best stories for ballets are those than can be *shown*, stories that require no elucidation at all in the written word. But stories inevitably have their complications. These complications were cleared up in the old ballets by pantomime. People could understand this when these ballets were created, for they were familiar with the mime vocabulary, but today, when that vocabulary has gone out of fashion, miming on the stage is often obscure to us and we aren't sure what is happening. Read the stories through, then, and in the theatre you will not be looking down constantly at an incomplete program note. You will be watching the stage.

Many people who go to the ballet, and not only newcomers, feel there is something suspect about ballets without stories—about dance ballets pure and simple. They think there is a hidden meaning they don't grasp. The real point is that they are trying to appreciate ballet intellectually. They expect ballet always to be like the theatre or literature or the movies, which, quite naturally, it is not. Ballet is like nothing so much as dancing. To appreciate it you have to watch it, not think about it. If you only think about it, you'll probably miss the next step and miss something you might have liked very much.

Don't hesitate to go to see ballet companies that you don't think are first-class. Only by seeing *all* the companies can you compare, analyze, and discover what you prefer.

Another thing I'd like to mention is this. Many of us are interested in reading ballet criticism in newspapers and magazines. This criticism can be informative and revealing but I think it is important for us, if we read critics, to read *all* of them, and then go to the ballet and see for ourselves. You will often find that critics radically disagree. How can you discover which one is right unless you see the ballet in question? It also happens very often that dance critics change their minds. Dance critics, like music critics, review the same pieces year after year; what they disliked one year they sometimes like another. If you have read a particular dance critic or music critic over the years, you will discover this to be true.

And, finally, no one can enjoy the ballet if he decides he will go only a certain number of times. If you go only occasionally, once or twice every few years, say, you will never be fully entertained. You must go as many times as possible, as often as you read a novel, as often as you go to the movies or the theatre, as often as you look at paintings or listen to a concert or an opera. We come to enjoy all of these arts through persistent exposure to what each has to teach us about the pleasures that life contains. If we neglect the ballet, we are depriving ourselves of one of the greatest of these pleasures. Naturally, we can live without art: we can eat and sleep and live by our senses alone. But throughout history man has never been satisfied with the necessities of life. He has sought entertainment and enlightenment through art and has become a happier being.

Part Three

A BRIEF HISTORY OF THE BALLET

Our word *ballet* comes from the Italian *ballare*, to dance, and it is to the courts of Italy at the height of the Renaissance that we trace the beginning of ballet as we know it today. Dancing as primitive ritual—as a form of hero worship and worship of gods, as glorification of the dead, as a means of celebrating the seasons and the elements—is fundamental in history. Dancing as a popular skill embodied in folk dances is familiar in every country. Dancing as a skill, as a refined human discipline, was developed in religious rites of Mediterranean countries and in the ancient Orient, where chosen persons were taught godlike gestures and movement in order to emulate and celebrate for the populace the drama of their common deities. In the choral dance of Greece, dancing as an art designed for entertainment grew out of the native ritualistic dance. Now the trained performer of a common ritual became the dedicated dancer who aimed to give pleasure to a nondancing audience.

Greek drama began with group or choral dances interrupted and embellished with storytelling. As the chorus of dancers began to sing and to participate in the action of the stories devised by poets, pantomime and meaningful movement evolved. The masks worn by the Greek chorus were a feature of the theatrical dance till late in the eighteenth century. The poet Aeschylus, whose plays were performed by two principal actors and a chorus, rehearsed his choruses in the postures, movements, and gestures proper to the dramatic situation. With his successors, Sophocles and Euripides, the importance of the chorus was proportionately reduced with introduction of a larger cast of characters, but a basic vocabulary of theatrically effective mimicry, attitude, and movement had been established.

What the Greeks achieved was extended by the Romans, who exploited the comic possibilities of mime and dance. The Romans combined the two with acrobatics and circus routines and used them to illustrate popular fables. Tumblers, jesters, and buffoons so humanized dancing that the ritualistic base of Greek tragedy was wholly forgotten.

The comic art of the Romans was reborn in sixteenth-century Italy by traveling players who embodied the *commedia dell' arte:* skilled popular comedians who improvised variations on stock characters—Pulcinella, Punch, Columbine, Pierrot, Harlequin, and others—in stock plots. The gestures, costumes, and characterization of these actors became comic archetypes for all of Europe, influencing many others—the dancers of Paris, the plays of Molière, the carnival puppet shows (*Punch and Judy, Petrouchka*) of the Western world.

While these troupes entertained the provinces of Italy and southern France, the capitals of the Renaissance saw splendid revivals of Roman opulence in the form of pageants and staged celebrations. The rulers of these capitals used every happy event—engagements, marriages, visits of notable persons, military victories—as an excuse for spectacular entertainment in poetry, painting, dance, song, and theatrical mechanics. Appropriate myths inherited from Rome were adapted for the particular occasion, depicted by artists, and danced by the masked members of the court. Interludes of dancing were performed at pageants between recitations and songs, between courses at banquets, and to accompany with appropriate representation the serving of rare dishes at great feasts.

Like the popular art of the *commedia dell' arte,* court dances also had special forms. The folk dances that the courts had sophisticated were further refined into precise floor patterns, simple set steps that required set preparations, and endings performed with elegant bows and flourishes. Popular court dances of this time were called *balletti* (diminutive of *ballo;* hence *ballet*); they were similar to the English morris dance. Castiglione, master of Renaissance manners, wrote in *The Courtier:*

"There are certain other exercises that can be practiced in public and in private, like dancing; and in this I think the Courtier ought to have care, for when dancing in the presence of many and in a place full of people, it seems to me that he should preserve a certain dignity, albeit tempered with a lithe and airy grace of movement; and although he may feel himself to be very nimble and a master of time and measure, let him not attempt those agilities of foot and double steps which we find very becoming in our friend Barletti, but which perhaps would be little suited to a gentleman. Yet in a room privately, as we are now, I think he may try both, and may dance morris-dances and brawls; but not in public unless he be masked, when it is not displeasing even though he be recognized by all." Within the aristocracy of the court a new aristocracy developed—the aristocracy of the best dancer.

Catherine de Medici introduced the new Italian pageantry to France. Under her influence, Italian musicians and dancing masters came to Paris and staged for the court spectacles consisting of vocal and instrumental music, spoken dialogue, pantomime, dancing, and mechanical effects. The combination of these elements produced the *ballet de cour,* or court ballet, the European model for costly entertainment. With the assistance of their ladies, gentlemen of the court performed *masques*—allegorical plays with poetry and dancing—and *mummings*—colorful dances performed by masked figures among dancers at court balls.

Toward the end of the sixteenth century, Catherine de Medici, with the assistance of an Italian musician turned dancing master, produced at her court an entertainment that superseded in extravagance and purpose all those previously seen in Europe. This work was called the *Ballet Comique de la Reine*. It employed all the familiar elements of the *ballet de cour* and Italian opera—music, singing, dancing, royal processions, declamation of verse, elaborate scenery and mechanical effects—but for the first time these elements were fused in a dramatic whole that made sense to the spectators: the disparate parts were not mere diversions at a court function, they represented a conscious design to entertain an audience with a unity of comedy, dance, music, and spectacle. The performance cost 3,600,000 francs, lasted for five hours, and was witnessed by some ten thousand people. Its success assured the future of dancing as a necessary part of regal entertainment. It was, in effect, the first ballet as we recognize the term today—a combination of music, dancing, plot, and design.

Seven years later there appeared in France a book that provided the first foundation for the establishment of dancing as a profession. Arbeau's *Orchésographie* (*The Writing of Dancing*) illustrated and gave directions for executing the popular court dances of the time. Arbeau also indicated the principles for the five basic positions of the feet that were to become the foundation of the classic dance. In an effort to teach the dances that had become so popular, it was necessary to arrive at principles upon which all teaching could be based: the limitations of the human body, how and in what directions it could move, and the fundamental steps that best prepared it for movement.

The popular dances of the continent had meanwhile become the courtly habit in England, where Queen Elizabeth appointed a gentleman to the post of Lord Chancellor because "he wore green bows on his shoes and danced the *pavane* to perfection." The poets Ben Jonson, Milton, and Campion, and the great designer Inigo Jones developed masques in imitation of the *ballet de cour*. The masques featured dancing by members of the court, but the real contribution England made to the development of ballet was in the antimasque, a pure dance that preceded the performance of the masque proper, danced by professionals. Ben Jonson thus addressed Queen Elizabeth in 1609:

"And because Her Majesty (best knowing that a principal part of life in these spectacles lay in their variety) had commanded me to think on some dance, or show, that might precede hers, and have the place of a foil, or false masque: It was careful to decline, not only from others, but mine own steps in that kind, since the last year, I had an *antimasque* of boys; and therefore now devised that twelve women, in the habit of hags or witches, sustaining the persons of Ignorance, Suspicion, Credulity, etc., the opposites to good Fame, should fill that part, not as a masque, but a spectacle of strangeness, producing multiplicity of gesture."

In France, dancing flourished at the court of Louis XIV, himself an accomplished dancer. In 1661 Louis XIV founded the first dancing academy in the world, an institution for the instruction of dancing that has continued down to the present day at the Paris Opéra. Under the direction of Beauchamp, the king's dancing master, and the Italian musician and dancer Jean Baptiste Lully, students were taught professionally, to perform on a stage. The great dramatists Molière and Corneille collaborated with Lully in the production of comedy and tragedy ballets that secured the admiration of court and public. The excellence of stage performance gradually superseded the court dances; the larger, freer movements possible in the theatre replaced the confined gestures of the ballroom. Louis Pécourt became the first *premier danseur*, the first dancer to excel in performances in a theatre. Soon women appeared as professional dancers for the first time.

Beauchamp specified the Five Positions of the classic dance, positions of the feet that became the prerequisite for a dancer's training at the French Academy and the instinctive basis for all performance. The positions are still the basis of ballet today. These positions are absolute in their anatomical authority: the ease with which they are taught to young students, the ease and security they allow the dancer on stage, and, most important of all, the variety of movement made possible by their use. They are as essential to ballet as fundamental techniques of sound structure are to architecture. The Five Positions, with their embodiment of the turned-out leg, distinguished ballet from all other forms of theatrical dance. Ballet dancing had now become a profession, one that could be taught and learned and mastered.

Now that there was fundamental agreement on the basis of the classic dance, there were quarrels about innovations of technique. While Lully in his years at the French Academy had devised dances that were complex in pattern and floor design, he had not considered dancing off the floor, dancing that aimed at elevation, at flight. His successor, Rameau, thought differently and encouraged his dancers to turn in the air and perform steps high off the floor. In Lully's time, when dancing was moved from the ballroom to the stage, it was quite natural for ballet to imitate the technique of dancing in a ballroom—where performers and spectators stood on the same level—but Rameau realized that on a raised stage the dancers were seen from an entirely different perspective by the spectators, that the dancers' feet were clearly visible for the first time, and, accordingly, that the dance must make an adjustment of technique to hold its audience. The conservative adherents of Lully, those who advocated a "horizontal" dance, contested the theories of the new, rebel "verticalists" of Rameau.

This contest between the Lullists and the Ramists contained the basic argument that runs throughout the history of ballet down to the present: the argument between "tradition" and innovation, between strict classicism and expressiveness, between pure dance and "literary" ballets, between ballet and modern dance. This argument was embodied in two popular dancers of the time: Marie Camargo and Marie Sallé. Camargo, champion of the new *danse verticale*, was a brilliant technician, praised for her airiness and strength. She was the first *danseuse* to perform the *entrechat-quatre*, to execute high *cabrioles* and jumps. To display her skill, Camargo shortened the conventional cumbersome ballet dress so that her agile steps might be seen. A great innovator, Camargo was also a traditionalist, interested in technique rather than the human and dramatic elements of the dance.

Camargo's rival, Marie Sallé, "muse of gracious, modest gesture," exemplified in her refined and gracious dancing a spiritual rather than technical elevation. Here the accent was on nobility of posture and deportment and on characterization of a particular part for dramatic effect. Sallé did not dance simply for the sake of dancing. Her most famous role, that of the statue beloved by Pygmalion, she devised for herself. Called a *ballet-pantomime* in opposition to the rigid and formal opera-ballets of the Paris Opéra, Sallé's dancing in this work was faithful to the Greek style of its story. Effecting another innovation in costume, Sallé let her hair down and over her corset and petticoat wore only a muslin dress "draped about her in the manner of a Greek statue."

Rameau's ballets at the Paris Opéra accommodated both the new technique and dramatic expression within the frame of the opera-ballet, a series of danced *entrées* connected by a threadlike plot. The *entrées* depicted dances in various countries—Turkey, Peru, Persia, America—which allowed for spectacle as well as for occasional dramatic interest in stories imposed upon the natives. With their great geographical variety and concern for imitation of native dances throughout the world, Rameau's ballets brought down to earth the mythological characters with which the dance had been preoccupied since the Renaissance.

Another dancer wanted ballet to go still further. After Rameau's death, ballet at the Paris Opéra degenerated to the point where each of its elements —dancing, music, story, and spectacle—seemed to exist for its own sake. The dancers' technical proficiency was displayed, with marked contempt for music, in ridiculous dramas. Jean Georges Noverre, a student of Louis Dupré, a great admirer of Marie Sallé and of the English actor David Garrick, wanted to unify the elements of ballet into a dramatic whole. He wrote, in ballet's first critical text, *Letters on the Dance and Ballets*, that poetry, painting, and dancing should be a "faithful likeness of beautiful nature," that dancing should be united with pantomime to ensure dramatic expression, and that such expression must be related directly to music. Working with such musicians as Christoph Willibald Gluck, whose reforms in opera were closely allied to Noverre's in ballet; with such dancers as Gaetan Vestris, first great classical dancer in Europe; with Marie Allard and Madeleine Guimard, superb mimes as well as dancers; and with the patronage of such notable persons as Marie Antoinette—Noverre successfully initiated reforms in ballets that were seen and applauded all over Europe. His ballets were danced in London, Vienna, Paris, Milan, and St. Petersburg. All of Europe delighted in the new *ballet d'action*—works in which dancers reflected in their movement and gesture the dramatic intention of plot and music. Among Noverre's students were Vincenzo Galeotti, who became ballet master at the Royal Theatre, Copenhagen; Charles Didelot, the Frenchman who became "the father of Russian ballet" at the Imperial Theatre in St. Petersburg; and Jean Dauberval, who, in *La Fille Mal Gardée*, created what was perhaps the first comic ballet.

One of Dauberval's pupils, Salvatore Vigano, extended Noverre's reforms in spectacular ballets produced in his native Italy. At La Scala, Milan, Vigano mounted works that unified music, dancing, and mime as Noverre had never been able to do. Mime, Vigano regarded as the expression of the "movement of the soul: it is the language of all peoples, of all ages and times. It depicts better than words extremes of joy and sorrow . . . It is not sufficient for me to please the eyes. I wish to involve the heart." Indeed, he regarded mime with such importance that the composer Rossini remarked to Stendhal, the choreographer's great admirer, that Vigano's ballets had too much pantomime and not enough dancing. Vigano's idea was the *choreodrame*, ballets in which Noverre's principle of dramatically expressive embodiment was seen in every dancer on stage, in the *corps de ballet* as well as in the performances of principal dancers. Within particular settings and plots, Vigano worked tirelessly to arrange dances appropriate to drama and score. Under his direction, La Scala became the greatest ballet theatre in all of Europe.

This pre-eminence of Italian ballet was sustained by the dancer, choreographer, and teacher Carlo Blasis, student of Dauberval, who wrote—in his *Elementary Treatise upon the Theory and Practice of the Art of Dancing* (1820) and in the *Code of Terpsichore* (1829)—the first lexicons of the classic dance. Here the basic theories of all the great dancers and choreographers who preceded Blasis were tacitly assumed in general instructions to pupils and ballet masters and were embodied in detailed, illustrated instruction on practice: the proper execution of positions, poses, movements, and steps of elevation—all the resources known to the classic dancer. Blasis' work has been the foundation of all instruction in the classic dance ever since. The classic disciplines he insisted upon in his teaching at La Scala were precursors of the instruction that later dominated the Russian Imperial School at St. Petersburg.

Founded in 1735 to teach court cadets the fashionable dances of Europe, the Russian Imperial School, adjunct of the Imperial Theatre, was directed by a series of French and Italian ballet masters, who produced in St. Petersburg the work of European choreographers and invited to the Russian capital foreign dancers to star in these works. The Frenchman Charles

Didelot was the first to establish the Russian school and theatre on a firm base. Didelot, student of Noverre, Dauberval, and the *premier danseur* Auguste Vestris, was appointed ballet master at St. Petersburg in 1816. He established at the Imperial School a consistent foundation of classical instruction and mounted such excellent ballets at the Imperial Theatre that the poet Pushkin was moved to say that in Didelot's ballets there was more poetry than in all the French literature of that time. After Didelot's death (1837) the Russian Theatre continued to flourish, but principally as an opulent setting not for Russian, but for the finest ballets and dancers of Western Europe.

In Western Europe of the 1830s, the supremacy of Italian dance technique combined with the Romanticism that dominated the other arts of the time to produce a new kind of ballet. Romanticism in ballet, as in the other arts, was a rebellion against classical subject matter, classical technique, and classical attitudes. The Romantic ballet extended the classical dance technique with daring innovations: girls danced on their toes for the first time, and new steps of elevation were devised to display voluptuous real-life heroines who by theatrical magic became idealized, unattainable creatures of wood and glade. Heroines of ballets were no longer characters from classical mythology: wronged peasant girls and sylphs displaced the Medeas, the Junos, the Aphrodites. Audiences rejoiced in the theatrical display of the beauty of the broken heart. Paris, again, and London were the ballet capitals of the world.

Marie Taglioni, creator of the wistful *La Sylphide*, became the first famous dancer Europe had ever known. The ballet *Giselle*, inspired by the Romantic poet Gautier, superseded Taglioni's vehicle in excellence of plot and dance, and enthralled audiences from St. Petersburg to Boston. Taglioni's contemporaries—Carlotta Grisi, the first dancer of *Giselle*; the Danish ballerina Lucile Grahn; the lively Fanny Cerito—appeared in a score of ballets on romantic themes, while the great Fanny Elssler, Taglioni's arch-rival, was so secure in her reputation that she could abandon the opera houses of Europe for two years and dance on tour throughout the United States. Elssler's phenomenal success in America in 1840–42 was typified by the reception tendered her by President Van Buren and his Cabinet at Washington and by the banquet given by members of Congress in her honor at the Capitol. In 1845 Jules Perrot, the Romantic ballet's finest choreographer and the one male dancer who managed to hold his own in this age of romanticism, staged in London a special dance for Taglioni and three of her rivals—Grisi, Cerito, and Grahn. The success of this *Pas de Quatre* obliged *The Times* to call the ballet "the greatest Terpsichorean exhibition that ever was known in Europe."

While the triumphs of these first great ballet stars increased the popularity of the art, the art itself began to suffer. Interest in all performances was centered on the stars and what they danced; people cared less and less about the music they danced to, the plots they acted, or the productions that displayed them. Taglioni or Elssler, alone, was enough. Prospective dancers and choreographers therefore saw little profit in remaining in Paris and London. In Russia, they knew, the czar's court required spectacular entertainment. And it could support it by the most bountiful treasury in Europe.

In the year Taglioni retired (1847), a young Frenchman, Marius Petipa, was engaged as a dancer at the Russian Imperial Theatre. Petipa was successful as a dancer in St. Petersburg; there he watched the work of the French ballet masters Jules Perrot and Arthur Saint-Léon as they entertained a new avid audience of aristocratic balletomanes. Then suddenly there was an opportunity to create a ballet of his own. In 1860 he had restaged the Perrot-Coralli *Giselle*, the romantic ballet that seemed certain to remain a permanent fixture in the Russian repertory. But ballet by this time required a new impetus, which Petipa discovered in a reawakened classicism. He devised for his ballet a mass dance on a tremendous scale, with spectacular stage effects. Beginning in 1862, with his first great success, a four-act dance extravaganza set in the desert, with pyramids and colossal palaces of ancient Egypt, Petipa succeeded Jules Perrot as ballet master to the Imperial Theatre. His influence was to dominate the Russian ballet almost up to the time of his death fifty years later. His supremacy survived the reigns of four czars, who delighted in the entertainment he provided their courts and in the universal model of excellence he caused the Russian ballet to become. Petipa created fifty-seven full-length, evening-long ballets, devised countless shorter *divertissements*, restaged seventeen ballets by other choreographers, and mounted ballets in thirty-four operas during his years at the Imperial Theatre.

St. Petersburg was now the ballet capital of the world. The French ballet master Petipa welcomed to Russia dancers and teachers from Italy, France, Germany, and Scandinavia; with their assistance he made the Imperial Ballet School the greatest in the world. Petipa's school provided the standard for the dancer's training, as his theatre was the exemplar for the dancer's performance. Foreign dancers who came to Russia for guest engagements introduced diverse technical elements from all of Europe: brilliant classicists, who had been trained in Italy under the disciplines founded by Blasis, contributed to the growth of a new style. This style was not so much Russian as polygenous. It was historic in its all-inclusiveness, in its gigantic assimilation of classic dance techniques as they were practiced in all of Europe. It produced, toward the end of the nineteenth century, great Russian dancers, who danced in such ballets as *Swan Lake* and *The Nutcracker*, works by the Russian choreographer Lev Ivanov, who produced them under Petipa's direction, and Peter Ilyich Tchaikovsky. Tchaikovsky was commissioned by Petipa to write the score for the ballet that turned out to be the masterpiece of both men. *The Sleeping Beauty*, Russian ballet music, as well as Russian ballet and Russian dancers, was the accepted standard throughout the Western World.

Petipa died in 1910. Some years before his death, the classical ballet he had perfected had passed its zenith; it began to disintegrate as its elements became disassociated. A young dancer and choreographer, Michel Fokine, who in 1905 created for the ballerina Anna Pavlova the short lyric dance *The Dying Swan*, rebelled against the omnipotence of "tradition." Like Sallé, Noverre, and Vigano before him, Fokine aimed at unification of dancing, music, and design. He asserted that dancing was interpretative, expressive. "The ballet must no longer be made up of *numbers*, *entries*, and so on. It must show artistic unity of conception . . . Ballet must have complete unity of expression, a unity which is made up of harmonious blending of the three elements—music, painting, and plastic art." Fokine's suggested reforms were rejected by his superiors at the Imperial Theatre. They were championed by a man who understood music, painting, and dancing: Serge Diaghilev.

Diaghilev wished to take the Russian ballet to Paris. In 1907 he had presented Russian music to Western Europe for the first time, and he now wished Europeans to admire what he knew to be the finest dancing in the world. He chose Fokine as choreographer to a company to be known as Diaghilev's Ballets Russes. Anna Pavlova, Tamara Karsavina, and Vaslav Nijinsky secured leave from the Imperial Theatre to be his principal dancers. His dancers, his designers, his musicians, were the finest in Russia.

On May 18, 1909, Diaghilev's Ballets Russes opened their first season in Paris. In the new ballets of Fokine, ballets like *Prince Igor* and *Les Sylphides*, and in the quality of the dancing, the music, and theatrical design, the season was an unprecedented success. This pattern of success continued the next year, with the Stravinsky-Fokine *Firebird*, and the next, with the Stravinsky-Fokine *Petrouchka*, and the next, with the Debussy-Nijinsky *The Afternoon of a Faun* and the Fokine-Weber *Le Spectre de la Rose*, and so on, season after season, year after year, for twenty years of dance entertainment based on an inviolable rule of uniform excellence in choreography, music, *décor*, and performance.

Paris was again the world capital of dance. Diaghilev's Ballets Russes provided a center of artistic endeavor such as Europe had not known since the Medici courts of the Renaissance. And Diaghilev, like the Renaissance princes, not only perpetuated established talent, he discovered, encouraged, and developed talent. He numbered among his principal female dancers Pavlova, Karsavina, Lopokova, Spessivtzeva, Dubrovska, Nemtchinova, Sokolova, Tchernicheva, Egorova, Nijinska, Danilova, and Markova; among the men, Nijinsky, Fokine, Vladimiroff, Bolm, Mordkin, Novikoff, Volinine, Cecchetti, Massine, Woicikowski, Idzikowski, Dolin, and Lifar. Among his composers were Stravinsky, Debussy, Ravel, Richard Strauss, Fauré, Satie, Respighi, De Falla, Prokofiev, Poulenc, Auric, Milhaud, Dukelsky, Rieti, Lambert, Berners, Sauguet, and Nabokov. His designers were such painters as Benois, Roerich, Bakst, Soudeikine, Doboujinsky, Larionov, Picasso,

Derain, Matisse, Braque, Gris, Utrillo, Miro, Tchelitchev, Di Chirico and Rouault. His choreographers were Fokine, Nijinsky, Massine, Nijinska, and myself.

Since the disbandment of Diaghilev's company following his death in 1929, his dancers and choreographers have influenced ballet throughout the world. Serge Lifar has been for many years ballet master at the Paris Opéra, which, with the Royal Danish Ballet at Copenhagen, continues the oldest traditions of teaching and performance in the free world. Ninette de Valois, a soloist with the Diaghilev company, founded a ballet company and an associated school in London which became in time the Sadler's Wells Ballet, the national company of Great Britain. Massine and I were the first choreographers of the Ballet Russe de Monte Carlo, founded in Europe in 1932. In America, I founded with Lincoln Kirstein the American Ballet, precursor of the present New York City Ballet. The American Ballet's complementary group, Kirstein's Ballet Caravan, produced, in addition to classical works, ballets based on native American material—*Filling Station, Billy the Kid, Yankee Clipper,* etc.—with choreography by such American dancers as Lew Christensen, Eugene Loring, and William Dollar and with music by American composers. The New York City Ballet, with its associated school, the School of American Ballet, represents the result of twenty years' work toward the achievement of excellence in classical performance.

The Ballet Theatre, founded by Lucia Chase and Richard Pleasant, grew out of the New York ballet school of Mikhail Mordkin. Fokine, who had staged many of his own works for many ballet companies, supervised productions of his ballets by the Ballet Theatre and created his last ballet for this company in 1941. The English choreographer Antony Tudor, who—like Frederick Ashton, principal choreographer to the Sadler's Wells Ballet—had been a student in London of Marie Rambert, joined The Ballet Theatre at its inception. Agnes de Mille and Jerome Robbins are but two of the native American choreographers whose work this company has produced.

No longer is any one place the ballet capital of the world. The most important center of activity has shifted, as before, with the finest teachers, the finest dancers, and with those who are able to advance the limits of the art. The history of an art that began in the courts of the Renaissance ends with ballet companies and associated schools in principal cities throughout the Western world. Ballet flourishes wherever there are great teachers and choreographers, talented dancers, and an interested audience.

I hope the foregoing has in some measure provided useful information for all who are interested in the ballet—the enthusiastic balletgoer, the student, and the teacher.

Part Four

CHRONOLOGY
OF SIGNIFICANT EVENTS
IN THE HISTORY
OF BALLET 1469–1953

Ballet, we have seen, is an art without nationality; it has a family history. The new ballets we see on the stage today come at the end of a long line of descent from the past. Dance has a living past in the dancers of today; its traditional theory of basic steps and movements is the foundation of its current practice. No one can learn to dance without a teacher, and that teacher was the student of an earlier master. In the eighteenth century, the Frenchman Noverre and the Italian Galeotti taught the Dane Antoine Bournonville, whose son Auguste was the master of the Swede Johannsen, teacher of the Russians Pavlova and Fokine.

The dancers, teachers, and choreographers we are familiar with today are thus offshoots of a great international family tree—living embodiments of a precise tradition. Ballet's history is a record of teachers and students: what the teacher handed down, what the student learned, what he carried forward and extended, what he rejected, what he changed. In the gradual unfolding of this story, we see how the contributions of different individuals in different countries move forward, seem to falter, then converge in the ballet we know today.

1469 Lorenzo de Medici, great patron of the arts, succeeds to the rule of Florence. His marriage to Clarice Orsini: grand procession, tournament; allegorical masque, executed by the foremost painters, poets, and sculptors of the time, depicts in song and spectacle the glories of antiquity.

1475 Grand tournament of Giuliano de Medici is held at Florence: scene, costumes, and dance figures commemorated in the *Birth of Venus, Mars and Venus*, and *Primavera* of Botticelli.

c.1500 Development in Italy and southern France of the popular court dance form the *ballo*, social dances performed in a ballroom or in the open air. The *ballo* is freer, more animated, than the other variety of dance popular at this time, the *basse danse* (low dance). Originally Italian, the *basse danse* was a carefully prescribed court dance, the ancestor of the minuet. *Balletti* is the diminutive of *ballo*, and it is from this word that we derive *ballet*.

1512   The *masque*, variation of princely Italian masquerades, is introduced in England, at the court of Henry VIII. Social, rather than theatrical or dramatic, at first, the *masque* later includes songs, speeches, introductory dance, general dance, and finale of speech and chorus.

1523   Robert Copland's *The Manner of Dancing Basse Dances After the Use of France* appears in England.

1533   Catherine de Medici arrives in France. Her marriage to Henry of Orleans (later Henry II) takes place: introduction of Italian pageantry to France.

c.1555   Baldassarino de Belgiojoso (Balthazar de Beaujoyeulx), Italian violinist, immigrates to France and becomes a member of the French Court: later develops French and Italian elements into the first modern ballet.

1558   Royal fete and ball is held on April 24 for the marriage of Francis, eldest son of Catherine de Medici, and Mary, Queen of Scots: spectacle with *"masques* and *mummeries,"* beginning of the *ballet de cour,* costly court entertainments consisting of vocal and instrumental music, spoken dialogue, pantomime, dancing, and mechanical effects. All dancers in these ballets wear masks. Ladies of the court participate, but principal roles are taken by men.

1570   Jean Antoine de Baïf, French poet, and Joachim Thibault de Courville, French musician, found the Academy of St. Cecilia in Paris to encourage the fusion of poetry, music, and movement after the manner of the ancients. Dancing to be in accord with music and song.

1571   Troupe of Italian comedians popularize in Paris the *commedia dell' arte* (Columbine, Harlequin, et al.), traditional native farces of Italy.

c.1575   Giovanni da Bologna's *Mercury*—inspiration for the *attitude,* basic pose of classic ballet. "On one occasion, performing the part of Mercury, I took, as I turned in my pirouette, the attitude of the statue of Mercury by Bologna."—Carlo Blasis, 1830.

1580   The history of ballet as we know it today begins on October 15, when Beaujoyeulx presents *Ballet Comique de la Reine* at the court of Catherine de Medici on the occasion of the marriage of Marguerite of Lorraine, the Queen's sister, to the Duc de Joyeuse: assimilation of French and Italian elements of dance, music, and spectacle into a coherent dramatic whole. To its creator, this work was called a *ballet* because it presents "a geometrical arrangement of numerous people dancing together under a diverse harmony of many instruments"; it is *comique* "for the lovely, tranquil, and happy conclusion by which it ends, by the quality of the personages involved, who are almost all gods and goddesses." Beaujoyeulx's musico-dramatic synthesis of Italian opera and French *ballet de cour* originates the school of French ballet and opera that is to serve as the model in Europe for two centuries.

1588   Jehan Tabourot, priest of Langre, publishes—under the pseudonym Thoinot Arbeau—*Orchésographie* (writing of dancing), *treatise in the form of a* *dialogue whereby all manner of persons may easily acquire and practice the honorable exercise of dancing*: illustrations and directions on the proper execution of dances of the time (pavane, galliard, gavotte, etc.), and establishment of principles for the five absolute positions of the classic dance (*see* Glossary). Arbeau's work provides the potential technical base for instruction in dancing and assures French supremacy in the initial development of ballet.

1597 Thomas Morley's *Plaine and Easie Introduction to Practical Musick* details the differences between types of music for dancing, calling the pavane "a kind of staid musick ordained for grave dancing" and the galliard "a lighter and more stirring kind of dance." The pavane, galliard, allemande, sarabande, polonaise, minuet, jig, gavotte, etc., were originally dance tunes that originated among the peoples of Italy, France, Germany, Spain, and Poland in the sixteenth century or before. These popular or courtly dances soon gave rise to a new form in music, as composers stylized the contrasting moods of the dances in the writing of *suites*.

1605 Ben Jonson, English poet and dramatist, and the architect Inigo Jones collaborate on the production of the *Twelfth Night Masque*: unrivaled scenic and dramatic effect.

1607 *Orfeo*, opera by Monteverdi, is performed on February 24 at the Academia degl' Invaghiti, Mantua: development of principles of *ballet comique* in musical work; first opera to use accompaniment of full orchestra.

1608 First antimasque, in *The Hue and Cry after Cupid*, Jonson-Jones, surrounds heroic figures with sportive dancers to amuse spectators with "antic faces" and "ridiculous gesture."

1625 Ballet in France regresses to nondramatic dances introduced by poems or songs.

1632 Jean Baptiste Lully (Giovanni Battista Lulli), musician and dancer, is born in Italy on November 29.

1634 First performance of *Comus*, masque by John Milton.

1641 *Prosperity of the Arms of France*, ballet by Cardinal Richelieu, performed.

1645 Cardinal Mazarin, successor to Richelieu as Prime Minister, introduces Italian grand opera to Paris: France absorbs Italian mechanical stage devices to increase the spectacle of ballet.

1645 Louis XIV, at age seven, first dances publicly.

1653 Louis XIV appears as *Le Roi Soleil* (the Sun King) in the *Ballet de la Nuit*, composed partly by Lully.

1658 "Tragedy and ballet are two species of painting in which what is most illustrious in the world is placed on view," writes Abbé Michel de Pure in *Idée des Spectacles*.

1661   Académie de Danse is founded by Louis XIV in a room in the Louvre, Paris: "Although the art of dancing has always been recognized as one of the most honorable, and the most necessary for the training of the body, to give it the first and most natural foundations for all kinds of exercises and amongst others for those of arms; and as it is . . . . many ignorant people have tried to disfigure the dance and to spoil it . . . we deemed it opportune to establish in our good town of Paris a Royal Academy of Dancing." On June 28, 1669, Louis XIV of France grants royal letters patent for the establishment of a theatre in which to present opera and drama with music: L'Académie de Musique et de Danse, the institution we know today as the Paris Opéra. Although the name of this institution has changed with different French regimes and it has occupied numerous buildings, the name on the Théâtre de l'Opéra in Paris is L'Académie de Musique et de Danse, representing almost three hundred years of uninterrupted history in teaching and performance.

1664   On January 29, in *Le Mariage Forcé*, Italian composer and dancer Lully begins collaboration with the French poet-playwright Molière; *commedia dell' arte* combined with the tradition of French court dancing in the creation of comedy ballets to incidental music. Louis XIV, Lully, and Pierre Beauchamp, first great French dancer, participate in performance.

1670   *Les Amants Magnifiques* is presented: comedy ballet by Molière and Lully in which the performers "by their steps, gestures, and movements, visibly expressed all things." On October 23 there is presented *Le Bourgeois Gentilhomme*, last collaboration between Molière and Lully: play includes overture, ten musical numbers, dialogue for soprano and contralto, a ballet in Act One (*Ballet des Nations*), and finale for solo and chorus. Lully dances at the first performance. Excerpt from the play: "All the ills of mankind, all the tragic misfortunes that fill the history books, all political blunders, all the failures of great commanders, have arisen merely from lack of skill in dancing. . . . When a man has been guilty of a mistake, either in ordering his own affairs, or in directing those of the State, or in commanding an army, do we not always say: so-and-so has made a false step . . . ?"

1671   *Psyche*, tragedy ballet by Molière, Corneille, Lully, and Quinault, presented on January 17.

1671   The Paris Académie opens on March 19 with *Pomone*, a *pastorale* with music by Cambert, dances by Beauchamp, and text by the Abbé Perrin, director of the Académie.

1671   Pierre Beauchamp, dancing master to the King, becomes first ballet master of the Académie. Dancing begins to be a profession, rather than a court pastime.

1672   Lully succeeds to the directorship of the Académie as composer, conductor, and manager; dancing school inaugurated under Beauchamp. Under Lully's direction, formal court dance is adjusted to the stage: larger, more open movements of the theatre replace small, confined gestures of the ballroom.

1672 Louis Pécourt, pupil of Beauchamp, makes his debut at the Académie, becomes *premier danseur*, dancing principal roles in ballets by Lully and Beauchamp. He was "handsome and well made," danced "with all possible noblesse," appeared always "with grace, justness, and activity," and was "so agreeable in conversation that the greatest lords took pleasure in his company."

1681 *The Triumph of Love* (Lully) presented on January 21 at St. Germaine en Laye, the first ballet in which women appeared as professional dancers. Ladies of the French court dance the first performance on this work (but it was later danced at L'Académie Royale, when Mademoiselle Lafontaine, first *première danseuse* in the history of ballet, made her debut).

1682 Père Claude François Menestrier's *Ballets Ancient and Modern* becomes the first published history of dancing.

1684 *An Arrow against Profane and Promiscuous Dancing Drawn Out of the Quiver of the Scriptures,* by Increase Mather, is published in Boston.

1687 Lully dies on March 22. In the fifteen years he superintended the Académie, Lully produced twenty grand operas in addition to other works and firmly established the new school of opera-ballet, in which music and dancing shared equally in the drama. Italian grand operas of this time give dancing a secondary place and include ballets only as *divertissements*. Lully, violinist and dancer, leaves French lyric drama so successfully formulated that Paris is the theatre capital of the world, a universally accepted model of teaching and execution.

1687 Beauchamp retires as ballet master; he is succeeded by Louis Pécourt.

1689 *Dido and Aeneas,* opera by Purcell, is performed by Josias Priest's Singing and Dancing Academy in London.

1697 Birth of Louis Dupré, *Le Grand Dupré,* great French dancer: a "rare harmony in movement earned for the celebrated Dupré the glorious title of 'Dieu de la Danse': and in fact this excellent dancer seemed a divinity rather than a man: the calm and flowing continuity of his every movement and the perfect co-ordination and control of every muscle made for a perfect ensemble."—Noverre.

c.1700 Pierre Beauchamp names the five basic positions of the classic dance (*see* Glossary). As a dancer, Beauchamp had also been a model for future technique in dancing; he was a virtuoso executant of *pirouettes* and *tours en l'air.*

1701 *Choreography, or the Art of Writing Dancing* is published in Paris. This early work on dance notation was edited by Raoul Ager Feuillet; it has been attributed to Louis Pécourt.

1705 Françoise Prévost succeeds Mademoiselle Lafontaine as *première danseuse* at the Académie. Rameau wrote that Prévost "put into one single dance all the rules we are able to give in our art and she puts them into practice with such grace, justness, and activity that she may be looked upon as a prodigy of her kind."

1707   Birth of Marie Sallé. Niece of the famous harlequin Francisque Moylin, and daughter of a tumbler, she is to endow her dancing with dramatic gesture and mimed expression and become a great *danseuse* of the century.

1708   At the château of the Duchesse du Maine, two celebrated dancers from the Opéra, Françoise Prévost and Jean Balon, perform the final scene of Act Four of Corneille's *Horace* as a pantomime. The scene is acted in silence, "through gestures and bodily movements, among which was not a single all-too-pronounced dance step": early introduction of dramatic mime into ballet.

1710   Marie-Anne Cupis de Camargo, celebrated French dancer of Spanish descent, is born on April 15; she becomes the principal rival of Sallé.

1712   *Manual*, by John Rich, provides a series of exercises for facility in dancing based on the five basic positions indicated by Arbeau (1588) and specified by Beauchamp (c.1700): beginning of a systematic foundation for the ideal execution of the classic dance.

1714   Birth of Christoph Willibald Gluck, German composer, the founder of modern opera.

1717   On March 2, John Weaver, English dancer and ballet master at the Drury Lane Theatre, London, presents a "new dramatic pantomime, after the manner of the ancient pantomimes," *The Loves of Mars and Venus*. This pantomime ballet with a plot is the first *ballet d'action* on record. Wrote Colley Cibber: "The fable of Mars and Venus was formed into a connected presentation of dances in character, wherein the passions were so happily expressed, and the whole story was so intelligibly told, by a mute narration of gesture only, that even thinking spectators allowed it both a pleasing and rational entertainment."

1721   *Anatomical and Mechanical Lectures upon Dancing*, by John Weaver, is published: establishment of an anatomical base for proper dance instruction. "Dancing is an elegant and regular movement, harmoniously composed of beautiful *Attitudes*, and contrasted graceful postures of the Body, and parts thereof."

1725   *The Dancing Master*, by Pierre Rameau, is published: descriptions of dances of the time and detailed instructions on the five absolute positions. "Dancing adds graces to the gifts which nature has bestowed upon us, by regulating the movements of the body and setting it in its proper positions. And, if we do not completely eradicate the defects with which we are born, it mitigates or conceals them. This single instance will suffice to explain its utility and to excite a desire to be skilled in it."

1725   Marie Sallé appears at John Rich's Lincoln's Inn Fields Theatre, London, in ballet-pantomimes. It was in England, rather than in the set, conventional pattern of ballet at the Paris Opéra, that Sallé could use freely the gestural dance that interested her. She was so popular, however, that the Opéra continually asked her to return. When she did so, the Opéra was obliged to produce the *ballets d'action* that she acted and danced with such expression. Thus popularity and intelligence combined to introduce a new kind of ballet to Europe.

1726 Marie Camargo makes her debut at the Opéra on May 5.

1726 First French dancing master is appointed to the Court of Denmark.

1727 Jean Georges Noverre is born on April 29.

1729 Gaetan Vestris is born in April, in Florence. He becomes the first *danseur* of his time, the first great classical dancer in Europe, a choreographer, mime, and ballet master; he is student of Louis Dupré.

c.1730 The *danse haute* (high dance) begins to replace the *danse terre à terre* (dance close to earth). The old court spectacles had been performed in rooms, with the audiences grouped about the dance area on raised platforms. In the theatre, the stage itself was raised and the audience watched from below. Lully's ballets, though making certain concessions to the theatre, still remained horizontal, describing dances on the horizontal plane of the stage floor as if it were still the ballroom and audiences were looking down on it. Rameau aimed at a vertical dance, where a theatre audience could be entertained by dancers who jumped and leaped. In the fierce controversy that raged between the Lullists and Ramists, the latter found great support in the popularity of the spectacular *danse haute* of Marie Camargo, who about this time shortened the traditional ballet dress in order that the audience might see the *entrechat* and other remarkable steps of elevation. Camargo is credited with introducing the ninety-degree turnout for dancers and the *entrechat-quatre* (see Glossary).

1734 Marie Sallé creates in London the ballet-pantomime *Pygmalion*. "She has dared to appear in this *entrée* without pannier, skirt, or bodice, and with her hair down; she did not wear a single ornament on her head. Apart from her corset and petticoat she wore only a simple dress of muslin draped about her in the manner of a Greek statue."

1735 Opening of the Imperial Dancing Academy in St. Petersburg, Russia, as the Empress Anna Ivanovna orders that all cadets be taught to dance in order to replace foreign artists at the Russian court. A Frenchman, Lande, is appointed director and an Italian, Francesco Araya, is engaged to teach the cadets Italian dances.

1735 *Les Indes Galantes*, opera-ballet by J. P. Rameau, is presented at the Opéra on August 23 with Dupré, Camargo, and Sallé.

c.1737 The works of Jean Philippe Rameau begin to replace those of Lully at the Académie. At this time, the original thirty-seven members of the company have increased to one hundred and forty-nine.

1738 Imperial St. Petersburg Theatrical Academy (now the Leningrad Choreographic Academy) is founded.

1743 Jean Georges Noverre, pupil of Dupré, makes his debut at the Opéra Comique, Paris.

1745 *The Princess of Navarre,* lyric comedy ballet by Rameau, libretto by Voltaire, is produced.

1745 On December 29, Jean Barthélemy produces in Berlin his recollection of Marie Sallé's *Pygmalion.* The statue is danced by La Barberina (Barberina Campanini), Italian *danseuse* who popularizes the Italian pantomime in European dance. She appeared at the Opéra, where Rameau arranged dances for her, and in London at John Rich's theatre, where she acquired knowledge of English pantomime. C. H. Graun composes for this production of *Pygmalion* music that substitutes for the conventional dance numbers a free score related directly to the action: the first score of this kind. Among the dancers in this production is Jean Georges Noverre.

1746 "It is up to poetry, music, and dance to present to us the image of human actions and passions," writes Charles Batteux, *Les Beaux Arts reduit à un même principe.*

1748 The Royal Theatre, home of the Royal Danish ballet, opens in Copenhagen.

1750 Noverre partners Camargo at Lyon.

c.1751 Noverre stages his first ballet, *Les Fêtes Chinoises (The Chinese Festivals).*

1751 Gaetan Vestris succeeds Louis Dupré as *premier danseur* at the Opéra.

1755 On February 5, Noverre signs contract with David Garrick to arrange dances at the Drury Lane Theatre, London. To Garrick, Noverre is "the Shakespeare of the Dance." To Noverre, Garrick is "the most handsome, the most perfect, and the most worthy of admiration of all actors; he may be regarded as the Proteus of our time, because he understood all styles and presented them with a perfection and truth which aroused not only the applause and praise of his countrymen, but also excited the admiration and encomiums of all foreigners. He was so natural, his expression was so lifelike, his gestures, features, glances were so eloquent and convincing, that he made the action clear even to those who did not understand a word of English."

1756 Marie Sallé dies. Writes her friend Noverre: "Mademoiselle Sallé . . . replaced tinsel glitter by simple and touching graces. Her physiognomy was noble, sensitive, and expressive. Her voluptuous dancing was written with as much finesse as lightness; it was not by leaps and frolics that she went to your heart."

c.1757 Gallini sees "the celebrated Dupré, at near the age of sixty, dance at Paris with all the agility and sprightliness of youth, and with such power of pleasing as if the graces in him had braved superannuation."

1757 "The dance still awaits a man of genius. It is in a bad state everywhere, for hardly anyone suspects the essence of it to be a kind of imitation . . . A dance is a poem. This poem should have its independent representation. It is an 'imitation' by virtue of the movements, an imitation which presupposes the collaboration of poet, painter, musicians, and pantomime-dancer."—Denis Diderot.

1760 On March 1, Noverre at Stuttgart, ballet master to the court of the Duke of Württemberg, begins reforms in the direction of the *ballet d'action*, pantomime ballet with definite plot, where dance is integrated with the action of the story.

1760 Auguste Vestris, great French dancer, son of Gaetan Vestris and the *danseuse* Marie Allard is born on March 27. Said his father, Gaetan: "Auguste is more skillful than I and the explanation is simple: Gaetan is his father—an advantage nature denied me." Auguste Vestris is credited with introducing the *entrechat-huit* and multiple pirouettes. He was the teacher of Charles Didelot, Jules Perrot, Carlotta Grisi, and Fanny Elssler, among others.

1760 Marie Allard makes her debut in June at the Opéra, Paris. Allard soon becomes a ballerina. She is a student of Gaetan Vestris.

1760 Noverre's *Letters on the Dance and Ballets* published in December in Lyon and Stuttgart: "Children of Terpsichore, renounce *caprioles, entrechats,* and overcomplicated steps; abandon grimaces to study sentiments . . . study how to make your gestures noble, never forget that is the lifeblood of dancing; put judgment and sense into your *pas de deux* . . . away with those lifeless masks, but feeble copies of nature; they hide your features, they stifle, so to speak, your emotions and thus deprive you of your most important means of expression; take off those enormous wigs and those gigantic headdresses . . . discard the use of those stiff and cumbersome hoops, which disfigure the elegance of your attitudes. . . . Lully's dance music is cold, tedious, and devoid of character . . . What was compatible then is no longer so . . . A well-composed ballet is a living picture of the passions, manners, habits, ceremonies, and customs of all nations of the globe, consequently it must be expressive in all its details and speak to the soul through the eyes; if it be devoid of expression, of striking pictures, of strong situations, it becomes a cold and dreary spectacle. This form of art will not admit of mediocrity."

1761 On June 12 there takes place at the Opéra the debut of Dauberval, afterward *premier danseur* and choreographer of the first comic ballet; he was a student of Noverre.

1761 *Don Juan*, "pantomime ballet in the manner of the ancients," with music by Gluck and choreography by Gasparo Angiolini (1723–96), is presented on October 17. This work, created independently of Noverre, claims to be the first of its kind. Its music and dancing are subordinate to a plot; Gluck's score is composed in terms of stage action.

1762   The *première* of Gluck's *Orpheus and Eurydice* takes place on October 5 at the Burg Theatre, Vienna. This opera epitomizes for music what the new *ballet d'action* of Noverre accomplished for dancing. Just as Noverre wished to replace the virtuoso dancer with action and meaningful gesture, Gluck in *Orpheus* broke the tyranny of the virtuoso singer and replaced casually connected solos with musical drama. The first production of *Orpheus* has ballets by Angiolini; a later production, ballets by Noverre.

1763   *Jason and Medea, ballet d'action* by Noverre, to music by Rodolphe, is produced on February 11 at Stuttgart with Gaetan Vestris as Jason.

1766   Double pirouettes are introduced in Paris by the German ballerina Anna Heinel.

1767   Noverre is appointed ballet master to the Imperial Theatres in Vienna, dancing master to Empress Maria Theresa and her family, and teacher of her daughter, Marie Antoinette; this is the beginning of his collaboration with Gluck.

1767   Birth of Charles Louis Didelot, French dancer, choreographer, ballet master, "father of the Russian ballet."

1767   The first performance of *Alcestis*, opera by Gluck with ballet by Noverre, takes place on December 26 at the Burg Theatre, Vienna. In his dedication of the opera, Gluck applies Noverre's doctrine to opera: "I shall try to reduce music to its real function, that of seconding poetry by intensifying the expression of sentiments and the interest of situations without interrupting the action by needless ornament. I have accordingly taken care not to interrupt the singer in the heat of dialogue to wait for a tedious *ritournel*, nor do I allow him to stop on a sonorous vowel, in the middle of a phrase, in order to show the nimbleness of a beautiful voice in a long cadenza."

1768   John Durang, first American to become famous as a dancer, is born on January 6.

1769   Salvatore Vigano, Italian dancer, choreographer, teacher, and ballet master —student of Dauberval—is born on March 25. "It is not enough for me to please the eye; I wish to interest the heart."

1770   Gaetan Vestris revives Noverre's *Jason and Medea* on December 11 at the Opéra, Paris, with Marie Allard. Vestris discards the mask customarily worn by dancers, freeing the features for expressive mime and the dramatic expression essential to Noverre's *ballet d'action*. A member of the audience later wrote of Vestris' performance: "The particular merit of Vestris was his grace, his elegance, his delicacy. All his *pas* had a purity, a finish of which one can have no idea today, and it was not without reason that they compare his talent to that of Racine."

1771   Noverre produces on October 17 a second version of his ballet *Les Jalousies ou Les Fêtes du Serail* at the Teatro Regio Ducal, Milan, to music by Mozart. The ballet performed between the two acts of Mozart's festival production is *Ascanio in Alba*.

c.1772 "Ballet is an action explained by a dance" appears in the *Encyclopedia* of Diderot and D'Alembert.

1773 Maximilien Gardel, *premier danseur*, discards his mask in performances at the Opéra.

1774 Noverre becomes ballet master at Milan.

1775 Royal Theatre, Copenhagen, engages Vincenzo Galeotti as ballet master, choreographer, and *premier danseur*. A student of Noverre, Galeotti remained active in Denmark until 1816. He built up a repertory of some fifty ballets which have been performed more than two thousand times.

1776 Gaetan Vestris becomes ballet master at the Paris Opéra.

1776 Revival of Noverre's *Les Caprices de Galathée* in November at the Opéra, Paris, with Madeleine Guimard, Marie Allard, and Le Picq.

1776 Ernest Theodor Amadeus Hoffmann, German writer, composer, lawyer, and masterful writer of romances, is born on January 24. Hoffmann wrote many imaginative and supernatural stories, of which only a few are contained in Offenbach's opera *Tales of Hoffmann*. The ballets *Coppélia* and *The Nutcracker* are based on two of Hoffmann's stories.

1776 Noverre succeeds Gaetan Vestris as ballet master at the Opéra in August; appointed by his former pupil, Marie Antoinette, now Queen of France.

1778 First performance of *Les Petits Riens* (Mozart-Noverre) at the Opéra, Paris, on June 11.

1778 August 3: Teatro alla Scala opens in Milan. Five ballets are produced the first year.

1779 *Mirza, ballet d'action* by Maximilien Gardel, with Gardel, Dauberval, A. Vestris, Guimard, and Allard, is presented in Paris. Act Three of this work takes place in America; it is the first ballet with an American scene.

1779 On May 18, Gluck and Noverre produce *Iphigenia in Tauris* in collaboration.

1780 Noverre becomes ballet master at the King's Theatre, London.

1781 On October 13, Mozart, writing on opera in a letter to his father, reaffirms Noverre's principles: "Why do Italian comic operas please everywhere—in spite of their miserable libretti? . . . Just because in them music reigns supreme, and when one listens to it all else is forgotten. Why, an opera is sure of success when the plot is well worked out, the words written solely for the music and not shoved in here and there to suit some miserable rhyme (which, God knows, never enhances the value of any theatrical performance, be it what it may, but rather detracts from it) . . ."

1783 First English translation of Noverre's *Letters* is published.

1783   The Bolshoi Theatre, until 1889 the center of Russian ballet, opens in St. Petersburg on October 5.*

1786   *La Fille Mal Gardée* (Dauberval-Hertel), probably the first comic ballet, is presented.

1786   *Les Caprices du Cupidon et le Maître du Ballet* (Galeotti) is produced on October 31 at the Royal Theatre, Copenhagen. This ballet has been in the repertory of the Royal Danish Ballet since its first performance; it is the oldest ballet in existence with its original choreography intact. Harald Lander revived the ballet for the Paris Opéra on February 27, 1952.

1792   Alexander Placide and his wife dance a ballet, *The Bird Catcher*, on January 25 in New York. John Durang, first professional American dancer, is in the cast.

1795   *Jason and Medea*, great *ballet d'action* by Noverre, is produced in St. Petersburg by his student Le Picq.

1796   *Flore and Zephire*, ballet by Didelot, is produced on July 7 in London: the first ballet in which a dancer is suspended on wire to simulate flight.

1796   *Danse*, by M. L. E. Moreau de Saint-Méry, is published in Philadelphia. Probably the first book on dancing published in the United States, *Danse* was freely quoted by Blasis thirty-four years later. Saint-Méry expressed the opinion that the principal object of the dance is "the same as that of music, the expression of sentiment and passions. A gesture is beautiful only when it depicts sadness, tenderness, pride—in a word, the soul."

1801   Charles Didelot becomes choreographer at the Russian Imperial Theatre. Pushkin, the great Russian poet, expresses the opinion that in Didelot's ballets there is more poetry than in all the French literature of the period. Didelot believed that ballet must have a plot; that dancers, in accordance with the action, must be able to solve their own problems, reconstruct the characters themselves: "A true dancer must be also a good actor and a poet at heart." His teachers were Auguste Vestris, Noverre, and Dauberval. Didelot is known as the "father of the Russian ballet."

1801   *The Creatures of Prometheus* (Beethoven-Vigano) is produced on March 28 at the Court Theatre, Vienna.

1803   Noverre's *Letters* is translated into Russian and Danish.

1804   Marie Taglioni, great ballerina of the Romantic era, is born on April 23.

1805   Hans Christian Andersen, Danish poet and fabulist, balletomane, is born on April 2. Andersen's fairy stories provide plots for many ballets.

1808   Gaetan Vestris dies on September 23.

*New Russian calendar dates are used throughout this book. Exceptions are those few instances where tradition or the preference of living persons dictates the use of the Old Style. Both Old and New Style dates are used in these few cases.

1810 Noverre dies on October 19.

1810 Fanny Elssler, Romantic ballerina, is born on June 23.

1810 Jules Perrot, great *danseur* of the Romantic ballet and its finest choreographer, is born on August 18; creator, with Jean Coralli, of *Giselle, Pas de Quatre*, etc. In Perrot's view, ballet must be filled with dramatic action and presented as a realistic reflection of life. He was responsible for the integration of dance and pantomime that made possible the dramatic ballet as we know it today. His teachers were Auguste Vestris and Salvatore Vigano.

1811 Théophile Gautier, poet, novelist, critic, guiding spirit of the Romantic Ballet, is born on August 31.

1812 The celebrated dancer and student of Dauberval, Salvatore Vigano, becomes ballet master at La Scala, Milan, and progress in the development of ballet shifts from France to Italy. Vigano's contribution was the *choreodrame*, or dance drama, a more complete development of Noverre's *ballet d'action* than had been realized in France. This was a dramatic spectacle that integrated principals, moving masses of dancers, and authentic backgrounds with music. His work anticipated Fokine's reforms and the mass spectacles of D. W. Griffith by a hundred years.

1815 Birth of Arthur Michel Saint-Léon, French dancer, choreographer, musician, and ballet master.

1816 Charles Didelot becomes first ballet master at the Imperial Russian Theatre. He remains in Russia until his death in 1837. In addition to the many excellent ballets Didelot produces in Russia, he establishes in the Imperial School the teaching methods and techniques that are afterward to make it famous.

1816 Antoine Bournonville, pupil of Noverre, succeeds Galeotti as ballet master and choreographer at the Royal Theatre, Copenhagen.

1819 Birth of Carlotta Grisi, ballerina of the Romantic era, creator of *Giselle*.

1820 Carlo Blasis' *Elementary Treatise on the Theory and Practice of the Art of Dancing* is published in Milan. The first complete work on dance technique, this book is still the primary text of classical dancing today.

1820 This is the approximate beginning of the Romantic ballet.

1821 Fanny Cerito, Romantic ballerina, is born.

1821 Lucile Grahn, Danish ballerina of the Romantic era, is born on June 30.

1821 Salvatore Vigano dies on August 10.

1821 Date of the first known print depicting a dancer *sur les pointes* (on toe). Dancing on *pointes* is the outstanding innovation in technique of the Romantic ballet.

1822   On February 6, gas lighting is first used at the Paris Opéra. The soft, misty quality of this lighting did much to support the ethereal scenes of the Romantic ballet.

1822   Marius Petipa, great choreographer and ballet master, the founder of Russian classicism, is born on March 24.

1822   Marie Taglioni makes her debut on June 10 at the Hoftheatre, Vienna, in a ballet created especially for her by her father, Philippe Taglioni: *The Reception of a Young Nymph at the Court of Terpsichore*. Another young dancer in the ballet who was also making her debut: Fanny Elssler.

1825   Birth of Augusta Maywood, first American ballerina to become internationally famous.

1825   The Bolshoi Theatre, Moscow, opens on January 18. The Moscow Ballet alone danced in this theatre until 1939, when it became the principal Soviet ballet theatre.

1826   Auguste Vestris gives his farewell performance at the Opéra.

1829   Auguste Bournonville succeeds his father, Antoine, as ballet master, choreographer, and *premier danseur* at the Royal Theatre, Copenhagen. Until his death, in 1879, Bournonville worked almost uninterruptedly in Denmark. He was the Royal Danish Ballet's greatest choreographic genius and also its finest organizer. He made ballet equivalent to opera and drama in importance at the Royal Theatre, developed Danish dancers, and enriched the Danish repertory with more than fifty original ballets. These works were not only romantic, in conformance with their time, but bright, comic ballets that depicted the life of the people. *Napoli*, his presentation of Italian life, is perhaps the finest of the ten ballets by Bournonville still performed in Copenhagen. A great dancer himself, the pupil of his father's friend Auguste Vestris and of Galeotti, Bournonville choreographed—in opposition to the French *ballet blanc*—for men as much as for women. Wrote Hans Christian Andersen: "When the Italian Galeotti died in Denmark, Terpsichore wept. Who was there that could supply his place as ballet composer? No one took his place; but a new one was born, who, like every true genius, made his own way—and that is Bournonville."

1829   Carlo Blasis' *Code of Terpsichore*, primary text for dancers, establishes fundamentals of the modern classic dance.

1830   The sylphide costume first appears, in Paris. This long, diaphanous ballet dress that reaches well below the knee, almost to the ankle, was named *post facto* for *La Sylphide*, the famous ballet created by Marie Taglioni in 1832. In its guise appeared many heroines of the Romantic ballet; the costume is still familiar in the second act of *Giselle*, in *Swan Lake*, and in *Les Sylphides*.

1830   Jules Perrot makes his debut at the Opéra.

1830 *Le Dieu et la Bayadère* (P. Taglioni-Auber-Scribe) is presented at the Opéra on October 13 with Marie Taglioni.

1831 Jean Coralli becomes ballet master at the Opéra.

1831 This is the probable date of the first *ballet blanc*, or white ballet, familiar today in *Giselle* (Act Two), *Les Sylphides*, et al., at the Paris Opéra.

1832 Marie Taglioni dances the title role in *La Sylphide* on March 12.

1832 *La Sylphide is* presented in London on July 26 at the Theatre Royal, Covent Garden, with Marie and Paul Taglioni.

1834 Birth of Lev Ivanov, first great Russian choreographer (*Swan Lake*, etc.).

1834 Edgar Degas, French painter of the ballet, is born on July 19.

1834 Fanny Elssler makes her debut at the Paris Opéra in September, in *La Tempête* (Coralli). Elssler's immediate and brilliant success begins at this point to challenge the supremacy of Marie Taglioni, whose rival she never ceased to be.

1835 Auguste Vestris, age seventy-five, partners Marie Taglioni in a minuet at a special performance at the Opéra on April 8.

1835 The first American performance of *La Sylphide*, by Céleste, takes place on April 15.

1835 Fanny Cerito makes her debut at the San Carlo Theatre, Naples. "There must be youth, and that I found in Cerito! It was something incomparably beautiful, it was a swallow flight in the dance, a sport of Psyche," writes Hans Christian Andersen.

1835 The first book of Hans Christian Andersen's *Fairy Tales* (*Eventyr*) is published in Copenhagen.

1836 Clément Philibert Léo Delibes, French composer, is born on February 21.

1836 Carlotta Grisi makes her London debut on April 12 in a *pas de deux* with her husband, Jules Perrot.

1836 Fanny Elssler appears in *Le Diable Boiteux* (*The Devil on Two Sticks*), ballet by Jean Coralli, at the Paris Opéra, on June 1.

1836 Auguste Bournonville stages *La Sylphide* for Lucile Grahn at the Royal Theatre, Copenhagen. This version, which had new music by the Danish composer Herman Lovenskjold, has been in the repertory of the Royal Danish Ballet since it was first produced.

1836 Théophile Gautier begins to write art and theatre criticism for *La Presse* in Paris.

1837 Carlo Blasis is appointed director of the Imperial Academy of Dancing and Pantomime at La Scala, Milan.

1837 Marie Taglioni makes her St. Petersburg debut on September 30, in *La Sylphide*. Taglioni remains in Russia until 1841.

1837 Augusta Maywood and Mary Ann Lee make their debuts in *The Maid of Cashmere* (*Le Dieu et la Bayadère*) on December 30 at the Chestnut Street Theatre, Philadelphia.

1838 Lucile Grahn makes her Paris debut.

1838 *La Sylphide* with Augusta Maywood in the title role and Mary Ann Lee as Flora is presented on March 17, at the Chestnut Street Theatre, Philadelphia.

c.1838 George Washington Smith, first American *danseur noble*, makes his debut at the Chestnut Street Theatre. Smith partners the American ballerinas Lee and Maywood, and Fanny Elssler. His popularity is such that he receives equal billing with all of his famous partners.

1839 Marius Petipa visits the United States with his father, Jean Antoine Petipa, in the ballet company of Madame Lacomte.

1839 *La Sylphide*, with Paul Taglioni and his wife Marie is presented on May 21, at the Park Theatre, New York.

1839 The American ballerina Augusta Maywood makes her debut on November 11 at the Paris Opéra.

1840 Carlotta Grisi makes her debut in Paris on February 28.

1840 Peter Ilyich Tchaikovsky is born on May 7/19.

1840 Fanny Elssler makes her American debut on May 14 at the Park Theatre, New York, in *La Tarentule* (Coralli) and a solo, *La Cracovienne*. Elssler's success is greater than that accorded any other European artist up to this time; she is received by President Van Buren, feted by Congress, and becomes the adored idol of millions.

1840 Fanny Elssler dances *La Sylphide* in New York on June 1.

1840 Marius Petipa first dances in Paris, at the Comédie Française, with Carlotta Grisi.

1841 In June, Fanny Cerito dances *La Sylphide* in London.

1841 Christian Johannsen, brilliant pupil of Auguste Bournonville, makes his debut at the Russian Imperial Theatre, on June 24, in a *pas de deux* with the ballerina Andreyanova. Johannsen later becomes *premier danseur*.

1841 First performance of *Giselle* (Adam-Perrot-Coralli), greatest of all the Romantic Ballets, takes place on June 28, with Carlotta Grisi and Lucien Petipa, at the Paris Opéra. Writes Théophile Gautier: "Carlotta danced with a perfection, a lightness, boldness and chaste and delicate voluptuousness which place her in the first rank between Taglioni and Elssler; as for pantomime she exceeded all expectations; not a conventional gesture, not a false movement; she was nature and artlessness personified. True, she has Perrot the Aerial for husband and teacher."

1842 Perrot is in London as dancer, choreographer, and ballet master; active there until 1848.

1842 Fanny Elssler dances *La Fille Mal Gardée* on July 1, during her last performance in the United States. The visit that had been scheduled to last only for a few months has been extended to more than two years.

1842 Marie Taglioni's farewell performance in St. Petersburg takes place on March 30.

1842 *Napoli*, masterpiece by Auguste Bournonville, is presented on March 29 by the Royal Danish Ballet. This ballet has been in the active repertory of this company ever since it was first produced.

1842 Auguste Vestris dies on December 5.

1843 Lucile Grahn makes her St. Petersburg debut in January, in *Giselle*.

1844 *Les Trois Graces* (*The Three Graces*), famous Romantic ballet print by Eugene Lejeune, is published in London on June 1. This lithograph is unique in its portrayal of three great dancers of the Romantic period: Taglioni as *La Sylphide*, Fanny Elssler as Florinda in *Le Diable Boiteux*, and Carlotta Grisi as Beatrix-Diane in *La Jolie Fille de Gand*. Elssler is the center and pre-eminent figure in the print—an acknowledgment of her supremacy over the older Taglioni and the younger Grisi. The identity of the designer and the accurate identity of all three Graces—overlooked for a hundred years—was not established until 1944 by George Chaffée, who related his findings in *Dance Index* (Vol. 3, Nos. 9–11).

1844 The American dancer Mary Ann Lee studies with Jean Coralli at the Paris Opéra.

1845 Taglioni, Grisi, Cerito and Grahn dance Jules Perrot's *Pas de Quatre* at Her Majesty's Theatre, London, on July 12.

1845 The Russian ballerina Andreyanova appears in Paris. Andreyanova studied with Taglioni when the latter visited Russia and in 1842 danced a version of *Giselle* in St. Petersburg. She was probably the first Russian dancer to appear in Paris.

1846 Taglioni, Grahn, and Cerito appear as the Goddesses, Perrot as Mercury and Saint-Léon as Paris, in *The Judgment of Paris* (Perrot-Pugni) at Her Majesty's Theatre, London, on July 23.

1846 *Giselle* is presented for the first time in America on January 1, with Mary Ann Lee and George Washington Smith, at the Howard Atheneum, Boston.

1847 Marie Taglioni retires.

1847 Mazilier succeeds Coralli as ballet master at the Opéra.

1847   Marius Petipa arrives in St. Petersburg as *premier danseur* at the Imperial Theatre.

1848   *Première* of *Faust*, fantastic ballet in seven scenes, ballet by Jules Perrot, is held on February 12 at La Scala, Milan. Fanny Elssler dances the first performance of this ballet; the American ballerina Augusta Maywood, the second. Maywood, who is to remain in Europe and found her ballet company, shares with Elssler the highest title a dancer can have in Italy: *prima ballerina e prima mima assoluta.*

1848   Fanny Elssler makes her Russian debut on October 22, in *Giselle.*

1848   Jules Perrot dances for the first time at the Russian Imperial Theatre on October 31. Perrot was ballet master at the Imperial Theatre from 1851–59.

1850   Enrico Cecchetti, dancer and teacher, is born on June 21.

1850   Lev Ivanov becomes a dancer at the Imperial Russian Theatre on March 2. Dancer, musician, and choreographer, Ivanov becomes second ballet master at the Imperial Theatre in 1855; as such he is chief assistant to Marius Petipa, who entrusts to him the choreography of *The Nutcracker* and almost the whole of *Swan Lake.*

1851   Carlotta Grisi makes her Russian debut on October 20, in *Giselle*; she remains in Russia until 1853.

1851   Last appearance of Fanny Elssler, in Jules Perrot's ballet *Faust*, on June 21, in Vienna.

1851   Cesare Pugni, Italian composer, is appointed official ballet composer at the Imperial Russian Theatre. In his many years in St. Petersburg, Pugni turns out music for more than three hundred ballets. This music is completely subservient to dance and possesses little dramatic interest. Only with the ballet scores of Delibes and Tchaikovsky does ballet become a coherent musical and choreographic whole.

c.1854   Carlotta Grisi retires.

1855   Fanny Cerito makes her St. Petersburg debut.

1857   Enrico Cecchetti, age seven, appears with his family in the Ronzani Ballet at the opening of the Academy of Music in Philadelphia.

1858   The Royal Opera House, Covent Garden, London, first opens in its present form. Since its reopening after World War II, Covent Garden has maintained two state-supported institutions: the Covent Garden Opera and the Sadler's Wells Ballet. Ballet was not regularly performed at Covent Garden until 1946.

1859   Arthur Michel Saint-Léon makes his debut at the Imperial Theatre, St. Petersburg, on October 19. Saint-Léon becomes ballet master and remains in Russia until 1867, when he is appointed ballet master at the Paris Opéra.

1860 The Maryinsky Theatre in St. Petersburg opens on October 14. This famous Russian theatre, today the Kirov State Academic Theatre of Opera and Ballet in Leningrad, was the home of the Imperial Russian Ballet from 1889 to 1939. Since the Bolshevik Revolution, the center of Soviet ballet has gradually shifted to Moscow and the Bolshoi Theatre, Moscow.

1860 Marius Petipa restages *Giselle* at the Russian Imperial Theatre, St. Petersburg, on October 20.

1860 Christian Johannsen begins to teach at the Russian Imperial School. Johannsen's fame as a teacher exceeds his fame as a dancer; what Petipa is to the theatre, Johannsen is to the classroom. From 1860 until his retirement, soon after the turn of the century, Johannsen is the master of all the great Russian dancers of this period. Pavlova and Fokine were but a few of his pupils.

1862 *The Daughter of Pharaoh* (Petipa-Pugni), first great success in Russia of Marius Petipa, is presented on January 30. This monumental spectacle, with scenes set in the desert, in pyramids, and in colossal palaces, introduces the mass dance on a large scale. Petipa stages the work in six weeks. With its success he becomes ballet master to the Imperial Theatre and begins that reign over Russian ballet that was to last almost until his death, nearly fifty years later.

1864 *The Humpbacked Horse* (Pugni-Saint Léon), first ballet with a Russian theme, is produced by the Frenchman Saint-Léon in St. Petersburg on December 27.

1865 Lucien Petipa becomes ballet master at the Paris Opéra.

1866 Paul Gerdt becomes *premier danseur* at the Russian Imperial Theatre. He is twenty-two years old. Gerdt remains a first dancer in St. Petersburg for fifty years, until his retirement in 1916. He is Franz in Petipa's revival of *Coppélia* (1884) and the prince in the first productions of *The Sleeping Beauty* (1890) and *The Nutcracker* (1892). In 1907 he appears as a young man in *Le Pavillon d'Armide* (Fokine-Tcherepnine-Benois) with two of his famous pupils, Anna Pavlova and Vaslav Nijinsky. As classical dancer, partner, and mime, he is regarded by many as the finest *danseur noble* ever to appear on the Russian stage. As a teacher, he is in large part responsible for the excellence of the Imperial School in classes for mime and supported adagio. Among his pupils: Pavlova, Fokine, and Balanchine.

1866 *The Black Crook* is presented on September 12 at Niblo's Garden, New York City. Marie Bonfanti and Rita Sangalli, both students of Carlo Blasis, are among the dancers who appear in this popular musical extravaganza, which runs for 475 nights.

1867 Saint-Léon becomes ballet master at the Paris Opéra.

1869 Nicholas Legat, dancer, teacher, and choreographer, is born on December 27 in Moscow. Although he is a fine dancer, Legat becomes important principally as an excellent teacher. At the Imperial Ballet School and, later, in

Europe, he trains many dancers who afterward become famous. Legat teaches in London after leaving Russia in 1914; the school he starts there is continued by his wife.

1870   The *première* of *Coppélia* (Saint-Léon—Delibes) takes place on May 25 at the Paris Opéra.

1870   Enrico Cecchetti makes his debut at La Scala, Milan.

1871   Birth of Carlotta Zambelli, ballerina, great teacher at the Paris Opéra.

1872   Serge Diaghilev is born on March 31.

1872   Théophile Gautier dies on October 23.

1875   The opening of the present Paris Opéra takes place on January 5. From the time of its founding in 1669, the Académie de Musique et de Danse has produced opera and ballet in twelve different buildings; this is its permanent home.

1876   *Sylvia, or the Nymph of Diana* (Mérante-Delibes) is first presented on June 14 at the Paris Opéra, with Rita Sangalli and Mérante.

1877   The first production of *Swan Lake* (Reisinger-Tchaikovsky) is presented on March 4 at the Bolshoi Theatre, Moscow.

1878   Isadora Duncan, American dancer, is born on May 27. "Man must speak, then sing, then dance. But the speaking is the brain, the thinking man. The singing is the emotion. The dancing is the Dionysian ecstasy which carries all away. It is impossible to mix in any way, one with the other."

1880   Michel Fokine, Russian dancer, choreographer and ballet master is born on May 8. "As a reformer, he is to the twentieth century what Noverre was to the eighteenth, for he has exerted a profound and beneficial influence in every branch of the art of ballet."—C. W. Beaumont.

1881   Anna Pavlova is born on January 15.

1882   Igor Stravinsky is born on June 17/29.

1882   Lev Ivanov is appointed *regisseur* of the Imperial Russian Ballet.

1883   The Metropolitan Opera House, New York, opens on October 22.

1884   Marie Taglioni dies in Marseilles on April 23.

1884   Fanny Elssler dies on November 27.

1885   The Italian ballerina Virginia Zucchi, pupil of Carlo Blasis, first appears in Russia. Zucchi's dazzling technique compels the Imperial Ballet School to balance the softer French style of dancing with the brilliant grace of the more vigorous Italian style in its instruction.

1885   Paul Gerdt celebrates his twenty-fifth anniversary on the Russian Imperial stage, in *La Fille Mal Gardée*.

1885 Lev Ivanov is appointed second ballet master of the Imperial Russian Ballet.

1885 Birth of Tamara Karsavina.

1887 Enrico Cecchetti, Italian dancer, is engaged by the Imperial Theatre in St. Petersburg on November 23. As a dancer, as one of the second ballet masters (1890), and, most importantly, as a teacher at the Imperial School (1892–1902), in Diaghilev's Ballets Russes (1909), and at his own school in London (1918), Cecchetti instructs and influences many great dancers: Pavlova, Karsavina, Nijinsky, et al.

1889 On April 25, the Maryinsky Theatre, St. Petersburg, becomes the center of the Imperial Russian Ballet. This famous theatre (now the Kirov State Academic Theatre of Opera and Ballet) remains the official home of Russian ballet until 1939.

1889 Olga Preobrajenska is graduated from the Russian Imperial Academy. She is ballerina at the Maryinsky Theatre for many years, until 1917, and teacher, in Paris, of Irina Baronova, Tamara Toumanova, Tatiana Riabouchinska, and many others.

1890 The first performance of *The Sleeping Beauty* (Petipa-Tchaikovsky) takes place on January 27 at the Maryinsky Theatre, St. Petersburg.

1891 Léo Delibes dies on January 16.

1892 Jules Perrot dies on August 29.

1893 Peter Ilyich Tchaikovsky dies on November 6/17.

1894 Hans Beck becomes ballet master at the Royal Theatre, Copenhagen.

1895 The first presentation of the complete *Swan Lake*, with choreography by Lev Ivanov and Marius Petipa, is given on February 8 at the Maryinsky Theatre, St. Petersburg, for the benefit of the Italian ballerina Pierina Legnani.

1895 A "class in perfection" is introduced at the Russian Imperial School for dancers who have been graduated and are dancing regularly at the Maryinsky Theatre. Christian Johannsen is the first teacher of this class, which is taken later by Nicholas Legat.

1898 Michel Fokine makes his debut on May 8 at the Imperial Theatre.

1899 Carlotta Grisi dies on May 22.

1899 Anna Pavlova makes her debut on June 25 at the Maryinsky Theatre.

1899 Isadora Duncan makes her debut in Chicago. This recital is not a success, and it is not until the following year, when she first dances in Paris, that Duncan's innovations are appreciated.

1899 The magazine *World of Art* first appears in St. Petersburg. Founded by Serge Diaghilev, Léon Baskst, and Alexandre Benois, this magazine gives

first expression to those ideas of modern art that are to dominate Diaghilev's
Ballets Russes.

1900   Vaslav Nijinsky enters the Imperial Dancing Academy in St. Petersburg
on September 1.

1901   Lev Ivanov dies; he was a Russian ballet master, dancer, and choreographer,
the choreographer of *Nutcracker* and *Swan Lake* (except for Act One and
Act Three, which are the work of Petipa). Associated with the Russian
Imperial Theatre from the time of his graduation from the Imperial School
in 1852 for almost fifty years, Ivanov remained inconspicuous because of
jealousies and theatre intrigue.

1902   Tamara Karsavina makes her debut on May 13 at the Imperial theatre.

1903   Anna Pavlova dances *Giselle* in St. Petersburg.

1904   Michel Fokine submits suggestions for reforms to the director of the Imperial Theatre: "Dancing should be interpretative. It should not degenerate
into mere gymnastics. The dance should explain the spirit of the actors
in the spectacle . . . it should express the whole epoch to which the subject of the ballet belongs. For such interpretative dancing, the music must
be equally inspired. In place of the old-time waltzes, polkas, pizzicati and
galops, it is necessary to create a form of music which expresses the same
emotion as that which inspires the movements of the dancer. The ballet
must no longer be made up of 'numbers,' 'entries,' and so on. It must
show artistic unity of conception. The action of the ballet must never be
interrupted to allow the *danseuse* to respond to the applause of the public. . . . Ballet must have complete unity of expression, a unity which
is made up of a harmonious blending of the three elements—music, painting, and plastic art." These suggestions are rejected.

1905   Michel Fokine creates the *pas seul Le Cygne* (*The Dying Swan*) for Anna
Pavlova in St. Petersburg; this becomes the best known of all Pavlova's
dances.

1905   Isadora Duncan makes her first appearance in Russia; her reforms in the
dance, her dedication to music, and her contempt for the close-fitting
costume and the ballet slipper in her improvised dances, are approved by
those who seek reform at the Imperial Theatre—among them, Michel
Fokine.

1906   Anna Pavlova becomes *prima ballerina* after a performance of *Swan Lake*
at the Maryinsky Theatre.

1907   Death of Lucile Grahn.

1907   Serge Diaghilev organizes a series of Russian concerts in Paris with the
assistance of Rimsky-Korsakov, Scriabin, Rachmaninoff, and Chaliapin.

1907   Fokine produces, for a charity performance on March 8 at the Maryinsky
Theatre, the ballet *Eunice*, dances in the manner of stylized movement

depicted on ancient Greek vases; the dancers appear in flowing tunics, barefoot.

1907 *Le Pavillon d'Armide* (Fokine-Tcherepnine-Benois), is presented on December 8 at the Maryinsky Theatre, with Pavlova, Nijinsky, and Paul Gerdt.

1908 *Chopiniana*, Fokine's first version of *Les Sylphides*, is presented on March 21, with Pavlova and Oboukoff.

1908 Vaslav Nijinsky is graduated from the Imperial Ballet School in May; he appears with Ludmilla Shollar in Fokine's dances in *Don Giovanni*.

1909 Diaghilev's Ballets Russes makes its first appearance, at the Théâtre du Châtelet, Paris on May 18: *Le Pavillon d'Armide* and *Prince Igor* (Fokine-Borodin-Roerich) create one of the most successful *premières* in history. This is the beginning of a new era in ballet, as Diaghilev makes possible the complete realization of Fokine's reforms and founds a ballet company dedicated to Fokine's ideal: unification of the three elements—music, painting, and dancing. Fokine is choreographer to Diaghilev.

1909 Diaghilev's Ballets Russes presents *Les Sylphides* on June 2, with Pavlova, Karsavina, and Nijinsky, at the Théâtre du Châtelet.

1909 Diaghilev appoints Enrico Cecchetti instructor to his Ballets Russes.

1910 Anna Pavlova and Mikhail Mordkin make their United States debut on February 28 in *Coppélia*, at the Metropolitan Opera House. "Her technique is of a sort to dazzle the eye. The most difficult tricks of the art of the dancer she executed with supreme ease . . . Grace, a certain sensuous charm, and a decided sense of humor are other qualities that she possesses. In fact, it would be difficult to conceive a dancer who so nearly realizes the ideal of this sort of dancing."—Carl van Vechten in the New York *Times*.

1910 *Swan Lake* is performed in England for the first time, in May, at the London Hippodrome, with Olga Preobrajenska as Odette and George Kyaksht as Prince Siegfried.

1910 *Firebird* (Fokine-Stravinsky) is presented by Diaghilev's Ballets Russes on June 25.

1910 Pavlova and Mordkin dance *Giselle* on October 15 at the Metropolitan Opera House. "Grisi is said to have been gently melancholy in it, but Pavlova was probably more than that. Her poetic conception of the betrothed girl's madness when she finds that her lover has deceived her, and her death, come very close to being tragic. It is almost impossible to describe the poetry of her dancing in the second act, where as one of the *Wilis* she engages in the wildest sort of measures under the forest trees."—Carl van Vechten in the New York *Times*.

1910 Tamara Karsavina succeeds Anna Pavlova as ballerina at the Imperial Theatre, St. Petersburg.

1910 Marius Petipa dies on July 14.

1911   Saison Russe is presented by Gertrude Hoffman in New York. Repertory includes first United States productions of *Les Sylphides* and *Scheherazade*. Gertrude Hoffman and Lydia Lopokova are the principal dancers. These versions of Fokine's ballets were not authorized by him.

1911   *Petrouchka* (Fokine-Stravinsky-Benois) is presented on June 13 in Paris by Diaghilev, with Karsavina, Nijinsky, Orlov, and Cecchetti.

1911   Diaghilev's Ballets Russes first appear in London on June 21.

1911   *Swan Lake* is presented in four acts on December 20 at the Metropolitan Opera House, with Catherine Geltzer, first dancer of the Moscow Imperial Opera, and Mikhail Mordkin.

1912   Nijinsky's *The Afternoon of a Faun* (Debussy) is presented by Diaghilev, Paris, on May 29.

1913   Anna Pavlova resigns from the Maryinsky Theatre; she never returns to Russia.

1914   In a letter to *The Times*, London, July 6, Fokine states the five principles of the New Ballet: (1) "Not to form combinations of ready-made and established dance steps, but to create in each case a new form corresponding to the subject, the most expressive form possible for the representation of the period and the character of the nation represented." (2) ". . . Dancing and mimetic gesture have no meaning in a ballet unless they serve as an expression of its dramatic action, and they must not be used as a mere *divertissement* or entertainment . . ." (3) "The new ballet admits the use of conventional gesture only when it is required by the style of the ballet, and in all other cases endeavors to replace gestures of the hands by mimetic of the whole body. Man can be and should be expressed from head to foot." (4) ". . . Expressiveness of groups and of ensemble dancing. In the older ballets the dancers were ranged in groups only for the purpose of ornament, and the ballet master was not concerned with the expression of any sentiment in groups of characters or in ensemble dances. The new ballet, on the other hand . . . advances from the expressiveness of the face to the expressiveness of the whole body, and from the expressiveness of the individual body to the expressiveness of a group of bodies and the expressiveness of the combined dancing of a crowd." (5) "Alliance of dancing with the other arts. The new ballet . . . does not demand 'ballet music' of the composer as an accompaniment to dancing; it accepts music of every kind, provided it is good and expressive. It does not demand of the scenic artist that he should array the ballerinas in short skirts and pink slippers. It does not impose any specific 'ballet' conditions . . . but gives complete liberty to their creative powers."

1915   Massine becomes choreographer to Diaghilev.

1916   The first American appearance of Diaghilev's Ballets Russes takes place at the Century Theatre, New York. The principal dancers are Pfanz, Bolm, Massine, Sokolova, Tchernicheva, Fedorova, and Cecchetti.

1916 Vaslav Nijinsky dances for the first time in the United States, in *Le Spectre de la Rose* and *Petrouchka*, with Diaghilev's Ballets Russes, on April 12 at the Metropolitan Opera House.

1916 The second New York season of Diaghilev's Ballets Russes opens on October 16 at the Manhattan Opera House with Nijinsky's *Til Eulenspiegel*. An American tour follows.

1917 *Parade* (Massine-Satie-Cocteau-Picasso) is presented by Diaghilev's Ballets Russes on May 18 at the Théâtre du Châtelet, Paris.

1917 *The Good-Humored Ladies* (Massine-Scarlatti-Bakst) is presented on April 12 by Diaghilev's Ballets Russes: the first major ballet by Massine.

1918 Enrico Cecchetti opens the Academy of Dancing in London.

1919 Nijinsky retires.

1920 The Royal Academy of Dancing is founded in London.

1921 The Fokine School opens in New York on January 1.

1921 Isadora Duncan is invited by the Soviet Government to open a school in Moscow.

1921 Diaghilev revives *The Sleeping Beauty* at the Alhambra Theatre, London, on November 2. Spessivtzeva, Lopokova, Egorova, and Trefilova alternate in the part of Princess Aurora. Pierre Vladimiroff is the Prince. Lopokova and Nijinska alternate as the Lilac Fairy. Parts of the fairies are taken by Dubrovska, Sokolova, Nemtchinova, Tchernicheva, Egorova, and Nijinska. Carlotta Brianza, the Princess Aurora of the original production of this ballet, is Carabosse. Stanislas Idzikowski and Lopokova dance the Bluebird *pas de deux* at the first performance. Ludmilla Shollar, Leon Woicikowski, and Anatole Vilzak are in the cast. This reaffirmation of the permanence of the classic dance fails with the ballet audience, which is accustomed to two or three ballets an evening, in the fashion made popular by Diaghilev himself.

1921 Bronislava Nijinska becomes choreographer to Diaghilev.

1922 On January 5, Enrico Cecchetti celebrates his fiftieth anniversary on the ballet stage by taking the part of Carabosse in Diaghilev's revival of *The Sleeping Beauty*.

1922 A *Manual of Classical Theatrical Dancing* (*Cecchetti Method*), by C. W. Beaumont and Stanislas Idzikowski, is published in London.

1923 "Dancing has forever been in existence as a spontaneous custom, a social discipline. Thus it is finally that dancing meets us not only as love, as religion, as art, but also as morals."—Havelock Ellis, *The Dance of Life.*

1923 *L'Ame et la Danse* (*Dance and the Soul*), dialogue by Paul Valéry, is published in Paris.

1924 Balanchine becomes choreographer to Diaghilev.

1924–25 Anna Pavlova and her company make their last American tour.

1925 *Petrouchka* is staged by Fokine for the Royal Danish Ballet on October 21 at the Royal Theatre, Copenhagen. With their careful attention to detail, respect for a choreographer's direction, and their scrupulous maintenance of tradition, the Royal Danish Ballet's production of this famous ballet is generally acknowledged to be the best in existence.

1925–26 Mikhail Mordkin and his Russian Ballet Company tour America.

1926 Martha Graham, dancer and choreographer, gives her first independent dance recital at the Forty-eighth Street Theatre, New York, on April 18. Like Isadora Duncan before her, Martha Graham has greatly influenced the theatrical dancing of her time, but more than Duncan—whose art was personal and inimitable—Martha Graham has developed in addition to a stage personality a new, nonballetic dance vocabulary expressive of inner tensions. This new system of dance can be imparted to others, can be taught with the same rigor as the classic ballet, and has become, under Martha Graham's tutelage, not only a contemporary contribution, but a lasting discipline.

1926 Ninette de Valois, former member of Diaghilev's Ballets Russes, establishes ballet school in London in May.

1926 Ballet Club (now Ballet Rambert), first permanent English company, presents at its first performance, on June 15, *A Tragedy of Fashion*, ballet by Frederick Ashton. Marie Rambert, the director of this company and its accompanying ballet school, was a student of Emile Jaques-Dalcroze and Cecchetti. Ashton, Tudor, De Mille, and Andrée Howard are a few of the celebrated choreographers who have studied under her direction.

1927 Isadora Duncan gives her last concert at the Théâtre Mogadon, Paris, on July 8.

1927 Isadora Duncan dies on September 14.

1928 *Apollo, Leader of the Muses* (Balanchine-Stravinsky-Bauchant) is presented by Diaghilev on June 12.

1928 Enrico Cecchetti dies on November 13.

1928 Ninette de Valois' Academy of Choreographic Art presents *Les Petits Riens* (De Valois-Mozart), on December 13, at the Old Vic Theatre, London.

1929 Serge Diaghilev in a letter to *The Times*, London, July 13, defends his Ballets Russes from charges that their dances are "extravagant, repellent, athletic, acrobatic": "The classical dance has never been and is not today the Russian Ballet. Its birthplace was France; it grew up in Italy, and has only been conserved in Russia. Side by side with the classical dance there has always existed the national or character dance, which has given the evolution of the Russian Ballet. I do not know of a single classical movement that was born of the Russian folk dance. Why have we got to take our inspiration from the minuet of the French Court and not from the Russian village festival? That which appears to you acrobatic is dilettante terminology for our national dance step. The mistake really, in fact, goes much deeper, because it is undoubtedly the Italian classical school which has introduced into ballet the acrobatic elements. . . ."

1929 The last performance of Diaghilev's Ballets Russes takes place at Covent Garden, London, on July 26. The program includes: *Le Bal* (Balanchine-Rieti-Chirico), with Danilova and Dolin; *Prodigal Son* (Balanchine-Prokofiev-Rouault), with Lifar and Dubrovska; *Aurora's Wedding* (Petipa-Tchaikovsky-Bakst), with Danilova as Aurora, Lifar as the prince, and Markova and Dolin as the bluebirds.

1929 Serge Diaghilev dies in Venice on August 19.

1930 *Capriol Suite* (Ashton-Warlock-Chappell), ballet based on dances described in Arbeau's *Orchésographie* (1588), is presented by Marie Rambert Dancers in London.

1930 The American *première* of Massine's ballet to Stravinsky's *The Rite of Spring* is presented on April 11 at the Academy of Music, Philadelphia. Martha Graham dances the leading role. The music is performed by the Philadelphia Orchestra under Leopold Stokowski.

1930 Anna Pavlova makes her last public appearance on December 13 in *Giselle*, with Pierre Vladimiroff, London.

1931 Anna Pavlova dies at The Hague on January 23.

1931 Ninette de Valois opens a ballet school at the Sadler's Wells Theatre, London, on January 31. The Sadler's Wells Theatre at the time is under the direction of Lilian Baylis, director of the Old Vic Theatre.

1931 The Vic-Wells Ballet gives its first performance on May 5 at the Old Vic Theatre, London, under the direction of Ninette de Valois. Other performances are given at the Sadler's Wells Theatre, and the history of the Sadler's Wells Ballet begins.

1932 René Blum and Colonel W. de Basil found the Ballet Russe de Monte Carlo; its choreographers are Balanchine and Massine.

1932 Harald Lander becomes ballet master to the Royal Danish Ballet.

1932 Constant Lambert, English composer and conductor, becomes musical director of the Vic-Wells Ballet and begins to conduct ballet performances at the Sadler's Wells Theatre.

1933 The first performance of *Les Présages* (Massine-Tchaikovsky-Masson), at Monte Carlo on April 13. This "choreographic symphony" to Tchaikovsky's Fifth Symphony portrays man's battle with fate; it is the first ballet to a full symphony.

1933   The Jooss Ballet makes its first United States appearance.

1933   The first performance of Les Ballets 1933 (under the direction of George Balanchine) takes place in June at the Théâtre des Champs-Elysées, Paris.

1933   The Ballet Russe de Monte Carlo gives its first Paris performance in June at the Théâtre du Châtelet.

1933   Serge Lifar and his Russian Ballets appear in the United States.

1933   The School of American Ballet is founded in October by Lincoln Kirstein, George Balanchine, Edward M. M. Warburg, and Vladimir Dimitriev.

1933   First performance in the United States of the Ballet Russe de Monte Carlo on December 22 at the St. James Theatre, New York. The program: *La Concurrence* (Balanchine-Auric-Derain), *Les Présages* (Massine-Tchaikovsky-Masson), and *Le Beau Danube* (Massine-Strauss-Polunin). Among the dancers are Alexandra Danilova, Leonide Massine, Tamara Toumanova, Tatiana Riabouchinska, Irina Baronova, Leon Woicikowski, David Lichine, Yurek Shabelevsky, and André Eglevsky.

1934   The first all-English production of *Giselle* is presented on January 1 at the Old Vic Theatre, London, by the Vic-Wells Ballet, with Alicia Markova.

1934   The School of American Ballet opens on January 2 in New York.

1934   *Fundamentals of the Classic Dance*, by Agrippina Vaganova (1879–1951), is published in Russia. This is the crucial text of present-day Russian ballet technique (translated into English by Anatole Chujoy, 1946).

1934   Ruth Page is appointed ballet director and *première danseuse* of the Chicago Grand Opera Company.

1934   Vic-Wells Ballet produces the first complete *Swan Lake* staged in England, with Alicia Markova, on November 20.

1934   The School of American Ballet presents Balanchine's *Mozartiana*, *Serenade*, *Alma Mater*, and *Transcendence* on December 6 at the Avery Memorial Theatre, Hartford, Connecticut.

1935   In March, the American Ballet, founded by Lincoln Kirstein and Edward M. M. Warburg, opens a two-week season at the Adelphi Theatre, New York, with a repertory of ballets by George Balanchine. Tamara Geva and Paul Haakon are guest artists in a company that includes Ruthanna Boris, Gisella Caccialanza, William Dollar, Charles Laskey, Eugene Loring, Annabelle Lyon, and Elise Reiman, among others.

1935   The Littlefield Ballet is organized in Philadelphia by Catherine Littlefield (1904–51): the first ballet company with an American director and American dancers. The following year this company becomes the Philadelphia Ballet. For this company, Catherine Littlefield choreographs a complete version of Tchaikovsky's *The Sleeping Beauty*.

1935 The American Ballet, under the direction of George Balanchine, becomes the resident ballet company at the Metropolitan Opera. Anatole Vilzak, Ruby Asquith, Harold and Lew Christensen, Erick Hawkins, Lillian Moore, and others join the company.

1935 *Dance: A Short History of Classic Theatrical Dancing*, by Lincoln Kirstein, is published in New York.

1936 *Lilac Garden* (Tudor-Chausson) is presented by the Ballet Club on January 26 at the Mercury Theatre, London.

1936 Ruth Page Ballets make their first appearance in New York on March 1.

1936 *Orpheus* (Balanchine-Gluck) is performed by the American Ballet on May 22 at the Metropolitan Opera House, with scenery and costumes by Pavel Tchelitchev.

1936 Ballet Caravan is organized in May by Lincoln Kirstein to provide opportunity for American dancers, choreographers, composers, and designers. Ballet Caravan tours the United States during three years, mounting new works by Lew Christensen, William Dollar, Erick Hawkins, and Eugene Loring to new music by Elliott Carter, Jr., Aaron Copland, Paul Bowles, etc. All the dancers, like those in the American Ballet, are students or graduates of the School of American Ballet; among them are Christensen, Marie-Jeanne, Caccialanza, Loring, and Danieli.

1936 *A Bibliography of Dancing* (Paul Magriel) is published in New York on August 2.

1937 The American Ballet stages a Stravinsky Festival on April 27 at the Metropolitan Opera House: *Apollo, Leader of the Muses; Card Game;* and *The Fairy's Kiss*—all with music by Stravinsky and choreography by Balanchine.

1937 The Philadelphia Ballet has a season at the Théâtre des Champs-Elysées, Paris, during the International Exposition: it is the first American ballet company to visit Europe.

1937 The San Francisco Ballet, with associated ballet school, is organized by William Christensen.

1938 *Billy the Kid* (Loring-Copland-Kirstein-French) is presented on October 16 by Ballet Caravan at the Chicago Opera House: the first successful ballet with an American subject portrayed in an American dance idiom.

1938 *Ballerina* (original title *La Mort du Cygne*), the first movie to deal in detail with ballet, is filmed in France, with Mia Slavenska and Yvette Chauviré. Many of the young students who appear in this film later become noted dancers.

1939 Nicholas Sergeyev's production of *The Sleeping Beauty* is presented by the Sadler's Wells Ballet on February 2 at the Sadler's Wells Theatre, London, with Margot Fonteyn, June Brae, and Robert Helpmann.

1940   Ballet Theatre's first performance takes place on January 11, at the Center Theatre, New York: *Les Sylphides*, *The Great American Goof* (Loring-Brant-Saroyan-Aronson), *Voices of Spring* (Mordkin-Strauss-Simonson). Among the dancers are Adolph Bolm, Patricia Bowman, Edward Caton, Lucia Chase, Karen Conrad, Leon Danielian, Agnes de Mille, Anton Dolin, William Dollar, Viola Essen, Nora Kaye, Andrée Howard, Hugh Laing, Eugene Loring, Annabelle Lyon, Dimitri Romanov, Nina Stroganova, Yurek Shabelevsky, and Antony Tudor. During its first season, Ballet Theatre presents eighteen ballets. Fokine stages his own ballets for the company.

1940   The Dance Notation Bureau is founded in New York for the purpose of recording ballets and dances in an intelligible dance notation.

1941   The American Ballet makes a South American tour. In its repertory are *Ballet Imperial*, *Concerto Barocco*, *The Bat*, *Billy the Kid*, *Time Table*, *Filling Station*, *Errante*, *Serenade*, *Apollo*, *Charade*, and *Pastorela*. Among the dancers are Marie-Jeanne, Lew Christensen, William Dollar, Nicholas Magallanes, Beatrice Tompkins, and Mary Jane Shea.

1941   Ballet Theatre makes its first transcontinental tour; Alonso, Baronova, Hightower, Markova, Osato, Robbins, and Skibine join the company.

1941   International Ballet is founded in England by Mona Inglesby. The repertory of this company includes the reproductions by Sergeyev of *Giselle*, *Coppélia*, *Swan Lake*, and *The Sleeping Beauty*.

1942   *Pillar of Fire* (Tudor-Schoenberg-Mielziner) is presented by Ballet Theatre on April 8 at the Metropolitan Opera House, with Nora Kaye, Hugh Laing, and Antony Tudor.

1942   Fokine dies on August 22.

1942   The first performance of *Rodeo* (De Mille-Copland-Smith) is presented by the Ballet Russe de Monte Carlo on October 16 at the Metropolitan Opera House, New York.

1944   The first American tour of the Mia Slavenska Company begins on January 3.

1944   *Fancy Free* (Robbins-Bernstein-Smith) is presented by Ballet Theatre on April 18 at the Metropolitan Opera House, New York.

1944   The first performance of Ballet International takes place on October 30 at the International Theatre, New York. The principal dancers are Viola Essen, Marie-Jeanne, André Eglevsky, and William Dollar. This company gives its last performance on December 23, 1944. Its founder, the Marquis George de Cuevas, established the Grand Ballet de Monte Carlo in Europe in 1947. This new company, which features many American dancers, returned to the United States for a four-week engagement at the Century Theatre, New York, November 1949, as the Marquis de Cuevas' Grand Ballet. The principal dancers are Rosella Hightower, André Eglevsky, Marjorie Tallchief, and George Skibine. This company returned to Europe in 1950; it is now known as the Grand Ballet du Marquis de Cuevas.

1945 The first season of Les Ballets des Champs-Elysées, in Paris. Its managing director is Roger Eudes; artistic director, Boris Kochno; ballet master and choreographer, Roland Petit.

1946 In London, the Sadler's Wells Ballet reopens the Royal Opera House, Covent Garden (closed as a theatre during the war), on February 20, with a performance of *The Sleeping Beauty*: Sadler's Wells Ballet, as the first permanent resident company at Covent Garden, becomes the national ballet of Britain.

1946 The first full evening of ballet by the Sadler's Wells Theatre Ballet is given on April 8 at the Sadler's Wells Theatre, London. It consists of *Promenade* (De Valois-Haydn), *Assembly Ball* (Howard-Bizet), and *The Nutcracker*.

1946 Ballet Society, a "non-profit organization for the advancement of the lyric theatre by production of new works," is founded in New York in July for private, subscription audience. Musical Director, Leon Barzin; Secretary, Lincoln Kirstein; Executive Manager, Frances Hawkins; Technical Director, Jean Rosenthal; Artistic Director, George Balanchine.

1946 Ballet Theatre opens its first overseas engagement on July 4 at the Royal Opera House, Covent Garden, London, with *Les Sylphides*, *Fancy Free*, *Black Swan pas de deux*, and *Bluebeard*.

1946 Ballet Society gives its first performance in New York on November 20. The program: *The Four Temperaments* and *The Spellbound Child*. Among the dancers are Mary Ellen Moylan, Tanaquil LeClercq, Beatrice Tompkins, Elise Reiman, Fred Danieli, Nicholas Magallanes, Todd Bolender, Francisco Moncion, and Herbert Bliss.

1948 Alicia Markova, Anton Dolin, and Mia Slavenska join the Ballet Russe de Monte Carlo on September 16 as guest artists for a season at the Metropolitan Opera House.

1948 The first performance of *Orpheus* (Balanchine-Stravinsky-Noguchi) is given on April 28, with Nicholas Magallanes, Maria Tallchief, and Francisco Moncion, by Ballet Society, at the New York City Center.

1948 The first public performance of Ballet Society takes place on April 29 at the New York City Center: *Renard, Elégie, Orpheus, Symphonie Concertante*.

1948 The first performance of Les Ballets de Paris de Roland Petit, at the Théâtre Marigny, Paris, on May 22.

1948 The Paris Opéra Ballet opens its season at the New York City Center on September 21.

1948 The first performance of the New York City Ballet, on October 11, as Ballet Society becomes the resident company at the New York City Center of Music and Drama. The program consists of *Concerto Barocco, Orpheus*, and *Symphony in C*. The Musical Director is Leon Barzin; General Director, Lincoln Kirstein; Lighting by Jean Rosenthal; principal dancers, Maria Tallchief, Marie-Jeanne, Tanaquil LeClercq, Beatrice Tompkins, Nicholas Magallanes, Francisco Moncion, and Herbert Bliss; Artistic Director, George Balanchine.

1948 *Cinderella* (Ashton-Prokofiev-Malclès), first full-scale, three-act English ballet, is presented by the Sadler's Wells Ballet in London on December 23.

1949 *The Dance Encyclopedia*, compiled and edited by Anatole Chujoy, is published in New York on March 21.

1949 The Sadler's Wells Ballet makes its first appearance in the United States on October 11 at the Metropolitan Opera House, New York.

1949 Jerome Robbins becomes associate artistic director of the New York City Ballet in November.

1949 *Firebird* (Balanchine-Stravinsky-Chagall) is given its first performance, with Maria Tallchief and Francisco Moncion, by the New York City Ballet at the City Center, New York, on November 27.

1950 Vaslav Nijinsky dies in London on April 8.

1950 The Sadler's Wells Ballet observes its twenty-first birthday in a gala performance at the Sadler's Wells Theatre, London, on May 15. At this performance, Ninette de Valois, director, dances the part of Webster, the maid, in *A Wedding Bouquet* (Ashton-Berners-Stein) and Margot Fonteyn takes the part in which she first appeared as a soloist, on December 4, 1934: Young Treginnis, in *The Haunted Ballroom*.

1950 The New York City Ballet opens its first overseas engagement at the Royal Opera House, Covent Garden, London, on July 10 with *Serenade*, *The Age of Anxiety*, and *Symphony in C*.

1950 Ballet Theatre begins its first European tour, in August, at Frankfurt, Germany.

1950 The first season of Festival Ballet opens in London on October 24, with Alicia Markova and Anton Dolin.

1951 Nora Kaye and André Eglevsky join the New York City Ballet in January.

1951 Jean Babilée and Nathalie Philippart are guest artists with Ballet Theatre at the Metropolitan Opera House, New York.

1951 Ballet Theatre opens its first South American tour on May 21, in Rio de Janeiro.

1951 Ballet Rambert celebrates its twenty-fifth anniversary in London on July 29. This company, under the direction of Madame Marie Rambert, has been in continuous existence longer than any other English company.

1951 Ballet Theatre School opens in New York on September 17.

1951 Sadler's Wells Theatre Ballet begins its first tour of Canada and the United States on October 5 at Quebec City, Canada.

1952   *The Classic Ballet* (Stuart-Dyer-Kirstein) is published on February 25.

1952   The first European tour of the New York City Ballet opens at the Gran Teatro del Liceo, Barcelona, Spain, on April 15.

1953   The New York City Ballet ends a three-month engagement at the City Center, New York, on January 25: the longest run of any ballet company in the United States.

1953   Second European tour of Ballet Theatre.

1953   First appearance outside Denmark of the Royal Danish Ballet—at the Royal Opera House, Covent Garden, London.

1953   Second European tour of the New York City Ballet.

1953   Third American tour of Sadler's Wells Ballet.

1953   Agnes de Mille Dance Theatre begins first tour of the United States.

The chronology of important events in the history of theatrical dance to be found in *Dance*, by Lincoln Kirstein (1935), is the master list upon which any chronology of the history of ballet must naturally be based, and I acknowledge my great indebtedness to it, as well as to the text of that monumental work. I am also indebted to numerous other sources, principal among which are: *The Dance Encyclopedia*, compiled and edited by Anatole Chujoy, the largest single collection of data on ballet in English; various contributors of articles to *Dance Index*, especially Lillian Moore, George Chaffée, Anatole Chujoy, and the late Dr. Artur Michel; numerous historical articles published in the indispensable magazine *Ballet*, which has unfortunately ceased publication; and the pioneer reasearches of C. W. Beaumont.

The scrupulous historical essays that appeared in *Dance Index* during that magazine's brief existence eloquently demonstrated that many writers on ballet have a cavalier tradition of carelessness and indifference to the accuracy of dates, names, places, and events. Insofar as possible, I have tried not to parrot previous errors and earnestly hope that, in the interest of accuracy, any readers who discern mistakes will be good enough to inform me of them in care of the publishers.

Part Five

HOW I BECAME A DANCER
AND CHOREOGRAPHER

A dancer's history usually begins at the age of eight or nine. I myself began to study dancing, in Russia, when I was nine. In my case, this was almost accidental. My father was a musician, a composer, and we were naturally a musical family. My brother played the piano, my sister played the violin, and from the time I was five years old, I, too, studied the piano. There was no idea that I should be a musician; I only studied music because my parents felt I should be missing something important in life if I knew nothing about it.

Many men in my mother's family had been in the army, and for a while it was thought that I would become one of the Czar's cadets. But one day my mother happened to be visiting the Imperial Ballet School in St. Petersburg. She had always loved dancing, and when one of the governors of the school suggested that she try to enter me, she agreed. After all, I could always go into the army if I didn't turn out to be good.

That was in 1914. In August of that year the Imperial School held its regular auditions for new pupils in St. Petersburg. These were auditions for the eight-year course in ballet, drama, and music. The final choice of which art the student would permanently pursue was made after he had learned something about each one. But these were not auditions in any real sense; we had never danced before, and there was very little they could tell. First, a doctor examined us briefly. He felt our muscles, listened to our hearts and our breathing, and sent us to the large auditioning room of the school. There were about a hundred and fifty boys seeking admittance and more than two hundred girls. In small groups, the boys and girls separately, we went in before the judges, who were seated at a table down at the end of the auditioning room. Karsavina was there, I remember. Even then I knew what a great ballerina Karsavina was and I was a little afraid. I thought I looked awkward.

The judges asked us to walk and observed our posture, our carriage. We knew absolutely no dancing and could not have executed a step if we'd been asked. The judges picked a few boys out of each group that came before them. I was picked out, but from the judges' manner I couldn't tell if this was because I was good or bad. We were told to go to another room, and after a long wait we were asked to come back. The judges watched us again, then divided the group, sending some of us to one side of the room. Again we waited. We had no idea who had been chosen or who had been eliminated. At the end of the day, they announced the names of those who had been selected as new students. I was one of seven or eight boys.

Until I actually entered the school, I didn't know whether to be pleased or not. Once in the Imperial School itself, I was decidedly displeased. I didn't like it. I was homesick, and the army seemed to me a much better idea than ballet.

The first year, we were all on trial at the school. Only if we passed that first year successfully would we be admitted as permanent students. I didn't care. All of us lived at the school, in Theatre Street, in St. Petersburg. We could go home only at Easter, Christmas, and during the summer; our parents could not visit us. The discipline was very strict: we all got up at the same time, washed at the same time (always in cold water, except on Friday before dinner), ate on a strict schedule, went to the same classes, and were sent to bed promptly at nine o'clock. We wore blue uniforms, with silver lyres on the stiff collar and on the cap.

And I did not like it. My fellow students knew this because I sulked so much. They didn't help matters by calling me "Rat" all the time. When I thought I couldn't stand it any more, I ran away. I knew my parents would be very angry, so I went to the home of an aunt who lived in St. Petersburg. She was understanding, but also she was firm with me. She took me back.

Still I hated the school. I was certain I had no aptitude for dancing and was wasting my time and the Czar's money. The only people who thought differently then were Olga Preobrajenska, the great *prima ballerina* at the Maryinsky Theatre, who was very kind to me, and my favorite teacher, S. M. Andreanov, who instructed me in classic technique.

Every day at the Imperial School we had the same schedule: ballet class, lessons in character dancing, classes in Russian literature, French, arithmetic, music (we all had to play some instrument), and religion. We also took fencing lessons. This was a curriculum similar to that of any fine European school, except for the ballet classes. I liked the classes in religion and music best, but still, even though I was admitted as a permanent student after the first year, I thought I was in the wrong place. I remembered that there were other departments at the Imperial School—drama and music— and thought that I might be better off there.

Then everything changed. What happened was very simple. In the first year at the school, we went only to classes; we were not associated with the Imperial Theatre, the Maryinsky, in any way. The second year, as was customary, we became a part of the theatre, dancing in large groups with the *corps de ballet.* I first danced on the stage of the Maryinsky in the garland dance in *The Sleeping Beauty:* the waltz in the first act. I also appeared as a cupid on one of the carriages in the final act. The Maryinsky was a beautiful

theatre, all blue and gold, and as children we were very excited about dancing on its stage, where almost any magical effect could be made: real waves,
scores of swimming swans, fire, and great cascading fountains banked in tiers.
We learned very early what it was to be a part of a theatre; the theatre became a home to us, a natural place to be.

The garland dance in *The Sleeping Beauty* was performed by scores of
people in the regular *corps de ballet* of the Maryinsky, and we children were
naturally unimportant, but that evening nevertheless changed my whole life.
At that moment I saw that others had been right about what was good for
me. I saw then what ballet was in terms of a theatre.

The Maryinsky production of *The Sleeping Beauty* was wonderfully
elaborate, a real spectacle, the kind of thing Hollywood tries to achieve in its
huge productions. Only here there was more magic. The Czar's treasury
could afford it! There were about two hundred and fifty dancers in the company; all were professionals. The first act of *The Sleeping Beauty* was marvelous in scenic effect: a huge garden with cascading fountains. When the
wicked fairy Carabosse appeared in the prologue, her great coach was drawn
by a dozen mice. Later, when she appeared in disguise and tricked the
princess into pricking her finger, her appearance changed completely. She
turned to the king and queen and said that the princess would die, and then,
miraculously, her disguise disappeared into the floor and they saw before
them the wicked fairy they had forgotten to invite to their daughter's
christening. It was fantastic—there she was, a bent old lady, harmless, and
the next moment her disguise had fallen through the floor and she was black
and shiny, the wicked fairy. Fire came up all over the stage and everyone
despaired. Of course, the Lilac Fairy then intervened and predicted that the
princess would wake up in a hundred years. Then the whole palace went to
sleep. From the stage floor, great trees and shrubbery arose and climbed
higher and higher, vines entwined about the colonnades of the garden, so
that the whole palace was overgrown and it was quiet, asleep.

Later, when the Lilac Fairy took the prince to the palace, there was a
wonderful panorama scene, not an interval with music, as this part of the
ballet is performed nowadays. The music was played slowly, as it should be,
and the Lilac Fairy guided her boat across the stage. The scenery moved
from left to right so that the boat really seemed to be moving over a lake
in an enchanted forest. Then, in the finale, where the Princess Aurora is
married, there was a spectacular apotheosis: the stage was deep and high, and
from high up in the back down to the center of the stage there was a great
flight of steps. On either side of the steps there was a flight of fountains,
which spilled over, one into the other, so that there was a continuous water-
fall. All the fairies were grouped on the stairs with their cavaliers, and they
and all the court bowed in tribute to the princess. It was beautiful.

And so I began to like dancing very much. I started to work very hard.
I wanted to dance more on the stage, and to do that I knew I had to be good,

very good. I was only ten, but I was experiencing with ballet the same kind of lesson I had learned with music.

When I first took piano lessons, I hated them, too. For two years the only thing that would make me practice was the thought of being sent to bed without my supper. Then, when I was seven, I learned a part of a Beethoven sonata. I didn't play it well at first, but well enough to hear how lovely it sounded. I loved it and wanted to play it well, so then it would sound even more beautiful. And now I was learning the same thing about dancing: it took work, but when you saw what the work could produce, you wanted to work very badly.

Ballet performances at the Maryinsky in St. Petersburg were given only twice a week, on Wednesdays and Saturdays. The rest of the week, the theatre was devoted to opera. All of us looked forward to the ballet evenings, when the official court carriages would come to the school and take us to the theatre for our appearances. Only when we were brought back to the school, at midnight, did we have our supper. We were so excited about going on stage at the theatre that, young as we were, we were not hungry until it was all over.

As a child, I danced in all the ballets in the Maryinsky repertory that required a large male *corps de ballet*: in the first real Russian ballet, *The Humpbacked Horse*; in the Petipa classics *Paquita* and *Don Quixote*; in *The Nutcracker*, where I began as one of the toy soldiers and gradually danced bigger parts—the king of mice, the nutcracker prince, and dance parts in the *grand divertissement*.

Someday I hope to produce *The Nutcracker* as it should be done. At the Maryinsky, the first act of this ballet was not merely a small family party with a miniature Christmas tree. There was an enormous Christmas tree with hundreds of presents under it. When the children had been sent to bed and little Clara tiptoed downstairs to rescue the nutcracker, her favorite gift, the stage picture changed completely. At the stroke of midnight, the toys under the tree came to life. The chief toy soldier became a general, challenging intruders. Mice invaded the room, and there on stage a great pitched battle between the soldiers and the rats took place. They fired muskets and shot off cannon balls of candy. Clara tried to help the soldiers, but only when her beloved nutcracker was transformed into a brave, handsome prince was the battle won. This kind of thing we do not see nowadays in revivals of *The Nutcracker*. People think of *The Nutcracker* as a "suite" rather than a ballet. First it was a ballet.

In the Maryinsky *Swan Lake*, too, there were marvelous stage effects. At the beginning of Act Two there was not just one swan swimming across the lake, as we see so often today: there were two dozen swans, gliding across what appeared to be real, rippling waves. Actually, each swan was secured to a long stick, which members of the Czar's Finnish regiment maneuvered underneath the stage between the rippling canvas waves. Later, when the twenty-four swan maidens appeared on stage, the audience didn't have to guess who they were: they had already seen them.

In another Maryinsky production, Mazilier's famous ballet *Le Corsair*, there was a real shipwreck. A gigantic ship was tossed high on the waves and completely demolished. The Czar's Finnish regiment worked again here, moving large sheets of canvas so that they undulated like storm waves. After the ballet was over, the soldiers formed ranks and drilled out of the theatre with impeccable military style, as if their regiment had just won honors at a parade.

I've gone into some detail here about the Maryinsky production for two reasons: first, to give some idea of the natural excitement these ballets had for all of us at the Imperial Ballet School; and second, because I find that people in general are very curious about what they call "Russian ballet." There used to be a time, until very recently, in fact, when people thought that *Russian* ballet was all there was. That was wrong, of course. Only because the Czar's treasury could afford it, only because the courts of the Czar in the nineteenth century required opulent entertainment, and because schools had been provided to train people to provide it, did it happen that in Russia there was a great period in ballet. The Czar's wealth created great theatres, schools were started to supply these theatres with dancers, and from all over Europe—the Frenchmen Didelot, Perrot, and Petipa; the Italian Cecchetti; the Swede Johannsen—ballet masters and teachers, dancers and musicians all came to embellish the Imperial courtly entertainment.

Contrary to the general belief, ballet was not taken very seriously by the Russian public. It was an entertainment almost exclusively for the aristocracy, among whom there were perhaps only a few gentlemen who were not primarily interested in what the ballerinas were doing after the performance. After the first performance of *The Sleeping Beauty*, Czar Nicholas I said condescendingly to Tchaikovsky, "Very nice." The Czar was familiar with every ballet in the repertory of his theatre and yet he had no idea that he had just heard the greatest ballet score the Russian theatre has ever produced. Like the rest of the Russian audience, he had a dilettante attitude toward ballet.

The Russians, as I have said, established ballet schools, and in these institutions the best teachers in Europe made great Russian dancers. All the influences—the French, the Italian, the Scandinavian—all the talent commingled to form in the nineteenth century in Russia the finest dancing academy in all the world.

By the time I first saw ballet at the Maryinsky Theatre, both Pavlova and Nijinsky had left Russia, never to return. But there were still in St. Petersburg many great dancers. Principal among these were Tamara Karsavina, our ballerina, and Pierre Vladimiroff, who had succeeded Nijinsky as *premier danseur*. We idolized these dancers and strove to perfect ourselves.

I worked very hard at the school, appeared in my first character role, a Spanish dance in Fokine's *Jota Aragonese*, in January 1916, and acted also on the stage of the Alexandrinsky, the Czar's dramatic theatre. At the ballet school we were trained in acting, too, and mime, where we learned the importance of stage gesture. We learned how different stage appearance was from ordinary life, how to work within theatrical disciplines to create illusion. One of my teachers, Paul Gerdt, appeared as a young man in Fokine's *Pavillon d'Armide* with two of his students, Pavlova and Nijinsky. Gerdt was then sixty-three years old, but from his stage presence he appeared as young as his students.

At the Alexandrinsky Theatre, I acted the part of the young student in Andreyev's *Professor Storitsyn*, among other roles, and at the Mikhailovsky, the Imperial Theatre for opéra-comique, I danced and acted in A *Midsummer Night's Dream* to Mendelssohn's music and danced one of the Furies in the Meyerhold-Fokine *Orpheus*. Like all other students at the school, I was almost oblivious to what was going on in the world outside. Few of us knew there was a war.

When Czar Nicholas II abdicated in March 1917, the Imperial Ballet School was closed down. I lived at my aunt's in St. Petersburg, waiting for the school to open again. I worked as a bank messenger, as a saddler's apprentice, and at nights played the piano for silent movies in neighborhood theatres. During the October Bolshevik Revolution later that same year, Lenin selected the balcony of the *prima ballerina assoluta* of the Imperial Theatre, Mathilde Kchessinska, from which to address the people. I remember hearing him that night. I had gone, with a group of my fellow students from the school, to see what was attracting the huge crowd. All of us thought the man on the balcony must be a lunatic. Then we were young; we did not understand the Revolution.

The Bolsheviks did not wish to reopen the Imperial Theatres: the theatres were, after all, aristocratic and "bourgeois" institutions. But Lunacharsky, the new Bolshevik Minister of Education, was a balletomane. He persuaded the Bolsheviks to use the Czar's old theatres for party meetings and for speeches to the public. Party members and the public were compelled to attend. In 1918 Lunacharsky further persuaded the Bolsheviks to allow the old Imperial Ballet Company and students of the school to perform *divertissements* in the old Maryinsky after these official functions were over. And so we danced again, this time in a "state" theatre, though it was the same Maryinsky, and the school was reopened. There was no heat, either in the theatre or at the school, and food and clothing were very scarce. On stage, in flimsy costumes, we could see our breath almost freeze; in the audience, people wore fur coats. At the school, we burned the polished parquet floors to keep warm and made trousers out of the draperies. The Czar's carriages, which had previously driven us to the theatre, were not available, and we had to walk to and from our performances.

We worked hard at taking up our studies again. A new course in Marxian history at the school seemed a small sacrifice for the resumption of training for our chosen profession. We were not paid, we were undernourished and ill-clothed, but still we studied and danced. When Lunacharsky came to take us to see Griffith's movie *Intolerance* in 1920, we still wore the remnants of our Imperial uniforms.

In 1921 I was graduated from what had become the Academy of Opera and Ballet (now the Kirov Academy of Opera and Ballet). I had been a government charge since I was ten years old, and the Bolsheviks, like the Czar before them, expected all graduates of state schools to remain in state theatres until they were pensioned. As an honor graduate, I secured good roles in the theatre's repertory.

This same year, 1921, I entered the Conservatory of Music in St. Petersburg. The famous composer Glazunov was then director of the conservatory. My interest in music had not diminished during the years I had spent learning the theatrical arts; rather, it had greatly increased. I had played the piano regularly at the school and on vacations, and it now seemed to me time to learn even more about music. For three years at the Conservatory of Music I studied theory, composition, and piano while I continued to dance in the state ballet company at the old Maryinsky. I wanted to be a fine pianist as well as a good dancer.

Meanwhile I had become interested in choreography. I do not know how to explain this interest. I had learned to dance, to move, I loved music, and suddenly I wanted to move people to music, to arrange dances. In 1920 I had arranged my first ballet, a short ballet in the Fokine style, to the music from Rubinstein's *La Nuit*, which was danced by my fellow students at th' school. The boys and girls who were in my ballet liked it very much, though its quality of movement was new to them. Our teachers did not like it at all. I saw immediately that I should never be able to convince the management of the state theatre to become interested in my work. I would have to present it myself.

This I did, in St. Peterburg, in 1923, in a program called "Evenings of the Young Ballet," which I organized with Vladimir Dimitriev, who has remained in Russia as a designer. In this program I was responsible for all the choreography. I tried to show the evolution of ballet in Russia from Petipa's classicism through Fokine's reforms to my own ideas of movement. The dancers were members of the state company who had been graduated with me. We had a hard time finding a place to put on this program, which was finally presented in the amphitheatre formerly occupied by the Czar's State Duma (Parliament).

The "Evenings of the Young Ballet" were popular with the dancers who performed them and with the young people in the audience, but they were not liked by the directorate of the state theatre. The director informed my dancers that they could not appear in my ballets and continue as members of the state company. We were therefore compelled to stop our performances, and I was obliged to arrange dances elsewhere.

At the Mikhailovsky Theatre I arranged the dances for Ernst Toller's *Broken-Brow*, devised pantomime ballets to the Milhaud-Cocteau *Le Boeuf sur le toit* and to Alexander Blok's poem *The Twelve*, and began work on a ballet set to Stravinsky's *Pulcinella*, which had already been staged in Western Europe by Diaghilev's Ballets Russes. I also arranged a dance scene for a production of Bernard Shaw's *Caesar and Cleopatra* at the Milhailovsky. (This was the opening scene, which I depicted as a cabaret. Later, when I knew English and could read Shaw in his own language, I saw what nonsense this was!)

All this time, I was still dancing at the old Maryinsky as a member of the state company. The modern ballets of the Diaghilev repertory were becoming a part of the traditional Russian repertory. These ballets excited me enormously: I loved their music and choreography and marveled at the imagination of a man like Serge Diaghilev, whose Russian company in France could produce so many masterpieces so consistently. Needless to say, no equivalent creativeness existed in the theatre at St. Petersburg.

In 1924 I thought it would be a good idea to take a small group of Russian dancers to Western Europe. We had some difficulty with the Soviet authorities, but in those days it was actually possible to leave Russia and the authorities thought the tour might well have propagandistic value. They consented, provided that we went to Europe on our summer vacation from the state theatre. We were called the "Soviet State Dancers." There were actually very few dancers—Alexandra Danilova, Tamara Geva, Nicholas Efimov, and myself. I was then twenty, the oldest of all. I arranged a number of ballets, among them pieces to the "Oriental Dance" from Mussorgsky's *Khovantchina* and a waltz of Kreisler's. We learned these dances perfectly and in June 1924 sailed from St. Petersburg (it had become Leningrad) on a German boat. We were bound for Berlin, where we had secured our first engagement.

In Berlin we danced with some success, then went on to perform in German watering places and at Mannheim. Then we accepted an invitation to dance at the Empire Theatre in London. From London we went to Paris. There we were fortunate enough to secure an audition with Serge Diaghilev, the genius impresario who had brought the Russian ballet to Europe fifteen years before and had caused the ballet capital of the world to shift from St. Petersburg back to Paris. Diaghilev had seen one of our performances; he liked our dancing and our dances. He invited us to join his Ballets Russes.

When I became ballet master to Diaghilev's Ballets Russes, I was twenty-one years old. I was humble in this position in the most famous ballet company in the world and sought to learn everything possible from Diaghilev, the man who had fostered Fokine and Nijinsky and commissioned from Igor Stravinsky that great composer's first ballet scores, *Firebird* and *Petrouchka*.

I had just arrived in Europe and, though I had learned European languages at the ballet school in St. Petersburg and knew the culture of Europe in general, I had much to learn.

Several years ago Anatole Chujoy's *Dance News* published an article of mine on Diaghilev to commemorate the twentieth anniversary of his death. What I said then seems just as true to me now:

> Perhaps it is only today, almost twenty-five years after his death, that all contemporary choreographers begin to realize the true proportions of the enormous artistic debt we all owe to Serge Diaghilev. If we analyze the work we have done since his death in 1929, we see that we are still following in his footsteps, still adhering to the principles laid down by him during the twenty years he guided the fortunes of his unique Ballets Russes. Were he alive today, Diaghilev would probably find a new direction in his beloved art form, a new approach to the creation and presentation of ballet. He was always twenty-five years ahead of his time.
>
> Diaghilev had the capacity to see not only the potentialities inherent in an artist, be he choreographer, composer, designer or dancer, he also knew what work, what style, what period, suited that artist best. Great though it was, his genius for discovery would not have been so overwhelming had he not had that innate and cultivated taste which alone distinguishes true artistic quality from a sense for novelty and craftsmanship.
>
> If I were to describe Diaghilev simply, I should say that he was a man of high culture. It so happened that he was a great ballet impresario, a patron of the arts, but he could just as easily have been a statesman, an ambassador: he could have held any post that required knowledge, intelligence, culture, taste. He was at home in world literature, music, painting and sculpture. He spoke three languages with the fluency and in the idiom of the native. Never a professional musician, he could read a musical score as one reads a book.
>
> Stravinsky has described Diaghilev's intimate musical knowledge in his *Autobiography* and Nicolas Nabokov, who also composed his first ballet for the Ballets Russes, has written of Diaghilev's great understanding of music in his book *Old Friends and New Music*. Never a choreographer or a dancer, Diaghilev knew what was exactly right and what was wrong about a particular ballet or in any portion of it. Never a painter, he possessed an unerring and intimate knowledge of art.
>
> These qualities made Diaghilev a creator, a real producer. He was not just the director or manager of a ballet company who guessed what the public would accept and what it would reject. He did not follow the public; the public followed him. He did not really care very much whether people agreed with him or not. What mattered to him was the work done by the best and most suitable choreographer, musician, designer and dancers. If they succeeded, their work was a success. Diaghilev so inspired the artists who worked under his direction that it is not too much to say that any ballet created for his company bore his personal stamp as well as that of the composer, painter and choreographer.
>
> Strangely enough, he did not interfere with work in progress. Before work began, he discussed projected ballets with their creators in great detail. We argued and recognized each other's points. Diaghilev

had great respect for artistic integrity. By the time actual work began on ballets, every phase of their production represented a collaboration between artists and their producer.

Even if we discount for the moment the fact that companies the world over are still using ballets created for the Diaghilev company (*Petrouchka, Les Sylphides,* etc.) and that much of what else there is in ballet today stems from the Diaghilev roots, we cannot escape the fact that it was Diaghilev who invented the formula of presenting three short ballets in one evening and thus made possible the presentation of ballet not only by big resident companies in the few opera houses of European capitals, but also by touring companies in big and small cities and towns in America and Europe.

If it can be said at all that one man took ballet from the thin aristocratic stratum of society and gave it to the people at large, Diaghilev was the man who did it. To Diaghilev's additional credit, one is reminded that he never attempted to lower the artistic standard of ballet to the level of those who had no prior knowledge, taste or appreciation of the art form. On the contrary, by constant and painstaking work to present ballet of the highest calibre to the people to whom ballet was new, he succeeded in elevating the people to the appreciation of ballet, in developing their taste and increasing their enjoyment.

Personally, I owe to Diaghilev my growth and development during the second period of my artistic life. The first part of it I owe to the Russian Imperial Theatre where I was brought up, to its strict discipline, to its classicism, the basis of all ballet, to its two-hundred-year-old tradition which instilled in me a love for ballet and a respect for its history and artistic principles.

The second period of my artistic life began in the Diaghilev company, where I learned to recognize what was great and valid in art, where I acquired the ability and strength to analyze a work of art on its true merits and where, finally, I learned to be on my own, to do what my artistic sense prompted me to do—in short, to be an artist. All this I owe to Diaghilev without any reservation.

For Diaghilev's company, beginning in 1925, I rehearsed the repertory and danced with the company in addition to creating ten new ballets. I don't think there's any question that *Apollo* (1928) was the most important of these, certainly the most important for me personally, for I regard this ballet as the crucial turning point in my artistic life. In the first ballets I choreographed for Diaghilev I had been successful, I think, but for the wrong reasons. *Pastorale,* for instance, which I arranged to music by Georges Auric in 1925, contained diverse types of movement—at least ten different types—whereas only one type was sufficient for the piece: the others should have been set aside and the one proper type developed. Stravinsky's score for *Apollo* taught me that a ballet, like his music, must have a restraint and discipline. Stravinsky's music had a wonderful clarity and unity of tone, and I saw that gestures, the basic material of the choreographer, have family relations, like different shades in painting and different tones in music. Some are incompatible with others: one must work within a given frame, consciously, and not dissipate the effect of a ballet with inspirations foreign to the tone or mood one understands it must possess. *Apollo* depicted Stravinsky's music visibly.

Prodigal Son and *Le Bal* (with Danilova, Nikitina, Dolin, and Lifar) were my last ballets for Diaghilev. A few months after the first performance of *Le Bal*, Diaghilev died in Venice. His company disbanded: there then came to an end the most important and entertaining twenty years of creativity in music and painting and dancing that Europe had seen since the Renaissance.

After some months had passed, I accepted an engagement as ballet master at the Royal Theatre, Copenhagen, with the Royal Danish Ballet, which, with the Paris Opéra, has the oldest continuous tradition of instruction and performance in the world. After this, I worked in London on my first musical comedy and in France helped to organize the Ballet Russe de Monte Carlo and staged for them their first new ballets: *La Concurrence*, *Cotillon*, and *Le Bourgeois Gentilhomme*.

My own company, Les Ballets 1933, was formed soon after this. This company performed in Paris and in London. It was during performances of Les Ballets 1933 that the painter Pavel Tchelitchev introduced me to the young American Lincoln Kirstein, who with Edward M. M. Warburg invited me to come to the United States to found the ballet school he knew was necessary if the classic dance was ever to flourish in America. We opened the School of American Ballet in New York on January 2, 1934, in studios that had been used in years past by Isadora Duncan. The school has become, over the years, the largest institution for the training of professional dancers outside the European state schools. Students from this school have danced in every American ballet company and in many companies in Europe. More specifically, they have been the basis for the founding of ballet companies that Lincoln Kirstein and I have directed. These companies have evolved and matured in the New York City Ballet. Morton Baum, Chairman of the Executive Committee of the New York City Center of Music and Drama, and the directors of that corporation invited Kirstein and me to found in 1948 this permanent, resident ballet company at the New York City Center. It is not for me to comment on the New York City Ballet: this would be like a father telling you about his own children. I can only invite you to come and see it, as I urge you again to see all ballet companies in New York and on tour throughout America.

Writing about ballet is difficult for me, even talking about ballet is difficult for me; if I were naturally a writer or a lecturer, and expressed myself well in writing and speaking, I should not be a choreographer. But I have tried to make clear a number of things in this book that will be of help to the audience and to the potential dancer. This book, however, as I have said elsewhere, is no substitute for the ballet you can see on the stage. Only by seeing ballet repeatedly in the theatre can you understand why it has entertained audiences for three hundred years and how it has given some of us happiness because we have been able to provide some of that pleasure.

Part Six

BALLET FOR YOUR CHILDREN

People often come to me and ask questions about dancing. They want to know if they should send their sons and daughters to ballet school, when to send them, how long it will take them to become dancers, and what chances they have for a career in ballet. Others ask about choreography: how I work, what I think of first when I am about to produce a ballet, whether choreography can be taught. In this and the following two sections I have answered these questions and many others that seemed to me important for students, dancers, parents of dance students, and—last but not least—the ballet audience.

Ballet must be seen to be enjoyed, but many of us are more easily entertained if we have in advance some information about an art that happens to be strange to us. Most people may want to relax and make no effort when they go to the theatre, but I think the answers to questions about a dancer's training, for instance, might help convince them that all art requires a certain amount of effort and ability on the part of the audience, too.

To ensure maximum clarity, I have arranged my views on ballet for your children, on dancers and choreography, in the form of particular questions and answers.

QUESTION: What ballets should children be taken to see?

ANSWER: Some people think that only ballets about puppets, such as *Petrouchka* and *Coppélia*, are good for children. They are, of course, but I think you will find that children enjoy almost all good ballet. A friend of mine, I remember, thought that a full program of four ballets would be too much for her five-year-old nephew to sit through; she thought the child would get bored and squirm. She decided that they would see only the first two ballets and then leave. But the child didn't want to go. He saw that all the other people weren't leaving and that there was obviously going to be more. He stayed for all the ballets and loved every minute of it.

Children enjoy ballets without stories as much as narrative ballets. If the ballet company is a good one and the orchestra good, they will love these musical ballets. We must understand that children are flexible; they have more imagination, more feeling for fantasy, than grownups. Grownups analyze. They come into the theatre and say sometimes, "This bores me, it's taking up my time"; or they compare, "My wife is better-looking than that girl"; or they complain that they see nothing on stage similar to everyday life. Children are open, freer, not so prejudiced. They have a natural ability to imagine things that ballet sometimes releases. The fascination life has for them is based on enjoying movement and change; ballet, in its idealization of movement, fascinates them. A storyless ballet, simply movement to music, they like almost instinctively. They will certainly like anything that is good, if we only give them the chance.

QUESTION: When should a child begin ballet training?

ANSWER: Children should begin to study when they are eight, nine, or ten years old—certainly not before they are eight. All you can really do with children before the age of eight is permit them to run around, dance a little, and sing songs. This, of course, is recreation and produces no real result. Before the age of eight, ballet training can actually be harmful. It is serious training and it is hard work physically. In ballet class the first thing we teach the children are the basic ballet positions, positions that are unnatural to them. Their hips, knees, and feet have to be turned out in certain directions. Because the bones and joints are still soft at this early age, we never force children into the basic ballet positions. If they can't do them perfectly, we wait. If you overtrain the small, undeveloped muscles of children, the muscles become hard and don't develop properly with the body and the child is apt to become deformed. So even when a child begins at eight, we are very careful. Very often a mother will come to me and say, "My child dances very well and she is musical too. I think she is another Pavlova." The child is perhaps four years old! In all probability someone has advised the mother that the child should study ballet, someone who wants to make money and naturally doesn't care what happens to the child afterward. If you take a child of four in a ballet class and train her seriously, you may please her parents but you will seriously harm the child. However, when a child is eight or nine years old, she can take a certain amount of direction and you can really begin to teach her.

QUESTION: What is the age limit for starting ballet training?

ANSWER: This really depends on the individual case—on the person's build and on the softness of his joints. Generally speaking, beginning students with professional theatre careers in mind should certainly start before they are fifteen years old—preferably earlier. If they start to study at fifteen, they will probably not be ready for the stage until they are over twenty, by which time most dancers have been professionals for some years. But I repeat, it depends on the individual case. Usually, after the age of twenty-two no satisfactory results can be obtained.

QUESTION: If you want your child to be a dancer, what is the best preparation before the child begins to attend ballet class?

ANSWER: I would suggest reading the child fairy stories—Grimm, La Fontaine, Gozzi, and many others—read them stories from Greek mythology and the stories of E. T. A. Hoffmann. Most people know Hoffmann's stories from the operetta by Offenbach, *Tales of Hoffmann*, but he wrote a great many other wonderful stories. The story of the ballet *The Nutcracker* is just one of them. And by all means read the stories of the great Hans Christian Andersen. And I don't mean Andersen's stories, or any others, as they are watered down, especially translated and condensed for children. Good fairy stories were always written for intelligent people. Children are more intelligent than many of us think. Mickey Mouse will interest a child for only a short time; you should move on to fairy tales. It is well to remember that if a child continues to be interested only in Mickey Mouse, it is probably because you have not introduced him to something new. Children like to move on to new, more complicated things. They don't like to be talked down to; they like it very much if you respect their capacity for new experience.

You should also play music for your child. If you don't play an instrument yourself, play records at home. Play them all the time; make music a regular thing around the house, like bathing and brushing teeth. Don't bother with jazz or swing or popular records; the air is filled with it from morning to night, and children will hear enough of it. Play anything good. Don't bother to tell the children what you are playing; soon they will remember, hum the music, and whistle it. They won't care what it is especially, but they will surprise you when they recognize it. Then go on to play other things.

Don't expect children to like the music you play at once, don't coax them, don't even ask their opinion, just play it. If you think Mozart bores children, you may find out that Mozart is just boring you. Children are not so prejudiced: they don't have the barriers to enjoyment that so many of us grownups have. Children are more aware, more teachable, more vulnerable to entertainment. They have their ears open.

QUESTION: Where are the best ballet schools in the United States?

ANSWER: Excellent schools with fine teachers are to be found all over America—in New York, California, Chicago, everywhere—not only in the big cities, but in smaller communities. New York is the center of dance activity in the United States—our ballet companies work in and out of New York and have schools there—and sooner or later, almost all dancers find themselves studying or working in New York, as all actors do. It often happens that dancers do not begin to study in New York until they have established some sort of reputation for themselves elsewhere and only continue their study in New York because it is convenient for their work.

QUESTION: If you had a son, would you send him to ballet school?

ANSWER: Yes. The people who ask me this question say they hesitate to send their boys to ballet school because they are afraid the boys will become "sissified" or perhaps will not develop strong, muscular bodies as they might in another activity. That isn't true. Male dancers must be very strong, not only for their own work but for partnering; their bodies must be flexible and they must have a great deal of endurance. This is the reason why many of our best dancers were good soldiers during the war. Of course, you can be strong and a "sissy" at the same time, but this has nothing to do with ballet: it is the person himself. We do not give ballet classes for boys and girls separately. They are together in class from the beginning. Perhaps if boys started to take dancing lessons early, they would appreciate the companionship and charm of girls even sooner than they ordinarily do!

QUESTION: How is a child selected for admittance to a ballet school?

ANSWER: About the only things you can judge a child on when she is eight or nine years old are her general appearance and her health. We can only tell whether a child's insteps are good, whether her limbs are in the right proportion, and whether they are flexible. We must be able to watch her in class, two lessons a week, for perhaps six months to come to a real decision. Also, at the beginning, talent is not always the first thing that a child shows. That might come much later, when she has learned to dance well enough to demonstrate talent. Some girls and boys at the beginning seem to be very good, but as time goes on it often happens that they just do not show progress or development. If they are satisfactory at the beginning and develop badly, we advise them not to continue.

It is good if a child is musical, if she knows how to keep time to music and reacts to it. But it often happens that it is impossible to make any judgment about this, too, until after some time has elapsed in training.

QUESTION: What is a child taught first at a ballet school?

ANSWER: At the beginning, each of the five ballet positions (see Glossary) is shown to the children and explained very simply and plainly. Then the children are placed facing the wall with both hands on the bar, so that their weight is evenly supported by both hands. Standing this way, they must first learn to stand in each of the Five Positions until they become completely familiar with them and can adopt one or another at will, but as yet without any connecting exercises. These first classes are taken slowly; children do these same exercises for a month or so and then they get used to it. Actually, an exercise is a memory of something, a spontaneous memory. Soon it becomes a part of your existence, of your body, and if you are trained well at the beginning, after a while you can move from one place to another in the right way without even thinking about it. The unnatural position, in other words, becomes natural. It's like reciting something. If you want to recite Shakespeare, you have to memorize. You repeat it for a hundred times perhaps, and then something happens in your brain. You can recite spontaneously.

The children's attention is drawn to correct posture at the beginning; they are taught to keep their backs straight, their shoulders down. Next they are taught to do *demi-pliés* (*see* Glossary, *Plié*) very slowly in each of the five positions, always paying strict attention to posture.

The training of children requires a long time, and trying to shorten it by hurrying the child does no good whatever. Children must be watched to see when they have had enough of each exercise. It is important never to strain them in order to speed their progress.

When the children are familiar with the Five Positions, they must learn how to change from one position to another by means of connecting movements. Next they learn *battements tendus* (*see* Glossary), beginning with the simplest: from first position to second position and back. They should be taught *battements* only in front, then only sideways, then in back, separately. All these exercises should be taught first with both hands on the bar, then with only one hand on the bar. At this point the children learn how the hand and fingers should be held. Then, away from the bar, in the center of the room, they are taught the arm positions.

QUESTION: Should parents watch their children in class?

ANSWER: No, or if they must, only very seldom, for it confuses things. The child's respect for his parent and his respect for his teacher are entirely different things, and until the child learns to dance well, I think it's a mistake to confuse the child with two kinds of authority. He will learn to respect his teacher and learn to dance much faster if parental concern is suspended during ballet class. At the School of American Ballet during a child's first two years, parents visit classes only once a month. We can all understand that parents are vitally interested in their children's progress, but when they have chosen a school and a teacher, they should trust their own judgment and have faith in the teacher.

QUESTION: How soon should girls studying ballet begin to dance on toe?

ANSWER: Children should not be allowed to dance on point until their fourth year of study—after they have completed three years of training. That is, if a child enters a school and begins regular training when she is eight years old, she is eleven before taking toe exercises. This period of preparation is vitally necessary because many foot and leg muscles must be developed properly before a child can dance on toe without injuring herself seriously. The child's soft bone structure may be irreparably harmed if she begins dancing on toe before she is ten or eleven. If a child of eight enters a school and takes daily lessons, two years of training will give her the proper preparation. No profit can come from permitting a child to dance on point before she is prepared. Her dancing future will be short and she will be harmed physically. Only competent teachers are in a position to judge exceptions to these rules.

QUESTION: Is toe dancing painful?

ANSWER: No, not if the proper muscles are trained well first. In good ballet schools we are always careful to do this. Naturally, at first the muscles ache from the unfamiliar movement, but to a dancer an aching muscle is a discovery: she knows that she is conquering something new.

If you have been to the ballet and seen dancers remain on stage for long periods of time in a difficult ballet, you have probably wondered at their physical endurance. Dancing, however, trains their muscles so that they are controlled or relaxed almost unconsciously. In a dancer's body there is no constant tension. Muscles must be relaxed until they are used. In modern choreography there are steps so fast that some muscles have to be relaxed instantly or the dancer will tire in a few minutes.

QUESTION: Can knock-knees and other defects be corrected at ballet school?

ANSWER: Some children are knock-kneed when they're very young, but by the time they are ten, their structure changes completely and they aren't as knock-kneed as you thought they would be. Then they can go on with their lessons, for we can control the appearance of the knees slightly. If the child continues to be very knock-kneed, it is best to give up the lessons. The parents of one little girl we had at our school were different sizes: the father was very, very tall and the mother very, very short. I guessed correctly that when the girl grew up, she would have very short legs and a very long torso. But she wanted to continue studying and did so until it was apparent that she had grown the wrong way. You can't do anything about a structural defect like this. You just have to wait, to hope, that the young children who start lessons when they are eight or nine will still be well proportioned when they grow up. I'm sure some parents think this is too big a chance to take, spending all that money when they can't be sure their children will develop correctly for a professional career. But this chance must be taken, for if the child does not start lessons soon enough, it will be difficult—if not impossible—for her to become a fine professional dancer.

QUESTION: How is discipline maintained in a ballet class?

ANSWER: This is a question parents often ask, and they are quite right to be interested in it. When children go to a strange ballet class with a new teacher, they are a little in awe of the instructor, quite naturally. But actually this makes them more anxious to follow directions, to repeat the positions and steps that the teacher shows them. If their parents directed them at home in this way, they would probably say, "No, I won't, I don't want to." Parents naturally don't want to force things; they think their children really don't want to and that they might cry. But the teacher doesn't care, even if the children do cry. He simply directs them, politely and firmly.

The teacher must direct his young pupils quietly: you can't scream and correct children all the time. You can scream once, twice, maybe three times, and the children will be scared and obey you; but if you yell at them any more, they won't be frightened. They'll get used to your yelling, and you'll find that you have to pretend not to see them misbehaving—so that you won't scream any more and embarrass your authority.

Children see everything. They certainly see how you react when you turn around suddenly and catch them misbehaving. They know you will think ill of them. But if you don't notice, they'll say to themselves, "*He* doesn't care, he looks straight at us when we're horsing around, we can do anything we want to!"

But to a certain extent with children in ballet class you can't notice everything. You have to pretend not to see some of their little tricks, because for a whole hour it's very hard to hold their attention. You can hold their attention by noticing their tricks only once in a while. Then be firm with them, and they will behave for a little while. The next week they are quieter and behave for longer periods of time. By the end of the first year they respect you. They behave like soldiers: they come on time, they know when to start, wait obediently for your directions, and, finally, when you tell them that the lesson is over and say, "Thank you," they acknowledge this with a bow which will be so important to them later when they bow gracefully on the stage. They become such good soldiers that they don't leave the class unless you do say, "Thank you."

You can't expect all children to like ballet classes. I certainly did not like them at first, and I think this is more or less true of most young pupils. Only gradually do they learn to like it. After some time has elapsed, they enjoy being able to do what they are told in class. They like the music the pianist plays for them to move to. First he plays music just for the sound, for rhythm and keeping time, but after a while he plays them little pieces. To look at the children, you'd think that they didn't know the difference, but they remember, they notice everything, they memorize music. Slowly they become trained to move well and to listen, and from a few steps and exercises they are able to do simple dance sequences. They watch grown-up dancers in other classes, admire them, and want to move beautifully too, by imitating with the little technique they have.

I think all children like the idea of dancing. If you tell them they're taking lessons to become something they don't know about, they don't listen to you. But dancing is different: they like it and somehow suffer through the lessons at first. It's like holding up a candy bar and saying to a child, "No, not yet, you must wait." They will wait, they will endure the lessons so that they can move brilliantly and beautifully. It is a natural thing for children to want to move well, to move well in time, to catch a baseball at the right moment, to hate to drop things. Dancing is a discipline that perfects this natural inclination: it gives us control over our bodies so that we are in a position to conquer space, so to speak, in given periods of time. Some music is very rapid, very complicated, and to move to it well is difficult, but the dancer is able to conquer the complicated time element of the music, she is able to move freely within the discipline of time.

Once we had at our school a child whose mother was a psychiatrist. The mother came to the school and wanted to know how the classes were run, how the children were made to behave, because at home she could do nothing with her own child. The mother watched her child in class, and this little girl—the little brat who at home was always doing the wrong thing—she was perfect! Like all the other pupils, she did exactly what the teacher said and enjoyed it. Afterward the mother wanted to know how this could happen. She said, "In my job I advise parents about their children. I'm supposed to know all about child psychology." She was told that it is a matter of knowing how to teach, when to notice things and when not to notice, and that children have a certain respect for what the teacher represents. For the child, the teacher is connected with a strange thing called the art of dancing, and the child knows that what she can learn from him is wonderful.

The respect that a child has for his teacher and the good manners she learns in ballet class are a very important part of the tradition of ballet, which is an aristocratic tradition. I use the word aristocratic here seriously, not because ballet is open only to an exclusive class of people, but because it is an exclusive art, practiced and completely understood only by those who are willing to spend a great deal of time and effort on it. The Greek word for aristocracy means the rule of the best, not the rule of an exclusive class. Ballet in this sense is a democratic art, open to all who are willing to work and to learn.

ABOVE: *Interplay*: John Kriza and Ballet Theatre dancers. BELOW:
Rodeo: John Kriza and Allyn McLerie and company in the Ballet Theatre
production.

ABOVE: *Corps de ballet* in the New York City Ballet's *Swan Lake*. BELOW: *Gaîté Parisienne:* Ballet Russe de Monte Carlo production.

©*Roger Wood*

Prodigal Son: Yvonne Mounsey and Francisco Moncion in the New York
City Ballet production.

LEFT: *The Cage:*
Nora Kaye and
Nicholas Magallanes
in the New York
City Ballet
production. BELOW:
Jean Babilée in *Le
Jeune Homme et la
Mort.*

Walter E. Owen

©Roger Wood

ABOVE: Alicia Alonso. BELOW: *Lilac Garden:* Tanaquil LeClercq and Hugh Laing, Nora Kaye and Brooks Jackson in the New York City Ballet production.

Serge Lido

ABOVE:
Divertimento:
Melissa Hayden,
Tanaquil LeClercq,
Maria Tallchief,
Diana Adams, and
Patricia Wilde in
the New York City
Ballet production.
LEFT: *Tyl
Ulenspiegel:*
Beatrice Tompkins
and Frank Hobi as
the Duke and
Duchess of Alba;
Jerome Robbins as
Tyl. New York City
Ballet.

Walter E. Owen

QUESTION: How many different classes are there in ballet schools?

ANSWER: Most schools are divided into different sections for beginners, intermediate, advanced, and professional classes, or classes equivalent to these distinctions. Classes for children are given separately. When a student has finished all the children's classes, she moves on to the regular classes. Students who have had previous study or experience are placed in the proper class after auditions.

QUESTION: Do students receive grades at ballet school?

ANSWER: Some schools give their children grades, but many promote students simply on the basis of their progress and ability in acquiring technique. Age has nothing to do with promotion, nor has the length of time spent in previous study. Promotion, in other words, is not automatic. It depends on the student's development. If a child has studied for some time and shows no aptitude for dancing, her parents should be so advised.

QUESTION: Should children practice ballet at home?

ANSWER: While practicing at home is not generally harmful, it actually does very little good; children should certainly not be made to do it. At home there is no teacher to watch and correct them; only in a class can they practice with real profit. It seems to me better if at home they think occasionally about their lessons and practice only the fine points they want to improve—hand movements and mime, for example.

QUESTION: Is it necessary for a student to continue her practice during long vacations?

ANSWER: It is not only unnecessary, it is inadvisable. If a serious student has been scrupulous about attending classes daily for nine or ten months of the year, rest and relaxation are recommended.

QUESTION: How many years of training are necessary before a beginner is graduated from a ballet school?

ANSWER: Usually, five or six years. The period is longer if the student has not attended class daily (Monday through Saturday for a minimum of nine months each year), shorter if his ability is exceptional. Because few students are likely to make their professional debuts when they are fourteen years old, this is an additional reason for not beginning to study until after the age of eight. It must be stressed, however, that few schools have any graduating system. No dancer really finishes going to school. Even if she is a ballerina in a ballet company, she still takes classes.

QUESTION: Is the public admitted to ballet classes?

ANSWER: No. Many schools allow visitors in class, and there is nothing wrong with this, particularly when the dancers have reached the professional point and are appearing frequently on the stage. But when the dancers are younger, it isn't such a good idea. Visitors distract the teacher and, most important, distract the students, who will naturally play to such an audience and are tempted to show off. Actually, visitors should be respectful and considerate and just ask politely if they may come, just as they would if they wanted to visit a class in a public high school.

QUESTION: Can students at a ballet school watch classes other than their own?
ANSWER: Yes, certainly. In fact they should be encouraged to do so. Most children who come to ballet class like to spend time afterward looking in on other classes. A young student who watches a professional class sees there the technique she is aiming for. This reinforces her ambition and makes her more eager to learn.

QUESTION: How do you tell whether or not a teacher is good?
ANSWER: This is certainly a problem that confronts parents as well as prospective students. It sometimes seems to me that there are more bad teachers of dancing than of any other art. There is a great tendency to take advantage of people's ignorance, for it is impossible to make a judgment about a teacher unless you know something about dancing. You can visit a ballet class, perhaps, and like what you see, but you can hardly tell if the teacher is training the children properly. Over the years bad teachers have devised many so-called methods, short cuts to fame; they invent nonsense about muscular knowledge to confuse and exploit those interested in ballet training. In engineering and medicine it's hard to fool people in this way, and there are laws to protect the public from collapsing bridges and quack doctors. In ballet training, however, where there is no great physical danger, there are no laws to protect you from fake teachers.

There are no short cuts, no new "methods" to become a good ballet dancer. There is only one way, instruction in the classic dance as it has been codified over a period of three hundred years. All able instructors teach ballet in terms of this universal tradition.

I think the best thing to do in seeking a good teacher is to ask the advice of a well-known professional, an experienced dancer. If you admire a dancer, find out where she studied from *The Dance Encyclopedia* or write to her. There are many fine schools, many wonderful teachers.

QUESTION: Are all ballet classes taught by the same instructor in a ballet school?
ANSWER: In smaller schools, yes, because it is necessary, but in the larger schools this is never the case. Teachers' schedules change throughout the year, and most students have a chance to benefit from the special knowledge and experience that each teacher naturally possesses. Such

a system exposes the young student to varied direction and tends to prevent him from unconsciously imitating one teacher.

QUESTION: Should dancers have stage experience while they are still studying?
ANSWER: Not until they have reached a stage of professional competence. Children who appear on the stages of state theatres in Europe are called upon to do only very minor roles: they are not allowed to take roles for which their learning and talent have not qualified them.

QUESTION: Do ballet schools provide room and board for students?
ANSWER: No, not unless these schools are attached to higher educational institutions such as colleges and universities.

QUESTION: Do some schools accept only professional dancers?
ANSWER: Most are open to all. Some schools, like the School of American Ballet in New York, are interested primarily in students who wish to become professionals; but this school also accepts serious students who do not have professional careers in mind. The state schools in Europe, of course, accept only those students who may graduate onto the stages of state theatres.

QUESTION: How do ballet schools in the United States differ from those in Europe?
ANSWER: There are private schools in Europe, but most of the famous schools are state-supported institutions associated with a state theatre. This is true in France, which has the oldest dancing academy in the world, in Denmark, and in Milan at La Scala; recently it has become the case in England. In Russia, the schools formerly supported by the Czars are supported by the Soviet regime. Each of these schools is attached to a ballet company financed by the state—the ballet of the Paris Opéra, the Royal Danish Ballet, and the Sadler's Wells Ballet, the ballet of the Bolshoi and Kirov state theatres, etc. Students are selected on a competitive basis, the government pays their way, and, after graduation, the student is obliged to spend a certain period dancing only with the state ballet company. It is axiomatic that if a student successfully completes the course, she will graduate onto the stage of the state theatre and become a permanent member of the state ballet company. Because these schools are state-supported, no foreign students are admitted except under extraordinary circumstances.

Since students in the state-supported European schools are chosen at a very early age, the curriculum consists not only of dancing in many cases, but includes also courses that students would be expected to take in ordinary schools—languages, literature, history, science, geography, and courses related to the other arts.

Students begin in these schools when they are about nine years old. In France, at the Opéra, the oldest ballet school in the world, the young students remain in the *classes supplémentaires*, first and second, for five years, then move on to the *classes des quadrilles*. The *corps de ballet* of the ballet company at the Opéra is selected from these groups.

The Paris Opéra ballet itself is divided rigidly into classes: *élèves* (apprentices), the first *quadrilles* (equivalent to *corps de ballet*), *quadrilles secondes coryphées* (dancers who perform in smaller groups than the *corps de ballet*, but who are not yet soloists), *petits sujets* (minor soloists), *grand sujets*, *premières danseuses* and *premiers danseurs* and, finally, *étoiles* (prima ballerinas and leading male dancers). Dancers remain in these divisions until they are promoted by the examinations that are given every member of the company every year. It is the usual practice for all dancers to perform two variations specified in advance by the directorate. The *étoiles* and *premières danseuses* and *danseurs* do not take part in the examinations. The examinations are judged by a jury of administrators, dancers, and teachers, which changes from year to year.

All the ballet schools in the United States are private; none are state-supported. This is, of course, also true of our ballet companies, which are not supported by public funds. A number of our ballet companies, however—the San Francisco Ballet, the New York City Ballet, and the Ballet Theatre, for example—have their own ballet schools, where the members of the companies take class scholarships alongside regular students. Here, of course, it is not axiomatic that successful completion of a course gives the dancer a job with the company associated with the school. Many schools provide scholarships. The School of American Ballet gives scholarships to about a hundred talented young people every year.

Part Seven

CAREERS IN BALLET

QUESTION: How are dancers selected for ballet companies?

ANSWER: By audition. The ballet master and other interested people in our ballet companies usually have these auditions when they need to replace some of their dancers or want additions to their companies. These auditions are held in New York and all over the country; the latter is particularly true of those ballet companies that travel.

Often, at an audition, the ballet master will ask the dancer to perform a variation that is familiar to her; then he may show her a dance she doesn't know and see how she performs it, because the one thing that the dancer may know very well is not the best clue to her real talent. Previous experience is good to have, but every year all our ballet companies take in new girls and boys whose familiarity with the stage is meager indeed.

Two of our American companies, the New York City Ballet and the Ballet Theatre, have their own schools, and it is mostly from these schools that new members of the companies are selected. This would be the ideal situation for every ballet company, for in this way—with a definite idea of what kind of dancer they desire—companies can train students within their own requirements. The advantage of this is obvious, of course—even before a student dances on the stage, she will have had, in class, a real idea of the company's style and artistic demands.

QUESTION: How tall should a dancer be?

ANSWER: Between five feet and five-feet-six inches for a grown-up girl. Grown-up boys can be taller, of course, between five-feet-six and six feet, but not over six feet. There are exceptions, but not many. If a girl is five-feet-eight, on toe she will be way over six feet tall and will look silly with any partner she dances with. Dancers who intend to be only soloists can naturally afford to be taller, because their greater height will not be distracting or ludicrous as they will not be with girls or boys of average height in the *corps de ballet*. I must point out, however, that tall or short dancers with distinctive personalities and abilities can certainly achieve success.

QUESTION: Should all dancers be musical?

ANSWER: It would be wonderful if they were. At some time in her life a dancer should play a musical instrument—the piano, violin, flute, any musical instrument. She may not have talent and may play badly, but this experience will make her participate in music: she will not always be passive in relation to it. She will understand something about what music is. That, like dancing, music is hard to perform well. If it isn't possible for her to play an instrument, she should at least know solfeggio: how to sing scales (do, re, mi, fa . . . etc.), how to read a little music and be able to sing from the notes.

But being musical, of course, is not just being able to play an instrument, even if you play it well. There are, for instance, many unmusical singers who can sing the proper notes, but who haven't the least idea what the song is all about. The dancer's relation to music is very similar to the singer's: an orchestra is accompanying what she does; she is always moving with the music. She can move to the music automatically, count to herself all the time, and never really listen. Afterward she won't remember the music, only the sequence of steps. Counting is necessary, particularly in learning a new ballet, where you are anxious to remember the precise moment for entrances, exits, and particular steps; but after these simple things are grasped, the dancer should not only count but should also listen very carefully. After all, there's no reason why the public should be obliged to sit and watch a dancer move to music that she thinks is dull. They will think it is dull, too. Perhaps being musical is something a dancer is born with—either she reacts to it or she doesn't—but I think that, with intelligent application, any student can develop certain sensitivities to music that will improve the quality of her dancing immeasurably. No advice will help her as much as going to concerts and recitals frequently and listening to as much music as possible.

If your children take piano lessons or learn to play some other musical instrument, it is proper to enforce a certain discipline about it for some time; but if after a few years a child shows no aptitude for the instrument, it is foolish to compel her to continue. She will begin to hate music and undo all your work. If she has studied for some time, acquired a certain skill and been exposed to what music is, and doesn't wish to go on with her studies, allow her to stop. If she really loves music, she will go back to it; if she doesn't like it, you will have done her no harm.

QUESTION: Should dancers go to college?

ANSWER: It would be nice if they could, but since students who wish to become *professionals* should be studying dancing every day, it becomes difficult. Serious dance students have—in addition to their regular ballet classes—classes in character dancing, modern dance, supported adagio, and so forth. This means that unless dance students go to college at night, or between their classes at ballet school, when they are no doubt tired from their work at dancing, they can't go at all.

There are many people who say that all dancers are stupid, and some give as a reason for this the fact that dancers are not properly educated. It would be nice if we could have complete dancing academies in America, where students could be taught an academic curriculum, music, and the other arts to complement their study of dancing; but we have no such institutions, and besides, I don't think it is true at all that dancers are stupid. My experience has been that they are, on the contrary, apt to be very intelligent. It is also my experience that there are many stupid college graduates. Intelligence is not entirely a matter of education.

QUESTION: Must all dancers first be members of the *corps de ballet*?

ANSWER: Usually this is the case. Directors of a ballet company who have not seen a young professional in school do not know how talented she may be until she has had a chance to display her gifts, and most young dancers are therefore engaged first for the *corps de ballet*. Many of them, also, are too young to be placed in anything else. If they evidence talent in the *corps*, they will soon be given larger roles. But it is only seldom that a member of the *corps de ballet* becomes a ranking soloist overnight. Ballet companies that are directly associated with their own ballet schools can watch students from day to day and discover soloists among them; these students need not be tried out in the *corps de ballet*. Most of the great Russian dancers became important soloists as soon as they were graduated, some before they were graduated. Tanaquil LeClercq, a ballerina of the New York City Ballet, began as a soloist and leading performer. But it is by no means "once in the *corps de ballet*, always in the *corps de ballet*." We must remember that André Eglevsky, *premier danseur*, joined the Ballet Russe de Monte Carlo when he was fourteen and was dancing leading roles six months later; that Alexandra Danilova began in the *corps de ballet* of the Maryinsky Theatre, advanced to soloist, and became a ballerina in Diaghilev's great Ballets Russes; that Alicia Markova took soloist roles in Diaghilev's company soon after she joined it at the age of fourteen; that Maria Tallchief joined the Ballet Russe de Monte Carlo as a member of the *corps* to become a soloist and a ballerina.

QUESTION: Is a dancing career incompatible with marriage?

ANSWER: By no means. Very often dancers retire when they marry, perhaps because they go to live with their husbands in places where there is little dancing or because they want to have large families, but many successful dancers continue their careers after marriage and their careers continue to be successful.

QUESTION: Must ballet dancers belong to a union?

ANSWER: There are several unions which a ballet dancer might conceivably join, depending on where the ballet company is performing. If the ballet company performs in a legitimate theatre or opera house, in all probability the dancer would join the American Guild of Musical Artists, because AGMA has agreements with virtually all companies who perform in these theatres.

QUESTION: How much are ballet dancers paid?

ANSWER: The minimum in 1953 was $87.50 a week for ballet dancers dancing in ballet companies. In 1942 the minimum was $41.50, and it can be seen that the dancer's pay has risen with the times; it will certainly continue to do so. Soloists and leading dancers are naturally paid much more than the minimum, but there is no established rule for their wages; it is a matter decided by the individual companies and the individual dancers. Still, it is obvious that no one ever pursued a dancing career to make a great deal of money. Leading singers and actors receive a great deal more money for their services than leading dancers. It's strange that this should be the case, for when actors and singers aren't regularly employed they can work at outside jobs and keep in practice by private study at night. The unemployed dancer, however, must attend ballet class during the day and work at her art constantly to keep in perfect condition. She seldom has either time or energy left for an outside job. The dancer between engagements is thus apt to be very poor. Even when they are working, I think it is safe to say that all dancers are underpaid or overworked, or both.

QUESTION: How long does a dancer's career last?

ANSWER: This is not an easy question to answer. Usually, nowadays, dancers appear on the stage by their late teens, often when they are sixteen or seventeen. It is even possible for dancers to become very famous before they are twenty. Some years ago, when I brought Irina Baronova, Tatiana Riabouchinska, and Tamara Toumanova to the Ballet Russe de Monte Carlo, they were all under sixteen. They were the "baby ballerinas" and became famous overnight.

By the time they are thirty, dancers have more or less reached their peak: they have acquired just about all the technique that is possible for them. But after they are thirty they can, of course, develop what they have learned and become greater artists still. The great dancers of the past—Pavlova, Karsavina, Spessivtzeva—we remember not as young girls, but as mature women, beautiful and gracious. Pavlova never retired; she was fifty when she died. Karsavina danced in public for the last time when she was forty-seven. It's up to the individual dancer. They can dance only occasionally when they grow older, and only gradually will audiences detect a change in them. Naturally, it is a happier thing if dancers retire before their audiences compel them to.

QUESTION: Should dancers have children?
ANSWER: Certainly. It does no harm whatever. Many dancers have children. Many dancers are also naturally unwilling to sacrifice a year out of their careers in order to have them. It depends on the individual.

QUESTION: Are sports good for dancers?
ANSWER: Only as an occasional pleasure. Dancers must take good care of their bodies. I would say that it is dangerous to skate, for instance. In skating, the knees bend a different way and the ankles are used differently. Playing football would be particularly hazardous. In fact, any game in which you would have to kick a ball would not be good. If a toe is injured, a dancer may have to give up dancing and all those years of study will be wasted. Tennis is all right, I suppose, for a little pleasure and if not pursued too strenuously. Actually, too much athletic activity destroys the finesse of a dancer's gesture. The truth is, of course, that dancers are so busy working at their art and are usually so tired from their studies that they seldom have the time or energy for sports.

Nathan Milstein, the great violinist, doesn't like to carry his violin because of the weight of the case. He must curve his fingers around the handle, and he feels that this strains them. It doesn't, of course, strain them seriously, and he would naturally be able to play well in any case; but he has some fine reaction in his hand that makes him think he won't be able to play with complete refinement. Horowitz, too, cares for his hands, as do all great instrumentalists. The principal instruments of a dancer are, of course, her legs, and she must respect them.

QUESTION: How is ballet training beneficial to those who do not intend to pursue professional careers?
ANSWER: Training in ballet strengthens the general physical condition of the body and develops the muscular system. It also gives complete control —poise, grace, and balance—to the body. Many people do not know how to enter a room gracefully; dancers do. Notice sometime that most people, when they are in a room with other people, often unconsciously turn around to look over their shoulders. Actually, they are self-conscious, ill at ease with their own bodies. They hesitate to turn their backs. These people control their faces well enough and imagine that grace consists largely of facial beauty. Dancers don't worry about people watching them from behind. They move unself-consciously; their grace is confident, an attribute of the whole body. For this reason, ballet

training is beneficial not only to those who intend to pursue professional careers, but to all people.

QUESTION: What careers are open to dancers after they retire?

ANSWER: Many of them become teachers. Certainly, experienced dancers who have appeared for many years on the stage are the best-equipped teachers. Many former dancers become ballet masters in our ballet companies. There they rehearse ballets, give classes, and preserve the artistic disciplines. Such a person must not only be an exceptional teacher, he must also have a good visual memory and be very musical. Others with talent become choreographers; perhaps they began to create ballets while they were still dancing. Still others continue to work in the theatre as character dancers and mimes. In this country we regard this as something of a comedown, but we really shouldn't. In the Royal Danish Ballet, for example, the dancers stay on in the company and are much respected. It is a wonderful thing to see a dancer who was once a ballerina doing a part such as the mother in *Giselle*. This sort of dancer is very familiar with the ballet and knows that the part is important. It is she and other dancers like her who hand down to younger people the old traditions, and not just in a gossipy way: they watch them rehearse, correct them tirelessly, make sure of every detail. In this way the original choreographer's intention is preserved, along with the steps he planned, and very old ballets survive intact. That is an exciting way for a dancer to pay her debt to her profession.

NOTES AND COMMENTS ON DANCERS, DANCING, AND CHOREOGRAPHY

Part Eight

NOTES AND COMMENTS ON DANCERS,
DANCING, AND CHOREOGRAPHY

QUESTION: What country produces the finest classical dancers?

ANSWER: Classical dancing isn't a nationalistic question, and for a very simple reason: it isn't nationalistic dancing. Native character or folk-lore has nothing to do with it. The ability to "turn out" properly, for example, has nothing to do with the country from which a dancer comes. Americans have a great deal of ability because their bodies are strong and also because they are a very musical people. Maybe it's because we hear music, all kinds of it, everywhere here. Children respond to this rhythmical music. They clap, dance, and develop rhythmical sense almost by nature. This sense of rhythm needs schooling, very good schooling; but with such a background in your students, you can develop very great dancers. In France there are also lots of strong, well-built dancers who are musical, and certainly the same is true of England, Italy, and other countries. In other words, people of all nationalities make wonderful classical dancers. The problem really narrows down to where the best schools are. Where you have the best teachers, you have the best dancers, no matter what their nationality.

QUESTION: Is there such a thing as purely American ballet?

ANSWER: In answer to this question and the two that follow, I'd like to paraphrase the comment that I made on these subjects in Serge Lido's *Ballet 2*, two years ago.

From the time ballet began, it has been influenced by *all* the countries where it developed, from Italy, to France, to Scandinavia, and it has adapted itself to the physical abilities of the different countries. The historical development of the art has been traced in another part of this book. I hope I have successfully shown that the classic dance is a fully developed art form, which has now become universal. It has a body of classified and organized techniques which will remain as the basis of the vocabulary of classical dance until such time as ballet is replaced by some other form of theatrical entertainment.

I think that if there is such a thing as purely American ballet, it is reflected not in style but in subject matter. For example, a ballet about cowboys might be called American, as a ballet about Sherlock Holmes might be called English, or the cancan might be called French. The latter case, however, is a question of national rather than classical dance.

QUESTION: Are there different styles of classical dancing for each country?
ANSWER: As for style of dancing for different countries, there are naturally some small differences in execution, but they are mainly differences of personality. For example, there may be ten different interpretations of *Swan Lake* or *Giselle* in England, France, Denmark, Italy, and the United States—all equally valid. Some people, whose taste is inclined toward the obvious, have come to expect certain stylistic clichés from dancers—as, for example, that the dancer should be warm and passionate—but a dancer does not necessarily have to be warm or passionate. Some people are readily inclined to look for the obvious on stage. There are two types of personalities, for example, which seem to be universally pleasing to audiences: one is the vampire, almost like a female Mephistopheles; the other personality is like the lyrical or the poetic one, often almost lethargic. Yet some very good dancers that I have seen in my life were beautifully cold, like birds with no warmth at all. Others were like Oriental queens; others, again, were like pure crystal. The technique of classical dance necessarily creates a certain uniformity in dancers, which has little or nothing to do with nationality, but which is certainly modified by the personality of the dancer. I am, of course, talking about dancers with talent. Talent is God-given: it is not given by a nation or a passport. A dancer must certainly have this gift, but the gift can manifest itself in forms as various as the universe. One cannot say that sunshine is better than shade, or that a glass of cold water is worse than a flaming chimney.

There are many so-called connoisseurs who try to dictate a certain style of ballet dancing, and they talk about a tradition that they never knew. Fortunately, this does not endanger the progress or development of ballet, because the real public—the people who sit in galleries, at a small admission price which most of them can ill afford—can distinguish good dancing from an inferior imitation of a style which was interesting a hundred years ago. Every performance demonstrates that this is the true ballet public, without prejudice or fake balletomanism.

I was brought up in St. Petersburg. The style of dancing there was very strict and precise. At the same time, in Moscow, six hundred kilometers away, the style of dancing was close to that of a circus performance. The Moscovites accused us in St. Petersburg of being cold, and we accused them of bad taste. History shows that the dancers and choreographers who later influenced ballet as a whole came mainly from St. Petersburg.

QUESTION: What is the future of ballet in America?

ANSWER: The future of ballet in America, as well as in the other countries, depends on the rise of new choreographers capable of furthering its development. A school of dancing is not enough. A school naturally perpetuates the technique, but it cannot lead to a new style in the ballet; nor can a new style of ballet be invented. Progress in any art is a slow and complex process, and therefore it cannot be generated by one person only. Many people are necessarily involved. In the field of ballet, it is not only the personality of the dancer and the art of the choreographer which achieve or create a style—one should not forget the composers. Delibes and Tchaikovsky are, I believe, as responsible for what is now traditionally known as classic ballet as its choreographers and dancers.

Any good company needs a professional choreographer, just as any good restaurant needs a good chef. If a ballet company does not develop successfully, the blame must be laid at the feet of its choreographer. If he was given all possibilities of choosing the best dancers, and if he was given the liberty to do what he wanted, he should not have failed in his task of achieving adequate results.

QUESTION: How does a choreographer originate his ballets?

ANSWER: This is a question I can only answer by telling you how I go about creating a new ballet, because, of course, different choreographers have different ways of proceeding with their work. When I am about to produce a ballet, I begin in one of two ways: either I begin with the idea and then look for suitable music, or I hear a certain piece of music which inspires me with an idea.

This idea need not be explicitly dramatic, as in a narrative ballet such as *Prodigal Son* or *Orpheus*; it need not have a written libretto. On the contrary, the idea might consist only in a *location*, a place, where I might wish dancing to take place, the particular people I want to dance there, and a special mood. *Cotillon* and *La Valse*, for instance, don't have plots, but they are dramatic in their casting, their dancing, and the mood which action and music evoke.

If I begin with an idea, I much prefer to have the music specially written for me and to be in constant touch with the composer while he is writing it. I try to tell him exactly what I want, and together we conceive the general mood and we time some of the dance sequences. I have found that most ballet composers like to have a definite timing for a ballet: they like to know when such-and-such occurs and how long it will last, whether a sequence is a dance sequence or a *pas d'action*, and so forth. Like novelists, they are interested in structure first. In this way, they can start to compose at any point in the ballet and not begin at the beginning. Working on the story ballets *Prodigal Son* and

Orpheus was a collaboration between the composers, Prokofiev and Stravinsky, and myself.

If I begin with the music, I familiarize myself with the score thoroughly and try to understand what the composer had in mind musically when writing it. When he wrote his *Concerto in D minor for Two Violins*, Bach had no idea of composing music for a ballet; but in listening to this music, it is possible to conceive of movement that harmonizes with the score. Actually, it seems to me that the music of Bach and Mozart is always very close to dancing. It would be wrong to say that all music should be danced, but I think the greatest music is never far from dancing. I agree with the poet who said that music rots when it is too far removed from the dance, just as poetry rots when it departs too far from music.

To familiarize myself thoroughly with a piece of music, I study the score and listen to it. If a piano transcription of the score exists, I play the piece over and over on the piano; if it does not exist, I make a transcription myself. Often I spend much more time learning a score than I do working out a ballet. The Mozart score for *Caracole*, for instance, I had in mind for three years, whereas setting the steps took only seven days.

There is always music that I wish to arrange dances to. Sometimes I make the ballets right away, if this is possible. One night, some years ago, the composer Alexei Haieff played me some pieces of his on the piano. I liked the music, but I didn't think of producing a ballet. Several days later, when this music kept running through my head, I wanted very badly to make dances to it. The result was *Divertimento*. If I were a poet, I'd probably have written a poem about what this music sounded like and looked like; but I am a choreographer, a dancer, and only in dancing do I express myself naturally. In other cases, I have known the music for many years and have kept it for the right moment. This was the case with *Symphonie Concertante*, music which has always seemed to me Mozart at his most beautiful; it was also true of *Symphony in C*, *Bourrée Fantasque*, and many other ballets.

Before beginning rehearsals, then, I have an idea of what the general scheme of a ballet will be. I never arrange any of the dances or movements until I actually rehearse the dancers. I discuss scenery and costumes with the designer, so that they will be in accord with the idea. I discuss the lighting, and I discuss the music with the composer and the conductor, but I don't discuss the ballet with my dancers unless we are doing a story ballet.

If the ballet has no story, there is no need to discuss their parts with the dancers in any detail; these parts the dancers work out by themselves, in individual practice. But in the case of a story ballet, I tell them what characters they are playing and what their relation is to the other characters.

Other choreographers, naturally, work differently. In working on story ballets, some choreographers spend lots of time talking to the dancers, explaining the story to them: the time the story took place, the history of that era, and so forth.

I have no fixed procedure. I don't come to rehearsals with any idea so definite and fixed that it can't be changed on the spot. I never write anything down. Often I try a step, or a series of movements, on a particular dancer and then I change it to something else. I indicate the steps first, and then the dancers repeat after me. It is very simple to mount a ballet using dancers you have worked with: they understand your smallest gesture and know what you want almost instinctively.

Sometimes I arrange the end of a ballet first; sometimes I commence in the middle. Rehearsal time is limited, and I can't always indulge in the extravagance of following the order of the music. If I have plenty of time, I work with each dancer until he or she is absolutely perfect; but the natural thing is for the dancers to want to practice the steps alone and perfect themselves. This they automatically do when there is little time, as in the case of *Prodigal Son*, which was produced in ten days in 1929, and with *Firebird*, which was produced in a week in 1949.

It has been my experience that dancers drop naturally into their parts; they gradually come to live them. Every detail is given: I show them every precise movement and the smallest mimed gesture and action.

QUESTION: Is it proper for the old classical ballets to be revived and revised by present-day choreographers?

ANSWER: Yes, I don't see why not, if the choreographers have respect for the original music and for the intention of the work as it has come down to us. This is a question that many people ask very seriously, as if it meant the life or death of ballet. They talk about tradition as a matter of remembering old steps accurately and reproducing them on the modern stage. The trouble is that no one can possibly remember all the steps of the ballets he saw years ago. A consistent form of universally intelligible dance notation has only recently been perfected.

What, then, do these people mean when they talk of preserving the classics in their original state? They mean, very simply, nothing at all. They don't know, nor does anyone else, exactly what those ballets were like. They just take the word of so-and-so that the old ballets, in fact, looked like such-and-such. But this is just one man's impression, and surely a faulty one: our memories are not as accurate as the movie camera.

We can naturally accept this man's word in part if the revivals he produces entertain us, but there is no use in deceiving ourselves into thinking that now, in the middle of the twentieth century, we are watching dancing and acting precisely as they were done in the nineteenth century. Those ballets—and their music—were changed radically and materially by dancers, conductors, ballet masters, and choreographers within the lifetime of their original creators.

It doesn't make sense to ask for the original, in short, if you have no idea of what the original was. People who always talk about tradition in a narrow, limited sense remind me of the story of the young Russian tenor who was to sing a leading part in a revival of an opera. During rehearsals, he was instructed to interrupt the dramatic action of one of his scenes and almost conceal himself at the back of the stage before he began to sing a difficult aria. The young tenor thought this was senseless and complained about it. But he was told that Mr. X, who had been very famous in this role, used always to interrupt the action in this manner and that he, too, must do so. The singer did as he was told, though he thought it was very foolish indeed. Some time later he asked the famous old tenor why he had changed the action of the opera. The old tenor was surprised and amused; he said, "Well, confidentially, I found that aria very difficult and I always needed to spit before I started to sing it, so I walked upstage a little and no one saw me."

QUESTION: Can anyone be taught to be a choreographer?

ANSWER: No. To be a choreographer, it is first of all necessary to be a dancer, a good one. This was true of choreographers in the past, as it is today; all our distinguished choreographers have been dancers of real quality. To become a good dancer, you must study at a ballet school for some years. Then you join a ballet company. This ballet company will dance good and important things, old ones and new ones, and there you will associate with conductors, musicians, and designers—as well as dancers. They advise you and you begin to learn. It's not, in other words, a matter of just learning how to dance and then starting to choreograph. You have to go through a period of preparation. If I told fifty well-trained dancers to move, to dance, to entertain me, they would not know what to do.

You must go through tradition, absorb it, and become in a way a reincarnation of all the artistic periods that have come before you. For instance, you must be able to know and feel how people acted and moved in Molière's plays, what sense of humor those people had, what their stage looked like. If you are going to do an Italian ballet set in a certain period, you try to go to Italy and become a part of that world. Then you put everything together—your dancing technique, your preparation in tradition, your knowledge of music, your ability—and something happens. A ballet is born.

Sometimes nothing happens. Then, I'm afraid, nothing can be done. There is no school where you can learn to be a choreographer. People can be advised about technique, they can be told to do this or that differently, but you cannot advise a person to be talented. He is born talented. It is a strange thing: your life is made somewhere, you are pushed in a certain direction, and you move that way.

There's no school that can teach choreography, just as there is no school where you can learn to be a novelist or a poet. Schools can give you technique, but from that point on you are on your own. At ballet school you can learn to dance, just as you can learn to write correct English and poetic meters in other schools, but that is only the beginning. Nothing really helps but the person himself, what inclination he has, what talent. We ought to remember the story of the famous English novelist who wanted to bring his son up to be a novelist, too. He worked with the boy, made him notice details in the way people acted, tried to teach him all the things he had learned with so much difficulty. He was deadly earnest about all this. His son turned out to be not a novelist, but a sheep farmer in Australia.

A choreographer must also be a teacher. I learned this myself when I did my first ballet, a composition in the Fokine style. I was fifteen years old and I taught this little ballet to eight boys in my class at the Imperial Ballet School in St. Petersburg. They were very good dancers. To make them stretch and extend themselves the way I wanted, I had to show them how to execute movements altogether new to them.

Choreographic movement is used to produce visual sensations. It is quite different from the practical movement of everyday life, when we walk, lift things, stand up, and sit down. Movement in choreography is an end in itself: its only purpose is to create the impression of intensity and beauty. No one intends to produce beautiful movements when rolling barrels or handling trains or elevators. But in all these everyday movements there are important visual dynamics if you look for them. Choreographic movements are the basic movements that underlie all gesture and action, and the choreographer must train himself to discover them. It's only natural that these basic movements will seem at first affected and artificial to the body that is accustomed only to the practical movements of everyday life. The object of the dancer's technical training is to enable him to perform—with perfect ease—choreographic movements, movements not limited by considerations of practical, daily life.

People in love all over the world have a certain attitude of sweetness and tenderness in the way they look and talk and touch. A choreographer notices this and finds movements to portray not the romance of A and B, but romance in general. A choreographer must see things that other people don't notice, to cultivate his visual sense. He must understand the stage space in a particular setting and how to fill that space with interesting movement; and to do this well, he must know music—know how to play it, preferably, and how to read it. For ballet is all a matter of space and time—the space on the stage, the time of the music to which the dancer moves.

The structure of a ballet must be tight, compact, like the structure of a building; good ballets move in measured space and time, like the planets.

The choreographer frees his mind from the limitations of practical time in much the same way that the dancer has freed his body. He turns not away from life, but to its source. He uses his technical proficiency to express in movement his essential knowledge. Talent, inspiration, and personality are not sources which come to an artist in a flash and go away; they are the accumulated results of all he has felt, thought, seen, and done—the stories he heard as a child, the art he has enjoyed, his education, and his everyday life—and are always with him, capable of being reached by his technical ability and transformed into dynamic designs of the utmost intensity.

If movement is the main means, possibly the only way, of presenting the art of dancing in its fullest significance, it is easy to understand the importance of connecting movements to each other with subtle care, yet at the same time emphasizing, by contrast, their continuity. For example, very brief and small movements to a fast or slow tempo—in every angle or degree of angle—are developed in relation to subsequent broad, large movements in the identical tempo, and increased from their use by one dancer to their use by many dancers. A kaleidoscope of such movements lives within the choreographer's brain, not yet, of course, set to any tempo. They are as yet only abstract memories of form. Of these, silence, placidity, and immobility are perhaps the most powerful forces. They are as impressive, even more so, as rage, delirium or ecstasy. When the body remains transfixed and immobile, every part of it should be invisibly tense, and even in relaxation there should be an inner muscular control.

The steps which a dancer has learned (and after he has studied about ten years with good teachers, he should have an impressive vocabulary of movements) are, when separate, devoid of meaning; but they acquire value when they are co-ordinated in time and space, as parts of the continual, rhythmic flow of the whole.

The student choreographer should at first work out simple technical exercises: for example, fitting eight bars of movement to eight bars of music. Many different interpretations may be given to music; there is no single meaning behind it which the listener must discover, and the choreographic student can fit any number of combinations of movements to the same eight bars of music. On the other hand, he can fit the same combination of movements to several different pieces of music. Or he can fit bars of movement to silence, which has a tempo of its own. But if he uses music, he must be sure to fit the movements to it completely.

There is a lot of talk about counterpoint in dancing. It is generally believed that counterpoint is based on contrasts. Actually, counterpoint is an accompaniment to a main theme which it serves to enhance, but from whose unity it must not detract. The only kind of counterpoint that I can see in dancing is the movements of arms, head, and feet which are contrapuntal to the static—or vertical—position of the body. For instance, in the *croisé* position the body is vertical—but one arm is raised, the other horizontal; one foot points forward, while the other supports the body; and the head is inclined toward one of the shoulders. All this is an accompaniment to the main theme, which is the vertical position of the body. In dancing one should not strive to achieve counterpoint by contrasting the movements of two dancers or two groups of dancers on the stage. This results not in counterpoint, but in disunity. (There is no need to apply musical terms to the dance; but if it is done, their meaning must be clearly understood.)

The eye can focus perfectly only on objects which are in the center of its field of vision. Those objects which are not head-on are seen clearly only because the observer knows and imagines what they are, while he focuses on the center object. If some new or different form is placed in the secondary part of a composition, the eye instinctively changes its focus and convinces itself of the identity of each individual form. And as vision is the channel through which the art of choreography reaches its audience, this inevitably results in confusion and a loss of attention to the main theme. But the eye can follow the movements of a large group of dancers if these form a harmonious pattern within its central field of vision.

It is impossible for choreographers to work very satisfactorily unless they are associated with a ballet company. You can compose music without an orchestra, but you cannot create a ballet without working directly with dancers.

In ballet companies, too, you learn many other things. When I was new in the Diaghilev company, I didn't know anything about Italian painting. I had just left Russia. Diaghilev took me to see pictures all over Italy. At first I was bored, but soon I became very interested: I saw that these pictures had a relation to other traditions I had absorbed, and I began to love them.

Choreography, finally, becomes a profession. In making ballets, you cannot sit and wait for the Muse. Union time hardly allows it, anyhow. You must be able to be inventive at any time. You can't be like the cook who can cook only two dishes: you must be able to cook them all.

Part Nine

GLOSSARY

straight line.

Familiarity with ballet terms is not really necessary when we first start going to the ballet. In fact, if we know too much about the terms, we'll be
watching to see what they mean in action and we'll miss most of the performance—it would be like knowing the meters of poetry before enjoying a
poem. But while familiarity with ballet phrases is not important at the outset,
it becomes important later on, after we have seen something of dancing.
When we go to the ballet often, we begin to remember different steps and
poses and want to know their names. That is only natural.

The most fundamental steps and positions—from the point of view of
the spectator—are described below; a number of additional terms, an understanding of which will increase the knowledge of inexperienced members of
the audience, are also discussed briefly. Because ballet as we know it was born
in France, French is the language of the vocabulary of the classic dance. As
such, it is ballet's international language, just as English is the universal language of sport and Latin the universal language of medicine.

BASIC POSITIONS

The five fundamental positions of the feet are learned by the ballet
student just as we all learn the alphabet. These positions constitute the basis
for all steps in the vocabulary of the classic dance and are learned by the
student at the very beginning, so that they become instinctive. These basic
positions were indicated by Thoinot Arbeau (1588), formally established by
Pierre Beauchamp, first ballet master at the Paris Opéra (c.1700), and set
down in writing by Pierre Rameau in *The Dancing Master* (1725). They
have been in constant use ever since, as the ideal foundation for exercises and
performance. Each of the positions features the characteristic that distin-
guishes the classic dance from all other forms of theatrical dance—the turned-
out leg. In ballet, each leg is turned out from the hip at an angle of 90
degrees, so that the feet form a single straight line on the floor. The five
absolute positions are performed with the feet flat on the floor, high on the
ball of the foot (*sur les demi-pointes*) or on the toes (*sur les pointes*).

FIRST POSITION: Heels are together; feet are turned out to make a single straight line.

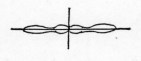

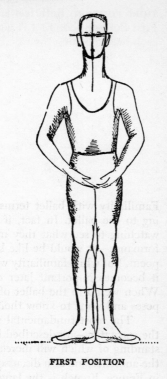

SECOND POSITION

FIRST POSITION

SECOND POSITION: Feet are turned out to form a straight line; heels are separated by a distance equivalent to one of the feet.

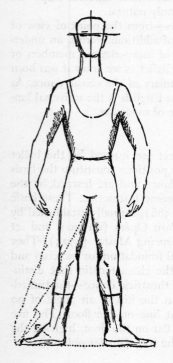

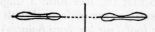

THIRD POSITION: Both feet are turned outward as in First Position; one foot is placed in front of the other, each heel touching the middle of the opposite foot.

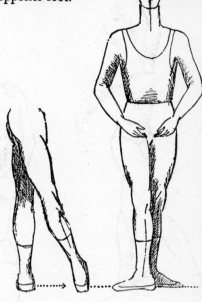

THIRD POSITION (RIGHT)
AND TRANSITION INTO
FOURTH POSITION (LEFT)

FOURTH POSITION: Feet are turned outward; one foot is placed in front of and parallel to the other at a distance of one foot. The toe of one foot is in line with the heel of the other.

FOURTH POSITION
FRONT VIEW (LEFT) AND
SIDE VIEW (RIGHT)

**FOURTH POSITION
CROISÉ**

**FOURTH POSITION
EFFACÉ**

**FOURTH POSITION
LEFT FOOT SUR LE POINTE**

FIFTH POSITION: Feet are turned outward; one foot is placed in front of the other, the heels and toes touching so that the big toe of neither foot projects: the feet are boxed in.

FIFTH POSITION

ADAGIO: As in music, a slow tempo: a dance in a slow tempo. The word is derived from the Italian *ad agio*, meaning at ease or in a leisurely manner. Adagios are danced by ballerinas and their partners. Adagios may occur in a ballet when the drama of the piece so dictates (*Swan Lake*, Act Two), as the central portion of a *grand pas de deux* (*Swan Lake*, Act Three), or simply as the music demands (*Symphony in C*, second movement). In adagio, the ballerina displays her beauty in slow, unfolding movements and sustained graceful poses. The principal quality of adagio is control.

Adagio is also the name for a section of any ballet class. Here the dancers practice—in the center of the room—slow, sustained exercises designed to give ease in the performance of dances that require balance, perfect line, and unquestionable authority in those who execute them.

The great Italian ballet master Carlo Blasis regarded the correct execution of adagio as the "touchstone of the dancer."

ALLEGRO: Dancing that is lively and fast, in comparison to adagio. All steps of elevation—jumps, *entrechats*, turns in the air, etc., are forms of allegro. An important quality of allegro is *ballon*, the ease with which a dancer remains in the air during a step in elevation and the ease with which he takes off and lands from a jump.

ARABESQUE: Set pose. In the most common form of arabesque, the dancer stands on one leg, with the other leg raised behind her and extended fully. The height of the raised leg is variable, as is the position of the arms.

BASIC ARABESQUE AND ARABESQUE PENCHÉ

ASSEMBLÉ: Literally, together. A step in which the dancer rises low off the floor, straightens both legs in the air, and returns to Fifth Position.

À TERRE: On the ground. *Par terre* is synonymous. Some dancers are called *terre à terre* dancers because they succeed best in steps that require no elevation, steps performed on the stage.

ATTITUDE: Basic pose of the classic dance, first described by Carlo Blasis (1829), who modeled it after the famous statue of Mercury by Bologna. In the basic attitude, the dancer stands on one leg and brings the other leg up behind at an angle of ninety degrees, with the knee bent.

THREE VIEWS OF AN ATTITUDE

BALLERINA: A leading female dancer of a ballet company. If the company is a large one, one or more principal ballerinas (*prima ballerinas*) stand at the top of the company's list of soloists. A dancer earns the title ballerina through years of hard work and by great dancing over the years in great roles. No matter what the standards of particular ballet companies, the dancer's lasting right to the title depends on continuous excellence in performance over a period of many years: we think of the great ballerinas of the past—Taglioni, Pavlova, Karsavina, Spessivtzeva—not as young girls, but as mature women. Few dancers possess the title ballerina with any secure permanence until they are thirty years old, at which time their native talent and artistry have usually been developed to the maximum. A ballerina is almost always associated with a particular role in a ballet—a role that has been created especially for her or a role in an accepted classic.

In the famous European ballet companies, which are state-supported and have their own ballet schools, the title ballerina (in France, *première danseuse*) stands at the top of a rigorous hierarchy. Beneath this pinnacle are arranged major and minor soloists, *coryphées* (dancers who perform in small groups), and the numerous members of the *corps de ballet*. Above the rank of *prima ballerina* there sometimes reigns the *prima ballerina assoluta*. It is interesting that in the history of the Russian Imperial Theatre this title was used only twice: by Pierina Legnani, the Italian ballerina who created the leading role in the Petipa-Ivanov *Swan Lake* (1895), and by Mathilde Kchessinska, who succeeded to the title after Legnani left Russia in 1901. In the early years of this century, Olga Preobrajenska, Anna Pavlova, Vera Trefilova, Lubov Egorova, and Tamara Karsavina were all ballerinas at the Maryinsky Theatre in St. Petersburg; Kchessinska was the only *prima ballerina assoluta*. This did not mean that Kchessinska was a better dancer than all the others; it meant simply that she was a maturer artist, with years of experience and excellent performance. The hierarchies in the European state theatres were developed as a means of periodic appraisal of personnel, as a way of adjusting salaries. Dancing in these theatres is like the civil service: you are promoted according to your ability and your experience, and seniority is naturally important.

In America, where we have no such system, there really seems little need to use the Italian words *ballerina*, *prima ballerina*, etc., to indicate ranks we don't have. Moreover, so many inexperienced and unimportant dancers call themselves ballerinas in America that the term has little meaning. All our fine dancers are stars of our ballet companies; when the word *star* is used, we have a better idea of something special. The male equivalent of the rank of ballerina is *premier danseur*.

BALLET: From the Italian *ballare*, to dance, via *balleti*, the diminutive form of *balle*, a dance-song.

BALLET BLANC (white ballet): Ballet in which girls wear long white gossamer costumes: *Les Sylphides*, *Giselle* (Act Two), etc.

BALLET D'ACTION: Literally, a ballet in which something happens: a ballet with a plot.

BALLET MASTER: In the early days of ballet, the ballet master was a choreographer, a man who designed or composed dances for a ballet company. In France and in Russia today, this is still the case. In England and America, the ballet master (or ballet mistress) is the person responsible for company instruction and discipline, the person who gives classes to all the company dancers, rehearses them in all ballets in the repertory, and assigns parts. He may or may not be a choreographer as well, though this is often the case. The name artistic director combines the jobs of ballet master and choreographer. In Diaghilev's Ballets Russes, the company choreographer was ballet master and the company instructor-disciplinarian was the *régisseur*.

BALLETOMANE: A ballet enthusiast: a person who attends the ballet regularly, has decided opinions about dancers, and is partisan about the type of ballet, music, etc., to be preferred above all others. In the ideal sense, the balletomane is one whose great love for ballet as an art transcends partisanship for the individual dancer and choreographer. It is to be regretted that the loud and long demonstrations of some balletomanes are sufficient to drive the newcomer from the theatre. Marian Eames has written: "Exactly who coined the word *balletomane* is not known. It would seem reasonable to assume that the behavior of the dance enthusiast was to blame for the selection of the ending *mane* rather than *phile*. Indeed, the dance enthusiast appears to have been frenzied to a degree in his devotion and often absurd. Yet his frenetic outbursts lacked the embarrassing hollowness of contemporary movie madness, for the idolatry lavished upon individual dancers was not born of a mere susceptibility to physical 'allure.' The adorer was moved by qualities and style which he could analyze and discuss; furthermore, his obsession with the art itself should not be confused with the easily bought allegiance of zealots who are beguiled less by the avowed object of their enthusiasm than by the glorious trappings which surround it."*

BALLON: A characteristic of *elevation* (dance in the air). The ease with which a dancer maintains in the air a position he normally holds on the ground; the ability to ascend lightly into the air and to land softly and smoothly. *Ballon* is the French word for *hand ball* and *balloon*; literally, it means *bouncing*. It is said that the term ballon was named after the French *danseur* Balon (active 1695), who possessed its qualities to a remarkable degree.

BARRE (or bar): The round horizontal bar secured around the walls of a ballet classroom or rehearsal hall at a height of about three-and-a-half feet. The bar is usually placed opposite the long mirrors in which the dancer can watch what he is doing. Every ballet class begins with exercises at the bar, the dancer holding the bar for support as the daily elementary and constantly repeated exercises are performed; the lesson continues with exercises in the center of the room.

BATTEMENT: A nickname for an action of the leg. For example, the *battement tendu* (stretched beating), where the dancer—in the simplest form of this exercise—stands at the bar and extends her foot in front of her on the floor, or sideways, or back.

BATTERIE: The master term that applies to all movements in ballet in which one foot beats against the other, or in which the two feet beat together. Two types of this movement are distinguished: *grande batterie* (large, high beating steps) and *petite batterie* (small beating steps executed at a lower elevation).

BRISÉ: Literally, a broken movement. A beating step of elevation in which the dancer rises from the floor, beats one leg against the other, and returns to the same Fifth Position—distinguishable from the *entrechat* in that only one leg beats.

CABRIOLE: A movement of *grande batterie*. The cabriole develops the *battement*—in which one leg moves away from the supporting leg and returns—into a brilliant step of elevation: here both legs beat together in the air. One leg swings up to an angle of ninety degrees, the other leg rises, meets it, and both calves are beaten together (the feet do not cross); the legs are fully extended, knees straight, toes pointed. Cabrioles are also executed at an angle of forty-five degrees from the floor; they can be performed in any direction—front, back, and to the side.

CARACTÈRE: The character dancer, or the dancer *en caractère*, performs national or folk dances—mazurkas, polkas, etc.—dances that are not performed on point. The dancer *en demi-caractère* performs popular dances such as the cancan, but may dance these on point; these are comic or semiserious dances, in other words, performed with some classical technique.

CHANGEMENT DE PIEDS (changing of the feet): Small jump from Fifth Position in which the dancer changes the position of both feet in the air.

CHASSÉ: Literally, chased. A sliding step: the dancer jumps low off the floor, lands, and the working foot chases the landing foot out of position. A *chassé*

*Foreword to *Russian Balletomania* by Anatole Chujoy, *Dance Index*, Vol. VII, No. 3.

embodies the same mechanical principle we see when we watch a horse canter. There the hind legs, moving together, displace the front legs.

CHOREOGRAPHER: Someone who makes dances. The word means, etymologically, someone who records dances. It has come to mean simply the person responsible for the design of movement in a ballet. It is inaccurate to say that a choreographer "writes" a new ballet—for no choreographer sets down on paper what he wishes dancers to do from one moment to the next—but this is sometimes said.

All good choreographers have been good dancers. But to be a good dancer, of course, is not necessarily to be a choreographer. The dancer wishes *to be moved*, the choreographer wishes *to move*. To combine the two inclinations successfully is rare, but rare indeed are great choreographers. The choreographer is best compared to the poet: he is a man who uses the material of the classic dance that has been developed over hundreds of years, just as the poet uses the language he writes in. Like the poet, the choreographer finds new ways of saying things.

CLASSIC: The word classic when applied to ballet is not the contrary of romantic. It applies to a rigorous basic vocabulary of steps and movements capable of infinite variation and a system of instruction that makes such variation possible for individual dancers. Classic ballets can be romantic, realistic, or mythological in subject matter. The classic dance is the dictionary of ballet and, as a method of instruction, it is also its grammar: basic steps and movements that must be learned and mastered if the student is to become an instrument of its possibilities. The classic dance is the fundamental material out of which new ballets are made; it constitutes the basic, instinctive knowledge that permits the dancer to perform them. As a system of instruction, the classic dance has been perfected through centuries of innovation and experiment. We know what is anatomically sound and physically possible. We know what must be taught first, how that must be learned so well that it becomes instinctive, what to teach next. We learn all this in schools, as dancers and teachers before us have learned it. Properly speaking, what we call the classic dance might be more easily understood if it were called the academic dance, after the academies in which it was evolved; but the word *classic* has come down to us, along with the tradition of the developed academic dance, and is now universally accepted. When we go to the ballet and see a ballet described as *classic* in the program, we know that the word doesn't imply something that is serious and perhaps not entertaining: classicism in dance is the basis for the finest entertainment.

CORPS DE BALLET: Dancers who appear only in large groups: the chorus, the backbone of every ballet company. Jean Georges Noverre (1759) advised the ballet master to "make your *corps de ballet* dance, but when it does so, let each member of it express an emotion or contribute to form a picture; let them mime while dancing so that the sentiments with which they are imbued might cause their sentiment to be changed at every moment." Until the present century, the function of the *corps de ballet* was merely decorative: as a group they embellished with their poses and did not distract from the performances of principal dancers. In dramatic ballets, they reacted with appropriate emotion to the dramatic situation (the death of Giselle, the huntsmen in *Swan Lake*).

The New Ballet of Michel Fokine, as he himself expressed it in 1914, "in developing the principle of expressiveness, advances from the expressiveness of face to the expressiveness of the whole body, and from the expressiveness of the individual body to the expressiveness of a group of bodies and the expressiveness of the combined dancing of a crowd." Every dancer in the crowd scene in the original production of *Petrouchka* (1911) had something to do at every moment, and each dancer was related in both action and reaction to the principals on stage. Ballet prior to Fokine was essentially linear: the stage was divided into parts where the *corps de ballet* danced, where the soloists danced, where the ballerinas danced, and these established patterns were seldom violated. With Fokine, movement on stage became orchestrated: each dancer on stage was an instrument contributing vitally to the general impression. Formerly it was only possible for a soloist to dance diagonally across the stage; now this is done by large groups of dancers: every dancer in such a group must be a soloist. Although every *corps de ballet* contains dancers of great talent who may eventually become principal dancers, and although it is wise for every soloist to have had experience in a *corps de ballet*, it is always possible in large state schools to discover talent early and not to permit it to idle long in the *corps*. This is the practice today with our ballet companies that are attached to schools. Talent is discovered early and used as soon as possible in appropriate roles. In ballet companies where the directors must first observe their new dancers in the *corps de ballet*, the *corps* itself becomes a kind of school, a testing ground, where talent is discovered. Experience in a *corps de ballet* gives a dancer invaluable lessons which are difficult to learn in any other way. Here she learns timing and precision; she learns also her relation to other dancers and other groupings of dancers on the stage. She learns, in fact, all the things that she must know to become a star.

DANCE (and danse): From the old high-German *danson*, meaning to drag or stretch.

DANSE D'ÉCOLE: Literally, dance of the school. The classic dance, the academic dance based on the Five Positions and turnout (*see* Classic).

DANSEUR NOBLE: A classical male dancer; partner of the ballerina in classical roles (Albrecht in *Giselle*, Siegfried in *Swan Lake*, etc.).

DÉVELOPPÉ: From the French word that means, literally, to develop or to unfold. A gradual unfolding of the leg as it rises from the floor and is extended fully in

DEVELOPPÉ À LA SECONDE

the air. As it is raised toward complete extension, the foot of the working leg passes (*passé*) the knee of the supporting leg.

DIVERTISSEMENT: A dance or a series of dances for simple diversion and pleasure. A *divertissement* may be a whole number, like *Aurora's Wedding*, which contains plotless dance excerpts from *The Sleeping Beauty*, or it may be part of a whole ballet, like the folk dances that celebrate Prince Siegfried's birthday in the third act of *Swan Lake* or the series of character dances that come in the last act of *Coppélia*. A *grand pas de deux* taken out of a ballet and performed alone without its surrounding plot is a *divertissement*.

ÉCHAPPÉ (from échapper, to escape or slip): Step in which the dancer's feet escape from a closed position to an open position as she jumps upward. The movement is brisk and vigorous.

ELEVATION: The ability with which a dancer rises from the floor to perform jumps, and the capacity to remain in the air in the midst of these movements. The *danse d'élévation* was first popularized by Marie Taglioni (active 1822–48); within living memory, Vaslav Nijinsky (active 1908–19) still serves as a model conqueror of the air.

EN ARRIERE: Backward
EN AVANT: Forward.
EN DEDANS: Inward.
EN DEHORS: Outward.

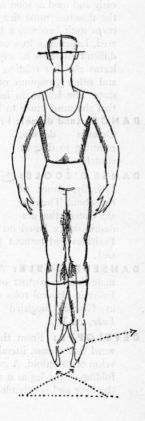

ENTRECHAT a, b

ENTRECHAT: Probably derived from the Italian *intrecciare,* to weave or braid. A beating step of elevation in which the dancer jumps straight into the air from *plié* and crosses his feet a number of times, making a weaving motion in the air. The term *entrechat* is compounded with numerals to indicate the number of movements of the legs: *entrechat-trois, entrechat-quatre, entrechat-cinq, entrechat-six, entrechat-sept, entrechat-huit.* Each leg moves once in a crossing: hence the term *entrechat-six* means six movements, or three crossings. *Entrechats* up

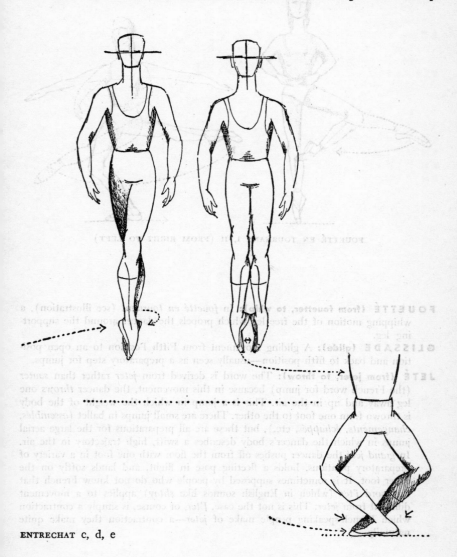

ENTRECHAT c, d, e

to *entrechat-six* are movements of *petite batterie*, small beatings; *entrechat-six* and above are movements of *grande batterie*, large beatings.

FOUETTÉ EN TOURNANT I, II (FROM RIGHT TO LEFT)

FOUETTÉ (from fouetter, to whip): In *fouetté en tournant* (see illustration), a whipping motion of the free leg which propels the dancer around the supporting leg.

GLISSADE (glide): A gliding movement from Fifth Position to an open position and back to fifth position—usually seen as a preparatory step for jumps.

JETÉ (from jeter, to throw): The word is derived from *jeter* rather than *sauter* (the French word for jump) because in this movement, the dancer *throws* one leg away and up in the air. This is a jump in which the weight of the body is thrown from one foot to the other. There are small jumps in ballet (*assemblés, changements, échappés,* etc.), but these are all preparations for the large aerial jumps in which the dancer's body describes a swift, high trajectory in the air. In *grand jeté* the dancer pushes off from the floor with one foot in a variety of preparatory positions, holds a fleeting pose in flight, and lands softly on the other foot. It is sometimes supposed by people who do not know French that the word *j'ter* (which in English sounds like *shtay*) applies to a movement different from *jeter*. This is not the case. *J'ter,* of course, is simply a contraction which French-speaking people make of *jeter*—a contraction they make quite naturally.

GRANDE JETÉ

LIBRETTO: The story line of a ballet; in a ballet without a plot, the idea on which the ballet is based. The ideal ballet story can be seen plainly and requires no extraneous explanation. The story of the *Prodigal Son* is a good example: once there was a boy who had everything, then he had nothing, then again he had everything.

NOTATION: The writing down of dances in a form sufficiently intelligible for their accurate reproduction. Dances were written down as early as the fifteenth century, but it is only recently—by the system devised by Rudolf von Laban—that the recording of dances and ballets has become universal (rather than arbitrary), accurate, and capable of the precision that permits them to be reproduced without the presence of the choreographer. The Dance Notation Bureau (founded in New York, 1940) has recorded many dances and ballets that have been faithfully reproduced on the basis of notation, and for the first time in dance history the copyrighting of choreography seems imminently possible.

PANTOMIME (from the Greek): Literally, all-imitating *pantomimos*. A dumb show of significant gesture, ballet's way of indicating intricacies of plot. The players in the original Roman pantomimes wore masks and could express themselves only with their bodies. These pantomimes portrayed mythic characters, gods and goddesses. The *commedia dell' arte* of Italy reduced these formal theatrical pantomimes into a popular burlesque with a permanent set of characters—Harlequin, Columbine, Pierrot, etc.—what has come down to us as the Punch and Judy show. The vocabulary of mime was gradually absorbed into ballet, as traveling Italian comedians visited France and as dancers and ballet masters required the dance to express human emotions and situations. While it was said of Camargo (active 1726-35) that "she danced to dance, not to stir emotion," it was said of her rival, Marie Sallé (active 1718-40), that she "replaced tinsel glitter by simple and touching graces. Her physiognomy was noble, sensitive and expressive." The acting and miming of David Garrick was an inspiration to the French ballet master Noverre, the "Shakespeare of the dance." The mime vocabulary is now unknown to most of us because it is no longer taught as it used to be. It is rarely used in modern ballets, but in the older ballets (*Giselle, Coppélia, Swan Lake, Sleeping Beauty*) mime was essential; as we watch the older ballets, a knowledge of some of its elements is essential for us.

Mime is limited. There are some things it is foolish to try to indicate in a ballet: you cannot indicate your mother-in-law and be readily understood. But within the limits of pantomime, much can be expressed. Noverre wrote: "Gesture is the countenance of the soul, its effect must be immediate and it cannot fail to achieve its effect if it is true. . . . Dancers, like actors, should devote themselves to depict and feel: they have the same object to attain." Here are a few important mime expressions seen in ballet:

YOU: Point to person with open hand (with pointed finger when angry).

BEAUTIFUL (or GIRL): Circle the face gently with the back of the hand, letting the back of the middle finger outline the face.

PRINCESS: Lift arms and hold hands just over top of head, as if enclosing a crown.

DANCE: Circle the hands around each other above the head.

KISS: Touch lips with finger.

LOVE: Hold both hands over the heart.

MARRY: Point to wedding-ring finger with index finger of right hand.

ME: Point toward self with middle fingers of both hands simultaneously.

KING: With a flourishing gesture raise the right hand above the head, indicating the feather commonly worn in the hats of the nobility.

QUEEN: Let index finger of right hand touch top of forehead at points where crown touches.

STOP: Hold up hand, palm out.

ANGRY: Raise arms above the head, elbows front, and shake fists.

SAD: Let fingers trace tears as they fall down the face.

WEEP: Hide face in both hands, or rub eyes with clenched fists.

BEG MERCY: Hold arms out, palms together, as if praying.

NO: Hold arms at the side, then cross them before the body in a definite gesture as the head shakes.

OBEY: Point to floor with decided gesture.

FORGET: Hold out hands loosely, palms up, and shake the head slightly.

REMEMBER: Touch the temple with the index finger.

FRIENDS: Clasp hands together on a level with the waist.

BLESS: With the hand, touch the head of the person blessed.

DIE: Bring arms up to the side of the head, then bring them down quickly so that the hands, fists clenched, are crossed in front of the body.

SLEEP: Incline the head against the back of the hands.

CHILD: With both palms down, raise the hands in three steps, as if measuring the height of a growing child.

THANK YOU: Inclining the head simply, bring one hand down from the chest, extending it toward the person thanked.

PAS: A pace, a formalized or measured step. The dancer's step, or *pas*, is very different from the ordinary step we take when walking: it is closer to the pace, which we take when we measure or consider something. A *pas* is a gesture of the whole body.

PAS D'ACTION: Action in dancing—that part of a dramatic ballet, for example, where the relation of the characters is clarified. A *pas d'action* is not pure dancing and not pure mime, but a combination of the two, an integral part of the ballet spectacle. It's similar to many moments in opera where characters—after suspending the action for a while and singing a quintet—turn again to each other and resume their dramatic relation.

PAS DE DEUX: A dance for two people. Although a *pas de deux* is any dance for two people, the usual, standard *pas de deux* consists of five parts: the *entrée*, in which the ballerina and the *premier danseur* make their appearance; the adagio, in which the *danseur* supports the ballerina in a slow, graceful dance; a variation of the ballerina; a variation of the *danseur*; and the coda, a concluding passage for both ballerina and *danseur* in which the dance is brought to a felicitous conclusion.

PAS DE TROIS: A dance for three people. *Pas de quatre* is a dance for four people; *pas de cinq*, a dance for five; *pas de six*, for six; and so forth.

PIROUETTE: A complete turn of the body on one foot. *Pirouette* used to be applied only to turns by men, while the term *tour* was reserved for turns by women. The terms are synonymous. Girls turn in pirouettes on *pointe*, boys on *demi-pointe*. Ideally, the body is vertical in pirouettes; the foot of the supporting leg remains in one place. The free leg can be lifted slightly off the floor, the knee bent, as in the most common form of pirouette; it can be raised in back, the knee straight, as in *pirouettes en arabesque*; or it can be raised in back, the knee bent, as in *pirouettes en attitude*; and so forth. Pirouettes have dazzled audiences since the history of ballet began, but multiple pirouettes were not introduced until 1766. At that time, three turns by a boy and two by a girl were considered spectacular. Turns performed off the floor are called *tours en l'air*.

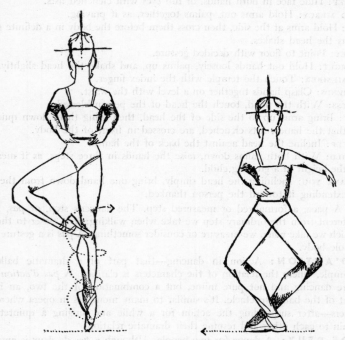

PIROUETTE I, II (FROM RIGHT TO LEFT)

PLIÉ (from plier, to bend): In the classic dance, this is a bending of the knees, the knees wide open, the feet turned outward. The function of the *plié* in the dancer's body is like the function of springs in an automobile: it is necessary for the development of elasticity. *Demi-plié* is a half, or small, bending; *grand plié* is a deep bending of the knees.

POINTE: The dancer *sur les pointes* dances on her toes. This innovation of the Romantic ballet (c.1820) is now universally used by female dancers in ballet: men stand on their toes only in certain Russian folk dances. If the dancer has been properly trained, dancing on point is neither painful nor uncomfortable nor damaging. Although the classic ballet is the only form of dance that uses toe dancing consistently, ballet existed long before toe steps were introduced; dancing on *pointes* cannot be called the single hallmark of ballet. Dancing on *pointes* is actually an extension of a basic feature of the classic dance: the straight line formed by the stretched leg and the pointing foot when the free leg moves from the floor. The ballet slippers of Marie Taglioni, who popularized toe dancing, were unblocked. The toes of ballet slippers were later blocked with glue, as they are today, to give the dancer additional support. Every dancer darns the exterior of the toe of her ballet slipper—not for support, but to provide security of position while she dances and to prevent slipping. Dancing *sur la demi-pointe* is on the half-toe, where the dancer is supported high on the ball of the foot and under the toes.

PORT DE BRAS: Movement or carriage of the arms.

RELEVÉ (from relever, to lift again): In ballet, the raising of the body onto *pointe* or *demi-pointe*.

RÉVÉRENCE: A deep bow.

ROMANTIC: Ballets that we call Romantic are a *kind* of classical ballet. *La Sylphide* (1832), which epitomized—until the masterpiece *Giselle* (1841)— what we recognize as Romanticism in ballet, was romantic in subject, temper, and mood; but both ballets expressed this, with innovations, in the vocabulary of the *classic* dance. Similarly, *Les Sylphides* (1909)—which embodies Romanticism in name, substance, and music—consists of classical steps and movements. What is classic in ballet is what has been developed over the years; what is romantic is a period through which that development passed. Romanticism in ballet, in other words, is not the opposite of classicism.

Romanticism was responsible for revolutionary innovations in classic technique and in the subject matter of ballets. Its desire for ethereal creatures caused dancers for the first time to rise on their toes, introduced the white ballet costume so familiar to us in *Giselle*, *Swan Lake*, and *Les Sylphides*, and caused the expansion of the dance vocabulary to meet the expressive requirements of elfin, unattainable heroines and heroes who aimed at—and so seldom secured— permanent happiness. As it contrasted real life with fantasy, the Romantic Ballet naturalized the pastoral theme that dominated earlier ballet. Where previously nymphs and shepherds were potential gods and goddesses, these pastoral characters now became realistic, only to escape later from realism's cruelty to supernatural kingdoms (Act II of *La Sylphide* and *Giselle*).

The heroes of the Romantic movement in ballet are: Théophile Gautier (1811–72), French poet, critic, and novelist, the librettist of *Giselle*; Jules Perrot (1810–92), dancer and choreographer, collaborator on *Giselle* and creator of the *Pas de Quatre*. Its heroine is its great ballerina Marie Taglioni (1804–84), creator of *La Sylphide*. The Romantic Ballet dominated the classic dance from about 1820 to 1870.

After this time, what we recognize as the great classical ballets—*Swan Lake*, *The Sleeping Beauty*, etc.—were created on the basis of a new uncovered, unconcealed technique and a more exacting dance discipline. Thus, unlike literature, music, and the other arts, ballet's great period of classicism came *after* the development of Romanticism.

ROND DE JAMBE: A rotary movement of the leg; the dancer describes circles in the air, or on the floor, with the pointed toe of the working foot. The *rond de jambe* is a basic exercise in the ballet class and a ballet step seen frequently on stage. The *ronde de jambe en l'air* is executed away from the floor.

SAUTÉ (from sauter, to jump): The word is used as a modifier to explain that a jump is involved in a step or pose: *sauté en arabesque, échappé sauté,* and so forth.

TOUR: *See* Pirouette.

TOUR EN L'AIR: A turn in the air. The dancer, standing in Fifth Position, rises from the floor from a *demi-plié*, executes a complete turn, and returns to original position. *Tours* may be doubled or tripled for spectacular effect, but three complete turns in the air is the maximum.

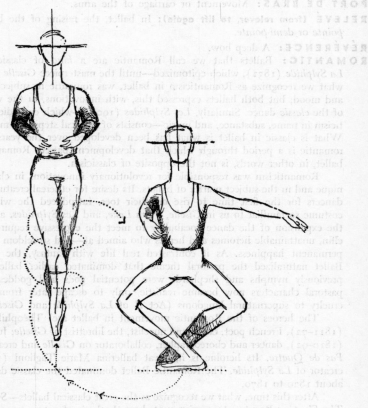

TOUR EN L'AIR I, II (FROM RIGHT TO LEFT)

TURNOUT: The distinguishing characteristic of the classic dance: knees that face frontward in a normal standing position are turned out from the hip at an angle of ninety degrees (*see* Basic Positions). Because dancers wore heels on their shoes at the time the five absolute positions were established, the complete ninety-degree turnout was not perfected until some time later. Complete turnout is not forced in beginning students.

TUTU: Ballet skirt; a nickname for *tunique*, tunic. The so-called Romantic tutu, which reaches to about twelve inches above the floor, was made famous by Marie Taglioni in the first famous Romantic ballet, *La Sylphide*; it is still familiar to us in *Giselle* (Act Two) and *Les Sylphides*. Gradually, however, with the perfection of dance technique, the tutu has been shortened to make the whole leg visible.

VARIATION: A solo, a dance for one person. Synonym: *pas seul.*

Part Ten

ANNOTATED SELECTION
OF BALLET RECORDINGS

The importance of music to ballet has been stressed by George Balanchine throughout this book. As a musician, I most heartily concur in this view. As a radio commentator on music, I can attest to its demonstrable value. Many times a week I receive requests asking that the music for such-and-such a ballet be played. Listeners have written me repeatedly that advance knowledge of music, and even a hearing of the music after they have been to the ballet has helped them immensely in their visual enjoyment of the dance.

I may be running the risk of reproach for the selections in the following pages, where you'll find my list of recordings of ballet scores you've been reading about. This is a list of personal favorites, for which a man must wrestle with his conscience rather than the record encyclopedia. With what I hope is a well-developed set of prejudices, I've tried to make the collector's choice a little easier. There are two or three recommended recordings for each work, though in some instances perhaps a dozen different versions may be available. Only when a score has been recorded just once do I undertake to list the recording regardless of whether it's good, bad, or indifferent (or difficult to obtain). Also bear in mind that not all ballet scores have found their way onto discs, at least not at this writing.

This list of records will have succeeded if the reader's enjoyment of ballet, both in the theatre and in recollection, is increased by a hearing of its selections.

JACQUES FRAY

THE AFTERNOON OF A FAUN
Claude Debussy: *Prélude à l'après-midi d'un faune*.
More than a dozen recordings have been made of this masterpiece. My favorites are in this order:
London Philharmonic Orchestra under Sir Thomas Beecham, Columbia 69600 (78); Philadelphia Orchestra under Leopold Stokowski, Victor

17700 (78); Philadelphia Orchestra under Eugene Ormandy, Columbia 12917 (78), 4-12917 (45), ML 2156 (LP), AAL 26 (LP).

THE AGE OF ANXIETY

Leonard Bernstein: *Symphony, for Piano and Orchestra* (after W. H. Auden).

Philharmonic-Symphony Orchestra of New York under Leonard Bernstein (Lukas Foss, piano), Columbia ML 4325 (LP).

EL AMOR BRUJO

Manuel de Falla: *El Amor Brujo.*

Among the many versions of this exciting score, a choice is hard to make. Decide between these two recordings: Leopold Stokowski conducting the Hollywood Bowl Symphony Orchestra with Nan Merriman as soloist, Victor LM 1054 (LP) or album WDM 1089 (45); or Carol Brice and the Pittsburgh Symphony Orchestra under Fritz Reiner, Columbia ML 2006 (LP). For the record, let us add that a version of the suite has been made by Enrique Jorda with the National Symphony Orchestra on English Decca. It's a very exciting recording, but the vocal numbers have been left out. Also, let's not forget to mention the Argenta version with the Paris Conservatory Orchestra on English Columbia, which is not yet released in the United States but has aroused great enthusiasm among the European disc reviewers.

L'AMOUR ET SON AMOUR

César Franck: *Psyché.*

Amsterdam Concertgebouw Orchestra under Eduard van Beinum, London LL 852/3 (LP). Chicago Symphony Orchestra under Désiré Defauw, Victor album DM 1122 (78), Bluebird LBC 1056 (LP) or album WBC 1056 (45).

APOLLO, LEADER OF THE MUSES

Igor Stravinsky: *Apollon Musagète.*

RCA Victor Symphony Orchestra under Igor Stravinsky, Victor album WDM 1424 (45) or LM 1096 (LP) (see *The Cage,* by same composer).

APPARITIONS

Franz Liszt music, arranged by Constant Lambert, orchestrated by Gordon Jacobs.

Two excerpts from the music providing the background for the work have been recorded by the author of the book, Constant Lambert. They are:

A. *Cave Scene, Mephisto Waltz No. 3.* Philharmonia Orchestra under Constant Lambert, English Columbia DX 1560 (78) or Columbia Entré RL 3056 (LP).

B. *Galop.* Same performers, English Columbia DX 1568 (78) or Columbia Entré RL 3056 (LP).

ASSEMBLY BALL

Georges Bizet: *Symphony in C.*
London Philharmonic Orchestra under Charles Munch, English Decca AK 1781/4 (78); Leopold Stokowski and his Symphony Orchestra, Victor LM 1706 (LP) or album WDM 1706 (45).

LE BAISER DE LA FÉE

Igor Stravinsky: *Le Baiser de la Fée.*
RCA Victor Symphony Orchestra under Igor Stravinsky, Victor LM 1075 (LP) or album WDM 1202 (45); L'Orchestre de la Suisse Romande under Ernest Ansermet, London LL 390 (LP).
Ansermet's version is excellent, but I still prefer the composer's recording.

BALLADE

Claude Debussy: *Six Epigraphes antiques* (orchestrated by Ansermet in the ballet production).
Up to now, no orchestrated version of this suite (for piano: four hands) has been recorded; but if you want to become acquainted with Debussy's lovely music, buy a recording of the work in its original form.
Norwood and Hancock, duo-pianists, Lyrichord LL 21 (LP); Gorini and Lorenzi, duo-pianists, Colosseum CLPS 1026 (LP).

BALLET IMPERIAL

Peter Ilyich Tchaikovsky: *Concerto No. 2, in G, for Piano and Orchestra.*
Liverpool Philharmonic Orchestra under George Weldon, soloist Benno Moiseiwitsch, His Master's Voice C 7607/10 (78) or Victor LCT 1127 (LP) or album WCT 1127 (45).
George Balanchine and many other musicians regard this concerto as far superior to Tchaikovsky's more popular First Piano Concerto.

LE BEAU DANUBE

Johann Strauss music, arranged by Roger Désormière.
London Philharmonic Orchestra under Antal Dorati, Victor album DM 414 (78).

BEAUTY AND THE BEAST

Maurice Ravel: *Ma Mère l'Oye.*
L'Orchestre de la Suisse Romande under Ernest Ansermet, London LL 388 (LP) (only complete recording of Ravel's original ballet score).

LES BICHES

Francis Poulenc: *Les Biches*.

Originally this was a ballet with songs (1924); Poulenc reorchestrated the score and arranged the music into a suite, omitting the overture and the vocal material.

Paris Conservatory Orchestra under Roger Désormière, London LL 624 (LP).

BILLY THE KID

Aaron Copland: *Billy the Kid*.

RCA Victor Symphony Orchestra under Leonard Bernstein, Victor LM 1031 (LP) or album WDM 1333 (45).

BOURRÉE FANTASQUE

Ballet made up of three compositions by Emmanuel Chabrier including:

A. *Marche Joyeuse*. Orchestre de la Suisse Romande, under Ansermet, London LL 696 (LP).

B. *Bourrée Fantasque* (originally a piano piece, orchestrated by Felix Mottl). Colonne Concerts orchestra under Louis Fourestier, Vox PL 7650 (LP).

C. *"Fête Polonaise"* from the opera *Le Roi malgré lui*. San Francisco Symphony Orchestra under Pierre Monteux, Victor 12-0978 (78) or 49-0517 (45); L'Orchestre de l'Opéra Comique, Paris, under Richard Blareau, London LS 647 (LP).

LA BOUTIQUE FANTASQUE

Selections by Gioacchino Rossini, arranged and orchestrated by Ottorino Respighi.

London Symphony Orchestra under Ernest Ansermet, London LL 274 (LP).

Decidedly superior to all other versions available.

THE CAGE

Igor Stravinsky: *Concerto in D for String Orchestra*.

RCA Victor Symphony Orchestra under Igor Stravinsky, Victor LM 1096 (LP) or album WDM 1424 (45).

CAKEWALK

Piano music by Louis Moreau Gottschalk, orchestrated by Hershey Kay. Philadelphia Orchestra under Eugene Ormandy, Columbia ML 4616 (LP).

Gottschalk, a nineteenth-century pianist matinee idol, was born in New Orleans of English and Creole parents. Chopin heard Gottschalk play in Paris and admired him a great deal. He was a pupil and friend of

Berlioz. Gottschalk composed many piano pieces in which he made use of Creole rhythms. A charming disc.

CAPRICCIO ESPAÑOL

Rimsky-Korsakov: *Capriccio Español.*
L'Orchestre de la Suisse Romande under Ernest Ansermet, London LL 694 (LP).

CAPRICHOS

Béla Bartók: *Contrasts for Violin, Clarinet, and Piano.*
Béla Bartók, pianist, Joseph Szigeti, violin, Benny Goodman, clarinet, Columbia ML 2213 (LP); Mann, Drucker, and Hambro are the instrumentalists on the Bartók Society 916 (LP).

CAPRIOL SUITE

Peter Warlock: *Capriol Suite.*
Boyd Neel String orchestra under Boyd Neel, London LL 801 (LP).

CARACOLE

Wolfgang Amadeus Mozart: *Divertimento No. 15, in B-flat* (K. 287).
NBC Symphony Orchestra under Arturo Toscanini, Victor LM 13 (LP).
A masterpiece performed in the grand style.

CARD GAME

Igor Stravinsky: *Jeu de Cartes.*
Berlin Philharmonic Orchestra under Igor Stravinsky, Capitol L 8028 (LP).

CARNAVAL

Robert Schumann: *Carnaval Ballet Suite.*
Philharmonia Orchestra under Robert Irving, Bluebird LBC 1025 (LP) or album WBC 1025 (45).
Irving's direction of this orchestrated collection of super-romantic piano pieces is excellent.

CHECKMATE

Arthur Bliss: *Checkmate.*
Royal Opera House Orchestra, Covent Garden, under Robert Irving, Columbia ML 4362 (LP).

CINDERELLA

Serge Prokofiev: *Cinderella.*
Royal Opera House Orchestra, Covent Garden, under Warwick Braithwaite (excerpts only recorded), Columbia ML 4229 (LP).

CON AMORE

Gioacchino Rossini: *three overtures.*
La Gazza ladra and *Il Signor Bruschino,* NBC Symphony Orchestra

under Arturo Toscanini, Victor LM 1044 (LP); *La Scala de seta,* Amsterdam Concertgebouw Orchestra under Eduard van Beinum, London LL 358 or LD 9023 (both LP).

The Toscanini recordings of these overtures written by our old friend "Il Signor Crescendo" are absolutely first-class.

CONCERTO BAROCCO

Johann Sebastian Bach: *Concerto in D minor for Two Violins and Orchestra.*

RCA Victor Chamber Orchestra under Franz Waxman, soloist Jascha Heifetz, Victor LM 1051 (LP) or album WDM 1136 (45).

Several recordings of this work have been made. My favorite is this version, in which the same violinist recorded both solo parts.

CONSTANTIA

Frédéric Chopin: *Concerto No. 2, in F minor, for Piano and Orchestra.*

George Sand wasn't the only woman in Chopin's life. Constantia Gladkowska was one of his early loves, and he composed for her the piano concerto to which the ballet is set.

NBC Symphony Orchestra under William Steinberg, soloist Artur Rubinstein, Victor LM 1046 (LP) or album WDM 1012 (45).

COPPÉLIA

Léo Delibes: *Coppélia.*

Many, many recordings of this ballet have been made. I am partial to the London version.

Paris Conservatory Orchestra under Roger Désormière (excerpts), London LS 183 (LP).

DANSES CONCERTANTES

Igor Stravinsky: *Danses Concertantes.*

RCA Victor Chamber Orchestra under Igor Stravinsky, Victor LM 1075 (LP) or album WDM 1234 (45).

DANTE SONATA

Franz Liszt's music, orchestrated by Constant Lambert.

Sadler's Wells Orchestra under Constant Lambert, with pianist Louis Kentner, English Columbia DX 967/8 (78).

DAPHNIS AND CHLOË

Maurice Ravel: *Daphnis et Chloé.*

L'Orchestre de la Suisse Romande under Ernest Ansermet, with the Motet Choir of Geneva conducted by Jacques Horneffer, London LL 693 (LP). This version is the only complete one of Ravel's magnificent ballet score, but the following versions of the two suites, extracted from the score by the composer, are also excellent.

Suite No. 1 only, San Francisco Symphony Orchestra and a Chorus of Women's Voices under Pierre Monteux, Victor album DM 1143 (78); *Suite No.* 1 (omitting Interlude for chorus) and *Suite No.* 2, Paris Conservatory Orchestra under Charles Munch, English Decca album EDA 29 (78); for those interested in *Suite No.* 2 only, NBC Symphony Orchestra under Arturo Toscanini, Victor LM 1043 (LP) or album WDM 1374 (45).

DESIGNS WITH STRINGS

Peter Ilyich Tchaikovsky: *Trio in A minor, Op. 50.*
Artur Rubinstein, pianist, Jascha Heifetz, violinist, Gregor Piatigorsky, cellist, Victor LM 1120 (LP) or album WDM 1488 (45).

FAÇADE

Sir William Walton: *Façade.*
London Symphony Orchestra under Robert Irving, London LL 771 (LP).

FACSIMILE

Leonard Bernstein: *Facsimile.*
RCA Victor Orchestra under Leonard Bernstein, Victor album DM 1142 (78).

FALL RIVER LEGEND

Morton Gould: *Fall River Legend.*
Philharmonic-Symphony Orchestra of New York under Dimitri Mitropoulos, Columbia ML 4616 (LP).

FANCY FREE

Leonard Bernstein: *Fancy Free.*
Ballet Theatre Orchestra under Joseph Levine, Capitol P 8196 or L 8197 (both LP).

FANFARE

Benjamin Britten: *Young Person's Guide to the Orchestra.*
Liverpool Philharmonic Orchestra under Sir Malcolm Sargent, Columbia ML 4197 (LP); not yet released—Amsterdam Concertgebouw Orchestra under Eduard van Beinum, supervised by Benjamin Britten, London LL 917 (LP).

FIREBIRD

Igor Stravinsky: *The Firebird.*
NBC Symphony Orchestra under Leopold Stokowski, Victor album DM 933 (78)—I prefer this version (hard to get, unfortunately) to the one made years ago with the Philadelphia Orchestra and also to Stokowski's most recent recording with an ensemble called "his Symphony Orchestra"; London Philharmonic Orchestra under Ernest

Ansermet, English Decca album EDA 30 (78)—I prefer this version to the one made more recently by this conductor with L'Orchestre de la Suisse Romande (LPS 300, easier to find); Philharmonic-Symphony Orchestra of New York under Igor Stravinsky, Columbia ML 4046 (LP)—The composer's own recording contains the greatest number of selections from the original score.

THE FOUR TEMPERAMENTS
Paul Hindemith: *Theme and Four Variations for Piano and Strings.*
Zimbler String Sinfonietta under Joseph Zimbler, with Lukas Foss, pianist, Decca DL 7501 (LP).

À LA FRANÇAIX
Jean Françaix: *Serenade for Twelve Instruments.*
Hamburg Chamber Orchestra under Eugen Jochum, Capitol L 8051 (LP).

GAÎTÉ PARISIENNE
Jacques Offenbach, arranged and orchestrated by Manuel Rosenthal: *Gaîté Parisienne.*
Boston Pops Orchestra under Arthur Fiedler, Victor LM 1001 (LP) or album ERB 13 (45).

GALA PERFORMANCE
Excerpts from works by Serge Prokofiev.
Piano Concerto No. 3, Dallas Symphony Orchestra under Antal Dorati, with William Kapell, pianist, Victor LM 1058 (LP) or album WDM 1326 (45); *Classical Symphony,* Boston Symphony Orchestra under Serge Koussevitzky, Victor LM 1215 (LP) or album WDM 1241 (45).

GISELLE
Adolphe Adam: *Giselle.*
Royal Opera House Orchestra, Covent Garden, under Robert Irving, Victor LM 1092 (LP) or album WDM 1397 (45); not yet released—L'Orchestre du Théâtre National de l'Opéra, Paris, under Richard Blareau, London LL 869 (LP).

LA GLOIRE
Ludwig van Beethoven, three overtures.
Coriolanus Overture, NBC Symphony Orchestra under Arturo Toscanini, Victor 11-9023 (78) or ERA 91 (45); *Leonore Overture No. 3,* NBC Symphony Orchestra under Arturo Toscanini, Victor LRM 7023 (LP) or album ERB 7023 (45); *Egmont Overture,* Boston Symphony Orchestra under Serge Koussevitzky, Victor LRM 7021 (LP) or album LRB 7021 (45).

GRADUATION BALL

Johann Strauss's music, selected by Antal Dorati.
Dallas Symphony Orchestra under Antal Dorati, Victor LM 1061 (LP)
or album WDM 1180 (45); New Symphony Orchestra under Anatole
Fistoulari, a complete recording of this work, London LL 883 (LP).

HAMLET

Peter Ilyich Tchaikovsky: *Hamlet, Overture-Fantasia.*
London Philharmonic Orchestra under Sir Adrian Boult, London LL
582 (LP).

THE HARVEST ACCORDING

Virgil Thomson: music derived from Virgil Thomson's works, including
his cello concerto.
Janssen Symphony of Los Angeles under Werner Janssen, with Luigi
Silva, cellist, Columbia ML 4468 (LP).

HELEN OF TROY

Jacques Offenbach's music, arranged and orchestrated by Antal Dorati.
Minneapolis Symphony Orchestra under Antal Dorati, Victor LM
22 (LP) or Album WDM 1381 (45).

L'HISTOIRE DU SOLDAT

Igor Stravinsky: *L'Histoire du Soldat.*
Instrumental Ensemble under Fernand Oubradous, with Jean Marchat
as the reader, Michel Auclair the soldier, and Marcel Herrand the devil,
Vox PL 7960 (LP)—only complete recording of this work; Instrumental
Ensemble under Stravinsky, with narrator, Columbia album MM 184
(78)—difficult to find.

ILLUMINATIONS

Benjamin Britten: *Les Illuminations.*
Orchestra of the Musical Arts Society of La Jolla under Nikolai Sokoloff,
with Alice Mock, soprano, Alco Y 1211 (LP); in preparation—a recording under the direction of the composer.

INTERPLAY

Morton Gould: *Interplay.*
Robin Hood Dell Orchestra of Philadelphia with Morton Gould,
pianist and conductor, Columbia ML 4218 (LP).

LE JEUNE HOMME ET LA MORT

Johann Sebastian Bach, arranged by Stokowski: *Passacaglia and Fugue
in C minor.*
Leopold Stokowski and his Symphony Orchestra, Victor LM 1133 (LP)
or album WDM 1512 (45).

JEUX

Claude Debussy: *Jeux*.
Symphony Orchestra of the Augusteo, Rome, under Victor de Sabata, Victor LM 1057 (LP) or album WDM 1276 (45).

JINX

Benjamin Britten: *Variations on a Theme of Frank Bridge*.
Boyd Neel String Orchestra under Boyd Neel, London LL 801 (LP).

JOB

Ralph Vaughan Williams: *Job, A Masque for Dancing*.
BBC Symphony Orchestra under Sir Adrian Boult, His Master's Voice DB 9024/8 (78).

KHADRA

Jean Sibelius: *Belshazzar's Feast*.
London Symphony Orchestra under Robert Kajanus, Victor album DM 715 (78).

LILAC GARDEN

Ernest Chausson: *Poème*.
London Philharmonic Orchestra under Sir Adrian Boult, with Yehudi Menuhin, violinist, His Master's Voice DB 9759/60 (78); Philadelphia Orchestra under Eugene Ormandy, with Zino Francescatti, violinist, Columbia ML 2194 (LP).

METAMORPHOSES

Paul Hindemith: *Symphonic Metamorphosis on Themes of Carl Maria von Weber*.
Cleveland Orchestra under George Szell, Columbia ML 4177.

THE MIRACULOUS MANDARIN

Béla Bartók: *The Miraculous Mandarin*.
New Symphony Orchestra under Tibor Serly, Bartók Recording Society BRS 301 (LP).
This ballet, the performances of which were banned several times in Europe because it shocked the so-called "*gens comme il faut*," has a fascinating score.

THE NUTCRACKER

Peter Ilyich Tchaikovsky: *The Nutcracker*.
A complete list of all the recordings made of this famous war horse would read like the telephone directory. In my estimation, the most satisfying version is the following:
Paris Conservatory Orchestra under Anatole Fistoulari, London LL 441 (LP). This record also includes portions of the score less frequently heard.

ORPHEUS
Igor Stravinsky: *Orpheus.*
RCA Victor Symphony Orchestra under Igor Stravinsky, Victor LM (LP) 1033 or album WDM 1320 (45).

LES PATINEURS
Music of Giacomo Meyerbeer, arranged by Constant Lambert.
London Symphony Orchestra under Robert Irving, London LL 651 (LP).

PETROUCHKA
Igor Stravinsky: *Petrouchka.*
London Philharmonic Orchestra under Ernest Ansermet, English Decca album EDA 2 (78)—this version is definitely better than the one made more recently with Ansermet's Orchestre de la Suisse Romande (London LLP 130, easier to find); Philharmonic-Symphony Orchestra of New York under Igor Stravinsky, Columbia ML 4047 (LP)—this is unfortunately incomplete.

PICNIC AT TINTAGEL
Arnold Bax: *The Garden of Fand.*
Royal Philharmonic Orchestra under Sir Thomas Beecham, His Master's Voice DB 6654/5 (78).

THE PIED PIPER
Aaron Copland: *Concerto for Clarinet and String Orchestra.*
Columbia String Orchestra under Aaron Copland, with Benny Goodman, clarinetist, Columbia ML 4421 (LP).

PILLAR OF FIRE
Arnold Schœnberg: *Verklärte Nacht.*
Philadelphia Orchestra under Eugene Ormandy, Columbia ML 4316 (LP).
For those who want to hear this work in its original form (sextet), I suggest the following recording, which was supervised by the composer: Hollywood String Quartet with Alvim Dinkin, viola, and Kurt Reher, cello, Capitol L 8118 (LP).

PINEAPPLE POLL
Sir Arthur Sullivan's music, arranged by Charles Mackerras.
Choose between these two recordings: London Symphony Orchestra under Robert Irving, Victor LM 1224 (LP) or album WDM 1653 (45); Sadler's Wells Orchestra under Charles Mackerras, Columbia ML 4439 (LP).

PRINCE IGOR

Alexander Borodin: *Dances of the Polovtsi* (from the opera *Prince Igor*).

My preference goes to Beecham's recording, which may be unavailable. The Van Beinum version is the next best.

London Philharmonic Orchestra and the Leeds Festival Choir under Sir Thomas Beecham, Columbia album MX 54 (78); London Philharmonic Orchestra and the London Philharmonic Choir under Eduard van Beinum, London LL 203 (LP).

THE PROSPECT BEFORE US

William Boyce's music, arranged by Constant Lambert.
Sadler's Wells Orchestra under Constant Lambert, Victor album DM 857 (78).

PULCINELLA

Igor Stravinsky: *Pulcinella*.
A new recording, conducted by Stravinsky, is in preparation by Columbia Records; Symphony Orchestra of Radio Berlin under Arthur Rother, Urania URLP 7093 (LP).

THE RAKE'S PROGRESS

Gavin Gordon: *The Rake's Progress*.
Royal Opera House Orchestra, Covent Garden, under Constant Lambert, Columbia ML 4229 (LP).

RODEO

Aaron Copland: *Rodeo*.
Ballet Theatre Orchestra under Joseph Levine, Capitol P 8196 or L 8198 (both LP).

ROMEO AND JULIET

Frederick Delius, selected compositions.
Over the Hills and Far Away, Royal Philharmonic Orchestra under Sir Thomas Beecham, Columbia ML 2133 (LP); *The Walk to the Paradise Garden* (from the opera *A Village Romeo and Juliet*), Royal Philharmonic Orchestra under Sir Thomas Beecham, His Master's Voice DB 9316/7 (78); *Eventyr*, Royal Philharmonic Orchestra under Sir Thomas Beecham, Columbia ML 4637 (LP); Prelude to the opera *Irmelin*, Royal Philharmonic Orchestra under Sir Thomas Beecham, His Master's Voice DB 9092 (78); *Brigg Fair—An English Rhapsody*, Royal Philharmonic Orchestra under Sir Thomas Beecham, Victor album WDM 1206 (45).
All this Beechamiana is superlative but some, unfortunately, are not easy to obtain.

LE SACRE DU PRINTEMPS

Igor Stravinsky: *Le Sacre du Printemps.*
Boston Symphony Orchestra under Pierre Monteux, Victor LM 1149 (LP) or album WDM 1548 (45); New York Philharmonic under Stravinsky, Columbia ML 4092 (LP); L'Orchestre de la Suisse Romande under Ernest Ansermet, London LL 303 (LP).

SCÈNES DE BALLET

Igor Stravinsky: *Scènes de Ballet.*
Philharmonic-Symphony Orchestra of New York under Igor Stravinsky, Columbia ML 4047 (LP).

SCHEHERAZADE

Nikolai Rimsky-Korsakov: *Scheherazade.*
No shortage of recordings of this indestructible war horse. Stokowski's showy version of the Arabian fantasy, narrative of fairy tale wonders told by Scheherazade to the Sultan Shahriar during a thousand and one nights is as good a job as one can hope for.
Philharmonia Orchestra under Leopold Stokowski, Victor LM 1732 (LP) or album WDM 1732 (45).

SCHUMANN CONCERTO

Robert Schumann: *Piano Concerto in A minor.*
Philharmonia Orchestra under Herbert von Karajan, with Dinu Lipatti, pianist, Columbia ML 4525 (LP).
Superb performance by a genius-pianist who is unfortunately no longer with us.

SCOTCH SYMPHONY

Felix Mendelssohn: *Symphony No. 3, in A Minor* (first movement omitted in this ballet).
Pittsburgh Symphony Orchestra under William Steinberg, Capitol S 8192 (LP).
However, my preferred recordings of the work was made some years ago by Dimitri Mitropoulos with the Minneapolis Symphony Orchestra, Columbia Entré RL 3017 (LP).

SERENADE

Peter Ilyich Tchaikovsky: *Serenade in C for Strings.*
Boston Symphony Orchestra under Serge Koussevitzky, Victor LM 1056 (LP) or album WDM 1346 (45); Philharmonia String Orchestra under Issay Dobrowen, His Master's Voice C 7722/5 (78) or Bluebird LBC 1021 (LP) or album WBC 1021 (45).

SLAUGHTER ON TENTH AVENUE

Richard Rodgers: *Slaughter on Tenth Avenue* (from the musical show *On Your Toes*).

This version is full-length. And the recording features a dozen other numbers from the show.
Orchestra under Lehman Engel, Columbia ML 4645 (LP).
Boston Pops Orchestra under Arthur Fiedler, WDM 1726 (78) and LM 1726 (LP).

THE SLEEPING BEAUTY

Peter Ilyich Tchaikovsky: *The Sleeping Beauty.*
Leopold Stokowski and his Symphony Orchestra, Victor LM 1010 (LP) or album WDM 1205 (45).
I prefer Stokowski's performance even though the Fistoulari-London recording is more complete.

SONG OF THE NIGHTINGALE

Igor Stravinsky: *Le Chant du Rossignol.*
Cincinnati Symphony Orchestra under Eugene Goossens, Victor album VM 1041 (78); in preparation—L'Orchestre de la Suisse Romande under Ernest Ansermet.
I wish Victor would reissue this beautiful recording on LP. Indeed, all of Stravinsky's great theatre music would be wonderful to have on records in complete form.

LE SPECTRE DE LA ROSE

Carl Maria von Weber: *Invitation to the Dance.*
BBC Symphony Orchestra under Arturo Toscanini, Victor 15192 (78) —this may be out of print; in that case, try Leopold Stokowski and his Symphony Orchestra, Victor LRM 7022 (LP) or album ERB 7022 (45).

A STREETCAR NAMED DESIRE

Alex North: Incidental music for the film *A Streetcar Named Desire.*
Orchestra under Ray Heindorf, Capitol L 289 or P 387 (LP).
The score used for the ballet is adapted and orchestrated by Rayburn Wright.

SWAN LAKE

Peter Ilyich Tchaikovsky: *Swan Lake.*
London Symphony Orchestra under Anatole Fistoulari, London set LL 565/6 (LP).
This version includes many portions of the work never recorded before.

LES SYLPHIDES

Frédéric Chopin: *Les Sylphides.*
I feel that Roger Désormière captures best the Romantic mood of this lovely *ballet blanc.* This may not be the flashiest version of the work, but it is the most poetical, in my opinion.

Paris Conservatory Orchestra under Roger Désormière, London LS 192 (LP).

SYLVIA
Léo Delibes: *Sylvia*.
Paris Conservatory Orchestra under Roger Désormière, London LS 184 (LP).

SYMPHONIC VARIATIONS
César Franck: *Symphonic Variations*.
Philharmonia Orchestra under George Weldon, with Robert Casadesus, pianist, Columbia ML 4298 (LP); Philharmonia Orchestra under Herbert von Karajan, with Walter Gieseking, pianist, Columbia ML 4536 (LP).

SYMPHONIE CONCERTANTE
Wolfgang Amadeus Mozart: *Sinfonia Concertante in E-flat* (K.364). I can't make up my mind between these two: Zimbler Sinfonietta with Joseph Fuchs, violinist, and Lillian Fuchs, violist, Decca DL 9596 (LP); Vienna State Opera Orchestra under Felix Prohaska, with Walter Barylli, violinist, and Paul Doktor, violist, Westminster WL 5107 (LP).

SYMPHONY IN C
Georges Bizet: *Symphony in C*.
It is hard to choose between these two; however, the Stokowski is easier to obtain:
London Philharmonic Orchestra under Charles Munch, English Decca AK 1781/4 (78); Leopold Stokowski and his Symphony Orchestra, Victor LM 1706 (LP) or album WDM 1706 (45); not yet released —L'Orchestre de la Suisse Romande under Ernest Ansermet, London LL 834.

THEME AND VARIATIONS
Peter Ilyich Tchaikovsky: *Theme and Variations* (from *Suite No. 3, in G,* fourth movement).
Philharmonia Orchestra under Nicolai Malko, Victor Bluebird LBC 1024 (LP) or album WBC 1024 (45) or His Master's Voice C 7826/8 (78).

THE THREE-CORNERED HAT
Manuel de Falla: *The Three-Cornered Hat*.
L'Orchestre de la Suisse Romande under Ernest Ansermet, with Suzanne Danco, soprano soloist, London LL 598 (LP)—complete recorded version of Falla's beautiful score.
A *must* on your list.

TIL EULENSPIEGEL

Richard Strauss: *Till Eulenspiegel's Merry Pranks.*
Boston Symphony Orchestra under Serge Koussevitzky, Victor album DM 1029 (78) or DV 1 (78); RCA Victor Orchestra under Fritz Reiner, Victor LM 1180 (LP).
To this writing, no recording has yet appeared which equals the Koussevitzky version of 1946—which may be hard to find.

UNDERTOW

William Schuman: *Undertow.*
The Louisville Orchestra under William Schuman, Mercury MG 10088 (LP).

LA VALSE

Maurice Ravel, two works.
A. *Valses Nobles et Sentimentales,* L'Orchestre de la Suisse Romande under Ernest Ansermet, London LL 795 (LP).
B. *La Valse,* San Francisco Orchestra under Pierre Monteux, Victor album DM 820 (78); Paris Conservatory Orchestra under Ernest Ansermet, London LL 22 (LP).
Too bad the old Koussevitzky recording of some twenty years ago is no longer available, because, in my estimation, it is a magnificent performance. I don't believe that a definitive recording of *La Valse* has yet been made. The ones listed above are the best to this writing.

Part Eleven

SELECTED READING GUIDE

Adventures of a Ballet Critic, Richard Buckle. Cresset Press.
The Analytical Concert Guide, Louis Biancolli. Doubleday & Company, Inc.
Art in Modern Ballet, George Amberg. Pantheon Books, Inc.
Artists of the Dance, Lillian Moore. Thomas Y. Crowell.
An Autobiography, Igor Stravinsky. Simon and Schuster, Inc.
Ballet, Arnold Haskell. Penguin Books.
Ballet, Photographs by Serge Lido.
Ballet Alphabet, Lincoln Kirstein. Kamin Dance Publishers.
Ballet Annual, Arnold Haskell, issued annually in London since 1947. A. & C. Black.
Ballet in America, George Amberg. Duell, Sloane and Pearce, Inc.
Ballet Lover's Companion, Kay Ambrose. Alfred A. Knopf, Inc.
Ballet Lover's Pocketbook, Kay Ambrose. Alfred A. Knopf, Inc.
Ballet Portraits, Maurice Seymour. Pellegrini and Cudahy.
Ballet Then and Now, Deryck Lynham. Sylvan Press.
Baron at the Ballet, Photographs. Collins; Morrow.
Baron Encore, Collins; Morrow.
The Bibiena Family, A. Hyatt Mayor. H. Bittner and Co.
A Bibliography of Dancing, Paul Magriel, editor. H. W. Wilson Co.
Blast at Ballet, Lincoln Kirstein. Published by the author.
Book of the Dance, Lincoln Kirstein. Garden City Publishing Co., Inc.
Borzoi Book of Ballets, Grace Robert. Alfred A. Knopf, Inc.
Chronicles of American Dance, Paul Magriel, editor. Henry Holt and Co.
The Classic Ballet, Muriel Stuart, Carlus Dyer, and Lincoln Kirstein. Alfred A. Knopf, Inc.
Complete Book of Ballets, C. W. Beaumont. G. P. Putnam's Sons.
The Complete Stories of Hans Christian Andersen, translated by Jean Hersholt. Heritage Press.
Milton Cross's Complete Stories of the Great Operas. Doubleday & Company, Inc.
The Dance, John Martin. Tudor Publishing Co.
The Dance, Troy and Margaret West Kinney. Tudor Publishing Co.
Dance and the Soul, Paul Valéry, translated by Dorothy Bussy. John Lehman.
The Dance Encyclopedia, Anatole Chujoy, editor. A. S. Barnes and Company, Inc.
The Dance Has Many Faces, Walter Sorell, editor. The World Publishing Co.
Dance News Annual, Anatole Chujoy and Winthrop Palmer, editors. Alfred A. Knopf, Inc.
Dancers and Critics, Cyril Swanson, editor. A. & C. Black.

Dance to the Piper, Agnes de Mille. Little, Brown and Co.

The Dancing Master, Pierre Rameau, translated by C. W. Beaumont. C. W. Beaumont, publisher.

Alexandra Danilova, A. E. Twysden. Kamin Dance Publishers.

Degas Dancers, Lillian Browse. Faber and Faber.

Isadora Duncan, Paul Magriel, editor. Henry Holt and Co.

An Elementary Treatise Upon the Theory and Practice of the Art of Dancing, Carlo Blasis, translated by Mary Stewart Evans. Kamin Dance Publishers.

Fanny Elssler, C. W. Beaumont. C. W. Beaumont, publisher.

Fokine, Lincoln Kirstein. British-Continental Press.

Michel Fokine and His Ballets, C. W. Beaumont. C. W. Beaumont, publisher.

Fundamentals of the Classic Dance, Agrippina Vaganova, translated by Anatole Chujoy. Kamin Dance Publishers.

A History of Ballet in Russia, C. W. Beaumont. C. W. Beaumont, publisher.

International Cyclopedia of Music and Musicians, Oscar Thompson, editor. Dodd, Mead & Co.

Invitation to the Ballet, Ninette de Valois. John Lane.

Invitation to Dance, Walter Terry. Tudor Publishing Co.

The Last Years of Nijinsky, Romola Nijinsky. Simon and Schuster, Inc.

Mary Ann Lee, First American Giselle, Lillian Moore. Dance Index, Vol. II, No. 5.

Letters on Dancing and Ballets, Jean Georges Noverre, translated by C. W. Beaumont. C. W. Beaumont, publisher.

Looking at the Dance, Edwin Denby. Pellegrini and Cudahy.

Alicia Markova, Anton Dolin. Hermitage House, Inc.

Mozart, Alfred Einstein. Oxford University Press.

Music in the Nation, B. H. Haggin. William Sloane Associates.

Music Since 1900, Nicolas Slonimsky. W. W. Norton and Company, Inc.

The New York City Ballet, Anatole Chujoy. Alfred A. Knopf, Inc.

The New York City Ballet, Photographs by Roger Wood. Phoenix House.

Nijinsky, Paul Magriel, Editor. Henry Holt and Co.

Nijinsky, Romola Nijinsky. Simon and Schuster, Inc.

Noverre, The Father of Modern Ballet, Deryck Lynham. British Book Centre.

Old Friends and New Music, Nicholas Nabokov. Little, Brown and Co.

Orchesography, Thoinot Arbeau, translated by Mary Stewart Evans. Kamin Dance Publishers.

A Pageant of the Dance and Ballet, Mark Perugini. Jarrolds.

Pavlova, Paul Magriel, editor. Henry Holt and Co.

Jules Perrot, Yury Slonimsky, translated by Anatole Chujoy. Dance Index, Vol. IV, No. 12.

Marius Petipa, Yury Slonimsky, translated by Anatole Chujoy. Dance Index, Vol. VI, Nos. 5, 6.

The Poetics of Music, Igor Stravinsky. Harvard University Press.

Reminiscences of the Russian Ballet, Alexandre Benois. G. P. Putnam's Sons.

The Renaissance in Italy, J. A. Symonds. Modern Library, Inc.

The Romantic Ballet, Théophile Gautier, translated by C. W. Beaumont. C. W. Beaumont, publisher.

The Romantic Ballet in London 1821-58, George Chaffée. Dance Index, Vol. II, Nos. 9, 10, 11, 12.

Russian Ballet, Adrian Stokes. Faber and Faber.
The Sadler's Wells Ballet, C. W. Beaumont. C. W. Beaumont, publisher.
The Sadler's Wells Ballet, Photographs by Roger Wood. Saturn Press.
Stravinsky in the Theatre, Minna Lederman, editor. Pellegrini and Cudahy.
Supplement to Complete Book of Ballets, C. W. Beaumont. G. P. Putnam's Sons.
Marie Taglioni, André Levinson, translated by C. W. Beaumont. C. W. Beaumont, publisher.
Tales of Hoffmann. Heritage House.
The Theatre Ballet of Sadler's Wells, Photographs by Roger Wood. Phoenix House.
The Theatre of Eugene Berman, George Amberg. Museum of Modern Art.
Theatre Street, Tamara Karsavina. E. P. Dutton and Co., Inc.
Three or Four Graces, George Chaffée. Dance Index, Vol. III, Nos. 9, 10, 11.
Tonight the Ballet, Adrian Stokes. Faber and Faber.
Twenty-Five Years of American Dance, Doris Hering, editor. Dance Magazine.
The Victor Book of Ballets, Robert Lawrence. Simon and Schuster, Inc.
The Vic-Wells Ballet, P. W. Manchester. Gollancz.
World Book of Modern Ballet, John Martin. The World Publishing Co.
World History of the Dance, Curt Sachs. W. W. Norton and Company, Inc.

Dance Index, a monthly periodical, New York, 1942–48, edited by Marian Eames, Baird Hastings, Lincoln Kirstein, Paul Magriel, and Donald Windham. Ballet Caravan, Inc.
Ballet, a monthly periodical, London, 1939–1952, edited by Richard Buckle.

SOME CURRENT PERIODICALS

Dance Magazine, a monthly periodical published in New York, edited by Lydia Joel.
Dance News, a monthly periodical published in New York, edited by Anatole Chujoy.
Dance and Dancers, a monthly periodical published in London, edited by Peter Williams.
The Dancing Times, a monthly periodical published in London, edited by Philip J. S. Richardson.

Index